The Harmonicon, Volume 3, Part 1

THE

A JOURNAL OF

Music.

VOL. III.

PART I.—Containing

Essays, Criticisms, Biography, and Miscellanies.

LONDON:

Printed for the Proprietors,

PUBLISHED BY SAMUEL LEIGH, No. 18, STRAND.

MDCCCXXV.

LONDON:
PRINTED BY WILLIAM CLOWES,
Northumberland-court.

CONTENTS OF PART I., VOL. III.

THE

HARMONICON.

No. XXV., JANUARY, 1825.

MEMOIR OF JOHANN LUDWIG DUSSEK.

JOHANN LUDWIG DUSSEK, or, as his countrymen name him, Ladislaw Dussek, was born in the year 1760, at Czaslau in Bohemia, a province which Dr. Burney justly calls the most musical in Germany, and who adds, that he knows no country where the art is more generally and successfully cultivated. The first-rate *composers*, however,—by which title we mean to designate those who are renowned for invention and for original genius,—have not been natives of Bohemia, the musical fame of which rests on its executive, rather than on its creative talent. In no part of Europe are to be found individuals who excel them as performers on wind-instruments; and for the piano-forte, the names of Dussek and Moscheles speak decisively as to their ability.

At the age of ten, Dussek was sent by a nobleman, a friend of his father, to one of the principal colleges in the university of Prague. During the seven years he remained there, he studied ancient and modern literature, but chiefly music, and profited much by the lessons of a Benedictine friar, who made him write every kind of exercise in counter-point. He had attained his nineteenth year, when he repaired to Brussels, and under the patronage of a gentleman at the court of the Stadtholder, gave a concert at the Hague in the presence of the whole court, which as much increased his reputation as his finances. Before he proceeded to Paris and London, he determined on a journey to the north of Europe, and had the good fortune to become acquainted with the celebrated Emanuel Bach, at Hamburg. Hence he departed for Petersburg; but on his way, Prince C. Radzivill made him such advantageous proposals, that he could not resist them, and remained with this prince two years, in the heart of Prussian Lithuania. He then returned to Berlin, and after a short stay, went to Paris, where he remained a long time. At the beginning of the French revolution he discreetly quitted that metropolis, and set out with all speed for London, where he continued till 1800. During more than a ten years' residence in this country, he shone as the greatest piano-forte player that had ever been heard; and it is difficult to determine whether he has since been surpassed in grandeur, brilliancy, and delicacy of taste. It is no ordinary praise of him to say, that many able judges have ascribed in part the great refinement of Cramer to the many opportunities he had of hearing his friend's exquisite performances on an instrument that afforded

them both so many triumphs, but has never yet produced them an equal.

While residing in this country, he married the daughter of Signor Domenico Corri, and, most unfortunately, both for himself and his art, entered into trade as a music-seller, in partnership with his father-in-law. He was in consequence obliged to leave England suddenly, and removed to Hamburg, where he remained above two years. He now repaired a second time to Berlin, and from a mere acquaintance, became the companion, and at last the intimate and confidential friend of Prince Louis Ferdinand of Prussia, who died so bravely for his country at Saalfeld, in 1806. This prince was well known to possess more talents than any other member of his family, independently of his skill on the piano-forte, and his elaborate and clever compositions for that instrument. On the death of his royal associate, Dussek wrote a Sonata expressive of his feelings on the occasion, under the title of an "Elegy." After a short engagement with the Prince of Isenburg, he entered into the service of the celebrated Talleyrand, Prince of Benevento, in which he continued to the end of his life in 1812.

His compositions, which reach Op. 77, are unequal, because many of them were produced by contract,—according to order, in mercantile language,—and were therefore adapted to the capacity and taste of the mob of players. But we know scarcely any composer who has given to the world so many things that are both good and popular at the same time: his Concertos, Op. 15 (The Plough-boy) and 22, (dedicated to Miss Collins,) together with his Sonatas, Op. 13, 24, and 31, and his many airs with variations, may be offered as instances. But his permanent fame must rest on his greater works; amongst which he is said to have held in the highest estimation Op. 9, 10, 14, 42, *Les adieux à Clementi*, and *Le Retour à Paris*, called here, the *plus ultra*, in opposition to, or perhaps in ridicule of Woelfl's well-known "*Ne plus ultra.*" His three sonatas, Op. 35, dedicated to Clementi, have always appeared to us to be his best work, as combining a greater portion of originality, science, and effect. His *Fantasia and Fugue*, inscribed to Cramer, is undoubtedly his most learned production, and for the profound musician it has many charms. There exists yet an Oratorio of his composition called the *Resurrection*, the words by the great poet Klopstock; and a mass which he wrote at Prague at the age of thirteen; but nothing is known respecting their merits.

The compositions of Dussek are all marked by a rich and ready invention, and a peculiarly delicate taste. Those of a gay kind show great brilliancy and freedom of melody; while his graver works, which were apparently produced *con amore*, display an entire command of all the stores of harmony, and great depth of feeling. Some very distinguished composers have modelled their best works after the originals of Dussek; and if morbid fashion, which is always panting after novelty, did not hold such despotic sway over the musical art, his productions would be now as familiarly known as they were twenty years ago.

LIST OF DUSSEK'S CHIEF WORKS.

Opera.
1. Three Sonatas for the p.-forte or harp, with accompaniment for viol. and vcello.
2. Three Ditto, for Ditto, and Ditto.
3. Three Ditto, for Ditto, and Ditto.
4. Three Ditto, for Ditto, and Ditto.
5. Grand Sonata.
6. "Petits Airs," with variations.
8. Three Sonatas.
9. Three Sonatas for p.-forte or harp, with accompaniment for viol. or vcello.
10. Three Ditto, for Ditto, and Ditto.
11. Duet for two p.-fortes.
12. Three Sonatas, dedicated to Mrs. Cosway.
13. Three Ditto, dedicated to Miss Jansen.
14. Three Ditto, with popular airs.
15. Concerto in E flat, with Plough-boy.
16. Three Sonatas with violin accompt.
17. Three Ditto, for Ditto, and Ditto.
18. Three Concertos.
19. Six Sonatinas for p.-forte and Violin.
20. Three Ditto, for Ditto.
21. The Rosary.
22. Concerto in B flat, dedicated to Miss Collins.
23. Three Sonatas dedicated to the Baronne de Dopff.
24. Sonata, dedicated to Mrs. Chinnery.
25. Three Sonatas, with Scotch airs.
26. Duet for two harps.
27. Concerto in F., dedicated to Mrs. Hyde.
28. Six easy Sonatas.
29. A Grand Concerto.
30. A Ditto Ditto.
31. Three Sonatas, and three Preludes, for p.-forte, and flute.
32. Grand Duo, à quatre mains.
33. Overture for two performers on one piano.
34. Two Sonatinas, for harp and flute.
35. Tre Gran' Sonate, dedicate al Muzio Clementi.
36. Duet, for harp and piano.
37. Sonata, for harp, arranged for p.-forte, by Cramer.
38. Grand Duet, for harp and piano, or two pianos.
39. Three Sonatas, dedicated to Mrs. Apreece.
40. Concerto Militaire, for p.-forte.
42. Fantasia and Fugue, dedicated to J. B. Cramer.
43. Sonata Harp, arranged for p.-forte, by Cramer.
44. The Farewell, a Grand Sonata, dedicated to Clementi.
45. Three Sonatas, for p.-forte.
46. Six Easy Sonatas.
47. A Sonata.
48. Duet, dedicated to *The Sisters*.
49. Concerto dedicated to Mr. and Mrs. Vidal.
50. Duet, arranged by Cramer.
51. Three easy Sonatas, for p.-forte and flute.
58. A Quintett, p.-forte, &c.
61. Elegy on the death of Prince Louis.
62. La Consolation, an Andante for p.-forte.
67. Three progressive Sonatas, for four hands on p.-forte.

Opera.
68. Concerto Notturno.
70. Concerto in a flat, dedicated to Viotti.
71. Six airs with variations.
72. Two easy Sonatas.
77. L'Invocation, Grand Sonata.
78. Posthumous-Rondo, for p.-forte.

The above list is collected from English and Foreign Catalogues, from Gerber, &c.; but owing to a want of uniformity in numbering the works of authors, both here and abroad, much error frequently ensues, and we fear that the foregoing is far from perfect.

MAYERBEER'S NEW OPERA,
IL CROCIATO IN EGITTO,
LATELY PRODUCED IN ITALY.
[From a Foreign Correspondent.]

A TRIUMPH of music, of a very unusual kind, has recently been obtained at Florence, in the production of Mayerbeer's opera, *Il Crociato in Egitto*; a work, say the critics, not composed of a motley collection of fragments, but forming an entire and connected whole; one of those effusions of genius which appear rarely in an age. It is considered as a happy amalgamation of the music of the German and Italian schools; as full of well-digested and profound harmonies, blended with a spirited and expressive melody.

This opera was first produced at Venice, where it obtained no less applause than at the latter place. The piece commences with a majestic overture; the introduction consists of a chorus of slaves, strongly expressive of their longing desire of liberty, and of their joy in again revisiting their native land; this is followed by a cavatina of the *prima donna*, (Adelaide Tosi) as *Palmide*, the daughter of the Sultan, who, with consoling words and gifts, appears as an angel of peace among these children of slavery. The music of this part is full of touching effects, perfectly expressive of the sentiment, and heightened by the instrumental part, which is admirably in unison with the voices. In this part an extraordinary effect is produced by an interchange of six trumpets, part of which are in the orchestra, and part on the towers of the holy city. This is succeeded by a chorus of female slaves, who sing and dance round the tent where *Mirva*, the little son of *Palmide*, sleeps, which is full of very charming movements. Another chorus of Emirs introduces the hero, *Armandos*, (Velluti,) who arrives with the olive-branch of peace; the cavatina which he sings, as well as the whole music of this scene, breathes the very notes of gentleness and peace. This is succeeded by a duet between Velluti and Reina, the tenor, which is exceedingly descriptive of a pacific disposition in the former, and disappointed rage in the latter. This interchange of feelings is happily expressed in the music.

There are also some romances in the first act, which, in order to be perfect, only require a more accurate adaptation of the parts, and a greater degree of brevity. The *finale* consists of a canon in five parts, and a chorus of warriors, full of power and dignity; in this it is doubtful which we ought most to admire, the beauty and expression of the song, or the power and admirably characteristic effects of the instrumentation. One of the chief excellencies of Mayerbeer's music is the respect that is always shown for the human voice; in the above chorus, the strong effects of the full orchéstra, and of two bands upon the stage, together with a very beautiful trumpet concerto, are truly overwhelming, but well managed; intervals occur in which the voices of the warriors calling to arms are finely contrasted with those of the timid female train, claiming the sacred rights of nature and love, and which are all allowed to be distinctly heard through these masses of harmony.

The second act, which is shorter than the first, rivals it in beauty. The parts principally admired are, a chorus of the Emirs, in the act of forming a conspiracy;—the quartett of the *Preghiera*, terminating in a sestett, which may stand a comparison with any music;—a chorus of Knights and Saracens, and a duet of great beauty, constructed entirely on the Italian model.

It is true that in Mayerbeer's music we sometimes meet with very uncommon phrases, which will not at once be either relished or understood; but when heard often, they enchant by their novelty and beauty, and strongly rivet the attention. It must be acknowledged by all, that the compositions of this master not only please the ear, but also express a language that speaks directly to the heart. His music may be compared to some of those grave-looking persons, who alarm us on a first introduction, but, upon closer acquaintance, charm us by the suavity of their manners, and the elegance of their conversation.

One fault we may be permitted to find with this composer, but it is a *happy one*, as Quintilian calls it, and this is, a redundancy of genius; if he possessed self-denial enough to retrench these exuberances, if he would bear constantly in mind that great law, *ne quid nimis*, his music might approach rapidly to perfection. It would have this immediate advantage, that his opera would be considerably shortened, and his hearers would not be deprived of an hour or two of their natural rest. Much praise was given to Mayerbeer for his *Romilda*, but in the present composition he has made a giant's stride. His *Crociato* ranks him with the greatest composers of the day, and will, in all probability, transmit his fame to posterity.

The singers rose in dignity with the music they had to perform, and never did Tosi and Velluti appear to greater advantage; their merit was the greater, as they had many difficulties, many new forms of melody and ornament, to contend with. The house was crowded to excess, and the public were more than pleased with the production; the applause was enthusiastic. At the conclusion of the piece the composer was summoned to make his appearance, and receive the congratulation of the house; nay more, the singers, and the scene-painter, Facchinelli, as well as the manager himself, were called forward to receive these honours, rarely indeed bestowed in the latter instances. But, to say the truth, the decorations, the scenery, and the whole paraphernalia of the opera, were in the highest degree splendid and full of good taste.

ON THE VELOCITY OF SOUND.

This is a subject which has engaged the attention of the greatest philosophers, and is highly interesting to really scientific musicians. We insert the following facts and inquiries, under the hope of drawing the attention of our readers to so important a subject.

The results have been deduced by Dr. Gregory from the experiments made by himself and others on the velocity of sound [*].

1. That sound moves uniformly; at least in a horizontal direction, or one that does not greatly deviate from horizontality.

2. That the difference in the intensity of a sound makes no appreciable difference in its velocity:

3. Nor consequently does a difference in the instrument from which the sound is emitted.

4. That wind greatly affects sound in point of *intensity*, and that it affects it also in point of velocity.

5. That when the direction of the wind concurs with that of the sound, the *sum* of their separate velocities gives the *apparent* velocity of sound: when the direction of the wind *opposes* that of the sound, the *difference* of the separate velocities must be taken.

6. That in the case of echoes the velocity of the *reflected* sound is the same as that of the *direct* sound.

7. That therefore distances may frequently be measured by means of echoes.

8. That an augmentation of temperature occasions an augmentation of velocity of sound, and *vice versâ*.

The inquiries with regard to the transmission of sound in the atmosphere, which, notwithstanding the curious investigations of Newton, Laplace, Poisson, and others, require the further aid of experiment for satisfactory determination, are, I think, the following, viz.:

1. Whether hygrometric changes in the atmosphere have much or little influence on the velocity of sound?

2. Whether barometric changes in the atmosphere have much or little influence?

3. Whether, as Muschenbrook conjectured, sound have not different degrees of velocity, at the same temperature, in different regions of the earth? And whether *high* barometric pressure would not be found (even independently of temperature) to produce greater velocities?

4. Whether, therefore, sound would not pass more slowly between the summits of two mountains than between the bases?

5. Whether sound, independently of the changes in the air's elasticity, move quicker or slower near the earth's surface than at some distance from it? (See Savart's interesting papers on the *Communication of Sonorous Vibration*.)

6. Whether sound would not employ a longer interval *in passing over a given space, as a mile, vertically upwards*, than in a *horizontal* direction? and if so, would the formulæ which should express the relation of the intervals include more than thermometric and barometric coefficients?

7. Whether or not the principle of the parallelogram of forces may be employed in estimating the effect of wind upon sound, when their respective velocities do not aid or oppose each other in the same line or nearly so?

8. Whether those eudiometric qualities generally (whether hitherto detected or not) which affect the elasticity of the air, will not proportionally affect the velocity of sound? and if so, how are the modifications to be appreciated?

---

* Cambridge Philosophical Transactions. MDCCCXXIV.

ON THE NATIONAL SONGS OF MODERN GREECE.

[Extracted from the interesting work recently published by M. Fauriel, entitled " *Chants Populaires de la Grece Moderne.*"]

If, as has been frequently observed, the manners, character, and genius of a people, are best learnt from their national songs, those of Modern Greece, of a nation in whose behalf so general an interest is at present felt,—cannot but be worthy of attention.

The National Songs of the Modern Greeks are the direct and genuine expression of their character and spirit; a species of poetry which does not live in books, which enjoys no factitious life, but breathes and speaks in the living mouths of her sons.

In all parts of Greece, every public event, however small its importance, or limited the sphere of its interest, becomes the subject of one, and frequently of several songs. Even the incidents of private life, when attended by any circumstances more remarkable than usual, seldom fail to find a poet to celebrate them, and a musician to adapt them to some characteristic air.

It is one of the peculiarities of almost all popular songs and airs, that the authors generally remain unknown; this is the case with the melodies of Modern Greece. But it is a remarkable circumstance, that the greater part of them are considered as the productions of blind itinerants, who are spread through all parts of Greece, where they represent the ancient rhapsodists with a fidelity which has something in it very striking.

In Greece there are no mendicants; every man capable of labour is expected to work, except he be blind; and even this exception is not apparent, for, in Greece, blind persons exercise a profession which renders them not only agreeable, but, in some respects, necessary, considering the character, condition, and lively imagination of the people:—this is the profession of itinerant singers.

Blind persons are in the practice, as well upon the continent, as in the islands of Greece, of learning by heart a number of popular songs, of every kind and period. Many of them acquire a prodigious quantity, and all of them know a great number. Furnished with these treasures of memory,—the only treasures to which such poets can generally lay claim,—they are always upon the march, traversing Greece in every direction, from the extremity of the Morea to Constantinople, from the Ægean to the Ionian Sea. They go from town to town, from village to village; a motley auditory is soon gathered round them, and they make choice of such songs as are suited to place and circumstance, and best calculated to awaken the generosity of the hearers, in order to obtain the trifling remuneration which constitutes all their revenue. These blind singers are to be met with more frequently in the villages, than in the towns. Wherever they come, they seem to give the preference to the uncultivated part of the population, which is always the most curious, the most greedy of strong impressions, and the least fastidious in the choice of the subjects offered to them. The Turks are the only persons who do not mingle in these groups; they pass by with an air of apathy or disdain. It is at the fairs, at the village feasts,—known under the name of Paneghyri,—that these itinerant singers are to be found, where they are sure of meeting with the greatest degree of encouragement.

They sing, accompanying themselves by an instrument with strings, which is played with a bow. This is exactly the ancient lyre of the Greeks, of which it retains the name as well as form. This lyre, when perfect, consists of five strings, but frequently it consists but of two or three; the sounds of which, as may well be supposed, have nothing very harmonious in them. These blind singers are generally found single; but sometimes also they unite in groups of two or more, in order to sing the same songs together.

These modern rhapsodists, being always on the move from place to place, always in quest of whatever can excite the imagination, or satisfy curiosity, nothing of interest can escape them; nothing of what is passing in the towns, villages, and country places. They take note of every thing, celebrate every occurrence, and through the medium of their songs, spread by degrees, throughout the whole of Greece, the renown of adventurous actions, and of the men by whom they were performed. These blind rhapsodists are, therefore, in fact, the chroniclers and historians, at the same time that they are the poets of the people; in this respect perfectly resembling the rhapsodists of Ancient Greece.

There is another very remarkable point of resemblance between the ancient and modern rhapsodists; the latter, like the former, are at the same time musicians as well as poets. Every blind songster who composes a song, composes the air to it at the same time. The composition of verse is to him but the half of his function as poet; to set his verses to music is indispensable for fulfilling the object and end for which they were made. It is true, that new words are sometimes composed to an air already known; but this is not ordinarily the case, for, generally speaking, every new song is produced and circulated with an air invented expressly for it.

Among these blind rhapsodists, there are, from time to time, found individuals gifted with the talent of improvisation. I heard of one in particular, who was living towards the close of the last century, in the small town of Ampelakia in Thessaly, in the neighbourhood of Mount Ossa. His name was Gavogannis, or John the Blind, who attained to a very advanced age, and gained a great reputation by the facility with which he *improvised* upon any given theme, as well as by the prodigious number of historical and other songs, with which his memory was stored. Having become rich, or at least comparatively so to his itinerant brethren, he afforded the rare example of a stationary rhapsodist. His visiters were numerous, as well to hear the songs of deeds of other days, as to propose subjects for his extemporaneous talent, for the exercise of which he was sure to be liberally rewarded.

Every Greek village celebrates annually the feast of its patron saint. On this occasion all the neighbouring villages repair thither. Song, accompanied by music, forms one of the most lively and most characteristic enjoyments of these meetings. It is there that these Homers of the day are sure of finding a numerous auditory, well disposed to feel all the varied expression of verse, the admiration of valorous deeds, or tales of tenderness and love. There can be no means more certain, and more rapid, of circulating these songs. A piece sung on one of these occasions, for the first time, is repeated on the morrow by eight or ten other villagers. In fact, it can easily be imagined, that songs sung in the midst of a great concourse of people, in the open air, amidst the gaiety of a feast, of which they form a principal ornament, and amidst that communion of joy and happiness which imparts a charm, even to the most common expressions, which cannot fail of making an impression not easily to be effaced.

Among the songs in question, some are composed with a view to be chanted to the accompaniment of a lyre, which is sometimes small, and sometimes approaches in size to the Welsh or Irish harp. Others are composed in order to be sung in dancing, which may be justly denominated *ballads*, in the strict sense of the word, as it was understood in the old Provençal poetry, though that meaning be now lost.

We shall present our readers with two specimens of these, one a sea-song, the other the farewell of a dying chieftain; and in order the more to identify them, we give the original Greek text. The hero of the first flourished about the beginning of the last century; the other was a Klephtic chieftain. Both these songs are said to be of great celebrity in Greece, and to be sung on almost all occasions. The reader will doubtless be struck by the great naïveté of the latter, highly expressive of

The ruling passion strong in death,—

of the aged chieftain, who imagines that even in his tomb it will be necessary for him still to enjoy the sweet illusion of waging war with the Turks, and of breathing the air of his native mountains on the return of spring.

ΤΟΥ ΙΑΝΝΗ ΣΤΑΘΑ.

Μαῦρον καράβι ἔπλεε 'σ τὰ μέρη τῆς Κασσάνδρας·

Μαῦρα πανιὰ τὸ σκέπαζαν, καὶ τ' οὐρανοῦ παντιέρα.
'Εμπρὸς κορδέτα μ' ἄλικην σημαίαν τοῦ ἐ̓ξῆκε·
" Μάινα, φωνάζει, τὰ πανιά, ῥῆξε τα, λέγει, κάτω |"—
" Δὲν τὰ μαϊνάρω τὰ πανιά, οὐδὲ τὰ ῥήχνω κάτω !

" Μή με θαρρεῖτε νεόνυμφην, νύμφην νὰ προσκυνήσω.
" 'Εγώ μ' ὁ 'Ιάννης τοῦ Σταθᾶ, γαμβρὸς τοῦ Μπουκοδάλλα.
" Τράχου, λεβέντες, ῥήξετε 'σ τὴν πρώραν τὸ καράδι·
" Τῶν Τούρκων αἷμα χύσετε, ἀπίστους μὴ 'ψυχᾶτε."—

Οἱ Τοῦρκοι βόλταν ἔρρηξαν, κ' ἐγύρισαν τὴν πρώραν.
Πρῶτος ὁ 'Ιάννης πέταξε μὲ τὸ σπαθὶ 'σ τὸ χέρι.
'Σ τὰ βούνια τρέχουν αἵματα, θάλασσα κοκκινίζει·
'Αλλᾶ ! ἀλλᾶ ! οἱ ἄπιστοι κράζοντες, προσκυνοῦνε.

ΤΟΥ ΙΑΝΝΗ ΣΤΑΘΑ.
JOHN STATHAS.

Topp'd by her floating flag of blue,
Across the waves a vessel flew;
Another vessel bears in sight,
Known by her flag of crimson bright.
    " Lower thy sail !" in conscious pride,
And lordly tone, the former cried.
" Lower thy sail to thee ! beware !
" For I the noble Stathas bear.
    " Think'st thou I am a timorous bride
" Who lays, when bid, her veil aside ?—
" Grapple her fast, my seamen brave ;
" Dye deep with Turkish blood the wave !"—
    The Turks brook not the haughty cheek,
But Stathas now is on her deck.
The waves are stained with crimson die,
They yield, and Alla ! is the cry.

Ο ΤΑΦΟΣ ΤΟΥ ΔΗΜΟΥ.

'Ο ἥλιος ἐδασίλευε, κι' ὁ Δῆμος διατάζει·

" Σύρτε, παιδιά μου, 'σ τὸ νερὸν, ψωμὶ νὰ φᾶτ' ἀπόψε.
" Καὶ σὺ Λαμπράκη μ' ἀνεψιὲ, κάθου ἐδῶ κοντά μου·
" Νὰ ! τ' ἄρματά μου φόρεσε, νὰ ἦσαι καπεταίνος·
" Καὶ σεῖς, παιδιά μου, πάρετε τὸ ἔρημον σπαθί μου,

" Πράσινα κόψετε κλαδιά, στρῶστέ μου νὰ καθήσω,
" Καὶ φέρτε τὸν πνευματικὸν νὰ μ' ἐξομολογήσῃ·
" Νὰ τὸν εἰπῶ τὰ κρίματα ὅσα ἔχω καμωμένα·
" Τριάντα χρόνι' ἁμαρτωλὸς, κ' εἴκοσι ἔχω κλέφτης·

" Καὶ τώρα μ' ἦρθε θάνατος, καὶ θέλω ν' ἀπαιθάνω.
" Κάμετε τὸ κιβούρί μου πλατὺ, ψηλὸν νὰ γένω,
" Νὰ στέκ' ὀρθὸς νὰ πολεμῶ, καὶ δίπλα νὰ γεμίζω.
" Κι' ἀπὸ τὸ μέρος τὸ δεξὶ ἀφῆστε παραθύρι,

" Τὰ χελιδόνια νά'ρχωνται, τὴν ἄνοιξιν νὰ φέρουν,
" Καὶ τ' ἀηδόνια τὸν καλὸν Μάην νὰ μὲ μαθαίνουν."

THE TOMB OF DEMOS.

The sunk was sinking in the west,
When Demos thus his sons address'd :
" My sns your evening meal provide,
" Then come and seat ye at my side.
    " Thou, Lamprakis, hope of my race,
" There ! take my arms and fill my place.
" My sons, my much-loved sabre take ;
" Cut boughs a verdant couch to make,
    " And when upon it I am laid,
" Go, call the priest my soul to aid.
" Full fifty years my land I served,
" Nor ever from my duty swerved.
    " Prepare my tomb, and make it large ;
" Place me in act the foe to charge ;
" And in it leave a passage free,
" Where spring's sweet bird may visit me,
    " And nightingales, whose notes may bring
" The tidings of returning spring."

[To be continued.]

ON THE MUSIC OF THE ASHANTEES AND FANTEES.

[Continued from page 291.]

The following is a translation of a long Ashantee Song, with little or no air. The men sit together in a line on one side, with their sankos and other instruments; and the women in a line opposite to them. Individuals rise and advance, singing in turn *.

1st. Woman. My husband likes me too much,
He is good to me,
But I cannot like him,
So I must listen to my lover.

1st. Man. My wife does not please me,
I tire of her now;
So I will please myself with another,
Who is very handsome.

2nd. Woman. My lover tempts me with sweet words,
But my husband always does me good,
So I must like him well,
And I must be true to him.

2nd. Man. Girl, you pass my wife handsome,
But I cannot call you wife;
A wife pleases her husband only,
But when I leave you, you go to others.

SPECIMENS OF VARIOUS AIRS.

No. 15. FANTEE AIR.   *For the Oompoochwa.*

No. 16. FANTEE AIR.   *For the Bentwa.*

No. 17. ASHANTEE AIR.   *For the Bentwa.*

No. 18. MALLOWA AIR.   *For the Violin.*

The music of Empoöngwa is, generally, very inferior to that I have before noticed. The enchambee, their only peculiar instrument, resembles the mandolino, but has only five strings, made from the root of the palm-tree: the neck consists of five pieces of bamboo, to which the strings are fastened, and, slipping up and down, are easily, but not securely tuned; it is played with both hands; the tones are sweet, but have little power or variety. Long stories are recited to the enchambee in the moon-light evenings, in a sort of recitative; a favourite one, is an account of the arts by which the sun gained the ascendancy over the moon, who were first made of coeval power by their common Father.

No. 1, (which I imagine commences in F major, and ends in G major,) is an Empoöngwa air, played on the enchambee. I do not know if the inversion of words is common in their conversation, as well as in their songs. A native envies a neighbour, named Engaëlla, who has ivory to barter with a vessel.

Amorill injanja Engaëlla; impoongee m'adgillinjanja.
A brass pan he has got Engaëlla; ivory I have got none.

Here again we find *me* answer to the personal pronoun, I.

No. 1. EMPOONGWA SONG.   *For the Inchambee.*

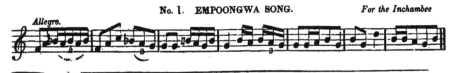

* I never heard this sung, without its recalling Horace's beautiful little dialogue ode, (9 lib. 3,) " Donec gratus eram tib'."

No. 2, in G major, is a song in which the men sing the air alone, and the women join in the chorus. It is an old one, and the subject the first appearance of a white man. One verse will be quite enough to satisfy others, and exculpate myself. At least half a dozen followed it.

Ma bengwoo   ma bengwa   baïï.
A fine strange thing, a fine strange thing, my mother.

Deboonga sai   camberwooma   mayennee.
Like the leaf of the fat tree *,   true I say,   so it is.

Sengwa moochoo,   baïï.
I make you look to-day, my mother.

Baï yangwan boonoo.
My mother fears this Fetish man.

My patience during a series of dull Empoöngwa songs, was recompensed by the introduction of a performer, as loathsome as his music was astonishing. It was a white negro from the interior country of Imbeekee; his features betrayed his race, his hair was woolly, and of a sandy colour, with thick eyebrows of the same; his eyes small, bright, and of a dark gray; the light seemed to hurt them, and their constant quivering and rolling gave his countenance an air of insanity, which was confirmed by the actions of his head and limbs, and the distortions of his mouth. His stature was middling, and his limbs very small; his skin was dreadfully diseased, and where it was free from sores, bore the appearance of being thrown on, it hung about him so loose and so shri-velled; his voice was hollow, and his laugh loud, inter-spersed with African howls. His harp was formed of wood, except that part emitting the sound, which was covered with goat skin, perforated at the bottom. The bow to which the eight strings were fixed, was consider-ably curved, and there was no upright; the figure head, which was well carved, was placed at the top of the body;

the strings were twisted round long pegs, which easily turned when they wanted tuning, and, being made of the fibrous roots of palm wine tree, were very tough, and not apt to slip. The tone was full, harmonious, and deep. He sat on a low stool, and supporting his harp on his knee and shoulder, proceeded to tune it with great nicety; his hands seemed to wander amongst the strings until he gradually formed a running accompaniment (but with little variety) to his extraordinary vociferations. At times, one deep and hollow note burst forth and died away; the sounds of the harp became broken; presently he looked up, pursuing all the actions of a maniac, taking one hand from the strings, to waive it up and down, stretching forth one leg and drawing it up again as if convulsed, lowering the harp on to the other foot, and tossing it up and down. Whilst the one hand continued playing, he wrung forth a peal which vibrated on the ear long after it had ceased; he was silent; the running accompaniments served again as a prelude to a loud reci-tative, uttered with the greatest volubility, and ending with one word, with which he ascended and descended, far beyond the extent of his harp, with the most beautiful precision. Sometimes he became more collected, and a mournful air succeeded the recitative, though without the least connexion, and he would again burst out with the whole force of his powerful voice in the notes of the Hallelujah of Handel. To meet with this chorus in the wilds of Africa, and from such a being, had an effect I can scarcely describe, and I was lost in astonishment at the coincidence. There could not be a stronger proof of the nature of Handel, or the powers of the negro.

I naturally inquired if this man was in his senses, and the reply was, that he was always rational but when he played, when he invariably used the same gestures, and evinced the same incoherency. The accompanying notes were caught whilst he was singing; to do more than set them down in their respective lengths, was impossible, and every notation must be far inadequate.

No. 2. EMPOONGWA SONG.

Andantino.

As regards the words, there was such a rhapsody of recitative, of mournful, impetuous, and exhilarated air, wandering through the life of man, throughout the animal and vegetable kingdom for its subjects, without period, without connexion, so transient, abrupt, and allegorical, that the Governor of the town could translate a line but occasionally, and I was too much possessed by the music, and the alternate rapture and phrenzy of the performer, to minute the half which he communicated. I can only submit the fragments of a melancholy and a descriptive part.

Burst of a man led to execution.

Yara yawa woo woo oh
Yawa wái yawa
What have I done? What have I done?

Bewailing the loss of his mother

Yawa gooba shangawelladi yaisa
Wo na boo, &c.
My mother dies; who 'll cry for me now
When I die? &c.

Pahmbolee gwoongee yayoo, &c.
Which path shall I seek my love?
Hark! I know now,
I hear her snap the dry sticks,
To speak, to call to me.

"Jiggledy, jiggledy, jiggledy, too too tee teo." often invaded or broke off a mournful strain; it was said to be an imitation of the note of a bird, described as the wood-pecker.

---

* The vegetable butter

No. 3. NOTES SUNG BY THE WHITE NEGRO FROM IMBERKEE.

FRENCH OPERA.

THE following notice has been issued by the administration of the *Académie Royale de Musique,* (The French Opera,) at Paris.

MEETING FOR THE PURPOSE OF DETERMINING THE PRIZES FOR LYRIC POETRY AND MUSICAL COMPOSITION.

Programme.—His Majesty, with a view to encourage Literature, and the art of Music, as it relates to the composition of pieces destined for the French Opera, decided on the 12th of October, 1824, that there should be an annual meeting, for the purpose of giving prizes for the two best works in the above classes.

First Prize of 4000 Francs.

This prize shall be awarded to the best lyric poem, in three or five acts, upon an historical, national, or imaginative subject.

The Second Prize of 2000 Francs.

This prize shall be adjudged to the best poem in one act, in the comic or pastoral style.

Conditions of the Competitions.—The style of the composition is not fixed, and the poets may adopt either the *chevaleresque,* or heroic, or that which has an affinity to comedy. The taste of the day may prefer a mixture of the two styles, as the success of many operas performed for some years past demonstrates.

A national subject may be purely historical. It may be also inventive, and without losing sight of the manners and customs of the age from which the plot is drawn. The administration will have pleasure in seeing our poets employ themselves in recalling, in such subjects as they treat of, the great actions and virtues of our kings, and the deeds that have honoured illustrious Frenchmen. But be the subject selected what it may, the first of all conditions will be, a respect for religion, monarchical principles, and morality.

Choregraphy being necessary, as well to the pomp as to the variety of performances, authors are invited to select incidents for the purpose of forming ballets. They are, however, apprized, that the administration, being obliged to limit the expense in getting up grand works, will not be able to accept such, whatever their merit may be, as will require too great a profusion of decoration, machinery, and costume.

Judgment and admission of works.—A jury, the formation of which shall be settled between this and the first of January, will pronounce upon the works sent to be examined, and will assemble in the Hotel of the Department of Fine Arts. The poems, in five acts, must be transmitted to the secretary for the above department before the first of May, 1825. Those in one act, before the first of February, in the same year.

The competitors will annex a sealed note to each piece, containing their names, titles, and residence ; and having a device, which must be repeated at the head of the manuscript.

The periods above stated will be punctiliously kept. The examination of the works and the decision of the jury will take place in the month that follows the two above-named periods.

The names of the successful authors will be published in the journals.

The pieces already accepted will be again submitted to a jury which will regulate the rank that they ought to hold. If the merit be equal, the preference will be given to the work of the oldest date.

The authors of the accepted pieces shall be free, on renouncing their acquired rights, to submit their works to competition.

Musical Composition.—Prizes equal to those awarded to the poems, shall be given to composers of music, according to the following rules :—

As soon as the poems deserving the prize shall be decided on, scenes shall be detached from them, and printed, in order to serve for the musical composition ; copies shall be delivered in at the office of the secretary of the Royal Academy of Music.

Composers who wish to compete for the prize, must transmit scenes set to music, within one month, if the poem be in one act, and within six weeks, if in three or five acts, after the opening of the meeting.

A musical jury will examine all the compositions sent, and decide by means of a ballot.

The composer who obtains the preference shall instantly be put in possession of the accepted poem. He will sign the engagement, under penalty of losing the prize, to transmit his finished score within four months after receiving the poem, if such poem do not exceed three acts, and within six months, if it is in five acts.

The prize shall be definitively assigned to the composer, after the fourth representation of the work, provided it be admitted by the musical jury that its success is undisputed, and that it has obtained the public suffrage.

Both French and Foreign composers shall be admissible as Musical competitors.

THE ROYAL SCHOOL OF MUSIC AND DECLAMATION IN PARIS.

Solemn distribution of Prizes under the presidency of M. the Viscount de la Rochefoucault.

Concert and Declamation.

M. le Viscomte de la Rochefoucault opened the sitting by a discourse, in which he congratulated the professors, the pupils of the school, and the director, M. Cherubini. This discourse was received by two rounds of applause. A passage in it appeared to announce that new and authorized measures for the promotion of the dramatic art are in preparation, which will raise the courses of declamation to the same degree of prosperity as those of musical study.

The distribution of prizes then took place. The successful candidates approached to receive their awards, in the midst of the applause of their fellow pupils, of their relations, and of the public, which always encourages rising talents, and participates in the joy of their triumph.

M. the Viscount de la Rochefoucault annexed to the prize of each pupil, a medal, on one side representing the impress of the monarch, and exhibiting on the other the elegant words in which that royal personage promised to uphold the institutions which his august brother had established.

Amongst the fortunate pupils who were more especially noticed and applauded, were young Alkan and Dejazet, both youths, who had obtained the first prizes for the piano-forte, and who have time sufficient before them to become first-rate practitioners on that instrument, should their talent grow with their growth.

The distribution of prizes was succeeded by a concert and by declamation. The concert was, as it usually is at the Conservatory, remarkable for the selection of its pieces, and the merit of the performers. The declamation excited, what it seldom does,—a feeling of interest.

MISCELLANEOUS.

THE new (Ninth) Symphony of Beethoven, composed for, and now in the possession of, the Philharmonic Society, is characterized, in a Vienna journal, as the *ne plus ultra* of this master's orchestral works, according to the unanimous opinion of the first-rate professors of that capital. In the last movement is introduced a *song !*—Schiller's famous *Ode to Joy,*—which forms a most extraordinary contrast with the whole, and is calculated to excite surprise, certainly, and perhaps admiration.

BLAHETKA, KALKBRENNER, MOSCHELES.

In the same report, which, by-the-bye, is more distinguished for bombast than any other quality, is drawn a singular parallel between the above piano-forte players, and, *mirabile dictu !* the palm of victory (*Siegespalme*) is given to Miss Leopoldine Blahetka, aged thirteen years only ; " as she combines the great qualities of both those masters, in addition to which she possesses some exclusively." Mr. Kalkbrenner, and Mr. Moscheles who visited Vienna nearly at the same time, about a year ago, are thus compared :—Kalkbrenner seems to have, with the same bravura, a greater share of " sentimentality," and Moscheles the finer tone, and more brilliancy.

Beethoven's Opera, *Mélusine,* remains in *statu quo ;* but J. N. Hummel has published a new opera, called *Mathilde de Guise.*

A posthumous work of the Abbé Vogler, a *Missa pro Defunctis,* is spoken of in all the musical journals of Germany in terms of the highest praise.

The widow of the late Nicolo Isouard is publishing a complete collection of the operas of Gluck, Sacchini, and Piccini, in score, under the title of " *Répertoire des Opéras Francais,*" though, singularly enough, the title does not contain one French name. The work has this motto, " On peut exploiter des mines précieuses dans les pays lointains ; mais n'oublions jamais les richesses que nous possédons."

J. Frey, another Paris music-seller, is about to publish, in a similar manner, at no very moderate prices, the

·scores of Mozart's operas, all of which have been brought out long ago, in most correct and elegant editions, by Simrock and Haertel, at a much lower rate. The score of *Figaro* in Frey's edition actually swarms ·with errors.

———

Signor Rossini announces likewise the intended publication of the scores of his operas, including, with those already performed, all that he is now composing, among which are named two comic operas. In addition to these are to be given to the subscribers with every opera. a book of Arietts, and Solfeggios, all by the grand Signor.
MM. Sauer and Leidesdorf are going to embark in a similar speculation ; their *Collection des Opéras de Rossini*, which they have advertised, will prove profitable only to the engravers and paper merchants.

———

The great Göethe, as he has been styled these twenty years past, has written a political satire, which Bierey has set to music, and the title of this singular joint production is this: Dämagogisch Gedicht von Göethe, fur eine Singstimme und *vier* Frösche, mit Pianoforte von Bierey, Breslau,—i. e., Demagogical Poem of Göethe for *Vox humana* and four Frogs, etc.
The words are extremely ludicrous, and, coming from Göethe, are, as a matter of course, quite original. His Excellency had better be more careful of the *four* great members of the *holy alliance.*

———

The French boast of having turned their *Code Napoléon* into verse ; but a German has achieved something much more wonderful. He has not only versified, but set to music, the whole Justinian Code of law ; and, what is more absurd, it is written with a serious view. The title of this nonsensical production is, *Römisch-Juristisches Gesangbuch. Leipzig*, 1824. Every particular chapter in the code is set to a popular melody ; for instance, the rights of persons to " *Life let us cherish,*" &c.

REVIEW OF MUSIC.

Te Deum, Jubilate, Sanctus, Kyrie Eleeson, Magnificat, et Nunc Dimittis. A Morning and Evening Church Service, *for Four Voices, with an Accompaniment for the Organ or Piano-forte, composed, and respectfully dedicated to all Choirs, by* Samuel Wesley. (Balls, 468, *Oxford Street, and* the Author, 16, *Euston Street, Euston Square.)*
English Cathedral music has hitherto required to be clad in the venerable garb of time, before it could obtain a cordial reception in our choirs. New composers are always suspected of a tendency to a kind of heterodoxy. Purcell, during his life, was thought too airy in his melody, too secular in his style, by most of the provincial churches that held an episcopal choir, and was obliged to yield to the grave counterpoint of Thomas Tallis, that
——— worthy wyght,
Who for long tyme in musick bore the bell,—
and the wailing strains of William Byrde, Richard Farrant, together with other erudite composers of the Elizabethan age, who had gained possession of the temples of worship. The masterly and charming works of Greene, Boyce, and Nares were, when first produced, declared by many to be only fit for the concert-room, and never got into general use till after their respective authors had been released from all those hopes and fears that a laudable desire for fame generates. Even now the excellent ecclesiastical compositions of Dupuis and Arnold are almost entirely confined to the royal chapel, for which establishment those works, and indeed all that we have alluded to, were officially composed.
Such being the fact, and the stimulous to the production of cathedral music being so weak, it ought to excite no wonder that so little is brought out ; in truth, it is only under peculiar circumstances, or when printed without risk by subscription, that any thing in the shape of fresh supply is offered.
The regulators of our various choirs have thus generally objected to the introduction of new music into their churches, on account of its alleged gaiety,— of its departing too widely from what they considered the standards of devotional harmony. But no such reasons can, we are persuaded, operate against the admission of the present service, for it is written according to the rules laid down in the practice, or the common law, of church composers: it is the production of one who evidently has studied Gibbons and Child, who is well acquainted with the less severe, but not less able, works of more modern masters, and has discerned the beauties of all. Hence an adherence to a style long established has been induced in Mr. Wesley, which has precluded any bold attempt at novelty, and led him into a few of those errors of emphasis that are so abundant in the early church musicians: but he has indulged in as much freedom from restraint as his well-considered plan allowed; in the *Jubilate* and evening service particularly, his Te Deum being more rigidly orthodox.
We regret that the author did not complete his work, by setting the Nicene Creed, which is sung in all cathedrals. The *Sanctus* and *Kyrie Eleeson*, both of which, on account of their brevity, should be most studiously written, are not so likely to please as the other parts of the service. We will here just observe, by the way, that Mr. W. has had the courage to correct the orthography of the word *eleeson*, which, being ἐλέησον in the Greek, (ἐλεέω,) should, in conformity to the rules of English pronunciation, always have been spelt with a double e, and not ei, as is usual. Whether this reform were now necessary, or not, may be a question.

Before offering a general opinion upon the merits of this work as a whole, we shall, in the impartial discharge of our critical duty, mention certain objections to some of its parts. In the *Gloria Patri* to the *Jubilate*, we meet with the chord of the 7th and 2nd in an extremely bare, crude state, and to our ears very cacophonous, though Dr. Blow might have enjoyed it much.—

An E flat in the penultimate bar of the same, is rather mystifying in a final cadence. In the second bar of the *Gloria Patri* to the *Magnificat*, the composer has placed himself in a dilemma, and, interpret the harmony as he

may, he will not be able to defend it by arguments drawn from either rule or effect. These, and one or two other blemishes that might have been pointed out, do not much surprise us in a work of considerable extent; such inaccuracies are often overlooked by their author, who, himself, would have been one of the foremost to perceive them in the composition of another person. The service possesses beauties that would hide numerous deformities, did they even exist: amongst its distinguishing qualities is the just expression of the words, wherein, had a man with so highly cultivated a mind as Mr. W. possesses failed, we should indeed have been disappointed, and one of our cherished theories would have been shaken. The fugal points, in which the full parts of the service abound, sing well, and are dexterously worked, particularly the peroration of the *Magnificat*; and some of the *verses* are replete with elegant, but simple harmony, which in performance must prove very delightful. With two examples of the latter we shall conclude this article. They are both for four voices—a soprano, alto, tenor, and base.

Slow. Soft Organ.

We be - lieve that Thou shalt come to be our Judge; We there - fore pray Thee, help thy Servants, whom thou hast re - deem-ed with thy pre - cious Blood.

The contrast of the following, after a strong, energetic passage, is very judicious and impressive.

Soft and Slow.

And hath ex-alt - ed hath ex - alt - ed the hum - ble the humble and meek.

and hath ex - alt - - - - - ed the

Tems Heureux, PETITE FANTAISIE *for the* PIANO-FORTE, *composed by* J. B. CRAMER, Op. 68. (J. B. Cramer, Addison, and Beale, 201, *Regent Street.*)

THIS divertissement, or *petite fantaisie*, as Mr. Cramer modestly calls it, is one of the most agreeable fruits of his genius that we have enjoyed for a long time past. It was certainly imagined in a favourable season, viewing it musically, and, judging by its suavity and calmness, we cannot but conclude that it was produced at a period of enviable moral tranquillity. So far, at least, the title is well chosen. It comprises five movements, four of which are very brief, and the fifth—or the third, in the order of arrangement—is a very charming original air, upon which the author has written six short variations, all of them strictly in character, but, notwithstanding, free from monotony, and in an engaging style. Though the extract may be thought a copious one, we shall take the liberty to insert the air in this place, as it may assist in drawing the attention of piano-forte players to the whole composition, which is exceedingly worthy the notice of all lovers of music, and is not, in point of execution, beyond the attainment of the great bulk of performers.

J. B. CRAMER'S SEQUEL *to his Celebrated Book of Instructions for the PIANO-FORTE, consisting of expressly composed and newly-arranged Pieces; each preceded by a short Prelude, fingered by the Author.* (J. B. Cramer, Addison, and Beale, 201, *Regent Street, and* Chappell and Co., 50, *New Bond Street.*)

WE congratulate all juvenile students in music on the publication of another work for their use, by so celebrated a professor as Mr. Cramer, and shall acknowledge that we have formed a very erroneous conjecture, if masters generally do not view its appearance with satisfaction, and introduce it among their younger pupils freely; for nothing flatters learners more than being set down to compositions that come out under a great name, a sort of flattery that commonly proves beneficial, by stimulating industry. But a more cogent reason for its use by teachers is, that it is calculated to inspire a pure taste, and to train the hand well for those efforts of a higher kind that are to follow.

We should say that the present work consists of six Sonatinas, were the term admissible into the nomenclature of the passing day, each of them, except the last, comprising three movements, and all accompanied by a short prelude. The author calls them *Pieces*, in compliance with the reigning fashion; so that to " speak by the card," we have here six pieces, each in three pieces. The popularity of these will not a little depend on the number of favourite airs woven into them, which, as may be supposed, are well selected, and skilfully incorporated with the various movements. Amongst them are, subjects from Haydn's symphonies; from Mozart's *Figaro, Zauberflöte,* and *Don Giovanni*; from Rossini's *Cruda Sorte,* and Weber's Overture to the *Freischütz*; from Corelli's *Follia d' Espagna,* and one of Handel's concertos; from Gluck, Pleyel, and Beethoven; together with parts of Clementi's *Chasse,* Viotti's Polacca, Arne's " Soldier tired," Scotch and Irish Melodies, &c. The work is fingered all through, and we hardly need add, in a manner that, except in few instances, will be received without hesitation, Mr. Cramer's authority being of great weight, and the excellency of his general system not to be disputed; for we judge of a tree by its fruits. Nevertheless it seems to us, that in the instances alluded to, his method will not quite accord with the rules and practice of many good masters, and that it will at least produce some discussion. This we shall not regret, for from the collision of opinions truth is sure to be elicited. The introductory Preludes are very useful, and if committed to memory, as they ought to be, being short, and simple in construction, may be rendered applicable to other compositions.

1. OVERTURE, alla Irlandese, *for the Piano-Forte, composed, selected, and arranged by* HENRY R. BISHOP, *Composer and Director of the Music to the Theatre Royal Drury Lane.* (Goulding, D'Almaine, and Co., *Soho Square.*)

2. INTRODUCTION and RONDO *for the Piano Forte, by* B. BLYTH, *Mus. Bac. Oxon* (Goulding & Co.)

3. IRISH AIR, *arranged as a RONDO for the Piano-Forte, with an Introduction, by* BURFORD G. H. GIBSONE. (Goulding and Co.)

MR. BISHOP has stooped a little, to put together what he might properly enough have named, a Medley-Overture; for this before us, *in the Irish manner,* is made up of at least nine popular Hibernian airs, scattered among three movements, forming altogether a piece of music that cannot fail of obtaining a very wide circulation, being got up with a view to please a large body of performers, particularly in the country and in schools, by its ease, simplicity, and—the nature of it being considered—we may add, good taste. Things like this are always in demand, and are generally produced by very incompetent persons: we are therefore glad when able masters condescend to employ themselves in such works of minor consideration, and rescue young practitioners out of the hands of those whose pseudo-compositions are not very likely to improve the feeling for music in youthful students.

No. 2, Mr. Blyth's Rondo, might have been called *le Papillon*, without any misnomer. It flutters about so, that it is very difficult either to find out if it have any design, or to trace its form; nevertheless it is very sparkling, and, if played by a light finger, that has a brilliant touch, will not be ineffective. The notes generally lay well under the hand, and a moderate player, having industry, may make a figure, and by no means a contemptible one, with this flighty rondo.

The Irish air chosen by Mr. Gibsone, is in itself the least meritorious part of his publication, for it is vastly common in phrase and style, and not wholly free from what savours of vulgarity; but he has introduced it in so elegant and charming a manner, and enlarged it with such musical judgment and taste, that he has converted an indifferent melody into a pleasant rondo.

1. " Venderlo sol bramo," *from Paer's Opera of Griselda, composed for the PIANO-FORTE, with* accompaniment for Flute, ad lib., *by* T. A. RAWLINGS. (J. B. Cramer, Addison, and Beale, 201, *Regent Street.*)

2. Favourite AIRS, *from Weber's Opera,* Der Freischütz, *arranged for the PIANO-FORTE, with an accompaniment for the Flute, ad lib., by* I. S. PEILE. *Books* 1, 2, and 3. (J. B. Cramer and Co.)

THE first of these publications is one of Paer's most beautiful airs, worked up into a short divertimento, and preceded by a good introduction of one page in length. The whole is rather brief, very familiar in manner, well arranged for the Piano-forte, and adapted to a numerous class of performers.

How many shapes is the *Freischütz* destined to assume? We can hardly imagine one in which it has not already appeared, except as a series of psalm-tunes; and we shall not be at all surprised to see it in the service of the church. " Why should the author of evil have all the good tunes to himself?" asked John Wesley, and immediately adapted one of his hymns to the song of *Nancy Dawson*. We hardly expected, when we first made this fine opera known to the public through the channel of the HARMONICON, that it would have put so many pens in motion, and consumed so many thousand reams of paper.

Mr. Peile has done little more than copy the airs, &c., as many had done before him; and the various adaptations are, most of them, so much alike, that it is difficult to distinguish one from the other. But in none that has come under our view, have we seen the beautiful and pathetic Cavatina, in A flat,—(see HARMONICON, No. XI.)—transposed into a key so foreign to it as that of A with three sharps, in which it now appears. Never have we met with anything of the kind half so injudicious.

C 4

It is only to be matched by the jerking *cadenza*, by which the fragment of the air given is joined—to what?—to a waltz !—to the very waltz printed in our Number IV. An amalgam of " The trumpet shall sound," and " Drops of brandy," would not have astonished us more. After this we cannot with reason complain of the mutilation which the cavatina has suffered ; for as little is retained, little is spoiled.

1. BRILLIANT RONDO *for the* PIANO-FORTE ; *the Subject in imitation of the celebrated Storm Rondo; composed by* M. C. WILSON, Op. 24. (Clementi and Co., 26, *Cheapside.*)

2. FANTASIA SCOZZESE *for the* PIANO-FORTE, *on the favourite airs of* The blue bells of Scotland, *and* Ye banks and braes of bonny Doon, *with an accompaniment for the* Flute, *ad lib. by* W. T. LING. (Gow and Son, 162, *Regent Street.*)

3. Le Sentiment d'Amour, *a familiar* DIVERTIMENTO *for the* PIANO-FORTE, *in which is introduced an admired* Irish Melody ; *composed by* J. MONRO. *(Published by the Author,* 60, *Skinner Street, Snow Hill.)*

THE admirable rondo by Steibelt has drawn forth three imitations that we have seen; perhaps there are many more. One of them was noticed in our review not long since. The present work is perceptibly modelled after *The Storm*, but not copied from that celebrated movement, and is a very clever composition, with a lively melody running through it, invigorated by some excellent modulations, and diversified by many brilliant passages, that require certain powers of execution, but are not unconquerably difficult for the better order of performers. One of these, in E flat, at page 3, is not the less classical for resembling in some degree an exercise by Cramer. We doubt whether imitations are likely to answer a composer's purpose, if he have profit in view : reputation undoubtedly is to be gained by such a publication as the present, and we shall hope soon to see some works more strictly original by the same author.

It does not follow that because everybody possesses the *Blue Bells of Scotland* by Griffin, and the *Banks of the Doon* by Steibelt, they should not be reset by as many as may choose to compete for public favour with those composers : on the contrary, we are glad to see others enter the lists ; for honourable rivalry, though now and then dangerous, is generally productive of some good. We have examined Mr. Ling's Fantasia without any invidious comparison, and wish that he had delayed the publication of it, not for nine years, according to the precept which Horace gives to poets, but nine months; he then most probably would have revised, and might have improved it. Parts of it are good, but the harmony in many places is rather erroneous, and not very pleasant to the ear ; for instance—

PAGE 8.

AND PAGE 11.

Altogether it appears to us, that Mr. L. would ultimately be better pleased with his own efforts, if he kept his manuscripts longer on his table, and sent fewer of them to the engraver.

The Irish air in Mr. Monro's divertimento is, " My lodging is on the cold ground," which is indeed very familiar to every body; and he has made no stranger of it by any of his additions. It is followed by the *Isleworth Waltz*, and would have been complete had it been preceded by the *Brentford-Butts March*.

1. Mnemosyne, *an* AIR *with* VARIATIONS *for the* PIANO-FORTE, *composed by* J. A. MORALT. (Monro and May, 11, *Holborn Bars.*)

2. ROMANCE, *with* Variations *for the* PIANO-FORTE, *composed by* AUGUSTUS MEVES. *(By the same.)*

3. INTRODUCTION, *and the popular French* AIR, " *C'est l'Amour,*" *arranged as a* RONDO *for the* PIANO-FORTE, *by* S. POOLE. *(By the same.)*

4. INTRODUCTION, *and the celebrated Irish Melody,* " The Bower of Eveleen," *arranged with* VARIATIONS *for the* PIANO-FORTE, *by* S. POOLE. *(By the same.)*

FROM the title of No. 1, and an inspection of the Air and its Variations, we are led to conclude, that Mr. Moralt is not a little indebted to memory for the materials of which his present production is composed.

The Romance by Mr. Meves is quite a bagatelle, and intended, we presume, for only very young performers.

No. 3 is an extremely easy adaptation of the French Air printed in the third number of this work, accompanied by an unvaried succession of triplets in the base ; but it is short, and may suit very young learners.

No. 4 pretends to something more than the former, by the same, and therefore compels us to say that it will not bestow on the Author any very splendid reputation as a composer.

BEETHOVEN'S OVERTURE TO EGMONT, *arranged for the* Piano Forte, *with accompaniments of* Violin, Flute, *and* Violoncello, *by* I. MOSCHELES. (J. B. Cramer, Addison, and Beale, 201, *Regent Street.*)

OF the music to Goëthe's *Egmont*, set by Beethoven, nothing is known in this country, except the overture, which was performed some years ago at the Philharmonic Society, and by its grandeur and originality excited the warmest admiration in all true connoisseurs of German music, and has never since failed to produce the same result. It was immediately arranged as a duet for the piano-forte by Mr. Watts, and widely circulated in that form. It is now adapted for quartett parties, to whom, in

present state, it will be a valuable acquisition; but it
ay be performed on the piano-forte, divested of the ac-
mpaniments, with very good, though certainly not with
ual, effect.

M. Moscheles has arranged this overture so as to omit
thing essential in the harmony: he could not make it
sy to execute, but has not crowded it unnecessarily with
tes, and it is in a very practicable form. The accom-
niments are free from all difficulty.

We shall not be expected to enter now into the merits
so well-known a composition; but as a specimen of the
anner in which it is arranged, and to give such of our
aders as may not happen to be acquainted with it, a
gle passage as a sample of the whole, we insert the fol-
wing few bars:—

1. HUMMEL's OVERTURE, Helen and Paris, *arranged for*
Two performers *on the* Piano-forte, *by* W. WATTS. (J. B.
Cramer, Addison, and Beale, 201, *Regent Street.*)

2. " Oft in the stilly night," *from Moore's National Melodies, arranged with* Variations *for* Two Performers *on
the* Piano-forte, *by* FERDINAND RIES, Op. 136, No 1.
(J. Power, 34, *Strand.*)

3. DUET *for the* Piano-forte, *selected and arranged from
the* Der Freischütz *of* C. M. von Weber, *by* SAMUEL
WEBBE. No. 1. (J. B. Cramer, Addison, & Beale, 201,
Regent Street.)

4. *A selection from C. M. von Weber's Opera*, Der Freischütz, *arranged as* DUETS *for* Two Performers *on the*
Piano-forte, *by* J. C. NIGHTINGALE, *Organist of the
Foundling Hospital.* Set 1. (Monro and May, 11, *Holborn Bars.*)

THE opening of Hummel's Overture, an *andante* of one
page, is an elegant and delightful movement, that must
succeed in pleasing all who have an excitable taste for the
art. Those whose feelings are not touched by it, may
be assured that they have no taste at all in music. The
rest of this composition, which is of course the greater
part of it, is a very brilliant *allegro*, in an extremely popular style, divested of those scientific modulations and
difficult passages that so frequently are found in the productions of this celebrated author, and quite adapted to
the most numerous class of amateurs. Indeed it is so
devoid of demisemiquavers and even semiquavers,—there
not being more of both together than of pages,—that it
looks more simple in construction, and more easy to execute, than it really turns out to be. This overture is very
well arranged, a praise that is due to all the publications of Mr. Watts; which consist wholly, we believe, of
adaptations.

No. 2 is an easy work by Mr. Ries. The air has all
the charms that tranquillity of strain can produce, and
the variations are in character with the subject; except
the second, a *vivace*, which is entirely out of place, and
will be at once discarded by those whose sentiments are
in unison with ours on this point. The rest of this duet
is very pleasing, and may be placed before almost any
performer.

Nos. 3 and 4 bring *Der Freischütz* once again into our
view. Mr. Webbe has chosen two subjects for his short
duet, that are less popular in their style than most of the
airs in the opera, but not without the peculiarity of character which distinguishes M. Von Weber from all contemporary composers.

Mr. Nightingale has selected the Jaeger, or Hunts-
men's, and the Nuptial choruses, together with the
March *; three of the most favourite pieces in the *Freischütz*, and has put them into an exceedingly easy form.

* See Numbers VI. and XXI. of the HARMONICON.

FOREIGN MUSICAL REPORT.

BERLIN.—The performances at the Opera during the present season have been *Il Barbiere*, by Rossini; *Die Waise und der Mörder* (the Orphan and the Assassin); *Die Hottentottin*, by M. Benelli; *Kiaking*, the music by Girowetz, the ballet by Titus; *Hamlet*, the music by K. von Miltitz; *Die Galeerensklaven*, by Schubert; *Jean de Paris*, by Boieldieu; *Preciosa*, by M. von Weber; *Die Unterbrochene Opferfest*, (the Interrupted Sacrifice,) by Winter; *Joseph en Egypte*, by Mehul; *Richard Cœur de Lion*, by Gretry; *Der Freischütz;* and *Die Falsche Prima Donna*, (the False Prima Donna,) by Ignatz Schuster.

The only novelty in this theatre, for so it may be called, was the revival of the celebrated and long-wished-for opera, the *Matrimonio Secreto* of Cimarosa. Too long have our boards been occupied by objects of inferior value, to the exclusion of many of the master-pieces of the art; and it is a subject of great satisfaction to the friends of genuine music, to see that the managers have had the courage to break through the general routine of stage performances, in order to make place for works of a loftier character. But, at the same time that we applaud the spirit which has led the conductors to revive this ornament of the old school, we cannot help offering a few remarks upon the manner in which it has been brought out. In the first place, we cannot agree with the director of the music relative to the time which he has chosen for the various movements of the opera; nor, in the next place, can we feel satisfied with the omissions that have been made, for instance, of the beautiful duet in C, in the first act, and particularly of the admirable tenor air in E flat, in the second act. Not satisfied with this, the three female singers also were allowed to spare themselves the trouble of learning the airs allotted to their parts in the second act, and we were obliged to rest satisfied with that of the Count only, with which we could have willingly dispensed. Hence we had the *Matrimonio Secreto*, without either soprano or tenor air! Could Cimarosa know this fact, he would not rest at peace in his grave. It is to be hoped that, for the future, the directors will be careful not to fall into blunders like these, which cannot but prove injurious to themselves, and offensive to the good taste of the public. No reasons can justify such liberties taken with a work of classical authority, whatever may be done in the instance of the ephemeral productions of the day.

MUNICH.—The last representation for the season, at the Royal Theatre here, took place in July. The whole of the representations given were thirty-seven in number. It cannot be denied that the *opera buffa* of the Italians, from its fire, its vigour, and the wonderful precision with which the performers act up to each other, possesses a charm peculiarly its own, as we have lately had occasion to witness in the performance of *Il Barbiere*, *La Cenerentola*, *L'Italiana in Algeri*, *La Repressaglia*, &c. But if we look at the serious operas, also, we see abundant occasion for the most exquisite enjoyment. If we had reason to be delighted with Signora Fenzi in the characters of *Semiramide*, and *Elcia* in the *Mosè*, we had no less cause to be satisfied, and even to be still more charmed, with Signora Lalande.

This great singer appeared in both the parts above mentioned, as well as in the character of Donna Anna, in *Don Giovanni*, of Ninetta, in *La Gazza Ladra*, as well as in the characters of *Elisabetta* and *Agilda*. Her expressive style of acting is no less admirable than her singing, and whenever she appeared, she was hailed with the most enthusiastic applause. The concerts given here have presented no novelties. If we might be allowed to venture our opinion, we should say that, admirable as is the manner in which instrumental pieces are performed, and judicious as is the selection made, including most of what is new, and all that is excellent in this department of the art, yet we could wish to see this taste rather less exclusive. Surely that noblest of all instruments, the human voice, might be allowed a more exalted place on these occasions, without being deemed an intruder!

DARMSTADT.—Four operas have been produced here, new to this place, *Climene*, by Kapellmeister Wagner; *Merope*, by Kapellmeister Mangold; *Der Freischütz;* and the *Olimpia* of Spontini. *Euryanthe* is also on the list of operas to be given.

BRESLAU.—This place possesses an able musician, in Kapellmeister Schnabell, and an excellent musical director in M. Berner, both of whom are indefatigable in their exertions for the interests of the art. There is here, besides an institution for church music, a *Singverein* (Song Association), by which occasional concerts are given. In the former, the town possesses a very superior organist in Berner; indeed he may with justice be said to rank among the first professors on that instrument of the present day. Kapellmeister Schnabel presides in the cathedral choir, where he has produced many masses of his own composition, which have been deservedly admired, particularly one in A flat major, which is remarkable notonly for the beauty of its song and splendid organ accompaniment, but also from the peculiarity of the circumstances under which it was composed. During the time this place was attacked by the French, the composer and his family were obliged for a time to seek shelter in a deep cellar, where he beguiled the melancholy hours by the composition of this mass.

In the vocal institution, M. Berner is the director, and gives instruction in song, as well as lectures upon composition. Besides this, M. Freudenberg has instituted an academy for music, upon a new system, which has created a great sensation here. The professor lately gave two public examinations of his pupils, in which satisfactory proofs were offered of the proficiency of the scholars in playing, as well as in composition. The first class, after affording a proof of their perfect acquaintance with the rudiments of the art, showed their practical knowledge by putting a given theme into four parts.

With respect to the concerts, they are led by both the professors, and are chiefly composed of amateurs and dilettanti. Every praise is due for the great correctness with which the music is given, but still it cannot be denied that the finish observable in the better orchestras of Germany, is here wanted; that delicate tint of colouring with which the different parts of a musical picture are made to harmonize together, and which, by happily blending softness and power, produces the perfection of the art. In the last concert performed here, Beethoven's symphony, entitled *Meerestille und Glückliche fahrt*, (The Stillness of the Sea and the Happy Voyage,) was performed with much effect, and in a manner that augured well for the future fame of

Breslau in instrumental music. It is to be regretted that there is not a single lady here to enliven these concerts by her voice, which cannot but seem dreary when that charm is wanting. Probably this defect may be owing to a want of good professors hitherto to give a finish to singing: but it is cheering to know that this defect will soon be remedied.

We must not forget to mention that M. Berner has been for several years past occupied with several interesting theoretical works, some of which we may hope shortly to see laid before the public. He is, besides, the author of various cantatas, and has produced many valuable compositions for the piano.

In the villages around Breslau, music is every where cultivated, particularly that of the sacred kind. Many of the churches have very respectable choirs, where some of the best compositions are occasionally attempted. Nothing is more common than to hear charming national airs in several parts sung by the peasantry, which prove a delightful solace to them after the labours of the day.

GRETZ.—Music continues to gain ground in this town, and to count in its lists an increasing number of votaries. The company of singers here is effective, and the following operas have been performed in a manner not unworthy of theatres of greater eminence: the *Italiana in Algeri, Jean de Paris, Otello, Il Barbiere di Siviglia, La Gazza Ladra, Der Freischütz, Joseph et ses Freres, Cenerentola,* and Paer's *Sargino.* With respect to this latter opera, we cannot but remark, *en passant,* that the whole composition is replete with truth and beauty, and is full of tender romantic effects, which were well preserved in the admirable acting of M. Yäger. The cantilena that reigns throughout this opera is delicious, and bears all the character of having emanated at once from the heart, and its colouring is that of a masterly picture drawn from nature herself.

MILAN.—There has lately appeared here a new opera from the pen of the young composer Soliva, entitled *Elena e Malvina.* This composer is already known by his opera *Il Capo di Ferro,* a composition which he produced immediately on quitting the Conservatory, where he had distinguished himself with much honour. Every one recognised in the young composer no common knowledge of music; his name became at once established, and his talents were immediately called into action in a foreign country. Arrived on the banks of the Vistula, he there ranked among the first professors, and, on his return to his own country, gave proofs that his time had been well employed, and that he was still more deeply skilled in the mysteries of the art. Of this abundant evidence was afforded in the opera abovementioned. Not that we mean to assert that the opera is of the first class, or even attractive as a whole, or that its originality is such as not to allow frequent imitations to be recognised; but the merit of a well-arranged combination of harmonies cannot be denied it, as well as many new forms of melody, and ornaments which are to be allowed a composer, provided they do not degenerate into extremes. In the introduction to the first act, the only objection that can be advanced, is its unreasonable length. The excellencies are conspicuous, in a terzetto, a duet, and in the finale, though not in an equal degree. The first act met with considerable applause, but the composer risked much in extending his subject to so unconscionable a length; for a space of two whole hours is surely enough to try the patience of the most indulgent audience. Composers, and all who exercise their talents for the amusement of the public, should bear strongly in mind, that the delight which, like eternal talkers, they feel in hearing themselves, without ever being fatigued, cannot be transferred to the hearers. We observed that this prolixity arose from a repetition of the same motivos, of which the composer seems so much in love, that he cannot for his heart separate from them. In this respect Rossini surpasses all his brethren. This prolixity might be pardoned, if it were limited to simple airs merely; but when it extends to duets, terzetts, quartetts, quintetts, &c., so that the principal subject is only served up again in a variety of shapes, the patience of the most indulgent is put to a test which it requires more than mortal endurance to support. Experience has taught us, that an act which exceeds an hour creates displeasure, one of an hour and a half fatigue, and above two hours ennui and disgust.

The second act has the advantage of being shorter than the first, but with the exception of the duet between Elena and Malvina, it did not produce any very great effect. The performers exerted themselves on this occasion in the most praiseworthy manner, particularly Madame Belloc, Signora Festa, and Signor Galli; the voice and acting of the latter is above all praise.

FLORENCE.—*Teatro della Pergola.* The company at present here consists of *Prima Donna,* Adelaide Tosi; *Musico,* Gio. Battista Velluti; *Tenor,* Domenico Reina; *Bass,* Luigi Biondini. The first opera given was Mayer's *Ginevra di Scozia,* in which, according to the very laudable and consistent practice, now so prevalent, many pieces of music foreign to the piece were introduced. But after all it did not please, and particularly as the principal singer, Velluti, was indisposed, and sung wretchedly out of tune. After this was given Mayerbeer's *Crociato in Egitto* [*], which was brought out by the master himself, and enriched with a new duet. This opera was received with great *furore;* during the first three evenings, the composer was regularly summoned to make his appearance at least four times during the course of the piece, in order to receive the congratulations of a very full house. The singers were also called to share the same tribute of applause; nay more, we are assured that, on the first evening, the *impressario* himself was destined to partake of the same honours.

Among the singers, the great favourite is the Signora Tosi, of whom the public form the greatest hopes, and who had the good fortune to enjoy, during a whole year, the instruction and advice of one of the greatest singers of the age, the Chevalier Crescentini. Her advantages are many, both as to voice and person; the former is of the soprano kind, impressive, sonorous, and of very considerable compass; the latter is full of beauty, accompanied with great grace and modesty of deportment.

Lord Burghersh, His Britannic Majesty's Minister at this place lately gave a grand fête here: part of the amusements consisted of an opera composed by himself, in which Signora Tosi, Signori Velluti, Reina, &c., performed.

VENICE.—The season here began with the *Zelmira* of Rossini, which, however, obtained but little success; it

* See page 2.

D 2

was followed by the general substitute of this composer's failures, *Il Barbiere*, which was very effectively performed, and succeeded in soothing the disappointment felt in the instance of the other opera. After this was given the *Adelina* of Generali, which is rather a favourite. But the great attraction has been the *Crociato in Egitto*, a new opera by Mayerbeer, and which was received with great *furore*. We shall find an early opportunity of giving more particulars of this masterly composition *.

AMSTERDAM.—We hear that a considerable improvement has been effected by an artist of this city in the French horn. He has contrived a mode, by which a transition into a variety of keys can be expeditiously effected. This was formerly managed by means of additional pieces which were screwed on or off as circumstances required; it is now effected without the necessity of having recourse to these means. This will be of great consequence in the orchestra, as it will prevent the interruptions necessarily attendant on the present method.

—— The German theatre in this city is ordered to be shut, by a decision of the authorities. A quarrel between two female performers has occasioned this measure. The last songstress engaged by the manager excited the jealousy of the *donna*, who had long held possession of the public favour. The partizans of these ladies became violent: an obstinate conflict took place in the theatre, and the sub-director of the local police, assisted by a great number of his agents, attempted in vain to quell the tumult: it became necessary, therefore, to introduce soldiers into the pit, and force the combatants out of the doors.—— The new singer, who was thus opposed, possesses real talent, and a brilliant voice; but she is a native of Holland, and the amateurs, most of whom are of German origin, refuse to listen to any performer who is not of that nation.

MALTA.—The celebrated Sigmund Von Praun—at present a Roman Count, and Knight of several orders, possessor of various prize medals, and member of several philharmonic academies—who, from his earliest years, attracted the attention of the fashionable world, by his acquirements, and his wonderful progress in the arts and sciences, has been equally successful in the field of music, and has acquired the reputation of being one of the first violinists of our time. He lately paid a visit to this island, and afforded the friends of music a great treat. He gave three concerts, two in the royal theatre, and one in the Palazzo Castiglioni. The loud applause with which he was greeted, was a proof of the enthusiasm which he had awakened in the audience. On the second evening, at the conclusion of a concerto which had called forth all his talents, a crown of laurel was contrived to be lowered down upon his head, and a printed ode, composed by the poet Cesare Vassalo, was circulated about the saloon. Some *dilettanti* have not hesitated to declare that, in the youthful Praun, Paganini has no mean rival of his fame. We learn that this artist is about to proceed on his musical travels.

PARIS.—The *Sacrifice Interrompu* having been frequently interrupted by the colds of M. Leon, the manager has struck at the root of the evil, by obtaining from the authors permission to suppress the part of the *Ecuyer*, which he performed. These gentlemen made no difficulty in acceding to the sacrifice, and, what is singular, the public has never perceived this double excision.

The dilettanti of the Louvois are all in rapture: Rossini is at last named manager of the *Théâtre Italien*. It is affirmed that the first act of authority exhibited by the *Maestro* was to propose an engagement to Madame Rossini, who offered no objection to its acceptance:—" *Women, be subject unto your husbands.*"

—— M. Cherubini has just given in his resignation. MM. Lesueur, Berton, and Boieldieu have given in theirs; we have reason to fear the departure of the latter for Russia. What in the meanwhile will become of the *Ecole Royale de Musique?* There is no other hope but in the interference of the august protector of the arts. An ordinance, which he has condescended to issue, is said to furnish a favourable augury in this matter.

—— In order to make M. Habeneck a proper compensation for the flourishing state in which he has left the Opera, in regard to the singing strength of the house, the *Minister de la Maison Royale* has just appointed him joint director with M. Cherubini of the *Ecole Royale de Musique*. He thus suddenly becomes the leader of the Lesueurs, Bertons, Boieldieus, Kreutzers, Baillots, Plantades, &c, It is moreover said, that M. Habeneck, impressed with all the importance of the place which he is about to occupy, has solicited permission from the minister to be admitted as a pupil into MM. Reicha's and Fetis' classes of counterpoint and fugue, and into that of superior composition under the control of MM. Berton, Lesueur, and Boieldieu*.

—— Zuchelli has appeared again in *La Cenerentola*, since his return from Italy. His excellent intonation and taste, the gaiety and originality of his acting, are as highly appreciated as ever.

—— The jury of the opera † have received unanimously the music of *Pygmalion*, composed by M. Halévy, a pupil of M. Cherubini, who gained a prize at Rome, and whose talents are full of the most brilliant promise. The authors of the words have added new characters to the lyric scenes of J. J. Rousseau, and introduced more action.

—— Signora Schiasseti has appeared in the character of *Isabella* in *L'Italiana in Algeri*: her success was great, but Mlle. Cinti is still remembered in the same with pleasure. Zuchelli is admirable in the part of *Mustapha*, and makes us forget Galli.

Curioni continues to perform, and has often appeared as *Osiride* in *Mosè*, with some success; but he is not very popular here as a singer. Mad. Mombelli, who pleases so much in the *Cenerentola*, does not produce any effect in the part of *Elicia*. The serious opera is not calculated for her voice.

—— M. Cherubini is about to revive a comic opera composed by him twenty years ago. The drama is to be written by MM. Scribe and Mellesville, who have already had joint interviews with M. Cherubini on the subject.

—— M. Habeneck, Director of the Opera, it is said, will soon be allowed to retire.

---

* This severe sarcasm will doubtless be understood by the English reader. (*Ed. Har.*)

† At the *Académie Royale de Musique*, the pieces offered to the theatre are examined and judged by a certain number of officers attached to the establishment, who form a *Jury*. This English word is now adopted in France.

---

* See page 2.

DER FREISCHÜTZ.

PARIS, Dec. 8.—The famous opera of Weber, the *Frei-schütz*, was yesterday brought out at the Odéon, under the name of *Robin des Bois.* It is unnecessary to dwell upon the absurdity of the work as a drama; the public here did justice to it, by condemning it. Of the music we must acknowledge that it should be heard oftener than once to be comprehended. The overture, some agreeable airs, and above all the chorus of hunters in the third act, were much applauded; but in general the pieces are long, and want melody.

[Such is the opinion which some of the Parisians have formed of this admirable opera! Our correspondent, however, condemnatory as he is of it on the whole, al-lows it more merit than most of the French journals dis-cover. And yet they can find nothing but *transcendent* beauties in *La Cenerentola*, and in *L'Italiana in Algeri!*

But upon the subject of this Opera, the French are not unanimous in opinion, as will appear from the following notice of it, written by a gentleman who unites in himself, what are rarely found in the same person, musical know-ledge and literary ability, and published in a Paris Journal of the most extensive circulation.—ED. HARM.]

"As to the music, there is but one opinion of its ad-mirable beauty and pure simplicity; the ear, accustomed to the noisy bursts and irregular accompaniments of Ros-sini, is sweetly and deliciously soothed by the gentlest concords, and by airs of combined harmony and melody, and yet suited to the situations. The composer, accord-ing to the example of Mozart, whom he appears to have taken for a model, never forgets that he writes for the stage, and rather endeavours to excite various feelings than to heap notes upon one another, thrown together al-most by mere hazard.

"If the music of the *Freischütz* can triumph over the words which it has to encounter, there is no doubt that it will be successful, and give rise to serious reflections amongst those musicians who have tied themselves to the chariot of Rossini. In this music, we may seek in vain for that contemptible profusion of deafening notes, for those unmeaning flourishes, and that continued use of the vulgar *crescendo*, which serve uselessly to swell out the scores of the Italian Orpheus. The Orchestra of the Ger-man master is full and well supplied; his musical edifice is placed firmly upon its foundation; and all the parts are scientifically finished, and not sacrificed to external ornaments.

"Still he knows how to do homage to grace, to that grace which in all the arts is inseparable from purity and real beauty of form; that grace which may be dis-cerned in the severe architecture of Greek and Roman ruins, and not that which allies itself with the irregular boldness of the middle ages; the grace, in short, of Gluck, of Haydn, and of Winter, of which so little is to be found in the works of Rossini. The overture to this Opera, which intimidates private piano-forte-players, is very fine, with the orchestra; and the learned author has introduced, with much art and felicity, the *motivos* of the different pieces in his work. The most remarkable of these are, an air for a tenor, full of fascination and sorrow; a de-licious duet for female voices, which might well be attri-buted to Mozart; a polacca, an admirable prayer, also for a female voice; a trio, and all the choruses, of which those of the hunters, and of the young companions of the bride, are especially worthy of notice.

"The finale of the second act is of a kind quite new,

and the musician has converted to his advantage, with all the boldness of genius, a situation which placed at his dis-posal only two singers and a subterranean choir. He appears even to have voluntarily imposed upon himself a further difficulty, by making one of the characters sing very little, and confining the other to recitative—all the interest is concentrated in the terrific infernal symphony, which paints wth irresistible force the convulsions of na-ture, shaken by the conflict of the contending powers, the resistance of the demons to a mortal armed with magic strength, and the disorders of living beings, and of the elements, on each new concession obtained by the conju-ration of the huntsman.

"Such is the impetuosity of movement in this passage, that it begins in C, and after having confounded the senses by a bold succession of all the modulations, and run through all the major and minor keys, it ends in A sharp; and yet all is connected with perfect art; nor does the composer seem to have felt a moment's hesitation, or difficulty. The rests in this symphony are not like several similar passages in Rossini, mere blank spaces in-terposed between different keys. Weber has no need of these petty artifices of a harmonist not sure of his science. These rests are destined to mark, by the vigorous chords which follow them, the casting of each bullet, as it is forced by magic from the infernal spirits."

MUSICAL FESTIVAL AT WAKEFIELD AND NEWCASTLE.

THE performances at Wakefield in October were really splendid; the selections nearly the same as those at York last year. The chorusses were admirably performed, and the best judges allowed that they had never been exceeded as to accuracy and spirit of execution. The receipts will barely cover the expenses, a result which was fully anticipated, and excited, therefore, no disappointment. The performers were, Mrs. Salmon, Miss Stephens, Miss Travis, Messrs. Braham, Vaughan, Terrail, Phillips, and Isherwood. Dr. Camidge was at the organ, and Mr. Knapton at the piano-forte. The leaders were Messrs. Mori and White.

The number altogether was—Principal vocal, 8; So-pranos, 24; Altos, 18; Tenors, 20; Basses, 24—94 *Vocal.*—Violins, 24; Violas, 10; Violoncellos, 8; Double Basses, 8; Wind Instruments, &c.—85 *Instrumental*; Total 179.

The NEWCASTLE MEETING did not go off very bril-liantly: Mr. Sapio, and M. and Mad. de Begnis were absent from ill health, and the chorusses were very mea-gre and inefficient. Madame Catalani was allowed to sing "He was despised" in the key of G; and "The Lord shall reign" was actually transposed into B flat, to suit her voice! This meeting was *farmed* by M. Valle-breque. The chief performers were Madame Catalani, Mrs. Salmon, Miss Stephens, Miss Goodall; Messrs. Terrail, Bedford, and Phillips. Organ, Mr. Thompson: Conductor, Sir G. Smart; Leader, Mr. Mori. The whole together amounted to only one hundred and eight per-sons, viz.

Principal Vocal, 9; Sopranos, 17; Altos, 8; Tenors, 12; Basses 18—64 *Vocal.*—Violins, 16; Violas, 4; Vio-loncellos, 5; Double Basses, 4; Hautboy, 1!! Other wind Instruments, 16—44 *Instrumental*; Total, 108.

D 3

EDINBURGH MUSICAL FESTIVAL,

FOR THE BENEFIT OF THE PUBLIC CHARITIES.

THIS festival took place in October last, commencing on the evening of the 25th, and terminating on the 30th. Three morning performances were given at the Parliament-house, and three evening concerts at the Theatre Royal. The former consisted of the *Creation*, the *Messiah*, and the *Mount of Olives*, together with a selection from the sacred compositions of Mozart, &c., and including the most admired songs, and the double choruses from *Israel in Egypt*, and *Judas Maccabeus*. The evening performances comprised some of the finest orchestral compositions, symphonies, overtures, &c., of Haydn, Mozart, Beethoven, Romberg, Rossini, Cherubini, and Weber: with solos, concertos, &c., by the chiefs of the various instruments.

The principal vocal performers were Madame Ronzi de Begnis, Miss Stephens, Miss Goodall, Miss Travis; Messrs. Braham, Vaughan, Bellamy, Phillips, Terrail, Swift, and Signor de Begnis. Mr. Yaniewiez led the band, occasionally assisted by Mr. Loder; and Sir G. Smart conducted. The numbers in the Orchestra were as follows:—Principal Vocal, 11; Chorus, 72; Violins, 21; Violas, 6; Violoncellos, 6; Double Basses, 5; Wind Instruments, &c., 16; Total, 137.

Sets of six tickets were sold at three guineas; single tickets, fifteen shillings.

The various performances gave, upon the whole, general satisfaction; but the grand festival at York last year, and the more recent one at Wakefield, had taught many of the northern amateurs, on the present occasion, to be somewhat fastidious; it was, therefore, discovered that the voices in the choruses were not well equalized, and that this important department did not produce effects so grand and striking as those which were fresh in the memories of many of the audience. A trashy song or two, and the eternal repetition of the same airs in London, and in the country, are very justly censured by a writer in an Edinburgh journal, where we find some excellent remarks on the above meeting. These, however, are mixed up with a little too much unction; and the detached notices of individual performers, which, by-the-bye, had appeared before, are quite *de trop*.

At a meeting of the Directors of this Festival, held on the 3d of Dec., the treasurer presented a detailed report of his accounts, of which the following is the result:—Receipts, 4,940*l.* 4*s.* 10*d.*; Expenses, 4,397*l.* 18*s.* 11*d.*; Balance, 542*l.* 5*s.* 11*d.*

❧ The Drama.

DRURY LANE THEATRE.

ON the first of last month, Mr. Sapio, a vocal performer who has been highly distinguished as a concert singer during the last four or five years, made his first appearance on any stage, at this theatre, as the *Seraskier*, in *The Siege of Belgrade*. The musical talents of this gentleman have for some time past been held in high estimation; his fame preceded him to the profession he has joined, and it devolved upon him less to acquire a new reputation, than to sustain that which he had already gained. His voice is a rich, low tenor, round in its tones, smooth, very musical, and powerful enough for any legitimate purpose. It has, perhaps, rather a tendency to the guttural, but this incli-

nation may be combatted, and finally overcome; we therefore do not set it down as an established defect. That which we always most admired in Mr. Sapio, was the chasteness of his style, and we trust that he will not now be led away by gallery applause to forfeit the good opinion which, for these qualities, he has gained with all real admirers and connoisseurs of song. " It would be curious indeed," says a judicious weekly paper, " if a singer, signalized in the concert room, by justness of conception, correctness of taste, and a freedom from the claptraps of violent transition and florid ornament, should be emulous of displaying them [the two latter] on the stage." Let him reject every invitation to indulge in meretricious finery that is offered him by the praise of those whose applause is censure; let him trust in the efficacy of that correct and finished style, for which he has hitherto been approved, and he will carry the public with him, even that portion of it which is now most deficient in real taste.

As an actor his pretensions are considerable; his speaking voice is clear and audible, and his delivery correct and impressive. His figure is good, and his deportment manly and engaging: there is a gentleman-like propriety in his tone and action on the stage which denotes the habits of good society; and this Mr. S. may be assured is not the least valuable of the many qualifications he possesses. His debut was most successful; he has at once taken the highest station, and is likely to maintain it. On the 12th Mr. Sapio appeared as *Prince Orlando*, in the *Cabinet*, and was quite successful. " Some called," says a daily paper, " for the *polacca* a third time, but the singer, with more good sense than singers usually evince, merely came forward, bowed, and retired. The manager, however, was determined to have it again; and the scene was left standing till his object was accomplished." On the 22d he performed the character of *Henry Bertram*, in *Guy Mannering*, and introduced " Oft in the stilly night," one of Moore's melodies, with great applause. A failure in a high note, in " Scots, wha ha' wi' Wallace bled," alarmed himself and his friends, but without any just cause. We hope, however, that it will induce him to economise his powers a little; we admire energy, but have no taste for mere physical force of voice.

COVENT GARDEN THEATRE.

One of the most delightful of Shakspeare's comedies, *As you like it*, was brought out in an operatical form at this house on Thursday, December 9th. This is really the most injudicious of all the attempts that have been made to convert Shakspeare's dramas into sing-song plays. In former instances there was something in the shape of excuse: the *Comedy of Errors* is extravagant, the *Two Gentlemen of Verona* is tedious and uninteresting; and even *Twelfth Night* is tiresome in scenes " where the actors are the laughers, instead of the audience." But in *As you like it*, the profanation is unpardonable: in fable, poetry, and incident—in variety and contrast of character, it is rich, almost beyond compare, and no play leaves on the mind a stronger impression of delight. Of the new music by Bishop, we shall soon have to speak in our review, we, therefore, will not enter upon it here. The pieces by Dr. Arne were those that carried away all the applause, and most deservedly they are admired. Two of them we have inserted in the musical part of the present number; they were enthusiastically received by the audience, and will always be heard with pleasure, because formed of materials that never fade.

THE

HARMONICON.

No. XXVI., February, 1825.

MEMOIR OF A. E. M. GRÉTRY.

Andrè Ernest Modeste Gretry (member of the French National Institute, Inspector of the *Conservatoire* of Music, and member of the Philharmonic Academy of Bologna) was born at Liége, the 11th of February, 1741. " The first lesson in music I received," says he, " nearly cost me my life. I was alone at four years old, when the boiling of an iron pot attracted my attention ; I began dancing to the music of this *drum ;* afterwards wishing to see how it was produced in the vessel, I overturned it into a very hot fire, and the explosion was so great, that I was scalded all over, and nearly suffocated. Ever since that accident my sight has been weak."

After his recovery, his father gave him, at the age of six years, a music-master, and wished to make him one of the children of the choir. " Since miserable children have existed, no one," he says, " was ever so miserable as I, abandoned to the power of the most barbarous music-master that ever lived."

Grétry afterwards relates an accident, which, he thinks, gave his mind a musical bias. We will pass his own words, observing, that Grétry is not a writer of the first rank. The same individual never possesses all the gifts of heaven, in an equal degree ; yet we are often struck by the tone of simplicity, candour, and good nature of his recitals.

" In my country, they tell children that God will not refuse them any thing they ask of him on the day of their first communion. I had for a long while resolved to ask him that I might die on the day of that august ceremony, if I were not destined to become an honest man, and one distinguished in my station. On that very day I was nearly killed. Having gone into a tower to witness the striking of *the wooden bells,* of which I had no idea, a beam, which weighed three or four hundred pounds, fell upon my head. I was knocked down senseless. The churchwarden ran for the extreme unction ; in the mean time, I came to myself, but I hardly recollected where I was ; they shewed me the beam that had fallen on my head. Never mind, said I, since I am not killed, I shall be an honest man, and a good musician."

After this accident, Grétry became habitually thoughtful ; his gaiety changed into melancholy, and music was the only balm that soothed his sadness. It is probable that the alteration in his character was produced by this casualty, and the change was, perhaps, propitious to his talent. He remarks, that all his life after he felt occasionally the effect of the concussion.

Grétry's father gave him a new preceptor in music, as gentle and kind as the other was rough and cruel. At this time a company of Italian singers arrived at Liége ; they performed the operas of Pergolèse, Galuppi, &c. " I took a part," says he, " in all the rehearsals and performances : there it was that I acquired a strong taste for music."

The young chorister, incited by these new lessons, made a rapid progress. His father perceived it, and begged his master to let the boy sing a motet the next Sunday. The account of this first triumph is still more touching than that of the day of his first communion. Grétry dared to acknowledge, in an age of *illuminati,* " my timidity had a support which was only known to myself. I had felt, for the last year, a devotion to the Virgin Mary almost amounting to idolatry ; and having for nine days implored her assistance, I was confident in the protection of heaven. The motet which I sang was an Italian air translated into Latin, an address to the Virgin, *Non semper super prata casta florescit rosa.* I had hardly sung four bars, when the orchestra softened itself to pianissimo, for fear of overpowering me. I at that moment darted a glance at my father, to which he returned a smile. The children of the choir, who surrounded me, drew back from respect ; almost all the singers left their seats, and did not even hear the bell which announced the elevation of the Host. I, at that moment, perceived my good mother in the church ; she wiped away her tears, and I could not restrain my own."

After having gradually advanced for some years, he ardently wished to go to Rome, then the country of music. His parents opposed it, on account of the bad state of his health. " But," said he, " if I go on foot, and beg on the way, my resolution is taken, I will abide by it." At length, in March, 1759, he was allowed to undertake the desired journey, being eighteen years of age.

On his arrival in Italy, his reflections do justice to that country and his own feelings. " After we had penetrated," he says, " a little way into the mountains, rocks, and glaciers, nature seemed suddenly to have changed her face. With what pleasure did I find myself all at once in a field enamelled with flowers ! It appeared as if some good genius had transported us from earth to heaven. I begged our guide to let me stop a moment to enjoy this delicious prospect ; but what was my rapture when I heard, for the first time, Italian melody sung by an Italian ? It was from a charming female voice, which transported me by its melodious accents. It was the first lesson that I received in music, in a country to which I had travelled for instruction. And this touching voice, with that plaintive expression which an almost vertical sun generally inspires; in short, those delicious and exquisite sensations that I sought at such a distance from my native soil, and for which I had quitted every thing, were found in a simple country girl !"

The first studies of Grétry at Rome were combined with circumstances which he details in a manner both interesting and agreeable. Among the latter we place the following :—" The fatigue of my journey and of the excursions I made in the environs of Rome, to view the precious relics of antiquity, threw me into a fever. When the physician of the village made his second visit, an old owl, named *Pizelli*, said to me in a grave tone, *Bisogna confessarsi,* ' you must confess yourself.' I went into a rage in maintaining to him that I was not so ill as to be afraid of dying. He departed in a passion, saying that the inhabitants of Liége had heads of iron.

" A young surgeon, whom they gave me as a companion, was insufferable ; our chamber he converted into something like a cemetery, and he once said to me, in a tender tone, ' Ah ! my friend, I have lost my *tibia; if* you die, perhaps you will permit me'——But I took care not to render him this service."

Nothing can be more natural, or more *naïf* than Grétry's account of his first visit to that author, to whom the French lyric theatre owes *Atys, Didon, Roland,* &c.

" I very much wished to see Piccini, who so well deserved his reputation. Two years ago he presented the theatre d'*Alberti* with *La Buona Figliuola,* and, what is rare for that country, it was continually performed during two years. A friend of mine, an abbé, offered to introduce me to the composer ; and presented me as a promising young man. Piccini paid me very little attention, and to say the truth, it was all I deserved. Happily, I did not want emulation; but what pleasure would the least encouragement from him have given me! I contemplated his features with a respect that would have appeared flattery, had my natural timidity allowed him to see what was passing in my mind. I immediately returned to my college, and having shut the door, wished to do every thing that I had seen done at Piccini's. I placed a little table by the side of the harpsichord, laid on it a book of music paper, and a printed *oratorio ;* I read the words, ran over the harpsichord, marked out the paper ready for my score; all this appeared to me very charming, and my delirium lasted for two or three hours. I should have been quite happy could I have believed myself Piccini. At length my air was finished, I sat down and played it over. But, oh misery! it was detestable ; I began to cry, and the next day, I sighing, returned to my study-book."

Grétry afterwards went over afresh the various lessons he had received from Casali, the only master he avows, and who thought his scholar too far advanced to require any further instructions. But it was necessary to reduce into order that chaos with which the teacher had filled the pupil's head. Grétry was passionately fond of the music of Galuppi, Piccini, Sacchini, but still more that of Pergolèse ; and was persuaded that he should never become a good musician, if he did not take declamation as his guide.

" I used such prodigious exertions to employ well the elements with which my head was full, that it overcame me. Experience had not yet taught me, that *the good artist is distinguished by his skill in correcting.* If I took pains to be simple, a crowd of ideas obscured my sketch. When I embodied the whole of these I was discontented ; I then retrenched, and was still less satisfied.

" This combat between judgment and fancy ; that is to say, between taste which would choose, and inexperience which did not know what to reject—this struggle was so violent, that it destroyed my health."

Was he then ignorant, who was benefitted by the lessons and works of all the great masters who then flourished at Rome ? No!—he possessed in the highest degree, judgment and taste, the first attributes of genius, and without which, nothing either good or beautiful can be composed ; the proof of which is, the combat to which he was a prey, and which made him sink under *such a prodigious exertion.*

After having heard at Rome some scenes of Italian operas and symphonies, he set to music the opera of *le Vendemiatrice.* The result of this *coup d'essai* was most brilliant. The author was covered with marks of distinction by every class of society, and a few days afterwards, many of the airs of that opera were sung in the streets of Rome.

Being recalled by his family, he quitted the capital of Italy, leaving in the hands of some of his countrymen, his psalms, masses, and lessons in composition.

He then proceeded to Bologna, where he was admitted a member of the Philharmonic Society ; but previously to obtaining that honour, he performed the usual exercise, by writing a fugue on a fragment of a *canto fermo,* taken by chance, in which the good Padre Martini assisted him with his counsel.

He afterwards went to Geneva, and undertook to instruct twenty female scholars, in order to provide for the expenses of his journey to Paris, and first residence in that capital. He wrote to Voltaire, entreating him to honour a young artist, just come from Italy, with a lyrical drama, to try his force in a language so enriched by his immortal productions. The aged poet sent him word that he could only answer his letter *de vive voix,* as he was too ill to write, but desired to see him as soon as possible. He had the next day a most gracious reception at Ferney; of which he gives an amusing account. M. Grétry in his youth, was interesting in his person, and pleasing in his manners ; Dr. Burney saw, dined, and conversed with him at Paris, three years after the period above alluded to ; and Voltaire, who treated him with great kindness, seems to have viewed him in a most favourable light. While he was at Geneva, he set his first French opera, *Isabelle et Gertrude,* which was so well received, that the audience called for him, after the manner of Paris.

Arrived and established in the capital of France, M. Grétry soon became connected with the principal literati of that city, particularly M. Marmontel, all of whose lyrical dramas were written to be set by the musician of Liége. The success of his compositions surpassed his most flattering anticipations, and his popularity was only inferior to that which Lully, Rameau, and Gluck had before enjoyed. Some of his operas are even now listened to with as much pleasure as they produced forty years ago, *La Caravane du Caire* particularly, which continues a stock piece, and is performed at the grand opera very regularly.

The subject of this Memoir became a warm partisan of

republican government, at the era of the revolution; and was the author of one, if not more, of those national airs which resounded in all parts of France, and alarmed every monarchy in Europe, at that eventful period. His political principles afterwards proved as pliant as those of his friends the *savans*, and he lived to accept the order of the Legion of Honour from as deadly an enemy to freedom as modern history can name. In private life, Grétry was an amiable character; he was frank, upright, devoid of envy, humane, and religious; his genius rendered him happy; his works display the lively emotions, the unspeakable delights which he owed to the art he cultivated. Fame heaped her favours on him; he was tenderly loved by his wife and his children; but here Providence placed a boundary to his felicity. Three charming daughters, whose filial piety distinguished them, even more than their talents, crowned his happiness during many years; but they all died successively, as they attained their fifteenth year. It is difficult to refrain from tears, while reading in his *Essais*, the language of profound grief in which the wretchedness of the father is expressed.

Grétry died at the Hermitage of Emile, Sept. 24, 1813, and was buried with great pomp in the cemetery of Mount Louis, close by Delille the poet, in a handsome tomb, upon which appears a simple inscription, in letters of gold, indicating the time and place of his birth, and the period of his decease.

No French composer ever obtained so widely extended a reputation as Grétry: for many years he was not only the great favourite of France, but enjoyed the triumph of having his operas performed, with unanimous applause, in several of the principal European cities. His *Zemire et Azor* was produced in London, both on the Italian and English stages; and on the latter, his *Richard Cœur de Lion*, as well as numerous selections from his various works, have been introduced with uniform success. In his native country, and in many parts of Germany, his dramatic compositions continue to be given, and some of them will never be superannuated, particularly the *Cara-vane du Caire*, which possesses merit that will always be appreciated by persons of real taste and discernment.

In 1780, he published at Paris, a work entitled *Mé-moires, ou Essais sur la Musique*, of which the French government, in 1793, printed another edition, in three volumes octavo. The first volume contains the musical life of the author, and observations on his operas, which are very useful to young composers. The two others treat of the *moral* and *metaphysic* of music. Most of his observations are those of an ingenious, thinking man, though a considerable share of personal vanity pervades all the volumes, and the whole work betrays a great deficiency of knowledge in what has been written on his art. It nevertheless, ought to be read with attention by the studious musician, who would not fail to draw from it much useful information.

The following is a complete list of the operas of Grétry, with the names of the authors of the words, and the dates of performance.

Le Vendemiatrice, at Rome, 1765.
Isabelle et Gertrude, at Geneva, 1767.

All the following have been performed at Paris, at the *Comédie Italienne*, or at the *Académie Royale de Musique*. At the *Comédie Italienne*, *Le Huron*, in two acts, words by *Marmontel*; 1769. *Lucile*, in one act, words by the same; 1769. *Le Tableau Parlant*, in one act, the words by *Anseaume*; 1769. *Silvain*, in one act, words by *Mar-*

montel; 1770. *Les Deux Avares*, in two acts, words by *Falbaire*; 1770. *L'Amitié à l'Epreuve*, in three acts, words by *Favart*; 1771. *Zemire et Azor*, in four acts, words by *Marmontel*; 1771. *L'Ami de la Maison*, in three acts, words by the same; 1772. *Le Magnifique*, in three acts, words by *Sedaine*; 1773. *La Rosière de Salency*, first in four acts, afterwards in three, words by *Pezay*; 1774. *La Fausse Magie*, in two acts, words by *Marmontel*; 1775. *Les Mariages Samnites*, in three acts, words by *Durosoy*; 1776. *Matroco*, in four acts, words by *Laujeon*; 1778. *Le Judgment de Midas*, in three acts, words by *d'Hell*; 1778. *L'Amant Jaloux*, in three acts, words by the same; 1778. *Les Evenmens Imprévus*, in three acts, words by the same; 1779. *Aucassin et Nicolette*, in three acts, words by *Sédaine*; 1780. *L'Epreuve Villageoise*, in two acts, words by *Desforges*; 1784. *Richard Cœur-de-Lion*, in three acts, words by *Sédaine*; 1785. *Les Mé-prises par Ressemblance*, in three acts, words by *Patrat*; 1786. *Le Prisonnier Anglais*, in three acts, words by *Desfontaines*; 1786. *Le Comte d'Albert, et sa suite*, in three acts, words by *Sédaine*; 1787. *Le Rival Confident*, in two acts, words by *Forgeot*; 1788. *Raoul Barbe-Bleue*, in three acts, words by *Sédaine*; 1789. *Pierre-le Grand*, in three acts, words by *Bouilly*; 1790. *Guil-laume Tell*, in three acts, words by *Sédaine*; 1791. *Callias*, in one act, words by *M. Hoffman*; 1794. *Lisbeth*, in three acts, words by *M. Favières*; 1797. *Elisca*, in three acts, words by *M. Favières*; 1799.

At the *Académie Royale de Musique*: *Céphale et Procris*, in three acts, words by *Marmontel*; 1775. *Andromaque*, in three acts, words by *Pitra*; 1780. *Colinette à la Cour*, in three acts; 1782. *L'Embarras des Richesses*, in three acts; 1782. *La Caravane du Caire*, in three acts, words attributed to *M. Morel*; 1783. *Panurge*, in three acts, words attributed to the same; 1786. *Amphitrion*, in three acts, words by *Sédaine*; 1786. *Aspasia*, in three acts, words attributed to *M. Morel*; 1787. *Denis-le-Tyran, maître d'école à Corinthe*, in one act, words by *Sylvain Maréchal*; 1794. *Anacréon*, in three acts, words by *M. Guy*; 1797.

ITALIAN MUSICAL LITERATURE.

A new edition has lately appeared of a work first published in 1821, entitled "*Discorso sulla Origine, Progressi e Stato Attuale della Musica Italiana, di Andrea Majer, Veneziano.*" The spirit and freedom of opinion, and exposure of the abuses that have crept into modern music, which mark this volume, have created a considerable sensation in Italy. We shall present our readers with an extract from the latter part of the volume.

"In the eighteenth century, an age during which the worst taste prevailed in the greater part of the other arts, music attained to a state of perfection. It alone remained uncontaminated by the general contagion, and succeeded in creating a new language, calculated, by originality and truth of melody, joined to the power of harmony and instrumentation, to attain the true object of the art—expression. In the annals of music, there does not appear, if I may so express it, any medium time (*tempo di mezzo*); in its rapid and sudden career, it started,—if I may be allowed a comparison drawn from a sister art,—at once from the coldness and stiffness of a

E 2

Gelasio and a Cimabue, to the grace and vigour of a Raphael and a Correggio.

"As to the *theoretical* branch of the art, the greater part of the writers of the eighteenth century saw the reasonableness of abandoning all vain and learned speculations relative to the music of the ancients, and of turning their attention to an analysis of the modern. After this period, schools were seen to spring up in every direction, among which the most celebrated were those of Naples, Rome, Florence, Bologna, Milan, and Venice."

The author then takes a rapid view of all the different kinds of music, and shows the progress which various composers made in each: he also gives an historical sketch of the different theatres; but the epoch in which he considers that music had attained the highest degree of perfection, is about the middle of the eighteenth century.

"The moment," continues he, "had arrived, in which nature had decreed to form, at a single cast, a host of eminent geniuses, who were destined to raise to the climax of perfection all the parts of music, and of the poetry of the lyric drama. And to begin with the latter, to mention the names of Zeno and Metastasio is to say every thing; but at the same time that these two writers were employed in perfecting the melodrama-seria, some poets of ability in Naples and Venice did their endeavours to render the same services to the musical comedy. Tullio, a Neapolitan, wrote the *Serva padrona*, immortalized by the music of Pergolesi; Lorenzi, a Neapolitan, wrote the the operas of *Fra i due Litiganti il terzo gode*, set to music by Sarti; the *Idolo Cinese*, by Buranello, and *La Pietra simpatetica*, by Palma. About the same period with the *Don Chisciotte* of Apostolo Zeno, appeared the *Socrate immaginario* of Galiani, and various *drammi buffi* of Goldoni, the most celebrated of which are *La Buona Figliuola*, *Il Filosofo di campagna*, and *Il Mondo della Luna*. At a more recent period, Palomba, a Neapolitan distinguished himself by his *Sposo di tutte, e Marito di Nessuno*, set to music by Guglielmi, and *I Zingari in Fiera*, and *Il Tamburro Notturno*, by Paisiello.

"Nor were our composers tardy in answering to the call of the muses. In Naples were seen a Scarlatti, a Vinci, a Leo, who created the *laws of melody*, and the *accompaniments of the dramatic air;* a Logroscino, who presented the first model of the musical buffo style; a Porpora, who gave the last degree of perfection to *prosody*, and to the pathetic *modulation of the recitativo;* a Durante, who preserving the unity of the *motivo* amidst a variety of modulations, gave the idea and the example of a perfect *duet;* finally, a Pergolesi, who enriched the musical language with a thousand original and sublime forms, both of melody and harmony, and succeeded in perfectly purifying it from its ancient dross. About the same period arose, at the other extremity of Italy, a Marcello, who taught the harp of David to resound anew, in strains sometimes soft and tender, at others majestic and sublime. Meanwhile, in a humble islet, near the city in which the last-mentioned composer flourished, arose a Galuppi, surnamed Buranello, a fruitful and universal genius, who succeeded in ornamenting theatrical music with a thousand new beauties; and diffusing around him the treasures of taste, of sensibility, and imagination, in almost every style, succeeded in obtaining a place in the first rank of modern Italian composers.

In the track of these greater luminaries appeared a host of other stars, some of which were scarcely inferior in lustre. To signalize them individually would exceed my limits, suffice it to mention the names of a Hasse, a Gluck, a De Majo, a Sacchini, a Piccini, a Trajetta, an Anfossi, a Sarti, a Guglielmi, a Cimarosa, and to terminate nobly this catalogue of glorious names, the immortal Paisiello."

Signor Majer next proceeds to a consideration of the causes that have led to the decline of music, which brings him to the third part of his treatise, "On the present State of Italian Music."

The following is a summary of the principal defects which our author observes in the music of the present time. "1st, A confusion of the different *genera* of music; 2d, the general triviality, and indefinite character of the *cantilene;* 3d, the accumulation of a hundred different *motivos*, saving the exact one suited to the subject; 4th, the intemperate use, or rather abuse, of the furious dithyrambic style, intent only upon astonishing the ear, without any ambition to touch the heart; 5th, the irregular and frequent starts in the *time* and *tone*, without their bearing any relation to the words; 6th, the tiresomeness of the thousand-times repeated cadences, varied only in the figures; 7th, the absurdity of the perpetual *obbligato* chorus; 8th, the charletanism and unworthy artifice of causing the violin parts to be executed by wind instruments, to seek to cover, by the extraordinary execution of the performers, the nudity of the *cantilene;* 9th, the other still more ridiculous practice of cutting melodial phrases into piecemeal, assigning a morsel to each instrument, as if the words of a discourse were to be pronounced by different interlocutors; 10th, the pedantry of noting down the smallest appoggiatura and cadence of the singing parts, transforming the spontaneous ornaments of song into a formal and scholastic *solfeggio;* 11th, the want of originality and of characteristic expression in the melodies, composed for the most part of variations upon the same subjects, to which all kinds of words may be adapted indifferently; 12th, the marvellous sonatas of the throat *(sonate di gola)* of modern singers, to the greater part of whom nothing in the world is wanting but a knowledge of the *portamento di voce*, of the proper method of taking the breath, of time and intonation! 13th, the ridiculous profusion of unmeaning and affected divisions, which destroy every idea of musical rhythm, and divide the bar into as many parts as suit the singer's caprice; 14th, the havoc which is made in the prosody, changing, as fancy directs, long syllables into short; the pausing and shaking upon the mute or nasal vowels, a fault which thirty years since, would not have been allowed to pass with impunity in the merest beginner; 15th, the introduction of a new mode of pronunciation, which divides the word suddenly into two parts, striking the last syllable with a rebound of the voice, not unlike the blow of a sledge-hammer, as *vendet-tàaaa, amor-èeee, campòooo;* 16th, the new mode of commencing the art of singing, without having first learnt to speak, which renders it impossible to guess in what language the actors are discoursing, and by which means the theatre is converted into an hospital for the deaf and dumb; 17th, the perversion of instruments, as to the nature of their several properties, and their relative place in the general scale; 18th, the whistling ottavino, the great drum, the Jannissary band, the whirlwind and tempest of the modern orchestra, in which the violin is made to counterfeit the flute, playing the chords upon the bridge, or striking them *pizzicati* with the finger after the manner of the guitar; 19th, the contrabasso, which is made to run flights of semiquavers; 20th, the wind-instruments, with their short and sharp sounds, which imitate the clucking of a hen; 21st, the sistrums, the cymbals, the timbrels, and the great drum, which deafen you with their stormy uproar, while the singers are accompanying the orchestra with all their might and main in arpeggios of three and five, of four and six, or go running up and down, like persons possessed, through all the degrees of the chromatic scale.— Such are the besetting sins of the music of the present day, and especially of the *melo-dramma seria*.

"As to the *opera buffa*, it is scarcely worth while even to name it, for it no longer exists. It is now several years since the *opera buffa*, and its attendant humour and merriment, have disappeared from our theatres. A malignant fever of the *sentimental* kind has invaded the minds of all. The public now-a-days frequent the theatres in order to attemper, with lacrymose farces and *semi-serious* dramas, the too lively transports of the general happiness that pervades all classes in Italy*. The moment your eye is greeted with the title *Buffo Serio* upon the bills of the Opera, all that remains for you to do is to recite the funeral oration of the arts, and of poor common sense."

Signor Majer proceeds in the same strain of complaint against the modern church music; and again returning to that of the theatre, he strongly expresses his disapprobation of the practice which prevails in the modern serious melo-drama of having, by little and little, omitted all the *recitativo parlante*; as if, he observes, in a dramatic action, it can be natural to suppose the whole of the personages to be in a state of strong excitement and passion from one end of the drama to the other.

Our author concludes by observing, that "the department of music in which the Italians at present excel, is that of the instrumental kind. Do we not see a Dragonetti capable of performing, even to a wonder, on the contrabasso the most difficult part of the first violin; a Paganini, who after having surprised the audience by one of the most difficult of his concertos, will repeat it from beginning to end on the single first string of the violin; a Schumatz, who also performs wonders upon the bassoon. It has been justly remarked, that when the facility of surmounting curious difficulties in the fine arts is considered as a merit, it is a certain characteristic of their decline."

ON THE NATIONAL SONGS OF MODERN GREECE.

[Concluded from page 5.]

NEXT to the war songs of the Greeks, the most remarkable are those of a domestic nature, which are numerous, and adapted to almost every situation of life. Our space will allow us to particularize two only of the most

* When it is remembered that Signior Majer writes at Venice, the bitter irony of this passage will be fully understood.

prominent—that on the departure for a foreign land, and the funeral song.

The domestic relations of the modern Greeks are more marked, more expressive of profound feeling, and attended with more ceremony and circumstance, than in any other country. To what cause may this be traced? Does it arise from the conformation and simplicity of their social state; or is it the oppression under which they live, that makes them feel more sensibly the necessity of clinging more closely to each other? Whatever the cause may be, certain it is, that all the most characteristic traits of the domestic usages of the Greeks furnish a proof of the fact; and under no circumstances is it seen more strongly, than in what usually passes at the departure of some member of a family to a foreign land.

Many causes oblige the young Greek to quit his home; and there is no event more painful to him than this temporary banishment. So attached is the Greek to his home, that to him every foreign land is a land of misery and exile, which he never names without the addition of an epithet (ξενημα), which is at once expressive of all that is most tender in regret, and most terrible in the anticipation of evil. In quitting his native place, and bidding adieu to his family and friends, he is not only in a state of uncertainty as to the possibility of his ever beholding them again;- he is also uncertain whether the Turks will permit him; whether they will spare the patrimony and lives, and, what is dearer than life, the honour of those whom he leaves in their power.

These observations will sufficiently explain the kind of ceremonial employed by the Greeks, in taking their farewell of those who are departing for a foreign land. On the day fixed for departure, the friends and relatives of the individual meet at his house, to partake of a farewell repast. When this is finished, the traveller sets out, escorted by his relations, and the whole of the guests, who accompany him to the distance of some miles.

On this, as on all other occasions in Greece, poetry and music are the organs through which are expressed the emotions of this interesting moment; the regrets and presentiments, both of him who goes and of those who remain. There are songs and music particularly adapted to this domestic ceremony, some of which are sung during the farewell repast, and others on the road, and at the spot where the final separation takes place. It is impossible for one who has not been witness of the scene, to form any adequate idea of the deep pathos and effect produced by these songs of exile. Some are of very ancient date, and have, from time immemorial, been common to the whole of Greece. Others are expressly composed for some individual occasion, sometimes by the traveller himself, at others by those who accompany him. Sometimes they are composed extempore by the mother, the wife, or the sisters of the individual who is quitting them. The following account of one of these affecting scenes is from an eye-witness, of my acquaintance.

In the district of Zagori, in the vicinity of Mount Pindus, lived a respectable family, to which belonged three brothers, the youngest of whom, by a very rare exception, was an object of aversion to his mother. After having borne for a long time, in silent and uncomplaining sorrow, her unjust rigour, the poor young man was obliged to set out for Adrianople. There was, according to custom, a farewell repast, which was numerously attended, and afterwards the whole of the guests accompanied the young traveller to the distance of four or five miles. The place where they halted, was at the foot of Mount Pindus, a spot of a very wild and savage aspect. Several pathetic songs, appropriate to the occasion, had already been sung; all was pensiveness and melancholy, when a circumstance occurred, which tended to render the scene doubly affecting. Suddenly ascending a part of the rock which overhung the road, the young traveller intoned a song which he had composed to a most pathetic air, appropriate to the occasion. He expressed, in the most touching manner, his grief at quitting his family, his country, and above all, his parting regret at not sharing his mother's affection. The young man's tone of emotion, the well-known justice of his complaint, the pathos of the melody, rendered doubly effective by the solitude and melancholy of the scene, penetrated every heart, and drew tears from every eye. The young man's mother was there; as the song proceeded, her emotion became extreme; and before it was finished, she burst through the crowd, threw herself round the neck of her son, covered him with kisses, and in the midst of sobs solicited his pardon for not having heretofore been a good mother to him: she promised to be so in future, and religiously kept her word.

The *Myriologia*, or funeral song, is of very remote antiquity. We see in Homer the whole family of Priam pouring their funeral sorrows over the corpse of Hector; and the custom has descended to the modern Greeks, in all its inspiration and originality.

These funeral laments last till the moment the priests come to convey away the body for interment, and is prolonged till the arrival of the funeral procession at the doors of the church. They are suspended during the prayers and psalmody of the priests, but are renewed again when the corpse is deposited in the earth. Nor do they terminate with the funeral; they are renewed on a variety of occasions, and during the whole year the female part of the family sing no other songs than those of a melancholy character.

Mothers are often heard to pour forth funeral laments over the infants of which death has robbed them; and these elegiac effusions are often of a very pathetic and graceful kind. The little innocent is regretted under the emblem of a delicate plant, of a flower, a bird, or any other pleasing object to which the fancy of the mother takes a melancholy pleasure in assimilating it.

The music to which these elegiac effusions are sung, approximates greatly in its general character to the Gregorian chant, but they have this peculiarity, that while other songs generally terminate in a low note, they finish in a high one. Another peculiarity is, that they are sung by women only, and are always produced extempore. It may well be supposed, that when this task, which custom imperiously demands, falls to the lot of a timid, ignorant, or uncultivated person, it demands a violent effort, a species of interior metamorphosis of the most extraordinary kind. It is requisite that at a given moment—at a moment when their ordinary faculties are confused or distracted by grief, they should suddenly acquire a power to which they were before strangers, of so regulating and modifying this grief, as to bring it under the control of poetry and music; and this, too, in presence of an innumerable crowd, who

are looking on, and expecting to catch emotion from theirs. Hence, it is by no means an uncommon thing to see women faint under the effort to which they have, as it were, wound up their powers. The following is a well-authenticated instance.

A woman of Metsoven, near Mount Pindus, at the age of twenty-five, had lost her husband, who had left her with two young children. She was a poor peasant girl, of great simplicity of character, and who had never given any indications of mind. Taking her two children by the hand, she advanced to the body of her husband, and began her myriologue by the recital of a dream which she had had some days before—a recital which she addressed to the dead body. Her manner was highly impressive, and the kind of recitative in which she sung it, expressive, in the highest degree, of agitation and solicitude. The beginning was as follows :—

Methought as I was busied with my domestic care,
A youth stood on my threshold, of fierce commanding air,
Adown his shoulders waving were wings of dazzling white,
And in his hand a naked sword, oh dread, appalling sight!
He sternly gazed upon me, then thus the silence broke :
"Is thy good man within?" All trembling, thus I spoke ;
"My good man is at home, and lulling on his breast
Our little weeping Nikolos, to soothe him into rest.
But pass not thou my threshold ; I prithee, youth, forbear,
Thy terrible demeanour my little boy would scare."
But vain were my entreaties, resistance was in vain,
The white-wing'd youth was resolute, and would an entrance gain.
He darted o'er the threshold, and plunged his cruel sword
Deep, deep within thy bosom, oh thou, my heart's sole lord !
There, too, is little Nikolos, thy hope, thy fondest joy,
At him the monster aim'd, but I saved our darling boy.

After this opening, the words of which, and the tone in which they were uttered, had made the by-standers shudder, some of whom looked towards the door, as if fearful of seeing the young man with the white wings ; while others gazed upon the little infant clinging to the knees of its mother—she threw herself, with convulsive sobs, upon the body of her husband.

With respect to the music to which these songs are sung, it appeared in general extremely simple, accompanied with a drawling kind of effect, and approximating nearer to plain-chant than to the music of the other nations of Europe. Their character always partakes of the plaintive, even when intended to celebrate the victories of their chieftains, or to convey sentiments the very opposite to the gentle and pathetic. On hearing them, one is tempted at once to pronounce that they must have been composed expressly to be sung among the mountains, and to be repeated and prolonged by the echoes, like the Ranz des Vaches of the Swiss Mountaineers.

With respect to the music of the rhymed songs, composed and sung in the greater towns, or the isles, it has more sweetness and unity of character, and betrays more artifice and contrivance. I heard many which were sung to Italian airs long since forgotten in Italy. The air of the mountain songs is frequently comprised in a single verse, usually in two, never in more. But the air, or more properly speaking, the couplet to the measure of which it is restricted, is frequently prolonged by the aid of words, which are arbitrarily introduced as a kind of burden, between the verses, and which, as being frequently altogether foreign to the subject, produce a very whimsical effect.*

The places and occasions in which the Greek songs of every kind, and of every part of Greece, may be heard to the greatest advantage, are in the Khans, or small Turkish inns at Constantinople, Odessa, &c., where the Greeks from the various provinces generally put up. On these occasions there is no other pastime than song. The old men usually set the example; the middle-aged, and afterwards the younger part of the company continue them; and not unfrequently the greater part of the night flows away, before the singers are tired of singing, or the hearers of listening to them. There each one yields himself up to the sweet emotions, awakened by the remembrance of his country, his family, and the spot that gave him birth; and each individual feeling tends to communicate an increasing impression to the whole. There, brought together by accident in a foreign land, the mountaineer of Ætolia, the inhabitant of Larissa, and the native of Scio, forget that they are any thing but Greeks: all those repugnances which belong to particular places, and particular modes of life, are suspended as if by enchantment. The mountaineer is not ashamed to yield to the tender emotions produced by the sweet accents of the poetry of the Archipelago, and the soft islander catches a momentary enthusiasm from the bravery and daring spirit of the heroes of the mountains.

The hero of the first of the two songs translated below, fell in an engagement with the Turks, in which the latter were commanded by the famous Jousouph, one of the generals of Ali Pacha, surnamed, by the Greeks, the *drinker of blood*, an epithet that appears to have been no figure of rhetoric. It would, perhaps, be proper to inform the reader, that it is a particular point of honour with the Greeks, not to allow their heads, after death, to fall into the hands of the Turks, who practise upon them every barbarous outrage. " My friends," said an expiring chieftain, "cut off my head, that our enemies may not bear it with them, to be exposed to the gaze of every passer-by. My enemies will see it, and their hearts will laugh with joy—my mother, also, may see it, and would expire at the sight."

The second song is founded upon a real anecdote; and it is to the two heroes mentioned in the text, that the noble resistance of Souli is principally to be attributed. It is added, that the moment the prayers for the dead were said for the six hostages, the indignant chieftains sallied from the church at the head of their chosen band, fell like lions upon the Turks, slew a great number, and forced the rest of the detachment to retreat.

ΜΑΡΤΥΡΟΙ ΤΟΥ ΣΟΥΛΙΟΥ.

Σύγκεφον μαῦρον σκέπαζε τὸ Σοῦλι καὶ τὴν Κιάφαν·
Ὁλημερούλα ἔβρεχεν, ὁλονυχτὶς χιονίζει.

Κ' ἀπ' τὸ Συστράπι πρόςχνεν ἕνας λιγνὸς λεβέντης·
Ἀπὸ τὰ Ἰάννινα πικρά, μαῦρα μαντάτα φέρει·

" Τὰ παλληκάρια τὰ καλὰ συντρόφοι τους τὰ χάνουν.
" Ἀκοῦστε, Φώτου τὰ παιδιά, τοῦ Δράκου παλληκάρια,
" Τὸ Δέλβινον τὸ ἄπιστον πρόδωσε τὰ παιδιά μας.
" Σ τ' Ἀλῆ πασᾶ τὰ ἔφεραν, τὰ ἕξ ἀραδ' ἀράδα.

" Αὐτὸς τὰ τέσσερά 'σφαξε, τῶν δυὸ ζωὴν χαρίζει,
" Τοῦ Δήμου Δράκου τοῦ υἱοῦ, καὶ τ' ἀδερφοῦ τοῦ Φώτου."
Κ' ἐκεῖνοι καθὼς τ' ἄκουσαν, βαρεὰ τοὺς κακοφάνη.
" Δίσποτα, τὸν πρωτόπαπαν ἐφώναξαν κ' οἱ δύο,

" Ψάλλ' ὅλων τὰ μνημόσυνα τῶν ἕξ παλληκαριῶν μας·
" Τὰ δυὸ, καθὼς τὰ τέσσερα, σφαγμένα τὰ μετροῦμε.
" Οὔτε ὁ Τύραννος ζωὴν τῶν Σουλιωτῶν χαρίζει·
" Οὔτε Σουλιώτης ζωντανὸς 'ς τὰ χέρια του λογᾶται."

THE MARTYRS OF SOULI.

On Souli's towers, and Kiapha,
The tempest beat, the deep snow lay;
When morning broke, a Souliot came,
Jannina's capture to proclaim.

"Our allies are our ruin—they
" Have dared our sacred cause betray;
" Ye sons of noble Photos hear,
" Ye sons of Drakos lend an ear.

" Six of our brethren are betray'd,
" The victims of the Pacha made;
" Those only who have pity won
" Are Photos' brother, Drakos' son."

The warriors heard the chief proclaim,
Deep sunk in grief, their kindred's shame;
Then cried, " Priest, be the office said,
" For all the six alike are dead.

" When Souliots win a Pacha's grace,
" They ill are worthy of their race.
" Who wear the chains that tyrants give,
" For us, at least, have ceased to live."

---

* The reader will at once call to mind the same effect as produced in some of the earlier Scotch songs, such, for instance, as " Up in the morning early."—*Note of the Translator.*

ΤΟΥ ΓΥΦΤΑΚΗ.   GHIPHTAKIS.

Διψοῦν οἱ κάμποι γιὰ νερὰ, καὶ τὰ βουνὰ γιὰ χιόνια,
Καὶ τὰ ἱεράκια γιὰ πουλιὰ, κ᾿ οἱ Τοῦρκοι γιὰ κεφάλια.

"Ἄρα τὸ τί νὰ γένηκεν ἡ μάννα τοῦ Γυφτάκη,
"Ποῦ ἔχασε τὰ δυὸ παιδιὰ, τὸν ἀδερφόν της, τρία ;

" Καὶ τώρα παλαβώθηκε, καὶ περπατεῖ καὶ κλαίει ·
" Μήτε 'σ τοὺς κάμπους φαίνεται μήτε 'σ τὰ κορφοβούνια."
" Μᾶς εἶπαν πέρα πέρασε, πέρα 'σ τὰ Βλαχοχώρια ·
" Κ᾿ ἐκεῖ τουφέκια ἔπεφταν, καὶ θλιβερὰ βροντοῦσαν.

" Μήτε εἰς γάμους ἔπεφταν μήτε εἰς πανηγύρια.
" Μόνον τὸν Γύφτην λάβωσαν 'σ τὸ γόνα καὶ 'σ τὸ χέρι.
" Σὰν δένδρον ἐῤῥαγίσθηκε, σὰν κυπαρύσσι πέφτει ·
" Ψηλὴν φωνούλαν ἔβαλε, σὰν παλληκάρ᾿ ὅττου ἦταν ·

" Ποῦ εἶσαι, καλέ μου ἀδερφὲ, καὶ πολυαγαπημένε ;
" Γύρισε πίσω, πάρε με, πάρε μου τὸ κεφάλι,
" Νὰ λὴν τὸ πάρ᾿ ἡ παγανιὰ, καὶ ὁ Ἰσοὺφ ἀράπης
" Καὶ μου τὸ πάη 'σ τὰ Ἰάννινα τ᾿ Ἀλῆ πασᾶ τοῦ σκύλου."

The mountains thirst for clouds, the plain
Parch'd by the sun, for cooling rain ;
The vulture for his prey, and more,
The Mussulman for Grecian gore.

" Where is Ghiphtakis' mother fled,
" Who wails, e'en now, two children dead ?
" Wand'ring amid the mountains wild,
" Seeks she her last, her fondest, child ?

" The sounds of war her ears assail,
" The gun loud thunders in the gale :
" Alas ! not now to celebrate
" The nuptial feast, the village fête.

" Then Ghiphtakis she wounded found,
" Stretch'd bleeding on the damp cold ground ;
" Thus lies the cypress, when the blast
" Its honours in the dust has cast.

" The foe is nigh ; strike home !" he said,
" And bear far hence your chieftain's head,
" Lest by the victor it be borne
" With joy, to glut his savage scorn."

A NEW MUSICAL INSTRUMENT,
THE SIRENIUM.

[From a Vienna Journal.]

M. JOSEPH PROMBERGER, of Vienna, has recently completed a new musical instrument, upon which he has been employed for several years, and to which he has given the name of SIRENIUM. It is of the piano-forte kind, but is distinguished from that instrument by its compactness and convenience of form, and more particularly by its internal improvements. It stands perpendicularly, and reckoning from the pedestal, does not exceed four feet in height. It has two ranges of strings, on which, by means of a peculiar preparation, its power of sustaining sound is brought to the highest degree of perfection, and its tones are so beautiful, clear, and full, that it is wonderful how so small a body, and strings of so short a compass, can produce such power. But the most extraordinary part of this invention is, that the sounding-board is moveable, and independent of the general frame-work : indeed, it is this peculiar feature that constitutes the great value of the instrument. It has also another peculiarity ; the hammer being separated from the key, whereby a certain advantage is gained over the English piano, besides allowing of the works being taken out with less danger of sustaining injury. The damper also is admirably contrived, and from the manner in which the instrument is constructed, the tuning likewise is rendered very easy ; and the double range of keys, instead of making this more complex, renders it in reality more simple.
The beautiful external appearance of this instrument makes it also an elegant and desirable piece of furniture ; and, at first sight, its destination would not be discovered, since no one would expect to find within so small a compass, a perfect piano-forte. The hinges, &c., are very tastefully arranged, and as they are interior, the division of the head-board is scarcely discernible.
We have no doubt that, from its compactness, its strength, firmness, and clearness of tone, and particularly from the durable nature of its mechanism, and the ease with which it can be tuned, it will be welcomed as a happy invention by many amateurs of the pianoforte ; and, in all probability, it will survive several of those shewy, noisy, and pompous inventions, which have surprised for the moment, but almost instantly fallen into oblivion.

NEW ORGAN AT BRISTOL.

To the Editor of the Harmonicon.

SIR,   *Bristol, December,* 1824.
As a lover of music I have been pleased at learning, through the medium of your pages, the progress of the art in other countries as well as our own ; and, being intimately connected with America, I was particularly gratified at observing in No. XXIV, page 222, some account of what our Trans-atlantic friends are doing, and at page 232, a description of two organs, one of large dimensions, lately built at New York. Perhaps the following account of an organ erected here, a few months ago, in the parish church of St. James, by Smith of this city, a native and self-taught organ-builder, may not be unacceptable to your numerous readers. The instrument possesses amazing powers ; I know not whether, in variety of effect, even that at York Minster exceeds it :

certainly there is no other in this kingdom which can vie with it. The height is 28 feet, width 16 feet, and depth 10 feet, and there are four rows of keys, besides two octaves of pedals from C C C.

CHOIR ORGAN, in a separate case, in front of the gallery, from c c to E in alt:
Stopped diapason,—Flute.
Dulciana,—Principal.
Fifteenth.

GREAT ORGAN, from c c to E in alt.
Open diapason,—Tierce.
Ditto,—Larigot.
Stopped ditto,—Twenty-second.
Principal,—Mixture, two ranks.
Ditto.
Twelfth,—Sesquialtera *. ►
Fifteenth,—Trumpet.
Ditto—Octave bassoon.

SWELL, from c to c in altissimo, four octaves.
Open diapason,—Cremona.
Stopped ditto,—Twelfth.
Principal,—Fifteenth.
Hautboy,—Tierce.
Trumpet,—Cornet †.

‡ BORROWED CHOIR ORGAN, same compass as great organ.
Open diapason,—Principal.
Stopped diapason,—Clarionet.
Flute.

PEDALS, from c c c, two octaves.
Open diapason,—Bassoon.
Stopped diapason,—Principal.
Double stopped diapason, lowest pipe c c c c.

The pedals are *of brass*, an invention of Mr. Hodges, the organist. Their great recommendation is, being brought nearer together, by which two octaves now take up less room than an octave and a-half formerly occupied. These are made to unite with either the great or choir organ, or both, at octaves; that is, the pedals being an octave lower than the keys, the lowest pedal takes the lowest key. There are six connecting stops, whose offices are as follows:

1. For uniting the swell in unison with the great organ.
2. Ditto,   an octave above with the great organ.
3. For uniting the great organ and choir organ.
4. Ditto,   the choir organ and swell.
5. Ditto,   the pedals to the great organ.
6. Ditto,   ditto,   choir organ.

in addition to these there are four *wind stops* for shutting off the wind at pleasure from either organ, of great use in case of ciphering; and also in producing a variety of effects not otherwise obtainable. There are also keys at the end of the swell row, for playing the pedal pipes with the hands; a great advantage to the performer who has not been accustomed to pedals; but these keys do not unite with the other rows. The borrowed choir organ is also without a connecting movement. The number of stops is *fifty*, and the combinations which may be effected by means of the different connecting stops, are almost incalculable. The effect of the *swell* when united to the great organ, is such as to lead even the most experienced organists who have heard it, to suppose that the whole organ is one immense swell. When the octave as well as the unison is added, it is almost overpowering. The

* A connecting stop for drawing the three preceding ones together.
† A connecting stop for drawing the preceding three together.
‡ So called being principally borrowed from the great organ, and to distinguish it from the small *choir* organ in front.

bellows are supplied by five feeders, worked by a revolving handle and crank, which move so freely, that a little boy has been found competent to the task of blowing during the performance of a full cathedral service. This instrument, of which I have attempted some description—and I assure you, Mr. Editor, that it is but a faint one,—must be heard to be fully appreciated. It was opened for the accompaniment of divine worship, on Sunday the second of May with complete cathedral service. The *Te Deum, Jubilate, Anthem,* and *Responses* in the morning service, and the *Cantate Domino* and *Deus Misereatur,* in that of the evening, were composed for the occasion by the organist, Mr. Edward Hodges. The choir, about twenty-five in number, consisted entirely of amateurs. Of their performance, or of the music itself, I shall only say, that both were such as to elicit the warmest approbation, and an unanimous request that the services of the day should be published, with which the author is about to comply; the public will therefore have an opportunity of judging for themselves, of his merits or defects as a composer of ecclesiastical music.

A considerable debt having been incurred in erecting a new gallery for the organ, and Sunday-school children, a musical performance was offered for the purpose of raising the necessary funds; accordingly, on Friday evening, the twenty-fifth of June, a grand selection from the works of Handel, Haydn, Beethoven, Pergolèsi, &c., was given at the church, and (with the exception of the leader, and two or three others,) entirely by *amateurs,* in number about fifty, who kindly volunteered their services. The performance completely answered the end in view: the debt incurred in building the gallery was thereby liquidated, and a numerous and most respectable assembly were highly delighted, at finding that Bristol possessed, within herself, so much musical talent. This city has been stigmatized as a place where the fine arts are neglected; where men are too intent on the accumulation of wealth, to pay any regard to those pursuits which have no direct tendency to that result. It has been repeatedly asserted, that a tolerable quartett could not be got up by residents within her walls; but with what little justice, the events of the evening alluded to have demonstrated. Bristol may be, and I fear is, deficient in professors; but while fifty resident amateurs can be brought together, almost by the influence of one individual, and while musical judges, who had the previous week attended the "Grand Festival" at Bath Abbey, are compelled to acknowledge, that in the performance of some of Handel's choruses, the amateurs were equal, and even superior, to the congregated host of regulars; they need not be afraid to attempt *quartetts,* or even "grand selections."

INJUNCTION AGAINST THE WORDS OF DR. ARNOLD'S
DUET IN No. XXV. OF THE HARMONICON.

WHEN we presented to our readers the beautiful Duet, by Dr. ARNOLD, printed in our last number, we little imagined that the genius of litigation could dispute our right so to do, or involve us in pains and penalties for an attempt to rescue from unmerited oblivion that delightful composition. Such, however, is the "glorious uncertainty" of the law, that an Injunction has actually been obtained in the Vice-

Chancellor's Court, to restrain us from printing, with the Duet in question, the words extracted from *Little's Poems*, although the music was actually set to those very words by Dr. Arnold in 1802, and in the same year sung upon the Haymarket stage, and published by Messrs. Caulfield, in a book containing all the music of the piece to which it belonged; from whose undisputed copy, and NOT from the work of any other person, the music and words printed in the HARMONICON were taken.

Scarcely, however, had our Twenty-Fifth Number appeared, when a claimant to the exclusive property in the poem, from which our EIGHT LINES had been taken, started forth in the person of Mr. Power, Music-seller, of the Strand, who most industriously circulated through the music-trade his determination to stop the sale of our Number; and before we had well recovered from the surprise occasioned by so unexpected a claim, our Printer and Publisher were served with notices of a motion in the Vice-Chancellor's Court. We were accordingly compelled to appear by our "Counsel learned in the law," to answer for the offence which we had so unintentionally committed.

The following is a brief report of the proceedings:—

Mr. STUART moved for an injunction to restrain the defendants from publishing in the HARMONICON, the words of a song composed by Mr. Thomas Moore, the copyright of which was the property of the plaintiff. The affidavit of his client set forth that a volume of poems by Mr. Moore was published in the year 1802, by Carpenter, of Bond-street. The name under which they were given to the world was, *Poems by the late* THOMAS LITTLE, Esq. The copyright of these poems was vested in the publisher, Carpenter, and remained wholly with him until he transferred certain songs selected from it to the plaintiff, by an agreement entered into in the year 1809. The songs were sixteen in number, and the song which was the subject of the present appeal to the Court was amongst the number. Mr. Moore and Mr. Power made a contract after this in 1811, and for certain considerations Mr. Moore assigned to Mr. Power his reversionary right in the music as well as the words of certain songs, and among these was included the song in question. It was sworn that the words of the song in the HARMONICON were part of those published in "LITTLE's *Poems*," and since published with music by the plaintiff. His client swears that he derived considerable emolument from the sale. It was evident that the words of the song in the HARMONICON were those published in the original poems, and he thought the plaintiff was clearly entitled to the injunction for which he prayed.

Mr. LORRAINE, for the defendants, opposed the motion. The affidavit of his clients stated, that LITTLE's *Poems* were published anonymously, and the preface to the first edition informed the reader that the author died in his twenty-first year, and added, that if he had lived longer his judgment might be riper and his mind more chastened. The death of the author was thus specifically put forward, and in the second edition it was repeated. As the law then stood, the copyright was vested in the author for the term of fourteen years. This term had elapsed, and his position was, that no claim made under an Act of later date, which extended the copyright to the author during his life, could hold good in this case, as the author's death was positively affirmed in the first edition, and studiously repeated in the second.

Mr. LORRAINE then said, it was sworn in the affidavit of one the defendants, that in the year 1802, soon after the publication of LITTLE's *Poems*, Doctor Arnold composed a Burletta, or Musical Piece, which was performed at the Haymarket Theatre, in August, 1802, called *Fairy Revels, or Love in the Highlands* [*]; in this piece the Doctor adapted, as a duet, from the

[*] A copy of the Book, containing the whole of the Music of the Burletta, printed and published in the year 1802, was produced in Court, and the words from which were found to be correctly copied.

Poems of Little, the song of—"*When time who steals our years away.*" The design of the HARMONICON was to communicate to the public the progress of music; and for the purpose of carrying that design into execution, it gave examples of various composers, and amongst them gave a specimen of the style of Dr. Arnold. They took this specimen from the *Fairy Revels*, and used the two stanzas of Little's song, originally used by the composer; neither music nor words were taken from the works of the plaintiff. This explanation, he was sure, would be sufficient, and his clients could not possibly be thought guilty of such a violation of copyright as would justify the granting of an injunction. The transgression, if it could be called one, was of so minute and trifling a description, that it neither demanded the protection, nor required the interference, of so solemn a Court. The original publication from which the song was taken consisted of three or four hundred pages; the part which his clients were accused of abstracting was composed of eight lines. This fact, and the circumstances under which the lines were taken, would bear out his clients. There was at all events one reason for which an injunction could not issue. It was long a settled point, that where the party had by any conduct or *laches* of his own, thrown any doubt upon his property, he could not succeed in any appeal he might make to that Court. He was bound to establish his right of property in a court of law. The prefaces to the two first editions, and the absence of all complaint respecting the Burletta of Doctor Arnold, in 1802, were circumstances fully sufficient to throw a doubt upon the right of property, and therefore, before the plaintiff could be heard in this Court, he should have his claim ascertained by a jury.

The VICE-CHANCELLOR was of opinion that an injunction should issue, to restrain the defendants from publishing those stanzas which were proved to be the plaintiff's property.

To the judgment thus given, it is of course our duty to submit; we have accordingly called in our Numbers, cancelled the leaves containing the objectionable stanzas, and reprinted the same Duet by Dr. Arnold, with words from CONGREVE adapted to the music.

We may perhaps be allowed to contrast the proceedings resorted to on this occasion, with our own conduct in the case of a very flagrant piracy recently committed on our work. Whole Memoirs, perfectly original, and which we had obtained at considerable pains and expense, were taken from us, without permission or acknowledgment; the piracy comprised nearly every one of the papers that had appeared up to the time of the publication of the piratical work, and the quantity of matter amounted to between 50 and 60 pages of small type in two columns. Not knowing the parties, we, as a matter of course, instructed our solicitor to proceed against the publisher of the work; but when we found that the original proprietor, and present publisher, had been deceived by the compiler of the work, and, (although responsible to us,) were themselves wholly unconscious of that piracy, we relaxed in our legal proceedings, and placing the question in the hands of a mutual friend, were content with the cancelling of the matter, and an acknowledgment of the arrangement in a temperately-worded Advertisement. We have REPRINTED EIGHT LINES which were set to Music, sung on the stage, and printed and published, upwards of two and twenty years ago; and for this offence have been exposed to the trouble and expense of a chancery proceeding, at the suit of an individual who has succeeded in proving that he purchased an interest in the said eight lines, SEVEN YEARS AFTER the publication of the work from which we copied them, but of which purchase we, in common with the whole world, were, from the very nature of the transaction, necessarily as ignorant as we are of the contents of his will, or the clauses in the lease of his house.

REVIEW OF MUSIC.

The whole of the Music in As you like it, *as performed at the Theatre Royal, Covent Garden, composed by* HENRY R. BISHOP; *to which are added, the three Songs composed for the above Play by* DR. ARNE. *The Poetry selected entirely from the Plays, Poems, and Sonnets of Shakspeare.* (Goulding, D'Almaine, & Co., Soho-Square.)

IN our last Number, under the head of *Drama*, we declared our sentiments without any reserve on the conversion into an opera of Shakspeare's *As you like it*, a play which ranks, deservedly, amongst the most delightful of his works, and that requires no adscititious aid to render it palatable in the present age, when its author is more generally understood, and more highly valued than at any period since the birth of his productions. We have now therefore, only to express our opinion of the manner in which Mr. Bishop has executed the task assigned to him, without again adverting to the metamorphosis, which we hold to be altogether indefensible in the present instance.

This publication comprises an overture and fourteen vocal pieces: three of the latter are Dr. Arne's beautiful and well known songs, "Blow, blow, thou Winter Wind," "When Daisies pied," and "Under the Greenwood Tree*;" all the rest are newly-composed by Mr. Bishop. The overture is of the genuine medley kind, made up of fragments of airs that are, or have been sung in all Shakspeare's plays; of unconnected bits from Purcell's music in Macbeth and the Tempest; from Arne's melodies in this very drama, and from those set by Bishop or selected by him, for the plays which he has already assisted in transforming into operas. The whole of it when kneaded and dove-tailed together, is, with the exception of an extremely good opening *andante*, not worthy of so able a composer, and infinitely below the occasion.

We will now consider the vocal pieces separately, according to the order in which they are performed and published.

The first that appears, a duet for two Sopranos, takes all its character from the key, A flat, and is not without merit as a composition, but discovers no novel trait.

The second, a song for *Rosalind*, recals to the memory the overture to Macbeth, though in a different measure. There is nothing very distinct or attractive in its air, but the accompaniment has some good ancient harmony in it, that suits well with the scene; for example—

Such passages remind us very seasonably of the madrigalists of Shakspeare's age. We cannot quit this song without observing, that it exhibits a new *mark* of measure, and it is not easy to guess why; for we assert that there is no difference between $\frac{6}{8}$, which is here employed, and common time, as hitherto designated by a C; therefore must condemn the throwing a fresh perplexity in the way of performers. It ought to be the study of sensible musicians to simplify their art, which is most unnecessarily complicated in its signs, and not to discourage those who pursue it as a delightful accomplishment, by the intrusion of another impediment.

The third piece, an interminable song given to *Celia*, is but indifferent. The words are ill adapted for music, and injudiciously chosen. The next is a glee for four male voices, in E flat, six-eight time, *Alla Caccia*, that is, in the hunting style, and very like all compositions of the kind. Then comes one of Arne's delicious songs, "Under the Greenwood Tree," to refresh us after the chase. The sixth is a comic song, given to *Touchstone*.

The seventh composition in order of publication is the beautiful sonnet, "Crabbed Age and Youth," set as a trio for *Rosalind, Celia,* and *Touchstone*. We cannot help being surprised that Stevens's admirable glee was not brought in here, for it would have been no difficult matter, in these days of dramatic violence, to produce a fourth person on the stage.

The eighth is Dr. Arne's exquisite air, "Blow, blow, thou Winter Wind." The ninth, a mediocre glee and chorus for four men's voices. A very pretty song follows this, "Oh! thou obdurate!" though the words are not very tractable in musical harness. This is succeeded by an air for *Rosalind*, in E, equal to the last in point of beauty, and superior as a union of poetry and music, beginning, "If Love had lent you twenty thousand Tongues." It is written for Miss Tree, and adapted to her low compass, going down to B continually; therefore not practicable by all female voices; but it may be transposed into G without suffering materially, and can thus be sung by any soprano.

Arne's playful, melodious, and charming song, "When Daises pied," is the twelfth piece; and here we notice an instance of squeamishness that amounts to downright immodesty, in the change of the common name of the plant, *Lady's-smock,* to *Lady's-frock!* Now, although it is not at the present day supreme *bon ton* to allude to this part of female attire, and we should be much surprised to hear, in any place, the homely Saxon word used voluntarily, in preference to the French term, which is become quite Anglicised; yet, as the former is perfectly inoffensive in itself, and has never before been objected to in its place, we cannot but disapprove the alteration. If every word in Shakspeare is to be at the mercy of capricious fashion, we may as well bid adieu at once to the writings of our great dramatic bard.

For the *Procession of Hymen* a lively and agreeable march and dance are introduced; after which the connubial God himself sings an air, set to the words, "Then

F 2

is there mirth in heaven," which is rather in the style of "*Bid me Discourse*," but very remote in degree of merit from this fine song.

The duty imposed on the critic is any thing but a pleasing one. We feel the force of this truth in mentioning the errors of accentuation which so often obtrude themselves on our notice in musical compositions, and from which the foregoing pieces are far from being exempt. In the Trio, " Crabbed Age and Youth," the accent is thus thrown ;

Age like win - ter, like win-ter bare.

in the same trio, we find

youth I do a - dore thee !

In the chorus, No. 9, the first words in the following line, " and having clim'd the steep-up heav'nly hill," are set as follows.

and having climb'd, and having climb'd the

The air, "Oh! thou obdurate!" shews similar inaccuracies, which are also observable in other places. But we gladly quit these, to notice a kind of new reading produced by emphasis, in the before-mentioned trio, in which Mr. Bishop has deviated from the usual mode, and, we think, with great judgment :

O my love, my love is young.

O! si sic omnia !

Les Charmes de Baden, RONDO PASTORALE *pour le* Piano-Forte, *par* CHARLES CZERNEY. Op. 45. (Boosey & Co., 28, *Holles-Street.*)

WE have here a very clever, pleasing rondo, by M. Czerney, rather less difficult than one or two other compositions by the same master that we have had to review, though in truth it seems to be a stubborn task for him to write music that is practicable for any but decidedly first-rate performers. We, therefore, felt ourselves uncommonly fortunate in being enabled to offer to our subscribers, the air that appears in this number, which is almost the only comparatively easy work by the author that has fallen into our possession.

This *Rondo Pastorale* occupies seventeen pages, including two allotted to the *introduzione*. Its motivo, which is remarkably buoyant and gay, is borrowed from part of the French air, " C'est l'amour," and well relieved by other subjects. The modulations are skilful, without being painfully *recherchées*, and a studied clear design is

traceable throughout the whole. The introductory part, an adagio in the *cantabile* style, shews great taste ; and the second subject of the Rondo (page 6, staff 1,) is beautifully expressive. Amongst other novel passages that are scattered in different parts of the rondo, is one that partakes of the nature of the double shake, produces nearly the same effect, and is easy to perform. We insert a single bar of it ;

gva alta. _____

We have only to regret that the author of this piece draws so largely upon the performer's powers of execution ; for not many will be found ready to answer the demand. Nevertheless this, like a few other things of the kind, may most advantageously be practised, and it must reward the student for the trouble bestowed.

THREE BRILLIANT WALTZ-RONDOS *for the* Piano-Forte *Composed by* J. N. HUMMEL, *Maître de Chapelle, &c.* No. 3. (Chappell & Co., 50, *New Bond-Street.*)

THIS is the third of a series of rondos, the two first of which were reviewed in No. xxiii, page 208, of our work. The present is in a much more familiar style than its forerunners, and the greater part of it, is so easy to execute, that most players may undertake it without apprehension of failure ; though there are some few passages in it that will demand from the majority of performers a little patient practice. This is a very charming rondo, full of melody, with a distinct and forcible rhythm, that leaves an impress on the organ of hearing. These are properties that all understand and feel : but it is not without other qualities that will recommend it to the learned in music ; the modulations are scientific, but not forced, as pleasing as ingenious, and are blended with the lighter parts with so much taste and judgment, that we shall be much deceived if it do not become a very general favourite.

A FAVOURITE WALTZ, *with* Variations *for the* Piano Forte, *Composed by the following Eminent Composers,* BEETHOVEN, C. CZERNEY, GÄNSBACHER, GELINEK, HUMMEL, KALKBRENNER, LEIDESDORF, LISZT, MAYSEDER, MOSCHELES, MOZART JUN., PIXIS, PLACHY, TOMASCHEK, WORZISCHEK. (Boosey, & Co., *Holles-Street.*)

IN our eighth number we printed a waltz by A. Diabelli of Vienna, which has been so much admired in Germany, that nearly all the composers of any fame in the capital of Austria have written variations upon it : Beethoven, our readers may recollect, composed no less than thirty three. A variation upon the same subject from each of the fifteen composers whose names appear in the above title, has been collected, and the whole together formed into one piece ; thus exhibiting in a single work the different styles of the masters who have contributed. Something like this was produced many years ago by Mr. Latour, who, wrote a number of variations on a given air, in imitation of the piano-forte composers residing at that time in London. It was an ingenious thought, and he executed it well, but still it only consisted of imitations; whereas the present is an aggregate of originals, and consequently much more interesting and curious.

Like most of the new publications that appear in Vienna, this offers no facilities to the great body of piano-forte players: it should rather be considered as an exercise, or an assemblage of examples, than as a piece to be performed merely for amusement. Indeed its length, twenty-five pages, will prove a bar to its general use in social parties. But as a study it is much to be recommended; the assiduous practitioner therefore will not regret obtaining a copy, and devoting some time to the overcoming of the formidable obstacles which it certainly presents.

Before quitting this article we must add, that we examined the contribution of *the son of Mozart* with a very anxious eye, but found nothing in it that indicated the genius of the parent: it is elaborate, and full of intentional difficulties, without effect, though shewing no want of scientific contrivance. This fact is more mortifying than surprising: it does not seem to be the intention of nature to make genius hereditary.

1. *The favourite* SCOTCH AIR, " Sandy lent the man his mull," *with an* INTRODUCTION, *arranged for the* PIANO-FORTE *and* FLUTE, *(ad lib.) by* T. A. RAWLINGS. (Gow & Son, 162, *Regent-Street*)

2. The Bridesmaids' Chorus, CARILLON RONDO, *for the* PIANO-FORTE, *composed by* AUGUSTUS MEVES. (Cramer, Addison, & Beale, 201, *Regent-Street*.)

BOTH of these are light compositions, full of pretty, easy passages, such as everybody can execute, and none will dislike. The Scotish air possesses a great deal of character, and will excite more or less of gaiety in all who hear it played with the spirit that the music of our northern neighbours requires.

The Bridemaids' Chorus, is The Fairies, published in the fifth number of the HARMONICON. Mr. Meves has mingled a great deal of what may be termed bell-music, —passages usually given by church-bells,—with this charming little piece from the Freischütz, and has made a perfectly easy, and a very agreeable compound of the two, and some few additions of his own.

1. The Parade, a MILITARY DIVERTIMENTO *for the* PIANO-FORTE, *by* CIPRIANI POTTER, Op. 17. (Gow and Son, 162, *Regent-Street*.)

2. The SICILIAN AIR, *on which is founded* " Home, sweet home!" *arranged with* Variations *for the* PIANO-FORTE, *by* J. C. NIGHTINGALE, *Organist of the Foundling*. (Halliday, 23, *Bishopsgate-Street*.)

MR. POTTER's divertimento consists of a march, with a trio, *alla Rossini*, and a quick step as a finale. All the movements are written with a view to general circulation, therefore facility is the first thing which the author has studied, and he has succeeded in his aim.

Mr. Nightingale has put some easy, but yet shewy, variations to the pretty Sicilian air, which constitutes,— not " on which is *founded*"—the popular air sung by Miss M. Tree. But we must observe, that as the melody

is quite of a plaintive kind, and the words set to it excite nothing but tranquil associations, quick variations upon it are altogether out of character.

A familiar VOLUNTARY *for the* ORGAN, *composed by* J. C. NIGHTINGALE, *Organist of the Foundling Hospital*. No. 4. (Monro and May, 11, *Holborn Bars*.)

THIS is a continuation of the series that we have mentioned before, and is well worthy the attention of all organists. The work is good, and singularly moderate in price. The present number is confined to four pages, comprising a soothing *andantino* for the swell, and a spirited fugue for the full organ. The latter may make a good exercise for the left hand, and is a brilliant movement for the noble instrument to which it is dedicated.

La Salle d'Apollon, *a collection of new and elegant* GERMAN WALTZES *for the* PIANO-FORTE, *composed by the most esteemed foreign authors.* Nos. 1 to 7. (Wessel and Stodart, 1, *Soho-Square*.)

THIS is a very elegant little work, in the style, but far superior in engraving and paper, of some pretty German publications. It is in octavo, and each number contains a waltz and trio in two closely-printed pages, in a small character, with a neat copper title,—for sixpence each! If this do not produce a sensation in the profession and trade, we shall be much surprised: such an attempt to reduce the price of music, and to sell it at a profit of only one hundred per cent., ought to be immediately resisted, surely, gentleman! In the meanwhile the name of Prince Ypsilanti, the composer of one of the waltzes, will bring this work into most alarming notice.

1. La Petite Ecossaise, AIR WITH VARIATIONS *for the* PIANO-FORTE, *composed by* JAMES CALKIN. (Lindsay, 217, *Regent-Street*)

2. L'Offrande au genie, DIVERTIMENTO *for the* PIANO FORTE, *by the same.* (Eavestaff, 66, *Great Russel Street, Bloomsbury*.)

3. WALTZ *for the* PIANO-FORTE, *by* M. C. WILSON. (Cramer, Addison, and Beale, 201, *Regent-Street*.)

4. FRENCH AIR, *with* Variations *for the* PIANO-FORTE, *by* THOMAS VALENTINE. *(By the same.)*

5. La Gracieuse, a DIVERTISEMENT *for the* PIANO-FORTE, *composed by* JOSEPH DE PINNA. *(By the same.)*

No. 1 is as simple and easy as the youngest or humblest performer can wish. Mr. Calkin certainly has not bestowed much time in search of original ideas for either his present air, or the variations to it.

The second is of a different description, and possesses considerable merit, particularly the *aria*, which shews both taste and knowledge.

No. 3 is a pleasant bagatelle. No. 4 is Le Troubadour du Tage, with three short variations and a finale: the whole forming an easy, pretty piece, of five pages.

No. 5 is put together with taste. In other respects what we have said of No. 1, may fairly and safely be applied to this production of M. de Pinna.

1. *The* OVERTURE *to* DER FREISCHUTZ *arranged for the* HARP *and* PIANO-FORTE, *with an accompaniment of* FLUTE *and* VIOLONCELLO, *by* N. C. BOCHSA. (Boosey and Co., 28, Holles-Street.)

2. Amusement for the Harp, *by* N. C. BOCHSA; Nos. 1 and 2. (J. B. Cramer, Addison, and Beale, 201, Regent-Street.)

3. Divertisement Ecossais, *by* T. A. RAWLINGS, *arranged as a* DUET *for the* HARP *and* PIANO-FORTE, *by* D. BRUGUIER. (Gow and Son, 162, Regent-Street.)

THE above overture by M. Weber is, in its present form, exceedingly well contrived for effect, and the accompanying parts are very easy to execute. It is here that M. Bochsa excels, his arrangements are almost always skilful, and do justice to the authors whose works he adapts, for he understands well the characters and powers of the various instruments he employs.

Both numbers of the " Amusement for the Harp" are easy, without being trifling. They have neither of them much pretence to originality, but are popular in their style, and well put together. The first has the fine air, Rosline Castle, introduced in it as a slow movement; and in the second appears Gluck's pathetic air, *Che farò senza Euridice?* both of them in a simple form and not distorted by any irrelative variations.

The third of these publications is a very easy arrangement of the pretty Scotish Divertimento composed by Mr. Rawlings, originally for the piano-forte only.

1. " Child of the Sun," SCENA *for a Baritone Voice, composed by* BURFORD G. H. GIBSONE. (Boosey and Co., and Clementi and Co.)

2. " What is Prayer?" *Composed for Three Voices, by* SAMUEL WEBBE. (Cramer, Addison and Beale, 201, Regent-Street).

MR. GIBSONE'S composition, which he terms a *scena*, —though he does not tell us from what dramatic poem the words are taken,—manifests a good deal of enterprise, and some ability ; but as to invention, the best but rarest thing in art, we have not been able to discover in it much of that irrefragable proof of genius. It must however be confessed, that there appears to be a necessary sameness in all English works of the cantata kind, written for a base or baritone voice, which no talent or industry can overcome. Dibdin gave a good receipt for the construction of an Italian bravura ; and, unless we are much mistaken, we could supply a formula for the compounding of a British base cantata.

This *scena* proves the author to be well acquainted with the great modern composers: that he has studied them with assiduity and advantage, his harmonies shew most clearly, and his instrumental parts partake of the same school ; but the air, which after all is the grand point, wants novelty, it resembles, without being in any way borrowed, a hundred other airs for a base voice. Let Mr. Gibsone, however, not be discouraged ; let him go on, and we think that he will have no reason hereafter to regret his perseverance. We do not recollect any great composer whose first, second, or even third work, gave him a niche in the temple of Fame.

Mr. Webbe gives no name to his composition, which therefore we venture to call a hymn for a soprano, tenor, and base voice, with a piano-forte accompaniment. It has a solemnity in it that is strictly in character with the words, and though not very new,—how little, alas,

can boast of this quality !—is elegant and soothing. The poetry of this is surely very beautiful ; but unfortunately it appeared in the newspapers when two or three of them were teeming with the false accounts palmed upon them, and with nonsense ; and the whole of what they printed being judged *en masse*, these stanzas were too generally condemned along with the wretched stuff to which they were joined.

1. SONG, " Pale the moon-beam shone," *written by* T. G. SMITH, Esq., *the music by* JOHN PURKIS. (Hedsoll, 45, High Holborn.)

2. DUET, " Hark ! those tones of music stealing," *with an accompaniment for the* HARP *or* PIANO-FORTE ; the words from BOWRING'S *Specimens of Russian Poetry; composed by* M. S. (Monro and May, 11, Holborn Bars.)

3. BALLAD, " The Dew-drop," *composed by* JAMES CLARKE. (Lavenu and Co., 24, Edward-Street, Manchester-Square.)

THERE is much to praise in the first of these vocal pieces, in respect to composition ; and a little to censure, as far as regards the setting of the words. The music displays a considerable share of fancy, and a strong feeling for bold harmony ; though the G flat in the last vocal staff of page 8 is rather daring. Mr. Purkis, in giving three quavers to the word " maniac," in exceedingly slow time, is not governed by the modern rules of orthoepy ; *ma-ni-ac* sounds very ill, at a period when the best speakers strive to press the word into two syllables, *ma-niac* ; and as Dr. Johnson's *mani'ac* is by universal consent quite exploded, it must not now be adduced as any authority. We object also to the breaks made by the accompaniment, in lines that ought not to be separated by rests : such errors in setting offend sensible hearers, and bring the art into discredit with those whose opinions ultimately will prevail.

The duet is an exceedingly pretty, unpretending little work, and though it will not strike by its originality, will please by its simplicity and ease.

The ballad contains the following lines complimentary to music;—

" And music is never so dear,
As when to its last notes we listen."

We often feel the justice of this assertion, while listening to a dull performance. But now and then, when coming in at the end of a guinea concert, the truth of the remark flashes upon us forcibly, though in a somewhat different sense.

The author of this air does not appear to have much respect for prosody, for he places the above preposition " to," on the accented part of the bar, and repeats it in the same way no less than three times in the space of five bars.

Analysis of the LONDON BALL ROOM: *in which is comprised, the History of the Polite Art, from the earliest period, interspersed with Characteristic Observations on each of its popular Divisions of Country Dances, which contain a selection of the most fashionable and popular ; Quadrilles, and Waltzes; arranged for the Piano-forte.* (Thomas Tegg, 73, Cheapside, and R. Griffin and Co., Glasgow.)

A RIGHT active man is Mr. Tegg, and most useful in his calling : he never puts his hand to any thing without proving his wish and means to do good. Lately he gave us an excellent work on chronology, and now he supplies us with one on choregraphy, both closely connected with nimble-footed Time; that, shewing how he slips away, and this, teaching how he may be kept.

There are some good treatises on dancing extant, but they are scarce, and most of them too elaborate. Noverre's is really a learned book, but it relates chiefly to the ballet, and theatrical branch of the art. Sir John Gallini's is more applicable to general purposes; this however is out of print, and a little too diffuse, the nature of the subject being considered.

The present work is well got up for popularity, containing much in a small space, and at a moderate price, compared to what is usually demanded for quadrilles, &c. We wish that the historical portion had been somewhat less diffuse, and the didactic part rather more extented, the author's objects would then have been, we think, more fully attained. These he states to be,—

"1st. To furnish the youthful part of the polite world with a Manual, which, without affecting to instruct them in the mode of acquirement, should, being instructed, supply them with the necessary materials for the practice of a rational and elegant amusement, in that situation, of all others without impeachment, the paternal roof. 2ndly. To take such a view of the History of the Art and its capabilities as may tend to remove the prejudices which may be entertained against it. 3rdly. To present to all the votaries of the muse a companion easy of access and correct in information."

A full third of the volume is occupied with a history of dancing, the modern application of the art, and a consideration of its utility. This is, of course, a compilation, but it is well compiled. Some directions for preserving the "etiquette of the ball-room" follow, which are as much intended for the instruction of the master of the ceremonies as of the public. Then begins the musical part of the work, which contains twenty-one country dances, six quadrilles, and nine waltzes, printed in type. The specimens are remarkably well selected, but the type is of the ancient and very imperfect kind.

"Country dances," the author tells us, "are the most popular, the oldest, and as capable of almost unlimited variety the best style of dancing that the English ball-room presents; they are considered to be of English origin, and as according in a remarkable degree with the genius of 'merrie England' we are inclined to that opinion, and till better reasons are exhibited we shall continue to consider them as national.

"The general character of this style of dancing is simplicity, ease, freedom, and liveliness, rather inclining to the mirthful than the graceful, and to cheerfulness than elegance."

Of that species of dance which for the present at least, has quite superseded the former, the author says, " Quadrilles are of novel introduction in this country, and we are indebted to the French for their revival, for they approximate so nearly to the dance termed the cotillion that design or invention cannot with justice be applied. They are danced in sets of eight, twelve, or sixteen persons, but the set of eight is best calculated for displaying the true spirit and the elegant graceful evolutions of this mode of dancing."

" The characteristics of the style are freedom, chasteness, and graceful ease. It will be obvious from the limited number of participators, that the quadrille is better adapted for the select few who compose the private assembly, (and for whose use this work is principally designed) than for the public ball, where too frequently the numbers prevent that selection we deem important.

" It is customary to play the first part of each tune prior to dancing to it, when it will commence with the second, unless it require the first to be repeated, with which also it usually terminates."

Last, though not least in general liking, comes the waltz, so vigorously assailed by some stern moralists, but which, nevertheless, keeps firm possession of the ball-room, unmoved by the anathemas of those who would check the social and innocent intercourse of the sexes, instead of encouraging its openness, and directing its influence. Of this German invention it is here observed, that " Assimilated with the country-dance, and partaking of its social character, it yet preserves its own peculiar features; the air, the movement, the graceful inclinations of the body and limbs, skilfully adapted to its expressive music, and keeping in unison with it, added to the various elegant positions, form, altogether, one of the most pleasing pictures the English ball-room presents."

FOREIGN MUSICAL REPORT.

VIENNA.—A new Opera Seria from the pen of Mercadante has been produced here, entitled Doralice, which, notwithstanding the exertions of the singers, proved little better than a failure. The opera was produced for the benefit of the Signora Eckerlin; and was brought out by the author himself, who comes to make some stay at Vienna. The effect of the whole was flat, and the only two pieces that pleased were an air in the first, and a duet in the second act; the latter is really a production of great beauty and originality. The overture, though noisy and full of pretension, met with but little applause. The same was the case with the first scenes, where there was but little to applaud, saving the excellence of the performers. The opening air of the hero (Signor Rubini,) served the singer as a scale upon which he was enabled to exercise all his powers of voice and variety of ornament, and as such met with its portion of applause; but as to originality of motive or management of subject, it was looked for in vain. The entrance air of the heroine (Signora Eckerlin,) though proceeding from beautiful lips, produced no impression, for it had some trifling drawbacks—a want of subject, and of every thing romantic; a character of music so well suited to the powers of this singer, and so naturally expected from the situations of the piece. The opening part of another air, sung by Donzelli, with its accompanied and expressive recitative, was much and deservedly applauded, and afforded ample scope for the powers of this admirable singer; in one part he reached the C in alt with perfect sweetness and precision. The air that followed was one of the favourites of the piece. The finale of the first act does not rise above mediocrity, and abounds with passages to which we are constantly tempted to bow as to old acquaintances.—The duet in the second act between Rubini and Donzelli, forms an exception to the rest of the music. It is full of sweetness, of an original cast, and enjoyed the advantage of being admirably sung; the applause was stormy, and both the singers and the maestro were called forward to receive the congratulations of the public. The concluding air of the Signora Eckerlin was of a piece with the rest of the work—weak and ineffective, and the finale, noisy, without energy and character. In a word, this composer must be allowed to be well versed in the technical branch of his art, and can get up a score cleverly enough, but in all his compositions there shines forth scarce one spark of real productive genius; scarce a trait of redeeming originality is found to animate the mass. But the greatest fault we have to find with Mercadante is the undisguised manner in which he imitates and borrows from the works of others, good and bad. Like the Boa Constrictor which devours indiscriminately all animals that come in its way, though it does not disdain the more delicate repast of a lamb or a fawn, so our author surrounds every thing with the gluten, with which his voracity supplies him, and thus swallows by wholesale.

VIENNA.—The other operas given here have been *Otello, Il Barbiere di Seviglia, Il Corradino, La Gazza Ladra,* and the *Elisa e Claudio* of Mercadante, which was received with considerable applause on the first representation, but which afterwards diminished in attraction.

BERLIN.—During the dearth which at present prevails in the field of creative excellence, our theatre here, under the direction of the indefatigable Spontini, is devoting its attention to the revival of the neglected beauties of the ancient school. The *Alceste* of Gluck has been brought forward with great effect, and every care has been taken by the composer above named, to have it given according to the true tradition of the movements; he has been for days together on the stage directing the orchestra and the performers in the attainment of this most desired object. The other masterpieces of this great ornament of the old German school are to follow in succession, and under the auspices of such a master, what may not the public expect! The other operas have been *Der Zögling der Nature* (The Child of Nature,) by Romani; *Preciosa; Belmonti und Constance,* by Mozart; *Der Bär und Der Bassa,* (the Bear and the Basha,) by Blum; *La Folie,* by Mehul; *Die Parias,* by Seidal; *Die Zauberflöte; Le Cantatrice Villane,* by Fioravanti; *Der Freischütz; Jean de Paris,* by Boildieu; *Kiaking,* by Girowetz; *Il Barbiere di Seviglia; Il Don Giovanni; Der Schiffskapitain,* (The Ship Captain,) by Blum; and on one evening was tried a selection in one act, of pieces from the *Ciro in Babilonia* of Rossini.

DRESDEN.—The management here has been very liberal this season in treating the public to a variety of dishes in the great music feast of the Opera. A long list of composers of various degrees of merit has been presented to us from Mozart to Rossini, from Rossini to Blum. The following is the bill of fare: *La Dama Colonello,* by Raimondi, three times. The music of this opera is light and ineffective. The truth of this seems to have been felt, if we may judge from the numerous airs and other pieces which it was judged necessary to introduce in it, not to mention a concertino with variations, given by Concertmaster Rolla, between the acts; *La Cenerentola,* three times; the *Maometto* of Winter, twice; *Tancredi,* once; *La Gazza Ladra,* twice; *Le Cantatrice Villane,* by Fioravanti, once; *Otello,* once; *Wie gerufen,* (the Arrival Apropos) by Paer, the music without power, an opera depending upon the good performance of the singers; *Euryanthe,* twice; *Preciosa,* three times; *Der Freischütz,* four times; *Die Entführung aus dem Serail,* twice; *Don Juan,* twice; *Die Zauberflöte* three times; *Jean de Paris,* by Boildeau, once; *Aschenbrödel :* Cinderella, by Isouard, once; *Il Sacrificio Interrotto,* by Winter, twice; *Cordelia,* by Kreutzer, once; *Rochus Pumpernickel,* by Blum, twice; *Die Rothekappe;* (The Red Cap,) by Dittersdorf, twice; *Nachtigall und Rabe,* Nightingale and Raven, by Weigl; *Fidelio,* by Beethoven; and *Le Chaperon Rouge,* by Boildieu.—Signor Rastrelli, (the elder composer of that name,) is engaged here as director of the Italian Opera.

MUNICH.—The novelty here has been a new opera from the pen of Pavesi, entitled *Egilda.* It was sustained by some of the first talent of the day, Signor Crivelli, Velluti, and Signora Lalande, and abounded with many strong theatrical situations; but after all it obtained but little or no success, which may in a great measure be attributed to this circumstance, that the music was not adapted to a German public, as all was done for the voice, and little or nothing for the instruments: the

latter appeared to be considered as merely assistants to the former; they were never allowed to maintain a prominent situation, or to tell their part of the story with effect. Add to this that the piece is full of reminiscences. Emboldened by the example of Rossini, modern composers seem to imagine that they can act thus with impunity: but in the present instance it was seen, that if relying upon the strength of his reputation, Rossini despises the ridicule poured upon him from every quarter, on account of this his besetting sin, yet that a composer of less note must not venture to take the same liberty. Pavesi tried it, and his piece fell to the ground. The other operas given during the season were, *Elisabetta,* twice; *La Gazza Ladra,* twice; *Il Don Giovanni,* four times; *Fidelio,* twice; in which latter difficult music, a new singer of the name of Devrient, acquitted herself to great advantage, and gives great hopes of future excellence; *Semiramide,* once; *Sophonisba,* once; *La Molinara,* three times; *Cosi fan tutte,* three times; *Otello,* twice; *Der Schnee* (the Snow-Storm,) four times;—the latter will, in all probability, be found here every season, with its attendant winter;—and *Il Mosè,* which had a long run.—The great attraction of the season has been the Signora Lalande, who was received on all occasions with great enthusiasm. This lady studied under Garcia, and afterwards became a pupil of Velluti. Power, taste, novelty in the ornaments of song, and an admirable delivery of the recitative, are proof of the good school from which she came.

STRASBURG.—The company here during the last season was very effective, nor have we ever witnessed a more brilliant and successful season, both at the French and German Opera. In the former were given *La Neige,* by Auber; *Otello,* by Rossini, and arranged in French by Castil-Blaze; *Valentine de Milan,* by Mehul; *La Valet de chambre,* by Carafa; *Le Caverne,* by Leseur; *La Flute Enchantée,* by Mozart; *Le Confidences,* by Nicolo; *Œdipe en Colone,* by Sacchini; *La Caravane;* Rousseau's *Divin de Village,* and *Pigmalion,* in which Madame Mariane Sessi made her appearance, and was received with great applause. She is a very chaste singer, and is likely to become a great favourite here.—At the German opera were given *Don Juan, Tancredi, Freischütz, Freischütz* twice; *Schweitzer-familie, Barbiere di Seviglia, Italiana in Algeri, Opperfest,* (The Sacrifice,) *Die Unsichtbaren,* by Eule; *Rochus Pumpernikel, Johann von Paris, Die Entführung aus dem Serail, Waisenhaus,* (The Asylum,) and *Daniel* or *Der Strassburger auf der Probe,* (the Strassburger at his wits ends.)

Among the Concerts of this season was one given in the theatre by M. Eugene Roy, the following was the announcement; "Flageolet solo des Fêtes de la Cour de France, compositeur de musique et artiste d'un des principaux theatres de la Capitale; *La Caprice des dames Parisiennes:* aussi divertissement, ou pot-pourri burlesque, tiré de l'opera, *Freischütz* de Rossini!! arrangé à grand Orchestre par M. Roy, tel qu'il a eu l'honneur de l'exécuter devant plusieurs Souverains, et récemment à la cour de S. M. Le Roi de Würtemberg, dont il a reçu les temoignages les plus flatteurs." But singular as this advertisement may appear, we must do M. Roy the justice to say that his performances on the flageolet are very extraordinary, particularly the effect of a prolonged echo which excited great admiration; in the dying falls of which, the tones were so faint that they were produced by the artist with his instrument quite beyond his lips.

—In church-music, we have had *Die Sieban Worte, (The Seven Words)* of Haydn, and a grand mass, by Beethoven, which were both given with great effect.—The music Institution under the superintendence of M. Baxmann, which is conducted on the principle of mutual instruction, proceeds in a prosperous manner. This indefatigable artist has succeeded in teaching his pupils, after a comparatively short instruction, what other professors have found it difficult to accomplish after long and laborious efforts;—we mean the art of singing at sight, and of writing down musical phrases, and whole compositions from hearing them only, and that with a facility that seems scarcely practicable.

WEIMAR.—The operas performed here during the last season have been *Tancredi*, *Il Matrimonio Secreto*, *La Molinara*, *Les Deux Journées*, *Jean de Paris*, *Cenerentola*, *Je toller je besser*, (The Folly), *Die beyden Blinder von Toledo*, (The Two Blind Men of Toledo), *Nacht in Walde*, (The Night in the Forest,) *Die Zauberflöte*, twice; *Entführung aus dem Serail*; *Freyschütz*, four times; *Sacrificio interrotto*, *Libussa*, *Count Gleichen*, twice; *Saalnixe*, (The Witch of the Saal). *Schewestern von Prag*, *Neue Sonntagskind*, (New-Sunday's Child,) *Fanchon*, *Bassa and Bär*, *Die beyden Galeeren sklaven*, (the two Galley-slaves,) *Jungfrau von Orleans*, (Maid of Orleans,) *Brant von Messina*, (Bride of Messina,) *Wilhelm Tell*, *Mädchen freundschaft*, and towards the close of the season, *Euryanthe*, twice. With respect to the latter opera, much might be said both in its praise and dispraise; many of its parts are good, many bad, and many between both. It is a general observation among performers, that the music of this opera ranks among the most difficult that has ever come before them. *Richard cœur de Lion* and *Ferdinand Cortez*, are in rehearsal.—Among the sacred music performed here, have been different Cantatas, by Homilius, Mozart, and Zumsteg, the Hallelujah from the *Creation* of Kunzan, a *Te Deum* by Hasse, Haydn's *Stabat Mater*, various masses by Haydn, and Mozart, the *Creation* of Haydn, his *Four Seasons*, and Handel's *Messiah*.—Among Concerts, the most remarkable have been those of Hummel, who has been received here with great enthusiasm.

GENOA.—This town has in its turn been visited by the incomparable Paganini, who excited no less enthusiasm in this, than in the other places through which he passed. His concerts took place in the *Teatro da Sant 'Agostino*, which was crowded in every part. It may not be uninteresting to know the exact arrangement of pieces selected by Paganini on those occasions. It is said that no one is more judicious in his choice than this artist, or, at least no one knows better how to adapt his selection to the taste of his audience; this list will, therefore, teach you to form a correct idea of the reigning musical taste in Genoa.

The first concert consisted; 1st, of an *Introduzione* by Asioli—but coldly received; 2nd, Cavatina from *Il Turco in Italia*, sung by Signora Pastori, *prima donna* of the *Teatro del Falcone*—obtained applause; 3d, *Concerto di un tempo* (an allegro movement) by Kreutzer,) executed by Paganini—was received *con furore*; 4th, *Aria buffa*, sung by Signor Coppini, *Buffo caricato* in the *Teatro del Falcone*—pleased much; 5th, Overture from the *Demofoonte* of Vogel; 6th, Cavatina from *La Gazza Ladra*; 7th, A Pot-pourri, composed and executed by Paganini—tumultuous applause; 8th, Duet from *Il Turco in Italia*; 9th, an Air from Rossini; 10th, Duet from the *Teobaldo ed Isolina* of Morlacchi; 11th, *Introduzione*, *Largetto*, e *Variazioni sul Rondo della Cenerentola di Rossini*, composed and performed by Paganini—*furore on furore*; 12th, *Finale a tutta Orchestra*.

The arrangement of the second concert differed but little from that of the first, except with respect to the introduction of two youthful claimants to public favour. The first was a Signora Bianchi, under twenty years of age, who was characterized in the bills as the little *virtuosa forestiera*, and who sang three airs; the other was a Signora Barette, who played a *Pezzo cantabile*, and a *Sonatina* upon the violoncello. They both experienced a flattering reception. The first has considerable powers of voice and execution; the latter is wonderfully gifted considering her age, which cannot be more than between twelve and fourteen. Paganini played another *Concerto di un solo tempo* by Rode, opening with an allegro movement in D minor and terminating with a *bravoura sonata* consisting of several pieces—the audience seemed to think this too long, a *Sonata militaire* for the G string, composed expressly for this occasion; as well as a *Larghetto a doppie corde*, e *Variazione sul tema*, "*Pria che l' impegno magistral proceda*", and an *Adagietto e Polachetta con Variazione*. But to describe the manner in which Paganini performed those various pieces is far beyond my powers. Those who have not heard him, will be able to form but a very imperfect idea of the unlimited command which he has of his instrument, of the brilliancy and originality of his touch, and of the magic effect which he knows so well how to produce by blending a kind of soft melancholy even with his most brilliant movement. An anecdote has been communicated to us, which is a proof of the extensive sphere of his attraction. A northern traveller and passionate lover of music, M. Bergman, reading accidentally the evening before in the journal at Leghorn, an announcement of Paganini's concert, lost no time, but instantly set out for Genoa, a distance of a hundred miles, and luckily reached the spot just half an hour before the concert began. He came with his expectations raised to the utmost, but, to use his own expression, the reality was as far above his anticipations as the heavens are above the earth. Nor could this enthusiastic amateur rest content with once hearing Paganini, but actually followed him to Milan, in order to hear him exercise his talents a second time.

The operas given this season in the *Teatro del Falcone* have been *Il Mosè* of Rossini, which was received with great applause; *Il Barbiere di Siviglia*, by the same, also very successful; *Il Don Giovanni*, *Elisa e Claudio* by Mercadante, so, so. Operas are alternately given in this theatre, and in the *Teatro da St. Agostino*; the latter is not only much larger but much better calculated for effect. With respect to the decorations and costume of these theatres, as well in the operas as in the ballets, which are of a mediocre class, they are far from being upon a footing with the performances, which are worthy of a better collection of properties. It is at the same time but justice to observe that the orchestra, which possesses several artists of merit, did its best to merit the favour of the public.

BOLOGNA.—A new singer has made her appearance here of great promise in the person of Signora Canzi. She made her debut in the *Barbiere di Siviglia*, and gave her part with great archness and effect, and displayed considerable powers of voice. She is likely to prove a great acquisition to the theatre, and in every representation rises in the public estimation. After one of her performances, the following Sonnet was thrown at her feet, attached to a crown of laurel.

"All Impareggiabile Cantante Signora Caterina Canzi, Prima Donna nelle opere esiguite nel Gran Teatro di Bologna.

"SONETTO.

"Eccelsa Donna, se ai soavi accenti
Spieghi la voce, ogni mortal tu bei:
Te sola ammiran le Felsinee genti,
E di gloria al tuo nome ergon trofei.
La grazie, onde se' adorna e li possenti
Modi, di che ti fer dono gli Dei,
Mostran e fra tue pene e ne' contenti,
Che figlia ai Nuni, e lor delizia sei.
E se l' obblio ricopre or queste or quelle,
Che al dir de' vati fur si care a noi,
E scessero quaggiù fin dalle stelle,
Alma non fia, che l' alto tuo valore
Possa obbliar, e degli accenti tuoi
Quel dolce suon, onde favelli al core.

"*Alcuni Ammiratori*   *Del Signora C. C.*"

[*Translated.*]

"To the Incomparable Singer Signora Caterina Canzi, Prima Donna in the operas executed in the Gran Teatro di Bologna,

"SONNET.

"O Lady, when in tones by feeling graced,
Thy magic voice steals soothing o'er the ear,
What wonder that Bologna's sons should haste
Some humble tribute to thy fame to rear!
But to the gifts of voice the powers divine
Have joined the winning charm of form and face;
Resolv'd a two-fold conquest should be thine,
By song to charm us, and subdue by grace,
Unlike the transient charmers of the day
Thy memory shall not lightly pass away,
Nor from our mind thy form and talent part:
When long, long years have fled, in memory's ear
Thy tones of melting sweetness shall we hear,
Thy voice persuasive, speaking to the heart.

"*Some Admirers*   *of Signora C. C.*"

GOTTENBURG.—The celebrated composer and pianist Ferdinand Ries, is at present here. It is said to be his intention in future to take up his abode in the neighbourhood of his native place—which also gave birth to his illustrious master Beethoven, and his friend M. Salomon—and in the bosom of his family, devoted at once to them, and to the art he cultivates with such success. His residence in this neighbourhood cannot but tend to promote the spread of the art, and increase the number of its votaries.

PARIS.—*The Journal des Modes*, in which the name of Rossini is eminent enough to be noticed, accuses this celebrated composer, of giving the ladies bad accompaniments, in piano-forte pieces. *Il maestro*, adds the critic of fashion, crowds and accelerates the movements towards the end of his *morceaux*, in such a manner, as to deprive amateur singers of breath. This is a very grave accusation, and one which without doubt, M. Rossini will answer.

———— *Théâtre Italien.* Since we last spoke of the *Théâtre Italien*, *Mosè*, *Nina*, and *L'Italiana in Algeri*, have been there performed. *Curioni's* singing in the first of these pieces, was very unequal; he is not so good in *Mosè*, as in *Otello*. *Mad. Mombelli* appears more bold than graceful; *Madlle. Cinti* more graceful than bold; and *Zuchelli* is, at once the most skilful and natural singer that can be heard. In *Nina* we hear and see no one but *Mad. Pasta*. It was not easy to succeed in this character at Paris, after *Mad. Dugazon* and *Madlle. Bigottini* who, without speaking or singing, was as pathetic as *Mad. Dugazon*. *Mad. Pasta*, without imitating either, has by this very means placed herself on a level with both these great actresses. The character which she gives to the madness of *Nina*, has more of exaltation in it than melancholy; but though we are moved less sensibly, we are not moved less deeply. *Mad. Pasta* sings the air *Il mio ben*, with admirable talent: but it is to the manner in which she sings it, that she owes the effect she produces. This piece is exceedingly well conceived; the expression and situation could not agree better. The above air, so simple and melancholy, is only a modulated declamation; the accent of nature is there. It is one of those pieces which cannot grow old; indeed this may be said of almost all the music of *Nina*. Paesiello has not composed any thing more simple and sweet.

———— It is said that Mad. Pasta is likely soon to give an incontestable proof of the conjugal felicity enjoyed by her husband and herself.

By a decision of the King, dated 26th November, some alterations have been made in the management of the *Académie Royale de Musique*, which had been revived by the ordinance of the 22nd of October, 1821. The management is committed to a director; an inspector general; a property-man; a stage manager, and a secretary. At the head of this establishment, is M. Desplantis, knight of Saint Louis, and an old officer of the army of the west. M. Habeneck, sub-director of *l'Ecole Royale de Musique et de Déclamation*, is elected conductor and leader, and the public will again hear with pleasure, the artist whose talent they have so often applauded. M. Kreutzer, after long and honourable exertion, is allowed to retire, and M. Gransire accompanies him. Amongst the persons engaged by the new administrations, the following are spoken of; M. Handry de Janvry, M. Henry, late of the accountant's department of the treasury, and M. Chauvin, one of the editors of *La Gazette de France.*

THE DRAMA.

DRURY-LANE THEATRE.

ON Tuesday, January the 18th, a new Opera, under the name of THE FALL OF ALGIERS, was produced at this theatre, written by Mr. C. Walker, the author of *Wallace*, and composed by Mr. Bishop, being the first work that he has set to original music, since his engagment at this house. The following are the characters, and the persons who represented them:

Orasmin, a Bey of Algiers,	. . . .	*Mr. Sapio.*
Admiral Rockwardine,	. . . . .	*Mr. Terry.*
Algernon Rockwardine,	. . . . .	*Mr. Horn.*
Timothy Tourist,	. . . .	*Mr. Harley.*
Cogi Baba,	. . . .	*Mr. Gattie.*
Mahmoud,	. . . .	*Mr. Brown.*
Hartley,	. . . .	*Mr. Mercer.*
Ben Brown,	. . . .	*Mr. O. Smith.*
Omar,	. . . .	*Mr. Comer.*
Selim,	. . . .	*Mr. Howell.*
1st Slave,	. . . .	*Mr. Webster.*
Amanda,	. . .	*Miss Graddon.*
Lauretta,	. . .	*Miss Stephens.*
Zaida,	. . . .	*Miss M. Nicoll.*
Almaide,	. . .	*Miss Carr.*

This Drama is made up of very slight materials, although its performance lasted four hours. Story, plot, or incident it cannot boast, and in situations, (according to the theatrical term,) it is lamentably deficient. The first act introduces *Algernon Rockwardine* to our notice, who details to *Timothy Tourist*, his servant, the story of his woes,—of his early marriage, and of his father's displeasure. *Timothy*, determining to lighten the load of captivity, commences taking notes, and resolves, when liberated, to publish an account of the gentle treatment of slaves, under the mild government of the Algerines. *Algernon's* wife, *Amanda*, is also a captive, and *Orasmin* falls deeply in love with her. He presses his suit, but in vain; *Algernon*, however, is within his grasp, and he is promised immediate freedom, if he will resign his wife into the arms of the Algerine. But the former, like most other scenic lovers, determines to sacrifice his life rather than comply, and *Orasmin* threatens him with instant death. At this critical moment the British fleet heaves in sight, commanded by the father of *Algernon*, when the Dey consents to the liberation of all the christian captives. *Orasmin* however determines to make *Amanda* his property, and refuses to obey his master's order: the bombardment of the citadel therefore commences, and in a few minutes *Amanda* is restored to her husband, and the Admiral has the pleasure of rescuing a son, whose fate he had long considered as utterly hopeless. There is also a love affair between *Timothy Tourist* and *Lauretta*, but *Cogi*, an old servant of the governor's, is smitten with her beauty, and has placed her as an attendant on *Amanda*, in the Harem, until a fitter opportunity occurs for making her his wife. She yields a pretended consent to his addresses, and he, in the excess of his love, gives her sundry jewels, which he had purloined from his master. These jewels she speedily transfers to *Timothy*, and aids his escape, by furnishing him with the cloak in which she herself was to have passed the guard, on her way with *Cogi*, to take shipping for England.

The *Siege of Algiers* is decidedly a counterpart of that dull drama, *The Siege of Belgrade*; but the latter is adapted to Martini's best, and very generally-admired opera, *La Cosa rara*; while the former is not one of Bishop's happiest efforts. The master is shown in every part of it, no doubt, but not in that airy, fanciful humour which generates popular melodies, or striking effects. Mr. Bishop has not written an overture to this opera, therefore that to Cherubini's *Anacreon* is performed: but the band is not powerful enough to give due effect to this splendid composition. The weakness is chiefly observable in the violins, which ought to be unusually strong to do justice to so grand a work; a work that is considered as the author's *chef-d'œuvre.*

To Miss Stephens and Mr. Sapio in the vocal department, and to Mr. Harley in the comic, whatever success *The Siege of Algiers* may experience, must be mainly ascribed. To their efforts the public did justice, though the injudicious attempts of friends to encore some pieces that did not strike the audience generally, were powerfully resisted. A song and a duet however were almost unanimously re-demanded, and merited the applause bestowed on them. But here we must stop, as, most likely, this opera will come under our notice in a printed form.

COVENT-GARDEN THEATRE.

THIS theatre has offered nothing to our notice of a musical kind that is new, since our last report. It is said that Weber's Melo-drama, *La Preciosa*, is getting up at this house, and we hope that there is truth in the rumour.

THE

OVERTURE, DANCES, MARCH, SONG, AND CHORUSSES;

IN THE MELO-DRAMA OF

$\mathfrak{Preciosa}$;

THE MUSIC BY

CARL MARIA von WEBER:

TO WHICH IS PREFIXED,

A ROMANCE (ON WHICH THE DRAMA IS FOUNDED) ENTITLED, THE

LITTLE GIPSY ;

TRANSLATED AND ABRIDGED FROM THE SPANISH OF

MICHAEL CERVANTES.

The Melo-drama of PRECIOSA was first produced about the year 1819, at Berlin, three years before the appearance of *Der Freischütz*. The principal part was written for Madame Stich, one of the finest women, and first actresses on the German Stage; the character of Preciosa gave her an opportunity of displaying her talents in Dancing and Singing, and also her skill on the Guitar. The words of the Opera are by M. Wolff, himself one of the first actors of the day. He has certainly not availed himself of all the interest with which the romance of Cervantes abounds, but the magnificence of the decorations, and the beauty and originality of the Music, atoned for the weakness of the drama, and it acquired a high degree of popularity in all parts of Germany, which still continues, more particularly at Hamburgh.

THE
HARMONICON.

No. XXVII., March, 1825.

PRECIOSA, OR THE LITTLE GIPSY,
A ROMANCE,

On which is founded the Melo-Drama Composed by Carl Maria von Weber;

TRANSLATED AND ABRIDGED FROM THE SPANISH OF

MICHAEL CERVANTES.

An old gipsy woman, who ranked high in her community, had brought up a little girl in the quality of her neice. She gave her the name of Preciosa, and instructed her in all the arts of the gipsy profession, especially in those of dancing and singing, which were objects of much importance in a lucrative point of view. In these she excelled to admiration; but at the same time her conduct shewed a decided superiority over the other girls of the troop, to whom her general manners and conversation presented a striking contrast. She even exhibited traces of good breeding, and of a superiority of mind far beyond her situation. Added to this, she was beauty itself. Neither the sun nor the air, nor all the severity of weather, to which these wanderers are exposed, had in the least tarnished the lustre of her beauty, or impaired the delicacy of her complexion. She also possessed great natural vivacity of manner, and a talent for wit and repartee; but though her conversation was playful and unreserved, her language never gave offence to delicacy; and such was the profound respect, strengthened by affectionate regard, which all the gipsy women, both old and young, entertained for her, that there was no one in the whole sisterhood, who presumed to say or sing any thing in her presence that was calculated to raise a blush. The old gipsy, her reputed aunt, was fully aware of the value of so precious a treasure, and acted like the eagle, who while she teaches her young ones how to fly, still keeps them within the reach of her talons. Wherever Preciosa went, she was always accompanied by the old woman, who sedulously impressed upon her the importance of making the most of her voice. Accordingly our young heroine was amply provided with a store of ballads, sarabands and *villanelles*, which she sung with wonderful grace. If the reader is curious to know from what source a constant supply of these useful materials were procured, we will inform him, that the old gipsy kept a number of poets in her pay; for, singular as the fact may appear, even in Spain, there were numerous sons of the Muses to be found, who were gracious enough to condescend to accept of money from the gipsies, in return for their compositions!

Preciosa received her first education in various parts of Castile, and when she had attained the age of fifteen, her pretended aunt carried her to Madrid, with a view to exhibit her talents, and to turn this treasure to the best account at the court, where, says the intrepid Cervantes, every thing is to be bought and sold, like fish or fowl, in the common market. Preciosa made her first appearance in the capital, on the festival of St. Ann, the patroness of the city. She entered by one of the principal streets, heading the other gipsy girls in a dance, to the enlivening sounds of the Biscayan tabour and the gay castagnettes. Her companions were decked out in gaudy finery, but Preciosa chose rather to appear attired with the utmost neatness and simplicity. All the dancers excited admiration, but Preciosa bore away the palm of applause. Indeed, she far outshone the rest, and possessed a charm of manner, and a marked superiority of air, that involuntarily attracted the attention of all who beheld her. The people flocked in crowds around her, and young as well as old, joined in manifestations of delight and encouragement. When the dance was concluded, she was requested to sing; this she did with unaffected grace: love and war formed the subject of her romance, and when it was ended, the air resounded with shouts of applause. After this the party proceeded to the church of Santa Anna, where, after dancing before the image of the saint, Preciosa sang a hymn in her honour. The hearers were all rapture. Heaven bless thee, child! said one. What a pity, exclaimed another, that she should be a gipsy; on my soul she merits a better fate, and deserves to be the daughter of a lord. Others were more gross in their remarks,—Oh, let the young baggage only grow up, said one, and she will steal more hearts than she will rob hen-roosts!

When this itinerant party were on the point of retiring a handsome young man availed himself of a favourable moment, made his way through the crowd, approaches Preciosa, presented her with a folded paper, whispered a few words of well-turned compliment, and disappeared, On reaching her home, Preciosa examined the enclosure, and found it to contain a song in her praise, and a carolus of gold. "It is somewhat extraordinary," said she, with her usual sprightliness, "to receive gold from a poet; such gifted beings have seldom much to give. If this be his mode of offering a song, may he copy the whole collection of romances ever composed, and present them to me one after another!" But in spite of this sally of wit, it cannot be denied that the elegance of the unknown poet's person, and the delicacy of his manner, excited Preciosa's curiosity, and left behind something of feeling to which she had before been a stranger.

After making a short, but profitable stay, in Madrid, the gipsy band quitted the capital, in order to pursue their adventures in some other place. As they pursued their way, they beguiled the time with the following lines, which they sung in chorus :—

Through forests—
Through greenwood forests around,
The echoes sound,
The merry echoes sound
As our jovial song
The deep woods along,
Comes mixt with the echoing horn's rebound.
Trarah, Trarah, &c.

The night, the night,
Throughout the livelong night,
Our watch we keep,
While the drowsy world's asleep,
While wolves are prowling
Our resting place round,
But start at the bay of the deep-mouth'd hound,
Wauwar! Wauwar, &c.

The world we roam,
The wide, wide world we roam,
Our ample home,
The world's our ample home,
While forests and valleys
Are loudly resounding
With songs from the earth to the welkin rebounding,
Holloo! Holloo, &c. *

They had proceeded only a few miles from the city, when in the midst of a pleasant valley they were overtaken by a person wrapped in a cloak, who said he wished for a private interview with the aunt of Preciosa, and the young gipsy herself. Accordingly, after a short consultation, it was agreed to hear what the stranger had to communicate, and they all three retired to a short distance from the company. No sooner were they alone, than the young man raised the beaver with which his face had before been partly concealed, and Preciosa was surprised to behold the young poet, who had presented her with the copy of verses, enclosing the carolus of gold. Addressing himself to the aunt of Preciosa, he told her that he was distractedly in love with her neice; that he had made many efforts to conquer his passion, but finding it impossible, had come to the resolution of devoting his life to her alone. Having made this declaration, he threw aside his cloak, and discovered on his breast the badge of one of the chief orders of Spain. He then proceeded to tell them that his name was Don Juan de Carcame, that he was an only son of one of the grandees of Spain, and entitled to a very large inheritance; but that all his fortune would be of no avail to render him happy, unless he could share it with Preciosa; that if they entertained a doubt of his sincerity, he was willing to submit to any test they might think proper to require; and in order instantly to give them some proof of the truth of his assertions, he presented the old

* These verses, and all that follow, except those beginning "When Preciosa's gentle touch," in page 41, were translated from the German, and adapted to the original music which appears in the subsequent part of this number, they were therefore produced under restraints that must apologise for any irregularities that may be found in them.

woman with a purse, containing a hundred crowns of gold, to be divided among the company.

The whole time Don Juan de Carcame was speaking, Preciosa listened to him with the most earnest attention; neither his person, his looks, nor his manners were disagreeable to her, and above all, his discourse and the earnestness with which it had been delivered, excited her most serious reflections. After a moment's pause, she requested permission of her aunt to address the knight. She began by assuring him, that though she was only a poor gipsy girl, that she had a soul above disgrace, and a virtue that was proof against all presents and promises. That to shew the sincerity of his professions, a more substantial pledge was necessary than his bare declaration. That she must in the first place ascertain whether he really was the noble person he proclaimed himself to be, and if so, that he must make up his mind to quit his father's house, and take up his abode among the gipsies for the space of two years, by way of probation.

The knight without hesitation accepted of the terms proposed; it was agreed that a party of the gipsies, with Preciosa at their head, should revisit Madrid the following day, in order to ascertain, by certain tokens given them by Don Juan de Carcame, the truth of the statement relative to his family, after which they were to repair to an appointed spot, at some distance from the capital, to await the return of their new companion, who, to prevent any suspicions from arising in his father's mind, was to pretend a journey to the north of Spain, where friends of his family resided. All this having been arranged, the knight took an affectionate leave of Preciosa, and returned to Madrid.

The following day, Preciosa, the old woman and a chosen party of the gipsy girls mounted their mules and revisited Madrid, in order, as had been agreed, to make the necessary enquiries respecting the family and connexions of Don Juan de Carcame. The particular street had been named to them by the knight, and the sign by which they were to know the house was a balcony with gilded lattice-work. On their way they were surrounded by a crowd who importuned them to dance, but so intent was Preciosa upon the object of her search, that nothing could divert her attention. They reached the street in question, and had not proceeded far down it, when they perceived the balcony which had been so particularly described to them. Standing there they saw a gentleman of about fifty years of age, who wore a red cross on his breast; by which distinction, as well as by the dignity of his deportment, it was no difficult matter to see that he was a person of high distinction. This gentleman no sooner perceived the gipsies, than he beckoned them to come in, assuring them that they should be handsomely recompensed. At this moment, three other knights joined the gentleman in the balcony, and they immediately perceived that one of them was Don Juan, who could not conceal his emotion at beholding his charming Preciosa. Encouraged by the invitation, all the party entered the gate and proceeded to the saloon, excepting the old woman, who purposely remained below, in order to gather from the servants something relative to the quality and expectations of Don Juan. As soon as the young gipsies entered the saloon, the elderly gentleman already described, exclaimed, "Doubtless that young girl," pointing to Preciosa, "must be the pretty gipsy girl who has been so much the subject of conversation here for some days past, and of whose wit and accomplishments so much has been said."—"Yes, it is she," returned Don Juan, "and without exaggeration she is one of the most beautiful creatures ever seen."—"Yes, they say so," said Preciosa, "and it shows how blind the whole world must be!"—"By the life of my little Don Juan," exclaimed the gentleman, "you are a thousand times more beautiful and charming than fame had reported; I say it without a word of flattery."—"And who is this *little* Don Juan, this son of your's?" inquired the young gipsy, with an arch demure look.—"Oh, the young knight who stands near you," said he pointing to the lover of Preciosa. "Well," cried the cunning gipsy, "I could have sworn that you were protesting by the life of some little Don Juan who could hardly run alone. Do you call this, pray, your little Don Juan? Why he is old enough to be a married man; and if I may be allowed to judge by some peculiar lines which I observe in his features, I do not think three years more will pass over his head, without his taking a wife, and that wife of his own choice too, or his mind must undergo a wonderful change." —"Then you have some skill in physiognomy" said one of the gentlemen.—"To be sure I have," returned Preciosa, "for what as a gipsy should I have been doing all this while in the world, if I had not possessed some little knowledge of the art, in order to be able to discover the tempers and dispositions of men? For instance, I know that Don Juan is of a very susceptible heart; he is disposed to jealousy, and he is also disposed sometimes to make indiscreet promises, which, he may, perhaps, find it no such easy a matter to perform. Heaven grant!" continued she, regarding Don Juan with an expressive look, "heaven grant he may not prove a deceiver!—Yes, on looking again, I see he is shortly to undertake a journey; but people do not always follow the route they profess to take. Perhaps, he may speak of going to the north, and yet it may be so ordered, that his journey may lay to the south: man proposes, but heaven disposes!"—"Strange to say, little gipsy," said Don Juan, somewhat disconcerted by Preciosa's frankness, and yet delighted at her ingenuity, "strange to say, that many things you have foretold concerning me, are perfectly correct; but I trust your suspicions as to my being a deceiver, will never be verified; I am sure, upon my conscience, that no such imputation has heretofore attached to my conduct. Yes, I am to undertake a journey, and I trust it will prove a prosperous one."— "I trust it may," said Preciosa; "but before you set out, allow a gipsy girl to offer you a little piece of wholesome advice. Young man, learn to moderate your passions, do not act precipitately; make no engagement that you do not fully mean to fulfil; detest falsehood, and—don't forget to give me something for having told your fortune." —"I thank you most sincerely," said Don Juan, "for your good advice. But there is one thing upon which you have dwelt, that mortifies me extremely; you have renewed your charge of doubting my sincerity; you would seem to insinuate that I am a deceiver. I must then protest my abhorrence of deception. Falsehood is debasing to all, and particularly to those who pretend to the rank of gentlemen in society. But you have asked me to recompense your gift of divination; I am ashamed to say I have not at this moment the means. It was but yesterday that I had an unexpected call upon me for my money, and I have exhausted all my allowance; but here is my father who will reward you in my place."

In the mean time the old gipsy entered, and said she must put an end to the conversation, for that they had much to do, and must depart for the country, before the nightfall. All the gentlemen entreated that they might be indulged with a dance. With this the gipsies complied; Preciosa took a Biscayan tambour, and led the dance with so much agility, lightness, and elegance, that the whole company was in an ecstacy of delight.

And here a little incident occurred, which we must not neglect to notice. Just as Preciosa was finishing the dance, she dropped a paper, which one of the gentlemen picked up and instantly exclaimed, "Oh charming! here is a madrigal, let it be read aloud for the good of the company." In fact, it was the copy of verses which had been presented to Preciosa by Don Juan, and which she had ever since kept treasured in her bosom. The father of Don Juan wished to look at it: it was handed to him, the turn of the thought pleased him, and he desired his son to read it aloud. This was a thunderbolt to poor Don Juan. But what was to be done; to refuse, would in some measure have been to criminate himself; therefore, with much stammering and agitation, he read aloud the following madrigal.

When Preciosa's gentle touch
Awakes the lute with forceful art,
The magic of the tones is such,
They steal unheeded to the heart.

And when her voice with dulcet sound,
Melodious strikes the raptured ear,
What sweet enchantment breathes around,
What pleasures gladden all who hear!

But though her voice possess such power
To lead at will the captive mind,
Yet claims this gipsy for her dower
Charms of a more resistless kind.

Her sparkling eye darts forth such ray,
Her beauty wakes such wild alarms,
That all must own her magic sway,
And kings be slaves of such bright charms.

Preciosa pretended to be very angry at the reading of these verses without her permission, but in secret she enjoyed extremely the confusion of Don Juan, and was delighted with this new proof of his love, for his embarrassment but too plainly revealed what was passing in his mind. Exchanging looks of tenderness, the lovers now bade a silent adieu, and the gipsies returned to their inn, mounted their mules, and returned to join their company, who had pitched their tents at the skirt of a wood, in order to pass the night.

Meanwhile Preciosa found that a revolution had taken place in her heart's affections; she was no more the same person, she felt that she no longer existed for herself alone, her heart was another's; but then that person was of a rank in life that made her startle at the contrast. Then too he was absent, and the alarming thought would dart through her mind, that he might not return; that she might never again behold him. She became thoughtful and melancholy; she sought to be alone, and the importunities of the old gipsy were now doubly annoying to her. At length the beldame fell asleep, and Preciosa profited by this moment to steal out alone. The evening was beautifully calm, and the moon rode in unclouded lustre. She wandered to a retired spot, and at a distance from the gipsy camp, and gave vent to her feelings in the following song.

When the gentle eve descending,
Brings a charm to day unknown,
When the moon her light is lending,
Sweet to wander forth alone.

H 3

Yet not lonely, thou art near me,
In this soft propitious hour;
How those looks, those accents cheer me,
Imag'd strong by fancy's power!

Absent far, in hours of gladness
Or of sorrow, think on me;
Trust me still, in joy, in sadness,
All my thoughts are still with thee.

The following day beheld the return of her lover. It was hailed with joy by the whole party, and the necessary preparations were made, without delay, for initiating Don Juan de Carcame into all the mysteries of the profession. One of the largest of their cabins was carpeted with turf, strewed with sweet herbs, and adorned with boughs and flowers. In the centre stood an elevated seat of cork-tree, on which the knight was placed, into whose hands were given a hammer and a pair of pincers, as emblematical of their arts. It was then agreed that the name of Don Juan de Carcame should be changed into that of simple André; and two gipsies thrumming a prelude on their guitars, he was called upon to show his agility in dancing, by cutting a caper or two. He was next ordered to uncover one of his arms, which was bound with showy silk riband, and then desired to wield two cudgels, which he did with great skill. These important ceremonials being concluded, the oldest gipsy of the band took Preciosa by the hand, and leading her up to the initiated, addressed him in a set speech. "We appropriate to you," said he, "the companionship of this our favourite maiden, who is the flower and ornament of all the gipsies in Spain. Consider maturely, and once for all, whether she be really the object of your choice, for we warn you that that choice once made, you can never again retract, and must be contented with your fate". He then entered into a long eulogium on the gipsy life, described its numerous advantages over a fictitious state of society, and drew a most animated picture of the gipsies' spirit of adventure, of the trials to which they are exposed, and of the undaunted courage with which they bore up against persecution and ill-fortune. "We are masters," continued the gipsy, warming with the inspiring nature of his subject, "we are masters of the fields and woods, of the mountains, springs, and rivers. The forests supply us with fuel unbought, the trees with fruit, the vines with grapes, the fields with game, the rivers with fish, and the hedges with the best and the whitest of linen. Early accustomed to hardship, we can scarcely be said to be sufferers. We sleep as soundly upon fresh straw, as others upon beds of down, and infinitely more to the promotion of our health; and by exposure to all the seasons, our bodies become covered, as it were, with a coat of mail, impenetrable to all the inclemencies of the weather. We become insensible to grief; we learn to despise torture and death; we ridicule all distinctions between the negative and the affirmative, except when it suits our purpose. The dazzling splendour of glory, the flame of ambition, and a certain ticklishness about honour, never affect us, though, to be sure, in this respect, we do but resemble many other fraternities. One of the great maxims of our profession is, that as the world is one great family, all things ought to be in common, and that the odious distinctions of *mine* and *thine* should be totally done away with. Hence, as members of this great family, we freely appropriate to our use such of its goods as come in our way, and of which we feel the natural want. It is true that the fictitious institutions of what is called

society, frequently interfere with this our great principle of action; but after all, what is its effect but to teach people a necessary degree of caution, and a laudable watchfulness over their property? Be assured, young novice," cried the venerable gipsy, raising his voice, while his eyes sparkled with animation; " be assured that you will derive inconceivable delight from a profession, which possesses infinitely more charms than you can as yet imagine. Indeed, what in the world can we picture to ourselves as more delightful, than to possess, without labour, all those things for which others waste the sweat of their brow! than to quit our houses in the evening destitute of every thing, and to return in the morning laden with every thing that the heart can wish! It cannot, however, be denied," added he, gradually lowering his voice, "that every question has its worst side: there are disagreeables belonging to every profession: it would be foolish for people always to look for fortunate days; the merchant cannot be always a gainer by his traffic: but it is also true to say that, in our profession, the good infinitely overweighs the evil; indeed, there is no kind of comparison between them. It cannot be denied that our way of life sometimes terminates all of a sudden at the gallows; but this only happens very, very rarely, and the misfortunes of a single individual ought not to dishearten all the rest of mankind. Besides, we have nothing to fear from a suffering brother; silence is one of the most sacred articles of our creed: in a word, we hold that a man may die a martyr, but never a confessor. No," exclaimed he, again raising his voice, "the fate of one individual ought not to put us out of heart. Because one vessel meets with a storm, and is wrecked, does it follow that others must not venture to sea? Would it be very wisely resolved, that the soldier should renounce the profession of arms, because, in the lapse of ages, a few millions have perished in the field? and if some of us are sentenced to tug at the oar, and to bear those little brands which are sometimes burnt into our shoulders, what, if things are considered in their real light, what should they be looked upon but as the staffs of our office, and the stars of our knighthood?" He concluded by again impressing on Don Juan's attention the necessity of a conscientious adherence to the principles and observances of the tribe, and of devotion to Preciosa, the acknowledged and affianced partner of his peregrinations. The inamorato replied at some length to the eloquent harangue of the aged orator, promising to remain true to the gipsy laws, and faithful to the lovely partner that they had consigned to him. When he had finished, the party again struck their guitars, and all joined in a song in praise of their newly initiated companion, André.

After a variety of adventures in this part of the country, it was determined that they should go and recruit the funds of their company in the province of Mercia, was a rich district, and where the party was not known. Accordingly, early on the following morning, they set out upon their march. A young colt was offered to André, but he refused it, declaring that he preferred proceeding on foot, in order that he might attend upon his young mistress, who was mounted on a sorry mule. These attentions were not lost upon Preciosa, who felt her love for André daily increase. The morning was fresh and delightful; the sun was rising in all his glory over the mountains of Mercia; and the matin song of a thousand birds resounded on every side. The moment was inspiring; the gipsies felt its influence, and as they moved briskly along, they sung with great glee and spirit, the following chorus:—

> We wake with sun,
> Our course to run,
>   O'er mountains and valleys afar.
> The crow of cock,
> Our 'larum clock,
>   Our watch-light the twinkling star!
> With merry song
> We march along,
>   No matter what country we roam;
> The world is wide,
> Let what betide
>   Wherever we come we've a home.
> Kind nature pours
> For us her stores,
>   And not over dainty are we;
> To refuse no gift,
> And to laugh at thrift,
>   Our maxims of wisdom shall be.

After a journey of a few days, during which the two lovers were inseparable companions, exchanging an abundance of tender expressions, and reiterating every hour their mutual protestations of eternal love, the company arrived at a town within three leagues of Mercia, and encamped near it. The band here, according to custom, distributed themselves into parties, and the more respectable among them, Preciosa, André, the old aunt, and two young gipsy attendants, entered the town, and took up their lodgings at an inn kept by a widow, who was reported to be very rich. She had a daughter between seventeen and eighteen years of age, named Carducia, who was of a very lively temper, rather good looking, and by no means of a bad taste. This young girl saw the gipsies dancing, and was much delighted with their grace and spirit, particularly with that of one of the inmates of her mother's house. This was no other than André, of whom she became so suddenly enamoured, that she was resolved not to let the very first opportunity pass of revealing to him her passion. No sooner was this hasty resolution formed, than she was all impatience to carry it into execution. She had not watched long for the young gipsy, before she saw him enter an inner-yard to look to his mule. As no one was near the spot, she at once accosted him, and without further preamble—"André," said she, having already learnt his name, "I am an only daughter, and shall inherit a good fortune; there are some persons who do not think me so disagreeable, and if I am fortunate enough to find favour in your eyes, there is nothing to prevent your becoming my husband. Answer me candidly, and if you are wise, do not suffer so favourable an opportunity to escape you; it is not every day that you will have the good fortune to find such a one." André remained confounded by the suddenness of the address, and the frankness with which such a declaration was made to him by the young, and not unhandsome, heiress. "You shall be satisfied," said he, the moment he had recovered from his surprise; "I will not keep you in suspense. To be candid with you then, my good Carducia, you have addressed yourself to a wrong person; my heart is pre-engaged, and no longer at my disposal. I have pledged my word to another, and our marriage is to take place the earliest opportunity; and to speak the truth, we gipsies never marry but with those of our own race. May heaven requite you for the favour you intended to confer on a poor gipsy, of which I am very unworthy, but even if I thought myself otherwise, and you were ten times as rich as you say you are, all would be unavailing to make me unfaithful to the word that I have pledged, which to me is more sacred than the obligation of an oath."

So utterly was Carducia confounded at this unexpected declaration, that she nearly sunk to the earth. She was not at all prepared for the rejection of so liberal an offer, and was about to remonstrate, when some other gipsies entered the yard, and prevented her. Filled with rage and disappointment, she immediately hurried away, breathing nothing but vengeance, and resolving to seize the first opportunity of carrying it into effect. André, who was not unacquainted with the female heart, and knew of what a disappointed woman was capable, like a wise and prudent man, was desirous of avoiding the impending storm by a hasty flight. He made known all that had taken place to the party, and entreated them to prepare to quit the town without delay. But if André had his views, Carducia, whose advances he had repulsed, had also hers. Jealousy and love are always upon the alert; she had contrived to gain intelligence of André's intended departure. As there was no time allowed her to renew her suit, she came to a resolution of arresting by force, him whom she was unable to detain by love. Seeing that not a moment was to be lost, her ingenuity was awakened, and love and vengeance supplied her with means which succeeded but too effectually. Amidst the confusion into which the gipsies were necessarily thrown by the suddenness of their departure, they could not look to every thing; and Carducia taking advantage of their embarrassment, got possession of André's leathern travelling bag, which she knew from the rest, and put into it various articles of value, such as a gold chain, a pair of rich coral bracelets, several rings, and other trinkets of her own. At length the gipsy band commenced their movements; but scarcely had they left the inn, when Carducia rushed into the street, and burst into the most tragical lamentations, exclaiming that the gipsies had robbed her, and carried away her jewels. The whole of the inhabitants of the village, with the Alcalde at their head, ran together at these outcries. The gipsies made a halt, and boldly asseverated to a man, adding some pretty round oaths into the bargain, that they had not taken a single thing, in proof of which they offered to open their baggage, and allow every thing to be searched. There was one among them, however, who was terribly alarmed at this proposal; for besides the splendid dress which Don Juan had laid aside on embracing the gipsy profession, she had certain other valuables in her baggage, which she was very anxious should not be exposed. But she was soon freed from her dilemma by the artifices of the designing Carducia, who after the baggage of one of the party had been examined, inquired which was the pack belonging to yonder fine dancer, pointing to André, for that she had twice observed him enter her room and perhaps he had her property. André burst into a laugh; but he did not laugh long, for what was his confusion, when, on opening his bag, the officers pulled out the whole of the stolen articles! All attempts at justification were vain; the Alcalde was unbounded in his reprobation, as well of André as of the whole party, and a soldier, one of his relations, who stood near him, roused André from the state of stupefaction into which this mysterious occurrence had thrown him, by a violent blow on the face, which nearly levelled him to the ground. It was then that the gipsy André vanished, and nothing was seen but the high-born spirit of Don Juan! His lofty nature could not brook the insult; he darted upon the brutal soldier, snatched his sword from its scabbard, and stretched him, to all appearance, lifeless at his feet. The enraged Alcalde sent for a strong guard, while the people ran furiously to the spot and seized the bold gipsy. Preciosa fainted away, and the unhappy lover, more solicitous to succour his mistress than to defend himself, quietly submitted to be seized by the populace, whom he could easily have dispersed, had not the love and the grief that overpowered all his faculties, prevented his making use of the soldier's sword which he held in his hand. André was immediately loaded with irons, and the Alcalde, who grieved for the fate of his relative, would have hanged him upon the spot without further ceremony, had he been invested with the power; but it was necessary to send him to Mercia, as this town was under its jurisdiction. All therefore that his fury could do was to expose the unhappy man to the insults of the rabble, and during the whole night to torture him with every kind of indignity.

The following morning the Alcalde marched off André and the rest of the gipsies, for they had all been made prisoners, under a strong escort to Mercia. The rumour of the affair had already reached this place, and the whole city flocked out to see the prisoners. Preciosa, whose beauty appeared still more interesting in the midst of her tears, attracted the admiration of all. The rumour of her charms reached the ears of the governor's lady, who felt so deep an interest in her fate that she desired to see her, and prevailed upon her husband not to suffer her to be imprisoned with the rest. Accordingly, Preciosa, as well as her reputed aunt, were, by the command of the governor, conducted to the house of the governor's lady. In the meantime, the unhappy André was thrown into a dark dungeon, with his hands and legs strongly fettered.

Preciosa had no sooner entered the room where the governor's lady expected her, than the latter received her with great kindness, embraced her with extraordinary tenderness, and rivetted her eyes so strongly upon her, that, without being able to assign any reason for it, she could not withdraw them again. "What is the age of this sweet young creature?" said she, addressing the reputed aunt of Preciosa. "Madam," replied the old woman, "she will be fifteen, in a month or two." "The very age," cried the lady, heaving a deep sigh "of my poor Constancia. Alas !" added she, "this young thing makes me sensibly feel that I am the most unhappy mother in the world; she renews a secret source of grief in my soul, which will not cease to flow till death has sealed it up for ever." In the mean while, Preciosa, who was overcome at being received with such unexpected kindness, had taken the hand of the lady and was bathing it with her tears. She now ventured to speak; she endeavoured to impress the mind of her protectress with a conviction of the innocence of the gipsy who was in prison. She protested with great earnestness, that the jewels which had been found in his baggage, had been placed there by a wicked artifice to ensnare him to his ruin; that as for the soldier who had been killed, he had drawn his destruction upon his own head by his imprudence and brutal conduct. "If you are pleased to feel any interest for me," continued she, kneeling, and in a tone of the most earnest supplication, "preserve my life by preserving that of the prisoner. Yes, my life depends on his! he is my husband, though just and honourable impediments have delayed our marriage, and our hands have not yet been

united at the altar. If money be necessary to obtain pardon, to appease the demands of the relations of the deceased, we are all of us willing to sell every thing we possess in the world. Oh, madam, you know what love is; you are married: pardon then the urgent solicitation of a wife who is virtuous, and who pleads for the life of a husband, whom she loves with all the devotion and tenderness of her heart."

During the whole of this address the eyes of Preciosa were rivetted on those of the governor's lady, while she held her hand fast locked in hers, bathing it with the tears that streamed from her eyes. The lady, who had listened to the whole with an interest and an emotion that were inexplicable even to herself, could not withstand the earnestness of the last appeal, and melted into tears. In the midst of this, the governor entered the room, and was not less struck with the singularity of the scene, than with the beauty of Preciosa, doubly heightened by grief. He inquired the meaning of all these tears; and the answer Preciosa made him was to release his lady's hands and run and embrace his knees. "Behold me at your feet," cried she, nearly exhausted by her grief, "to crave the pardon of my husband; or rather to demand justice for him at your hands, for he is innocent; his misfortune and his natural greatness of soul are his only crimes. But if his evil destiny should pursue him even to death; if the fatal sentence of the law must be passed upon him, at least, let me be permitted to die in his place; and if such a willing sacrifice be not sufficient, at least, sir, do but suspend his sentence for a few days; for I despair not to be able to produce proofs of his innocence. Heaven will always protect those who are only criminal because they have not the means of defending themselves." The governor was so astonished at the force and justness of such reasoning in a young girl, that he was not able to utter a word in reply, so utterly was he absorbed in admiration.

During this touching scene, the old gipsy woman stood lost in thought. She seemed pondering over something of importance, and her bosom appeared to labour with some mighty secret, which embarrassed her greatly, and which she could not bring herself to disclose. At length, appearing to gain resolution, she approached the governor, and begged permission to withdraw for a few moments, adding: "With your permission, sir, I will explain an important mystery, which will more than surprise you, and convert your grief into joy; although," said she, muttering in a under voice, "what I am about to disclose may prove fatal to myself." Saying this, she rushed out of the apartment, leaving them confounded at her words. During her absence, Preciosa redoubled her tears and supplications, and above all entreated respite. Her object in the last request was to gain time that she might apprize the father of Don Juan of all that had passed. She saw that it was the only expedient left for delivering him, though with relation to herself it was the most fatal alternative she could adopt, for it was in reality nothing less than to renounce for ever the hope which she had so fondly cherished, of one day becoming the wife of Don Juan.

The old gipsy was not long before she returned. She entered with a small casket under her arm, and entreated the governor and his lady to withdraw with her for a moment into another room, as she had something of great moment to disclose to them. The governor, who had no other idea than that she had some theft to dis-

cover, which might in some way or other affect the present case, complied, and they retired into an adjoining room. No sooner were they alone, than the old woman threw herself upon her knees, and said ; "If the joyful tidings I am about to impart, does not merit your pardon for the crime of which I am come to confess myself guilty, then I am ready to suffer every punishment you may please to inflict; but first," added she, "let me ask you whether you know these jewels ?" producing the casket which contained the jewels of Preciosa, and presenting them to the governor. He declared he had no knowledge of them. "Then," said the old woman, placing a paper in his hand, "this will inform you to whom they belong." The governor hastily opened it, and read as follows.—
" The name of this little girl is Donna Constantia de Azevedo y de Menesses; her mother is Donna Guimar de Menesses, and her father Don Ferdinand de Azevedo, Knight of the order of Calatrava: she disappeared on the day of the Ascension, at eight o'clock in the morning, in the year 1595. The little girl had on these jewels, which have ever since been carefully preserved in this casket. "

The lady of the governor had no sooner heard the name of Constantia, than hastily seizing the casket, she opened it, and recognised the jewels, which she covered with kisses; but so overpowering were the feelings of the moment that she sunk into a swoon. When she recovered, she addressed the old gipsy:—"Alas !" cried she, in a transport of joy mingled with fear; "and where is the mistress of these jewels, or I should rather say, the dear child to whom they belong ?" "You ask me where she is ?" said the old woman ; "where but in your own house. The young gipsy girl, who has already drawn so many tears from your eyes, is their mistress ;—she is your daughter—your beloved Constantia. It was I,—with remorse I confess it,—it was I who stole her from your house in Madrid, the very day and hour mentioned in that paper. Can you have clearer proofs than these ?" "Yes," exclaimed Donna Guimar, rushing with a mother's tenderness into the room where she had left Preciosa, and where she found her surrounded by the whole household, who were attracted thither by her beauty and the interest they felt in her fate,—"yes, there are proofs even stronger than these;" so saying, she hastily bared the neck of Preciosa, and found a natural mark, with which she knew her daughter to have been born, and which had gradually increased as she had grown up. She then overwhelmed her with caresses, and taking her in her arms, flew into the apartment where she had left her husband. "Yes," cried she, "it is, it is our long lost daughter ! Every thing convinces me of the fact ; nay, were there no other evidence, the extraordinary presentiments which nature herself dictated, the very moment I beheld her, would be a sufficient testimony." "Yes," cried the enraptured husband ; "I felt the same presentiments with yourself; it is our beloved, our long lost daughter, whom heaven has restored us by a miracle, and for which we can never sufficiently express our gratitude."

Preciosa was perfectly bewildered by this extraordinary scene ; ignorant of what had passed in the adjoining room, she was lost in astonishment at the overwhelming endearments lavished upon her by Donna Guimar and her husband, who almost stifled her with their embraces. But when she became sufficiently composed to comprehend what had passed, no language can describe her emotions of gratitude, wonder, and rapturous delight.

The governor wished, for the present, both his wife and her daughter Constantia to keep the affair secret ; he enjoined the old gipsy to do the same, assuring her that he granted her his free pardon. He added, that the joy of having recovered his daughter completely recompensed him for all the anguish he had felt in losing her, and that there was but one thing that still rendered him unhappy, which was the reflection that she should have been affianced to a gipsy, a thief and a murderer. "Ah ! sir," said Preciosa, interrupting him, "he does not merit any of these epithets ; it is true that he has been the cause of this man's death, but so gross and brutal was the soldier's conduct, that he could scarcely expect any other than the fate which has befallen him. The name of murderer, sir, applies only to those who assassinate in ambush, and not to the man who draws his sword in defence of his honour, as this cavalier has done."— "Cavalier!" exclaimed the governor, "what is this prisoner then not a gipsy ?" Here the old woman gave a brief account of the history of André. She said that he was the son of Don Francisco di Carcame, a knight of the order of St. John, an honour which he himself also enjoyed. She added, that she had preserved the dress which he had laid aside on becoming a member of the gipsy band ; and she gave them an account of the contract and agreement that had been entered into between Preciosa and Don Juan, on whom she was most lavish in her praises, though not more so than his merits justified.

The governor and his lady were not less surprised at this recital, than they had been at the adventure of their daughter. The former ordered the old woman immediately to go and fetch the dress of Don Juan, which she did, and shortly after returned, accompanied, by a gipsy, who had had the especial charge of it. During the old woman's absence, the father and mother of Preciosa asked her a thousand questions, to all of which she replied with so much good sense, grace and naiveté united, that she could not have done otherwise than command their affection, even had she not been recognised as their daughter. They pressed her most earnestly to tell them, whether she really felt a sincere regard for Don Juan. The question embarrassed her at first, but, at length, she acknowledged that her attachment was of the warmest and most sincere kind, being founded at once upon love and gratitude ;—love for his virtues and amiable character, and gratitude for his condescension in having humbled himself so far as to become a gipsy for the love of her. That she felt it a duty to make some return for the extraordinary sacrifice which he had made ; but that, nevertheless, this feeling should never exceed the bounds which their consent and approbation should think fit to prescribe. "Let us talk no more of this, my dear Preciosa," replied the father, "for it is my wish that you should ever retain that name in memory of our having once lost you, and happily recovered you again. I am your father, you are my daughter ; and be assured that I shall neglect nothing to procure you an alliance worthy of your birth and your virtues." Preciosa sighed deeply at hearing these words, and her mother, full of penetration, saw clearly the depth of her attachment for Don Juan. The governor also made the same observation in his mind, and continued : "Your destiny my daughter is fixed. Don Juan is of a distinguished family ; his love for you cannot be otherwise than sincere ; heaven has certainly formed you for each other, and it is not for us to oppose its designs. In the mean time I must direct my attention to the poor Don Juan, who is suffering in prison; but till I find a proper opportunity of publishing his innocence, I enjoin the strictest silence on this subject." Saying this, he embraced Preciosa, and went to visit Don Juan, in order to put in execution a project which he had conceived, of ascertaining whether the affection of the prisoner for his daughter was sincere.

He accordingly repaired alone to the prison in which Don Juan lay, loaded with irons, and on reaching it, learnt with great satisfaction that the soldier, who had been supposed to be mortally wounded, had recovered, and was pronounced out of danger. On entering the cell in which the prisoner lay, he ordered a skylight to be opened, in order to have an opportunity of surveying his countenance more attentively, and assuming a stern aspect, thus addressed him: "You see before you the chief judge of the city; I am come to examine you on the subject of the crimes of theft and murder with which you are charged. But first of all, I wish to ascertain whether it be true, that a young gipsy girl, who belongs to your party, and who is at present in my house, be your lawful wife?" Don Juan no sooner heard these words, than a suspicion flew across his mind that the governor had become enamoured of Preciosa and had her conveyed to his house, in order to try and persuade her to become his own. He manifested great uneasiness, and replied in an agitated manner, "That if the gipsy girl had declared herself to be his wife, she had been guilty of no falsehood, for that, if in one sense, she was not his wife, in another she certainly was." "It is true," replied the judge, "that she has simply said she was affianced to you, and I can well believe it; for though eventually it matters but little to me whether you be married or not, it was necessary that your answers should strictly correspond. This young girl, who in consideration of her extreme beauty deserves that I should grant her some small request, when not in opposition to my official duty, seeing that there was no hope of your escaping the sentence of the law, has so earnestly importuned me to permit your espousals to take place before the execution of your sentence, that I have almost come to the resolution of granting her request."—"Ah! if it were permitted me to mingle my prayers with hers," said Don Juan, "it would be the only favour I should have to ask at your hands. I feel that if this were granted to me, I should have nothing to regret in the loss of life; conscious that I die innocent, solely for having been actuated by the just indignation of the moment to punish a coward who had insulted my honour, that honour, which belongs to every state and profession."—"I see you are desperately in love, with this little creature," said the governor.— "Yes, sir, I do love her with all a husband's tenderness," said Don Juan; "with a love more sincere than language can describe; and I sum up all the happiness I expect upon earth in exchanging with her my plighted faith, and receiving her hand before I die. Let this be done, and I welcome with joy any fate that may await me, however severe."—"Well," replied the governor, scarcely able to restrain his feelings at this proof of genuine love, "this very day, you shall have your request." Accordingly, at the appointed hour, (for so the governor had arranged it,) Donna Guimar, a father confessor, Preciosa, and some domestics, met in one of the apartments of the prison. Don Juan was introduced, laden with chains, and pale from exhaustion, confinement, and agitation of mind. Preciosa, who was ignorant of

what was to take place, uttered a scream at the sight of him, trembled violently, and would have sunk in a swoon, had not her affectionate mother come to her support, and soothed her with the assurance that all was intended for her happiness, as well as that of the object of her affections. All were struck at the contrast of feelings exhibited on this occasion; Preciosa in tears and agitation, Don Juan overwhelmed by his feelings and melted at the view of Preciosa, while the governor and his lady were all composure and even cheerfulness.

After a few moments of profound and painful silence, Don Guimar desired the priest to make the necessary arrangements for performing the ceremony of marriage between the gipsy man and the little gipsy girl. The priest said he could not undertake to do it, as the forms of the church, which were indispensable, had not yet been complied with. "The ceremony must then be postponed," said Don Guimar; "and this interruption will be the means of delaying the punishment of the criminal; because, as my honour is engaged that he shall marry this little gipsy, I must see the requisite forms of the church complied with to that effect. And," continued he, addressing the prisoner, "I draw the most favourable omen in your behalf from this delay. But tell me honestly; should fortune prove favourable in this instance, and at the moment you are mutually exchanging vows with this little gipsy, should your pardon be pronounced, in which character would you wish to estimate your happiness? Would it be as the gipsy André, or as the knight, Don Juan de Carcame?" What was Don Juan's astonishment at hearing himself addressed by his own name! But this surprise did not prevent his answering the question, with his usual candour and nobleness of feeling. "I find," said he, "that Preciosa has not been able to preserve secrecy, and that she has disclosed who I am. Never mind; I will not falsify my own heart. Were I permitted to taste the happiness which you promise, I should be a thousand times more happy than if I were the master of the world. With her, and with her only, I centre every wish of my heart, every hope and comfort on this side the tomb."—"Don Juan," said the governor, "I can contain no longer. I pronounce you innocent. I have heard all; I have the happiness to acquaint you that the soldier, who was thought to be mortally wounded, has recovered, and there is no longer any fear for his life. Preciosa shall be yours; and in possessing her, allow me to say that you possess all that I myself hold dearest upon earth. Yes, in giving you the hand of Preciosa, I give you Donna Constantia de Menesses, my only daughter, who if she is equal to you in love and sincerity, is not beneath you in birth and connexions,"

Don Juan, at hearing these words, could scarcely persuade himself that he was not under the sweet delusion of some pleasing dream, from the enchantment of which the terrible reality might yet awake him. The affectionate caresses of his Preciosa, and of his future parents, however, soon convinced him of the blissful reality.

The union of the two faithful lovers took place shortly after, with the entire approbation of the father of Don Juan. Never had Mercia witnessed a day of more general joy and festivity, for the story of the Two Gispies had become familiar in every mouth. Balls and fireworks closed the happy day, and long years still beheld the wedded fair in the possession of increasing happiness.

THE DRAMA.

KING'S THEATRE.

Though the parallel may appear rather ludicrous, yet we cannot avoid comparing this theatre to some fen-farms, which, if productive once in every four or five years, pay enough to enable the tenant to bear the losses he sustains during the unsuccessful intervals. Now and then we have a good season at the Opera House, but it comes about as often as a fine summer, once in an Olympiad, and helps us in our musical chronology, as the celebration of certain games assisted the Greeks in marking the periods of their history.

The last season will long be remembered in the annals of this theatre ; the patronage of the beau-monde was never more lavishly bestowed, and the receipts have seldom been exceeded ; yet the performances were unsatisfactory, and a heavy list of debts, which will never be discharged, were left, to the serious injury of numbers of deserving persons, and, we may almost say, to the disgrace of the nation itself. But let the blame of all this fall on the right head, on Signor Benelli, who, without any one qualification for the office, undertook the management of the establishment, encumbered it with extravagant engagements, in order that he might profit by the commissions he received on them, involved the whole theatre in confusion, and then decamped, after having raised money here, as he had done in various other places, by every sort of means, and without the most distant prospect, or the slightest intention of ever paying his creditors a single farthing in the pound.

In consequence hereof, the lease of the King's Theatre for the only remaining year granted by Mr. Chambers, has been thrown back on the hands of Mr. Ebers, who, to protect himself against the injury which he would unavoidably suffer were the house not opened to the public, has again embarked in the enterprise, and commenced his undertaking by circulating in the fashionable world the following note :—

King's Theatre, February 1st, 1825.

" Mr. EBERS begs leave most respectfully to acquaint the Nobility and Gentry, Subscribers to the Opera, that, encouraged by the advice, and supported by the patronage, of many Personages of the Highest Rank, he has resumed the Lease of the KING'S THEATRE for the present Season, and that it will be opened on Tuesday next, the 15th of February, under the direction of Mr. AYRTON.

" The following Performers have been engaged during the short interval that has elapsed since the Theatre returned into the hands of MR. EBERS ; and under the very peculiar circumstances of the Establishment he hopes that the annexed list of those with whom arrangements have already been made, and of others with whom treaties are pending, will be considered as a pledge that the Italian Opera will loose none of its lustre during the approaching Season.

" *For the Opera*—Madame Ronzi de Begnis, Madame Vestris, and Madame Caradori ;—Signor Garcia, Signor Curioni, Signor Begres, Signor Remorini, Signor Porto, Signor Crivelli, Signor Di Giovanni, Signor Rubbi, and Signor De Begnis.

" The Chorus will consist of Thirty-six Voices.

" Leader of the Band, Signor Spagnoletti ; Composer and Conductor, Signor Coccia ; Poet, Signor Stefano Vestris.

" *For the Ballet*—Monsieur Charles Vestris, Madame Ronzi Vestris, Monsieur Coulon, fils, Mademoiselle Legros, (to whom engagements have been sent.) Monsieur Le Blond, Mademoiselle Julie Aumer, Mr. Boisgerard, Mr. Venafra, Mr. Bertrand ; Mademoiselle M. Gladston, Mademoiselle Le Court, Mademoiselle O'Brien, Mademoiselle L. Colson, Mademoiselle Laura, Madame Spitalier ; with an improved and augmented Corps de Ballet.

" Principal Ballet Master, Monsieur Aumer ; Second Ballet Master, M. Boisgerard ; Leader of the Ballet, Mr. Rophino Lacy.

" Principal Scene Painter, Signor Zara ; Stage Manager, Mr. Kelly ; Assistant Stage Manager. Mr. Di Giovanni ; Secretary and Treasurer, Mr. Allan.

" Mr. Ebers is in treaty with Mademoiselle La Croix, for the Ballet. A treaty is also nearly concluded with Madame Pasta."

The theatre, however, did not open on the appointed day, on account of the illness of a principal performer ; and when, at length, all persons engaged were ready to make a commencement, the Lord Chamberlain, at the instance of the Secretary of State for the home department, interposed his authority, and suspended the license that he had granted, till the building, which rumour stated to be in a very unsafe state, should be surveyed by Messrs. Soane and Smirke. After a careful examination of the premises, these gentlemen reported that it would be necessary to make considerable repairs in the north wall, which would require about three weeks to complete. In consequence of the unavoidable delay thus occasioned, Mr. Ebers, at the pressing desire of many subscribers to the opera, has, it is said, been induced to engage the Haymarket theatre for the first few nights, and there to give such operas and ballets as the limited dimensions of that stage, orchestra, &c., will allow, till the more splendid and appropriate building is prepared for the reception of the public. We believe this report to be true, though we cannot vouch for its correctness, as no announcement to such an effect had been made when our present Number went to press.

DRURY-LANE AND COVENT-GARDEN THEATRES.

No new musical drama of any kind has been produced at either of these houses since our last report ; but both theatres have exhibited real scenes that are sufficiently humiliating to the nation ; scenes that must be attended by many evil consequences, but which we hope may be followed by one good effect, and teach us to estimate the comparative morals of other countries with rather more liberality than we have hitherto exhibited in judging of foreign habits and manners.

ORATORIOS.

These Performances are to be divided between the two winter theatres this year. They commenced at Covent-Garden on Friday the 18th of last month, when a considerable portion of Judas Maccabæus was performed, together with a miscellaneous act. Some parts of the fine oratorio of Handel were well executed ; others were much less fortunate, and upon the whole we cannot bestow much commendation on this evening's entertainment ; which, nevertheless was not entirely without amusement, for the *Superintendent* of the oratorios at Covent-Garden, thinking, we are bound to conclude, that the various forces in the orchestra wanted more generalship than either the leader or conductor, (two able men) could bring into the field, and perhaps not unwilling to make a little display, posted himself in the very front of the action, where, brandishing a truncheon in his hand, he laboured hard to make the troops move together : but he strove in vain ; they were, very likely, raw, they probably wanted drilling ; and moreover, to confess the honest truth, as this was the first time that the *superintendent* had ever essayed to command, it is possible that he did not inspire the ranks with so much confidence as he seemed to feel in himself, or as they might have felt in a veteran.

The chief performers at the Covent-Garden Oratorios are, Miss Paton, Mrs. Bedford, Miss Love, Miss Graddon, Messrs. Braham, Sapio, Pearman, Bellamy, &c: The leader is Mr. Mori, and the conductor Mr. Wesley.

PHILHARMONIC CONCERTS.

Previously to the re-commencement of these concerts, the Philharmonic Society had three private meetings in the months of January and February, for the purpose of trying, with the full orchestra, new compositions, and deciding on their fitness for public performance. Amongst these were, a symphony by Mr. Cipriani Potter, an overture by Mr. Goss, Weber's overtures to *Precioaa* and *Euryanthe*, and a Grand Symphony recently composed for the society, by Beethoven. All of these we shall

I 2

THE HARMONICON.

have to notice when they are regularly before the public. But much curiosity having been excited by the latter composition, from the pen of so great a master, we shall anticipate in part our regular criticism on it, by observing, that it manifests many brilliant traits of Beethoven's vast genius; that it embodies enough of original matter, of beautiful effects and skilful contrivances, to form an admirable symphony of ordinary duration: but that unfortunately, the author has spun it out to so unusual a length, that he has "drawn out the thread of his verbosity finer than the staple of his argument," and what would have been delightful had it been contained within moderate limits, he has rendered wearying by expansion, and diluted his subjects till they became weak and rapid. When we add that the time which it is calculated this composition will take in performing, cannot be much less than an hour and twenty minutes, our readers, though they have not heard it, may almost judge for themselves of its inadequacy to fix the attention of any audience, or to produce such an effect as the admirers of Beethoven must earnestly wish.

The first concert of this season was given, at the Argyle Rooms, on Monday, February 21st. The following is the programme of the performance.

ACT I.

Sinfonia, in B flat, Op. 60 . . . . . . Beethoven.
Duetto, "Far calzette," Mad. Ronzi di Begnis and Sig.
  De Begnis . . . . Mosca.
Quintetto, two Violins, two Violas, and Violoncello,
  Messrs. F. Cramer, Oury, Moralt, Lyon, and Lindley . Mozart.
Scena ed Aria, "Deh, parlate," Mad. Ronzi De Begnis,
  (Il Sacrifizio d'Abramo) . . . . . . Cimarosa.
Overture to Euryanthe, (never performed in this
  country) . . . . . . Carl Maria von Weber.

ACT II.

Sinfonia, No. 11 . . . . Haydn.
Recit. and Air, "In splendour bright," Mr. Sapio . . Haydn.
Pot Pourri, Violin Obligato, M. Mori . . Spohr and Mayseder.
Duetto, "La ci darem," Mad. Ronzi de Begnis and
  Mr. Sapio . . . . Mozart.
Overture in D . . . . B. Romberg.

Leader, Mr. KIESEWETTER.—Conductor, Sir G. SMART.

The two sinfonias performed in this concert, are less known than most of the other orchestral compositions of the same authors. That by Beethoven has few traits that strike generally, and at once, but possesses much to please the true connoisseur; it is written carefully, and betrays none of those eccentricities that are often at variance with established rules. The other, which is the eleventh of those composed for Salomon's Concerts, is much more airy and popular in its style; the andante of this, in G, is one of the most elegant of Haydn's productions; how beautifully the first violins sing the melody,—

how ingenious and effective the accompaniments of the other instruments,—and how masterly the climax! Haydn, says a modern writer on music, begins to be laid on the shelf; an assertion in which we cannot acquiesce. Grant it, however, to be true, he is only where Milton has long been placed, by a majority of those who are denominated well-educated persons. But do the real admirers and judges of poetry and music consign either of these great geniuses to darkness and dust? certainly not, for true taste recognises a standard, and is never swayed by fashion. We admit that in the indulgence of a sense, satiety may be produced, and indiscreet zeal is too apt to force a composer before the public so often, as to excite an ennui that is frequently mistaken for a change in opinion.

Bernard Romberg's fine overture we have more than once had occasion to notice, in our remarks on these concerts. The novelty of the evening was the overture to Weber's grand romantic opera, Euryanthe, a very bold, imposing composition, in which the author again shews how plentifully he is stored with original ideas, and how well he understands musical effect. To comprehend thoroughly the present work, it must be often heard, and herein it differs from the overture to the Freischütz, which stikes at once: indeed the latter is the superior production of the two, though we are not disposed to compare them invidiously; both proceed from the mind of a great master. The charming quintett of Mozart, had ample justice done it by Mr. F. Cramer: the strong feeling it excited, and the applause which every now and then murmured from each auditor, shewed that, whatever state musical taste may be in elsewhere, it is in full vigour among the subscribers to the Philharmonic Concerts. We cannot pass this without mentioning in terms of praise, Mr. Moralt's judicious performance of the viola part. The violin pot-pourri displayed all Mori's talent on this instrument; the composition is of no ordinary kind, though we are heartily tired of the meagre air Partant pour la Syrie, which is embodied in it. The comic duet, sung admirably by Signor and Madame De Begnis, is one of the best things of Mosca that we ever heard. The productions of this modern composer are generally very flimsy, and only fit for the minor Italian theatres. The scena of Cimarosa is one of the finest of his works, and was sung with vast energy and true feeling. Mr. Sapio, who was literally called out of his bed to supply the place of Signor Garcia, proved that his powers are soon awakened into action. In the hurry of the moment it is difficult to make a good choice, otherwise, doubtless, Mad. De Begnis and himself, would have found something less common than La ci darem la mano, which looses half of its effect when removed from the stage.

The whole performance proved the unabated excellence, and the enthusiasm of this fine band. While the Ancient and Philharmonic Concerts last, and are properly managed, music will be in no danger of sustaining any permanent injury from the caprices of fashion; although there will always be some to cry out, that Handel is gothic, and Haydn superannuated.

THE

HARMONICON.

No. XXVIII., APRIL, 1825.

MEMOIR OF PETER WINTER.

PETER WINTER, a veteran in his art, and the ablest living dramatic composer in Germany, is one of the few living dramatic composer in Germany, is one of the few eminent German musicians who have lived to see the liberation of their country from the oppressor's yoke, and its return to the halcyon days of peace. Winter has also had the personal good fortune of being in the service of a prince whose greatest pride is the patronage of the fine arts. The enlightened king of Bavaria—whose capital is so illustrious from the large assemblage of brilliant talent in all departments of literature and art, which has gradually gathered there—was not merely satisfied with placing Winter, his principal musician, above the every-day difficulties of life, but he also rewarded his merits with high honours and dignities, by first conferring knighthood on him, and then raising him to the rank of nobility.

Peter von Winter, chapel-master royal to the king of Bavaria, and Knight of the Order of Merit, was, according to several German biographers of the latest date [*], born at Mannheim, in the year 1755; other writers, however, namely, Gerber, Choron, and some English biographers, state him to have been born at Munich, in the year 1758. His father was a brigadier in the Palatine guards, and it was probably owing to this peculiar employment that he could take little share in the education of his son; but as he evinced at an early age strong symptoms of a natural genius for music, he was placed under the court musician Mair, to acquire the first rudiments of that art. His instrument being the violin, he subsequently took lessons from W. Cramer, the father of Messrs. J. B. and F. Cramer, who was first violin at the court of Mannheim, from 1750 to 1770; and under this excellent master, he made such rapid progress, that he was admitted into the elector's orchestra at the early age of ten. Here he soon distinguished himself on several instruments, but more especially on the violin, which had ever been his favourite.

The higher department of the art, harmony and composition, he studied, as far as the latter can be taught, under the far-famed Vogler; and no mean reputation accrues to the venerable Abbé, when upon the list of his pupils are found three such names as Winter, Carl

M. von Weber, and Mayerbeer, the justly-admired composer of the opera *Il Crociato in Egitto.*

Winter had by this time risen so high in the estimation of his sovereign as a musician, that in the year 1775, at the opening of the German theatre at Mannheim, he obtained the honourable appointment of director of the orchestra. This situation he also retained at Munich, when the elector's court was removed from Mannheim to that capital. Lipowsky states, that in the year 1788, the elector Carl Theodor appointed Winter his chapel-master, and that he at the same time desired him to compose, for the carnival at Munich, the opera of *Circe,* which, however, was never performed.

The first compositions that made Winter's name known, were his *Ballets.* After these had stamped his reputation, he began to write concertos, symphonies, quartettos, and many pieces of church music; by these various musical exercises, he not only acquired great readiness, and a tact for composing, but also that particular skill in the management of instrumental accompaniments, and the treatment of vocal parts, which render his finest productions so characteristically beautiful.

The master whom Lipowsky names as having initiated Winter into the arcana of his art, and as having finished his musical education, prior to his many professional journeys into foreign countries, is Salieri, styled by him the first classical chapel-master in Europe.

But although Winter travelled much, both in his own and other countries, yet Munich always was his principal home, and the city to which he was most attached. His musical wanderings have, indeed, been so frequent, and of such extent, that he may be said to have past *years* on the high-roads of the continent; and if the immense number of his works be considered, it is difficult to imagine how he found time for either, much less for both of these pursuits. He has several times visited Italy at the invitation of the theatres of Venice and Naples; several times Paris, and once London. His first professional tour in Italy occurred in the years 1792 and 1793; and then it was, and not till then, that he became thoroughly acquainted with vocal music. It has been remarked, however, that he always retained his own peculiar style of composition, and he composed pieces in the same original manner at Paris as he did in London, Venice, Naples, and other cities, with the least possible sacrifice to the taste of the public, and the spirit of the age.

---

[*] The authority for this date which we most rely on, is the following:—Baierisches Music-Lexicon, von F. J. Lipowsky, Munich.

Between 1796 and 1798, he visited Vienna, where, *Das unterbrochene Opferfest* (The Interrupted Sacrifice,) allowed by the unanimous consent of critics to be the best of his operas, and indeed of his numerous works—was brought out. The gay Viennese, to whom whatever is light, joyous, and easy, is always more acceptable than the grave and the profound, considered that beautiful opera to be " too pathetic," and it did not, therefore, at first meet with the success, which it has so decisively acquired since, on the stages of almost every capital in Europe.

In the month of January, 1800, his grand serious opera of *Montalban* was performed for the first time at Munich ; and in the summer of 1801, he resided during six months at Paris. Early in 1803, he made a second journey to that capital, for which, in the course of the preceding year, he had written his next best opera, *Tamerlan*, to French words. *Choron* in speaking of this magnificent production, characterizes Winter as " *un compositeur énergique, riche, abondant, dramatique, et toujours local dans sa musique et dans ses motives.*"

After a short stay at Paris, he came to London. Here he remained till the end of the year 1804, after having acquired the highest honour and reputation by the operas *Zaire, Proserpina, Calypso, Castor and Pollux ;* and by the extremely successful ballet of *Orpheus.*

In 1806, he once more took the road from Munich to Paris. In March, 1817, the journals of Venice announced his departure with regret, softened, however, by a promise to furnish two serious operas for their theatre. Of those which he afterwards wrote for Italian theatres, and Italian tastes, none was so well received as his *Maometto,* an *Opera seria,* produced but a few years ago.

In speaking of Winter generally as a composer, it must be allowed, that from many years' experience and study, he possesses in particular, a profound knowledge of whatever belongs to the *voice ;* and that he understands better how to adapt compositions to its compass and power, than any other living composer. His last voluminous work, published only a few months ago, *A Treatise on Singing,* in 3 vols. folio, shows with what diligence he must have applied himself to this important branch of the musical art. As a dramatic composer, he has been deservedly extolled for grandeur of declamation, and effective instrumental accompaniments. Many of his airs in the *Opferfest,* in *Proserpina,* and *Tamerlan,* vie in beauty with the most favourite productions of Mozart ; and in several of his overtures may be discerned much of the spirit and fire of Beethoven.

The catalogue of his works cannot fail to create surprise. Gerber, whose dictionary comes down only to 1813, enumerates thirty operas (including *Calmal*), and since then he has produced several new pieces. Besides these, he has written many grand masses, *Offertoria, Graduales, a Requiem,* twelve or more grand *Cantatas,* among which *Timoteo, or the power of music,* is most celebrated ; concertos for single instruments, overtures, orchestral symphonies, including the celebrated grand symphony with chorusses, for the solemnization of the battle of Leipsic, 1813, not to enumerate at least two hundred other pieces—single songs, serenatas, quartetts, quintetts, and septetts, for stringed and wind instruments ; which prove him to be no less industrious, than he is productive and full of genius.

This venerable man, with seventy winters on his head, is yet in health, and in active possession of his fine faculties. He still resides at Munich, where his great name, well known throughout Europe, is as fresh and flourishing as ever.

LIST OF WINTER'S WORKS.

I. FOR THE CHURCH.

1. Missa, for 4 Voices, and Orchestral Accompaniments, MS. Traeg. Vienna.
2. Graduale, ditto, ditto.
3. Offertoria, ditto, ditto.
4. *Die Pilger auf Calvari,* Oratorium, written for Munich.
5. *Bettulia Liberata,* Oratorium, 1792, for Venice.
6. *Die Auferstehung,* (The Resurrection,) Cantata, MS.
7. *Die Erlösung des Menschen,* (The Redemption,) with a subjoined *Stabat mater.*
8. A Requiem ; by far the best of his compositions for the Church.
9. Pastoral-Mass, Munich.

II. FOR THE THEATRE.

1. *Bellerophon,* Melodrama for Mannheim, 1787.
2. *Helena und Paris,* for Munich.
3. *Psyche,* German Opera.
4. *Circe,* Opera seria for Italy.
5. *Leonardo und Blondine,* Melodrama, to the text of Bürger.
6. *Cora und Alonzo,* ditto.
7. *Armida,* Melodrama with Chorusses, in 3 acts.
8. *Der Bettelstudent,* (The Poor Student,) Operette, Vienna.
9. *Orpheus,* Pantomime with Songs.
10. *Das Hirtenmadchen,* (The Shepherdesses,) Operette.
11. *Sherz, List, und Rache,* (Mirth, Cunning, and Revenge,) Operette.
12. *Cato in Utica,* Opera seria, for Venice, 1791.
13. *Antigone,* Opera seria, for Naples, 1791.
14. *I Sacrificj di Creta,* Opera seria, 1792, for Venice.
15. *Armida und Rinaldo,* Melodrama, for Vienna, 1793.
16. *I Fratelli rivali,* Op. buffa, 1794, for Munich.
17. *Ogus, osia il Trionfo di bel Sesso,* Opera buffa, 1791, for Prague.
18. *Die Sommerbelustigungen,* (The Delights of Summer,) Ballet, for Berlin, 1795.
19. *Das unterbrochene Opferfest,* (The Interrupted Sacrifice,) Operette, Vienna, 1796. This Opera has been arranged in Germany, for nearly all instruments, a proof of its popularity in that country.
20. *I due Vedovi,* Opera buffa, 1796, Vienna.
21. *Die Thomasnacht,* Operette in 2 acts, 1795, for Bayreuth.
22. *Die Pyramiden von Babilon,* as the second part of the *Zauberflöte.*
23. *Eliso,* Opera for Vienna, 1798.
24. *Das Labyrinth,* ditto ; one of his most successful works.
25. *Der Sturm von Shakspeare,* for Munich, 1799.
26. *Maria von Montalban,* Opera seria, 1800, Munich.
27. *Tamerlan,* Opera, with French words, for Paris, 1802, where it was received with great applause.
28. *Castor und Pollux,* Italian words, for London, 1803.
29. *Der Frauenbund,* (The Female Union,) Opera, for Munich, 1804.
30. *Colmal,* Grand Opera, for Munich, 1809.
31. *Die Blinden,* Opera von Holbein, 1810, is much praised.
32. *Calypso,* Opera Seria, for London.
33. *Proserpina,* ditto, ditto.
34. *Zaira,* ditto, ditto.
35. *Maometto,* ditto, written a few years ago for Italy, and received with the most flattering applause.
36. *Etelinda,* one of his latest Operas, performed at Milan.
37. *Die Pantoffeln* (the Slippers), Opera, performed at Hamburgh without success.
38. *I due Valdomiri,* also one of his latest Operas, performed at Milan.

39. *Gibblas in der Räuberhöle*, Ballet, for Berlin.
40. *Der Tod Adams*, (The Death of Adam,) Ballet, for Munich.
41. *Arianne*, Grand Opera.

III. For the Chamber.

1. *Pigmalione*, Cantata.
2. *Piramo e Thisbe*, ditto.
3. *Die verlassene Dido*, (Dido Deserted,) ditto.
4. *Vortiger*, ditto.
5. *Hector*, ditto
6. *Agnes de Castro*, ditto.
7. *Henri IV.*, ditto.
8. *Bayersche Lustbarkeit*, (Bavarian Merriment,) ditto.
9. *Der Französische Lustgarten*, (The French Pleasure Garden,) ditto.
10. *Die Hochzeit des Figaro*, Cantata.
11. *Andromaque*. ditto.
12. *Prague et Philomele*.

All these were composed before 1793.

13. *Die vier Tageszeiten*, (The Four parts of the Day,) Cantata.
14. *Die Macht der Töne* (Timotteo), ditto., Ital. and German, to Dryden's *Alexander's Feast*; one of his greatest works in this class of compositions.
15. *Germania Friedens Cantata*, (The Peace of Germany.)
16. *Gesange beim Clavier*, in 8 Parts; Munich.
17. *Three Cantatinas*, Ital. and Germ.
18. *Nine Canzonettas*, ditto.
19. *Quatuor*, for voices ditto.
20. *Gesang auf den Tilsiter-Frieden*, (Song on the Peace of Tilsit.)
21. *Patriotisches Lied*, with Orchestra.
22. *Preisgesang der Musik*, (A Musical Prize Song.)
23. *6 Canzonettas, Duette, Terzette, &c.*, Ital. and German.
24. *6 Airs Italiennes*, avec paroles allemandes, 2 Viol., Alto. e. Vello.
25. *Freude schöner Götterfünken*, (Hymn to Joy,) for 4 Voices, with Piano-Forte.
26. *Die Musik*, for 4 Voices, with Piano-Forte.
27. *Phantasie der Liebe*.
28. *Das Waldhorn*, vierstimmiger, Gesang, with Piano-Forte.

IV. Instrumental Compositions.

1. VI. Concerti à Viol. princ., e Orch.
2. Concerto à Oboe princ., ditto
3. Concertino à Viol. Clar. Cor de Bassetto, e Fag. princ., e accomp. di 2 Viol., Viola, e B.
4. Rondo con Variaz., à Viol. princ., 2 Viol., 2 Fl., 2 Cor., V. e B.
5. III. Sinf. à gr. Orch., Op. 1, 2, 3, Offenbach.
6. Quatuor, p 2 Viol., Alto et B., Op. 5, Un. 1900.
7. III. Quint., p 2 Viol., 2 Alto et B., Op. 6, Leipz. 1802.
8. Sestetto, p 2 Viol., 2 Corn., Alto et B., Op. 9.
9. Trois nouv. Quat., p 2 Viol., Alto et B., Paris.
10. Septuor, p 2 Corn., Clar., 2 V., Alto et B., Op. 10, Leipz.
11. Sinfonia concert., p V., Clar., Fag., et Cor., &c., Op. 11.
12. Six Entreactes, Liv. 1, 2.
13. *Grosse Schlachtsymphonie mit Chören*, (Battle-Symphony,) in commemoration of the battle of Leipzig, 1813. *Vollstandige Singschule*, in 3 Vol. folio, in Germ., French, and Italian, Mainz 6 Schott.

To the above may be added at least Thirty more pieces in different kinds of composition, either published within the last five years, later than the biographies from which this catalogue has been compiled, or still possessed by Winter in manuscript. Among these are about twelve orchestral overtures, and various pieces for the voice, with orchestral accompaniments.

MUSICAL GLEANINGS IN AFRICA.

From Major Laing's Travels in Western Africa [*].

Major Laing, who was sent by Sir Charles M'Carthy, in the year 1822, on a mission to the King of the Soolima country, for the purpose of establishing a commercial intercourse between that kingdom and Sierra Leone, has just published a most amusing and interesting account of his travels to that distant and hitherto unexplored country. The route of the enterprising traveller lay through the Timannee and Kooranko countries, and from thence to Soolimana; regions which had never before been visited by a "white man," and accordingly every page of his journal teems with new features of savage life, facts and observations relative to manners, customs, and scenery, or incidents of personal interest and adventure, which constitute the peculiar charm of works of travels in unfrequented countries.

Much as we have been delighted by the perusal of this highly interesting journal, we must of course confine our observations to such parts of it as relate to the subject to which the Harmonicon is exclusively devoted; and we therefore proceed to collect the accounts and observations of Major Laing relative to the rude music, and incidentally to the dances, of these hitherto unvisited children of Africa.

In describing the customs of the Timannees, Major Laing says:—

Dancing is a favourite amusement among the Timannees, but it is accompanied with neither grace nor exertion; the musicians (if they may be so called) stand in the centre, while the men and women, mixed indiscriminately together, dance round them, but with little change of place, as the movements are principally confined to the head and upper parts of the body. The women are not unfrequently indelicate in their attitudes; which, as they are entirely encouraged by the men, is not to be attributed as a fault to them.

Among these people

There are four trades or professions, to which conjointly is given the appellation of Nyimahalah; they rank in the order in which they are enumerated, and consist of the *fino*, or orator; the *jellé*, or minstrel; the *guarangé*, or shoemaker; and the *noomo*, or blacksmith; all of whom are high in the scale of society, and are possessed of great privileges. They travel throughout the country unmolested, even in war; and strangers, if of the sable hue, are always safe under their protection. The guarangé and noomo earn their livelihood by the exercise of their respective trades; the fino by his oratory and subtlety as a lawyer; and the jellé by singing the mighty deeds and qualifications of rich men, who, in his opinion, have no faults. Like the minstrels of old, they are always at hand to laud with hyperbolical praise the landlord of a feast, and headman of a town.

During his short stay at Kooloofa, our traveller says—

About nine in the evening I retired to rest, and in a very few minutes closed my eyes in slumber, which the good inhabitants

* Travels in the Timmanee, Kooranko, and Soolima Countries, in Western Africa. By Major Alexander Gordon Laing.—With Plates and a Map. 1 vol. 8vo. Murray.

K 2

of Kooloofa were termined I should not long enjoy; for, out of compliment (as they informed my boy) to the first white man who had ever set foot in Kooranko, they commenced such a din of drums, flutes, and various other instruments, accompanied with dancing and singing, which was kept up all night, that sleep was banished from my pillow till daylight.

At Seemera, in the Kooranko country, Bee Simera, the king of the place, paid him a very high compliment:—

At parting, he sent his griqt or minstrel to play before me, and sing a song of welcome; this man had a sort of fiddle, the body of which was formed of a calabash, in which two small square holes were cut to give it a tone; it had only one string, composed of many twisted horse-hairs, and although he could only bring from it four notes, yet he contrived to vary them so as to produce a pleasing harmony; he played at my door till I fell asleep, and waking at day-break, his notes still saluted my ears, when finding that his attendance would not be discontinued without a douceur, I gave him a head of tobacco, and told him to go home and thank his master.

A day or two afterwards, the major, having the good fortune to stand very high in the king's estimation, was informed by his sable majesty "that he had ordered some of his people to dance for his (the major's) amusement;" this royal entertainment is thus described:—

In a few minutes, a man beating a big drum with his right-hand, and playing with the thumb of the left, armed with a thimble, upon a conical-shaped piece of hollow iron slung from the fore-finger, and followed by a crowd of women, entered the yard; when commenced a most grotesque kind of dance, in which there was more action than elegance, and more labour than grace. The dancers scarcely moved their feet, but made up for their deficiency in that respect by twisting their bodies into attitudes completely serpentine, and giving a continual motion to their heads; they brandished in the right-hand a large knife, and in the left a tomahawk, with great dexterity. They were followed by successive couples, each displaying their activity in a manner which was rather distressing than agreeable to witness; the female by-standers encouraging them by clapping their hands, and evincing by acclamation and gesture their unqualified approbation. The amusement was kept up with unabating vigour till the close of day.

At Nyiniah, says Major Laing, among other civilities, the head man of the town

. Paid me a visit early in the morning, attended by his chiefs and his principal griot*, the latter of whom sung loudly the praises of his master, whom he represented as the richest and most hospitable man in the whole country. He sung "of the white man who came out of the water to live among the Kooranko people; the white man ate nothing but fish when he lived in the water, and that was the cause of his being so thin. If he came among black men, he would get fat, for they would give him cows, goats, and sheep to eat, and his thirst should be quenched with draughts of milk."

* Jellé-man, or minstrel.

At Woorowyah, the major and his party rested to recover the fatigues of their journey. On their way to this town, they narrowly escaped being murdered for the sake of the merchandise which they carried with them; a plot to effect that diabolical purpose having been laid between the head-men of the two towns through which the route lay. The cool, prudent, and determined conduct of Major Laing prevented the commencement of the work of treachery; and the gratitude of a discharged Negro from the late Royal African Corps diverted the party destined to make the attack, out of the road through which the travellers passed; time was thus gained, and the party arrived at the town without being molested. The intended murder and robbery was, however, known at Woorowgah; and the women, disappointed in not participating in the spoils of the destined victims, gave vent to their disappointment in their songs, and apostrophized the "white man" and his riches in a way by no means agreeable to the feelings of their auditor.

In the evening (says the major) dancing commenced, accompanied with songs from the females, the tenor of which did not entirely please me. They sang "of the white man who had come to their town; of the houseful of money which he had; such cloth, such beads, such fine things had never been seen in Kooranko before; if their husbands were men, and wished to see their wives well dressed, they ought to take some of the money from the white man." I am not certain how this might have terminated, if Tamba*, who still accompanied me, had not mixed with the singers, and being well known among them, answered them by a counter song. He sung of "Sierra Leone; of houses a mile in length filled with money; that the white man who was here had nothing compared to those in Sierra Leone; if, therefore, they wished to see some of the rich men from that country come into Kooranko, they must not trouble this one; whoever wanted to see a snake's tail must not strike it on the head." Tamba's song was listened to and applauded, and my money remained unmolested.

Pursuing their journey, the party arrived at Kamatoo, where they "found the whole of the inhabitants crying and howling bitterly, it being the commencement of their custom on the death of a chief who had been slain in battle" with a neighbouring state.

The lamentable howling of the mourners was continued all night, and at daylight was superseded by music, which lasted with little interruption during the whole of the day and succeeding night; some of the instruments were skilfully handled, and sent forth most melodious sounds; and the vocal performers, who I learned were jellé-men from Sangara, far surpassed the uncouth squalling of any of the attempts I had hitherto heard on the part of an African. The deep tones of a large ballafoo resounded through the still morning air in a manner truly solemn; I awoke early, and lay listening for upwards of an hour with pleasure to the music which rung on my ears like magic,

* Tamba is the discharged negro before mentioned; he had, since his return to his native country, assumed the profession of jellé-man, or minstrel, and in this capacity rendered the major a second essential service, displaying in both instances the most grateful devotion to his former masters.

and I might have been thus entranced much longer, had it not been for the unpleasant sensations of a parched skin, headach, and chilliness, too faithful harbingers of the approach of fever, with which I was attacked.

At length the party reached the place of their destination, the Soolima country, in which they were most hospitably received, and soon welcomed by the special messengers of the king, who sent forward a party, headed by his own son, to conduct the travellers to Talaba, the capital of the kingdom, and the royal residence. The king received them in the kindest manner, and during their stay in his capital, continued to them the most benevolent treatment. On their arrival at the town, a grand military spectacle took place, in which sham fights were performed by large bodies of horse and foot soldiers, under the command of Yarradee, the king's brother, who was the War-Master, or principal military chief of the country.

While these warlike movements were going forward (says the major), another set of people were by no means idle ; consisting of above one hundred musicians, who playing upon divers instruments, drums, flutes, ballafoos, harps of rude workmanship, with many other kinds which it would be tedious to enumerate, kept up a din sufficient almost to crack the tympanum of ordinary ears, and which compelled me to fortify mine with a little cotton; two fellows, in particular, with crooked sticks, kept hammering with provoking perseverance, and with the violence of blacksmiths at the anvil, upon two large drums which stood about four feet high, in shape similar to a chess-castle turned upside down ; their only desire appeared to be that of making a noise, and in that I suppose the chief art consisted, for the harder they beat the more applause they obtained. A nod from the king at length put a stop to this clang of steel and din of drums, and I was flattering myself with the hope of being permitted to retire to the apartment allotted for me, but my motion was interrupted by the king, who said I must hear something more. Being again seated, a jellé, or singing man, elegantly attired in the Mandingo costume, his wrist and elbows ornamented with bells, and beating on a sweet-toned ballafoo, the notes of which he ran over with taste and velocity, stepped out, and after playing a sort of symphony, or prelude, commenced a dialogue in song with some persons who did not appear at first, but who afterwards joined him.

Jellé.—"There is a white man come from afar, come from the very salt-water, that a Soolima man has never seen. Let us do him honour, for he has come to shake hands with the great Assana Yeera, the powerful in war. Let us do honour to Assana Yeera, and shew the white man that he is great, and that his people love him, because he is good. Where are my wives to join me in the song ?"

(Voices answering of the Wives, who had not yet appeared.)

"We are here, but we fear the white man's skin ; we fear his greegrees will kill us, if we dare to look upon him ; none but men can behold him ; the woman fears him too much*."

Jellé.—"Come out, my wives, and see the white man, come out and do him honour ; his greegrees are strong, it is true, but then he is good, and has walked to this country to do us good."

Wives entering.—"Then we come, but we must shut our eyes, for we never yet looked upon a man with a white skin ; we come to do him honour, we come to sing to him of the great Assana Yeera, renowned in war ; and of the heroic Yarradee, his valiant brother."

The jellé-man was now joined by ten women, fancifully dressed out in fine cloths, bracelets of party-coloured beads encircling their wrists and ancles, and having their hair ornamented with shells and pieces of cloth ; drawing up behind Yarradee, the jellé began a lively air in praise of that chief, in which he was joined by the females, who bawled till every vein in their throats was distended with blood ; in my life I never heard the female voice raised to such a pitch ; it was absolutely terrific ; I expected every moment that a blood-vessel would burst, especially when the measure was long, and the attempt to continue vociferous to the last without drawing breath, brought blood enough into the throat to have almost created suffocation ; I was much distressed, and certainly not amused, and was happy when the clamour ended. The words which they sung were the following, and, as I was informed, are rehearsed on all public occasions before Yarradee, to commemorate an advantage gained by that warrior over his inveterate enemies the Foulahs, at a time when an army of 10,000, headed by Ba Demba, laid siege to Falaba.

Song.

"Shake off that drowsiness*, O brave Yarradee! thou lion of war ; hang thy sword to thy side, and be thyself.

"Dost thou not behold the army of the Foulahs ? Observe their countless muskets and spears, vying in brightness with the rays of the departing sun ! They are strong and powerful, yea, they are men ; and they have sworn on the Alkoran, that they will destroy the capital of the Soolima nation.

"So shake off that drowsiness, &c.

"The brave Tahabaeere, thy sire, held the Foulahs in contempt ; fear was a stranger to his bosom. He set the fire-brand to Timbo, that nest of Islamites ; and though worsted at Hericot, he scorned to quit the field, but fell, like a hero, cheering his war-men. If thou art worthy to be called the son of Tahabaeere,   "Shake off that drowsiness, &c.

"Brave Yarradee stirred ; he shook his garment of war, as the soaring eagle ruffles his pinions. Ten times he addressed his greegrees, and swore to them that he would either return with the sound of the war drum†, or with the cries of the jellé‡. The war-men shouted with joy—'Behold ! he shakes from him that drowsiness, the lion of war ; he hangs his sword to his side, and is himself again.'

---

* The Soolima females conceal their faces when they either eat or drink in the presence of men ; they never venture to take even the smallest unauthorized liberty.

* Yarradee is remarkable for natural listlessness and inactivity.
† In triumph.
‡ The jellé people are always employed to sing at the death of any great man.

" 'Follow me to the field,' exclaimed the heroic Yarradee, 'fear nothing ; for let the spear be sharp or the ball swift, faith in thy greegrees will preserve thee from danger. Follow me to the field, for I am roused, and have shook off that drowsiness. I am brave Yarradee, the lion of war ; I have hung my sword to my side, and am myself.'

" The war-drum sounds, and the sweet notes of the balla encourage warriors to deeds of arms. The valiant Yarradee mounts his steed, his head-men follow. The northern gate * of Falaba is thrown open, and a rush is made from it with the swiftness of leopards. Yarradee is a host in himself. Observe how he wields his sword. They fall before him—they stagger—they reel. Foulah men! you will long remember this day ; for Yarradee 'has shook off his drowsiness, the lion of war ; he has hung his sword to his side, and is himself.' "

While the Jellé and his wives were vociferating these words (for I can hardly call it singing, as, although the air played on the ballafoo was both melodious and in good time, the voices kept neither time nor measure), Yarradee proudly threw himself into various pantomimic attitudes, suitable to the expression and at the conclusion giving a loud shout, made a rush forward, and being followed by his war men en masse, represented the part which he had performed in reality with so much success among the Foulahs about fourteen years before. This part of the performance being finished, he stepped forward singly, and with sword in hand opposed himself to twelve musketeers, who made repeated attempts to fire at him, but in vain, the priming always burning in the pan, Yarradee at the same time laughing and shaking his greegrees+ in token of defiance ; at length overcoming them all, and making them kneel at his feet, he commanded them to discharge their muskets in the air, which to my great surprise they did, and not a single musket missed fire.

These ceremonies being concluded, the major retired to the hut prepared for him, making his way through a whole defile of wondering women and children. " I believe," says he, " I was more than once addressed by the curious, in order that they might hear me speak, for when I answered ' Alla baraka,' they would shout, ' Kumulo, Fooroto Kumulo!' ' He speaks, the white man speaks !' "

The news of my appearance was soon spread abroad, and the yard was forthwith crowded with dancers, musicians, and singers; among the latter of whom I was not a little annoyed to behold the females whose stentorian lungs had so stunned me in the morning, and I was obliged not only to submit to a repetition of Yarradee's war-song, with their diabolical chorus (which is a favourite air among the Soolima musicians), but to pay them for their trouble ; otherwise, according to Musah ‡, I should have had a bad name amongst them, and nothing is more dreaded by an African than a bad name from the jellés. The sound of the balla was beautiful, as also the recitation by the singing men, but the din of the chorus roared forth by the women was savage in the extreme. After the war-song of Yarradee, they sung for

nearly half an hour of the wars between the Soolimas and Foulahs, a few sentences of which were translated to me as they were caught by my interpreter ; and are as follows :—

SONG.

"The men of the Foulah nation are brave. No man but a Foulah can stand against the Soolimas. The Foulahs came to Falaba with 30,000 men ; they came down the hills like the rolling of a mighty river ; they said, Falaba men, pay, or we will burn your town. The brave Yarradee sent a barbed arrow against the Foulahs, and said you must slay me first. The fight began ; the sun hid his face ; he would not behold the number of the slain. The clouds which covered the skies frowned, like the brow of the Kelle Mansa. The Foulahs fought like men ; and the ditch around Falaba was filled with their slain. What could they do against the Soolima Lion? The Foulahs fled, never to return ; and Falaba is at peace."

As soon as the Amazons had finished their song, a droll-looking man, who played upon a sort of guitar, the body of which was a callabash, commenced a sweet air, and accompanied it with a tolerably fair voice. He boasted, that by his music he could cure diseases ; that he could make wild beasts tame, and snakes dance ; if the white man did not believe him, he would give him a specimen ; with that, changing to a more lively air, a large snake crept from beneath a part of the stockading in the yard, and was crossing it rapidly, when he again changed his tune, and playing a little slower, sung: " Snake, you must stop ; you run too fast, stop at my command, and give the white man service." The snake was obedient, and the musician continued: " Snake, you must dance, for a white man has come to Falaba; dance, snake, for this is indeed a happy day." The snake twisted itself about, raised its head, curled, leaped, and performed various feats, of which I should not have supposed a snake capable ; at the conclusion, the musician walked out of the yard, followed by the reptile, leaving me in no small degree astonished, and the rest of the company not a little pleased that a black man had been able to excite the surprise of a white one. On my retiring to the interior of my dwelling, the dancing commenced, the noise of which deprived me of rest till a late hour; and on my awaking in the morning, I found, by the sluggish beat of the fatigued drummer, that some, more reluctant than others to break up an amusement which daylight alone puts a stop to among Africans, had not yet discontinued their exertions.

With this extract we take our leave of Major Laing's very sensible Journal of his Travels to the Soolima Country, a work which we can confidently recommend to our readers as one of the most interesting and amusing modern books of travels which has fallen under our observation.

* The gate which looks towards Foulah.'
+ Fetishes, or charms.
‡ The guide and interpreter.

DISCOVERY OF ANCIENT GREEK TABLETS RELATIVE TO MUSIC,

OF A DATE 709 YEARS BEFORE THE CHRISTIAN ERA.

By PROFESSOR MURCHARD, of Berlin.

The doubtful character of all known accounts relative to the music of the Ancient Greeks, and the obscurity in which the subject is consequently involved, render interesting, in a peculiar degree, the discovery of two documents of high antiquity and unquestionable authenticity, with the particulars of which we here present our readers.

The documents to which we allude are two metal tablets, on which is engraved in ancient Greek, an account of a Music Feast at Ephyræ, (Corinth,) in the third year of the Sixteenth Olympiad, or in the year before Christ 709, by Lasus, of Hermione. An important addition to the History of Ancient Greek Music is thus furnished, interesting alike to the antiquary and to the lover of the art, and which throws more light upon its nature and character in those early ages, than all the labours of the numerous writers upon this subject.

The following account, with the comments and historical memoranda attached, is given by the celebrated PROFESSOR MURCHARD, of Berlin, whose nephew, M. KRAUTMANN, was the fortunate discoverer of these interesting relics of antiquity.

Frederick Krautmann quitted the university of Heidelberg at the moment when the present state of Greece first attracted the attention of Europe. Being a young man of an enterprising and adventurous spirit, he determined upon joining the cause of liberty in Greece; and accordingly departed for that country, and fought under the standard of Colocotroni. Circumstances brought him to Gerema, the ancient Corinth, in the neighbourhood of which city he had frequent opportunities of making short excursions. Inspired by the thought of being upon classic ground, he determined on directing his attention to the numerous relics of antiquity in Corinth and its neighbourhood; more particularly with the view of collecting inscriptions towards an elucidation of the history of this part of Greece.

One evening, attended by a faithful Greek servant, he had sauntered to a small grove of olive-trees, to the south-east of the Acropolis. Having prolonged his ramble further than usual, and becoming fatigued, he threw himself upon a bank to rest. They were both unarmed, and as at the distance to which they had strayed from the town, they might be exposed to some sudden attack, he ordered his servant to cut down a young olive plant, in order to provide them with the means of repelling any assault. The servant, a powerful fellow, vainly attempted to pull up the plant by the roots; but, being resolved not to be foiled in his object, he removed with his hands the earth about the root of the plant. Mr. Krautmann, who had not observed what the man was doing, was suddenly aroused by the exclamation of his servant; " Master, here is an iron pot in the ground." Mr. Krautmann instantly sprung forward, assisted the man in removing the olive-tree, and in the cavity formed by the loosening of the roots, discovered the upper part of a metallic vessel embedded in the earth. By their united exertions, they removed it from its place, and cleared it from the earth that adhered to it.

It proved to be an amphora of metal, about two feet high and one broad, and was hermetically sealed. No words can describe the delight of the youthful antiquary. Favoured by the darkness of the night, they bore home the treasure in safety; on the way something was observed to rattle within the vessel. The moment he had reached his apartment, Mr. Krautmann hastened to discover the contents of the amphora. Nothing remarkable could be recognised on the exterior, except the body of verdigris with which it was incrusted, and which bespoke its antiquity. Every attempt to open it proved fruitless, and he was obliged to retire to rest with the mortification of not being able to effect his purpose. In the morning, the necessary instruments were procured, and Mr. Krautmann proceeded to work with great caution, and in order as little as possible to injure the vessel, he determined to saw off the lid, which was accordingly done. Through this aperture two detached tablets were observed; his curiosity was doubly excited, and he did not hesitate for a moment to sacrifice the amphora, in order to come at the precious contents. After much labour and time, the body of the amphora was sawed in two, and the treasures it contained were brought to light. The sides of the vessel were an inch in thickness, and hence it may well be imagined that the operation was not effected without much difficulty. By what means these tablets were originally enclosed in the vessel, and how it was hermetically sealed without damaging them, are questions which I leave to the connoisseur. With inconceivable joy, Mr. Krautmann found that the tablets contained Greek inscriptions, which were sharply and plainly engraven in the metal. Being no unskilful philologist, he immediately proceeded to decipher them, and upon the tablet designated by an Alpha, found the following title.

" LASUS, THE SON OF EUPOLIS, OF HERMIONE, RECOUNTS TO POSTERITY THE MUSIC-FEAST OF EPHYRÆ."

Shortly after, Mr. Krautmann returned to his country, brought safely with him these precious relics, and deposited them in the hands of his learned uncle, Professor Murchard.

The two tablets are formed of an unknown metal, of a colour between green and gold. As Ephyræ was afterwards called Corinth—the reason for which will be shortly seen from the tablets themselves—I do not think I am hazarding too bold an opinion, if I assert, that these tablets are formed of the metal known by the designation of Corinthian, a chymical analysis of which will now become possible. Florus and Pliny seem to have given a just description of it, when they represent it as consisting of a mixture of gold, silver, and copper. Such indeed is its appearance, and not that of brass; and, therefore, the learned mineralogist Reil is wrong in his conjectures on this subject. Both the tablets are a foot and a half in height, eight inches in breadth, and a quarter of an inch thick. The characters run from right to left, and take a sloping direction. In some few places, the verdigris has eaten away some of the letters, yet, except in two places, it has been found practicable to fill up the lacunæ, and these do not, from the context appear to be of any great importance.

I now proceed to give a faithful translation of the first tablet, inserting a few observations in such places as appear to require elucidation. After the heading lines, as given above, the first tablet runs literally as follows:

" In the third year of the fourth Olympiad, in the reign of king Telestes, the Heraclite, there was in Ephyræ a meeting of many men and maidens skilled in song. There were also many actors there, and players on the flute and cythara, for the people and the king were joyous, and loved in their hearts the god-like art of song."

This very beginning deranges the results of historical researches which had cost long years of toil; for, supposing Troy to have been destroyed 1184 before Christ, and that Telestes was reigning 500 years later in Peloponnessus, it would follow that Gatterer, and the more modern writers, and particularly v. Raumer, are wrong in fixing the first Olympiad 776 before Christ, but that Petavius was perfectly right in placing it in 777. It is also further proved, by the introduction to this tabular inscription, that the ancients really reckoned their Olympiads according to the sovereign, king, or archon, &c., but by no means continued to reckon them according to chronological order.

" But there were also present at Ephyræ, Pherekydes of Patræ, the giver of the rhythm (PΥΘΜΑΓΟΣ) and Damon of Cyrenæ, who instructed the scholars."

The word here translated giver of the rhythm signifies, as will be seen in the sequel, nothing more than music-director. Damon of Cyrenæ being here mentioned as contemporary with Telestes, shews the fallacy of the opinion heretofore entertained, that he was a contemporary of Socrates, 422 before Christ, which would make him above two hundred years old. How nugatory our struggles after truth are frequently found to be !

" But Damon gave instructions in the Hypocritic music."

(Unfortunately no explanation is here afforded.)

" There was besides in Ephyræ, Pyrene, the daughter of Teresias, skilled in song, and admired throughout the whole of Hellas and the Peloponnessus. When the Choragi had spoken, she sung in the Hypolydian and Hypomixolydian modes. But Pherekydes had improved the Epigonion, and invented the ninth and tenth tones, but the tenth is called Antibypate."

We here become acquainted, for the first time, with a songstress, who lived 700 years before Christ. I had imagined that I before knew what Hypolydian and Hypomixolydian meant, but I now feel convinced that I am ignorant about the matter, for it is afterwards said that Pyrene, the daughter of Teresias, sung the Hypopotamon *, which had never before been heard of. Now it is supposed by the moderns that the Hyperbolaion of the ancients was our A above gamut. If this were correct, then Pyrene must have sung to E in alt, in which case it is not easy to divine how this tone could have created such

admiration in all Greece, as it lies perfectly within the compass of a female soprano voice, and our soprano singers sing a full octave higher. Hence, it is much more probable that the Hyperbolaion of the ancients was the tone of B or C in alt; for that the tone of F in alt, or G in alt, should have caused such astonishment is much more likely. Now, in the Hypolydian and Hypomixolydian modes the Hyperbolaion does not occur at all, and yet Pyrene sung in these modes, and, therefore, five tones higher than the Hyperbolaion !—Epigonium, according to its very etymology, signifies a stringed instrument, which was set upon, or held between the knees. Further on we shall find that it resembles our violin. —What is meant by the ninth and tenth tones, heaven only knows.

" Lastly, there was also at Ephyræ, Lasus, the son of Eupolis. The same was sent for from Hermione by king Telestes. For Lasus had written many works on the musica, (ΜΟΥΣΙΚΑ) which is a compound of poetry, eloquence, sculpture, painting, dance, and the art of singing, as well as that of the playing of the flute, and of stringed instruments. But this latter art was called by distinction musica. Lasus had also written the lives of many great singers and players on the cythara; and Kypsiles was the greatest player on the cythara of that time."

Here we find Lasus making some mention of himself, of whom nothing till now was known, except that he flourished 600 years before Christ, and had written something theoretical upon music. The errors of chronology are again very sensibly felt in this passage ; but of still greater importance is the discovery that, at the time of Lasus, under the term musica, not philosophy and grammar, but the combined idea of all the arts was understood, and that as the Greeks had no distinct word for music, they employed the collective term musica to signify music in particular. We also see that Lasus was the musical Plutarch of the Greeks. What a loss to the art that his works should have perished ! That Kypsiles was the most celebrated player of the cythara of his time, is also an interesting notice; but of still greater importance to the philologist is the circumstance, that from this name, as well as from the ancient name of Corinth (Ephyræ), as well as from many other passages in these tablets, it is sufficiently evident that the letters Z.H.Υ. were already known in the time of Lasus ; and, therefore, that those writers who have maintained that Simonides of Keos, who lived much later, viz., 467 years before Christ, was the first inventor of these letters, have been greatly in error.

" But Telestes, inasmuch as many singers, and players on the cythara, as well as dancers and actors were present, and as his throne was splendid, commanded Pherekytes to prepare a great feast in honour of music (ΜΟΥΣΙΚΑ.) But Pherekytes obeyed, and expeditious messengers hastened to Hellas, and to Peloponnessus, to invite all renowned artists and umpires, and many people from all countries, to Ephyræ. For, at the command of the king,

---

* How beautiful and appropriate is this designation; Hypopotamon signifies something which lies on the other side of the river, and, therefore, is not to be attained to.

all took a part in the feast who loved musical contests. ΑΓωΝΕΣ ΜΟΥΣΙΚΟΙ."

" But soon there came Terpander from Antissa, Ibykos from Rhegium, Kypsiles from Mitra, and Thamyras the Thracian, to Ephyræ, to assist at the feast. And Terpander was the inventor of the barbiton, and of the new signs of tone; Ibykos was the inventor of the sambuca, and Thamyras the inventor of the Dryopian mode."

Here our chronological premises are again suddenly disarranged; for Ibykos of Rhegium had till now been considered as having flourished about 550 years before Christ, but Thamyras, or, as the learned Herrman calls him, Thamyris, is even mentioned by Homer; now, may not the authentic document lying before us tend to strengthen the new-formed theory, that no such person as Homer ever existed, and that the works which bear his name are the productions of a much later period; or, supposing the Homerides to be the real authors, could have been produced only in the seventh century before Christ? Again, if Terpander was the inventor of the signs of tone, how could it have been Pythagoras? The Dryopian mode is the same as the Dorian, for Doris was anciently called Dryopis.

" Now, when they were all together, the town could not hold the assembled multitude, for there were many people from all countries. But Telestes ordered the people to repair to the mountains. There they made merry, for the king was hospitable, and feasted the people. And many sacrificed in the mountains to the God who guides the steeds; hence, the Isthmian games were repeated this year. ΤΟΥΤΟ . ΓΑΡ . ΕΛΛΗΣ-ΠΟΝΤΟΥ. ———— ΑΚΟΥΕΣΘΑΙ . ΟΝΟΜΑ."

The people went into the mountains;—by these mountains may probably be understood the range of hills that cross the isthmus between the Morea and the main land; for it is expressly said that the people sacrificed to the God who guides the steeds, (Neptune), and that the Isthmian games were renewed: now it is known that the Isthmian games, in honour of Neptune, took place here.—The Greek words above quoted, indicate a lacuna which I am unable to fill up.

" But Telestes had caused an amphitheatre to be erected in a meadow near the town, for the entertainments of the evening. The same was extremely spacious, and had room for the many thousands of men that had assembled. But on the Kathedras sat the maidens and the matrons.

" Now, when Pherekydes had arranged every thing as had been commanded him, the people hastened there, and the feast lasted from that time forward full eight days."

Hence it cannot be maintained that women were not accustomed to be present at the spectacles of the

ancients; but, at the same time, it is evident that the men are here mentioned as being separated from the women, and it would even seem as if the women did not sit at all in the amphitheatre, but in a place (the Kathedræ) which was separated from it; for had it been included within the amphitheatre, the latter must have been of an enormous size. However, it is possible that only women of the better classes were admitted.

[To be continued in our next.]

FOREIGN MUSICAL REPORT.

VIENNA.—On occasion of the birth-day of his majesty, the opera of Der Schnee, and the grand ballet of Psyche were commanded, between which Haydn's Hymn for the Emperor was sung by the whole of the company, and received with every demonstration of patriotic feeling. The great attraction of the season has been Rossini's Mosè in Egitto, which was cast with great power. Considerable judgment has been shewn in making the opera terminate with the very effective Preghiera, and in leaving the catastrophe of Pharoah's host to the imagination of the spectators. Indeed, the finest machinery in the world, aided by the most powerful music, could not cover the absurdity of such a spectacle. On the merits of this composition so much has been said, that any remarks from us would be altogether superfluous; suffice it to say, that nowhere has Rossini given so undeniable a proof of what his powers are capable, when he has the courage to follow the native impulse of his genius, unbiassed by the fashion of the moment.

The other operas of the season were Die Falsche Prima Donna, in which M. Blumenfeld gave the part of the pseudo-Catalani with very great effect; his soprano falsetto is of the most extraordinary kind, and enables him to imitate this great singer in a manner that is altogether astonishing. The Donna del Lago, in which the celebrated Signor Comelli-Rubini appeared to great advantage in the character of Malcolm Græme. Der Sänger und der Schneider, (the Singer and the Tailor), an opera founded on the well known anecdote of Farrinelli. Der Thurm von Gothenburg, (the Town of Gothenburg, by D'Allayrac, &c.

———— A grand ballet was produced by M. Vestris at the Karnthnerthor theatre, entitled Alcine; the music selected from various masters. About twenty years since, a ballet of the same name delighted all Vienna, not so much by the excellence of the dancers, as by the exquisite music of the great Weigl. May we not be permitted to ask, why such genuine treasure of the art should be allowed to lie buried in the dust of the archives, while modern trash is forced without mercy upon the public? Would not the directors of opera establishments find their account in every way, by reviving such music, rather than bringing forward other compositions, merely because they are new?

———— Among the concerts that have taken place here the most remarkable were the four Quartett-subscription Concerts given by professor Schuppanzigh, in which ample justice was done to some of the master-pieces of Haydn, Mozart, Beethoven, Spohr, Onslow, the two Rombergs, &c. In these meetings the celebrated Carl Czerny, presided at the piano.

———— With this season concludes Sigr Barbaja's engagement here, but at the request of the musical public it is to be prolonged another half year, at the end of which term, it is said the Italian Opera is to close altogether. But this is almost impossible, for it has taken such deep root among us, that it would be universally felt as a privation of something almost necessary to our very existence.

———— Preparations are making for the musical celebration of the approaching nuptials of the Crown Prince of Aus-

L

tria, with the Princess Sophia of Bavaria. On this occasion Sig. Mercadante is to produce a new opera, and a cantata for the occasion, on which he is now said be to busily employed, doubtless, tacking together his work from all the compositions of the best Italian masters, and by way of a contrast, and of something particularly new, we do not despair to hear a part of Haydn's concluding chorus of the *Creation*. All the great Italian singers are engaged to sing on this occasion, the Court Kapellmeister, Eybler, is said to have already completed a new *Te Deum*, which is to be produced at this solemnity.

BERLIN.—On occasion of the celebration of the birth-day of his majesty the King of Prussia, was performed *La Neige*, by Auber; a new Festive March by Spontini; and a *Cantata* in honour of the day, by the same master; all of which were received with great applause.

The only novelty of the season has been a new opera entitled *Cardillac*, the music by Kapellmeister Schneider. This is a subject of a terrific kind, and the music is entirely in character with the poetry of the piece, and displays throughout the hand of a master.

This was followed by *Don Juan*, *Ferdinand Cortez*, *Il Barbiere*, *Le Nozze di Figaro*, *Hieronymus Knicker* by Dittorsdorf, a very favourite comic opera, which has continued to delight the public here for more than thirty years past; *Der Freischütz*, *Die Falche Prima Donna*, music by Ignatz Schuster; *Ein Abend in Madrid*, (An Evening in Madrid,) the music by J. P. Schmidt; *Das Geheimness*, (The Secret,) by Solie; *Il Matrimonio Secreto*; *Alphonso und Leonora*, by Sor; *Le Rentier*, by Boyeldieu; *Der Reisende Student*, (The Travelling Student,) by Winter; *Le Fête Champetre*, by Boyeldieu; *Gioventù di Enrico V.* by Morlacchi; *Tancredi*, *La Gazza Ladra*; and *Margarita d'Anjou*, by Mayerbeer. With respect to the last-named composer, one of the Berlin Gazettes has the following remark. "It is surely to be regretted that Mayerbeer has heretofore exerted his superior talents for strangers only, and not for his native country. Can this have arisen from any neglect or indifference on the part of his countrymen? Let us yet hope that some German director will call upon him to display his genius in the composition of a German opera, that he may fairly compete for the palm of triumph, on the same ground with some of the kindred spirits of his native country. And let us hope that this will be done before the flower and freshness of his genius have been poured forth in the adornment of themes for other lands. While Germany possesses a native genius of this class, capable of adorning her stage with the master-pieces of his talent, how melancholy a spectacle is it to see that stage usurped by the trivial, and sometimes contemptible, productions of foreign composers!"

———— Two concerts given by Moscheles here, before his departure, were among the most splendid that Berlin has witnessed for many years. With respect to this great pianist, we will not say a word relative to mechanical difficulties conquered by him with perfect ease, as these may be vanquished by almost all, who labour in earnest to attain their object. What we would dwell upon is, his sylph-like facility, and the bold, but playful, character of his style; the most difficult series of tones flit away, not as if the strings had been struck by the key and the finger, but as if they had been swept by the passing breeze, whence accents so new, so varied, so expressive, arise, that even amateurs the most difficult to be pleased, are forced into admiration.

With respect to this professor's compositions; many of them, being written in great haste, and in moments snatched from his continual occupation, cannot be supposed to possess superior merit, but on the present occasion we were delighted to hear two concertos of real excellence; *viz.*, in E flat major, and G minor. There is a greatness of ideas, and such a high and poetical instrumentation in the Adagio,—a movement in which *all* virtuosi do not excel,—that the beauty of the composition can for a moment make us forget even this performer himself. It is with no common feeling of regret, that we reflect how long it may be before we are again enchanted with this artist's

performance. Virtuosi may be compared to comets; they are not stationed like composers in the centre of a circle of which they are the life and soul; they are not governed by common laws; their course is wild and eccentric, they excite a momentary astonishment, and then sweep away into vast distances, from which their return is not to be calculated.

MUNICH.—The new theatre opened the 2nd of January, when the king and his family went, and the receipts were very considerable; his Majesty commanded that they should be distributed amongst the poor. A prologue, a cantata, and the fairy ballet of *Cendrillon*, composed the entertainment.

NAPLES.—The last novelty brought forward in this city, before the closing of the theatres on account of the death of the king, was a grand historical ballet from Sir Walter Scott's novel of *Kenilworth*, the music by PACINI, and the action, dances, &c., by the celebrated Gioja. This ballet is full of character, power and beauty. The finest scenes of Sir Walter's story have been woven together with great judgment. The episodic dances are full of spirit, character, and picturesque effect. The Scotch dances are well managed, and pleased extremely; the dance of the Nereïdes at the feast given by Leicester to Queen Elizabeth, is a picture not unworthy of the genius of Guido; and the warlike dances of the Britons, Romans, Saxons and Normans, are like some of the bolder works of Michael Angelo, with occasional touches of the pencil of Raffaello. The music was of a higher character than that usually adapted to spectacles of this kind, and was marked throughout with numerous beauties, and great characteristic effects.

MILAN.—The *Maometto* of Rossini has been attempted here but without success. The following remarks we quote from one of the Italian journals. "History informs us of two Mahomets, one the founder of Islamism, the other the conqueror of Negroponet; the serious opera has also its two Mahomets, the first from the pen of Winter, the second from that of Rossini. Whoever bears the one in mind, will scarcely condescend to think of the other. The air of Galli, which would be heard to greater advantage with a simple accompaniment than with a full orchestra, as well as the eternal *Stretta* of *Zoraide*, would, if placed in the scale against a single musical phrase of Winter, in his celebrated Invocation, be sure 'to kick the beam:' the former is every-day music, the latter is eternal. If such be the case, the question may naturally be asked, why, instead of producing music merely because it was new, recourse had not been had to the neglected scores of Winter, which could not have failed to delight all the true lovers of music? Was it for the purpose of affording Galli an opportunity of appearing on the stage on horseback? Yet we cannot help thinking the singer's vanity might have been gratified at a lower rate, than by the sacrifice of good taste. The *Maometto* of Rossini did not please at Vienna, where it was first produced; why then seek to force it down the throats of the public here, especially when it is known that the father of this deformed offspring has been heard to express his dissatisfaction at the child of his own fancy?"

———— Four composers have during the present season entered the arena of the theatre of this city, to dispute the palm of musical glory, Rastrelli, Nicolini, Soliva, and Pacini. Of the first of these we can only say that he has youth and nothing before him; from the second both the one and the other are fied never to return; he has sunk into a mere scribbler of notes, an eternal blotter of music-paper, an exhauster of the patience and good-nature of the public. The third of these composers, Soliva, came off with some share of glory; but the fortunate musician was Pacini, who has before reaped no common laurels in his *Barone di Dolsheim*, and who on the present occasion obtained a decided success in his serious opera entitled *Isabella ed Enrico*, which was hailed with unanimous applause. This success was the more flattering, in proportion as the disadvantages he had to contend with were the greater; by the term disadvantages, we do not mean the competition he had to sustain with his rival composers, but the task was not so easy to enter into the field of contest with such music as *Tancredi*, *Agnese*, and *Il Don Giovanni*,—pieces which at this itme occupied the theatre of this place. The overture was brilliant and at once bespoke a favourable attention. In the first act the favourite pieces were an *aria* and *scena*, a duet, and the finale, which was full of powerful effects. In the second act, also a duet, a tenor air, and a concerted piece, without particularizing several minor beauties, which mark considerable originality of talent, and great command of the resources of his art. The music improved upon us at a third hearing, and if there were any defect which our calmer judgment would be disposed to criticize, it was in parts of the accompaniments which were too noisy. The author, like Rossini, betrays too great a fondness for the trumpet and the trombone, and appears to think he can never give his hearers too much for their money. There were also many misplaced and feeble passages which served only to impede the march of the action, and diminish the interest of some of the situations of the piece. But these blemishes were not sufficient to outweigh its numerous beauties, and the new and charming melodies that were scattered throughout; and in adverting to them, we are influenced solely by a wish to offer a useful suggestion to this composer, relative to his future efforts.

———— The *Maometto Secondo* of Rossini served as a debût for a new French singer, of the name of Favelle, who was very favourably received; but not so the opera. In spite of all its stage effect, and the introduction of horses into the bargain; in spite of the great drum, introduced in a *recitativo obligato*, in one place, and *violini pizzicati* in another, all would not do. The good Milanese pronounced it plainly and roundly to be *un vero errore*. With the exception of a *preghiera* in the first act, the whole is poor in song, and barren of ideas. But if these are wanting, the hearer is treated in their stead with boisterous choruses, janissary bands introduced on the stage, and a fury of instrumentation in the *recitativi obligati*, before unexampled.

If it be recollected that, in the space of fifteen years, Rossini has composed twenty-seven operas, and six *farsi*, (pieces in one act;) that the greater part of them are quietly laid at rest for ever, and of the *farsi* but one, (the *Inganno felice*,) still known to the public, and that of his later operas in particular, the greater part have come almost still-born into the world, it assuredly ought to act as a hint to the composer, that it is time to let his talents lie fallow for a time, in order to gain energies for future productiveness.

The *Maometto* was followed by *Torvaldo e Dorliska*, also by Rossini, which shared a somewhat better fate than its predecessor, for it is much more in his better manner, and abounds with melody and song.

The *Donna del Lago*, aided by the talents of the Pesaroni, who performed the part of Malcolm with great energy, was reproduced this season with considerable effect. A judicious amendment in the finale of the first act, was the omission of a dozen trumpets, which formerly overpowered the singer, and before which, like Jericho of yore, the opera was nearly falling to the ground on the first representation. The part of the heroine was sustained by the Signora Garcia, but though she sung the opening air with much effect, she did not succeed upon the whole. With respect to this air, some Parisian critics have objected to the too frequent repetition of its motivo. No such blame would have existed, had such a repetition been from the pen of a great master. Has not Mayerbeer, in his *Esule di Granata*, from four single notes formed an entire and excellent stratum? was its continued repetition ever thought tedious? by no means. Have the eternal repetitions of the principal ideas in the music of Haydn been ever deemed wearisome or misplaced? on the contrary, they have been thought by real judges to constitute one of its greatest charms, and to act as a kind of emphatic impression of the subject.

Semiramide, by the same composer, followed. It was received with the same applause as last season.

Nothing can be more remarkable than the advanced posts of the Rossinian horde, which besiege the orchestra, the greater part of whom quietly doze out the principal part of the opera, and are only awakened at proper time into activity by the plaudits of their colleagues, and return the echo with half-shut eyes. Into what a mechanical affair has not applause degenerated in the present day! At the very same hour, nay at the very same minute of each returning day, one bears the same hands clapping as well in the opera as the ballet: it would seem as if the great clock in the proscenium of the Scala had been expressly stationed there for the purpose of enabling ourselves to ascertain this curious fact, and those said gentlemen to know the precise moment when their hands are to be set in motion.

Such have been the operas given this season, and frequently with one act from one opera, and another from another alternately.

Of the music of the grand ballet of *Sesostris*, all that can be said is, that it is, entirely of the modern school of music of that kind; so far from having any thing of an Egyptian cast about it, the principal dance is to a waltz movement. Signor Taglione has made his Egyptians move in steps perfectly French; besides this we have another instance of modern good taste; the stage is, as in Rossini's *Maometto*, on more than one occasion crowded with horses and Janissary bands. If such strong stimulants are continued, and found necessary to satisfy the gross taste of the public, adieu to the orchestra, and to the charms of song: in a word, when all that belongs to such gorgeous spectacles is exhausted, to what is recourse to be had next?

———— The celebrated Paul, for the ballet, was engaged at a very considerable sum, but his dancing was not exactly to the taste of the public here; he therefore, fell very opportunely sick after two or three nights, and appeared no more.

———— Those who are well versed in such matters, hint that the new direction of Mr. Glossop, will, at the close of this his first season, find a rather serious deficit, although in some instances he has introduced a certain degree of economy. Once for all we would remark, that it might be well for this Director if he possessed a little more firmness of character, and did not suffer himself to be led by the singers, and would show a better choice in the selection of his operas. It is a great pity that drums and trumpets are allowed to chase away the *opera buffa*, for which the Italians have so natural a turn.

We shall shortly be able to give you some particulars of the forthcoming opera of *Caraffa*, the appearance of which is looked forward to with a considerable degree of curiosity.

———— We have the honour of having at this moment among us Signor Giuseppe Antonio Augusto Benelli, late Impressario of the Italian opera in London. It is to this worthy man that Rossini is indebted for the ample pockets-full of English guineas which he carried away with him from that liberal capital; though it is said that it required immense persuasion on the part of Giuseppe Antonio Augusto Benelli to persuade him to undertake the journey. After making a melancholy bankruptcy in the British capital, filling the pockets of others, and *expending every farthing of his own handsome property which he had embarked!!* he is now here looking out for some fresh speculation, and as *his honour and integrity (!!)* are so well known and *so justly prized*, we doubt not of his speedy success.

VENICE.—Coccia's opera of *Clotilda* has been produced at the teatro St. Luca, for the purpose of introducing to the public a new singer in the person of Fanny Ayton, who met with considerable success in the principal part, and is likely to become a great favourite with the public. Her voice possesses great sweetness and flexibility, but is defective in strength.

PALERMO.—On occasion of a visit of the Duchess of Parma to this place, a *Cantata* was written in her honour, by the celebrated GENERALI, and performed at the theatre. This master is engaged here as *Maestro di Capella*. It was recently reported that this composer was dead, but we are happy to find this opportunity of contradicting the report.

L 2

TURIN.—A new opera was recently produced here on the theatre of the Prince Carignan of Savoy, entitled *La Pastora*, the music by the Neapolitan Maestro, NICOLO VACCAJ. It was very favourably received, and the composer, who, according to custom, assisted at the three first representations, was hailed with repeated and enthusiastic applause. We hope to be able shortly to give further particulars of this composition.

TRIESTE.—We were condemned to witness here another melancholy failure of an opera, as we had done before at Vienna; with this difference, however, that the *Didone* of Mercadante at least retained the greater part of the recitative of Metastasio, but in the *Themistocles* of Pacini, only a few scattered lines of this great poet were allowed to be heard among the new, but worthless rhymings of some modern versifier. This poetical crime is not less atrocious than the musical one, for the composer and the corrupter of the text have shewn a kindred mind, and were both punished by the contempt of the public. In addition to this, the virtuosi of the establishment inserted in Pacini's opera a number of extraneous pieces, which however they might be favourites with them and their own coterie, were by no means so with the public, who expressed their discontent in no equivocal manner. But to compensate for all this, we are promised the *Crociato* of the celebrated MAYERBEER, which is looked forward to with great expectation.

ROVIGO.—The season here opened with GENERALI's opera *I Baccanali di Roma*. In producing it here, recourse was had to a method now become but too common, and by which several works of merit, not to say some of the greatest masterpieces, have been so disfigured, as scarcely to be recognised again; we mean the custom of introducing pieces in operas not originally belonging to them. But in the present instance, those interpolations were managed with so much judgment, and so well contrived not to interfere with the general march of the action, that the public rewarded the attempt with general approbation.

The favourite singer here is the Signora Antonietta Caleazzi, who in the present instance had a very arduous task to fulfil, of which she acquitted herself to great admiration. Critics speak of her genuine and beautiful tenor voice, and the judgment and good taste that mark both her acting and singing. The orchestra here is very powerful, and admirably conducted by the able leader Signor Gaetano Zocca, of Ferrara; indeed the whole management of the chorusses, &c., reflects great honour on the establishment.

ESTE.—We are sorry to announce that the theatre here has fallen a prey to that devouring element, whose rage few of the greater theatres of Europe have escaped. During the performance of the grand ballet *L' Incendio d' Aquileja ordinato da Attila*, one of the scenes caught fire, and so rapidly did the flames spread, that the dancers were obliged to escape in their light attire; and so great was the alarm in the orchestra, that several of the musicians left their instruments behind them. Fortunately no lives were lost on this melancholy occasion.

PARIS.—The new measures which have been taken at the *Théâtre Italien*, have not yet produced the expected result; the

increase of exertion which they impose upon the performers is not compensated by a corresponding benefit. It is even probable that Monday's representations will always be to empty benches; the very means which have been adopted to induce the public to come, will be the cause of their staying away.

By announcing that Mondays would not be included in the days of subscription for the season, but that they would be reserved for occasional subscribers and for amateurs, they have thrown discredit upon this day.

A person who goes into the pit, and exposes himself to be suffocated, on one of the three fashionable days, disdains to use a box for Monday, because to be seen at the Italian opera then, is to compromise, to degrade oneself. Monday at the *Théâtre Italien*, is what Saturday is at the *Opera Française*, the day for the citizens. The increased price of the boxes has not produced a corresponding increase of profit. The effect of this measure is to force many into the pit, who find the boxes too expensive, and to chase from the pit, those who cannot submit to pay three francs, (2s 6d.,) when they have for so long paid only thirty sous, (1s. 3d.,) for it cost no more to hear Viganoni, Mandini, Rafanelli, Rovedino, and Morichelli, in the operas of Paesiello, Sarti, Martini, and Cimarosa.

The pit began to hiss this innovation; it is no longer so, but the managers gain nothing thereby. The amateurs have changed their rage into sullenness, and have deserted the house; and little pains have been taken to induce them to come back. It is not by varying the performance, or increasing their stock of pieces, that they will succeed; and indeed this stock is becoming poorer every day. Not only *Elisabeth*, *Le Turc en Italie*, and *Le Barbiere di Scviglia*, have disappeared, but those pieces which are performed the most frequently, are not the most approved. We have waited for many weeks for *La Dame du Lac*, a composition both original and melodious, which has, at last, taken its proper rank in the public estimation, and which is liked better every time it is heard. We have not heard *Zoraide* for many months, and indeed by the extraordinary manner in which the parts are distributed, they have deprived both the pieces and the performers of the greatest part of their charm. Does not the part of *Donna Anna* do as much injury to Mlle. Monbelli, as she to it? And Mlle. Schiassetti, beautiful as she is, does she not deprive the *Italiana* of the very charm it takes from her? There is little wisdom in these ladies thus to misapply their talents, and little firmness in the directors to suffer them.

—— The manager of the Italian Opera in London, is endeavouring to detach from us the charming Pasta; he holds out to her the allurements of a most enormous salary, and the payment of the debt due to her from the *regisseur*, Benelli. Sig. Curioni is preparing to depart for London, and it is thought that Mlle. Monbelli is also anxious to go thither.

—— M. Rossini has been defeated in his design of bringing out M. Mayerbeer's opera, *Il Crociato in Egitto*, in such a way as to endanger its safety. The composer himself lately arrived in this city, and immediately represented his case to the minister, who, handsomely ordered that the German Amateur-Musician should be allowed to cast all the characters, and produce his work in his own manner. He has, therefore, most prudently, reversed all M. Rossini's arrangements, and he will now, consequently, stand a fair chance of success.

REVIEW OF MUSIC.

AMICITIA, a SONATA for the PIANO FORTE, with an accompaniment for Flute or Violin, (ad libitum) Composed, and dedicated to I. Moscheles, by his friend, J. B. CRAMER. (J. B. Cramer, Addison and Beale, 201, Regent-street.)

WITH unfeigned pleasure do we again sit down to review a work by this ingenious, elegant, and intelligible composer, who so thoroughly understands the character, and so accurately estimates the powers of the instrument for which he chiefly writes. In Mr. Cramer's productions we neither observe that glitter which is generally employed to hide a poverty of invention, nor those extravagant passages of degradingly-mechanical execution, which serve only to conceal the want of expression ; but we find that good taste which arises from a strong musical feeling, and from a full recognition of the sovereignty of harmony ; a taste that is not fleeting, like the ultra fashionable works of the day, but which existed, under different forms, more than a century ago, and will, perhaps in other shapes, exist as long as the art is cultivated, because founded on an immoveable basis.

This Sonata is adapted from a quintett which is about to appear, and is in every way worthy of the celebrated performer to whom it is inscribed. It certainly demands great practical skill, and must not be attempted by any but players of a high order: it requires strength of hand, quickness of finger, and above all, that peculiar and impressive touch which so few have been found able to imitate. It is in four movements ; the first in E major, slow ; the rest in the same key, Allegro ; the third an Adagio, in B major, and the last a brilliant Rondo, of course in E major. The following is the subject of the Allegro, which is worked with spirit through eight pages:—

The adagio will be improved by the accompaniment of the continuous sounds of a bowed instrument : on this account it seems to us that we shall like it better in its original form as a quintett. The rondo opens in a very sparkling manner, but the master-passion of the composer—the passion for the expressive—continually peeps out in the midst of the assumed gaiety. As an instance of this, we extract the subjoined beautiful passage, wherein the ancient style is so happily revived, bringing with it all those recollections of classical music that, we fear, so few in the present day are enabled to enjoy. It is an andante, expressivo, occurring in the middle of the movement, and with which we conclude this article:—

1. FOUR RECREATIONS *for the* Piano-Forte, *by* J. N. HUMMEL. Book 2. (J. B. Cramer, Addison and Beale, 201, *Regent-street.*)

2. *A collection of* NEW GERMAN WALTZES, *composed for the Piano-Forte, by* I. MOSCHELES. (Chappell and Co., 50, *New Bond-street.*)

THE first of these is one of those useful publications that we are always glad to see, and most willing to commend: it will assist materially in smoothing the rugged path that learners have to beat, and is sanctioned by a name of the highest musical celebrity. These recreations contain eight easy movements, which will gratify and at the same time improve the young student, accomplishing a most desirable end, by converting the toil of practice into the enjoyment of a pleasure.

The above remarks are quite applicable to the new German waltzes of M. Moscheles, which are as good and pleasing as they are practicable. They are seven in number, five followed by one trio, and the remainder by two. The increasing number of easy works by good composers looks well; if young players are to be condemned to the painful druggery of learning the trash that is too often placed before them, because it is not difficult, it must be obvious to all, that not only the taste of such persons can never be well trained, but that disgust must soon supervene. But let it not be understood that we mean to mention this publication by M. Moscheles as one that is only adapted to those who cannot achieve better things: it undoubtedly offers facilities to a very moderate description of performers, but it is worthy the notice of all, and is as fit for the accomplished piano-forte player, as for those who are only in progress towards that high degree of improvement to which some arrive.

———

VARIATIONS, *in an easy style, in the favourite Finale in the Melo-Drama,* La Fée de France, *for the Piano-Forte, composed by* CHARLES CZERNY. Op. 52. (Boosey and Co., 28, *Holles Street.*)

M. C. CZERNY is beginning to learn, that publishing for a few mechanical players is an unprofitable employment; he is therefore reducing his compositions to the humble level of such performers as only wish to give pleasure to those that have a real taste for music, properly so called; such as have no more desire to master the difficulties that are sometimes contrived, than an elegant dancer has to figure on the slack rope. These six variations are a proof of the reformation which, we begin to hope, is taking place in the present author's opinions; they are attainable by all players of tolerable abilities, are written with some taste, and a due consideration of the nature and capabilities of the instrument. The air itself is of a very familiar kind, and, though rather trite, has something in it that will catch the attention.

---

1. SEVEN BRILLIANT VARIATIONS *for the* Piano-Forte, *to a Theme of* Rossini, *composed by* FRANCIS LISZT. (Boosey and Co., *Holles Street*.)

2. IMPROMPTU BRILLIANT, *for the* Piano-Forte, *on Themes of* Rossini *and* Spontini. *Op.* 3. *Composed by the same.* *(Published by the same.)*

THE author of these two publications is the juvenile wonder that has astonished all the connoisseurs in Europe by his performances, during the last two or three years, and has often been mentioned in different parts of the *Harmonicon.* In these pieces he has only noted down some of the brilliant passages of execution that he has often, in various shapes, practically displayed, and which pleased as extraordinary feats, though they are neither likely to gratify thus combined and offered as a musical composition, nor to find many who will take the trouble to practice them: they shew a taste that mature age will, we sincerely hope, very much improve; but they certainly manifest a knowledge of the art that is perfectly surprising in a boy of only twelve, or at the utmost, thirteen years of age.
Of the above two compositions, we prefer the *Impromptu*, consisting of themes from *La Donna del Lago*, and *Armida* of Rossini, and the *Olimpia* and *Fernand Cortez* of Spontini. The times of these are indicated by the metronome, though not quite clearly. The note whose length the pendulum vibrates, should be stated.

Selection of Piano-Forte Music, *composed by* L. VON BEETHOVEN. *Nos.* 1, 2, 3, *and* 4. (Gow, and Son, 162, *Regent Street.*)

JUDGING from the first four numbers of this work, it is likely to prove an excellent selection from the best compositions of the great German master. The first is the elegent air, *Quant' è piu bella*, from Paisiello's opera, *La Molinara*; the second, the theme in G; the third the admirable sonata in A flat, dedicated to Prince Lichnowski, in which is the sublime *Marcia Funebre*, printed in the fifth number of the *Harmonicon*; and the fourth is the popular melody, *Nel cor piu non mi sento*, also by Paisiello. These are all well brought out, but, considering that the publishers have no copyright to purchase, the prices are too high.

---

1. L'Amitiè, FANTASIA *for the* Piano-Forte *in which are introduced* Three Favourite Airs; *composed by* J. A. MORALT. (Cramer, Addison, and Beale, 201, *Regent Street.*)

2. Le désir de Plaire, DIVERTIMENTO *for the* Piano-Forte, *composed by* JAMES CALKIN. (Gow and Son, 162, *Regent Street.*)

3. MASONIC AIR, *with Variations for the* Piano-Forte, *composed by* WILLIAM CALKIN, *Organist of Arundel Church.* (Gow and Son.)

4. DIVERTIMENTO, *for the* Piano-Forte, *in which is introduced* Bishop's *admired Duet,* "I love thee;" *by* T. VALENTINE. (Goulding, D'Almaine and Co., 20, *Soho Square.*).

THESE compositions are all very easy in execution, and adapted to performers who have learnt music from one and a half to two years, according to their different degrees of aptitude.
The first is marked by that good taste which generally distinguishes Mr. Moralt's publications. The two French airs, *Malbrouk*, and *Ah! vous dirai-je maman*, introduced by him, are common enough, certainly, though the former may, perhaps, be not very much known to all the present generation.
Mr. Calkin's divertimento consists mainly of a rondo pastorale, which is very agreeable in effect, and need not be disdained by superior players. It is, however, too long for the quality of its subject, and the prudent master or performer will curtail it.
Of the masonic air we cannot say much; it is very feeble, and the variations on it partake of the nature of the theme. Ten pages are really too much to devote to such materials.
The Divertimento, No. 4, has the advantage of No. 3, in being modestly short; in other respects it is on about the same level.

---

1. FANTASIA, *in which is introduced the* Bacchanalian Song *and* Jager Chorus, *from* Weber's Opera, Der Freischütz, *arranged for the* Piano-Forte, *by* CAMILLE PLEYEL. (Cramer, Addison, and Beale. 201, *Regent Street.*)

2. INTRODUCTION and VARIATIONS *for the* Piano-Forte, *in* Weber's Jager Chorus, *by* J. LORD. *(Published by the same.)*

3. The FREISCHUTZ RONDO, *consisting of the* March, *and the most favourite Airs in* Weber's *celebrated Opera; arranged as a* Divertimento *for the* Piano-Forte, *or* Harp, *by* C. ARNOLD. (Bedford Repository, 45, *Southampton Row, Russel Square.*)

4. RONDO, *on a favourite Theme from* WEBER'S Freischutz, *for the* Piano-Forte, *composed by* J. A. TATTET. (Gow and Son, 162, *Regent Street.*)

5. The OVERTURE *to* EURYANTHE, *newly arranged for the* Piano-Forte; *composed by* C. M. von WEBER. *(Published by the same.)*

6. OVERTURE *to* PRECIOSA, *composed and arranged for the* Piano-Forte *by* C. M. von WEBER. (Cocks and Co., 20, *Princes Street, Hanover Square.*)

7. *The beauties of* WEBER'S *celebrated Melodrama*, PRECIOSA, *composed and adapted for the* Piano-Forte, *by the Author.* *(Published by the same.)*

FROM the day when we first made known to the public M. von Weber and his *Freischütz*, up to the present moment, every music shop in London has poured it forth, in all possible shapes, till the town is almost inundated by it.
Camille Pleyel's fantasia we have placed first, because it decidedly takes the lead of all the rest, and is a clever composition, but rather difficult.
No. 2. by Mr. Lord is well adapted to the hand, and also to the instrument, though somewhat lengthy.
No. 3 is very short, easy rondo, combining the march, the hunter's chorus, the waltz, and another air; with a lithographic print, well designed, as a title-page.
Mr. Tattet's Rondo is the charming air in the finale

to the last act; which is the same as the subject in G in the overture.

The overture to Euryanthe, No. 5, is not judiciously arranged, for it is here rendered more awkward to execute than the edition published in Germany, in which the convenience of the performer has not been very sedulously studied. Of the overture itself we have more than once spoken. It is a most masterly work.

The overture to *Preciosa* is in the possession of all our subscribers, and does not require any further notice here. The Beauties also of the same melo drama, No 7, are only, in part, what have been published in the *Harmonicon*.

---

1. " *Audivi Vocem de Cælo*," a MOTET, *composed on the lamented Death of the* Rev. Thomas Rennell, B.D., *Vicar of Kensington, and inscribed to his Memory by* WILLIAM HORSLEY, Mus. Bac. Oxon. (Welch and Hawes, 246, *Regent Street*.)

2. " What is prayer," *composed for a Single Voice, with an* Accompaniment *for the* Piano-Forte, *by* WILLIAM HORSLEY, Mus. Bac. Oxon. (Birchall and Co., 140, *New Bond Street*.)

CANONS, were formerly much used in the compositions of the church, and were introduced, it is said, as a check upon that lighter and more fanciful style which a vivid imagination might otherwise have indulged, in writing music that demanded gravity of manner.

As, however, it was soon found that this simplicity might be accomplished without an adherence to rules that put genius in fetters, canons were no longer necessary; though, by way of exercise to young contra-puntists, the study of them in the schools may be, and frequently is, of service.

There is a great variety of canons. Those by augmentation and diminution, and working in contrary motion, are probably the most difficult of construction; but those in most general use are the 3 in 1, and 4 in 2. The first of these consists of one subject only, given to three voices, the bass and upper part moving in precisely the same intervals, so as to constitute the same melody; and the middle part forming also the same melody, only taking it in the dominant, or fifth of the key. Such a canon is *Non Nobis Domine*. The canon 4 in 2 is in four parts and embraces two subjects; the upper and middle voice, and the bass and alto, or second treble, forming two distinct melodies in strict interval, yet the whole constituting a complete and correct harmony. This *appears* to be more complicated than the three voice canon, but we have our doubts whether musicians in general think so.

After a careful examination of the motet now before us, we are enabled to bestow upon it almost unqualified praise. There are some trifling drawbacks on the general effect; but in the very best canons there will, and must necessarily be, a hitch or two somewhere, especially where the subject is so lengthened as in the present instance. In the fifth bar, page 2, there is a little clashing of notes that is not very agreeable; and in the first bar of page 3, we greatly regret that we cannot have some note in the tenor, instead of the rest;—the treble and alto alone produce a meagre and *disappointing* effect. Upon the whole, notwithstanding, this is an admirable specimen of the canon 4 in 2. The subject is highly

expressive of the sentiment, and is at once devotional and funereal, and from the holding note upon the word *requiescant* to the close, uncommonly solemn and affecting.

In our twenty-sixth number we remarked on the beauty of the verses, " What is prayer?" &c., which, the more we know of them, the more we discover their poetical merit and strong feeling. In setting such words, it was impossible for a man of M⁻. Horsley's judgment to indulge in that free melody which is applicable to sentiments of a less serious nature; the subject pointed out to him a boundary, and he has not attempted to exceed the prescribed limits. Hence in this hymn,—as we venture to call it,—much of what, musically speaking, is termed pleasing, with respect to air, must not be looked for, but in lieu of this quality, we have a most correct, and suitable adaptation of the notes to the words, affording to the singer every opportunity of expressing the poet's meaning with a heightened effect, and of giving such a colouring to his ideas as must render them more striking and impressive. To religious people, of whatever sect, and to those who like sacred music, this hymn will really prove an acquisition; and the young composer, —(we might have added, also many old ones,)—may study it most advantageously, in order to learn how possible it is to set words without obscuring their meaning, or sacrificing their accent.

---

1. " Here's the vow," BALLAD, *sung by* Mr. Sapio, *composed by* DR. JOHN CLARKE, *(of Cambridge)* (Goulding and Co., Soho-square.)

2. " Farewell to thee, Scotland!", *the poetry by* Sir James Webster Wedderburne, *suggested by the author's departure for Italy*: *the music composed by* HENRY R. BISHOP, *composer to the Theatre Royal, Drury-Lane.* (Golding and Co.)

3. DUET, " At Summer's Eve," *for two trebles; the poetry from* Campbell's Pleasures of Hope, *with an accompaniment for the piano-forte; composed by* WILLIAM H. CALLCOTT. (Birchall and Co., 140, *New Bond-street*.)

IT is not the lot of a composer to be always successful. Dr. Clarke has certainly been more often so than most of his contemporaries; he has given to the world many proofs of talent, that will be known and admired long after the present and succeeding generations have passed away. But this ballad will not go down to posterity, we surmise; it has no faults, but shows no traits of novelty, and probably is now as little esteemed by the author as by us.

The poetry of No. 2 ought to recommend it, though the air alone will not do much in the way of a good introduction. The fine national feeling, the strong local attachment displayed in the words, should we think, have imparted more warmth to the composer than appears in his present publication, which is rather tame for the subject, and without any apparent attempt at originality: though it must be granted that the melody, were it new, would not be unpleasing. In the first symphony there is a bar too much, an error which may be remedied by beginning the vocal part on the third quaver of the eighth whole bar, and omitting the ninth bar altogether. We much recommend all of our readers who purchase this song, to have recourse to the measure here recommended, for nothing in music is more distressing, except singing out of tune, than a fault in rhythm.

We were·glad to see again the name of Callcott as a living composer; it raises up a thousand agreeable reminiscences, and excites a hope that the father may revive in the son. This is, probably, Mr. W. Callcott's first attempt, and as such we will not examine it very closely. We advise him not to be over-hasty in publishing his early productions, for no man is *au fait* till he has blotted many quires of paper, and not to be anxious to appear before the world till his compositions have received the *imprimatur* of an able-judging professional friend.

A Selection of FRENCH MELODIES, *with symphonies and accompaniments, by* W. EAVESTAFF: the words by W. H. BELLAMY, ESQ. No. 1. (W. Eavestaff, 63, *Great Russell-street, Bloomsbury-square*)

THIS is the first number of a work which is intended to make known to. the purely English amateur of song, the national airs of our Gallic neighbours, which, as we have often observed in our publication, possess a degree of, merit that is as stoutly denied as unblushingly profited by, in the case of many composers amongst our own countrymen. How excellent some French melodies are, the subscribers to the Harmonicon have already had many opportunities, and will have many more, of judging; though we have generally thought it advisable to give them in their native language, which is so well known to all who cultivate music as an accomplishment, that we have considered a translation as quite supererogatory.

This is the first number of six, to which the collection is to be extended: it contains three airs, one whereof is also arranged as a duet; the whole making four vocal pieces. The melodies now published are well chosen, if simplicity were the object chiefly in view, and have very appropriate accompaniments. The work is in quarto, and brought out with great neatness and care.

The poetry, though it does not exhibit much imagination or fervour, is smooth, and far from inelegant; but its best praise, as part of the present work is, that it is well adapted to the music, and though it may not astonish by its vigour, will please by its good taste. As a specimen of it, we insert the following, set to the third melody.

> Tell me not of life's decay,
>   Here to-day and gone to-morrow;
> While I bask in pleasure's ray,
>   What know I of sorrow?
>
> While the flowers are round me blowing,
> Beauty's eyes with fondness glowing,
> Nectar from the goblet flowing,
>   What know I of sorrow?
>
> While the sun shines warm and bright,
> I will sport without repining;
> Time enough to think of night
>   When the stars are shining.
>
> While the light guitar is sounding,
> Bright forms o'er the green turf bounding,
> Ev'ry joy the scene surrounding,
>   Who can think of pining?

1. " On pense à toi," ROMANCE, *à Maria Stuart; paroles du* COMTE DE LA GARDE, *mises .en musique par le* MARQUIS DE SALVO. (Bedford Repository, 45, *Southampton Row.*)

2. " La Leçon inutile," ROMANCE; *paroles de Comte de Lagarde; musique par le* MARQUIS DE SALVO. (*Published by the same.*)

3. " Le Soldat Laboureur," ROMANCE, *par* ROMAGNESI. (*Published by the same.*)

4. " Le depart du jeune Grec," *musique de* GARAT. (*Published by the same.*)

5. " Embarquez-vous," *chansonnette, par Monsieur* AMEDEE DE BEAUPLAN. (*Published by the same.*)

6. " Le Chant des Chasseurs," *written and arranged to the Hunter's -Chorus in* Der Freischütz, *by the* COUNT DE LAGARDE. (*Published by the same.*)

BOTH of the romances, No. 1 and 2, shew talent, but talent that requires the aid of a little scientific knowledge, and more cultivation.

No. 3 is a spirited air, *alla marcia*, by one of the cleverest of the many good composers of this kind of music that are now living in Paris. No. 4 is in the same military style, but very inferior in all respects to the former. Perhaps the author thought, reasonably enough, that war and harmony are at variance, and having elected the first for his subject, he must reject the last as an accompaniment.

The chansonnette, No. 5, has given us much pleasure; it begins in the minor, and ends with a few bars in the major with excellent effect, and to those who like good French music we recommend this air. All the above fine vocal pieces are embellished by very well-drawn lithographic frontispieces, illustrative of the subject; a custom that is gaining ground fast in France, though we only view it as a sort of excuse for the high prices charged for a couple of pages of engraved music.

No. 6, the hunter's chorus in the *Freischütz*, is certainly not improved by being reduced to a one-part song. There are many specimens of harmonized airs to be found in every music shop in London; here is an instance of an unharmonized quartett.

---

1. DUO, *pour* PIANO-FORTE *et* GUITAR, *composé par* LEONARD DE CALL. Op. 105. (Wessel & Stodart, 1, *Soho Square.*)

2. Philomèle, *Recueil d'Airs, arrangés, avec accompagnemens Progressifs, de* GUITARE, *par* GEO. HOURI DERWORT. No. 17. (*Published by the same.*)

3. The Cabinet for the SPANISH GUITAR, *containing the most admired Vocal and Instrumental Pieces, by eminent Foreign Composers. Nos. 1, 2, 3, and 4.* (Eavestaff, *Great Russell-street, Bloomsbury.*)

WE cannot help thinking it strange that any composer should have achieved his 105th opera, without our having met with his name before. Nevertheless, the fact is before us; and facts are proverbially stubborn. This duet consists of two adagios following, and by way of a finale, an andantino. The whole is perfectly easy, and to slow-moving fingers, may, perhaps, prove very agreeable.

The present Number of *Philomèle*, is M. Lafont's

Romance, *Si tu m'aimais.* The air is charming, and the accompaniments, both for the guitar and piano-forte, are excellent.

No. 8 is one of the most elegant and moderate-priced little works we have ever beheld. Each number contains four pages, in octavo, of engraved music, comprising an air with variations, and a French song for a soprano voice, with a guitar accompaniment, together with a neatly-etched frontispiece; the whole sewed up in a smart looking cover,—and all for one shilling! The work is to be continued monthly; and amateurs of the guitar will not be doing themselves justice, if they do not at least look at this praiseworthy work.

---

1. GRAND POT-POURRI *upon the Overture, Waltz, and nine favourite Airs in "* Der Freischütz," *for the* PIANO-FORTE *and* FLUTE OBLIGATO, *by* HENRY KOHLER. (Cocks and Co., 20, *Princes-street, Hanover Square.*)

2. *Vive le Roi, ou* God save the King, *en* FANTASIE *et Variations pour la* FLUTE, *avec accompagnement de* Piano-Forte *ou* Harp, *par* C. N. WEISS. (Lindsay, 217, *Regent-street.*)

3. FANTASIA BRILLANTE, *for the* FLUTE *and* PIANO-FORTE, *including the Bridesmaids' Song and Cavatina from* Der Freischütz, *by* C. N. WEISS. Op. 77. *(Published by the same.)*

4. *Three favourite Airs selected from* Der Freischütz, *and arranged as* SOLOS *for the* FLUTE, *with brilliant Variations, by* H. KOHLER. (Lindsay, 217, *Regent-street.*)

5. Flore, *Recueil des pieces les plus favorits et agreable, pour la* FLUTE SEULE, *par divers auteurs celebres.* No. 4. (Wessel and Stodart, 1, *Soho Square.*)

KOHLER is a name of importance amongst flute players; the present is one of his best works, and includes all the most popular things in Weber's opera. This Fantasia must have two expert performers, to whom, and to all admirers of good German music, it will be sure to prove interesting.

M. Weiss' first publication is rather astounding; the very title-page, which we have prudently abridged, prepared us for something out of the common way; and certainly the variations on our national anthem required due preparation. These are dedicated to George IV.: should his Majesty perchance see them, he will surely exclaim, " God save us!—can this be God save the King?"

The Fantasia soars not quite so high; its themes are not so illustrious as that in which the author erected his other work, and he has therefore been more tranquil in descanting on them. A tolerably good flutist may profit by this publication, the accompaniments of which only requires a moderate performer on the piano-forte.

No. 4 is for the flute only, and not so difficult as the same author's work mentioned above. The airs here published are, the *Bridesmaids' Song,* the *Jäger Chorus,* and *Through the Forests.*—See No. XXI. of the *Harmonicon.*

No. 5 is a continuation of the work before noticed. This Number contains an adagio of Keller, and a Fantasia by Kulau.

NOTICE OF FOREIGN MUSICAL LITERATURE.

Le Haydine, ovvere lettere sulla vita e le opere del celebre maestro Gius. Haydn, di Guiseppe Carpani. Edizione seconda, riveduta ed accresciuta dall ' autore. Padova, 1824.

THE first edition of these interesting letters upon Haydn, relative to which we have given some particulars, (*vide* HARMONICON, vol. I., page 124,) appeared in Milan in 1822. It has a pleasing portrait of Haydn, and engravings of the various medals that have been struck at various times in his honour. The present edition is enriched with an appendix, containing various particulars concerning Rossini.

Le Rossiniane, ossia lettere musice-teatrali, di Giuseppe Carpani. Padua, 1824, with a portrait of Rossini.

THIS consists, for the greater part, of a collection of such articles relative to Rossini, as have appeared from time to time from the same pen, in various Italian journals. It contains first, letters on the Venetian theatre; secondly, an answer to the observations of the Berlin Gazette of 1818, respecting the *Tancredi* of Rossini; thirdly, observations on the *Freischütz* of Weber; fourthly, on the concert given by Rossini in Vienna; fifthly, letter on *Zelmira* *; sixthly, appendix to this letter, on the variety and mixed character of style, and on musical language (an entirely new article); seventhly, answer to an article in the Milan Gazette, against *Zelmira*; eighthly, answer to an article in the same on *Zoraide e Ricciardo.* Signor Carpani is an enthusiastic admirer of Rossini, and it is not difficult to divine the object of these articles. The above-mentioned new appendix, No. VI., which fills eighteen pages 8vo., is intended as a refutation of the objections that have been made to Rossini, that his operas have all but one and the same colouring, and are marked by no distinctive style and character. Signor Carpani begins by saying, that as yet there exists no code of a general musical rhetoric; that the variety of the characters of nations where song is cultivated, is the principal obstacle to any fixed and determinate system, and that the true rhetoric, as well as the true æsthetic of music, are as yet to be sought for; and how is it possible to find it, when even the language itself does not exist. " Where is the note that expresses God, life, death, man, wife, &c.? How can it be positively determined that such a particular passage belongs to the buffo, to the heroic, or the pastoral? I challenge any one to shew me such a passage or accompaniment as will express such or such a phrase or sentiment, and no other. Music may represent the effects of mind, but it cannot represent the causes, and still less particularize them, (*renirne ai particolari.*) Musical passages or phrases serve for every style: it is not their character, but their succession and connexion which give it its variety;" neither can the writer see how expression and variety of style can be effected by instrumentation or accompaniment: he, finally, maintains, that harmony is but an accessary in music; that the limits of style are so undeterminate,

---

* It was from this letter, which first appeared in the *Biblioteca Italiana,* that our extracts, vol. II., page 126, were taken.

that even the most learned composers have erred in this respect, and that, therefore, the usual indulgence shewn to others, ought also to be extended to Rossini. At the conclusion he proves, that even if a sanctioned musical language were possible, still it were not at all to be wished, as in this manner music, divine as it is in its nature, would, by this most fatal acquisition (*fatalissimo acquistio*,) cease to be a fine art, and bereft of its charm and life, would belong merely to those that are mechanical. In a long note, it is also maintained, that music particularly acts upon the physical powers of man, &c.

The *Corriere degli Spettacoli*, of which we have already spoken as having made its appearance in Bologna, has ceased, and in its place appears, in an elegant form, an interesting journal under the title :—

Cenni Storici intorno alle Lettere, invenzione, arti, commercio, et spettacoli teatrali dell' anno, 1824. Parte prima. Bologna.

THE last numbers contain a series of critiques upon STENDHAL's *Life of Rossini*, whereof two editions have appeared. After some observations on the manner in which the French get up their books, and upon the two portraits of Rossini and Mozart, which head these volumes, the Italian Editor gets very angry at the author's presumption in bringing Rossini in comparison with Mozart. This passage is the more remarkable, as it occurs in a volume printed in Bologna, where Rossini received his education and first musical ideas. " However high the esteem which the writer feels for his *protagonista*, would it be right for him to couple this composer's name with that of the man who has filled the world with his fame? And what comparison can there be between a composer, however fortunate in certain works composed for the theatre, and the author who by the power of his genius has subdued the world, and will make future ages respect his name? Who will say whether the glory of Rossini is destined to survive himself; and whether, after some few years, fashion, who is as absolute an arbitress of music as she is of female dress, may not cry up some other composer, who has tossed out for himself a path altogether different from that of the idol of our day?" How true and candid this! When in Stendhal's LIFE it is remarked, that " the compositions of Mozart are of a melancholy, and those of Rossini of a brilliant, character; that Mozart was but twice in his life gay, and that in his *Don Giovanni*; that Rossini was just as often melancholy as Mozart was gay; that one paints love as felt in Germany, and the other as in Italy; that Mozart paints, brooding in silence over its object, unhappy love, Rossini the more fierce and violent passions:" the author observes in reply, " that the author may be in the right with respect to Mozart, as perhaps his passions were of a tender and melancholy nature, but that with respect to Rossini, his character was too well known to allow any argument upon the subject. If a passion must be felt before it can be expressed, how could Rossini succeed in painting the deeper feelings of love, which he had never felt—if he has laughed and still continues to laugh at those who are the votaries of this passion?" This critique is not yet concluded, and at the rate the author has advanced, it will yet be some time before it be so.

THE ANCIENT CONCERTS.

FIRST CONCERT, 1825.

Under the Direction of his Grace, the Archbishop of York, for His Royal Highness the Duke of Cumberland. Wednesday, March 2nd, 1825.

ACT I.

Overture.		
Chorus. O come let us sing.		
Air. O come let us worship.	(Anthem.)	Handel.
Chorus. Glory and worship.		
Glee. When winds breathe soft.		Webbe.
Recit. Thrice happy king.		
Song. Golden columns.	(Solomon.)	Handel.
Recit. My arms.		
Air. Sound an alarm.	(Judas Maccabeus.)	Handel.
Chorus. We hear.		
Movement.	(From his Lessons.)	Handel.
Song. Tears such as.	(Deborah.)	Handel.
Trio. Fall'n is thy throne, O Israel!		
Recit. First and chief.		
Air. Sweet bird!	(Il Penseroso.)	Handel.
Chorus. Lord, thou art gracious.		Marcello.

ACT II.

Overture and Dead March.	(Saul.)	Handel.
Duet. Te ergo quæsumus.		Graun.
Recit. Be comforted.		
Song. The Lord worketh.	(Judas Macc.)	Handel.
Quartett. Prepare, then.	(Semele.)	Handel.
Recit. Relieve thy champion.		
Song. Return, O God of Hosts.	(Samson.)	Handel.
Concerto, 2nd.	(Oboe.)	Handel.
Recit. Alas! I find.		
Song. Guiltless blood.	(Susanna.)	Handel.
Monody. Forgive, blest shade.		Callcott.
Coronation Anthem. Zadok the priest.		Handel.

WE had occasion last season to go very much into detail in our reports of these concerts ;—our observations, this year, will not occupy so much of the reader's attention, as we shall pass over such performances as we have mentioned in former numbers, confining ourselves, for the most part, to such *novelties* as we may be fortunate enough to fall in with.— We trust that this optimistic will not prove unsatisfactory. On Wednesday, the 2d of March, the Archbishop of York treated us again with the opening of last year ;—we say *treated* us, because the anthem ".O come let us sing" is one of those noble efforts of genius. that cannot be too often repeated*. Than Handel's heavenly song, "O come let us worship," and Vaughan's chaste and feeling singing, nothing can be more delicious. After the "soft breathing" of the *old winds*, we were favoured with an air from Solomon, not particularly striking, but we hailed it as a novelty, and as it introduced to our notice a new performer, and one of considerable promise.— Miss Wilkinson is, we have been told, a scholar of Mr. Greatorex's ; her voice a low treble, clear, but not yet arrived at that fulness and flexibility which time and practice will doubtless give it.— To suit its quality and compass, her second song was far better chosen than her first ;—she did great justice to " Return, O God of Hosts," but the " Golden columns" had rather a *leadenish* effect upon our ear ;—besides, where was the necessity for giving Miss Wilkinson a *tenor* song to sing, when there are so many contr'alto airs by Handel which would have suited her so much better ?—This young lady will, unquestionably, under the tuition of her able master, prove a great acquisition to these concerts ; and we would recommend her to turn her attention speedily to Storge's scenes in the oratorio of *Jephtha*. Mr. Sapio's " Sound an Alarm," was an alarm indeed !— We will not be so ungracious, on this gentleman's first appear-

* We missed, however, the fair Lancashire Choir;—not even Miss Travis was in her place ; and the trebles, with the boys only, were as much too feeble and inefficient, as they were before too powerful.—*Some* of the ladies, at any rate, we hope to see back again.

ance in this concert room, as to treat him with *all* our rigour; but we earnestly advise him to recollect, in future, that *singing* before an Ancient Concert Audience is one thing, and *shouting* to the one shilling gallery of Drury Lane Theatre another,—his alteration of the time in the song, too, completely destroyed its simplicity and energetic effect.—These stratagems to shew off the voice, at the expense of the composer, are scarcely tolerated on the stage: on occasions like the present they are totally indefensible. Mr. Sapio's duet with Miss Stephens, was a performance much more creditable to him;—but the part was still too high for his voice, and the continual rise from his full tenor tones to the *falsetto* had a very feeble effect: should this gentleman be finally engaged, we recommend, with due deference to the noble directors, that his talents be confined to the *Italian* school.—There he will be always at home, and, we doubt not, always respectable.

Mr. Phillips is another candidate for an Ancient Concert engagement, and we very cordially congratulate him upon the strong and favourable impression he produced, by his performance of the evening, upon the minds of his auditors; particularly in his last song, "The Lord worketh wonders," in which he was chaste, clear, and animated. There is a want of depth and fulness in his tones, which defect, however, time and practice will, we doubt not, remedy; but he is neither deficient in compass nor flexibility of voice; and, what is better, has an accurate ear. When this young gentleman has got the better of a little provincial coarseness in his manner of accenting his words, his singing will be still more pleasing;—in short, it will be his own fault if he be not, in process of time, though not exactly a second Bartleman, perhaps found to approach very near to him. We will say nothing about Mrs. Salmon's "Sweet Bird." We *must* presume that she was indisposed! We gratefully thank the most reverend director for a *novelty* which followed; we never heard a more magnificent display of Marcello's powers! The modulations varying on the points of imitation had a wonderful effect, and the *coda* we have seldom heard equalled even by Handel himself. Our old enemies, the drums and trumpets, were more clamorous than ever; but there is no help for it. Ling was very respectable in the 2nd oboe concerto, and indeed, now that we have lost poor Griesbach, is decidedly the best performer on the instrument left us. Miss Stephens sung her song from *Susannah* delightfully; it is in these tender and pathetic airs that she excels: when she has to strain her voice in loud and elaborate passages, her tones are (we do not like to use the word *coarse*) any thing but sweet.

We had nearly forgotten the quintetto from *Semele*;—it had *novelty* at least to recommend it,—but we have been favoured with more striking novelties from Handel.

Well, three *new* singers and three *new* performances to begin with, look well.

SECOND CONCERT.

Under the direction of the Earl of Derby, for his Royal Highness the Duke of Cambridge. Wednesday, March the 9th, 1825.

ACT I.

Opening of Grand te Deum.		*Graun.*
Duetto. Qual anelante.		*Marcello.*
Anthem. Sing unto God.		*Dr. Croft.*
Song. What though I trace.	(*Solomon.*)	*Handel.*
Concerto 9th.		*Geminiani Corelli*
Recit. acc. Deeper and Deeper. }	(*Jephthah.*)	*Handel.*
Song. Waft her, angels. }		
Chorus. Lift up your heads.	(*Messiah.*)	*Handel.*
Recit. Let eternal honours. }	(*Judas Macc.*)	*Handel.*
Song. From mighty kings. }		
Recit. March, Air, and Chorus. Glory to God. (*Joshua.*)		*Handel.*

ACT II.

Overture and Minuet.	(*Iphigenia.*)	*Gluck.*
Sestett and Chorus. This is the day.	(*Anthem.*)	*Dr. Croft.*
Glee. Oh Nanny!		*Carter and Harrison.*
Song. Softly rise. }	(*Solomon.*)	*Dr. Boyce.*
Chorus. Ye southern breezes. }		
Recit. Spoea—Euridice' }	(*Orfeo.*)	*Gluck.*
Song. Che faro senza }		

Chorus. For unto us a Child. }		
Pastoral Symphony. }	(*Messiah.*)	*Handel.*
Recit. acc. There were shepherds. }		
Chorus. Glory to God. }		
Song. Honour and arms.	(*Samson.*)	*Handel.*
Glee. Here in cool grot.		*Earl of Mornington.*
March and Cho. Crown with festal.	(*Hercules.*)	*Handel.*

WITH the bill of fare for this evening was presented the following notice:

Hanover Square, March 9, 1825.

"The subscribers are respectfully informed that Miss Wilkinson is prevented singing this evening by sudden and severe indisposition. In consequence, Mr. Vaughan will take her part in the duet of 'Qual anelante,' and, instead of the recit. and air, 'Che faro,' and the song, 'What though I trace,' Miss Stephens will sing the recit. and air, 'Farewell, ye limpid streams,' and Mr. Phillips the recit. and air, 'Shall I in Mamre's fertile plains.'"

We were sorry for it, not only on Miss Wilkinson's, but on poor Phillips's account, to whom, instead of the song in Orfeo, was given another of Bartleman's most impressive performances:—this is not quite fair;—airs of this description are, at present at least, quite beyond his powers, and we should have thought it would have been obvious to those who are more capable of judging on the subject, and on whom the business of choosing the songs to be sung by this very rising performer devolves.—As to "Honour and Arms," we do not hesitate to affirm that, Bartleman excepted, we never heard it given with greater accuracy and spirit;—he fully understands his points, we would only advise him to be less exuberant, in future, in his cadences; these are at all times difficult to manage with effect, and should be quite let alone till the voice and judgment are completely formed.—Mr. Phillips has been brought forward two years at least too soon, and we lament the circumstance much, because the public do not always mark the progress of improvement, and encourage it accordingly.

We were glad to see the Lancashire ladies in their places again, and Miss Travis, was, as usual, pleasing and judicious in the part she sustained in the opening of Graun's "Te Deum." —"Qual anelante," was exceedingly well sung, and certainly lost none of its effect by Vaughan's taking the second part.—Miss Stephens was feeling and delicate, as she always is, in "Farewell," but we think the orchestra always drag the beautiful burst into the major key;—the contrast, on every account, should be marked with greater animation. In the last movement of the 9th Concerto, Dragonetti surprised, we confess, more than he pleased us, by playing the violoncello part on the double bass: —the *occasional rasp* of his mighty bow is very well, but a quick succession of them has a disagreeable, and even a ludicrous effect.

Mr. Sapio *tried*, at any rate, to give expression to the bitter woes of Jephthah, but we can only give him credit for his exertions: it will *not* do, the stage and the concert-room must be separately considered;—besides, Mr. S. may, with very little practice, so far soften down his Italian manner of pronunciation as to avoid vulgarisms,—"Fauther," for "Father," is sad work.

The "Mighty Kings" of Mrs. Salmon was, we are grieved to say, like her "Sweet Bird," on a former night, a complete failure; we have heard her, on former occasions, sing out of tune, but not continue so, with grating pertinacity, from the commencement to the conclusion of her song, which was the case this evening. How are we to account for this break?—We will suspend our opinion a little longer. The magnificent chorus from Joshua was admirably sustained both by voices and band; as to the trumpet performer, (Harper we believe is his name,) there may possibly have been as good, but there never could have been a completer master of his very difficult instrument.

Vaughan's "Softly rise," in the second act, was rich and soothing; a beautiful specimen of the pure English school of singing; we would advise some *other gentlemen tenor singers*, if they *must* imitate, to take Vaughan for their model.

Upon the other pieces performed we have nothing material to remark: we can add nothing to what we have already *said* repeatedly of their respective merits. The concluding chorus was, however, more judiciously chosen than is too often the case. "Crown with festal pomp the day," is, indeed, so exactly what it ought to be for sending the worthy *Ancients* to their carriages, that we wish it was always reserved for that purpose.

PHILHARMONIC CONCERTS.

SECOND CONCERT, Monday, *March 7th.*

Act I.

Sinfonia in D.	*Mozart.*
Song, Mr. Phillips, " Haste, nor lose the favouring hour," (Der Freischütz)	*Weber.*
Concerto Oboe, Mr. Vogt, (his first performance in this country)	*Vogt.*
Trio, " The flocks shall leave the mountains," Miss Stephens, Mr. Sapio, and Mr. Phillips (Acis and Galatéa)	*Handel.*
Concerto in G, Piano-Forte, Mr. Potter (never performed in this country)	*Beethoven.*

Act II.

Sinfonia, in C Minor	*Beethoven.*
Aria, Mr. Sapio, " Il mio tesoro," (Il Don Giovanni)	*Mozart.*
Introduction and Variations, Corno obbligato, Mr. Schuncke (his first performance in this country)	*Schuncke.*
Scena, Miss Stephens," Softly sighs,"(Der Freischütz)	*Weber.*
Overture, *Preciosa*	*Weber.*

Leader, Mr. Mori.—Conductor, Mr. Attwood.

With the exception of the two symphonies, the second concert was very unequal to the first, and, indeed, inferior to most that have been given by the Philharmonic society. To these orchestral compositions by Mozart and Beethoven, we have paid many a sincere and just tribute of praise ; both were now executed with the spirit and precision that mark the instrumental efforts of this fine band ; and the Overture to Weber's *Precio a* is very original and pleasing. The concerto of Beethoven was well played by Mr. Potter, who shews an excellent feeling for music of this high class ; but it was not prudent to introduce it in an evening, when two other concertos were put in the programme. At the institution of this society, it was a fundamental law, that no concertos should be allowed. An occasional relaxation of the severity of this was discreet, and almost necessary. A new instrumental performer has a right—particularly if a stranger—to have an opportunity of displaying his talent once, in some piece in which he alone is to be conspicuous. But between wisely deviating from a rule sometimes, and breaking through a salutary regulation thrice in an evening, there is a wide difference ; the one is a proof of judgment, the other of unsteadiness. It was very right to allow M. Vogt to exhibit himself in what he conceived the most advantageous manner; but M. Schuncke should have been reserved for another night, and Beethoven's piano-forte concerto ought to have been heard when no other single instrument was to make a display. M. Vogt, the first hautbois at the French opera, or *Academie Royal de Musique*, executes more on his instrument than any *oboeist* that we have ever heard ; but his tone is thin, and somewhat harsh: he has the fault of French singers, he forces the tones till they become hard and disagreeable. M. Schuncke is a good horn player, but not equal to Puzzi.

The vocal portion of this concert, after excepting Handel's trio—much out of its place here—was very inferior indeed. To give things that are almost nightly performed at the English theatres, and with scarcely any change in the singers, is a sign of poverty that we did not expect to witness, and indicates, we conclude, that the managers are not at all aware of the vast abundance of new vocal music, of the highest merit, that is weekly appearing in Germany and elsewhere: not to mention the shelf-loads full of excellent pieces by the greatest masters, that, with a little industry might be produced.

THIRD CONCERT, Monday, *March 21st.*

Act I.

Sinfonia, Letter T.	*Haydn.*
Terzetto, " Tutte le mie speranze," Mad. Caradori, MissGoodall,& Mr. Vaughan(*Davide Penitente*)	*Mozart.*
Quartetto, two Violins, Viola,and Violoncello,Messrs. Spagnoletti, Oury, Moralt, and Lindley	*Mozart.*
Song, Mr. Vaughan, " Why does the God of Israel sleep," (Samson)	*Handel.*
Quintetto, Flute, Oboe, Clarinet, Horn, and Bassoon, Messrs. Nicholson, Vogt,Willman, Platt, and Mackintosh	*Reicha.*
Recit. ed Aria, Mad. Caradori, " Per pietà," (Cosi fan tutte)	*Mozart.*
Overture, *Les deux Journées*	*Cherubini.*

Act II.

New Grand Characteristic Sinfonia, MS., with Vocal Finale, the principal parts of which to be sung by Mad. Caradori, Miss Goodall, Mr. Vaughan, and Mr. Phillips (composed expressly for this Society)	*Beethoven.*

Leader, Mr. F. Cramer.—Conductor, Sir G. Smart.

Haydn's symphony in E flat, which is enumerated amongst his old ones, because produced antecedently to the twelve composed for Salomon, is a beautiful specimen of its author's genius for invention, and elegance of taste: there is a purity in it, both as to construction and effect, that must always recommend it to the student who diligently analyses, and to the public who attend only to its performance. The andante was encored. The overture to *Les deux Journées*, which many consider as Cherubini's chef d'œuvre, has before been noticed as it deserves in this work. Both of these charming instrumental pieces were received with genuine applause.

The new symphony of Beethoven, composed for, and purchased at a liberal price by, this society, was now first publicly produced. In our last number we mentioned it, and we see no reason for altering the opinion we there offered. We must, however, correct our statement as to its duration. At a rehearsal, where so many interruptions occur, it is next to impossible to ascertain exactly the length of a piece: we now find this to be precisely one hour and five minutes ; a fearful period indeed, which puts the muscles and lungs of the band, and the patience of the audience, to a severe trial. In the present symphony we discover no diminution of Beethoven's creative talent; it exhibits many perfectly new traits, and in its technical formation shews amazing ingenuity and unabated vigour of mind. But with all the merits that it unquestionably possesses, it is at least twice as long as it should be ; it repeats itself, and the subjects in consequence become weak by reiteration. The last movement, a chorus, is heterogeneous, and though there is much vocal beauty in parts of it, yet it does not, and no habit will ever make it, mix up with the three first movements. This chorus is a hymn to joy, commencing with a recitative, and relieved by many *soli* passages. What relation it bears to the symphony we could not make out ; and here, as well as in other parts, the want of intelligible design is too apparent. In our next we shall give the words of the chorus, with a translation ; in the present number our printer has not been able to find room for them. The most original feature in this symphony is the minuet, and the most singular part, the succeeding trio,—striking, because in duple time, for which we are not acquainted with anything in the shape of a precedent. We were also much pleased by a very noble march, which is introduced. In quitting the present subject, we must express our hope that this new work of the great Beethoven may be put into a produceable form ; that the repetitions may be omitted, and the chorus removed altogether ; the symphony will then be heard with unmixed pleasure, and the reputation of its author will, if possible, be further augmented.

We have only time briefly to notice the other parts of this concert. The terzetto, from an almost unknown work of Mozart, is beautiful, and was admirably performed. The quartett by the same was indeed delightful, and Spagnoletti did it justice. Mr. Vaughan's choice of " Why does the God of

Israel sleep?" was not fortunate; it is quite beyond his physical power, and out of his style. Mad. Caradori sang the aria from *Cosi fan tutte* with more delicacy than effect: But we regret to leave off by saying, that the quintetto for wind instruments, by Reicha, was, by the whole room, thought unworthy of the place, and of the performers engaged in it: its dulness for a short time might for once have been endured; but its extreme length, added to its almost unparalleled barrenness of every thing either scientific or pleasing, rendered it one of the most intolerable pieces that we were ever condemned to hear.

ROYAL ACADEMY OF MUSIC.

A CONCERT of vocal and instrumental music, for the benefit of this Institution, was performed at the Hanover-square rooms, on Friday the 25th of March, by the pupils of the Institution. The following is the programme of the pieces given:—

PART I.

Symphony	(*Jupiter.*)	*Mozart.*
Quartetto, "Lo star-led chiefs."	(*Palestine.*)	*Dr. Crotch.*
Quartetto, Violins, Viola, and Violoncello.		*Mozart.*
Serenata, " Oh notte soave."		*Paer.*
Military Concerto, Piano-Forte.		*Dussek.*
Finale to the First Act of *Il Tancredi.*		*Rossini.*

PART II.

Overture	(*Anacreon.*)	*Cherubini.*
Quintetto, " Santo, oh Dio."	(*Cosi fan tutte*)	*Mozart.*
Solo, Flute		*Tulon.*
Air, "Nunzia ognor."		*Blangini.*
Sestetto, "Sola, Sola."	(*Il Don Giovanni.*)	*Mozart.*
Overture.	(*Der Freischutz.*)	*Weber.*

There was much talent shewn at this concert, and the performance did credit to the masters, as well as to the gentlemen of the committee. We wish success to this establishment, and therefore recommend the managers to revise their plan, and, particularly, to purify it from any person in the shape of a teacher whose character and example may injure the morals of all the young people who are likely to be under the tuition of such a person. We have received a letter on the subject, a kind of commentary on an article that appeared in a Sunday paper, distinguished for its humour, which we hope to be able to insert in our next number. Unfortunately we could not make a corner for it in the present.

THE ORATORIOS.

THESE Lent Concerts, divided between the two theatres, filled very well, and were conducted at a moderate expense. The new composition of Weber, produced by Mr. Bishop at Drury-Lane Theatre, is an unequal work; much of it shews the original genius of the author, while parts of it are rather obscure and tedious. The other composition by the same, was delayed so long at Covent Garden, that we had no opportunity of hearing it. There is a general feeling that these performances are protracted to a most unreasonable length, often five hours and a half, a period which is enough to exhaust the patience of the most determined *fanatico* alive. The motive is, doubtless, a legitimate one, and a spirit of rivalry compels one house to give as much for money as the other; but a reform by mutual agreement would be beneficial alike to the public and the performers.

MADAME CATALANI'S CONCERTS.

DURING the last month, this celebrated singer has given four concerts, on Thursdays, at the Argyle Rooms. The first and second were not very fully attended; the two last were filled almost to suffocation. The chief performers were, Madame Catalani, Mrs. Salmon, Mr. Sapio, and Signor Remorini. It is Madame Catalani's intention to give four more after Easter.

THE DRAMA.

ITALIAN OPERA.

THE architects of the Board of Works having determined that very considerable repairs, and the entire rebuilding of the north wall, were necessary at the King's Theatre, Mr. Ebers, *ad interim,* engaged the Haymarket Theatre for the performances of the opera. It opened on Tuesday, the 1st of March, with Mozart's *Nozze di Figaro.* The boxes are separated by temporary partitions, and the pit and gallery are in communication, the latter taking the name of the Balcony. The entrance into the pit is made by sacrificing the centre front box, which is converted into a passage, and a short double staircase descends from it in a very convenient manner. The orchestra is enlarged by taking, in addition to it, one row of the pit, and the major part of the band is thus accommodated.

This summer theatre is certainly not favourable to music, owing to the number of breaks in the fronts of the boxes, and the many cavities, in which the sounds are lost. The tones are no sooner uttered than they expire; they fall as it were dead from the mouths of the singers, and that beautiful blending which a very slight resonance produces, is wholly wanting. This may be in some measure also attributable to the curtains that divide the boxes, which are likely to operate unfavourably in so small a space, though in a larger area they have less influence.

No sooner were the doors of this temporary Italian Theatre prepared to move on their hinges, when the principal tenor, Sig. Garcia, was attacked by one of his hoarsenesses, and rendered incapable of performing. A new opera was then to be got up, which was no sooner ready than Mad. de Begnis, the *prima donna*, fell ill, and was rendered useless to the establishment for upwards of a fortnight. Recourse was then had to the *Barbiere di Siviglia*, in which neither of these personages was wanted. This, and a thousand former instances of the kind, should operate as a hint to managers of the foreign theatre, to engage principal performers conditionally, so that when real illness, or approaching age, or caprice, prevents their exerting their talents, their salaries should be suspended. On the 19th of March, a new Opera *semi-seria*, in one act, was produced for the first time in London; and by a composer, Generali, whose name was before unknown to the theatre. The title of this is *Adelina*, and the characters are:

VARNER, *Father of Adelina*	-	-	Sig. Remorini.
ADELINA	- - - - - -	-	Mad. de Begnis.
CARLOTTA, *another Daughter of Varner*,			Mad. Caradori.
ERNEVILLE, *Lover of Adelina*	-	-	Sig. Garcia.
DON SIMONE, *Schoolmaster*	-	-	Sig. de Begnis.
FIRMINIO, *Servant*	-	-	Sig. G. Crivelli.

The story is originally Florian's, and the subject of his novel *Chlorine.* It was converted into a short, sentimental piece, called *Lisbeth*, for the French stage, whence the dramatic part of the present opera is taken. The *Father and Daughter* of Mrs. Opie, *Agnese*, and *Clari*, are all from the same source, and the history of the latter may be considered to be nearly the same as that of the present opera. The music is very good throughout, though not of the highest order, and is exactly calculated for a small theatre. The most remarkable part of it is, that it has afforded Rossini much *materiel* for his *Barbiere*, and *Gazza Ladra.* The resemblance, or rather identity, is so striking, that a critic, sitting near to us in the pit, said, "This Generali has taken his best subjects from Rossini." The former composer assisted his more fortunate, and indeed more gifted, contemporary in his early works: it is said Generali is still living, though it is commonly supposed that he died a few years ago.

On Saturday the 26th, *L'Italiana in Algeri*, is to be produced. But as our work goes to press before that day, we must speak of this revival in our next. The King's Theatre will, it is understood, be re-opened on Tuesday, the 12th of April.

DRURY-LANE AND COVENT-GARDEN THEATRES.

Both these theatres succeed so well with their old pieces, that no fresh effort has been made to bring out anything new. The *Freischütz* continues to draw crowds at each house: a proof of the taste of the middling classes for what is really good in music.

MEMOIR OF Dr. ARNE.

AMONG our native composers, there is no one who, next to Purcell, claims a higher distinction than Dr. Arne. His genius, like that of his illustrious predecessor in the art, had a decided influence upon the national taste, and tended to settle and establish that *manner*, which, with more justice than any other, may be denominated *English*.

Thomas Augustine Arne was the son of an eminent upholsterer, of King-street, Covent-garden *, and was born on the 12th of March, 1710. He received a good education, being sent by his father to Eton, with a view of his being brought up to the profession of the law. But his natural bias for that art which was destined to render him so great an ornament to his country, disclosed itself in his earliest youth, and is said to have interfered with those studies, which, in the estimation of men of calculating minds, are of far higher importance. His first musical means and performances were not, however, the most propitious. Some of his fellow-students were heard to declare, that they had but too good reason to remember his predilection for music at this period, for, that by means of a miserable, cracked, common flute, he used to torment them everlastingly, interrupting their studies by day, and their repose by night.

On quitting Eton, this passion for music grew more

* The father of Dr. Arne had for his sign the *Crown* and *Cushion*. He has the credit of being the original projector of the performance of Handel's compositions to English words. Mr. Arne is said to have been the Political Upholsterer delineated by Addison, in the *Tatler*, and was probably also the person who perished so deplorably in the Fleet Prison : for in *The Tatler*, he is not only mentioned as a bankrupt, but, in a report read in the House of Commons, on the 2d of March 1728, it appears, that a Mr. Edward Arne, upholsterer, being in the tap-room of that prison, was suddenly seized without the least provocation, and forced into a damp, nauseous, and unwholesome dungeon, without fire or covering ; where, through excessive cruelty for the space of six weeks, he lost his senses, and died.

On the Report of this Committee, John Huggins, the warden of the Fleet, was tried for murder, but acquitted. James Barnes, his agent, by whom this outrage was committed, fled, and was never tried. However, the Lord Chief Justice Raymond was of opinion, that, had he been on his trial, and the fact proved against him, he would undoubtedly have been found guilty of murder, having certainly exceeded his duty, and being guilty of a breach of that trust which the law reposed in him, and being therefore answerable for all consequences. Various other cruelties, exercised about this time, gave rise to this Committee, which the humane Thomson has celebrated in his *Winter*, line 359 to 388 :

"And here can I forget the generous band," &c.

strongly upon him, and he sought every means of gratifying it. Of this the following anecdote, as heard from his own mouth, will be a sufficient testimony. Frequently, when his finances were low, he was tempted to avail himself of the privilege of the domestics of the nobility, by borrowing a suit of livery, and stealing into the upper gallery of the opera, a part of the house at that time appropriated to this purpose. At home too, his ingenuity devised the means of pursuing his favourite study. Well aware of the parental displeasure which he should incur, should the secret of his devotion to the art transpire, he clandestinely procured an old spinnet, and conveyed it to a room on the attic story, where, after cautiously muffling the strings with a handkerchief, he would practice during many a live-long night, while suspicion and the family were lulled asleep. And fortunate was it for the young musician, that he escaped detection, for his father is represented as having been a passionate man, and, had he discovered how his son passed his time, would perhaps have thrown the instrument out of the window, and not impossibly the player after it.

The luckless moment at length arrived, when he was to commence serving a three-years' clerkship to the law. What a chilling announcement to the youthful and ardent votary of the god of song! Though nature and inclination made him feel the impossibility of his ever cooling down into a special pleader, yet a sense of duty would not allow him to oppose his father's will. He, therefore, dissembled his repugnance, and to all appearance applied seriously to the study of the profession : but, alas! Coke was forced to give place to Corelli. Besides applying himself with redoubled diligence to improve his execution on the spinnet, as well as to acquire a knowledge of thorough bass, he contrived to procure the important advantage of Festing's * instructions on the violin.

* Michael Christian Festing was a pupil of the great Geminiani. He filled the place of first violin at a musical meeting chiefly composed of noblemen and gentlemen performers, who met on Wednesday nights, during the winter season, at the Crown and Anchor Tavern in the Strand. On the building of the Rotunda in Ranelagh Gardens, he was appointed sole conductor of the musical performances there. By his zeal and indefatigable exertion, he also contributed very essentially to the establishment of the fund instituted for the support of decayed musicians and their families ; and, for several years, discharged, without any remuneration, the office of secretary to that excellent institution. He died in 1752.

N

Under this master he made so rapid a progress, that not many months after his application to that instrument, he was enabled to lead a chamber band at the house of an amateur who gave private evening concerts. It happened that Arne's father was invited to one of these musical soirées, and his astonishment, not unmingled with indignation, may be imagined, when he beheld his son, the hopeful young lawyer, in the very act of playing the first fiddle. It was some time before his anger could be appeased; but, at length, cool reflection and the apparent desperation of the case, determined him to indulge this pertinacious bent of nature, and afford his son every opportunity of turning his talents to the best account. The ponderous volumes of law were accordingly ousted from his apartment, to make room for a selection of the best musical works; and being now at liberty to practise without restraint, the tones of Augustine's violin bewitched the whole family. Having discovered that his sister was not only fond of music, but had also a very sweet and touching voice, he undertook her musical education; and so rapid was the progress she made under his able instructions, that she was soon qualified for a public singer. The style in which she acquitted herself in Lampe's opera of *Amelia*, induced her affectionate tutor to prepare a more brilliant character for the display of her abilities. Accordingly, though at that time only eighteen years of age, he set to music Addison's opera of *Rosamond*, in which, while the future celebrated Mrs. Cibber represented the heroine, the younger brother of the composer acted the part of the page*. The piece met with a very warm reception, and was performed ten successive nights, the last being for the benefit of the composer.

The success of this production was too encouraging to permit the ardent mind of so young a candidate for fame to remain inactive. He shortly afterwards tried his power in a burletta, and fixed on Fielding's *Tom Thumb*. This piece, which was originally brought forward under the title of *The Tragedy of Tragedies*, was now transformed into *The Opera of Operas*, and re-produced at the new theatre in the Haymarket "set to music *after the Italian manner*, by Mr. Arne, Jun." The reception of this effort was no less favourable than that of the former. At the second representation, the Princess Amelia and the Duke of Cumberland were present; the sixth was honoured by the presence of the Prince of Wales, and the eighth had among its auditors the younger princesses.

These two pieces possessed sufficient merit to establish Arne's reputation as a dramatic composer; but the music of *Comus*, produced in 1738, evinced powers of a more lofty kind, and astonished and delighted every judge of original air, and elegant composition. In this Mask he introduced a style, unique, and perfectly his own. Without pretending to the loftier energy of Purcell, or the more majestic dignity of Handel, it was vigorous, gay, and natural, and possessed such strong and distinctive features as to form an æra in English music. There is a character of grace, a flowing, sweet, and lucid style of melody about it, which captivates the ear by the simplicity of its motivos, and satisfies the understanding by the eloquence of its expression, and the truth of its emphasis.

In the year 1740, Arne married Miss Cecilia Young, a vocal pupil of the celebrated Geminiani, and a performer of considerable eminence. In 1742, they went to Ireland, where the husband as a distinguished composer, and the wife as a celebrated singer, were kindly and honourably received. After remaining two years in that country, they returned to England, and he formed an engagement with the proprietors of Drury Lane Theatre, for himself as composer, and Mrs. Arne, as serious singer. Here he produced his *Britannia* and the *Judgment of Paris*, both Masques, *Thomas and Sally*, an afterpiece, and *Eliza*, an opera. On the death of Gordon, the first violin, he accepted of the situation of leader of the orchestra. His hand was at this time enfeebled by rheumatism, but he gave proofs of the goodness of his school, and by his skill surpassed every other performer on the violin who had preceded him in that situation.

In the summer of 1745, the proprietor of Vauxhall Gardens having resolved to add vocal to instrumental performances, Mrs. Arne was engaged as principal singer. This change opened a new field for the display of Arne's powers, in the composition of ballads, dialogues, cantatas, duets, and trios, many of which, after enlivening this pleasant evening-retreat, spread through the whole kingdom, and charmed universally, by their elegance, sweetness, and simplicity*.

In 1762, after producing, besides the operas and pieces above named, the two oratorios of *Abel* and *Judith*, Doctor Arne,—for during this interval the university of Oxford had honoured him with the degree of Doctor of Music,—ventured upon the new and arduous task of composing an Anglo-Italian Opera,—an Opera consisting of songs, duets, and recitative, without any spoken dialogue. The drama he selected for this purpose was the *Artaserse* of Metastasio, a composition admirable in the original, but much of its brilliancy and power were lost in the English translation, which was wholly executed by himself†. It was in the music of this piece that he first quitted that simple and natural cast of melody, which in his *Rosamond*, *Comus*, and other compositions, had universally attracted and pleased. The risk, therefore, which he ran in thus suddenly changing his whole style and manner was great; but his boldness was triumphant, and his success complete. It must, however, be allowed, that the nature of his undertaking admitted of one resource, and of that he very liberally availed himself. As it was intended that the style of the new piece should assimilate to that of the Italian, abundant opportunities of imitation were afforded him, which, while they had the effect of imparting to the

* Among the numerous compositions produced by Arne for Vauxhall Gardens, no one was more admired and continued longer a favourite of the public, than the little diaglogue of *Colin and Phœbe*, the words by Moore, of the well-known *Fables for the Female Sex*.
† Baker, in his *Companion to the Play House*, mentions this transaction in very disrespectful terms, though he extols the music. Viewed as a literary effort, it is certainly not entitled to any praise beyond negative praise; but when compared to many subsequent dramatic productions of professed authors, it may very fairly be considered as a superior work. Let the candid critic place the verses of *Artaxerxes* by the side of nine-tenths of the lyrical attempts which are to be found in the theatrical writings of the present age, and he will be obliged to admit that, thus paralleled, Arne may almost be said to shine as a poet. Dr. Arne was the author both of the words and music of two comic operas, *The Guardian Outwitted*, and *The Rose*; the former produced in 1764, and the latter in 1778. Neither of these were successful.

* This drama, meritorious in its poetry, and delightful in its music, was first performed March 7, 1733, at Lincoln's-Inn-Fields. The characters were cast as follows: the *King*, Mrs. Barbier, *Sir Trusty*, Mr. Leveridge, (the composer); *Page*, Master Arne; *Messenger*, Mr Corfe; *Queen*, Mrs. Jones; *Griseldini*, Miss Chambers; *Rosamond*, Miss Arne.

whole an air of novelty, ran no risk of detection from a play-house audience. The original performers in *Artaxerxes* were Tenducci, Peretti, and Miss Brent, the Doctor's pupil, who did ample justice to the instructions of her master, and became the favourite singer of that period. The piece was received with an enthusiasm new to the English stage, and had an immense run; and, when ably performed, is still, and will ever continue to be, listened to with rapture.

The fame of Dr. Arne was now established on an immovable basis; yet he still continued to compose with unwearied diligence, and, between the period of 1762 and 772, were produced, his opera of the *Fairies*, his music to the tragedies of *Elfrida* and *Caractacus**, by Mason; his additions to Purcell in *King Arthur*; his dramatic songs of Shakspeare set to music, and his compositions for the Stratford Jubilee.

But though such success attended Dr. Arne's secular productions, his compositions of a sacred kind were altogether as unfortunate; he was always a loser whenever his oratorios were performed. And yet it would be unjust to say that they did not merit a better fate. But circumstances were against them; Arne had to contend with the gigantic strength of Handel, and the consequence of such a competition was, that he was never able to have his music so well performed. This great competitor had always at his command a more numerous and chosen band, a better organ, on which he shone with such unrivalled excellence, and better singers. But the compositions themselves are full of beauty, and though, by the side of this great master of his art, Arne's chorusses dwindle into comparative insignificance, yet his melodies are frequently admirable.

This charming musician died of a spasmodic complaint, on the 5th of March, 1778, and was buried in the Church of St. Paul, Covent Garden.

Of the general character of Dr. Arne's music, it has been observed, that if the melody were to be analyzed, it would appear to be neither Italian, nor English; but an agreeable mixture of Italian, English, and Scotch. But, except the opera of Artaxerxes, and some few of his airs that form designed imitations of the Scotish style, no compositions are more purely English than the vocal productions of this master. It has, with an equal degree of confidence, been asserted, that he was not a sound contra-puntist; but every candid adept in the science of harmony will vouch for his erudition as a theorist, and his skill in modulation and harmony. Unlaboured simplicity and liquid sweetness are the natural characteristics of his music, not loftiness and grandeur; and it has been remarked, that if ever he compromised his gracefulness, it was where he affected a dignity or force, not natural to his genius. But his powers, if not gigantic, were animated and striking, as well as pleasing and simple; and on proper occasions, vigorous and brilliant. The air in *Rosamond*,— *Rise, glory, Rise!*" displays a fire and a nobleness, to

which few English contemporaries could pretend. Among the more impressive examples of delicacy and tenderness, we could instance his " *Vain is Beauty's gaudy flower*,"— " *When in smiles the fair appears*,"—" *Gentle youth, oh, tell me why*," and the air, " *To keep my gentle Jessy*," introduced in the *Merchant of Venice*; to these may be added the well known melody of " *Where the bee sucks*," which has long proved the indispensable ornament of Shakspeare's *Tempest*.

Of instrumental compositions Dr. Arne has left us only few, but they are sufficient to prove, that it alone required a more constant exercise in that province of composition, for him have to become as equally conspicuous there, as in the vocal department. Besides his well known overtures, he composed several sets of Sonatas for violins and other instruments, and a suite of harpsichord lessons, which are not deficient in merit and beauty.

It is no common title to praise, in this bright and permanent ornament of the English theatre, that during the fourscore years that elapsed between the death of our British Orpheus, the immortal Purcell, and that of Arne, no candidate for musical fame, among our countrymen, challenged and obtained the high and universal admiration conceded by his countrymen to the productions of the composer of *Comus* and *Artaxerxes*.

LIST OF DR. ARNE'S WORKS.

Rosamond, an Opera.
Alfred, a Masque, (by Thompson and Mallet.)
Comus, a Masque, (altered from Milton, by Dr. Dalton.)
Eliza, an Opera.
Thomas and Sally, a Burletta.
Britannia, a Masque.
The Songs in " As you like it."
———————— " The Merchant of Venice."
Arcadian Nuptials, an Opera.
King Arthur,   Ditto.
Elfrida,   Ditto.
Caractacus, a Musical Drama.
Artaxerxes a serious Opera.
The Guardian outwitted, comic do.   ⎫ Written, as
The Rose, a comic do.   ⎬ well as com-
The Contest of Beauty and Virtue, a Melodrama ⎪ posed by
A Pasticcio.   ⎭ Dr. Arne.
Phœbe at Court, an Opera.
The Sacrifice, or *Death of Abel*, ⎫
Judith,   ⎬ In the Oratorio style.
Alfred the Great,   ⎭

In addition to these he wrote, and published in collections under various titles, an immense number of cantatas, songs, catches and glees, which were sung at the different places of public amusement. His songs in the *Lyric Harmony* display exquisite taste, and are deemed the standards of the true genuine English ballad. In WARREN's *Collection of Catches, Canons, and Glees*, are several compositions by Dr. Arne, of which Cunningham's elegy on the death of Shenstone, " Come Shepherds, we'll follow the hearse," deservedly ranks as one of the finest speciments extant of the class of music to which it belongs. It was sent in as a candidate for the prize gold medal given by the Catch-Club, in 3769, and failed of success, Dr. Aylward's rival glee, "A cruel fate," a very inferior work, proving the victor. Dr. Arne shewed his resentment by never again entering the lists as a competitor for the prize. He had, however, previously obtained seven medals, for three Glees, three Catches, and a Canon. Dr. Arne was also the reputed author of *The Cooper*, a musical entertainment, published in 1772, and *Don Saveiro*, a Musical Drama, in 1750.

* Unfortunately, the music of this piece was never printed. Its story is as follows : the MS. was left in the hands of the Doctor's son, Mr. Michael Arne, by whom it was sold to Harrison, a bookseller in Paternoster Row. This man becoming a bankrupt, the compositions were resold or lost. This is the more to be regretted, Dr. Arnold, who had perused the score, described it as containing some of the brightest and most vigorous emanations of Dr. Arne's genius. May some lucky chance yet bring it to light !

ROSSINI AND THE OPERA SINGERS, *versus* WEBER AND GERMAN MUSIC.

(From a Dresden CORRESPONDENT.)

OUR theatre has been almost wholly occupied of late by Rossini's music, to the exclusion of the works of our native composers. The German Opera seems sunk into its winter sleep; the long promised *Euryanthe* has been given here but once. What is the cause of this? Why should this genial production of our great Weber be condemned to oblivion?

Those who have an opportunity of seeing behind the curtain, will be able to trace the cause of this neglect not to the public, but to the singers, whose cabals and finesse have a deeper influence upon a composer's success than the world generally imagines. These people have been so long used to the light, the often repeated and repeating strains of Rossini, that they are become quite spoiled. The music of the modern idol of Italy, is of such a nature as to be readily learnt by the singer, and one of his operas serves as an introduction to a knowledge of all the rest. Not so the music of Weber and other profound masters; being drawn from the human heart, and marking all its variety of feelings, its character is ever varied, and requires to be studied with deep attention. Now, it is this very necessity that makes our singers shun the task. No doubt the same causes that have operated against the success of *Euryanthe* in our theatre, have also had their influence elsewhere; how are we otherwise to account for the apparent neglect with which this striking and characteristic music has been received? Perhaps there never was an opera upon which so great a variety of opinions has prevailed; but it is to be regretted that no able analysis of the music has yet been given, beyond the general remarks which have casually been made upon it. This opera has been reproached with a want of melody. What an assertion! Is not the whole, from the introduction to the finale, replete with melody in the true sense of the word? Do not the numerous airs, duets, &c., contain the most beautiful, effective, and truly dramatic melody, emanating from the very soul of feeling? Some of the all-knowing critics asserted, " that it was too full of research, and abounded with evident attempts at effect." Now I cannot help being of opinion, that if there are marks of research, there are also evidences of something good having been found. Weber is so favoured a child of genius, that the materials of song are ever ready in his mind, without the necessity of labour and study. These critics recognise the *effects* resulting from such research; but provided we are furnished with the beautiful in song, we are not very fastidious as to the mode in which it has been produced, but enjoy excellence as we find it.

In addition to this, it has been remarked that the present opera is no *Freischütz*. Seldom has a more matter-of-fact assertion been made, for can there be any thing in the world more distinct than the character of these two operas; would our consistent critics have Adolar sing like Max, Lysiart like Caspar, Euryanthe like Agatha, and Eglantine like Annette? What a contrast of persons, time, and situation!—It has been asserted in a public Journal, that Weber had been heard to declare that he regarded his *Euryanthe* merely in the light of a musical essay. Even if such had been the case, if in some circle of his friends the composer had dropped such

an expression, we may set it down as a proof of that modesty which is commonly the attendant of genius. I have but one word more to add, which is, that if this opera were performed with the spirit and power requisite to do it justice, it could not fail of a success equal to its merit.

DISCOVERY OF ANCIENT GREEK TABLETS RELATIVE TO MUSIC.

OF A DATE 709 YEARS BEFORE THE CHRISTIAN ERA

By PROFESSOR MURCHARD, of Berlin.

[Continued from Page 55.]

" Now the feast took place as follows: on the first day the Hymettian dancers performed, and the priests sang the NOMOI. For the feast was sacred."

These few lines would afford materials for a whole volume, and yet such a volume might not suffice to solve the doubts to which this passage gives rise; for who is able to explain what is meant by Hymettian dancers? That there was Hymettian honey, and why it was so called, is known. If we were to say that Hymettian dancers, were dancers from Mount Hymettus, then it might be justly remarked that, according to a notorious fact, inhabitants of the mountains are never the best of dancers. It appears more natural to suppose that the dances here spoken of were of a religious kind, since Jupiter, as is well known, had the appellation Hymettius, and therefore, it may easily be supposed that persons belonging to his religious rites were called Hymettian.— It will be remarked that in this passage of the text, a kind of introductory festivity seems alluded to. " The priests sang the νομοι:" after much research, I have not ventured on a translation of this word. It evidently implies certain religious songs, which were not changed; or of a ritual nature, which were essential, and not to be omitted; for νομος signifies law. According to Claudius Ptolomæus [*], the term νομος was used by the Greeks to signify a hymn to Apollo. Boethius, however, is of opinion that the etymology of the term νομος is to be traced to the circumstance of the laws being at an early period, before the invention of the art of writing, set to music, and sung by the people, in order that they might be more strongly impressed on the memory. But in the times of Telestes, this practice could no longer have obtained, because the art of writing was then known; and, therefore, the priests mentioned in the text could not have sung subjects appertaining to matters of law.

" On the following day the players and dancers, and the performers on the flute and cythara, acted a tragedy. This was called *Theseus*, and Telestes the Heraclite had ordered it. Hence there was great splendour in the dresses, and in the images ranged there. But, for the performances of the strophes, Damon of Cyrenæ had invented new modes for the players on the flute, and Kallias of Ephyræ for the antistrophes, for the players on the cythara. Also the part which was to be spoken

[*] Lib. III. Cap. iv. §. ii.

by the Choragia, was now sung in the Phrygian mode, this having been first preluded to them by the players of the cythara and flute; and this was a new invention of Lasus, the son of Eupolis. But Pherekydes lived in the greatest enmity with Damon of Cyrenæ, for the one envied the other, for both were celebrated. Now while the flute players were playing to the strophe, Pherekydes flattered the people; and the people whistled upon little pipes. But Damon of Cyrenæ went forth and wept."

Here again we have much that requires elucidation. Lasus makes mention of the splendour of the images exhibited at the performance of the tragedy; but no mention is made of decorations. May not these images have supplied the place of decorations, and may not the latter have been implied by the former? How desirable would it be that our learned Böttiger should make his researches on these interesting points! especially as this excellent Archæologist has already in his work "Ideen zur Geschichte der alten Malerie," (Ideas for a History of Ancient Painting,) started this very question, though he has not attempted a solution of it.—From the subsequent lines of this passage, we see that the Chorus in the tragedy of the ancients sung the strophe according to a given form, and did not merely recite it. It is said to have been an invention of the time of Telestes, and is mentioned as being alternately accompanied by instruments. A later passage of the inscription leaves no doubt as to the fact that the Greeks were acquainted with harmony, much as the moderns have called the fact in question. After the instruments had accompanied the Chorus, and then played a kind of interlude, the leaders of the Chorus sang in the Phrygian mode. According to Apuleius [*], this mode was employed in preference, for songs of a serious and solemn character. This is in accordance with our document, for the Choragi, as the announcers of the decrees of fate, could recite or sing in no other than solemn and sustained tones.—Further on we read, that Pherekydes and Damon, as being both celebrated, cherished great enmity one towards the other. We are forced to acknowledge that, two thousand four hundred years ago, the world was exactly the same as at present, and we might be tempted to exclaim, C'est tout comme chez nous!—the same jealousies among artists, the same envy, the same cabals, the same nationality, the same tricks to obtain popular favour.

"On the third day of the music feast at Ephyræ, there was represented a tragedy, after the old manner. And, when the Choragi had spoken, the chorus sang in the Hypomyxolidian mode; and the Chorus consisted of men, youths, boys and maidens. But Pyrene, the daughter of Teiresias, sang the Hypopotamon, which had never before been heard, since it lies five tones higher than the Hyperbolaion. And all the people clapped their hands aloud, so great was the joy that reigned in the hearts of all the hearers. But King Telestes caused to be presented to the divine songstress a costly set of jewels as a gift. For the like had never before been heard."

With respect to the Hypomixolydian and the Hypopotamon, I have already given my opinion above [*]. It is particularly remarkable that Lasus should twice observe of the Hypopotamon, that it had never been heard before. It must, consequently, have been extraordinarily high. It is also stated that the Chorus consisted of men, youths, boys, and maidens: that the Chorus sang is also mentioned. Hence, how can it be any longer doubted that the ancients, in the time of Lasus, were perfectly acquainted with the varieties of the human voice, and that they combined harmoniously the bass, tenor, treble, and descant? For it is in the highest degree probable that the men sang the bass, the youth the tenor, the boys the treble, and the maidens the descant. The opinion that among the ancients, female parts were played by men, is therefore contradicted, as it is certain. from the above text, that in the Chorus, at least, there were female singers. But King Telestes caused to be presented to the divine songstress a costly present;—hence we see, that it is not our age alone that is entitled to the epithet enthusiastic; that it is not with us alone that singers are idolized: the ancient Greeks also were enthusiasts, and were not less lavish of their θειος, (divine) than we are, since even on a swine-herd they once bestowed this glowing epithet. It is not a Catalani alone that has received costly presents from royal hands; the days of Grecian glory can also reckon its art-loving monarchs.

"Now when the fourth day was come, the great musical contests took place, and Telestes awarded to the conquerer a golden branch of palm. But Pherekydes began the contest, and sat himself down before all the people, and played the Epigonion. For he had improved the same; and he stretched four strings over a small piece of wood, and played on them with a smooth stick. But the strings sounded so, that the people shouted with joy."

Here we are made acquainted with the nature of the musical contests of the ancient Greeks. The very existence of such contests is a proof that the Greeks must have had a more cultivated music, than our musical antiquarians seem to have been heretofore inclined to allow. A concert in which a whole people participates, is assuredly rather more important than our musical soirées, which, in some respects, may be said to appertain less to music, than to conversation and to the refreshments of the evening.—To the conqueror was decreed a branch of fir. But whence comes it that the laurel is not mentioned? Strabo and Euclid are too minute on this point to leave any doubt as to the fact, that the laurel was the plant placed upon the brow of the musical victor. Probably, in the Peloponnessus, and on the Isthmus, the fir was substituted in place of the laurel, for Herodotus mentions that, at the Isthmian games the brow of the victor was wreathed with a branch of fir.—According to the description here given, the Epigonion would appear much to resemble our violin or violoncello. Imperfect as, according to this description, the instrument would seem to have been, Pherekydes must have possessed all the requisite qualifications of a good performer, since the tones which he knew how to produce from his rude

---

[*] De Asino Aureo, Edit. Ruhnkin, cum not. vari. 1786, Lib. IX. Cap. 6.

[*] See Harmonicon for April, p. 56.

instrument, were capable of delighting, even to rapture, the assembled multitude.

"Upon that, Damon of Cyrenæ contested for the prize. Now he sang with his scholars in the new Dryopian manner. And the people shed tears. But when Kypsiles touched the strings, there was again joy in all hearts. After this Ibykos of Rhegium sang to the Sambuka; but Thadmis, the Phœnician, struck with great art the Krotalon. At last there followed Terpander of Antissa, and the same played the Barbiton, and in such a manner that all the people clapped their hands in loud applause. Now when the umpires consulted, they unanimously awarded the prize to all the competitors. But Telestes, the Heraclite, was obliged to distribute much gold from his treasure."

I have not ventured to translate the names *Sambuka* and *Krotolon*. That the Sambuka and the Barbiton are not the same instrument, as has heretofore been imagined, is evident from this passage, otherwise in being thus mentioned together with another instrument, the fact would certainly have been remarked. Krotolon has usually been translated *plectrum*. What an indignity offered to those great models of every excellence, the ancients, to introduce among their musical instruments the plectrum! What would a Viotti have said, to have heard his fiddle-stick mistaken for his cremona? It is evident that it cannot have been a plectrum, otherwise it would not have been itself struck upon, but have been used to strike upon some other instrument. In order to assume a place in musical contests, the Krotolon must have been an efficient instrument; possibly it might have been an agreeable sounding instrument, with bells or chimes. By the way, it is to be regretted that Aristoxenes gives no account whatever of this instrument, in his description of Ancient Greek instruments.

"But now when the fifth day was come, a much greater number of people were assembled there. Now the fifth day was the most beautiful and remarkable in all the feast. For Pherekydes, the giver of the time, had invented a new method for all the flutes and cytharas together. But all those skilled in music, who could play on the flute, or the cythara, had assembled, in order that all might play together in the new method, and they were, full 800 in number. After the Rythmagos had ranged them in order, he appointed secondary givers of the time, with white staves. But they stood facing the morning, mid-day, evening, and midnight. Pherekydes had stationed himself in the centre, and had placed himself on a high seat, waving a golden staff, and the players on the flute and cythara were placed in a circle round him. Now when Pherekydes with his golden staff gave the signal, all the art-experienced men began in one and the same time, so that the music resounded afar, even to the sea. And Pherekydes had arranged it so, *that*

tones differing from each other came together in such a manner, that therefrom a harmony arose."

This text needs no comment. Whoever would now persist in disputing the fact of the Greeks having cultivated instrumental music and harmony, must first of all attempt to invalidate the authenticity of the documents before us. Here then is it, for the first time, stated in clear and simple words, that through the consonance of altogether-varying tones, harmony was produced. And what an orchestra this at Ephyræ! We thus see that the Greeks knew the effect of strong and voluminous music, and that Pherekydes was an experienced and observant director, since he required no more than four sub-directors to regulate his 800 musicians. He showed great judgment in ranging the musicians in a circle round him, as in this manner, all the extreme lines of his grand orchestra were equidistant from him.

"But this music sounded very masterly. For when all the flutes and cytharas had played together, the flutes singly took their turn, and then again the cytharas alternately. Now, while all this was going on, the Rythmagos beat with his staff up and down; and from this have arisen the terms arsis and thesis. At the conclusion, they again sounded altogether. But there were there of flutes, the Lydian, Dryopian, and Phrygian flutes; the horn, the Celtic and Paphlagonian Salpinx; also the Syrinx, and Bombyx: of Cytharas, were celebrated the Sambuca, Barbitos, Trigonon, Phorminx, Lyra, Magrepha, Pektis, Chelis, Epigonion, and Simicon. But the Simicon was played with a bow. Also were here played the Krotalon, the Tympanon, and the Sistron. *But the Rythmagoi beat with the staves in equal movement, in order that all might keep together.*"

Here then we have a proof that the Greeks had symphonies like ourselves, and that the mode of composing with an interchange of stringed and wind instruments is the most ancient. Then that under the term flutes all kind of wind instruments, and under that of cytharas all stringed instruments are implied, is so evident from the context of this passage, as to admit of no dispute. Lasus reckons among the flutes the horn as well as the salpinx or trumpet; and why should it appear too over-strained to suppose, that under the terms Lydian, Dryopian, and Phrygian flutes, our common flute, the elegiac Chalyme, and the Clarionet, may be understood? Are not all these instruments considered by us as merely individuals of the same genus? I am well aware, that according to modern writers, the term Bombyx signifies the ancient Chalyme, but how then did it happen, that some centuries ago, the Bombards were designated by the same term? Caspar Bartolinus, in his learned Treatise, *De Tibiis Veterum*, chap. 6, describes the Bombyx as a large wooden instrument, curved in the form of a worm, with the observation, that its name Bombyx, (silk worm,) was derived from this its form. Hence, in all probability, the Bombyx of the ancients was our Serpent. Again, Lasus comprehends, under the term Cythara, all those instruments that had strings. But it would be leading me too far from my subject, to particularize all the stringed instruments of the ancients, especially as Meibomius* has so minutely examined this subject. I cannot, however, permit the present opportunity to pass without observing, that it is impossible the Semicon could have had five and thirty strings, as is stated in the *Musicalishes Lexicon* of Koch, for had such been the case, it could scarcely have been practicable to play it with a bow. The Semicon of the Greeks must, therefore, have been a kind of violin. Lastly, how comes it that Lasus introduces under the head Cythara, the Magrapha, since it appears incontestible from the Talmud and the sacred writings, that this instrument, which was employed by the Hebrews in divine worship, was of the wind kind. Its very etymology bespeaks its Hebrew origin. We further learn from the text, that the Greeks were well acquainted with time. Lasus could not, in this respect, have expressed himself more clearly than he has done in the above passage. Here, too, we have a clear dèfinition of the terms *arsis* and *thesis*. Rousseau, in his *Dictionnaire de Musique*, under the articles, " battre le mesure" and " Arsis," observes very incorrectly, that the Greeks designated the accented part of the bar by raising the hand, and the unaccented by the beat of the head; he also adds that Scarlatti used this method of giving the time; but, for my part, at least, I frankly acknowledge that I cannot understand Rousseau's meaning in these passages.

" Now, when this new mode of performance was concluded, a prodigy happened at Ephyræ. For on a sudden there appeared a youth, who mingled with the men skilled in song, and the same was of divine aspect. But he was called Korinthos, and no one knew whence he came. The same said to the people, that he had invented a flute more powerful than all flutes and cytharas, over which it held the mastery. But Korinthos called his flute ΠΟΜΟΡΑ, and the same was made like a slender hollow column. At the top was a large golden opening, and the sounding head was artificially inlaid with golden chased work, and formed like the capital of a column. Now, when Korinthos had intoned it, there resounded an unknown tone, deep and strong, even as when the waves of the sea beat upon the shore. And he played it in the manner of Pherekydes, and it sounded like — — — TE. ΑΓΝΟΕΙΝ. But Korinthos called the deep tone, which carried the whole new method, the Hypantiproslambanomenon."

It is one of the properties of human nature, to suppose that there is some supernatural agency in those occurrences which lie beyond our comprehension. This is particularly the case in regard to the common people, of which we see an example in the case in question.—An unknown, and possibly modest, artist, brought some new and beautiful invention, and having secretly withdrawn, in order to shun the praises and proffered rewards of the people, it was at once imagined that the band of the gods was visible in the occurrence, and that possibly the youth himself was some god in disguise. Perhaps Lasus had another and

more profound meaning in this passage; for we shall immediately see that what the unknown youth brought with him as a present, was the fundamental bass. Now, if all melody and harmony be nothing without the fundamental bass, and if they derive their value and character from this alone, is not the bass then really the very soul, the enlivening principle of music ? And was it not then a truly Greek idea to endeavour to prove the bass to be of divine origin ?—It is evident that the instrument of Korinthos could have been nothing else than the contrabassoon, for this instrument resembles a hollow column, and its metal funnel may without any great stretch of fancy be compared to the capital of a column, and if the instrument of Korinthos was of uncommon length and thickness, such a comparison would be still more natural. Lasus expressly says, that the tone was so strong, that it " carried" all the other instruments. What a bassoon! What a fundamental bass must this have been! The tone A, as is well known, was called by the Greeks, Proslambanomenos. Now, if Korinthos called his deepest tone Hypantiproslambanomenon, then this tone must, by means of this *anti*, and the *hypo*, which bespeaks something still higher—have been the A of 32 feet.—Here occurs the second lacuna in the text.

" On the sixth and seventh days, the method of Pherekydes was repeated, for the people would hear nothing else, and they threw down to the youth wreaths of flowers. But Korinthos upon that disappeared, and left his Pomora behind him in Ephyræ.

" Now after this, Telestes, the Heraclite, gave to the columns of his palace the form of the Pomora, and ordered that the same should be called, after the youth, Corinthian columns. And so has it been " done since that time."

Let me be allowed to add one more remark ; may not the Bass-pommer, which was still in use some centuries ago, have derived its name from the Pomora ? But I would particularly bespeak attention to the circumstance from which sprung the name " Corinthian columns," since it naturally leads to this second conclusion, that from the adoption of this order of columns, the name of Ephyræ was laid aside, and this town obtained the name of the columns for which it was so famous.

" On the eighth day, the Hymettian dancers performed, as at the commencement of the feast, and the priests repeated the NOMOI, in order that the feast might finish in a sacred manner. And the people remained yet a long time at Ephyræ, till at length they dispersed themselves.

" Now thus was the music-feast at Ephyræ, in the third year of the fourth Olympiad of the reign of King Telestes, the Heraclite."

[Such is the conclusion of the first tablet.]

---

* *Collectio Antiquæ Musicæ Scriptorum, Septem.* Edit. Amst. 1652, Tom. VII., Lib. 2, Cap. 6.

NOTATION FOR THE HORN.

To the Editor of the HARMONICON.

SIR,   *Cambridge, Feb. 20.*

ALLOW me, through the medium of your widely-circulated publication, to ask of musical composers, the reason of an inaccuracy that has appeared to me to exist in this method of writing the Scale of the Horn. It is well known, that the tones of this instrument are identical with those produced by the harmonic divisions of a string, and accordingly we should expect them to be, in the natural key,

C, C, G, C, E, G, B♭ (false) C, D, E, &c.

Now, I believe that the first of these notes is never used, although it is evidently *the* note of the instrument *par excellence*, answering to the whole open string on the violoncello for instance. This, however, I should not so much wonder at, as it is difficult, perhaps *nearly* impossible, to produce it in the usual keys.—*Quite impossible* it is not, as I have, though but a young performer, sounded it in the high B flat key, and in A.—What I wish to know is, why, if this note is not meant to be used, it should be written instead of its octave, taking the trouble to put ledger lines under the bass clef, when the proper place is the second space. I have before me at this moment the 2nd Horn part of Beethoven's overture to *Fidelio*, in which the following passage occurs:

Here the break in the written scale is most glaring; the tones are meant, I presume to be continuous, and yet the author goes at once from G in the treble to the twelfth below it in the bass. You will tell me that it is the custom to write Horn music an octave higher than it is played, for the same reason I suppose as in the case of the Guitar—it is more convenient.—Then I ask, why, if they do this in the treble, they alter their practice in the bass; or rather, why they adhere strictly to what may be, perhaps, the original notation in the latter case, having, for the sake of convenience, parted from it in general?

You will oblige me, and I dare say other persons, by giving a fuller account, if possible, of the Invention mentioned in your last number, by which the key of the Horn may be changed without the clumsy expedient of putting on a different crook. I have often thought this might be effected by giving two or more turns to the slide, or *coulisse*, and I suppose this might equally be applied to the Trombone—it would only be drawing out four or six tubes at the same time instead of two.

If you can insert these remarks you will oblige,

Your humble servant,

H. C.

AN ENQUIRY INTO THE ORIGIN OF THE NATIONAL ANTHEM,

"GOD SAVE THE KING."

FROM "AN ACCOUNT OF THE GRAND MUSICAL FESTIVAL AT YORK," by JOHN CROSSE, Esq., F.S.A., F.R.S., &c. &c. &c.

THE intimate connexion subsisting between the national vocal music and the morals, the customs, and the history of a people, has been allowed by the wisest of men in all ages, and the saying of an eminent writer, that it matters little who makes the laws of a country, provided care be taken who writes its songs, was dictated no less by moral than by political sagacity. It is natural to desire to see our national songs collected, and to know something of their origin, but it is a singular circumstance that both the author and the age of our most justly celebrated and widely adopted one should have hitherto eluded all research, and almost baffled conjecture itself. We have no expectation of being able to settle a point, which can probably be decided only by some fortunate discovery, and not by any suppositions, however ingenious; yet, it would not be right to pass over *God save the King*, without making some mention of the various statements which have been put forth respecting it. Many of our readers probably are not aware, that Mr. Richard Clark published in 1822, *An Account of the National Anthem*, &c., in which he attributes it to the reign of James I.* Having, however, possessed ourselves of most of the copies of the tune mentioned by him, and referred to the different notices of it in several works, previous to the appearance of his book, we shall endeavour to condense some account of it within the compass of a note†, which we are not without hope will be found to be generally interesting.

It is commonly allowed, that the earliest printed copy that is known is that at p. 252 of the *Gentleman's Magazine*, for October, 1745, where it is entitled, *A Song for two Voices*, as sung at both play-houses; and in the table of contents, *God save our Lord the King*, a new song. The words there given consist of the three verses precisely as above printed, with the exception that "*sing*" has been substituted for "say," in the last line but one. It next occurs in the *Thesaurus Musicus*, published not long after that period, and has been reprinted in this original state, both by Mr. Clark and Dr. Kitchiner.

About the year 1795, the attention of the public was turned to the discovery of the author of this song, in consequence of its being claimed by George Savile Carey, as the production of his father Henry Carey, which claim he industriously maintained, not without the hope of obtaining some pecuniary recompense from the King, as is apparent from the account of his journey to Windsor, in his *Balnea*. The claim was acquiesced in by Archdeacon Coxe, in his *Anecdotes of J. C. Smith*, Handel's amanuensis; by Mr. S. Jones, in the *Biographia Dramatica*; and by Mr. D'Israeli, in his *Calamities of Authors*. The latter gentleman, however, in the *Gentleman's Magazine* for August, 1814, expresses his opinion that Carey only adopted the music, and applied the song by the change of a single word "*George*" for "*James*." Certain it is, that neither Carey's early poems, his *Musical Century*, in 1737 and 1740, nor his dramatic

* Of this contemptible book we have spoken, in the terms that it merits, in the Fifth Number of the Harmonicon, Vol. I. p. 67.—(ED.)
† The whole of this very able essay appears in the shape of a note in Mr. Crosse's work.—(ED.)

weeks, collected in 1748, contain the least notice of the words or the tune; and as G. S. C. was born in 1743, in which year his father unhappily put an end to his own life at the age of 10, he could not have received any personal information from him. Yet, after all, it is probable, that we owe the revival of them both to Carey, or there is the positive evidence of J. C. Smith, who assured Dr. Harington, in June, 1795, that Carey "came to him with the words and music, desiring him to correct the bass, which he accordingly did, and that it was intended to form part of a birth-day ode—and a writer in the *Gent. Mag.* for 1796, Suppt. pt. ii., asserts, that he heard *God save the King* sung at a tavern in Cornhill, by Carey, about the year 1740. As Carey died in 1743, it is thus pretty certain, that the epithet "*new*" in 1745 is not strictly correct; neither can . Mr. Galliard's assertion, that it was produced by Carey in 1745 or 6, be considered to prove any thing more, than that he was instrumental towards its becoming popular at that time, when its performance is thus described in a letter to Garrick by that dramatic enthusiast, Benjamin Victor, dated Oct. 1745. "The stage, at both houses, is the most pious, as well as most loyal place in the three kingdoms. Twenty men appear at the end of every play; and one stepping forward from the rest, with uplifted hands and eyes, begins singing, *to an old anthem tune*, the following words, *O Lord our God arise*, &c., which are the very words and music of an old anthem that was sung at St. James's chapel, for King James II., when the Prince of Orange was landed, &c."—(*Victor's Letters*, vol. i., p. 118.)—Now it must be admitted, that this passage is a proof, that *God save the King* was then believed by some to have been composed in honour, and sung in the reign, of the last of the Stuart monarchs; and in corroboration of this belief, there is a weighty body of traditionary evidence. Dr. Burney, in the fullest account of Carey that we know of, in Rees's *Cyclopædia*, says, "We have urgent reasons to believe, that it was written for King James II., while the prince of Orange was hovering over the coast. And when he became King, who durst own or sing it? We are certain, that in 1745, when Dr. Arne harmonized it for Drury Lane, and C. B. himself) for Covent Garden, the original author of the melody was wholly unknown." He also told the late Duke of Gloucester, that he knew the words were not written for any King *George*; and when in his 87th year, he informed a friend of Mr. D'Israeli, that he well remembered its introduction in 1745, when it was received with so much delight, that it was re-echoed in the streets. At that time," says he, " I asked Dr. Arne if he knew who was the composer; he said he had not the least knowledge, nor could he guess at all who was either the author or the composer, but that it was a received opinion that it was written and composed for the Catholic chapel of James II., and as his religious faith was not that of the nation, there might be a political reason for concealing the names of all those who contributed to give interest to the catholic worship."—(*Gent. Magazine*, August, 1814.)—Dr. Arne, it may be remarked, was himself of a Roman Catholic family, in which such a tradition was likely to be preserved.—Dr. B. Cooke supposed it to be the composition of Dr. Rogers, who died in 88—, and told E. J. (probably. Edward Jones, *Gent. Magazine*, Feb. 1796,) that he remembered to have heard the tune sung when he was a boy, to the words of *God save great* JAMES; and Dr. Byrom, of Manchester,

who was born in 1691, informed Mr. Lloyd, of Holme-Hall, that the song was first written "*great* CHARLES."—(*Gent. Magazine*, December, 1814.)—Dr. Campbell's assertion, that it was sung at the coronation of James II., and G. S. Carey's admission, that it was attributed by some to the time even of James I., are of little moment, except so far as they testify the prevalence of a general opinion of its early date.

In 1814, Mr. Clark published, *The words of the most favourite pieces*, &c., from which his account of *God save the King* being copied into the *Gent. Magazine*, Mr. D'Israeli and other correspondents were led to renew the discussion of 1795 and 6. Pursuing the hints that were thrown out, and having observed in Dr. Ward's *Lives of the Gresham Professors*, p. 205, these very words, affixed as the title to No. 5 of the contents of a volume of organ music by Dr. John Bull, then preserved in the library of Dr. Pepusch, Mr. C. was induced to search the records of the Merchant Tailors' Company, respecting the entertainment given by them to King James I., on July 16, 1607, as is supposed, in congratulation for his escape from the gunpowder-plot. It certainly appears, that on that occasion, Ben Jonson was employed to write, and Dr. Bull to compose, something in honour of the King, which was sung by the gentlemen of the Chapel Royal; and Mr. C. endeavours to shew, that our present song was the very one then produced and performed. He does not, however, seem to be aware, that the wish to dine with the company originated with the King, and that the report of the attempt to assassinate James on the 22d of March, in that year, although he quotes Jonson's sonnet upon it, was productive of the greatest confusion and dismay; and, coming so quickly after the discovery of the powder plot, was an additional circumstance, particularly calculated to call forth expressions similar to those of the song. Indeed, a letter written by the Earl of Kent, on the occasion, speaks of there being " just cause to sounde forth God's praise, together with incessant prayers for his Highnes' *longe, happie, and prosperous raigne over us.*"—(See Gifford's *Jonson*, vol. viii., p. 179.) —Yet, whatever coincidence may exist between the words of contemporary documents, such as the Prayers for the 5th of November, &c., and those of *God save the King*, all reasoning founded on the conjectured identity of the tune with that so called by Dr. Bull, has been utterly exploded by the publication of the latter by Dr. Kitchiner, in his *Loyal and National Songs of England*, from the original MS. in his possession ; transcribed into modern notation by the late Mr. E. Jones. Dr. K. observes, that it is a ground for the organ on four notes, with 26 different basses, totally unlike the modern air; but, after reviewing the above particulars, we are far from agreeing with him that there is nothing but " mere hearsay evidence, and vague conjecture, that the words or the music as now sung had been either seen or heard previous to October, 1745." *

Let us now consider the various attempts to establish a Scotish as well as a Jacobite origin for this celebrated piece. Mr. Pinkerton, in his *Recollections of Paris*, vol. ii., p. 4, says, that " the supposed national air is a mere transcript of a Scottish anthem," in a collection printed at Aberdeen in 1682. In this bold assertion he, no doubt, alludes to a work which excited some interest a few years ago from this imagined discovery, *Songs and*

---

* See Harmonicon, No. V., page 67, for a review of Dr. K.'s book.

Fancies, to 3, 4, or 5 parts, &c. Printed by John Forbes, 3d edition, 1682—(1st edit., 1665. 2d edit., 1666.) Mr. Bindley's copy of the *Cantus* part only of this work, No. 2264, was sold by Mr. Evans, in Feb. 1819, for £11.; and again in April, 1823, No. 1124 of Mr. Watson Taylor's catalogue. Mr. Perry's copy, No. 1923, was sold in March, 1822: both of these copies we have consulted, but have never heard of any of the other parts being known to be in existence. A transcript of the 9th song, in the minor key of G., is given by Mr. Clark, and certainly it may, by curtailing and altering a little, be made to resemble our present air; probably, however, even this is not Scottish, as the work is chiefly composed of " choice Italian songs and new English ayres."* An edition of this book is also, doubtless, the one referred to in the *Proceedings of the Highland Society of London*, p. 63, where it is supposed, that the original words were Scottish, and in favour of the house of Stuart. Two stanzas are, likewise, there given, which are very remarkable: the first of them is substantially the same as our present common version, and the other contains a prayer for the *true-born* Prince of Wales, and a second restoration of the family. These verses, which are cut on an old drinking-glass, preserved at Fingask, the seat of P. M. Thriepland, Esq., certainly appear to belong to a period not later than 1715, and another copy of them is cut on a glass in the possession of the representative of the Bruces of Clackmannan. Now, admitting the genuineness of these Scottish fragments, which does not appear to be doubtful, they afford tolerable evidence of an earlier date than 1745. In confirmation of this, we find Mr. Hogg, at song No. 24, of the second volume of his *Jacobite Relics*, presenting us with six stanzas, entitled, *The King's Anthem*, which, he says, "is the original of the anthem now so universally sung, which has changed sides, like many staunch Jacobites, and more modern politicians, when conveniences suited." Mr. H. gives us also "another of

* From a copy of *Forbes's Cantus*, now lying before us, we print the hymn alluded to, (or the IXth Song, as it is called,) which, from its resemblance to *God save Great George our King*, seems to have some near connection with it ; but whether, as the prototype, or as a kind of imitation, we cannot pretend to determine.—*Editor of* THE HARMONICON.

Re - mem - ber,   O thou man,   O thou man,

O thou man,   Re - mem - ber,   O thou man,

thy time is spent : Re - mem - ber,   O thou man,

how thou *was* dead and gone, and   I did

what   I can ; there - fore re - - pent.

the same," (No. 24,) in a song of six stanzas to the same tune, beginning " *Britons, who dare to claim*," and mentioning *Dutch Politics, Hanoverians, and Charles the son of James*. He does not assign any date to either of these songs, but asserts, that the music was undoubtedly composed at a later period than they appear to have been; which, considering the peculiar metre, we think altogether improbable ; but of the nature of Carey's claim he is evidently ill-informed, supposing him to have added the accompaniments. We are unwilling to prolong this account by quoting them at length, but we think the reader will agree with us, on referring to them, that the first two stanzas of No. 24, may fairly be ascribed to the time when James II. was on the throne, from the prayer which they contain, " *God send a royal heir*," and bless king and queen, that a royal progeny from them may reign to all posterity. The third verse, mentioning *Prince Charlie*, and *George* ; and the fourth, speaking of the family who are in *Italy*, with the rest, are certainly additions after the Revolution. We shall only further observe, on this part of the subject, that the first and second lines *God bless, and God save our Lord, the King*, of Mr. Hogg's *King's Anthem*, remarkably agree with the *title* in the *Gent. Mag.* for October, 1745, although the words "*our Lord*" do not occur in the song itself as there given, but are altered into " *great George*;" which, we think, strongly points out Mr. Hogg's as the old and partially known version, alluded to by Dr. Arne, as written for James the Second.

Having stated thus much in illustration of the origin of the words, the little that is known respecting the music, previous to 1745, may soon be recounted. A writer in the *Gent. Mag.* for March, 1796, asserts, that the tune, " which evidently furnished the subject of it, is to be found in a book of harpsichord lessons by H. Purcell, published by his widow," and is in four parts. Vague as this reference is, its accuracy is worth ascertaining.—Besides Rogers and Purcell, the air has been attributed to Anthony Young, the father, and to Anthony Jones, the grandfather, of Mrs. Arne ; but, if either of them had been the composers, Dr. Arne would assuredly have been acquainted with the fact. Some have even ascribed it to Handel, and we are in possession of a transcript from a copy bearing the date of 1689, with the name affixed of Vaughan Richardson, whose master, Dr. Blow, was the author of the catch, *God preserve his Majesty, and for ever send him victory, and confound all his enemies*. But the earliest known copy certainly appears to be the one in four parts, without words, and entitled *God save our noble King*, which is taken from an old book, once the property of the celebrated Thomas Britton, the musical small-coalman, who died in 1714, and now in the possession of J. S. Hawkins, Esq. F. S, A., son of Sir J. H. This curious volume has the following memorandum on the title-page, "Deane Monteage, given to him by his father, 1676," on which it may perhaps be deemed fanciful to remark, that Bishop Montagu, as Dean of the Chapel-Royal, was one of those who, with Bird, Bevin, Gibbons, &c., sung "melodious songs" at the dinner to King James, in 1607. Higher than 1676, the air has not yet been traced. We can scarcely forbear to mention, as some compensation to the memory of Carey, for denying his claim to the authorship of this song, that Mr. D'Israeli has bestowed much greater praise upon his works, as well for their poetry as their patriotism, than they have met with from other writers;

but with the painful addition, that, although he was a principal founder of the *Fund of decayed Musicians*, when he was found dead he had only one halfpenny in his pocket. The mother of Mr. Kean, the actor, it may be added, was the daughter of G. S. Carey.

As might naturally be expected, the additions which have been made to this national song, on various public occasions from time to time, have been tolerably numerous. The two earliest of these are of the same date as the revival of the tune itself,—a stanza in honour of Marshal Wade, (who was appointed to the command of the army in October,) and four stanzas in the *Gentleman's Magazine* for December, 1745, entitled "an attempt to improve the song " *God save,*' &c., the former words having no merit but their loyalty," and beginning thus, *Fame let thy trumpet sound.* These words, with a different tune to them, are given by Dr. Kitchiner; who, omitting the latter part of the above title, and forgetting that he has himself ascribed the words and music of another song to Mr. Webbe, strangely conjectures from their general similarity, that "they were all three the production of some loyal subject, who desired no other reward than the gratifying consciousness of having served his country." At least as early as 1754, the received words were rendered into Latin, as appears from a copy given in the *Gent. Mag.* 1795, Suppl., pt. ii. But the next English words that we meet with are five stanzas, written by the Rev. W. D. Tattersall, for the 1st of January, 1793, and published with the air, harmonized by Dr. T. S. Dupois. On the 15th of May, 1800, his late Majesty having been shot at by James Hadfield, at Drury-Lane Theatre, the following stanza, said to have been written on the spot by the Right Hon. R. B. Sheridan, was sung by Mr. Kelly at the end of the farce, when it was enthusiastically encored by the agitated but delighted audience. In the *Gent. Mag.* for 1800, it is, however, stated to have been produced, *impromptu*, originally at Quebec.

> From every latent foe,
> From the assassin's blow,
>   God save the King!
> O'er him thine arm extend,
> For Britain's sake defend
> Our Father, Prince, and Friend;
>   God save the King!

We find this national song in the books of the *Ancient Concert*, for March, 1801, where it was sung with a supplemental stanza, imploring health for his Majesty; in which year also the return of peace was hailed with additional verses at Manchester; and probably Mr. Webbe's lines, above mentioned, beginning *Welcome to Britain's Isle*, may be referred to the same period. Two stanzas, on the occasion of the King's illness, by G. Children, Esq., sung at Tunbridge, by Mr. Sale, appear to belong to the year 1811. On the visit of Queen Charlotte to the City national schools, on April 29th, 1818, being her last appearance in public, two stanzas, written by E. L. Swift, Esq., were sung by the children, in which her Majesty joined; and in the *Philanthropic Gazette* of July 8th following, are four stanzas, adapted to a time of peace, and to the use of schools. Lastly, the accession of his present Majesty has drawn forth three additional verses from the pen of George Colman, Esq., the second of which is, perhaps, the only one among those enumerated that at all deserves being annexed in perpetuity to the original. Several attempts have been made to adapt the air to hymns for divine

service, but it is too deeply connected with political and secular associations, notwithstanding the modern custom of describing it as the national *anthem*, ever to prove acceptable in a church.—Nevertheless, its effect, wherever it is performed, would be sensibly improved were it to be sung in a slower time, and with more reference for the name of GOD, than it usually is ; and that it was thus performed in 1745, we have the testimony of Lady Lucy Meyrick, as given by Miss Hawkins, in her *Anecdotes*, that as Mrs. Cibber then sung it, " it was a perfect hymn."

Much more successful, as well as better directed, have been the efforts to introduce this specimen of English music into other countries. We learn from the *Tour in Germany*, before quoted, that it has been adopted by the Weimarese, the Saxons, and the Prussians, as their national tune ; and that, upon the occasion of the King's paying a visit to the theatre at Berlin, when the writer was in that city, the whole immense audience burst forth in "*Heil dir im sieger kranz,*" the Prussian *God save the King*, sung to our notes. "The Austrians," it is justly observed, "were perfectly right not to borrow from foreign treasures, when they had Haydn to compose their ' *Got erhalte Franz den Kaiser;*' but the Austrian hymn, with all its melody and sweetness, has too much of the psalm in it ; it wants the manly, majestic, full-hearted boldness of the strains in which we are accustomed to express, not more our respect for our monarch, than our own national pride." This very character of Haydn's air recommends it to our notice, as admirably calculated for the morning performances at a musical festival ; and, if furnished with appropriate words, more strictly sacred than those of *God save the King*, it might be adopted by us as properly a *national anthem*, not less suited to divine service on public occasions, and to musical festivals, than the other is to the secular concert-room. A copy of the original score of Haydn's hymn in seventeen parts, as sung in the Imperial Chapel at Vienna, for which we are indebted to the kindness of Madame Catalani, is now lying before us ; and nothing can exceed the effect of its performance as we have heard it done by a tolerably large band, especially in the chorus in the seventh and eighth lines, given alternately *fortissimo* and *piano*, and ending with the latter, in the most subdued and affecting manner.

In conclusion, we shall enumerate a few instances in which *God save the King* has been skilfully interwoven with, or introduced into, other works. Mr. Webbe, happening, in the year 1789, to hear a person in the street sing this song in the key of D., whilst some gentlemen in the room with him were performing a glee in B. minor, was prompted thereby to write the glee *My pocket's low*, in which the upper part consists of the air in the former key, while the words of the three lower parts are set in B. with two sharps and two accidental sharps ; and, in the glee of *British sentiments*, inscribed to Mrs. Billington, after the subject has been led off in common time by the three under voices, the first part of the national tune is brought in by the *soprano*, still preserving four crotchets in a bar. Mr. Attwood has, with no less ingenuity than propriety, introduced it in the symphony to his *Coronation Anthem*, and Mr. Clementi has done the same, we are told, in a very scientific manner, and with the happiest result, in a *national symphony*, performed at the *Concerts Spirituels* of 1824. In Mr. George Onslow's quartetts, however, is a still earlier instrumental arrangement, apparently constructed on the model of Haydn's quartett, No. 77, in Op. 76, containing the hymn for the Emperor. It forms the *adagio* movement to No. 1. of his Op. 9, dedicated to M. Boucher, and was composed before 1814, in which year we procured it in Paris, and heard it privately performed in London, by the late Mr. Salomon, by whom it was greatly admired.

ROSSINI'S *"MOSÈ IN EGITTO,"* IN VIENNA.

[*From a Correspondent at Vienna.*]

.... AFTER a variety of delays, with the causes of which I need not acquaint you, as it is not likely they would very strongly awaken your interest, we have at length had the satisfaction of hearing Rossini's delightful opera, *Mosè in Egitto.* The characters were thus powerfully cast :—

FARAONE, *Rè di Egitto*	Sig. Lablache.
AMALTEA, *sua consorte*	Signa. Dardanelli.
OSIRIDE, *erede del trono* . . .	Sig. David.
ELCIA, *Ebrea, sua segreta moglie.*	Signa. Fodor Mainville.
MOSÈ	Sig. Ambrogi.
ARONNE	Sig. Ciccimara.
AMENOFI, *sorella di Aronne* . .	Signa. Unger.
MAMBRE	Sig. Raucher.

The singular phenomena presented by the operas of Rossini, the admirable creations of genius and fancy, the splendid traits of masterly talent, ranging in singular contrast by the side of things of a very common-place nature, and even these copied and re-copied by the master himself,—these phenomena, with which all his operas abound, are also conspicuous in the *Mosè.* It is true that this master is rich in felicitous ideas, that he knows the happy art of combining them into a finished whole,— as, for instance, in the admirable *Introduzione* to the opera which forms the subject of my present remarks,—and, consequently, he claims and receives the homage of my sincere admiration ; but, at the same time, I must confess that I am wholly at a loss what judgment to form of the singular contrasts by which his compositions are marked, where the feeble and the insignificant are so often seen placed immediately by the side of the powerful and the expressive. Rossini is a master that can paint single parts of a subject, individual portions of a picture, with admirable skill, but who is altogether defective in that sustained tone, that uniformly characteristic touch, that general keeping, which bespeak the master, the founder of a new school. We are naturally prompted to ask ourselves this question ;—How is it possible that one and the same master should produce compositions so unequal one to another, and hastily commit them to the judgment of the musical world ? The greatest masters have their moments of weakness, but his are so glaring and so frequent, that we naturally inquire ; Does, on these occasions, his faculty of creating so far abandon him that he is unable to invent new ideas, and is obliged to take up again with old ones, many of which he has absolutely worn threadbare ? And yet when we observe more closely the copious spring of his ideas, whence gushes a constant stream of enchanting melodies, of high wrought and effective harmonies,—when we notice the magic skill with which he conjures up the most beautiful forms, though, it is but too true, to fade quickly again into empty air ; when we observe how in his accompaniments he sports with the most beautiful colours, and, by means of

a succession of new lights, creates new shades in pleasing and endless diversity ;—yes, I say, when we consider all this, it would be little less than folly to attempt to deny this master his claims to genius.

Another phenomenon which is frequently observable in the world of composers, does not hold good in the instance of Rossini ; I mean the instance of a composer, who, among the many works which he has produced, can boast but of a solitary instance in which genius shines forth in its native lustre, while in all the rest its aid has deserted him. Have we not many instances of masters who, in their first or second great work, have given proofs of so powerful a genius, as to afford the world room to anticipate a series of productions equally marked by talent and excellence, and yet who appear in such creations to have at once so far exhausted the resources of their genius, as to leave all their subsequent works void of that heaven-descended fire, which imparts to the inert mass its warmth and vitality, and without which, the works of the master are but as so many cold and inanimate statues, the mere products of labour and indefatigable industry. We have seen several examples of this, in men, who may not inaptly be compared to the aloe, whose first blossoming is followed by its decay. But, however, Rossini cannot be ranked with this class ; for the works which he has produced are so numerous, and marked by so great a diversity of character, that they are entitled to be considered as individuals of a different genius.

The inequality which marks his productions, and to which we have before alluded, is to be traced to the circumstances in which they were produced. The composers in Italy can boast of advantages, which are denied to those of Germany. The former execute all their works according to the order of the *impresario,* and at a stipulated sum. But where among us shall we find the theatres which thus enter into engagements with composers, in order to supply the musical wants of the public? In Italy, the *impresario* makes his engagement with the composer, to produce his opera within a stated period, in order to meet the exigencies of particular seasons. Now, it is according to this criterion, that the fair estimate and real valuation of the productions of Rossini should be made. For it is possible, that the composer may have proceeded in the composition of the first part of his opera with the greatest diligence, and in conformity to the impulse of his genius, and, in this way, may have produced individual parts of a work which may have surpassed, and even left far behind all his previous labours. But suddenly the spirit of the *impresario,* haunting him like a restless ghost, enters the composer's chamber, presents before his eye the contract which he has signed, binding himself to the production of an opera within a given period, and in a menacing attitude, demands the fulfilment of his engagement. Those who know how the freedom of the mind is fettered, and its spontaneous exertions crippled, by a state of feverish anxiety, lest a work should not be completed within the period stipulated, will not be surprised when we assert, that there are very celebrated masters, and those too who are quite *au fait* in matters of this kind, and yet who have been so distressed by this harassing state of the feelings, as to find all the faculty of invention frozen up, and the powers of fancy so crippled, as to be unable to write a single line. If we figure to ourselves the gay and genial Rossini in a situation like this, he who has ever been used to contemplate life but on its sunny side, and to yield to the happiness of the moment, reckless of the future, we shall have no difficulty in conceiving how readily the Italian maestro will have had recourse to his own store of materials ready at hand, employing without ceremony such portions as he finds convenient for the despatch of the work which presses on his hands.

Like another Procrustes too, he is ingenious in adapting the music of others to the dimensions which his fancy, or rather his convenience, has planned; by this process the works of other composers are brought ready to his use; all he has to do, is to reduce what he finds too long, to the requisite size, and *vice versâ :* nor is the matter so difficult as a novice in matters like these might suppose; sometimes it is effected simply by changing an ascending melody into a descending one, or the contrary. Who, within the last years, has not heard of such chopped and changed music, and how great a portion of old and musty spirit has been distilled into some semblance of the essence of *Der Freischutz?* But these are chiefly the artifices of minds of an inferior order, who from necessity are led to steal from the rich man's table; hence, such a charge becomes a deeper reproach to the highly-gifted Rossini.

With respect to the *Mosè*, it had the advantage of being admirably performed throughout; the charming Fodor was powerfully supported by the talents of Lablache, Ambrogi, and David. The pains and labour bestowed on the production of the piece were immense. The rehearsals of this exceedingly difficult music, had been numerous, and at length had become so irksome, that not only the music-director, M. Weigl, but the whole of the performers, male and female, had waited with no less impatience for the promised delivery from the plagues by which they were oppressed, than did the children of Israel for theirs by the hand of Moses. But this meritorious endurance and persevering spirit were more than compensated by the complete success of the piece. The universal feeling is, that the worthy music-director, Weigl, and the whole of the artists, have gained themselves fresh laurels by the admirable manner in which this opera was brought forward.

The enthusiasm excited by the *Introduzione,* the duet in the second act, the *Scena* of Madame Fodor in the third, and the *Preghiera* at the conclusion of the piece, was the highest reward which can await the higher efforts of art. The great effects of this opera depend upon a proper attention to the lights and shades of the music, and a due distribution of the *piano* and *crescendo,* the *forte* and *fortissimo;* and in the instance before us, all these important points were carefully attended to, and reflect the highest credit on the music-director.

It is an undeniable fact, that, without a good and intellectual performance, the highest and most finished production of art would appear tame, and be deprived of half its beauty and dramatic effect; while on the contrary, it has the power to uphold, and to impart a splendour to, productions of a mediocre class: a truth, of which we have recently had a striking instance in this city, in the *Doralice* of Mercadante, which was almost entirely upheld by the powerful talents and exertions of the performers.

In order that a performance may be perfect, all party spirit should be banished, all personal jealousies should sink before a noble zeal for the real interests of the art. It is thus only that justice can be done to the great productions of men of genius.

FOREIGN MUSICAL REPORT.

VIENNA.—On occasion of the marriage of the Arch-duke Francis with the Princess Sophia of Bavaria, a new opera was produced here entitled *Le Nozze di Telemaco ed Antiope :. Azione lirica, in due parti.* The music of this piece is selected from various authors, by Sig. Maestro Mercadante, together with dances analogous to the piece, by Sig. Ventris. The characters were thus powerfully cast, including the whole strength of the company: *Ulisse, Rè d'Itaca,* Sig. Lablache; *Penelope, sua moglie,* Signa. Comelli Rubini; *Telemaco,* Sig. David; *Idomeneo, Rè di Salente,* Sig. Ambrogi; *Antiope, sua figlia,* Signa. Fodor Mainville; *Minerva,* Signa. Ekerlin; *Mentore,* Signa. Ciccimarra; *Marte,* Sig. Donzelli; *Venere,* Sig. Dardanelli; *Apollo,* Sig. Rubini; *Grandi, Sacerdoti; Popolo d'Itaca; Guerrieri; le Deità del Olimpo; Le Muse; Le Grazie: il Comercio: L'Agricultura: le Arti, &c.:*—all this sounds very grand and imposing, but the reality was very poor and meagre, a mere combination of heterogeneous matter, a thousand times heard, and a thousand times criticised. On this splendid occasion the Emperor and the whole court were present.

This was followed by a new opera, by the same composer, entitled *Il Podestà di Burgos.* The same observations we made in our last on Mercadante's *Doralice,* may be applied to the composition before us. Only two airs in the piece obtained any approbation, and this was owing in no small degree to the talents of Madame Fodor, and Signors Rubini and Lablache. The story is a miserable farce, and the composer has given almost the whole subject *parlando,* and neglected the real *cantilena ;* an error into which, perhaps, the great success of similar passages in the *Matrimonio Secreto* have betrayed him; but in the modern composer, where do we find the playfulness, the spirit, the gaiety, the brilliant and appropriate accompaniments, of the great Neapolitan master?

On the same occasion Rossini's Canzonetta, entitled *L'Addio ai Viennesi,* was sung by David, but did not make any impression.

When there is a dearth of new pieces at our second-rate theatres here, recourse is had to a singular medley entertainment, respecting the good taste of which we leave our readers to decide. The following is one of these amalgamations: First was given a short fairy opera in one act, entitled *Der Kurze-mantel,* (the Short Mantle,) with the following *bonbons* for the dessert: 1st, a duet from *Doralice,* sung by Donzelli and Rubini; 2dly a *Pas de deux,* danced by Madlle. Heberle and M. Samengo; 3dly, a *Pas de trois,* by Madlle. Vaquemoulin, Ramacini, and M. Hullin; 4thly, a duet from *Elisabetta,* sung by Signa. Dardanelli, and Sig. Donzelli; 5thly, an aria from the *Don Juan,* sung in an enchanting manner by Sig. Rubini; 6thly, a *Pas de deux,* danced by Madlle. Brugnoli and M. Rosier. The whole was a compound of art and grace. Double prices, a full house, and uproarious applause!

Among the other musical entertainments of this place, was a grand Concert, for the benefit of the public benevolent institutions, which was crowdedly attended. The bill of fare on this occasion was as follows: 1st, Beethoven's overture to *Fidelio;* 2nd, Cavatina from the *Gazza Ladra,* sung by Ambrogi; 3rd, a brilliant Rondeau for the piano, composed and performed by M. Benedict; 4th, a duet from Mayer's *Adelasia ed Aldermo,* sung by David and Donzelli with great applause; 5th, Variations for the Flute, composed and executed by Professor Janusch of Prague; 6th, a duet from *Tancredi,* sung by the Signoras Fodor, and Comelli-Rubini, which was received with thunders of applause; 7th, the *Chorus* from Weber's *Euryanthe;* 8th, Overture from Catel's *Semiramis;* 9th, a Terzetto from Mercadante's *Apoteose d'Ercole;* 10th, Polonaise for the Violoncello by Romberg, performed by M. Fränzl; 11th, an aria by Raimondi; 12th, Duet from Fioravanti's *Musicomania,* sung by Mad. Fodor, and Sig. Lablache, and received with great enthusiasm; 13th, aria from Mosca, sung by David with great power and expression; 14th, the *Preghiera,* from *Mosè in Egitto.* The programme of this concert is presented in full, in order that it may serve as a criterion to the reader in judging of the reigning taste of this city.

In sacred music, the most striking novelty has been a new *Requiem* from the pen of Kapellmeister Wittasek. Of this composition, nearly the first which the author has given to the public, the critics speak in terms of unqualified approbation. By one it is pronounced worthy of ranking by the side of all the master-pieces of this kind, and that its lustre will not be obscured even by the immortal work of Mozart himself. The whole is described as breathing a spirit of patriarchal simplicity, as being replete with song admirably adapted to the sacred character of the text, and as clothed with a highly appropriate and expressive accompaniment. The parts that produced the greatest and most decided effect, were the *Dies Iræ*, the *Benedictus*, and the concluding movement, *Requiem æternam*, which were all marked by distinctive beauties, though all in the same solemn and impressive style.

BERLIN.—The only novelty that our boards have lately had to boast is the opera of *Cardillac*, the music by Kapellmeister Schneider, but it is not likely to add much to the laurels lately gained by this composer. With the exception of one or two short pieces, and some instrumental parts to introduce pantomimic action, there is but little to show the hand of the master. The story is good, but the poet has not been very successful in his part of the work, an evil that is not unfrequently felt severely by the musician, and which sometimes proves the wreck of better music than the present performance has to boast. This was followed by *Don Juan*, the *Cortez* of Spontini, Rossini's *Barbiere di Siviglia*, *Le Nozze di Figaro*, and the revived comic opera of *Hieronimus Knicker*, the music by Dittersdorf. Thirty years ago this was a very favourite piece with the good people of Berlin, and its comic beauties appear to be no less relished by the present musical race, for its appearance was hailed with very great enthusiasm. The music is gay and characteristic, and full of airs which have been long familiar to the ear, though now beginning to give way to more brilliant favourites. Indeed what popular music can now stand its ground against the attractions of *Der Freischütz?* There was also produced a Musical Potpourri, in one act, entitled, *Die Schneidermamsells*, (The Lady Tailors,) a pleasant little piece, with some good music by Angely.

——— Among our concerts, the most brilliant was that given by M. Möser, on which occasion was produced here, for the first time, Beethoven's grand Symphony in C minor, which, with its spirited allegro, graceful andante, gay minuet, and imposing finale, was given with great spirit and effect. M. Möser played a new concertino, by Mayseder, with very characteristic variations to the beautiful air *La Barcarola;* he also accompanied on the violin obbligato a scena and air from Mayerbeer's opera of *Margarita d'Anjou*. What is principally admired in M. Möser's performances is his firm sustained bow, united to great ease and brilliancy of execution. On the same evening M. Meschelos delighted us with a new Rondo, executed by him with his usual power, on that instrument of which he reigns as one of the greatest masters of the day.

CASSEL.—Our opera company have been very industrious this season; we have been treated with the following performances, which were given with a splendour, spirit, and effect, highly creditable to the directors of this establishment. *Der Freischütz*, four times; *Schweizer-familie, Jean de Paris, Aschenbrödel* (Cenerentola,) *Roth-käppchen* (Chaperon rouge,) *Calif de Bagdad, Tancredi, La Gazza Ladra, Il Barbiere di Seviglia,* by Rossini; *Sointags Kind* (The harmed Child,) *Oberon, Karlo Fioras, Don Juan, Zauberflöte, Ferdinand Cortez, Le Petit Matelot,* by Gaveaux, newly revived here; *Lodoïska* by Cherubini; *Faust* by Spohr; and lastly *Euryanthe* by Weber, twice.

Der Freischütz continues with unabated spirit. On one occasion, during its performance, the Grand Elector engaged the whole of the house for the military, who had been assem-

bled at this place for the grand review. What with the terrors of the stage, and the whiskered fierceness which the whole house displayed, the scene was truly terrific, so much so indeed, that we do not wonder at the almost total absence of ladies on this fearful occasion.

The *Faust* of Spohr was new to our boards, and produced considerable effect. It was extremely well brought out; the singers, the chorus, and the orchestra, all appearing studious to surpass each other. Of all the operas of this now celebrated composer, the present appears to be growing the most popular. The music is full of powerful effects, and admirably adapted to the character of the subject. We cannot, however, withhold an expression of regret to see that more has not been made of Goethe's wonderful subject, or rather, that the subject had not been put into the hands of a person more experienced in stage business and situation.

With respect to Weber's *Euryanthe*, it was not received with the applause that was anticipated from a production by the author of *Der Freischütz*. The latter still continues the great favourite here. That, on the first representation of the former, it was heard without any mark of applause, was a matter of course; the Elector was present on occasion of his birth-day, and it is the etiquette to receive personages of this exalted rank with silent applause. But that on its second performance, the approbation should have been so cold and reserved, does appear to us very extraordinary, considering the numerous beauties with which the piece abounds. The general opinion here is that the author has sunk beneath the feebleness and insipidity of the story, upon which he had the ill-fortune to labour. It were to be wished that composers in general would be somewhat more circumspect in the choice of their subjects. Experience daily teaches us that, with the great multitude—upon whom, after all, the success of theatrical productions in a great measure depends—the poetry, or at least the story, is an object of primary consideration. But it cannot be denied, that Weber has produced in this composition much that is new and masterly, and there is no doubt but its success would have been more decided, had he not alarmed the singers, and overloaded the orchestra with too many difficulties. With respect to the accompaniments, a comparison between this composition and one of the operas of Mozart—the *Don Giovanni* for instance—which in this respect is the model *par excellence*, would be highly interesting. In the present opera, Weber's power is principally shown in the choruses and concerted pieces.

NAPLES.—Our theatre, under the management of Mr. Glossop, goes on but very indifferently. The principal operas given, were the *Zelmira* and *Tancredi* of Rossini, as well as the *Teobaldo ed Isolina* by Morlacchi; but neither of them obtained any decided success. This, by the partisans of the Rossinian school, was taken in high dudgeon, particularly with respect to that great object of their worship, the *Tancredi;* and the want of success was at once set down to the account of the singers; and to say the truth, there was some foundation for such an assertion. It is said that, for certain, Signor Barbaja is to resume the management next season, as the court is by no means satisfied with the present administration; and it is said, that in the contract of Mr. Glossop, especial provision is made in one of the articles, that if Mr. Glossop should not give satisfaction, direction of the said theatre should terminate after the expiration of one year.

The celebrated violinist, Paganini, appeared here recently, and gave a concert. On this occasion his name was announced in the bills as *Filarmonico*, a term which gave occasion to serious debates amongst the cognoscenti in this place; some considered it as an appellation of modesty; others took it in a contrary sense: at all events, it was considered as a little dash of affectation.

MILAN.—The latest novelty produced here has been an opera from the pen of Paccini, the subject of which is taken from Grecian story. *Themistocles* being condemned to banishment, flies from his ungrateful country, and seeks refuge in the states of his chief enemy, Xerxes, to whom he surrenders with noble confidence, and who not only receives him with joy, but is even desirous of giving him the chief command of his armies against Greece. This illustrious man, however, prefers death to the dishonour of fighting against his country, unjustly as that country has treated him; and by this generous example of self-devotion, produces such an effect on the mind of Xerxes, that he breaks the vow of eternal enmity which he had made against the Athenians, and concludes a peace with them.

To this truly noble subject, lyric poetry is indebted for one of its most memorable efforts, in the drama of METASTASIO; a poem which has stimulated the talents of the young Paccini; though in the present instance we are sorry to notice such glaring departures from the great original. This composer has, in this opera, attempted to realize a favourite project, which is no less than an attempt to recal the recitative to that character and expression which was formerly heard from the lips of the great masters of the art of singing, and which formed the genuine musical declamation. In the part of Themistocles, in which this attempt is chiefly exemplified, a Signor Bonaldi, a singer of but second-rate talents, obtains that applause which is often denied him in airs and duets.

This opera was evidently produced in favour of a singer, who, after an absence of several years, had excited a general interest and desire to hear her once again; for it could not certainly be said that the excellence of the music had determined the choice of the piece. The Pesaroni, in the character of Xerxes, makes us forget the dissimilarity that exists between her, and the idea we are led to form of this great king, our attention being exclusively engaged by her song, in which nature and art have combined to subdue the soul by beauty, sweetness, and power. We do but repeat what is already known, when we say, that the highest purity of sound, a flexibility, without effort, an extremely soft modulation, a perfect trill, and a distinctness of pronunciation, all combined in an inimitable mezzotinto, entitles this singer to the praise of being a genuine mistress of her art. If any fault is to be found, it is that she injures her simplicity by too great an endeavour after the curious embellishments of art. This defect was particularly visible in the opening air of Xerxes, which the composer had doubtless written expressly to shew her vocal powers; but when these ornaments are not carried to excess, and the beauty of her voice is allowed its full and natural play, it must be acknowledged that the organ of Pesaroni is enchantment itself.

With respect to the opera, the composition is weak, and the accompaniments meagre and ineffectual, and we seek in vain for any great originality of ideas. The author has availed himself of the ornaments of Rossini, without any attempt at disguise. Two airs and a duet, however, have merit, but their success cannot be denied to have been owing in a great measure to the superior talents of the artists by whom they were executed.

With regard to Paccini himself, we are sorry to learn that, from the ill state of his health, he has been obliged to come to the resolution of writing no more for the stage. We however hope, that after renovating his health by some years of retirement, we may be enabled to hail the re-appearance of this young composer, who has already by his precocious talents given no unpromising hopes of future excellence.

———— The following is the list of our opera company: *Prime Donne*, Signa. Pesaroni, Signa. Favelli, Signa. Garcia, Signa. Albesti, and Signa. Biagioli; *Seconde Donne*, Signa. Francini, Signa. Sacchi; *Primi Tenori*, Sig. Bonoldi, Sig. Verger, Sig. Dupont; *Secondi Tenori*, Sig. Biscottini, Sig. Bonaldi, (younger brother of the singer of the same name;) *Bassi*, Sig. Galli, Sig. Filippo Galli, Sig. Vasolli, Sig. Poggioli, and Signa. Pesaroni, a contralto who performs in male characters; her style, is of the cantabile kind, and according to the opinion of the best professors of singing and cognoscenti of Italy, is the first singer now in the world. It is true that Fodor

and Pasta have been extolled in all the foreign journals as the *non plus ultra* of the art. But with respect to Mad. Fodor, the composer Caraffa, who engaged her for St. Carlo himself, asserted that she ranked second to the Pesaroni, and, though the powers of Mad. Pasta are great and commanding, yet it must not be forgotten that her pleasing person tells much in her favour. But with Pesaroni the case is quite different; though unable to boast of any exterior attraction, either in person or features, and with a voice by no means of the first class, yet what refinement of art, what soul in her commanding song, how finely shaded all her performance! But beyond the cantabile—which, however, is the true touchstone of a singer's excellence—we cannot deny that this lady has some defects, which in the estimation of calmer judges than the Italians, might detract considerably from the high reputation which, in other respects, she has acquired. With respect to Signa. Favelli, she has tolerable power of voice, and upon the whole, may be called a good singer, but her articulation is so bad that the ear cannot catch a single word of what she is singing; a fault, for which, in our opinion, nothing can atone. She also occasionally throws out a bold trill, but it is not always the most judiciously employed, and does not produce the best effect. With the Garcia every one was enchanted at the first public rehearsal; in the moment of enthusiasm, it was declared that nothing equal to her voice had been heard since the days of Marchesi. And to say the truth, in the beginning, her beautiful, clear, and flexible soprano voice, combined with great distinctness of pronunciation, created a great sensation.

But this excellent voice began soon to get out of tune, and it was observed, that though the Garcia was capable of performing much that was great, yet that she was not at home in many important branches of her art: therefore the star of her fame was obscured. Perhaps the size of our theatre might have been the cause why her voice thus suddenly lost its tone; indeed so vast an interior requires lungs of brass, and has proved the wreck of many a promising debutante. But we trust this may prove only a temporary failure, and that her beautiful gift may yet be restored to her, to enable her to rival the fame of the great Correa, of whom she is said to be a relative. With respect to the younger Galli, he is in figure, voice, song, and action, the very miniature of his brother. If we shut our eyes, we might imagine we heard Galli behind the scenes; if we close our ears, we can suppose him acting in a diminutive size.

———

PADUA.—During the season of the great fair here, Mayer's favourite opera of *Rosa bianca e Rosa rossa* was given, which pleased much; it was followed by the *Semiramis* of Rossini, which was new to this place, but did not excite any very lively interest. The other operas during this season, in the towns in the vicinity of this place, were as follows; at Brescia, have been given the *Donna del Lago*, and Mayer's *Rosa bianca*, both of which pleased, and were well performed, particularly the former, in which Lalande, Lorenzani, and the tenor, Winter, produced a great effect. At Bergamo was also given the *Donna del Lago*, in which Madame Balloo displayed her talents to great advantage. At Sinigaglia was given Mercadante's *Andronica*, in which Crivelli and Pastori obtained well-earned applause. In Lugo, the same opera, in which the chief character was admirably sustained by the *prima donna* Landiah In Vicenza, Mercadante's *Didone* was given, in which Cecconi and Canzi appeared to considerable advantage; it was followed by Rossini's *Aureliano in Palmira*.

———

CREMONA.—The theatre here, of the burning down of which an account has been given, has been rebuilt with additional splendour, and opened with Mayer's opera, *La Rosa bianca*, which was followed by several of the more popular operas of Rossini. The company is effective.

REVIEW OF MUSIC.

1. Ero, an Italian Cantata, for one voice, *with an accompaniment for the* Piano-Forte, *composed by* Signor Maestro Coccia. (J. B. Cramer, Addison, and Beale, 201, *Regent Street.*)

2. Calipso, Cantata a Voce Sola, *coll'* accompagnamento *di* Piano-Forte. *Musica del Maestro* Mle. Carafa. (*Vienna, presso* Artaria *e Comp.*)

The Cantata,—by which is to be understood. a piece of music for one voice only, wherein recitatives and airs are blended together, and accompanied by a single instrument,—was very common till towards the end of the last century, when it fell into disuse, and was superseded by the *scena*, which in some respects it resembles, though it is essentially different in many points. The best of the early *cantata* were produced by Alessandro Scarlatti, (the father of Domenico,) one of the most original composers of Italy ; but Handel, Marcello, the Baron D'Astorga, Pergolesi, and others, followed in the same line, and gave to the world several that were much admired in their day. England, during the short life of her great musical genius, Purcell, was inferior to no country in this species of music ; "*Mad Bess,*" "*From'rosie bowers,*" and "*Let the dreadful engines,*" have never been exceeded in beauty of melody, in force and accuracy of expression, or in originality of thought : indeed, we are much inclined to add, that they are without an equal, even up to the present moment ; though we are quite

alive to the vast merit of Haydn's *Arianna a Nasso*, and Mozart's "*Ch' io mi scordi di te !*"

The author of the first of the above cantatas, a Neapolitan by birth, and well known in Italy as the composer of many excellent operas, is now conductor of the orchestra at the King's Theatre. The present specimen of his talents makes us regret that he has not yet been called upon to furnish an opera, which a professor in his station generally engages to produce ; though, the state of the establishment for the last two or three years being considered, he is, perhaps, fortunate, in not having exposed himself to the injury which he might have sustained during such a period of anarchy.

The subject of Signor Coccia's cantata is the history of Hero and Leander. The beautiful priestess of Venus anxiously expects the arrival of Leander ; a tempestuous night ensues, and her solicitude increases ; morning discovers the fate of the youth of Abydos, when, urged by despair, she plunges into the same grave that has entombed her lover. All the various states of passion which the story implies, are judiciously expressed in the different movements of this composition, but without any extravagance ; without any attempt to describe in musical sounds what they are incapable of representing : good sense, and a full knowledge of prosody, mark the setting of this cantata. The music is bold and energetic, partaking more of the character of the German than of the Italian school, which will be seen in the following example, extracted from the introduction :—

Hero, with a mind agitated by gloomy presages, appeals to the gods to relieve her from such agonizing doubts. Her invocation is preceded by the annexed most beautiful and classical harmony :—

The episodiacal address to the dove, at page 19, is in the best Italian style of ornamented melody, and charmingly contrasted to the other parts of the cantata; when performed by a singer of taste, it will never fail to produce an effect on auditors who possess a real feeling for vocal music.

Signor Caraffa has made his name popular by a single air, *Aure felici.* Of his other compositions, scarcely any one, out of the many that have come into our possession, will be heard of a year or two hence. But he has plenty of time before him, abundance of opportunities for distinguishing himself, and, it is said, much industry; we may therefore reasonably hope, that the author of a melody so original and enchanting, has not exhausted himself in a solitary effort. His present work is founded on the story of the departure of Ulysses from the island of Calypso. There is a constant attempt made throughout the whole of this piece to produce effect, but without success; we find in it no additional proof of that talent for invention which appeared in the air above mentioned, and though the composer has aimed at harmonies in the modern style, yet he has not been successful, unless the subjoined passage, from page 7, be considered as an instance:

There are some Rossinian passages in this cantata, but they are quite allowable, so far as the right and title of the composer of Pesaro is concerned; for he has taken the only flower of value in Caraffa's wreath, and applied it to his own purpose, without any acknowledgment.

J. B. CRAMER'S 25 NEW AND CHARACTERISTIC DIVERSIONS, *Composed for the Piano-Forte, and Dedicated to his Pupils.* Op. 71. (Cramer, Addison, and Beale, 201, *Regent Street.*)

WITH Mr. Cramer's two books of exercises for the piano-forte, all musical proficients are so well acquainted, that it is quite superfluous, in naming them, to add one word to the praise which they have so universally, and so deservedly obtained. We mention that admirable work here, simply for the purpose of stating, that the present publication may be regarded as a synopsis of it, because containing many of the most essential passages in the eighty-four studies, modified and condensed into a small compass. But we would on no account wish to deceive our readers by leading them to imagine that these *Diversions* are calculated with a view to supersede the Exercises; though they may answer the purpose of those who are such economists of time and money, as to pause ere they enter upon a work in two large volumes, and to hesitate before they embark in an expense of between two and three pounds.

The intention of this publication is, to instruct the far-advanced practitioner in the various styles of piano-forte playing; to equalize the power of the fingers, and unite them in the *legato* manner; to teach the two principal kinds of touch, the light and the firm; to accustom the performer to the crossing of the hands, and to the occasional striking of two keys with one finger; to give a facility in executing passages of quick syncopation, &c. Each of the five and twenty diversions has

a name indicative of the composer's object; thus the third which is designed to shew the best means of sliding a finger, is entitled *Il Sdrucciolare,* (*sdruccioloso* would have been a better word); the thirteenth, for giving a firm and brilliant shake, is called *The united Couple;* the second, for equalizing the power of the fingers, is named *Les deux Amis;* and these titles afford the author sometimes an opportunity of being jocular: for instance, the twenty-third he denominates *The gilded Toy,* which is a provoked and excellent burlesque of "the *modern* style of adagio performance, and slide of double notes." Here Mr. C. gives us about eighty-seven notes in a bar, amongst which are several double-double-double demi-semiquavers! This reproof, from a master who knows as well as any musician living how to produce the best effects from Piano-forte music, is seasonable and just, and will, let us hope, operate as a check on the impolitic practice, the stupid pedantry, of which a few living composers are too often guilty.

Some of these pieces are very beautiful, particularly *The Rivulet,* a smooth, flowing andante, meant to initiate the learner in the art of playing in three and four parts, one of these parts being in florid counterpoint. To render this description more clear to some of our readers, we insert the two first bars of the piece:

The twenty-fourth, named *I pensieri dolenti,* abounds in "expression and feeling," which are what the author intends to inculcate. The last, "The Author's [*i. e.* Mr. Cramer's] dream," is a specimen of exceedingly good harmony, and, by bringing all the fingers into use at the same time, effects what he intends.

As *Nullius addictus jurare in verba magistri* is our rule,—we have no motto—we do not hesitate in differing from Mr. Cramer in his manner of fingering some passages in this work. We shall mention only two instances; the first is in the above quotation, and second is in the third *diversion,* page 7:

We feel ourselves called upon, if not to condemn both methods, at least to recommend all masters who may use the present publication, to exercise their own discretion occasionally, by making such alterations as their judgments shall dictate. We have no reserve in saying, that in the latter case our own fingering would have been, 1 × 1 2 3 4 × 1 × 2; and herein we are borne out by the rules of another great master. We ought to state, however, that the last bar is extracted from the example of *sliding the finger,* and that, perhaps, the author would not use the same fingering in ordinary cases.

We have thus minutely examined this work, not only on account of the reputation of its author, but because we are persuaded that it will necessarily get into that general circulation which it merits.

ANCIENT CONCERTS.

THIRD CONCERT.—*Under the direction of the Earl of Darnley. Wednesday, March the 16th, 1825.*

ACT I.

Overture.	*(Pastor Fido.)*	*Handel.*
Anthem. O sing unto the Lord.		*Handel.*
Madrigal. O'er desert plains.		*H. Waelrent,* 1590.
Song. Rasserene il mesto ciglio.		*Gluck.*
Double Chorus. He gave	*(Is. in Egypt.)*	*Handel.*
Recit. No more in Sion.		
Song. Wise men, flatt'ring.	*(Judas Macc.)*	*Handel.*
Concerto, 7th.		*Corelli.*
Song. Quel bricconcel.		*Piccini.*
Song. Why do the nations.		
Chorus. Let us break.		
Song. Thou shalt break.	*(Messiah.)*	*Handel.*
Grand Cho. Hallelujah		

ACT II.

Concerto, 4th.	*(Oboe.)*	*Handel.*
Selection from Acis and Galatea.		*Handel.*
Glee. A gen'rous friendship.		*Webbe.*
Duetto. Un flume di pace.	*(Psalmo XLVI.)*	*Marcello.*
Overture and Requiem.		*Jomelli.*
Song. Lord to thee.	*(Theodora.)*	*Handel.*
Double Chorus. Gloria Patri.		*Leo.*

We were too well pleased with the performance, generally, of this Concert, to complain of its want of novelty: the duet " O worship the Lord" was delightfully given by Miss Stephens and Vaughan, and the whole anthem, indeed, very ably sustained in all its parts. Miss Wilkinson we were happy to see in her place again; she sang " Rasserene" very chastely, and with more confidence, apparently, in her powers; there is great richness in some of her tones, and we think that the songs, &c. hitherto chosen for her have been very judiciously selected; whether by her master, Mr. Greatorex, or the director of the night, we cannot say. Mrs. Salmon *has been* very ill,—she sung "Wise men flattering," however, very admirably, in a more subdued tone of voice than is usually the case, and with less flourish and decoration, and we trust this is not in consequence of continued indisposition. Mr. Sapio executed his song (by no means an easy one) in much better taste than on former occasions, and we sincerely hope he is beginning to forget the galleries and slips of Drury Lane Theatre altogether. Mr. Phillips is not quite a Polyphemus yet, but his performance, especially in his recitative, was very spirited, and his conception of the character quite accurate: another year will bring him nearly up to the mark. We were much pleased at his not hazarding the low F at the words " capacious mouth;" he could only have taken it in a voice so feeble as to have rendered the effect ridiculous, and he showed his good sense, as well as his diffidence, in rising to the upper note. The trio was admirably sung. The Italian duet did not display Miss Wilkinson's style and voice so well as the air from Theodora, which she gave with great force and feeling. The Requiem was finely performed, as usual. As to the sublime "Gloria Patri" of Leo, brought in as it was, amidst the motion and whispering of departure, when the attention, however anxiously given, must be necessarily distracted, its effect was partly lost, from its situation. We have already so strongly and repeatedly deprecated this violence to good taste and feeling, that we fear the grievance to be irremediable; we once more, however, implore, with great deference and respect, the noble directors, the most reverend one in particular, to give this matter their serious consideration, and we trust they *will* be disposed to think, that a " *Gloria Patri*" of any description, and by any composer, should only be introduced when it can be heard in the stillness, and with the reverence due to the subject. How many *good* choruses of Handel there are that would be more suitable to such an occasion! If our humble remonstrance does not now succeed, we have done,

ACT I.

Overture to the Occasional Oratorio.		*Handel.*
Psalm XXXIV. (N. V.) Through all the changing scenes.		
Recit. acc. I feel.		
Song. Arm, arm, ye brave.		
Chorus. We come!	*(Judas Macc.)*	*Handel.*
Trio and Cho. Disdainful.		
Song. O Lord! have mercy upon me.		*Pergolesi.*
Concerto, 4th.	*(From his Trios.)*	*Martini.*
Song. Let the bright Seraphim	*(Samson.)*	*Handel.*
Glee. With sighs, sweet rose.		*Dr. Callcott.*
Recit. acc. Justly these evils.		
Song. Why does the God.	*(Samson.)*	*Handel.*
Recit. acc. But bright Cecilia.		
Air and Grand Cho. As from.	*(Dryden's Ode.)*	*Handel.*

ACT II.

Overture to Henry the Fourth.		*Martini.*
Kyrie Eleison, from a Service.		*Jomelli.*
Song and Cho. The trumpet's.	*(Dryden's Ode.)*	*Handel.*
Trio and Cho. See the conqu'ring.	*(Judas Macc.)*	*Handel.*
Concerto, 4th.		*Corelli.*
Luther's Hymn.		
Song. What though I trace.	*(Solomon.)*	*Handel.*
Glee. Peace to the souls of the heroes.		*Dr. Callcott.*
Recit. Rejoice, my countrymen.	*(Belshazzar.)*	*Handel.*
Chorus. Sing, O ye heavens!		

FROM the *occasional* overture *constantly* performed, we beg to pass to " the changing scenes of life," of which we have only to remark that it was a less striking, and a less serious psalm tune than any we have yet heard. His Grace the Archbishop seems to be of opinion that it is introduced in a *proper,* though not exactly the properest place. To *such* authority we must, perforce, submit; poor Hamlet did the same—

" But break my heart—for I must hold my tongue."

Phillips continues his successful career, and we cordially congratulate him; for though much, and deservedly applauded, his manner is marked with that becoming deference and total absence of self-conceit which gives an additional interest to his performance. His scene from *Judas* was perfectly understood; sufficient depth and fulness of voice must be the work of time, but there is no deficiency in point of energy or flexibility. Miss Wilkinson's "O Lord, have mercy" was given with great pathos —but why must she sing *bass* and *tenor* songs? "He was despised" would have been surely a fitter companion for " What though I trace." However, she sung both airs exceedingly well; indeed no singer of the present day could have conveyed the expression of the words more chastely or feelingly. Cramer's *Cantabile* in Martini's 4th Concerto we cannot pass over in silence, though we have heard it so often; a more delicately-touched and highly-finished performance it is impossible to conceive. Then as to Miss Stephens; we were quite astonished at the force she displayed, and with all due discretion too, in " Let the bright seraphim" and " As from the power." These are not the kind of songs best calculated for her, but she sung the two very trying and difficult airs above mentioned as well as we ever heard Mrs. Salmon in her best day. We very deeply regretted the absence of this lady; we fear from severe indisposition. It was an arduous undertaking for Vaughan to give the proper effect to the very difficult song, " Why does the God," and yet he did; so far at least as spirit, feeling, and a clear articulation could give it. The physical strength was certainly wanting, but we have heard voices of far greater power tear the air to tatters.

We have heard far more striking specimens of Jomelli's Church music than the Selection that opened the 2d Act: there is an interspersion of *fiddle-diddle* accompaniment through the graver passages, strangely incompatible with the religious sentiment of the subject, particularly in the last chorus: it is too light and orchestral all the way through, and the " Amen" is tacked, as it were, to the " Cum sancto spiritu" in an abrupt and undignified manner, very unusual, and quite unworthy of the splendid talents of this great composer.

We conclude our remarks on this Concert, by re-urging the remonstrance submitted (respectfully, we trust), to the noble directors in our last critique. What can be said for the Introduction, at the very beginning of the second act, of the *clanging* chorus in Dryden's Ode,—in which there is neither interest nor dignity, and which Handel only designed for a noisy contrast to the "soft complaining flute,"—and leaving to the very last, one of the most sublime emanations of his genius! If there had been one period of the evening fitter to be selected for commanding the attention than another, it should have been dedicated to "Rejoice, my countrymen," and the glorious chorus which follows; but, lo! it is made the *signal* chorus for the carriages to draw up, and the company to depart.

FIFTH CONCERT.—*Under the direction of the Earl of Fortescue. Wednesday, April the 13th, 1825.*

ACT I.

Overture.	*(Esther.)*	Handel.
Chorus. Your harps.	*(Solomon.)*	Handel.
Glee. Since first I saw.		Ford.
Scene from Tyrannic Love.		Purcell.
Song. To God our strength. }	*(Occ. Oratorio.)*	Handel.
Chorus. Prepare the hymn. }		
Song. Gratias agimus.		Guglielmi.
Concerto, 4th.	*(From his Solos.)*	Geminiani.
Song. Brave Jonathan.		
Chorus. Eagles were not. }	*(Saul.)*	Handel.
Song. In sweetest harmony. }		
Chorus. O fatal day!		
The Passions.	*(Solomon.)*	Handel.

ACT II.

Overture.	*(Ptolemy.)*	Handel.
Recit. To heaven's Almighty. }	*(Judas Macc.)*	Handel.
Song. O liberty! }		
Chorus. Sing unto God. }		
Song. Where e'er you walk.	*(Semele.)*	Handel.
Chorus. Blest be the hand.	*(Theodora.)*	Handel.
Concerto, 2d.		Martini.
Recit. Sposa! Eurydice! }	*(Orfeo.)*	Gluck.
Song. Che farò. }		
Madrigal. Flora gave me.		Wilbye.
Chorus. Blessed be the Name.	*(Anthem.)*	Dr. Boyce.

We were a little disappointed in the selection of this evening, because we always look forward to Lord Fortescue's bill with great expectations. The Overture, Opening Chorus, Madrigal, and Scene from Tyrannic Love have been so often commented upon, that a repetition of remark would be entirely useless. Mr. Phillips sang the fine song from the Occasional Oratorio with a correctness perhaps a little overstrained; we do not like too much ornament and cadenza, but, on the other hand, a too sudden close has not a good effect; and simplicity may sometimes sink into tameness. In the quick movement he was sufficiently alive; but the first part was a heavy affair. The chorus (with the exception of the *hammering* repetition upon the words "The timbrel hither bring," which we never could relish), is highly spirited and characteristic.

We do not think that any length of time or practice will enable Miss Wilkinson to give effect to "Gratias agimus." It is a song in every respect unfit for her; Mr. Greatorex, very probably, thinks so too.

We were glad to see Bellamy again; for with all due deference to Mr. Phillips's rising talents, and confidently predicting the excellence to which he will arrive, he certainly could not, at present, have given "Brave Jonathan" in the style and with the feeling of our veteran performer.

The scene from Saul was, as usual, finely executed; Miss Stephens might have been more impressive in her beautiful song, but we must make allowances for this "never-ending still beginning" of it, beautiful though it be.

"The Passions" were given in all their full characteristic colouring; but Vaughan appeared to sing with effort, as if labouring under a cold. The finest chorus, "Draw the tear from hopeless love," we have heard much better performed: the chorus singers were without confidence, and unsteady.

Mr. Sapio acquitted himself very respectably in "O liberty." May he continue thus *moderato*, but—he has made it up with Elliston.

Mrs. Salmon has not certainly the art to give effect to a song with which she herself is not pleased; so we pass on to the chorus from Theodora—a very fine one, and when it has been more practised, will be better performed. The best chorus singers that can be collected will lose, by degrees, the useful requirement of reading music at sight, when they have ceased the practice of the art. There is scarcely a chorus performed at the Ancient Concerts that the present choir could not sing as well

without the book as with it. Miss Wilkinson's air from the Orfeo of Gluck was charmingly sung. Here she was quite at home; with a little more confidence, however, there would be, what is still wanting, a little more animation.

In Wilbye's beautiful Madrigal, Mrs. Salmon sung with feeling and effect: the truth is, she was interested in the composition.

We endeavoured to hear, and pay the attention due to Dr. Boyce's very admirable anthem, but it was all in vain: the rising of one-third of the company to get to their carriages, and save five minutes, at least, of their most precious time, rendered it impossible to listen to this masterly and affective composition.

PHILHARMONIC CONCERT.

FOURTH CONCERT, *Monday, April 11, 1825.*

ACT I.

Sinfonia in E flat	Mozart.
Recit. and Air, " Deeper and deeper still," Mr. Sapio (Jephtha)	Handel.
Concerto Piano-forte, Mr. Neate (never performed in this Country)	C. M. Von Weber.
Aria, Miss Stephens, " Gratias agimus tibi," accompanied on the Clarinet by Mr. Willman	Guglielmi.
Overture, *Olimpia* (never performed in this Country)	Spontini.

ACT II.

Sinfonia Pastorale	Beethoven.
Aria, Signor Remorini, " Largo al factotum," (Il Barbiere di Seviglia)	Rossini.
Concerto Violin, Mr. Kiesewetter	Mayseder & B. Romberg.
Duetto, Miss Stephens and Mr. Sapio, " Ah se de' mali miei" (Il Tancredi)	Rossini.
Overture, Anacreon	Cherubini.

Leader, Mr. Spagnoletti.—Conductor, Mr. Bishop.

In my remarks on this Concert, I trust that I shall be exonerated from any malevolent intention of detracting from the merits of either the individuals performing, or the music selected, further than is essential to the true ends of criticism, by pointing out the imperfections, and thereby adding my endeavours to those of the immediate Directors, towards ultimately rendering truly excellent that which is already so superior, in most respects, to every thing of the kind in this country. The first symphony (one of my most esteemed favourites) was most admirably performed, with the exception of a trifling misconception of the *tempo giusto*; the introduction being tediously slow and heavy, while the two allegro movements were as much too fast. This is a fault for which I hardly know how to point out a remedy; and it is the more to be regretted, because a source of annoyance in a great majority of the performances, that would otherwise prove so high a treat to the lovers of the science. My observations on this head apply equally to the symphony of Beethoven in the second Act, in which the Peasant's Dance was played so rapidly as to destroy the intended expression, and make it a more appropriate accompaniment to an exhibition on the tight-rope. This was the more evident, from the distressed manner and difficulty with which the wind instruments were hurried through it. I fear that these errors will stand little chance of correction, so long as the leader, whoever he be, shall deem it unnecessary to study the character of the movements. I am in the habit of seeing a gentleman at the piano-forte as *Conductor*; what his duties are, I will not presume to determine, but would strenuously recommend that he, having perhaps more leisure than the leader to peruse the score, and judge how far it may be possible to execute the various passages at a certain speed, would occasionally suggest some amendment on this point, and thereby relieve himself from the suspicion of holding a sinecure. Indeed, let the duty devolve upon whom it may, a more strict observance of the composer's intentions, in many passages, would convey the sentiment, or poetry, of which this composition is characteristic, in a very different manner to the minds of the hearers. The orchestra, in the slow movement, should be kept in better subjection, and drilled till they understand a *real piano*; they would then produce that light and shade,—so indispensably necessary, but so seldom heard,—which constitutes one of the most captivating charms of music. A better management of the drums in the storm would have produced a much more appalling idea of thunder; and a greater precision in the execution of the short passages given to the violins, (apparently imitative of the lightning) would have rendered the imitation less incomplete. Added to which, the doing away with that perpetual and insufferable nuisance of marking the time by stamping, striking the bow on the desk, and, when the slowness and length of the measure will not afford sufficient opportunities for either of these, the barbarism of marking the subdivisions of a long note with the bow, is a " *consummation devoutly to be wished.*" We may be thought fastidious in this particular, but we feel assured that those who are less inclined to quarrel with the evil, must have become reconciled to it from habit and constant recurrence, as we are told those who take up their abode next door to a coppersmith, may, after a while, cease to be disturbed by his hammer. These and other similar interruptions have more than once induced me to wish that music could be divested of bars, and rendered legible by some contrivance less likely to produce the Gothic noises which now disturb the heavenly feelings such harmonies, if heard without, would give rise to.

Signor Remorini seemed labouring as though his song was too high for his voice, nor did we think it well suited for the occasion, though so excellent in the opera for which it was composed.

Mr. Neate's Concerto was owing to an imperfection in the piano-forte, necessarily deferred till the second act. The Composition reminded me strongly at times of passages in *Der Freischütz.* The march, and latter movements are charming, but as a whole, it is not remarkably striking.

Miss Stephens's " Gratias agimus" was delightfully sung, and as finely played by Mr. Willman on the Clarinet. The cadence, like all double cadences that I have been unlucky enough to listen to, was highly applauded ; it would therefore perhaps be presumption to offer the remarks which I should otherwise have ventured upon, with regard to these tasteless deformities. Mr. Kiesewetter played in his usual style of excellence ; his performance, which is always dignified and expressive, was nevertheless rather deficient in quantity of tone, arising, probably, from a defect in his violin. I should have been more gratified had he played the Concerto in its original form, instead of attaching the Rondo of B. Romberg to it.

Of the Overture by Spontini, there is little to be said, having few claims to notice on the ground of originality. If noise constitute music, it must take the *place d'honneur* of most of its contemporaries ; but this ingredient, like black in a picture, if not sparingly used, fails to produce the desired effect.

[*For the above notice, we are indebted to a Correspondent.*]

THE DRAMA.

KING's THEATRE.—The return of the Italian Opera to this Theatre, on Tuesday the 12th of April, was a source of high gratification to all lovers of music ; the Haymarket, well as it is constructed for the purposes intended, is in no way calculated for grand lyrical representations.

The indisposition of Madame De Begnis delayed the performance of *Pietro l'Eremita* till Saturday the 23d, when it was revived in a very perfect manner. The characters are now thus distributed :

Noraldino, Sultan of Egypt, *(Faroane)* Sig. REMORINI.
Orosmane, Son of Noraddino, *(Osiride)* Sig. CURIONI.
Ismeno, Minister of the Sultan *(Mambre)* Sig. G. CRIVELLI.
Pietro l'Eremita, Leader of the Crusaders, *(Mosè)* Sig. PORTO.
Lucignano, a General of do. *(Araone)* Sig. BEGREZ.
Fatima, the Sultana, *(Amaltea)* Madame CARADORI.
Agia, daughter of a noble Crusader, and secretly married
 to *Orosmane* *(Elcia)* Mad. RONZI di BEGNIS.
Costanza, wife of *Lucignano* *(Amenofi)* Mad. CASTELLI.

This is the *Mosè,* the oratorio by Rossini, altered in name, scene of action, and period, so as to render it admissible on our stage. We have in the above list, added the original names of the characters, for the convenience of those who possess foreign editions of the opera. As we shall endeavour to notice this work in our next review, we shall only state here, that it was now given in a most efficient and perfect manner ; all the performers, as well in the orchestra as on the stage, exerted themselves to do justice to a piece that contains so many specimens of scientific composition, and some such admirable musical effects. The union of the two departments, the vocal and

instrumental, was very remarkable on this occasion, and the result was proportioned to the attention bestowed, and the efforts made by all parties. Signor Curioni appeared for the first time this season, in the present opera. His arrival will relieve the management from many difficulties, and afford so slight pleasure to the frequenters of this theatre, with whom he is, deservedly, a great favourite. Mad. De Begnis as *Agia* quite surpassed herself ; never did she appear to so much advantage. Madame Caradori acted the part of *Fatima* with a little too much diffidence, but her singing was an ample atonement for any histrionic deficiencies. Remorini, for whom the part was written, made every thing of it that was possible, and the deep, majestic voice of Porto, gave what may almost be termed sublimity to the prayer at the commencement of the opera.

DRURY-LANE THEATRE.—On Monday, the 4th of April, a new afterpiece, under the title of *Abon Hassan, or the Sleeper Awakened,* was produced at this theatre, the music by Carl Maria Von Weber, adapted to the English stage by Mr. T. Cooke.

DRAMATIS PERSONÆ.

The Caliph Haroun Alraschid	MR. BEDFORD
Abon Hassan	MR. HORN
Zabouc	MR. HARLEY
Mesrour, the Grand Chamberlain	MR. BROWNE
The Sultana Zobeide	MRS. ORGER
Zulema	MISS GRADDON
Nouzamoul	MRS. HARLOWE.

Abon Hassan has given mortal offence to the Caliph of Bagdad, by uniting his fortunes to those of *Zulema,* who has rendered herself equally obnoxious to the Sultana on account of her marriage with *Hassan.* The young couple, thus deprived of their patrons' favour, are reduced to great extremities, and determine, by the advice of *Zabouc,* to counterfeit death, as their only means of living. The stratagem is accordingly adopted, and *Hassan* betakes himself to the palace, where he finds the Caliph in a particularly good humour, to whom he relates a fictitious tale of distress and the death of *Zulema.* The monarch is touched by the recital, orders him two hundred sequins wherewith to inter his deceased spouse, and six new wives from his own storehouse, by way of consoling him, and effectually repairing his loss. In the mean time, *Zulema* has been playing off an equally successful hoax on the Sultana, by whom she also is supplied with money ; but *Zobeide,* not having any husbands to spare, does not offer to comfort her protegée with even a single one. The pecuniary wants of the young people are thus supplied ; but these are interrupted, as was to be expected, in the height of their gaiety, by the appearance of the *Grand Chamberlain* and *Nouzamoul,* dispatched by the monarch and his spouse, who, on comparing notes, were rather mystified by the contradictory statements of husband and wife. Accordingly these functionaries appear for the purpose of ascertaining the real ghost ; but disagreeing in their subsequent representations, having been deceived by the alacrity and adroitness of *Zabouc,* the Caliph and Sultana arrive in person to investigate the case. An explanation takes place, &c. &c. &c.

Is there one of our readers so unfortunate as not to know, that all this is from the immortal *Arabian Night's Entertainments?* No!—and we, perhaps, have been indiscreet in affording the space which the above outline fills. The piece has proved decidedly successful, for the story is excellent, and the music,—though it does not, as that of the *Freischütz,*

" Come on the sense like sounds from other spheres,
 Heard by the spirit,—not the body's ears"—

is light, original, and pleasing. Of the latter, however, we leave our readers to judge for themselves, for most of it is given in our present number.

COVENT GARDEN THEATRE.—On the 8th of April, a play in three acts, interspersed with music, named *The Hebrew Family, or a Traveller's Adventure,* was brought out at this theatre ; but after a languid existence of a very few nights, it was "heard no more." The music was a heterogeneous *melange,*— some good, some bad, but much in a state of neutrality that entitles its bearers to pity. The piece is dead, and its faults shall, for us, lie buried with it. Some of the music survives, and if it challenge our notice, we shall have an opportunity of examining it in our future critical columns.

THE
HARMONICON.

No. XXX., June, 1825.

MEMOIR OF JOSEPH WEIGL.

For nearly thirty years the operas of Weigl have not only honourably maintained themselves on the principal stages of Germany, but some of them are to this day as great favourites as those of Winter, Himmel, and Weber, if not of Mozart. This alone, considering the influence of time upon musical taste, sufficiently proves their intrinsic goodness; and Mr. Weigl, who is yet numbered amongst the living, must be considered as belonging to that small class of German musicians, who have ventured to soar to the more lofty regions of dramatic composition, and succeeded in the arduous undertaking.

Joseph Weigl, maître de chapelle and director of the orchestra in the Imperial Theatre at Vienna, was born in that city in the year 1765. His father, who had some reputation as a good violoncello player, instructed him in the rudiments of musical science; but fortunately he was shortly after placed under a much greater master, the famous Albrechtsberger, who had more or less share in the musical tuition of nearly all the great musicians of the Vienna school, and who was at that time in Germany, what the Padre Martini was in Italy. After he had been properly grounded by this master in the principles of harmony and composition, he was transferred, according to the usual practice, to Salieri, for the vocal department, or for the *application* of the rules he had so lately learned. That young Weigl had profited by, and was deserving of the instruction of two such great men, is sufficiently proved, by their highly honourable testimonies respecting " his diligence in the cultivation of the finest natural talents for music, whilst under them." Still more flattering was what Joseph Haydn, his godfather, addressed to him in 1794, after the representation of his first opera, the *Principessa d'Amalfi*. " When I had the pleasure of becoming your godfather, I implored Providence to give you a great musical talent. My prayers were heard. It is a long time since I have heard any music with such enthusiasm, as yesterday I did your *Principessa d'Amalfi*. It is rich in ideas, sublime, full of expression; in short it is a master-piece. I took the warmest share in the just applause which was paid you. Continue, my dearest god-child, always to pay attention to this genuine style; that foreigners may again see what Germans can do."

Immediately after he had finished his studies under Albrechtsberger and Salieri, he proceeded on a professional tour to Italy, and these produced several operas,

which were received with extraordinary applause, particularly at Milan. After his return to Vienna, where he had passed by far the greatest part of his life, and written most of his operas, he received the honourable situation of Director of Music at the Imperial Opera. Towards the end of the year 1815, he made a second journey to Italy, in consequence of an engagement with the Milan Theatre La Scala. Though he had here to encounter a most severe contest with Paër, Rossini, and S. Mayer, who were prepared by their happiest productions to dispute with him the victory, his semi-serious opera, *L'Imboscata*, was so well received, that in the first three representations he was called for at the close of each act; and this favourite piece continued to be given to the end of the season. After this he returned again to his native town, no more to leave it, but to enjoy, in the midst of his countrymen and friends, that life of independence which he entirely owes to his talent and industry.

As a musical character, and particularly as a writer of operas, almost his only works, it is difficult to compare him with other composers, his style being so entirely his own, and so strictly original. He is, in music, what Gessner is in poetry: he shines most in the idyl and the pastoral, a species of vocal composition which is rarely cultivated, even in Germany, but for which Weigl seems to have been gifted by nature with a peculiar fitness. The innocent, the insinuating, and gentle gaiety, and all the softer emotions of the mind, are much better suited to his genius, than the higher aspirations of grandeur and sublimity. Two kinds of style are clearly discoverable in his works. His earlier productions are eminently distinguished by freshness of colouring, by a natural charm, and by beauty of melody, to which qualities they principally owed their success in Italy. To these belong the *Principessa d'Amalfi*, his *Amor Marinaro*, (The Corsair in Love,) the beautiful music to the *Uniform*, and to the melodrama, *The Youth of Peter the Great*, besides several excellent *ballets*. An entirely new style, the character of which has been described as a sort of " insinuating sentimentality," is found in his *chef d'œuvre*, *The Swiss Family*, which has continued to be performed, with very few interruptions, ever since 1809, when it came out at Vienna, and still is played with undiminished popularity.

In the Operas *Das Waisenhaus*, (written in 1808,) and *Der Bergsturz von Goldau*, (in 1812,) predominates the same character as is found in *Die Schweitzer-Familie*.

Carl Maria von Weber called this style,—which owing to the favourable reception of the last-mentioned operas, became very general in Germany,—a sort of " ingenious, yet effeminate velvet painting ;" (" eine weibliche Sammetmahlerei,") an opinion which conveys as much censure as praise. This celebrated musician gives Weigl, at the same time, the highest credit for an uncommon richness in the most pleasing musical ideas, and above all, for that soundness and purity of style, which, as he says, has become so predominant in the Vienna school through the works of Mozart and Haydn. " Most striking," continues Weber, in the *Dresden Abendzeitung*, No. 134, " are Weigl's predilection for the triple time in music ; his fondness for making the violin always express the principal melody ; his apparent endeavour to give whatever ideas he turns to music as melodiously *rounded* as possible ; and to fulfil more by these means, than by correctness and purity of declamation,—all that is required for *scenic* effect. For serious dramatic music, he does not seem to possess a congenial talent, and his Opera *Hadrian* by no means bears the stamp of that greatness which the subject so justly demands. This was probably the reason why it so little succeeded. On the other hand, his oratorios, (for instance, *La Passione di Giesu*,) are composed in a dignified and masterly manner. But very lately, the magic of his flattering and pleasing melodies has anew shewn itself, in the little melodrama, *Die Nachtigall und Rabe*, (The Nightingale and Raven.) For the chamber he has written very little. It deserves, however, to be mentioned, that he has a distinguished talent for leading or conducting any opera in which he feels himself interested." Thus far Carl Maria von Weber.

We now proceed to give a list of his principal works :—

LIST OF JOSEPH WEIGL'S COMPOSITIONS.

I. OPERAS AND CANTATAS.

1. *La Principessa d'Amalfi*, Opera buffa. 1794.
2. *Venus and Adonis.*
3. *Der Strassensammler*, (Street Collector.) Operette in one act.
4. *Giulietta e Pierotto*, Opera buffa at Vienna. 1795.
5. *Eugene II., der Held unserer Zeit*, (Eugene II., the Honour of our Time,) in honour of the Archduke Charles, at Vienna. 1797.
6. *Il Solitari*, Opera buffa, performed at ditto. 1797.
7. *L'Amor Marinaro*, Opera buffa. 1798.
8. *La Caffetiera Bizzarra*, ditto, Vienna.
9. *Il Pazzo per Forza*, ditto, ditto.
10. *L'Academia di Cisolfauto.*
11. Overture and Entre-actes to the *Fürstengrösze*, (The Renowned Prince,) together with three other Overtures.
12. *Die Pilger*, (The Pilgrim.)
13. *The Uniform*, Opera buffa for Vienna ; one of his best works.
14. *Die Verwandlung*, (The Metamorphosis,) Operette in one act.
15. *Das Waisenhaus*, (The Orphan Asylum,) a German Opera written for Vienna, 1808, and received there with universal applause. The music is like the story, full of naiveté, and is written rather in the Italian than in the German style. Without being very full of harmony, or rich in bold modulations, it abounds in pleasing and simple melodies.
16. *Die Schweitzer-Familie*, (The Swiss Family,) In three acts. Vienna, 1809. This Opera has been the principal foundation of Weigl's celebrity as a lyric or pastoral composer.

17. *Adrian von Ostade.*
18. *Der Bergsturz*, (The Mountain Tomb,) Opera in three acts, Vienna, 1815. This Opera also deserves to be particularly distinguished, for the popularity it has obtained abroad.
19. *Das Dorf im Gebirge*, (The Village in the Mountains.) A German Opera.
20. *Des Iahrmarkt zu Grünewald*, (The Fair of Grünewald.)
21. *L'Imbostata*, for Milan.
22. *Die Iugendjahre Peter des Grossen*, (The Youthful Days of Peter the Great.) German Opera.
23. *Das Petermännchen.*
24. *Daniel in der Löwengrube*, (Daniel in the Lions' Den.) For Vienna, 1817.
25. *Nachtigall und Rabe*, (The Nightingale and the Raven,) a pastorale from the French of Lafontaine ; for Vienna, 1818.
26. *Der Einsiedler auf den Alpen*, (The Hermit of the Alps.) Opera.
27. *Francisca von Foix*, ditto.
28. *The Emperor (Kaiser) Hadrian*, Opera for Vienna.
29. *Il Rivali di se stesso*, for Dresden.
30. *Il Ritorno d'Astrea.* Cantata.
31. *Vestas Feuer*, (The Festival of Vesta.) Opera for Vienna.

II. BALLETS.

1. *Die Reue des Pygmalion*, (The Repentance of Pygmalion.) 1794.
2. *Richard Cœur de Lion*, 1795.
3. *Der Raube der Helene*, (The Rape of Helen.)
4. *Die Zerstörung der Stadt Troja*, (The Destruction of Troy.)
5. *Alonzo e Cora.* 1797.
6. *Die Vermählung im Keller.* (The Wedding in Keller.)
7. *Das Simbild des Menschlichen Lebens.* (The Emblem of Human Life.)
8. *Alcina.*
10. *Der Tod des Hercules.* (The Death of Hercules.)
11. *Alceste.* 1802.

III. MISCELLANEOUS VOCAL COMPOSITIONS.

1. *Kriegslieder*, (War Song,) Von Collin.
2. *Der Oestreichische Grenadier*, (The Austrian Grenadier.)
3. *Music to die Weihe des Zukunft*, (The Happy Return.)
4. *Sieg des Eintracht*, (The Triumph of Harmony,) an allegorical cantata, by Castelli.
5. *La Passione di N. S. Giesu Christi*, a Grand Oratorium for Vienna. This is one of his finest productions.
6. *Vier Lieder*, (Four Songs,) Von Reissig.
7. Cavatine, *Come potrei mai vivere.*

IV. FOR THE CHAMBER.

Three Trios for Hautbois, Violin, and Violoncello. These are the only instrumental pieces of Joseph Weigl, to be met with in the Musical Catalogues of Germany.

NOTICES OF REMARKABLE MUSICAL PERFORMANCES IN FOREIGN COUNTRIES.

From the *Account of the Musical Festival at York, in 1823. By* JOHN CROSSE, Esq., F.S.A., &c., &c.

The following are some of the most remarkable musical musters on record :—

At an interview between Francis I., King of France, and Pope Leo X., at Bologna, in 1515, the united musicians of the establishments of both those munificent princes formed a large body, the number of which is not mentioned.

On the cessation of the plague at Rome, in the early part of the 17th century, a mass by Benevoli, for six choirs, was performed in St. Peter's, by more than *two hundred* singers, arranged in circles within the dome, the sixth occupying the summit of the cupola. The organ only was employed.

Lulli's *Te Deum*, composed for the recovery of Louis XIV., in 1686, (by beating the time to which he lost his life from a mortification,) was afterwards performed at Paris, on the recovery of his eldest son, by *three hundred* musicians.

In 1723, most of the great musicians of Europe being assembled at Prague, to celebrate the coronation of the Emperor, Charles VI., as king of Bohemia, an opera, composed by Fux, was performed in the open air, *by a hundred* voices, and *two hundred* instruments; all the principal singers were of the first class. Burney's *German Tour*, Vol. ii. p. 177.

At the funeral of Rameau, at Paris, in 1767, a solemn service was performed by the united bands of that city: and at that of Jomelli, at Naples, in 1774, *three hundred* musicians attended, and contributed to the expenses.

The Musical Institution, at Vienna, similar to our Musical Fund, was formed about 1773, and executes Oratorios twice a year, in Advent and Lent, with a band of near *four hundred* vocal and instrumental performers, the profits of which are about 500*l.* each time.

The *Creation* was performed to an audience of 1506 persons, by *one hundred and sixty* musicians, at Vienna, in 1805, in honour of the author, who was present until the end of the first part; when, overcome with age and emotion, he retired, and bade adieu for ever to music and the world. There was also a performance in honour of Haydn, at Vienna, about the year 1811, of which some account was given in the newspapers of the day, stating, that the band consisted of from *seven to eight hundred* musicians. Of this remarkable assemblage, which is the only one that rivals the Abbey meetings, no details have fallen in our way, but the fact has been confirmed to the writer, whilst this sheet was in the press, by the kind communication of the present Empress of Italian song.

Bands of *two hundred*, or more, musicians, are not very uncommon in Italy and Germany; but nothing equal to the last Abbey Festival is to be found in the continental annals. An entertainment of a peculiar nature, though only consisting of *one hundred and twenty* performers, given to the Emperor Joseph II., in the Rezzonico palace, at Venice, deserves notice, however, on account of its singularity. It comprised all the girls in the four conservatorios, under the direction of Bertoni, uniformly and elegantly dressed. Every kind of instrument, and every species of voice, including double basses, wind instruments, vocal tenors, and basses, were supplied by young female hands and female throats on this remarkable occasion.*

ON MUSICAL EDUCATION.

[*From the French of* M. GRÉTRY.]

THERE is no truth that should be more frequently, and certainly no one that can be more profitably, repeated to the student than this:—" That it is by observing and following nature, that the imitative arts are brought to perfection." It must, however, be at the same time remem-

---

* In our next a review of Mr. Crosse's Work will appear.

---

bered, that all the modes of following nature are not equally good. Every passion, every character, has a variety of features; and, according to the subject treated, and the situation presented, there is always one which will claim the preference over the rest. Hence the danger of imitating even a good production, if that production be itself but an imitation; this copy of a copy cannot but feebly reflect the lively sentiment with which the man of genius was animated. In a word, if in his productions the artist imitate only the works of man, his labours will perish, whereas the nearer he approximates nature, which is imperishable, the nearer he approaches immortality.

There is nothing that would tend more to the happiness of my declining days, than to be able to point out to the young artist the path he ought to follow; to inspire him with a confidence of being able to attain the object in view; to awaken in his breast a spirit of emulation which no checks, no discouragements, can cool. Whatever the road he had marked out for himself, whatever the peculiar bent of his genius, I should wish to encourage him in the race, by pointing out the prize that awaits him at the goal. In a word, I should wish to convince him of this important truth,—that his talent must be directed to some particular branch of excellence, to which he should limit his ambition, for that, of all delusions, the most fatal is the presumption of being able to attain to universal perfection.

But, it may be urged, is it not according to the more or less active nature of his being, according as his organization is more or less favourable to the science which forms the object of his pursuit; is it not after having called all his faculties into activity, and tried every kind of excellence, that the young artist succeeds in selecting that which is best adapted to him? In some respects this is true. Such is the course which many have followed in reaching the term of their studies; but it is not the best. It requires a mass of dispositions, which do not fall to the lot of all the aspirants to excellence, to enable them to surmount the dangers by which this method is attended. We may rest assured, that many talents which would have attained perfection, have been destroyed in the very bud of their promise, from an ignorance of the means of giving them a due direction, and of forming them according to models of acknowledged excellence. It will not be denied, 1st, That a young man is often thrown, almost at hazard, into the hands of an ignorant master, who has no pretension either to taste or discernment; and that, unfortunately, whatever this master does, whatever he esteems, admires, and prefers, will, in this pupil's regard, become the model of perfection to which he will aspire. Is it not melancholy to see that, in such a case, every step he takes towards the point of imaginary perfection, is but an aberration from the right line! 2ndly, That the pupil, ere yet scarcely initiated into the science, may fall into the hands of some pedant, who by dint of checking the sallies of genius, and of moulding nature, as he terms it, may render both the one and the other contemptible. 3rdly, That he may fall into the hands of some coterie, some knot of partisans of a particular species of bad taste, who recognise nothing as good beyond their little contracted sphere of excellence. 4thly, That if he frequent the society of the amateurs of noisy music, of the grand effects of harmony, of a curious complication of chords, he will be persuaded into the belief that this is the only course he ought to adopt. 5thly, That if circumstances should throw him in the way of church music, either in Germany or Italy, where he will bear little else than fugues, learned counterpoint and figured song, it is much to be feared that the happiest disposition for painting the passions, for creating felicitous melodies, would remain smothered beneath these scientific masses. 6thly, That if he should labour for the theatre, and it should fall to his lot to try his talents on some meagre and ill-digested subject, which affords no exercise for the imagination, he will believe himself destitute of talent. 7thly, That, if after having composed good music to an unsuccessful poem his music should be treated with neglect, he will think that he has deceived himself, and wish to change a manner that is good, for one which is inferior.

When the pupil has been sufficiently instructed in the principles of the art, a good master will choose the favourable moment for reasoning with him upon the grounds and nature of the art itself, in order to determine him in the choice of what is excellent; he will demonstrate to him what is the excellent of all times and places, in opposition to that which depends upon fashion, or is upheld by the mania of particular times and particular men. Nothing will tend more effectually to determine the pupil's mind, and convince him of the certainty of a real standard, in opposition to that which is uncertain and the product of circumstances, than an examination of the method pursued by those masters who have obtained celebrity, and a consideration of the reasons why such a style and character of music has constantly maintained its ground, while others have suddenly sunk into oblivion, or insensibly fallen into neglect, after enjoying their hour of celebrity.

Convinced of the truth of such observations, the pupil would be prompted thus to reason with himself: " Yes, I now begin to see which is the true road to excellence; by following it, I shall, according to the means with which nature has endowed me, approach nearer to perfection, and shall no longer run the risk of being led astray by that which has only the semblance of truth. If I have talent, I may hope to obtain that reputation which will not perish with the fleeting breath of popular applause; and without aspiring to perfection, I may reasonably hope to have made some advances in the path of excellence, and leave behind me some memorials of industrious and not ill-directed study, by which those who succeed me may possibly profit."

There are two roads which conduct to celebrity in the arts and sciences, that of theory and that of practice. Theory is science, is speculation pursued as nearly as possible to mathematical exactitude, from which results a code of laws. Practice consists in the employment of these rules, modified so as to produce the most pleasing effect, and brought into action by being applied to some determinate object which the artist wishes to describe. In all cases, it is doubtless necessary to possess more or less of the theory of an art, before proceeding to the practice of it; but we may also devote ourselves exclusively to theory, and become learned, without ever reducing the elementary rules to practice, without ever employing them to the end for which they were made.

But let us consider, whether by dedicating too much time to the theory of the arts, particularly those which administer to our pleasures, we may not estrange ourselves from the very object which these arts have in view. If in our days too great an ambition has been shewn to appear learned, if a curious complication of harmony has been too studiously sought, to the detriment of genuine melody, it is surely time to return to that noble simplicity which is the very soul of art; it is surely time to change our system, by consulting our feelings, which reproach us with having run into excess. Yes, let the youthful votary of the art be persuaded of this important truth—that the more we affect learning, the more we shall depart from the true, the touching, and the beautiful. I do not fear to assert, that the smallest original air is preferable to the most ingenious and scientific complication of harmony. The author of a beautiful air has done something for our enjoyment; the author of a series of calculated harmonies has surprised us, has led us into a labyrinth, from which we are generally anxious to extricate ourselves as quickly as possible. The real amateur, the true musician, will ever hold it as a principle, that it is only those who are strangers to the soul of melody, that will show an exclusive preference for the laborious system of harmony. No; harmony is but a beautiful problem, of which song is the solution.

One of the first objects, therefore, of a good master, will be to teach his pupil to construct melodial phrases, and to unite them with grace. He does this from a conviction, that the art of constructing captivating melodies is the art par excellence. The very reverse of this is the method usually pursued by masters of composition, who begin by giving a bass, upon which they make the pupils construct a melody. But it will be found, that the result of such a method is not a melody properly so called; it is the product of a bass, and, according to the best masters, the song is good if it proceeds in a contrary movement to the bass, if consecutive fifths, double octaves, and the intervals termed *irregular* be avoided, &c. Why then give the pupil a bass, which can only produce a formal melody, an artificial production, a mechanical song, in which sentiment is out of the question? No, a good master will pursue the very opposite method to this: he will teach the pupil to compose a melody, in which taste and feeling have a share, and which will assuredly be susceptible of a bass; he will be cautious not to impede the free march of feeling; he will habituate the pupil to the creation of easy and pleasing melodies; he will teach him to regard the bass, the harmony of accompaniments—in a word, the scholastic part—in the light in which they ought to be considered, namely, as the support of the melody, as the pedestal of the statue. What, indeed, can be more ridiculous, than to occupy the pupil's time in the erection of pedestals, without ever speaking of the statues?

But it may be said, if the pupil has genius, he will afterwards naturally proceed to the production of sentimental melody. I would answer, no; he will not do so, unless urged by the force of nature herself. And why should not the system of education have been sedulous from the very beginning, to follow the course which nature herself spontaneously suggests? Our system of education chains down the pupil to the mechanical branch of the art, at the very time he ought to be exercising his talents upon that which is essential; I call it the essential part, because it is thence that all our pleasures result. Having first of all fixed the ideas respecting melody, I am aware, that in order to form a finished composer, a painter of the passions, recourse must necessarily be had to the study of counter-point;

but then there will be nothing to fear; song, the essential branch of the art, will have taken deep root, and harmony and counter-point will come at a favourable moment to foster its growth, and impart to it its necessary strength. Heretofore masters appear to have been more solicitous with regard to science than to song; on the contrary, it were to be wished, that harmony should ever be considered as the assistant, as the support of song; and that the most effectual method of becoming a good harmonist, is, in the first instance, to have the mind deeply imbued with the essence of melody. Let this art, which is justly entitled to the name of *sentimental music*, be once developed; let the pupil be taught to analyze his feelings, to give a satisfactory reason why such a particular note in such a particular situation produces so powerful an effect, making our bosom either thrill with delight, or shudder with horror, and it will be seen what a progress will be made in the real art of music!

Never let us doubt of the important truth, that it is melody alone which can guide us secure through the labyrinth of modulated chords; that it is she alone who can keep us within the bounds marked out by good taste; that when melody ceases to be pleasing, we are arrived at the point at which science ought to stop. A good master, therefore, will make his pupil compose the most pure and simple airs, and proceed to the art of modulation, before he attempts to initiate him in the mysteries of thorough bass. He will make him compose airs of a passionate and terrible kind, progressing into a variety of modes. He will be under no apprehension of his producing a medley not susceptible of an accompaniment; for he has already taught him that song must be his guide throughout. He will not, therefore, make incoherent errors; it is only the ambition of passing for learned, that betrays us into the commission of sublime blunders like these. According to this principle, let us suppose that the pupil begins a subject in C major, he will afterwards pass into G, into D, and into A; he will be made to pause and remark the note which has made him quit the key in which he began, and conducted him into these different modes. It will be observed to him; " You were in C; you touch the F sharp, the leading note of G, you are therefore in G; you touch the C sharp, you are therefore in D, &c." Always obliged to be *cantabile*, observe what his course will be. If he commence his air in C major, and the train of his impressions at the moment be of the tender and pathetic kind, he will change his key, descending by fifths into the minor mode. If, on the contrary, after commencing in C major, his feelings should be of a joyous cast, or, mounting to the region of sublime ideas—should he be prompted to sing of the glory of heroes, he will ascend by fifths into the major mode. If in modulating, he should fall into an error—and he will fall into a thousand before he becomes an adept in the art— he should be told; " You have committed a grand error against rules; for in this place you are no longer *cantabile*." It should then be pointed out to him, in what respect he has erred against rule; and the key should be pointed out to him into which he ought to have progressed; but he should never be told with that coarseness which is but too common among masters; " You are ignorant, Sir;"—but " you have been betrayed into an error here." And if you destine your pupil to be a painter of the passions, permit him to make some blunders; it will make him more conscious of his strength afterwards.

In this manner it is, that instinct or sensibility will lead your pupil to science; while it may be set down as a principle, that science would never have led him to that melody which is the result of sensibility. When these happy dispositions have been superinduced; when the mind of the pupil is thoroughly imbued with song, and skilled in the art of modulation, then is the happy moment to render him a composer, for *composition*, in the strict sense of the word, signifies the art of making several parts move together. Then it is that he may be taught to form a scholastic theme of two, three, or more parts upon a given bass; for then, as before observed, there will be nothing to be apprehended; song, the essential part, will be predominant in all his compositions, and harmony and counter-point will now come at the happy moment, to impart to them additional force, and strengthen their expression.

In order to render more clear the reasoning here pursued, I would class the talents of composers as follows:

1st. The harmonist, without the faculty of melody;

2nd. The melodist, without the science of harmony;

3rd. The melodist, who is also master of harmony.

The harmonist who possesses not the faculty of melody, but who occupies himself in researches upon the theory of the art, doubtless merits our esteem; he calculates, he prepares the materials which await the vivifying touch of genius; but such a one runs the risk of being forgotten when the man of genius has exhausted these materials, when he has enlivened them with song, and imparted to them those accents of passion which render them indestructible.

The melodist without the science of harmony, is a child of nature. There is no one of his accents but produces an agreeable sensation; he has the gift of pleasing the multitude, who are solicitous only to be pleased, without troubling themselves about science. Even the man of science is constrained to love him, and experiences in listening to his accents a charm which pierces through the scientific coating in which he is enveloped. Yes, those melodial phrases which imprint themselves on the memory, which haunt us night and day, are the genuine treasures of music, in the same manner as those fortunate verses which are short in words, but comprehensive in sense, constitute the reputation of the poet.

The master melodist, who at the same time possesses a thorough knowledge of harmony, is the musician *par excellence*; but how rare to find a man in whom these great requisites are equally balanced! It is sensibility that produces melody; it is the patient study of harmonial combinations that constitutes the learned man: to conciliate the two faculties is a task more than difficult. Let the youthful artist consult his own feelings, and be studious to follow nature; let him build his music upon melodies that are pure and expressive, and they will possess a character of truth which must survive all the vicissitudes of fashion. Let him emulate the truth and melody that reign in the declamations of Pergolese, the tender and angelic song that breathes throughout the compositions of Sacchini, the expressive harmony that prevails throughout the scores of Gluck. Study to preserve your melodies so pure, and to render the phrases so correspondent one to the other, that their impression may be instantaneous, and the effect of the whole be seen at a glance. It is thus that they will charm the fancy, and produce so indelible an impression on the imagination, as never again to be effaced. Such is the case with respect to all the great master-pieces that remain to us. In some of their lesser details they may have partly grown out of date, but their broader features possess a character of nature and truth, which bid defiance to the influence of times and fashions.

To the Editor of the HARMONICON.

London, May 4, 1825.

SIR,

The following observations which I lately met with in the *Quarterly Journal of Literature, Science, and the Arts**, I have transcribed and sent to you, as they may probably prove interesting to the scientific readers of the HARMONICON.

I am, Sir,

Your very obedient Servant,

R. D.

ON THE OSCILLATIONS OF SONOROUS CHORDS.

In a science of such universal interest as music, which is the object of discussion, not only of the musician, but of the mathematician and the natural philosopher, it is remarkable what a discordance of opinion there exists with regard to those sounds called harmonics, and even with regard to the oscillations of sonorous chords. The following interesting theorem removes all obscurity from these subjects.

If any two sonorous chords, A and B, be so placed, as that the oscillations of one shall cause the air to act upon the other, as in all stringed musical instruments, and if A oscillates m times, while B oscillates n times, m and n being any whole numbers prime to each other; then, if either of these chords, as A, is put in motion, the action of the air will divide B into m equal parts, each of which will oscillate n times, while A oscillates only once.

This theorem is the base of the theory of harmonics. It was deduced from a property demonstrated by Lagrange, in Sect. 6. *Mec. Analytique*, that a vibrating chord is susceptible of being divided into any number of equal parts, each of which would vibrate as if isolated. It affords a refutation of (what geometers seemed not absolutely to doubt) the assertion of Rameau, that every fundamental note in music is accompanied with its octave, twelfth, and seventeenth. It proves that, whether a sonorous homogeneous chord of uniform solidity has one, two, or three species of vibrations, these oscillations being necessarily performed in equal times, it cannot produce but one single note at a time. It is remarkable, that while the illustrious geometer just named had the proof of the fallacy of the received theory of harmonics before him, he was framing an hypothesis to account for its truth.

MEYERBEER, AND *IL CROCIATO IN EGITTO.*

Trieste, March, 1825.

THE celebrated opera, *Il Crociato in Egitto*, is rapidly making the tour of Europe. This composition has been the means of raising M. Meyerbeer into a reputation scarcely less sudden than that procured for M. v. Weber by *Der Freischütz*. After having been brought forward in most of the principal theatres of Italy, it has within the last two months been produced here, with a splendour hitherto unknown to the theatre of this place, and received with an enthusiasm almost unprecedented, even in this land of vivacious feeling.

The opera had been for some time expected; it was known that more than usual attention had been bestowed, in order to enable it to be brought forward with all the perfection possible; that the zeal of all parties, united to that of the composer himself, who had paid a visit to Trieste, expressly with a view to superintend its production, was unremitting; that there had been no less than thirteen full rehearsals, and as many separate ones of the choruses. Expectation and impatience were therefore on the tiptoe, and its appearance was at length crowned with unanimous and tumultuous applause. I shall not easily forget the enthusiasm which this moment produced, an enthusiasm which a calmer review of the merits of the piece has fully justified. For myself, I frankly acknowledge that of all the operas I ever heard, the music of *Il Crociato* has touched me most, as well by the novelty of its motivos, as by the sweetness of its melodies, and the grandeur and lofty character of its accompaniments.

As I am of opinion that *Der Freischütz* is the first of modern German music, so is *Il Crociato* the first of the modern Italian: or rather I would correct myself and say, that of all living composers, Meyerbeer is the one who most happily combines the easy, flowing, and expressive melodies of Italy, with the severer beauties, the grander accompaniments, of the German school; to which I would add, that he unites the still greater merit of painting the various feelings of the heart with perfect truth, and of carefully adapting his orchestral effects to the character of the melody which they are made to illustrate and enforce.

The means of the theatre here are but limited, and the liberality of the management has not always been a subject of praise; yet on the present occasion, the facilities found for the production of the *Crociato* astonished every one, and the efforts made seem to have surprised even the artists themselves; they could have arisen only from that enthusiasm which can supply many wants, and make up for many deficiencies.

The journals of this part of the world are full of rapture; they declare that both singers and orchestra rivalled each other in their exertions, and entered entirely into the soul and spirit of the great composer, who happily for them had been present at all the rehearsals to direct their energies, so that the minutest beauties of the piece were brought fully into view. The management is said to have spared no expense, no sacrifice, in order to produce it with a splendour deserving of the composition.

To complete all, the poet Rossi, the author of the poem, was at Trieste, and by actively co-operating with the composer, succeeded in impressing the singers, and particularly the chorus, with the force of the sentiments they had to utter, and of making them enter into the spirit of the situations of the piece, many of which are full of real theatrical effect. How fortunate would it be if all theatres enjoyed these important advantages! at all events, more might certainly be done in this respect than has usually been attempted; too often the artists have been left to their own caprice, or to accidental means of comprehending the spirit of the poetry, and the force of the situations. By the way, we cannot let this opportunity pass of remarking, that the poem of Rossi is by far the best of its kind that has appeared in Italy for many years; the style is good, and in excellent keeping with the interesting nature of the action.

From what has been said, it will be seen, that in order to do justice to this opera, considerable depth of stage, and splendour of decoration is required, effective choruses and performers, together with an energy of action corresponding to the striking situations of the piece; for on these, after all, much of the effect of the music will necessarily depend. The following were the singers who sustained the principal characters here: the *soprano*, Signora Canzi; the *mezzo-soprano*, Signora Carolina Bassi; *contr'alto*, (which was not effective,) Signor Villa; *primo tenore*, Signor Tacchmardi; *basso*, Signor Bianchi.

The choruses,—a wonder for Italy,— went off admirably, though, upon the whole, too feeble for the situations. The soprano parts are particularly defective in Italy generally, and yet we are led to believe that the children here sing almost before they can walk; whereas, with the exception of Naples and Milan, there scarcely can be found a chorus with soprano voices. With very few exceptions, the orchestra was perfect, and executed the music in its true spirit and time. No idea can be formed of the warmth with which the opera was received. Meyerbeer was called upon the stage no less than four times at the close of each act; the singers also enjoyed their full share of honour. After the performance, the composer was met at the door of the house by an immense concourse of people, who came prepared with bands of music, and lighted torches, and accompanied him to his residence with tumultuous acclamations. He was then obliged to show himself at the balcony, amidst the roar of a thousand *evvivas*, the clang of trumpets, and the deafening roar of drums:—no very judiciously-chosen compliment by the way, wherewith to greet this creator of sweet harmonies.

After partaking of some refreshment he was invited to repair to the Cassino, where he was accompanied in the same manner as before, and on reaching this place, he was installed in due form, and crowned with laurel, in the midst of a tumult of applause, and a riot of acclamation, of which those only who have witnessed it can form any adequate idea. This uproarious meeting did not disperse till four in the morning. Another honour, less riotous, but more grateful, was also shewn to the composer, in a public dinner given him by the principal people of the town; nor on this occasion was the poet Rossi without his share of honour; he was placed in a conspicuous situation near the composer, and greeted with the approbation which his merits deserve. From the more exalted loungers in the Cassino, to the ragged idlers on the quays, nothing is talked of, but Meyerbeer and the *Crociato*; favourite pieces of the music are

hummed in every direction, and the favourite romance is in every mouth *. In a word, the magic of this modern music has effected more wonders on the shores of Etruria, Adria, and Illyria, than ever was done by the art in days of yore.

P. V.

ON THE MUSICAL DRAMA.

[From a Paris Journal.]

SINGING is heard upon all the theatres of Paris, *La Comédie Française* excepted; nor is it satisfactorily proved, that Melpomene and Thalia are not sometimes heard to utter there a kind of semi-lyric declamation. Never was the saying of Mazarin more rigorously true: Voltaire expressed his astonishment, that the French could sit out three hours of music; were he still living, he would feel no hesitation in confessing, that without singing, they could not exist a single day.

The same was also the taste of the people of antiquity. Music formed the delight of the greatest kings; David could no more separate himself from his harp than from his sling; Alexander, after subduing the world, was desirous of learning to play on some instrument; Socrates could not discover that wisdom was incompatible with music; Nero was more tenacious of the beauty of his voice, than of all the prerogatives of absolute power. Our ancestors also were fond of the song; I find an incontestible proof of this in the treaty of peace made by Clovis with Theodoric, king of the Ostrogoths in Italy. In one of the articles it is stipulated, that the latter should be obliged to send into France an excellent player on the guitar. Dagobert, the same to whom

Le bon saint Eloi
Disait; O mon roi,
Votre majesté, &c.

fell violently in love with a nun whom he heard singing in the choir; Louis XII. composed little ariettes, and the grave Louis XIII. himself, noted down one, which is to be met with in the *Musurgia* of Kircher. Was it not Queen Elizabeth's wish to be lulled into her last long sleep by the sound of instruments? So many examples, the number of which I should find no difficulty in augmenting, justify the taste of the French for music, and are an excuse for their entertaining, in this respect, the opinion of the master of M. Jourdain, who assures us "that without it a state canot possibly exist."

The Greeks were of the same opinion; they considered harmony as the image of good order in government. Full of this idea, they made a decree that nothing should be changed in their music. Woe to the rash man who should dare to propose any innovation! He was at once anathematized, and his name was added to the list of criminals of the state. Hence it is seen that the Greeks had their *Société de Bonne Musique*, the same as we have our confraternity *De bonnes lettres*. Our national character will not permit us to imitate the example of the Greeks on this point, for, rather than remain stationary in the art, we should have overturned twenty governments, in order to have enjoyed the liberty of changing

<hr>

* For this composition, see p. 138 of the Music in the present Number.

our music twenty different times. Happily there has been no necessity of recurring to extremes like these: our musical revolutions have been successively operated without any other disorder, than some smart fisty-cuffs dealt out in quick time, and some wigs torn off in irregular cadenzas.

Honour! a hundred times honour to the dilettanti who, at a memorable period, risked their ears and noses in order to raise Gluck and Piccini to the worm-eaten thrones of Lulli and Rameau! It is they who prepared the way for the appearance of a Mehul, a Cherubini, a Grétry, a Daleyrac, a Nicolo, a Berton, a Boieldieu, who, by their learned harmonies and sprightly melodies, have proved, that in spite of all the eloquent sarcasms of a celebrated philosopher, the French could also have their music. Perhaps it would have been wise to stop there, and not to have forgotten the important truth that, *le mieux est l'ennemi du bien;* but, attainted with *Garatism* even to the third degree, our singers have been ambitious only of warbling, and our composers being constrained to write for birds, came at last to consider our lyric theatres as so many aviaries.

The principal movers of this great musical revolution have, doubtless, been the buffoons of Italy, who having had the address to bring themselves into fashion, have succeeded in making the public believe, that out of their theatre there is no salvation. Since that fatal moment our great composers have broken their lyres, and abandoned the French scene to all the wild furor of the *point d'orgue,* the *crescendo,* and the roulade. Our young musicians, seduced by the rage of the day, have sought for nothing but ultramontane inspirations; and our poets too, infected with the same spirit, have established their Parnassus at Berthelemot's, and set about rhyming prose more desperate than the following passage of an Italian Opera:—

" O ma charmante meûnière,
Tu m'a moulu le cerveau
Tu m'a reduis en farine,
Tu me pétris en gateau,
Tu me cuis à la sourdine
E m'avales d'un morceau *."

These verses naturally lead me to speak of the operas at the *Odeon ;* the success of which cannot possibly be called in question.

Rossini, Winter, and Weber divide the public favour, and in vain do Corneille and Moliere strive to make their voices heard; they are overwhelmed by the din of trombones and contra-basses. The question on this point is settled. The second *Theatre Francaise* is no more; it has fallen before the blast of the trumpets of the new Joshuas, and upon its ruins we already behold the rising walls of a temple to the God of *Italico-Germanico* harmony. The present might, perhaps, be the proper place to examine with what degree of right Melpomene and Thalia have been chased from the sanctuary assigned them as their property, by a royal ordinance; but this argument would carry me too far. I will return to my subject.

* Oh my charming maid of the mill,
Thou hast ground my brain to meal,
Thou to finest flour has brought it,
And into a cake hast wrought it,
And when baked so nice and brown,
Swallow'd at a mouthful down.

In all the critiques which I have constantly launched against the *pasticci* of M. Castil-Blaze, I have never pretended to deny the advantages which our young composers may derive from the study of the scores of foreign composers; on the contrary, I am persuaded that no musical work can be appreciated, till it has been heard; a simple reading will not suffice in music as in literature, and in spite of all the talent of our musical judges, they too often pronounce an opinion in the dark. In as far, therefore, as the Odeon affords us an opportunity of judging of the compositions of foreign masters, it is a useful institution, and serves at once to promote the interests of the art, and the enjoyment of the public; but from the moment its directors are determined no longer to keep within the limits prescribed by taste and good sense; when it is to be nothing but the same thing over and over again; to-day Rossini, to-morrow Winter, the next day Weber, there is an end of French music. Again, if we must have Weber, Winter, and Rossini, let us have them pure and genuine, not changed and garbled as fancy or caprice may dictate. Unhappily it is more easy to imitate the defects than the good qualities of men of genius; and in this respect, it is not difficult to anticipate the result. The danger is not imminent I will allow; the company of singers at the Odeon is not yet sufficiently strong, or so organized, as to afford any just cause for alarm; but the moment may arrive when our fears may not be groundless. Then will it come to pass, that attacked on both banks of the river, the French Muse will infallibly see her last asylum invaded, and will have no other resource left than the street musician, and his barrel organ.

But be it as it may, let not the young artist be disheartened; let him not lose sight of what one of our masters, and he no common man, has observed relative to this subject. "The real sublime of every work," says Gretry, " is truth; upon that fashion can have no lasting influence. A sparkling pretender to excellence may eclipse for a moment the merit of men of ability; but it will not be long before the public will blush in silence at having been deceived, and fresh homage will be rendered to the native charms of truth."

CONCERTS OF M. HUMMEL AT PARIS.

M. HUMMEL has almost surpassed the expectations to which his great reputation had given rise. The three pieces which he executed at his first concert excited even enthusiasm. One of them, the *Rondo Brilliant,* has been seldom heard with accompaniments, which are of extraordinary beauty, and afforded great delight. His new Concerto is still more remarkable on account of its science and grace.

The execution of M. Hummel is free, chaste, and in perfectly good taste; he does not strain to astonish. Many performers have more pretension, and, if we may use the term, more emphasis in their playing, but they seldom produce the effect he does. Mlle. Schiassetti and M. Bordogni were well received. An extempore performance by M. Hummel, although rather too long, shewed the surprising skill and facility of invention by which he is distinguished. Amateurs will long remember this agreeable musical evening.

The rooms of M. Erard, large as they are, cannot

contain the crowd of amateurs who wish to attend the concerts of this celebrated musician.

The extemporaneous performance at the end of the second concert which he gave last Friday, produced an astonishing effect upon some of the spectators. *Madame Pasta* surpassed herself in Gluck's cavatina in *Orfeo*, " *Che faro senza Euridice ?*"

The third concert given by M. Hummel was attended by great numbers. This distinguished composer again proved himself worthy of his reputation, and of the success of the two former concerts. The sonata for two performers, executed by Kalkbrenner and Hummel, appeared learned and original. An adagio in the old style, if it had lasted much longer would have fatigued the auditory. Interminable cadences, and shakes of a quarter of an hour long, may prove the skill of the performer, as a minuet well danced displays the ease and grace of Mlle. Noblet and M. Albert; but these ornaments of the old school, to be at all bearable, should be short. However, a very delightful rondo succeeded this musical minuet; and its charming light style was more apparent from the contrast. M. Kalkbrenner took the upper part, and M. Hummel the second. It was easy, to those amateurs who were a little experienced, to perceive and appreciate at once, the effect produced by the union of the brilliant and elegant manner of the former, with the free and easy style of the latter. The vocal part of this concert was composed of an air by M. Paër, sang by Madame Marconi; and a tezzetto, by the same master, sung by Madame Marconi, Mlle. Dorus, and M. Lavasseur; and another air by Paër, sung by Mlle. Dorus, who received some applause. A trio by Hummel, performed by Baillot, Norblin, and the author himself, was singular and learned, and on this account was approved by composers. M. Vimercati received the same applause for a very different sort of merit,—he executed a concerto on the mandoline. True connoisseurs are inclined to allow but little to the mere conquest of difficulties.

The composition of M. Vimercati was not in good taste. Why has he not dedicated to the harp, or even to the guitar, the immense time which he must have employed upon the mandoline, an ungrateful instrument, whose sharpness he will never soften, and whose dryness cannot be overcome. A theme from Mozart, Handel, and Weber, on which M. Hummel performed some variations, gave him an opportunity to introduce one of the most brilliant extempore pieces ever heard. We cannot enough admire this instantaneous creation, this facility of producing in a moment, music, as pure in style, and as brilliant, as if it had been polished in the study of the composer after long consideration.

SOME ACCOUNT OF M. MEYERBEER,

The Composer of *Il Crociato in Egitto.*

M. MEYERBEER is the son of one of the richest bankers of Berlin, named Beer*. At a very early age he evinced a remarkable talent for music, and at ten years old performed a concerto on the Piano-Forte, at a public concert given at Berlin, for the benefit of the charitable institutions of that place, on which occasion, their Majes-

* *Meyer* among the Jews—for of that community was this composer's family—is a prænomen; instead therefore of writing his name Meyer Beer, he has joined the two.

ties of Prussia were present. His master on this instrument was the famous Lanska. He began the study of composition at a very early period under Bernhard Anselm Weber, first Kapellmeister at Berlin, and afterwards under the distinguished Zelter. Being more advanced in age, he completed his musical education under C. M. von Weber, both being nearly of an age,—about 35. At Munich he composed his first opera, called *Jephthah's Rash Vow*, to German words. The reception which this obtained, encouraged him to cultivate his favourite art with increased zeal. He accordingly proceeded to Italy, where he adopted more of the Italian style, and produced several compositions, of which the most successful were his operas of *Romilda e Costanza*, *Emma di Resborgo*, and, last of all, his master-piece, *Il Crociato in Egitto.*

Meyerbeer being a man of very considerable fortune, does not compose from pecuniary motives, but altogether in the spirit of an amateur; the profits arising from his productions he has hitherto bestowed upon the most deserving of those who performed them, and in other acts of generosity.

THE YORK FESTIVAL.

THE Second Yorkshire Grand Musical Festival is fixed to take place on the 13th of September, and three following days, in York Minster; there will also be Concerts on the first three evenings in the New Rooms,—the building of which was noticed in the Harmonicon for July, 1824,—which will be led by Messrs. Kiesewetter, Mori, and Loder, respectively. Mr. F. Cramer leads the Morning Performances, and the whole will be conducted by Mr. Greatorex,—assisted by Mr. Camidge, Dr. Camidge, Mr. White, and Mr. P. Knapton. The Cathedral band will consist of upwards of 600 vocal and instrumental performers, and the Concert Orchestra of 140 to 150 instrumentalists. The choruses are to be delivered to the singers in June, and a rehearsal of them is to take place on Saturday the 10th September, which will ensure more correctness in the new pieces than has usually been attained at country meetings, at the same time that the pressure of numbers upon the roads will be somewhat more widely dispersed.

The first morning's performance will commence with the JUBILATE of Handel, composed for the peace of Utrecht, without any introductory symphony; thus producing the effect of all the voices and instruments at once upon the ear, the want of which is lamented by Dr. Burney in his *Account of the Commemoration.*

The 102d Meeting of the three Choirs, takes place at Hereford, in the preceding week to that at York.

The Derby Meeting follows that of York in October.

MISCELLANEA.

IN those places where musical contests are carried on with violence and animosity; where there are more critics and theorists than composers and practitioners, it is not to be expected that the public taste can become very refined, or the fancy and enthusiasm of musicians be much encouraged or enlivened.

A RAGE for universality, or for gain, tempts many composers to quit the road which nature and art have destined for them, and to enter on another, where they are sure either to be bewildered, or to become so destitute of the necessary requisites for travelling through it, as to be obliged to rob and plunder every one they meet.

The composer, who to genius unites soundness of judgment, will not lavish upon common and trivial occasions, what should be reserved for extraordinary purposes. He will leave to fops and pedants in the art, all that alarms, astonishes, and perplexes; he will let no other arts be discoverable in his compositions, than those of pleasing the ear, and of satisfying the understanding.

Dr. Burney, after hearing the compositions of a German, in which, though great art and contrivance were perceptible, yet the modulation was natural, and the melody smooth and elegant, exclaimed: "As much art as you please, Sir, provided it be united with nature; and even in a marriage between art and nature, I should always wish the lady to wear the breeches."

The Abbé Morelet, in his work Sur l'Expression Musicale, has the following just and beautiful remark. "A finished air of the pathetic kind is an assemblage of various accents, which have, at different times, escaped from souls endowed with sensibility; it resembles the painting of Zeuxis, which pourtrayed the Goddess of Beauty by an assemblage of the most exquisite traits of loveliness the painter could select. It is thus that the sculptor and the musician concentrate dispersed beauties, and succeed in inspiring us with that delight which nature could not of herself, unaided and unassisted, impart."

An author, speaking of the famous quarrel between the partisans of the ancient and modern music, has the following remark. "If after having read all the authors upon music that came in my way, from Aristoxenes to M. Rameau, I were permitted to state the impression that has been left on my mind, I would do it in three words. The Ancients are the fathers of music; they left behind a numerous offspring, the greater part of whom did not know their own parents; and the other part, still more ungrateful, refused to know them."

The composer Vivaldi filled, at the same time, the functions of priest and of maestro di capella. A remarkable instance of absence of mind is related of him. As he was saying mass in a crowded church, the musician's mind wandered from the sacred subject, and was busy amidst the creations of his fancy. Totally absorbed by the brilliant conceptions of the moment, which he was fearful of losing, what did the good priest do? He quitted the altar, to the no small amazement of the congregation, hurried to the sacristy, and scratched down the precious motivo upon the margin of a missal. He then returned quietly to the altar and finished the interrupted sacrifice. This abberation of fancy had, however, well nigh cost poor Vivaldi very dear. Some of the scandalized auditory made this pardonable irregularity of the musical priest, a subject of accusation to the Holy Office, but the Inquisition, with a lenity not always found at that tribunal, dismissed the complaint with indifference, for doubtless in the eyes of the successors of Torquemada, a madman and a musical virtuoso were one and the same thing.

Musical paradoxes may be advanced and defended, with all the force of logic and the powers of persuasion; but at last it will, in all probability, be found, that common sense, habit, and prejudice will not leave the decision either to reasoning or eloquence, but insist upon having a vote upon the occasion.

The grumblers, the laudatores temporis acti, are a very ancient family. Aristotle, Plato, and others, in the most flourishing period of music in Greece, are full of their lamentations for the corruption of the art. It is more than probable, that those philosophers, like certain modern amateurs, exaggerated the evils of which they complain. In music more than in any other

thing, men are apt to be influenced by the force of reminiscences, and are tempted to call that the decay of the art which is frequently nothing else than the decay of their faculties, and the effect of age, which steals on imperceptibly, and blunts the finer edge of sensibility.

J. Schultze has written a treatise De Usu Musicis, &c., which appeared under the fictitious name of J. J. Weidenero; the eighth division of the work has the whimsical title, Cantores amant humores.

Inventions, says an Italian writer, make the tour of the world, and at the place which they reach the last, generally leave some memorial behind them. The only specimen I ever saw of the Tromba marina (the Trumscheit of Luscinio, as described by him in his Musurgia,) was at Tornia, upon the northern shores of the Gulf of Bothnia. It appeared to have been preserved with great care, and was in the possession of a merchant, but no one knew how to use it.

It is reported here (Berlin), that M. v. Weber has just completed the first act of his new opera of Oberon, which he has been engaged to compose by the direction of one of the theatres of London. As a literary production, the poem he has to work upon, has been stated to be a very meritorious composition, full of dramatic situation and effect.

There has just appeared in Leipsic, Shakspeare's Lieder, mit Begleitung des Piano-forte in musick gesetzt, von Fr. von Boyneburgk, (Shakspeare's Songs set to music, with piano-forte accompaniments.) It is spoken of as a work possessing great merit, and abounding with original and effective melodies.

Rossini's opera of Armida has just been published by Breitkoff and Härtel, of Leipsic, the whole handsomely printed in lithography.

Beethoven is still active; he has just completed two new Quatuors, which are shortly expected to be given to the public.

Schubart, in his work entitled Æsthetic der Tonkunst, (Æsthetic of Music), has given it as his opinion that the Jews Harp might be so far improved as to admit of Concertos being played upon it, and for this opinion he was not a little ridiculed. But strange, as it may appear, the idea of this fanciful writer has in a certain degree been realized. A. M. Eulenstein, from Heilbronn, has invented a new instrument, or rather improved the little instrument already spoken of, which he calls the Mouth Harmonica, on which he has been performing various pieces of music to the astonishment and delight of numerous private circles. After much study, and by much ingenuity, he has succeeded in obtaining from this insignificant instrument, which in its vibrations usually produces consonants only, four entire octaves in the major scale, and hence he can give melodies, not only with ornamental passages, but even with entire variations. As the tone is formed by the mouth, this instrument unites the powers of the common harmonica with the modifications which the human breath is capable of imparting to it. According to M. Eulenstein, it cannot be played in the minor mode, because the vibrations form the major third, but it produces the minor sixth, which always proves an inconvenience to the performer in the major tones. This gentleman has studied thorough bass, in order to extend and perfect his powers on the instrument. He is a very modest, unassuming young man, and meets with much encouragement.

An advertisement recently appeared in a German newspaper, for a gentleman's servant. Among other indispensable requisites, it was stated, that he was neither to sing nor whistle any part whatever of Der Freischutz!

Mr. Ferdinand Ries is at present engaged in composing an opera, which has been written expressly for him by Mr. George Soane, author of Faustus and other dramatic works.

FOREIGN MUSICAL REPORT.

VIENNA.—The only piece given here this season that can be entitled to the name of novelty, was *Le Cantatrice Villane*, an opera buffa by Fioravanti, which was admirably performed by Signor Lablache, and the Signoras Sonntag and Dardanelli. The *ensemble* was masterly, and the piece was received with considerable applause. The other performances have been *La Molinara* by Pasiello, six times; *Nachtigall und Rabe* by Weigl, once ; *Le Lazrione d'una Vedova* by Generali, three times ; *Cordelia* by Kruitzer, once ; *Alle fürchten sich*, (They all Fear), by Isouard ; *Das Hausgesinde* (The Domestic), by Fischer, twice ; *der Gebesserte Lorenz* (The Lorenzo Improved), by Eulenstein ; and *Cenerentola*, three times.—Among the concerts the most remarkable was that given by Professor Schunke and his two sons, who performed wonders on the horn, as well as on the piano. The elder, thirteen years of age, gave Hummel's grand Concerto in A minor, with a precision, taste, and feeling, which is not rarely surpassed. *God save the King*, with variations, performed on the horn by the father and the younger son, was a surprising performance, and called forth a burst of applause.

Our veteran Weigl had a very successful benefit, on which occasion his favourite opera of *Die Schweitzer-familie* was represented.

BERLIN.—The greatest novelty that has excited the attention of the musical world here has been the revival of Sacchini's *Œdippe*, that wonder of the last age. It was produced with considerable spirit, under the direction of the celebrated Spontini, who has already shewn great judgment in the manner in which he has revived some of the masterpieces of the old school. The great difficulty on these occasions is to know the true movement of the different parts of music, to which no positive indications have been left by the composers. In the present instance, so much attention was bestowed on this point, that all the old cognoscenti,—which, by the way, is saying a great deal, —appear to have been perfectly satisfied. Accustomed as we have been to the more perfect orchestra, formed since the days of Mozart, the music of the older school frequently appears meagre and unsatisfactory, and yet how is this evil to be remedied ? A Mozart might venture to give additional accompaniments to the *Messiah*, but where are we to find the superior musician, the master-mind that would venture upon the same task with respect to the masterpiece of the last age ? No wonder therefore that this opera could scarcely be said to have found a public, and that its run was not what the management had anticipated. We think that the principal reason of this may be, the too great formality and uniformity that prevails throughout the airs, duets, &c., a uniformity from which the taste of the time did not allow the composer to depart. Almost all his airs seem cast in the same mould, principal passage, collateral passage, and then entire *reprise*, like the first allegro and other determined forms of the sonata.

DRESDEN.—The *Zelmira* of Rossini was lately produced at the theatre here for the first time, and was received with moderate applause. This opera is another proof, among the many, of how much Rossini is capable, with a due direction given to his talents, and had he been solicitous rather to consult the real wants of art, than to be flattered into self delusion by the empty applauses of his frivolous countrymen. Driven by circumstances to hasty composition, he has rummaged without scruple in the scores of all the masters both ancient and modern,

and appropriated as much to his own use as he found convenient ; and yet, in spite of all this, we must acknowledge that he possesses so ample a fund of his own, that he might with profit draw upon it if he would. The characters were well cast, and the piece excellently supported throughout.—At length *Jessonda* has been produced here. After the expectations that had been raised by the fame which this opera of the ingenious Spohr had obtained in Leipsic and Cassel, we were at length amply gratified, and are happy to bear testimony to the merits of this composer. The overture, the duet, chorus of soldiers, and air of the heroine, in the second act ; the chorus of priests and air, in the third act, were the parts that pleased the most. It has been observed of this opera that it possessed the peculiar merit of having made no attempts at effect, but sought to attain its object by simple and natural melody, enforced by appropriate accompaniments.

The other operas given have been Seyfried's *Der Waise und Der Mörder* (the Orphan and the Murderer), twice ; *Der Freischütz*, twice ; Weigl's *Nachtigall und Rabe* (Nightingale and Raven), once ; *Die Entführung aus dem Serail*, once ; *La Cantatrice Villane*, once ; *Tancredi*, three times ; *Ricciardo e Zoraide*, three times ; *La Gazza Ladra*, twice ; *La Giovantù d'Enrico V.*, by Morlacchi, four times ; *Margherita d'Anjou*, by Meyerbeer, twice ; and Rossini's *Italiana in Algeri*, twice.

WEIMAR.—The interests of music were never better consulted here than during the last season. It is with satisfaction we can state, that the utmost unanimity prevails between the members of the theatre and of the court chapel ; and under such circumstances, even from performers of moderate talents, much may with justice be expected ; how much more then from artists of the merit which this place has the good fortune to possess. The following list of the performances of the season will show that there has neither been any want of industrious exertion, nor of judgment in the selection of the pieces performed—Cimarosa's *Matrimonio Secreto*, twice ; *Libussa*, *Cenerentola*, *La Follie*, *Die Schwestern von Prag* (The Sisters of Prague), *Der Freischütz*, six times ; *Bär and Bassa*, twice ; *Der Wassertrager*, (the Watercarrier), *Das Neue Sonntagskind*, seven times ; *La Molinara*, *Tancredi*, twice ; *Die Zauberflöte*, twice ; *Jean de Paris*, *Count von Gleichen*, twice ; *Das Opferfest*, *Die Saalnixe*, the first time produced ; *Fanchon*, *Die Entführung aus dem Serail*, twice ; *Euryanthe*, three times ; *Ferdinand Cortez*, twice ; *Le Nozze di Figaro*, *Richard Cœur de Lion*, twice ; *La Clemenza di Tito*, *Den neuen Gutsherrn* (The New Tenant), *Camilla*, twice ; and *Don Giovanni*, once.

STUTGARD.—A new romantic opera in three acts, entitled *Der Bergkonig*, (The Mountain King), the music by Kapellmeister Lindpaintner, was produced here, and was very favourably received. The critics commend the composition as containing many very charming melodies, worthy of the former fame of this composer, of whom we have before had occasion to speak with praise. The overture was full of new and striking effects, and was loudly encored, as well as several of the airs and a chorus. The composer was called for at the conclusion of the opera and received the warm congratulations of the public. It cannot be denied that in the composition of this piece, both the poet and the composer had an eye to the *Freischütz*, and appear rather to have sought a resemblance in many parts than to have avoided it. The decorations and the mode in which it was brought out was creditable to the management.—The season has been a very active one. Besides the above new composition, we had *La Rappesaglia* of Kapellmeister Stuntz, three times ; *Mosè*, *La Neige*, Shubert's *Galeerensklaven* (Galley Slaves), *La Clemenza di Tito*, *Così fan Tutte*, *Otello*, *Cenerentola*, *La Dama Soldato*, *Schweitzer-familie*, *Verwandlungen* (The Metamorphosis), *Preciosa*, *Tancredi*, *Freischütz*, *Mark Antonio*, *Medea*, *Le Chaperon Rouge*, *Barbiere di Seviglia*, *Don Juan*, and *La Gazza Ladra*.—Another novelty here also was the revival of *Salomons Urtheil* (The Judgment of Solomon), the music by Quasins, which has long been laid on the shelf. The music is of a very masterly kind, though somewhat antiquated in its forms. Some of the marches contained in the piece are worthy of notice, as well as a prayer by Solomon, a movement full of touching effect, with an accompaniment by two violoncellos obbligati, which is very tender and soothing ; it was called for with great eagerness, and was repeated, together with some other of the pieces.—Among the numerous concerts given here, there is one which I cannot let pass without a particular notice. It was of an historical kind, arranged by Kapellmeister Lindpaintner, in which study and amusement were both happily consulted. It was in three parts, with four pieces in each part arranged as follows :

I.   Marenzio 1556. Lulli 1633. Handel 1685. Jomelli 1714.

II. Haydn, Mozart, Viotti, Winter.

III. Spohr, Rossini, K. M. v. Weber, Spontini.

This praiseworthy and judicious idea was very happily realized, and excited the liveliest interest in all the lovers of music. It is a practice which deserves imitation, and it would even seem advisable that in every concert the pieces should be arranged in their chronological series, by which the historical character of the music might be more exactly ascertained, and the different schools be preserved distinct from each other. Such an arrangement would not at all be found to interfere with variety, on the contrary, as in the instance before us, the contrast of pieces was much more striking than if they had been selected from contemporary composers only.

MUNICH.—In order to avoid a dry repetition of names, we shall in speaking of the theatrical peices of the season particularize those things only which can lay claim to some degree of novelty. The favourite opera *La Neige* was followed by *Le nouveau Rentier*, an opera by Boieldieu, which did not however long maintain its ground, and *Le count Armand*.—The Italian opera management was satisfied with giving no new peices during the greater part of the season, till at last came *L'Abitrator del Bosco*, the music by Pavesi. The plot of the piece is good and well sustained throughout — praise to which but few things of this kind can lay any pretension. The music is of a pleasing but not very characteristic kind, and one of the airs by Rubini was warmly encored. An air of Mozart was introduced in the piece, and stood like a vigorous plant among the sickly shrubs by which it was encompassed. Signora Schiasetti who is now regarded as the no-unworthy rival of the Pasta, has been replaced here by Signora Casagli, a very accomplished singer with a high soprano voice. A Signora Vecchi is also rising rapidly into reputation here ; she performed the character of *Tancredi* in a very effective manner, and showed a good school and great flexibility and sweetness of voice.—In church music, a great impression was made on the public by the performance of a grand posthumous mass of that extraordinary and eccentric man the Abbé Vogler. It was like all the compositions of this master, of a desultory kind, but yet full of such powerful effects as to excite general admiration.

BREMEN.—The last musical half year of this place has contained more of interest than any preceding year, so rapidly does the reign of music spread amongst us ; concert has followed concert, opera has succeeded opera, and numerous have been

the artists that have visited us in the course of their musical travels. The operas given have been the following : *Tancredi*, *Don Juan*, *Jean de Paris*, *Die drey Sultaninnen*, (The Three Sultanas) by Süsmeyer. *Il Sacrifixio Interrotto*, *Otello*, *Entführung aus dem Serail*, *Barbiere di Seviglia*, *Der Freischütz*, *Il Flauto Magico*, and *La Molinara*. *Euryanthe* was also well performed by a full orchestra in a concert given by the *Gesang-verein* (Song-society,) and called forth great and deserved applause. In sacred music we have had the *Tod Jesu* of Graun, Haydn's *Creation*, and Handel's *Messiah*, all under the direction of Professor Riems, whose zeal and devotion in the cause of the art deserve every praise.

MAGDEBURG.—Music, which since our grand festivity has rather languished among us, has resumed fresh vigour with the return of spring, and we have been visited by numerous artists of eminence, who have delighted the lovers of the art with many judicious selections of most of the favourite pieces of the day, as well in the concert room, as in sacred music. The favourite piece of the season, and which has been repeated in every direction, was Göethe's celebrated song *Kennst du das lande*, set to music by Mühling, which is a lovely melody, admirably expressive of the sentiments of this far-famed song. The accompaniment is very charming, and the effect of an echo produced by two horns quite magical. This song has already exercised the musical talents of numerous composers, and lastly of the great Beethoven himself*, but we do not hesitate to risk our opinion that M. Mühling has been of all the most successful in rendering the spirit and character of the poetry.

VENICE.—Since the *Crociato* of Meyerbeer the taste of our amateurs has been spoiled for music of a second-rate kind, but we cannot always enjoy the treat of such excellency. The *Crociato* was succeeded by an opera that pleased much in Milan, but which failed here altogether ; this was the *Elisa e Claudio* of Mercadante. It had been mended, altered, and patched with new pieces, but all would not do, it was played to empty benches, notwithstanding the excellent acting of that improving actress, Fanny Ayton, who may now be said to be naturalized in Italy, and who promises fair to be a distinguished ornament of our lyric theatre.

MILAN.—The latest novelty of our lyric boards has been a new semi-seria opera of Caraffa, entitled *Sonnabulo*, the success of which was but very moderate, though full of very pleasing things. But whence this want of success ? The cause is evident. Rossini in his numerous, indeed too numerous compositions, has exhausted every description of *crescendo*, *agitato*, *mosso*, *grave*, and all the family of dissonances, indeed every combination of which the seven musical notes are capable, and having done so, he constantly draws upon himself and is pardoned, as the materials are his own ; and, bad or good, he has founded a school of his own.

There is a peculiar fire and character about him even in his very errors, which redeem in a certain degree his failings, and make him everywhere a favourite. Not so with those who, led away by the taste of the times, imitate this great idol of the day. Reminiscences are pardoned in Rossini, but not in his imitators, and among these imitators is Caraffa. It is to be regretted that this composer should have suffered himself to sink into an imitator, as he has the materials of originality within him, and wants only confidence and industry to bring them into effect. There were parts in the present opera which proved this truth beyond the power of contradiction. We might instance, in particular a duet, by Galli and Pesaroni, and a Cavatina by the latter, in the first act, an air by the younger Galli and the finale of the second, each of which was marked by passages of distinctive merit, and yet which fell off at the close, and became

---

* For this Song see HARMONICON No. XXVI.

quite Rossinian. When will our composers quit this imitation of imitation, and return to nature and truth? Caraffa, we repeat, is a composer of talent, let him trust to his native energies, let him seek for that originality which will entitle him to the genuine esteem of his contemporaries, if not the applause of later days.

MILAN.—One of Cimarosa's comic operas has recently been revived here, entitled *Giannina e Bernardone.* This is a very pleasing composition, and its appearance was hailed with great delight; among the pieces that called down the greatest applause, were the celebrated quartetto of the first act, and a duet introduced in the second act, composed, as the report goes, by Generali. The comic character of Bernardone, was admirably presented by the Buffo Parlamagni, a performer who is rising rapidly into public favour, and his daughter gave the part of Giannina with great playfulness and good taste. These two may be called the real pillars of this opera, in which, on account of the weakness of the instrumentation, many alterations have been made; with what success and in what taste, we may be able to form some opinion, from the fact of the first flute-player having been allowed to introduce a little concerto of his own composition in the midst of the quartett above named, and which lengthens the piece nearly half an hour. This season, which has been under the management of Mr. Glossop, may not unaptly be termed the season of splendour and poverty. Splendour in regard to the singers, dancers, decorations, dresses, &c., but with respect to the music, poverty in the real sense of the word. Four old operas by Rossini, to which a temporary interest is contrived to be imparted by means of new bands on the stage, and a troop of horses to render the action more piquant; one still more out of date by Paccini, and a grand ballet, with music by the Neapolitan Maestro di capella, Luigi Carlini: *summa summarum*—all Rossini, over and over again. It is true that the flattering hope was held out to us in the early part of the season, that we might expect to enjoy the *Il Don Giovanni*, but, alas, the pleasing illusion was destroyed, and, most probably, for more reasons than one. As long as the singers are allowed to rule with absolute power the *repertoire* of the theatre, and will only show off on their own hobby horses, it is impossible that theatrical music can make any advancement. The evil should be checked in time. It were a consummation devoutly to be wished, that all directors of great theatres would act in unison, and regain that authority, without which neither the public can expect to enjoy good music, nor the meritorious composer to have his deserts made known. Last spring a Signor Galli, a well-known partizan of Rossini, was selected to fill the place of principal music director of the Scala. From such music directors, good Lord deliver us! However, I have the pleasure of being personally acquainted with Mr. Glossop, and know him to be a zealous votary of Mozart; and that it is his intention to bring out all the operas of Mozart, from the first he composed to his *Idomeneo*. It is to be hoped that no intrigues behind the curtain will prevent him from carying this laudable intention into effect.

PARIS, *April 28.*—After a long illness, which attacked the seat of the voice, M. Donzelli appeared last Tuesday in the character of *Otello*, in which he should be more moderate, he would then both sing and act better, without fatigue, and would produce a greater effect. The efforts which he made occasionally spoiled one of the sweetest voices we ever heard. The continual passion to which he abandoned himself, prevented him from being as impressive as he would be if he occasionally altered his manner. Garcia was miserably defective in the same way. It is by skilfully passing from calmness to agitation, from the most absolute dejection to the most terrible fury, that Talma produces so great an effect, he occasionally releases the spectators from their attention, and they pardon him for making them sometimes tremble, as he often leaves them to weep. But perhaps the faults which we here notice are more to be attributed to the peculiar circumstances in which M. Donzelli was placed on Tuesday, than to him. Perhaps he thought that his powers were not great enough, and in attempting to increase them, produced the exaggeration of which we complain. But let him be assured, that he is not one of those who fail from want of power. The spirit of justice dictates the above observations; we will now add, that as a singer M. Donzelli displays great skill, and as an actor a rare sensibility, and that he has not lost any of the reputation he obtained in Italy. That this is the public opinion was proved by frequent and unanimous applause. This was one of the best performances which we have seen for a long time, at this theatre. All the actors surpassed themselves, even including Madame Pasta, which would have seemed impossible.

PARIS.—The ancient quarrel between the *bâton* and the violin is not yet settled at the royal academy of music. After certain observations, launched forth in some of the journals, like pilot-balloons to discover which way the wind blows, it appears that, in the orchestra, the violin is to be reinvested with the government. It seems however to us, that the leader of a numerous musical army, will encounter great difficulties, if at the same time he must attend to the singers; to his own particular troops; to the score, and at the same time, draw those pure sounds from an instrument which ought alone to claim all his attention. But MM. Habenek and Valentino, whose talents are so well known, are the most proper persons to decide to which the sceptre belongs. We only wish to observe, that a general should direct his army, and rarely fight himself.

Signor Veluti, the celebrated-soprano, has set out for London. He is so little of an admirer of what the *Rossinistes* so much approve, and so unwilling to coalesce with the *gran Maestro*, that any engagement with him here was impossible.

M. Meyerbeer's opera, *Il Crociato in Egitto*, has now been in rehearsal more than four months at the *Théâtre Italien*, and its performance is again postponed till it is more fit for representation. We have had nothing new at the Italian Opera for nearly nine months!—The time is arrived that should give birth to something.

REVIEW OF MUSIC.

OLYMPIA, A GRAND OPERA, *in three Acts, by the* CHEVALIER SPONTINI. (Schlessinger, *Berlin.*)

THIS opera, which was first produced at Berlin, has excited so much attention in Germany, and indeed on the whole continent, that an analysis of the composition, and some remarks on its merits, have been asked for by many of our readers.

It was on the banks of the Sebeto that this composer's genius first displayed itself, and where he made so astonishing a progress in the science of harmony, that his fame filled not Italy alone, but spread throughout the whole of Europe. It was on the banks of the Seine that his genius became matured, and that he composed his two great works, *La Vestale* and *Ferdinand Cortez*, which filled all connoisseurs with admiration, who recognised in these classical compositions a legitimate disciple of the school of Gluck and Mozart, whose various qualities he has, in a great degree, combined.

The poem on which this music is built, is Voltaire's well-known tragedy of the same name.

The overture, which forms a real, characteristic prologue to the piece, commences with a grand *allegro marcato* and a warlike air; after a few chords which repeat the first motivo, a change takes place into an *andante religioso*, a melody full of effect, with which the composer concludes the grand chorus of the 7th scene.

This is succeeded by a repetition of the *allegro marcato*, in a well-marked crescendo. The bass movement is very striking, and from these four principal motivos, the whole grand overture is composed. Immediately after this follows the introduction, consisting of a chorus of people and warriors, which is very pompous and imposing.

From the joyous movement, a transition takes place to a *maestoso marcato*, containing the recitativo obligato of the high priest :

Maestoso marcato.

VIOLINI.

VIOLA. BASSI.

Then follows a march in B major, which announces the arrival of Cassander, Antigonus, and followers. In the same rhythm the two former sing a duet, in the middle of which is an andante with chorus. Then comes a prayer to the gods, in which the warriors swear unity and amity ; this is one of the most original pieces of the opera, and of very powerful effect.

The air of Cassander, to the words *O Souvenir épouvantable*, is in the grand style, and full of deep feeling. The manner in which he has painted in notes the feast of Alexander, and the treason that has prepared the poisoned cup, is full of vivid effects. While the wind instruments are made to express the joys of the festivity, the violins and violas designate by chromatic passages the treachery that is stealing upon the security of the banquet hour. Then follows the air of Olympia, *Près d'un amant si tendre*, in which the music bears the character of innocence and simplicity ; and in the melodious duet which follows, the sentiments of two tender lovers are admirably expressed. After this is a religious march, of a real touching character, which shows very powerfully the hand of a master, as may be observed from the following subject :

FLAUTI.

VIOLON-CELLO.

This music requires but to be heard to be duly appreciated. In this there is a triple chorus, wherein the ingenious composer has expressed three distinct sentiments; that of religion in the chorus of priests and priestesses, the tenderness of love in the hero and heroine of the piece, and the rage and fury which Antigonus harbours in his breast against the two lovers. The movement is admirable in its effect, and reminds one of the happiest efforts of Mozart.

After a feast with dances, the music of which is very original, Statira enters veiled, and sings an *andante sostenuto*, highly expressive of the deepest emotions of grief. The surprise, the alarm with which she surveys Cassander, the supposed murderer, could only be given with such truth and reality by the genius of a Spontini. The exclamation " Cassander!" followed by a burst of the orchestra; the chorus uttering in astonishment, *Quel cris d'horreur, et quels accents!* is productive of an effect altogether overwhelming. To harmony like this we may well apply the words spoken by the famous Scarlatti on another occasion ; " This indeed is music—music which shakes the soul, and will not let the most insensible sleep." The finale is also full of energy and mingled passion; and dull indeed must he be, who is not touched and aroused by its powerful appeal to his feelings.

We now come to the second act. The scene represents a gloomy vale, in which the solemn rites of the avenging Diana are celebrated. A propitiatory sacrifice commences; then a chorus of priests and priestesses, in F minor, with a very original accompaniment; the melodial effect is much heightened when the priestesses join in the major mode. This passage displays great knowledge of stage effect, and cannot fail to touch the feelings.

The scena of Statira, which is expressive of inconsolable grief, and the despair of the unhappy widow of Alexander, is a really classical and admirable composition, beginning with the words, *Oh deplorable mere, O Deux, quel et mon sort!* The ritornello in F minor already expresses her melancholy situation; the complaining wind instruments enter, and strengthen the single passages, according to the passion of the moment, whether of grief, of melancholy, or of despair. Then follows the air, *Implacables tyrans, ennemis de mon sang,* which is full of character and expression; the following is the motivo.

Allegro impetuoso.

There is throughout the whole of this movement, such power, originality, and truth, that the effect is truly electrical.

The third act commences with a ritornello, allegro agitato, expressive of the anxiety of Olympia, as to her destiny. The priest whom she consults, raises her hopes, and her sorrows are converted into joy; which is heightened into ecstacy, at the sight of her lover Cassander, who appears, sword in hand, prepared to enter the lists against the faithless Antigonus. Here is introduced a duet, which is not the least among the numerous beauties of the opera. The contrast of feelings exhibited on the scene, during the combat of Cassander and Antigonus without, is of the most masterly kind. This is a subject on which many composers have exercised their skill, but in our opinion, never has it been so successfully treated as in the present instance. Antigonus is vanquished, mortally wounded, and before he dies, reveals the innocence of Cassander; the whole of which is described in a *picture of tones* of the most powerful and expressive kind: the variety of modulation, the sudden change of time from quick to slow, the progression from the major to the minor mode,—all are replete with passion, and mark the hand of a great master. With what nature and truth is not the rage, despair, and finally relenting spirit, of the dying Antigonus depicted! This

scene is followed by another of a triumphal kind, in which a march of a very spirited and original character introduces Statira, who gives her hand to Cassander, whose innocence has been fully shewn. A general chorus, of a lofty character, terminates an opera which, assuredly, deserves to rank among the first productions of the age. It is not sufficient that this opera be heard to discover its merits: the score must be studied by the connoisseur, in order fully to develope the merit of the composition.—[*From a Correspondent.*]

AN AIR *for the* PIANO-FORTE, *the* VARIATIONS *composed for, and dedicated to* HER ROYAL HIGHNESS THE PRINCESS AUGUSTA, *by* GEORGE ONSLOW. Op. 28. (Boosey and Co. Holles Street.)

THE name of Onslow as a composer is not unknown to our readers; we have given some specimens of his talent in our collection, which, in themselves, are sufficient to prove him a man of real genius, and we shall endeavour to find other opportunities of corroborating the fact. The present is an elegant air, in A, *andante, quasi allegretto,* full of taste and feeling, with eight variations, which are not in the modern style of extravagant execution, but temperately written, practicable to moderately good performers, and pleasing to all. The first variation, —a succession of double notes, in thirds, for the left hand—is that which we prefer, the others are not so much distinguished by their novelty, or so striking in their effect. Mr. Onslow has in this work shewn little of that learning in harmony which most of his other compositions display; he has studied to be agreeable and accessible, and has succeeded. The price he has set upon it, four shillings for twelve pages, is surely higher than good policy would dictate; however it is well brought out, and worthy of the illustrious Personage to whom it is dedicated.

---

1. A Second DIVERTIMENTO *for the* PIANO-FORTE, *by* FERDINAND RIES. Op. 117. (Birchall and Co. 140, *New Bond Street.*)

2. NINTH FANTASIE *for the* PIANO-FORTE, *on the most favourite Themes in* Weber's opera, Der Freischütz, *composed by* FERD. RIES. Op. 131. (Boosey and Co. Holles Street.)

THE first of these opens with a larghetto in A flat,— the favourite key of the day,—in a charming manner, which leads to an allegro moderato in E flat, a very comprehensible motivo, well relieved, and modulated, not in an exceedingly original style, but with the judgment that Mr. Ries usually shows on all points where a practical knowledge of the science ought to be exhibited. This movement passes into a third, in the former key, in which the time is accelerated into an allegro molto, and thus terminates the piece with much brilliancy. This Divertimento may, as to the ability required in the execution of it, be classed with the air of Mr. Onslow: it is composed, not by any means for the vulgar, nor for the dull mechanical pedant, but for the many who have acquired a certain command of the instrument, and have a taste too good to be satisfied with common airs rendered more tiresome by a string of common variations.

The fantasie, No. 2, is rather more complicated in its structure than the preceding; which, indeed, from the nature of its themes, was to be expected; for it would be as difficult to put the music of the *Freischütz* into a simple form, as to reduce a diophantine problem to the rule of three. Mr. Ries has chosen the best and the most popular of the airs in Weber's grand opera for his present purpose, and woven them together with the address of an excellent master, and with a proper feeling for the original composer;—except in one instance, where he has transposed the fine cavatina into A, from A flat, the original and characteristic key, an act of barbarism of which we should not have supposed so good a musician, and so sensible a man could be capable. Surely he must, by this time, have learnt the difference between the contemplative sobriety of shade, and the gay brilliancy of sunshine; two things not more opposed than the key in which the author has written this exquisite air, and that into which the present adaptor has transferred it. This fantasie is long, but not difficult, and to those who are not already supplied with the *Freischütz* in many different shapes,—if any such are to be found,—it will prove a useful purchase.

THE ENIGMA, VARIATIONS *and* FANTASIA *on a favourite* Irish Air, *for the* PIANO-FORTE, *in the style of five* Eminent Artists; *composed, and dedicated to the originals,* by CIPRIANI POTTER. (Boosey and Co., *Holles Street;* Mechetti and Co., *Vienna.*)

NOT having the penetrating talent of an Œdipus, we have in vain essayed to solve this enigma, and to assign to the " five eminent artists" those variations in which their styles are imitated. We cannot help thinking that Mr. Potter, unknown to himself, has satirized the taste of some of the very modern piano-forte composers,—Hummel, Czerny, and such as delight in splitting demisemiquavers into halves and quarters; who study to render music difficult and repulsive in most of their compositions, and to load the market with crudities and impossibilities. Mr. Cramer has well exposed the same in his late work, the *Characteristic Diversions,* noticed in our last, and, with the able co-operation of the author of the *Enigma,* we hope that the desirable end of bringing into disrepute such glaring absurdities may finally be accomplished. There is a great deal of elegance in parts of this publication, which we cannot help thinking, are too good to be employed in a satire of the kind.

ALLEGRO DI BRAVURA, *composed for the* PIANO-FORTE *by* D. SCHLESINGER. Op. 1. (J. B. Cramer, Addison, and Beale, 201, *Regent Street.*)

THIS is the first of a series of *Allegri di Bravura,* (an affected title, by the bye,) and shews a vast deal of patient industry, if not of native genius. It is a study, meant to display not only what the author can write, but what he can play, and is, we presume, published rather with a view to making himself known, than with any hope of an extended and profitable sale. Mr. Schlesinger was a pupil of Mr. Ries, to whom he dedicates this, his first work; he therefore has bestowed labour in it commensurate to the respect which he feels for his master, and has paid his teacher the compliment of not only proving himself to be one of his disciples, but one of the most zealous, the most *ultra* that he can boast.

1. A DIVERTIMENTO, *in which is introduced* Mozart's *admired air,* The Manly Heart, *composed for the* PIANO-FORTE, *with an accompaniment for the* FLUTE, *(ad lib.)* by CAMILLE PLEYEL. (Cocks and Co. 20, *Princes-Street, Hanover Square.*)

2. INTRODUCTION *and* VARIATIONS *to the celebrated* Spanish Air, Cancion del Tragala, *for the* PIANO-FORTE, *composed by* J. Mollwo. (The Author, 6, *Charles Street, Soho Square.*)

3. THREE FANTASIAS *to a favourite Spanish Song, for the* PIANO-FORTE, *composed by the same. (The same.)*

To transpose from one very characteristic key to another altogether unanalogous to it, seems to be the prevailing fancy of modern arrangers. No sooner had we quitted Mr. Ries's Fantasie, than we took up M. Camille Pleyel's Divertimento, in which we find the beautiful duet in the *Zauberflöte,* in E flat, transposed into G, without the slightest excuse; for the whole piece might just as well have been in the former, as in the latter key, in respect to the author's general purposes, and infinitely better in point of effect. Passing by this great error in judgment, the present publication gives a pleasing instrumental form to Mozart's beautiful vocal duet,—a duet that many years ago, was sung everywhere and on all occasions, was chaunted in churches, danced at balls, marched to by regiments, harped, fiddled, and piped, till, like all popular music, it was so hacknied, so continually dinned into the ear, that it became actually tiresome, was laid aside, and is now almost forgotten, and ready to be re-produced as a new thing. M. Camille Pleyel has not made his adaptation of it difficult; it will suit most people, and the flute accompaniment is an agreeable addition to it.

Mr. Mollwo's variations, No. 2, are brilliant, and require an agile, neat performer. The air is national in its character, and animating. The *Introduzione* is a little after the school of Rossini, and ineffective.

The *Three Fantasias* on one theme are in rather a familiar style, and, with the exception of a few bars occasionally introduced, are very easy to perform.

1. INTRODUCTION *and* VARIATIONS, *with* FLUTE *Accompaniment,* (ad lib.) *on an admired Air composed by Mr.* Shield, *by* T. A. RAWLINGS. (Goulding and Co., *Soho-square.*)

2. DIVERTIMENTO, La belle Bergere, *for the* PIANO-FORTE, *with a* FLUTE *Accompaniment; composed by the Same.* (Clementi and Co., *Cheapside*).

THE first of these has a spirited introduction of three pages, leading to Mr. Shield's beautiful air, " From the white-blossomed sloe," upon which four variations are written, and a coda added; the whole executed in very good taste, except the fourth, *alla polacca,* a style that is as remote from the character of the melody, and from all the associations which a recollection of the words gives birth to, as a hornpipe is from a psalm tune. Let the performer then omit this, and the rest of the piece will be worth possessing, will suit nearly all practitioners, and please almost every hearer.

The second, a pastoral divertiment, is very simple in construction,—as from its title was to be expected,—and easy in execution. It is a harmless bagatelle, in all things except the price, which, considering the quantity and quality of the composition, has very little of pastoral moderation about it.

MOZART'S SIX GRAND SYMPHONIES *newly arranged for the* PIANO-FORTE, *with Accompaniments for a* FLUTE, VIOLIN, *and* VIOLONCELLO, *by* MUZIO CLEMENTI. No. 1. (Clementi & Co., 23, *Cheapside*).

IN our former numbers we have noticed two of Mozart's Symphonies arranged by Mr. Clementi, forming a part of the series of which this is numerically the first, though the third in the order of publication. The present is in E flat, the most popular of the six composed by the great master, and therefore, probably, the best. As it is evidently Mr. Clementi's design, in these arrangements, to lose as little as possible of the effects intended by the author, he has never sacrificed any notes of the score for the purpose of rendering his adaptation more easy to the performer: hence, this number, as also the former ones, requires a good piano-forte player, with a powerful hand; for considerable force and a wide stretch are demanded in almost every page of the symphony.

MOZART'S *celebrated* AIR, "Non piu andrai," *varied for the* PIANO-FORTE, *by* J. P. PIXIS. Op. 70. (Clementi & Co., *Cheapside*.)

THIS is an ingenious and pleasant amplification of the fine air in the opera of *Figaro*. A short introduction leads to the theme, and the latter is followed by five variations, the fourth of which is masterly, and the whole are brilliant, though very attainable by tolerably good players. M. Pixis is now one of the favorite composers and performers of the imperial city of Vienna : he seems to have good sense enough not to render all his publications impracticable to amateurs ; a merit of which many of his fellow citizens and brother professors cannot boast.

THE HEBREW FAMILY.

1. DUET, "Tell, pretty cousin," *Sung by Miss Tree and Miss Cawse, in the play of* The Hebrew Family ; *composed by* THOMAS ATTWOOD. (Clementi and Co., *Cheapside.*)
2. SONG, "When beauty courts the pensive mien," *Sung by Mr. Sinclair in the same. By the same.* (Clementi and Co.)
3. RECT. and AIR, *Sung by Miss Tree in the same. By the same.* (Clementi and Co.)
4. SONG, "Care! fly far," *Sung by Miss H. Cawse in the same. By the same.* (Clementi and Co.)

THE HEBREW FAMILY failed, as we stated in our last number; but its want of success is mainly attributable to the feebleness of the drama, and in some degree to the want of interest in part of the music introduced into it: though in justice to all the composers engaged in the work, we must say, that the weakness of the plot, and the deficiency in wit in the dialogue, were enough to render abortive any attempt in an auxiliary department

VOL. III.

to bolster up the play. Else could such compositions as these now before us have proved unavailing ?—We fearlessly assert, that, supported by a few other pieces of equal merit, they would have sufficed to keep alive, for a season, any drama possessing aught of the vital principle, on which they had been engrafted.

No. 1 is an animated conversation-piece; the motivo a very engaging melody, and the whole admirably well adapted for dramatic effect. No. 2 is a song in two movements, an andantino in G minor, followed by an allegretto in G major ; the latter in the polacca style, and a little à la Rossini, with some divisions in it for those who like

"———— To gargle in their throat a song."

No. 3 is what the Italians would call an *aria di bravura*, full of laborious passages, and not intended for ordinary amateurs to execute. It is an imitative song, very cleverly composed, and, though banished from the stage by the condemnation of the piece to which it belonged, likely to become a favourite in concerts. The introductory symphony is extremely good, and shewy, without being difficult for the accompanist.

No. 4 is in a very popular style, and, if our recollection does not deceive us, was called for a second time at the theatre the few nights that it was performed. An exceedingly promising little girl, Miss H. Cawse, gave great effect to this gay air by her manner of singing it, so that the chauntress and melody together excited vast applause. We should object to the accent of some of the words in this, if we thought that they had been intelligible to the composer, or were worthy of criticism : such poetry is quite common at present on the English stage, where nonsense verses are now uttered without exciting a shrug, and expected by the public as a matter of course.

---

1. DUET, "Busy, curious, thirsty fly," *sung by Mr. Braham and Mr. Lacy, composed by* J. EMDIN, ESQ. (Goulding, D'Almaine, and Co., 20, *Soho-square*.)
2. SONG, "The Sailor's Return," *by a* YOUNG LADY. (J. B. Cramer, Addison, and Beale, 201, *Regent-street*.)
3. SONG, "Fair Geraldine," (*in the Spanish style*,) *by* JOHN BARNETT. (*Published by the Same*.)
4. "Not a drum was heard," *set to music by* JOHN BARNETT. (Mayhew and Co., 17, *Old Bond-street*.)
5. BALLAD, "Still let me love," *the words by Lord Byron ; composed by* G. WARE. (Cramer and Co., 201, *Regent-street*.)

THE first of these, though recently published perhaps, must have been one of Mr. Embdin's early compositions, for it contains inaccuracies that do not appear in his later productions ; at the same time it shews invention, the soul of music, as of all the fine arts.

We wish much success to the young lady who has tried her strength in the second of these vocal pieces, but recommend her to read the words of her next song with more care. The fair composer has, by rests, broken what little connection there was in the words that she has set, and thereby actually given a new sense to some of the lines.

S

Mr. Barnett must have intended, in the third of the above, to exemplify bad accent: we scarcely ever saw so successful a lampoon on many of our modern vocal composers, as his present production exhibits.

No. 4 may also be considered as a didactic work, the object of which is, to illustrate the rules of harmony by shewing what is to be avoided. Here we have consecutive octaves in abundance, and sevenths rising to the octave to be resolved, &c. ; then by the arrangement of the rests, the verse is made to express the *burial*, not the *turning*, of the sod with the bayonets ; as well as other things, which the poet never dreamt of. All this will prove a good lesson to young composers; but as there is much feeling, and a laudable struggle at novelty in parts of the song, we regret that the examples of *errata* were not reserved for some other purpose.

Mr. Ware has studied the words of his ballad carefully, and expressed them with taste.

FOREIGN MUSICAL LITERATURE.

TRAITE SUR LA HAUTE COMPOSITION, by ANTONIE REICHA, Professor of Music in the Conservatore at Paris. 2 Vols.

THE work here given to the public is a continuation of the same author's works, entitled *Instructions sur l' Harmonie*, and *Traité sur la Melodie*. These three works form the most complete series of musical instruction that has yet appeared. As the well-earned reputation which M. Reicha enjoys, is sufficient to create an interest respecting any work proceeding from his pen, we shall give an outline of the contents of this work.

The first book treats of the *ecclesiastical modes*, and their accompaniment ; of the *severe style ;* of *double chorusses ;* of *harmony* according to the new style ; of a *new theory* of the solution of dissonances. The first book is an indispensible appendix to the science of practical harmony; it also serves as a natural introduction to the books that follow.

The second book treats of *counterpoint*, and of its employment.

The third book, of *imitations*, and *canons* of every kind.

The fourth, of the *fugue*, in all its kind, and modes of employment, as well in the old as in the modern school.

The fifth, of the various modes of accompanying the *vocal fugue* with the orchestra; of the various modes of treating the subject in fugues, of the *fugue phrasée*, of the employment of the matter of the fugue in the various kinds of musical productions.

The sixth and last book, treats of *musical ideas*, of the *poetry of music*, of the *exposition of the ideas*, of the *developement of the ideas so exposed*, of the *form* or *plan of musical compositions, most proper for the developement of the ideas*, and lastly of various objects which have not before been treated of in works on composition.

Besides the numerous examples introduced for the illustration of the text, there also occur in the course of the work more than fifty complete pieces of engraved music, in which all the subjects treated are practically represented. The clearness and precision with which all this is executed, bespeak the learning, diligence, and skill of the Professor. Though there already exist several works which treat of these various subjects, there is

none which combines them all in one point of view ; and what confers the highest value on the present publication is, that it brings under the eye of the composer all the practical knowledge of the present day, of which he stands in need. The question here is not to know the rules relating to counterpoint, in canons or particular imitations, but the more difficult and rare art of rendering such arts of counterpoint available.

ESSAI SUR LA MUSIQUE, *ses Fonctions dans les Mœurs et Sa veritable Expression, suivi d'une* BIBLIOGRA-PHIE MUSICALE, *par* M. P. LAHALLE. (Roussilon, Paris).

THIS work is divided into twelve chapters, of which the following are the titles : *Prolegomenes, Argument, les Faits, Suite et Résumé des Faits, Analyse, Systeme, Deduction des Doctrines Précédantes, ou la Musique Moderne, Genie National, Bornes de l'Art, la Poesie de la Musique, Quelques titres Secondaires, Epilogue.*

This short summary is sufficient to convey a clear idea of the nature of the present work, but the author himself has explained it more fully in his preface, which is written in a very sprightly style. He had at first entitled his work *Philosophie Musicale*, the real title, in fact, suited to the work : but he was prevailed upon by his bookseller to change the denomination, under the assurance that it was not suited to the public of our time. It is not improbable, however, that both the author and the bookseller had their reasons for this alteration.

This work neither treats of the principles of acoustics and mechanics as applied to the musical art, nor of the theories of harmony, counterpoint, composition, or accompaniment ; but merely of the nature of music, abstractedly considered, as forming no unimportant part of that great whole, to which the ancients gave the name of philosophy.

Combating such principles as are false, though sanctioned by time and fashion, the author re-ascends to causes, analyzes them with care in order to demonstrate their effects ; examines the nature of the passions in order to discover the expression which is suited to each ; considers the power of music in various points of view, both as insulated, as united with painting and poetry, and, in certain peculiar situations, as operating on both mind and body.

M. Lahalle has slightly touched upon the curious subject of the relations existing between music and painting, and from the talent discoverable in the little he has written on this point, we regret that he has not investigated the matter more deeply. It would not have been difficult for him to find strong arguments in favour of his system. It has been pretended that music like painting, is capable of presenting real imitations, and that insulated from every accessory, even that of words, and rendered by instruments only, which could present neither allusion nor local colouring, its real expression might be rendered comprehensible. This error is victoriously refuted by the author of the present work ; but there is an infinity of other pretended relations, which it might not have been less useful to combat and overthrow. For, with the exception of the progression of musical tones, which are perfectly similar to the progression of the tones of colours, painting and music do not appear to us to have any relation to each other.

On this subject an anecdote is related, which, if it be not a mere invention, tends less to prove the contrary of this proposition, than the originality, or the pitiable delusion of a celebrated painter. Mengs had long been at work upon a picture, the subject of which was the Annunciation. One day, a friend of his stole into his room unperceived, and found him singing away at a furious rate. Astonished at seeing him so merry within a very short period of his wife's death, to whom he was very tenderly attached, he inquired the reason of his merriment. Oh! pray do not interrupt me, said Mengs, I am singing a Sonata of Corelli, as I am desirous of painting my picture in his style.

Hence has arisen a system as absurd as it is ridiculous, and which its partisans can defend only by refusing to those who refute them, the blessing of being possessed of perfect organs, and a soul sufficiently sensible to perceive those finer gradations of shade, which, say they, it is more easy to feel than to express.

In his last chapter, M. Lahalle gives a very clear, though very precise résumé of his work, which, to sum up all in a word, is admirable both as to style and matter.

It is full of new views of his subject, which are presented with neatness and even elegance ; many assertions of the writers of the day are ably refuted, and yet with due modesty and reserve. There can be no doubt but that the public will justly appreciate the merits of this performance, to which we shall possibly have occasion hereafter to refer. The *Essai sur la Musique* is followed by a short treatise upon *Musical Bibliography*. The author has shewn great research, as well as discernment, in the manner in which he has arranged a list of references for the materials of a *General History of Music*. It were to be wished that M. Lahalle would fill up the outline he has given. We know no one who appears better qualified for the task, one of the greatest difficulties of which he has surmounted in the treatise before us. We trust that he will meet with due encouragement for writing the history of an art, the nature and essence of which he has explained with so much talent and good taste.

THE ANCIENT CONCERTS.

SIXTH CONCERT.—*Under the Direction of the Earl of Derby. Wednesday, April the 20th, 1825.*

ACT I.

Overture.	*(Otho.)*	Handel.
Song. Lord, remember David.	(Redemption.)	Handel.
Scene from the Oratorio of Joshua.		Handel.
Song and Chorus. Vengo a voi.		Guglielmi.
Concerto 2nd.		Corelli.
Duet. Here shall soft Charity repair.		Dr. Boyce.
Chorus. Te gloriosus apostolorum.	(Te Deum.)	Graun.
Song. Pious orgies.	(Judas Maccabeus.)	Handel.
Double Chorus. The Lord shall reign.	(Israel in Egypt.)	Handel.

ACT II.

Overture.	(Ariadne.)	Handel.
Selection from the Oratorio of Saul.		Handel.
Song. Dove sei.	(Rodelinda.)	Handel.
Concerto 4th.	(Opera 4th.)	Avison.
Song. I know that my Redeemer.	(Messiah.)	Handel.
Introduction and Chorus. Ye sons of Israel.	(Joshua.)	Handel.
Ode. Blest pair of Sirens.		J. S. Smith.
Double Chorus. From the consort.	(Solomon.)	Handel.

AFTER the pleasing overture to *Otho* (the gavotte by the way, was wofully dragged) Mr. Sapio favoured us with a song of

Handel, the best we think he has yet sung; and we were glad to find that his return to the theatrical boards had not made him unmindful of moderation in the orchestra of Hanover Square. The scene from Joshua was very sweetly opened by Miss Stephens, but we think, as a whole, that it is not very striking, especially with the omission of the only air which gave it variety and animation, viz., " Hark, 'tis the linnet!" Why the duet was preferred, which is really mere common place prettiness, we cannot imagine, unless Miss Stephens had a fancy to try whether the lower tones of her voice could not charm us equally with her high notes :—we should have been better pleased, we confess, to have seen and heard her *on the wing*. There was not much to boast of in what followed;—Mrs. Salmon did her best with it, but Guglielmi appears to have been attending throughout the song, as well as the chorus, more to the fiddles and basses than to the choir ; the voices are accompanying the instruments, rather than the instruments the voices.

Dr. Boyce's duet was a rich treat ;—a more beautiful composition of the kind we do not know, and Vaughan and Phillips sang it delightfully. There is no part of Graun's Te Deum that is not striking ; the selection from it this evening was not perhaps the best that could have been made, but it was very well performed ; the music is too light and airy for the loftiness of the subject. Miss Wilkinson's " Pious Orgies" was altogether a very affecting performance ;—she must, however, bear in mind, that animation is requisite to give the full effect to the most serious, as well as joyous airs. The marvellous chorus from Israel in Egypt closed the act well.

The magnificent chorusses that open the Oratorio of Saul, may be ranked among Handel's finest productions, and we should have been better pleased to have had them by themselves, without the " Daughters of the land," though led by Miss Stephens herself. " Welcome, welcome," to the tinkling of that *thing* which we believe is called a dulcimer, was miserably flimsy and ineffective, so immediately following the sublime Hallelujah!—Miss Wilkinson's " Dove Sei," was very chastely given ; it is exactly the description of air to which she should adhere, and in which she will always excel. " I know that my Redeemer," was most feelingly sung by Miss Stephens, and it is one of those divine melodies of Handel,—perhaps the most so of any,—that cannot too often be repeated. When we say that Stafford Smith's conception and execution in the setting of Milton's sublime ode, is equal to the poetry, we think he will be satisfied with our panegyric. It is, in truth, a very extraordinary composition—superior, of its kind, to any thing we have ever heard.

We do not absolutely quarrel with the winding up this time, but why not always the " tyrants" or something in which the trombones and double drums may be all in all ? Would that it *were so*.

SEVENTH CONCERT.—*Under the Direction of the Earl of Fortescue. Wednesday, April the 27th, 1825.*

ACT I.

Overture.	(Atalanta.)	Handel.
Funeral Anthem.		Handel.
Recit. When He is in His wrath.		
Song. When storms the proud.	(Athalia.)	Handel.
Chorus. Oh, Judah! boast.		
Recit. acc. Ah! perche.		
Song. Il caro ben.	(Perseo.)	Sacchini.
Chorus. May no rash intruder.	(Soloman.)	Handel.
Concerto 10th.		Corelli.
Recit. acc. Me, when the sun.		
Song. Hide me from day's.	Il Penseroso.	Handel.
Glee. As now the shades of eve.		Dr. Cooke.
Chorus. No more to Ammon's god.	(Jephthah.)	Handel.

ACT II.

Overture.		
Chorus. O the pleasures.		
Recit. 'Tis done!	(Acis & Galatea.)	Handel.
Song. Heart, the seat.		
Chorus. O God! who in thy heav'nly	(Joseph.)	Handel.

Recit. Brethren and friends.		
Recit. acc. O! thou bright orb. }	(Joshua.)	Handel.
Chorus. Behold! the list'ning sun.		
Concerto 12th.		Corelli.
Song. Verdi prati.	(Alcina.)	Handel.
Chorus. Venus laughing.	(Theodora.)	Handel.
Madrigal. Dissi all' amata mia.		Luca Marenzio.
Song. Oft on a plat.	(Il Pensieroso.)	Handel.
The Hundredth Psalm.		

THE spirited Overture that opened the present Concert, and in which Mr. Harper's unrivalled trumpet was brought most nobly into play, did not at all prepare us for the Funeral Anthem, all beautiful though it be: we should not like to be transported suddenly from a Military Review or a Coronation Procession to a gothic cemetery by moonlight—and yet, with a temper congenial to either scene, there is much to admire. "When storms the proud" is a fine song, but it is too much for Phillips—when he has to encounter the lower F or even G, he reminds us a little of what is vulgarly called snarling—his upper notes are, on the contrary, clear and mellow, his ear very correct, and he is always animated. We do not think that the songs generally chosen for Miss Wilkinson are chosen well; she has not yet acquired the finish, the polish, (if that be a better word) for the recitative and air of this evening. The Nightingale Chorus very properly introduced "Hide me from day's garish eye," which (for the truth we must speak) we have heard Miss Stephens sing very much better, and now that we have begun to scold, we must proceed to mention a fault she is too apt to commit, and that is her adding to, or substituting her own, for the composer's note in the melody she is warbling; few of Handel's slow airs will bear the slightest change or addition, and the delicious song under our present notice, the least of any.

We find the noble Director still enamoured of silence and shade; Dr. Cook's glee was charmingly sung, but Mr. Jenkinson's drumsticks in the chemosh chorus quickly dissolved the "magic spell:" the fine fugue was completely destroyed by them, and why?—Handel has, properly enough, introduced trumpets in his Oratorio Score, but we see nothing of Drums, common or kettle. We shall dispose of the Second Act without much comment, passing merrily over the "plains" as usual, and ——here however we must quit the cheerful mood, to express our deep regret at the continued indisposition (for we are loathe to attribute her frequent failures to any other cause) of Mrs. Salmon; but the song allotted for her this evening is in itself difficult, and full of those sustaining, as well as gliding passages which require great strength and compass of voice; Mrs. Salmon should have had a less arduous task assigned her.

Of the two chorusses which followed, the first is, beyond all comparison the best, though the "listening sun" has his merits, too. We don't like the musical pun that Handel has condescended to make by means of the trumpet and oboe each in its turn standing still,—and he seems to have been a little ashamed of it himself towards the close of the chorus, for the holding note is suddenly discontinued. Now, this, on the other hand, we do not approve; the idea once adopted, should have been preserved throughout. Miss Wilkinson's "Verdi Prati" was as it should be, but really we are as weary of it as the "laughing Venus" which followed:—and, by-the-by, we are not quite sure that the words of this heathen chorus are exactly consistent with ancient decorum.

Luca Marenzio's madrigal again—and what wonderful charm there is in the same, we are quite at a loss to discover. "Oft on a plat" is not so well calculated for Sapio's voice and style, he sang the song, however, with feeling; after which we made a hasty retreat to avoid being chorussed out by the 100th Psalm!

EIGHTH CONCERT.—Under the Direction of the Earl of Darnley. Wednesday, May the 4th, 1825.

ACT I.

Overture.	(Rodelinda.)	Handel.
Frost Scene.	(King Arthur.)	Purcell.
Duet. Qual anelante.		Marcello.
Glee. Deh! dove.		Dr. Cooke.

Recit. But who is he? }	(Joshua.)	Handel.
Song. Awful, pleasing Being.		
Chorus, O Father, whose almighty.	(Judas Macc.)	Handel.
Concerto 11th.	(Grand.)	Handel.
Selection from Alexander's Feast.		Handel.

ACT II.

Selection from Alexander's Feast.		Handel.
Song. Resta ingrata.	(Armida.)	Sacchini.
Concerto 11th.		Geminiani Corelli.
Recit. If I give thee.		
Song. Let me wander. }	(L'Allegro.)	Handel.
Chorus. And young and old.		
Round. Wind, gentle evergreen.		Dr. Hayes.
Selection from Israel in Egypt.		Handel.

UPON the eighth concert there is scarcely any thing to remark that we have not remarked before. The only performances in the first act are the "Deh dove" of Dr. Cooke, and the beautiful song from Joshua: of the first we cannot speak too highly: there is an interesting variety in the whole of this motet, and the parts are put together with that admirable skill in vocal arrangement for which this distinguished master in the English school is so justly celebrated. Miss Wilkinson did not exactly satisfy us in "Awful, pleasing being." It is well adapted to the quality of her voice, but there was no animation, and without animation, without the expression of a varied feeling in every bar, this fine invocation is totally lost.

We really think that Vaughan, as well as his admirable condjutor Mr. Lindley, have abundant merit in keeping their eyes open, and performing so well as they do, the "Lydian measures." How deadly sick of it they must both be!—

In the Second Act, Phillips was particularly happy in "Revenge, revenge!"—Since Bartleman's performance we have never heard it given with so much fire and feeling; the second part of this song, beginning "Behold a ghostly band" is eminently beautiful, but requires very finished singing. Miss Wilkinson pleased us more in Sacchini's air than we expected; it is a charming song, but it demands much force of expression; Miss W. has therefore the more merit in executing it so successfully. We have wandered by the "Hedge Row Elms" so often that we are really quite tired of the scene, varied and sweet though it be; Miss Stephens, we suspect, would as soon "wander" any where else, too. The Round was indeed a novelty!—though certainly not in its place; it is so beautiful in itself, and was so beautifully warbled by the Syrens Three that we must needs praise. And then—what a concluding chorus! In justice, however, to the worthy Ancients, they did not treat, with their usual bustle and inattention, the glorious Selection. —We saw no symptoms of either, till within a few bars of the very last chorus, when they relinquished, with evident regret, even so small a portion of this sublime composition.

NINTH CONCERT.—Under the direction of His Grace the Archbishop of York. Wednesday, May the 11th, 1825.

ACT I.

Concerto, 5th.	(Grand.)	Handel.
Psalm XVIII.	(St. Matthew's Tune.)	Dr. Croft.
Cantata. Nel chiuso centro.		Pergolesi.
Glee. 'Tis the last rose of summer.		(Irish Melody).
Song. Odi grand ombra.		De Majo.
Concerto, 1st.	(Opera 3d.)	Geminiani.
Recit. What blissful state! }	(Alex. Balus.)	Handel.
Duet. O what pleasures!		
Trio and Chorus. Sound the loud timbrel.		Avison.
Recit. acc. O worse than death. }	(Theodora.)	Handel.
Song. Angels, ever bright.		
Song. Vouchsafe, O Lord! }	(Te Deum.)	Handel.
Solo and Chorus. O Lord in thee.		

ACT II.

Overture.	(Sosarmes.)	Handel.
Glee. Mark'd you her eye		Spofforth.
Military Symphony. }	(K. Arthur.)	Purcell.
Song and Cho. Come if you dare.		

Song.	Ombre! Larve!	(Alceste.)	Gluck.
Duet.	Caro! Bella!	} (Julius Cæsar.)	Handel.
Chorus.	Ritorni ormai.		
Concerto.	(From Select Harmony.)		Handel.
Song.	Lascia amor.	(Orlando.)	Handel.
Chorus.	Let none despair.	(Hercules.)	Handel.
Glee.	If o'er the cruel tyrant Love.		Dr. Arne.
Recit.	Divine Andate!	} (Bonduca.)	Purcell.
Duet and Chorus.	To arms.		

WE do not like to pass by the Fifth grand Concerto quite unnoticed ; it was, as usual, very spiritedly performed, and as we cannot (hinc illæ lacrimæ !) be gratified, once in a way, with a Symphony of Haydn or Mozart, the grand and oboe Concertos of Handel ought to hold their station. Miss Wilkinson was not effective in " Nel chiuso Centro" and the succeeding air, and we are sorry to observe that there is, as yet, no perceptible improvement either in this young lady's voice or style: we equally regret to give another opinion which we have hitherto withheld, because we could not give it rashly ; her ear is decidedly defective ; and though it be an imperfection which care and constant practice may, and, we hope, *will* remedy ; yet care and constant practice will alone do it. If Miss Wilkinson be called upon at every Concert, to undertake those powerful and trying Italian recitatives which were laborious exertions even to the late Mrs. Billington, or Mrs. Salmon, in their best days, there is an end to *gradual* practice, and consequently gradual improvement, but *bavaura* is not Miss Wilkinson's style, and never will be.

The most reverend Director seemed determined to try of what . " stuff" (somewhat " perilous," too,) our little friend Vaughan was "made of : " "Odi grand ombra" would be a trying song for Braham, with all his power and flexibility ; it is certainly *not* a song calculated for Vaughan, yet he sung it chastely, and with spirit and feeling, and was most ably supported on the bassoon by Mr. Mackintosh, who, if he be not quite so finished a performer as his admirable predecessor, Holmes, follows very closely at his heels. We were not left exactly in a " blissful state" after "pleasures past expressing," we do not recollect any song or duet of our great Composer's, that has less claim to attention.—" Sound the loud Timbrel" is a mawkish tantararara piece of business in our opinion ;— however, it seemed to give great delight, and was received with vast applause.— What can we say about the " Angels ?"— Phillips's " Vouchsafe" was very charmingly sung ;— with feeling without vehemence, with correctness without sluggishness ;—in short, he reminded us of Bartleman, and what can we say more ? The heavenly chorus which followed would have completed our treat, if it had not been so dismally dragged.— Mr. Greatorex is, without any comparison, the ablest conductor of Choral Music, and of Handel's in particular, in this country ; we think, however, that he is too apt to lean towards the *adagio* in almost every composition of which he has the direction.

We do not remember to have heard the Overture in Sosarmes, often at these Concerts,—the fugue is very pleasing and animating.—Upon "Marked you her Eye," " Come, if you dare," and "Caro and Bella," we have really commented so often, that we are quite tired of the subject :—Purcell's inspiring strain produces a fine effect upon the stage, and he composed it for action, not for a Concert Room.—After the Concerto, the last movement of which is singularly airy and fanciful, Phillips outdid his usual outdoings in " Lascia amor."—It is in itself an admirable song, full of fire and point, and it was given by this very rising vocalist with correspondent excellence.—The song was followed by one of those chorusses which cannot be heard too often ;—It is what we should distinguish as one of Handel's *melodious* chorusses, and we are much indebted to Greatorex's *taste* and judgment for the occasional *breaks* into piano during the performance, which produce a most pleasing effect.—Often as we have heard the most animated, perhaps, of all our immortal Purcell's *bursts*, yet we can never hear it without delight, and it must be confessed that though the action which *should* accompany the music as in the former case be wanting, the effect produced by the Ancient Concert band is still inspiring in a very great degree.

PHILHARMONIC CONCERTS.

FIFTH CONCERT, *Monday, April 25, 1825.*

ACT I.

Sinfonia, No. 5		Haydn.
Scena ed Aria, " Tu consoli"		Garcia.
Quartetto, two Violins, Viola, and Violoncello, Messrs. Mori, Watts, Moralt, and Lindley		Mayseder.
Aria, Madame Caradori Allen, " Al più dolce, e caro oggetto" (L'Inganno felice)		Rossini.
Overture		A. Romberg.

ACT II.

Sinfonio in D		Beethoven.
Aria, Signor De Begnis, " Agitato da smania funesta" (I Fuorusciti)		Paër.
Fantasia, Violoncello Obbligato, Mr. Lindley		B Romberg.
Terzetto, " Quel sembjante, e quello sguardo," Madame Caradori Allen, Signor Garcia, and Signor De Begnis (L'Inganno felice)		Rossini.
Overture, Zaira		Winter.

Leader, Mr. Loder.—Conductor, Mr. Clementi.

HAYDN's symphony, the fifth of the twelve composed for Salomon's Concerts, is not so well known as most of this matchless set ; opening in a minor key it is less calculated to strike common ears than those which commence more brilliantly, but to the real amateur it is full of charms, which though they do not burst out into sudden splendour, unfold numberless beauties gradually, and permanently please. How delightful the andante of this piece, in E flat—how exquisitely beautiful the subject, and how skilfully managed. There is a noble simplicity in the whole of the composition that forms a fine and instructive contrast to some of the laboured productions of the present day. Beethoven's symphony, the first in Cianchettini's edition, one of his earlier works, is full of spirit and meaning, and was written when his mind was rich in new ideas, when he had not to seek for novelty in the regions of grotesque melody and harshly-combined harmony. We have here a larghetto in A, that speaks a language infinitely more intelligible than the majority of what are called vocal compositions have the power to express: the great elegance and beauty of this movement obtained a very general encore.

Romberg's and Winter's Overtures, both of a high order, have more than once been noticed in our pages. The quartett by Mayseder was admirably performed by Mori, and by the dancing gaiety of its manner produced an effect that pleased the majority of the audience. But this is a style of composition that has no longevity in it, and will expire nearly at the same time that the present tie of the cravat is exploded. Lindley's Fantasia was, in point of execution, a delicious enjoyment : where, if we were to lose this unrivalled performer, should we find his equal ? and, nevertheless, how are his talents rewarded ? the humblest Singer that appears at these concerts is more highly remunerated than the first Violoncellist in the world.

Of the vocal portion of this performance it is only possible to speak in terms of the strongest disapprobation, with the exception of a song by Paër. That the music of Rossini's very worst opera should be allowed a hearing at the Philharmonic Concerts, is a proof of neglect in those who selected or suffered it, that makes us tremble for the credit of the Society under whose name and sanction these performances take place. Not less reprehensible are the managers for allowing a singer to produce any composition of his own before an audience amongst which there are so many true connoisseurs. M. Garcia's music may suit very well a few fashionable parties, where Mozart, Haydn, and nearly all that is good, are excluded, but it is certainly not calculated for the Philharmonic Society.

We had the pleasure to see the venerable, but still vigorous, Clementi, conduct this concert. How this justly-celebrated composer must have enjoyed the symphonies !—How he must have laughed in his sleeve at the vocal music placed before him ! But he is a philosopher, and perhaps considered the one as a contrast to the other, as the highest and the lowest specimens of the art he has so long adorned.

SIXTH CONCERT, *Monday, May 9, 1825.*

Act I.

Sinfonia in D	*Mozart.*
Duetto, Signor Curioni and Signor De Begnis, "All' idea di quel metallo," (Il Barbiere di Seviglia)	*Rossini.*
Concerto Piano-forte, Mr. Peile	*Moscheles.*
Aria, Miss Paton, "Di piacer." (La Gazza Ladra)	*Rossini.*
Overture, "L'Alcalde de la Vega" (never performed in this country)	*Onslow.*

Act II.

Sinfonia, No. 8	*Haydn.*
Aria, Signor De Begnis, "Madamina," (Il Don Giovanni)	*Mozart.*
Septetto, for Violin, Viola, Violoncello, Double bass, Clarionet, Horn, and Bassoon, Messrs. Loder, Moralt, Lindley, Anfossi, Willman, Schuncke, and Mackintosh	*Beethoven.*
Duetto, Miss Paton and Signor Curioni, "Ricciardo che veggo," (Ricciardo e Zoraide)	*Rossini.*
Overture, Fidelio	*Beethoven.*

Leader, Mr. Kiesewetter.—Conductor, Mr. Potter.

THE symphonies in the sixth concert were, as usual, performed with a spirit and accuracy not to be found elsewhere; in England at least. That by Mozart is one of the most animated of his orchestral works. Haydn's, in B flat, written for Salomon's Concerts, is a perfect picture to the ear, if the expression may be allowed; the author intended it to represent to the imagination a village fête, the commencement of which is retarded by a thunder-storm: all are creeping about to find shelter; the tempest then abates, and the festivities begin. A second clap of thunder suspends the gaieties, and consternation again reigns: but the heavens soon recover their serenity, and the rural sports suffer no further interruption.

The overture to *L'Alcalde de la Vega*, a French opera now performing with great success at Paris, composed by George Onslow Esq., is a masterly composition, with strong claims to the merit of originality, and effective in performance. The author may be classed as one of the Beethoven school, the disciples whereof are remarkable for their ardour and constancy in pursuit of novelty; in the attainment of which, however, few are successful, the major part only finding enough of it to mystify themselves, puzzle their auditors, and bring some reproach on the style itself. But Mr. Onslow is a brilliant exception; he is a true genius, and, in all probability, would have discovered a path for himself, had not his illustrious precursor lived to point out the way. The overture to *Fidelio* is one of those very original works that invite troops of composers to attempt similar flights. We need not say how unequal to the adventurous task are the vast majority of those who soar so high.

Mr. Peile executed a concerto of Moscheles with ability; but this performance was a direct violation of one of the fundamental laws of this society. The concertos of Mozart and Beethoven, being orchestral pieces, are exceptions to the rule: and when a composer himself, whose high talent pleads something of an excuse, wishes to appear in one of his own works, a deviation from established usage may be palliated; but to allow any performer to break violently through a law of such vital importance to the well-being of the institution, is to shew, either great weakness in those who sway the sceptre, or the influence of favouritism. The septetto of Beethoven, one of the most ingenious and delightful of his works, was performed in a manner that almost reached perfection. The new horn, M. Shuneke, is a man of high talent, which he exhibited in this piece most distinctly.

The vocal part of this concert was perhaps a degree better than that of the fifth, though still exceedingly uninteresting. The first duet was well sung, but has been heard to satiety. The same must be observed of "*Madamina*." Miss Paton may be ambitious of singing Italian airs, but the ambition of the managers should prompt them to adapt the music to the talent of the singer. Miss Paton in an English ditty,—we include under this term Scotish and Irish,—is charming: in Italian she is a stranger in a foreign land, received kindly, but not at home.

THE DRAMA.

KING'S THEATRE.—The opera of *Pietro l'Eremita*, mentioned in our last, continued to draw full houses to this theatre,—though once it was actually obliged to be represented without Madame De Begnis, the *prima donna!*—till the arrival of Madame Pasta, who, after as much negociation with the French Government as would have sufficed for the exchange of a colony, suddenly appeared in London on Saturday, May 7th, and on the following Tuesday, performed the part of *Desdemona* in Rossini's *Otello*. The audience she drew, and the plaudits she received, fully justified the management of the Italian Opera, in the high terms granted to this admirable singer and actress: the house was filled with people of the upper ranks, who all seemed eager to testify their opinion of her merits. On Friday the 20th *La Semiramide*, by Rossini, was brought out; *Semiramide*, Madame Pasta; *Arsace*, Madame Vestris; *Idreno*, Signor Garcia; *Assur*, Signor Remorini; *Oroe*, Signor Porto, &c. This opera had been announced for the previous Tuesday, and was postponed, owing to some misunderstanding between Mr. Ebers and Madame Vestris, in which it did not appear that the latter was to blame. The public, with sufficient reason, resented the change of performance, and so much disapprobation was manifested at the drawing up of the curtain, that the performance was delayed upwards of an hour. The tumult was, however, at length appeased by the appearance of the Director on the Stage, who explained the cause of the substitution of *Otello* for *Semiramide*, and the former was allowed to proceed.

The spirit shewn by the public on this occasion will, we earnestly hope, operate as a broad hint to the *entrepreneur*, and act on the performers as a salutary lesson. The high prices paid to a few, two or three, of the latter, instead of warming their zeal in the service of the theatre, too often raise their notions of their personal importance, and seduce them into a neglect of their duty. It is said that one of the *Signori* engaged here, has exhibited most decided symptoms of insubordination throughout the whole season; and contributed much, by refusing to attend a rehearsal, to the delay in the production of *La Semiramide*. Why was he not shewn up at once? If the arrogance of such people do not receive some check, not only the public at large, but the body of Italian performers themselves will ultimately suffer. The great majority of these are respectable, well-conducted artists, who do their duty faithfully, and are as much respected in private society, as they are approved by the public; but one neglectful, refractory person getting amongst them, is always found to be sufficient to interrupt the proceedings of the concern, and throw a discredit on all engaged in it.

We have entered so much at large into the merits of Madame Pasta, and devoted so much space to the examination of *La Semiramide*, in former numbers, that it is quite unnecessary to add anything further upon either subject here. Before this present number is published, *Nina*, Paisiello's favourite opera, will have been performed for Madame Pasta's benefit, and also the *Tancredi* of Rossini. We shall notice both in our next.

DRURY LANE THEATRE.—A new Opera, under the name of *Faustus*, has been produced since our last; the music not by Spohr, but by Bishop and others. We must defer our notice of it till next month.

COVENT-GARDEN THEATRE.—Nothing new has appeared here during the last month; the Theatre fills without the aid of novelty.

THE
HARMONICON.

No. XXXI., July, 1825.

FOREIGN MUSICAL REPORT.

VIENNA.—Paer's celebrated opera *Agnese* was recently revived here, and the characters cast with great power, as will be seen by the following list: *Agnese*, Signora Fodor; *Uberto*, Signor Lablache; *Pasquale*, Signor Bassi; *Ernesto*, Signor Rubini. The piece was most admirably performed, and produced an effect here which we have rarely witnessed. Amateurs agree in ranking this opera among the best of Paer's compositions, and it presents difficulties in the execution which are not easily surmounted. This was followed by Rossini's *Bianca e Faliero*, which was produced for the first time in this place, but did not produce any great effect, from the circumstance that all the principal pieces were already familiar to the public through the medium of the Concert room.—At the *Theatre an der Wien*, the only novelty has been a new fairy opera entitled *Nuraddin, Prinz von Persien*, the music by Kapellmeister Riotte. The story is taken from that inexhaustible mine for the dramatic writer, the "Arabian Nights Entertainment," and with respect to the music, it is of a pleasing kind; several pieces were encored, particularly a duet and chorus, which possessed considerable beauty.

In sacred music, the pieces given this season have been Weigl's Oratorio *Das Leiden unsers Herrn Jesus Christus* (the Sufferings of Christ) and another on the same subject by August Berg, but the latter produced no great impression.

Grillparzer has produced his new Tragedy, entitled *Ottokar*, which has had considerable success; one of the booksellers of this place purchased the MS. from the author for the sum of 2000 florins, (about 200 pounds sterling.) We mention this tragedy on account of the overture composed to it by Seyfried, in which various Austrian national melodies were introduced with great effect, as well as other incidental vocal pieces of considerable merit.

BERLIN.—Our opera here is acquiring fresh force under the conduct of our celebrated Spontini, who perseveres in devoting unremitted attention to the reproduction of the classic music of the great masters of the old school. Gluck has revived in all his glory, and preparations are making to give the remainder of his master-pieces, which have so long laid upon the shelf. The latest among the other revivals has been Weigl's comic opera entitled *Die Uniform*, which has not appeared upon the scene above these twenty years. Its appearance was hailed with joy by all the lovers of genuine and characteristic music, and after several representations, it still continues to be heard with delight, and many of the pieces are constantly encored.—The novelty at the lesser theatre has been a piece entitled *Die Rückkehr des Kosaken* (the Return of the Cossacks), from the Russian of Prince Schachowskoi, which pleased by the agreeable character of some of the national airs with which it was enlivened. The other pieces that continue the great favourites of the season, though of very opposite characters and different degrees of merit, are Sacchini's *Œdipus auf Colonus*, Spontini's *Ferdinand Cortez*, and Rossini's *Tancredi*.

Among the concerts of the season, the most remarkable was that given for the benefit of the excellent institution of this place for decayed musicians. On this occasion, among other pieces of merit, was given Winter's celebrated Cantata entitled, *Timotheus, or the Power of Music*, and Romberg's *Lied von der Glocke* (Schiller's poem of the Bell.) The meeting was numerously attended; and the objects of the charity fully complied with.

There has appeared at this place a publication of an important nature in a musical point of view, entitled, *Versuche über die Schwingungen gespannter Saiten, besonders zur Bestimmung eines richerer Maasstabes für die Stimmung,* ("Essay on the Vibrations of distended Strings, particularly with a view to determine a more positive standard for Tuning") by E. J. Fischer, Professor of the Academy of Sciences. This volume contains many curious experiments and facts relative to acoustics, which will doubtless be found very useful in the formation of that desideratum of science, a complete theory of acoustics.

DRESDEN.—The opera season here commenced with Cherubini's favourite opera of *Faniska*, which to all the lovers of characteristic music always proves a high treat. The grand air in the second act created quite a furore; this air is a specimen of melody and accompaniment which the French composers of the present day would do well to imitate. The other operas were *Euryanthe, Otello, La Neige, Don Giovanni, Mercadante's Elisa e Claudio*, which, notwithstanding all its imitations, is full of pleasing effects, and indicates no mean talents; *L' Inganno felice*, and *Il Theobaldo ed Isolina* of Morlacchi.—A new German opera, the poetry by Kind, the author of the poem of *Der Freischütz*, the music by Marschner, was lately produced, entitled *Der Holzdieb* (the Wood-stealer,) which was attended with considerable success. It abounds with melodies and concerted pieces of no common character, and is likely to prove a favourite piece. *Jessonda* also still continues here in all the flourishing success of last season.—It has been remarked, that of late the musical world of this place has divided itself into two parties, the first of which is all for v. Weber and his music, and the other for that of the Italian school. The latter party is very powerful, and from the admirable manner in which the Italian operas are given, appears daily to acquire strength. This conflicting spirit may lead to results important to the musical interests of this place. We shall have occasion to revert to this subject before long.

LEIPSIC.—Since the last report which I gave you from this place, our music has been confined to concerts, vocal and instrumental. Among the former the Subscription Concerts were particularly strong, and in the two meetings the following master-pieces were given; Beethoven's Symphony in A major; Ditto of Feska No. 1, E flat major; by L. Spohr, No. 1, E flat major; by Beethoven No. 4, B major; Military Symphony by Haydn; by Mozart in E major; by Bernh. Romberg, E flat major; and Beethoven's Pastoral Symphony. In overtures—the Concert—Overture by B. Romberg; Overture of *Medea*, by Cherubini, do. by Sigis. Neukomm; Overture to *Jessonda*; Overture by Andr. Romberg; and Beethoven's Overture to *Coriolanus*.—On occasion of the Birth-day of the King of Saxony, an additional concert was given, in which were introduced the Jubilee Overture of C. M. v. Weber, and the solemn hymn *Domine Salvum fac*, by music-director Schultz.—In the vocal concerts, the chief pieces given were Schiller's *Die Macht des Gesanges* (the Power of Song,) set to music by Andr. Romberg; Scena, chorus and march from *Idomeneo*, Goëthe's *Meerestille*

und glücklich Fahrt, by Beethoven; *Polymelos Prussischer National Lieder*, by J. N. Hummel, an air from *Emma di Resburgo* by Meyerbeer, which was loudly encored, as was also an air from Nicolini's *Annibale'en Bithinia*, "Quanto l' empia fortuna."
——A concert was also given by M. Buschmann of Gotha, in which he introduced an instrument of his own invention, called the *Terpodion*, which singularly combines the effects of the piano with those of wind instruments. It is of great power, and admirably calculated for giving the various shades of the *crescendo* and *decrescendo* with a perfection of which perhaps no other instrument is capable. But there is an advantage which it possesses peculiar to itself, *viz.*, that the tones of sustained chords can at the same time be fully and distinctly given *staccati*, and be employed in conducting the melody. It is most particularly adapted to the chamber and the chapel, as choral and figural passages can be given on it with great ease and effect. We feel assured that if this instrument were once introduced into the musical world, a distinction to which it is well entitled, there would very soon be no want of compositions written expressly for its tenor and character. We understand that this ingenious mechanist intends to travel, in order to exhibit his invention.
——In sacred music we have had here, for the first time, Schneider's Oratorio, *Die Sündfluth*, (The Deluge) which was given for the benefit of the institution for poor and decayed musicians. It was well attended, and the object of the meeting amply fulfilled, but the music did not produce the entire effect which was anticipated.

PRAGUE.—This city continues to keep up its ancient musical reputation, and is always select in its list of stock pieces. The attraction of the season has been a Signora Arrigani, who made her debût in the character of Agatha, in *Der Freischutz*. Her voice is of a very superior quality; she shews the goodness of her school in every part of her singing, and bids fair to become a favourite singer. Weber's *Sylvana* was revived for the purpose of introducing another new singer, but the experiment did not succeed, indeed the recollection of the success which the famous Madame Grünbaum obtained in this piece, two seasons ago, rendered it impossible for any singer of second-rate talents to succeed after her. The operas that followed this were *La Clemenza di Tito, Il Don Giovanni, Tancredi, Il Barbiere di Seviglia* and *Le Nozze di Figaro.*—The genial opera of *Faust* was again brought upon our scene. This opera, independent of its high value as a product of art, possesses a particular interest for Prague, as having been produced here for the first time in 1816, under the auspices of the ingenious M. v. Weber. It had been finished in 1814, but had found obstacles for its production elsewhere, and at length had the good fortune to be ushered into the world on a stage that had witnessed some of the most splended triumphs of the genius of Mozart. In the very overture we recognise the hand of a master; it is a genuine preface to the dark tale of " Faust," and paints the internal workings of this terrible mind. A golden thread of melody runs through the whole texture of the piece, and binds the whole together with admirable art and beauty, while the harmony is of the purest kind, and the accompaniments full of character, energy, and originality. The painting of the varied situations of the piece are all of a masterly kind, and if defective in any thing, it is in the general good keeping. The music however presents many difficulties for the performer, and, in the present instance, we were sorry to see that these difficulties were not surmounted with the same spirit and facility as on former occasions; indeed many of the characters were so supported as to leave much to be wished for.—We are happy to announce that the Society for the promotion of music in Bohemia is making a rapid progress. We learn that thirty-nine new students have been admitted on its lists; viz, thirteen for the violin and viola, three for the violoncello, three for the contrabass, and four for each of the common wind instruments. One of the conditions of this institution is that the pupil must not be under ten years of age, and not above fifteen, and must have already acquired some elementary knowledge of music, but particularly of song, in order that some estimate may be formed of his musical talents.

BREMEN.—The lyric theatre of this place has unfortunately of late not kept pace with its former fame; various causes might be assigned for this falling off, but we shall not enter upon them at present. But few regular artists of merit belong to the operatic establishment, and the public have to depend for their musical enjoyments upon such travelling artists as circumstances bring to this place. The operas given at intervals have been *Der Freischutz, Le Nozze di Figaro, Der Schiffskapitain, Il Barbiere di Siviglia, Camilla, Das Waisonhause, Fanchon, Il Don Giovanni, Preciosa, Cenerentola*, and *La Clemenza di Tito;* a list which is wonderfully full considering the circumstances above alluded to, and which makes the defect still more to be lamented, as it is evident there is no want of encouragement on the part of the public.
A grand concert was given in the opera-house, in commemoration of the victory of Leipsig, on which occasion was given with considerable effect a new grand military symphony by Schmidt, entitled *Die Schlacht bey Grossbeeren* (the Battle of Grossbetren), of which the critics speak very favourably.

MAGDEBURG.—In a dramatic point of view, this place has, for some time past, been a perfect desert; but for this dearth of the lyric drama, ample atonement has been made by the numerous concerts that have been given here, unprecedented, as well in number, as in the richness displayed in the selection of pieces, among which were some of the highest and most difficult compositions of the present day, all of which were executed in a style in the highest degree creditable to the taste and industry of this city.

MILAN.—The new *Impress* and fresh company have caused a great attraction to the theatre here lately, but the charm of novelty once over, it was found that there was but little to gratify curiosity. The two new pieces were not successful; first, Taglioni's new Ballet, *Bianca di Messina*, and next Caraffa's new Opera, *Il Sonnambulo*, in which there was but little that was new, though much of old materials to which a gloss of novelty was attempted to be given. In fact, at the present moment, it is no little risk for a composer to write an opera, except indeed he be gifted with a richness and fertility of fancy far above the common. Rossini, as all the world knows, has brought to the highest finish the crescendo, the cabaletta, every species of cadence and modulation, every kind of variation and musical trickery, Janissary music, &c., and has made them the chief support of his operas—we say finish, because they all existed before his time. Now, if a composer has no other resources than these, the cry immediately is, that it is Rossini that has been plundered or imitated, a charge that has been confidently brought against Mosca and Generali, though it is well known that these composers trod out the path for Rossini, and that he has made free with their labours to an extent that is hardly credible. On the other hand, if recourse is had to other means, the composer may be sure beforehand that he will displease the greater proportion of the public. And yet, after all, we must contradict our first assertion, and be allowed to declare, that nothing, perhaps, is more easy than to compose an opera :—a little mechanical adroitness, some few piquant new melodies (no matter whether they be the property of others or not) to be wrought up into cabaletti and arias; here and there some beautiful passages of harmony from the German school, in order to give the piece an air of learning; contrasts without number, even at the expense of common sense; noise, in order to keep the hearer awake,—and you have a modern opera cut and dried.
The *Sonnambulo* of Caraffa possesses some pieces of a masterly kind, but which are not remarkable for their novelty. It was given only four times. The miserable nature of the plot, and the bombast of the poetry, may possibly have contributed to the ill success of the piece. The audante movement of the overture was much admired for its beauty and expression. In this opera Caraffa has taken the heroic resolution of doing away with the Janissary bands; if he should adhere to this determination in all his future operas, the *Sonnambulo* will form a striking epoch in the Italian opera of the present day ; not but what we should regret the effect this would have on a

host of musicians who would thereby be reduced to the workhouse.

After the fall of the *Sonnambulo* there was a *da capo*. *Semiramide* was most frequently given; the opera next in order was the *Donna del Lago*, which had a tolerable run; and then came the *Torvaldo e Dorliska*, which enjoyed a very short reign. The *Semiramide* pleases here above every thing; many of the Milanese critics consider it as the finest production of their favourite, and find it full of new and effective music; of which kind they particularly name the introduction and duet in the first act, and Galli's grand scena in the second. It would not, however be difficult to point out the sources from which Rossini has derived much of the music of this opera. A Venetian marquis, a great coguoscente, was lately heard to declare in company, that he had it from Rossini's own lips, that the music of the first brilliant chorus of the introduction was taken from a Hungarian ballet, entitled *Das Volksfest in Kisbar*, (the Rural Feast in Kisbar); it is also maintained that the Neapolitans, in the second act, is not Rossini's own : but all these trifles are pardoned and overlooked in the child of fortune.

FLORENCE. — *Teatro della Pergola.* The new opera, *Le due Duchesse*, by Celli, made a *fiasco ;* on which Mercadante's *Elisa e Claudio* was produced, and met with considerable applause. The *Crociato* of Meyerbeer also continues to be received with the same *furore* which its first appearance excited. This opera is in preparation for the theatres of Lucca, Padua, Leghorn, Bologna, Turin, and indeed of every theatre in Italy of any note.—Lord Burghersh gave at his own residence an opera composed by himself, entitled *Fedra*, which was performed by the principal singers of the opera. It was followed by a ball, and the whole entertainment was of the most splendid kind. The Florence Gazette says of the music, that it is composed *con isquisito gusto, e somma intelligenza dell' arte*, (with exquisite taste, and with the highest knowledge of the art.)

THE ANCIENT CONCERTS.

TENTH CONCERT.—*Under the Direction of the Earl Fortescue, Wednesday, May the 18th, 1825.*

ACT I.

Overture.	(*Pharamond.*)	Handel.
Quartet and Chorus. Then round about.		
Recit. Relieve thy champion.	} (*Sampson.*)	Handel.
Song. Return, O God of Hosts.		
Chorus. O filial piety !	(*Hercules*)	Handel.
Song. Sin not, O King.	(*Saul.*)	Handel.
Concerto 1st.	(*From his Solos.*)	Geminiani.
Madrigal. The silver swan.		Orlando Gibbons.
Recit. Sposa—Euridice!	} (*Orfeo*)	Gluck.
Song. Che farò		Gluck.
Solo and Quartet. In my distress.		Marcello.
Quartet and Chorus. We will rejoice.	*Anthem*	Dr. Croft.

ACT II.

Overture.	(*Semele.*)	Handel.
Motet. Qui pacem amatis.		Steffani.
Chorus. Juravit Dominus.		Leo.
Recit. Vieni.	}	
Duetto. Alma mia.	} (*Admetus.*)	Handel.
Chorus. The people shall hear.	(*Israel in Egypt.*)	Handel.
Recit. acc. Crudele !	}	
Song. Ho perduto.	}	Paisiello.
Chorus. Envy, eldest born.	(*Saul.*)	Handel.
Concerto 5th.	(*Op. Second.*)	Martini.
Chorus. Avert these omens.	(*Semele.*)	Handel.
Madrigal. Stay, Corydon.		Wilbye.
Song. Praise the Lord.	(*Esther.*)	Handel.
Anthem. Sing unto God.		Dr. Croft.

WITH Lord Fortescue's last selection we were a little disposed to quarrel ; but, for the present, we cannot sufficiently express our gratitude. It was, indeed, a rich treat, and nothing maukish

to interrupt our satisfaction from the beginning to the end.— And yet we are obliged to speak a sad truth ;—" A very heavy Concert" was the general whisper, and a terrible yawning was succeeded by a very perceptible *yearning* after "O, Nanny !" or some such delicious *morceau* as a little relief from *ennui.*—At this rate the ancient concert never can be the sterling entertainment it once was under the superintendence of our late good old King, and will dwindle, at last, into "The ladies' amusement," as some facetious editor has entitled a collection of pretty glees.

The spirited overture to Pharamond was followed by that exquisite chorus from Sampson, which we have lauded over and over again, and are still pleased to laud. Miss Wilkinson in "Return O God of Hosts" was admirable !—These are the songs for her, and the feeling manner in which she sang was, to us at least, a convincing proof that she felt confident in her powers to do this fine air justice. Then followed a noble chorus from Hercules, to which, when the chorus singers are more perfect, justice may be rendered ;—they were in a sad state of *égarement* this evening. We confess to a little of the *sombre* in "Sin not, O King" and the "Silver Swan" coming so immediately after ;—but perhaps it was for the sake of contrast, and to introduce Madame Pasta with more splendid effect. —It must be confessed that, in some parts of her performance, this fine singer exceeded our most sanguine expectations ; but in others she was much too declamatory, and seemed entirely to have lost sight of the concert-room: when she descended from such exalted regions, and fell into tender warbling, nothing could be more delightful.

We were not very much interested in Marcello's Quartet, but the glorious chorus which followed made ample amends.— We do not recollect to have heard it performed before, and it was creditable to all parties concerned that it was so admirably sustained throughout.—We regret that any portion of this magnificent anthem was omitted ; the trio that follows the first movement is beautiful and impressive, and the concluding chorus "Some put their trust in chariots," whilst it is animated in the highest degree, is strictly devotional, and excites those sentiments of gratitude to the divine giver of all good which the distinguished composer intended.

The second act opened with the strikingly original overture to Semele, and the old and deserved favourite "Qui Pacem Amatis."—Leo's "Juravit Dominus" was a novelty, and a magnificent one ; at the close, however, there is a blot which turns in an instant what had been the ne plus ultra of sublimity, into downright pantomime. We allude to a little jiggish symphony which is brought in during a pause of the voices.—It is the capering of Punch, interrupting the solemn march and rapt emotion of the tragic muse ; but such anomalies are not unfrequent, we grieve to say, among the Italian composers of church music, even the old ones.

The Duet from Admetus was another novelty, and one of great character and originality, and it was moreover exceedingly well sung.—Then followed the *heaviest* of the *heavy* chorusses of Handel (according to ancient concert language in general) "The People shall hear." A composition which for imagination and contrivance, and for characteristic sublimity, the great master has never excelled, and very, very rarely equalled !—

Madame Pasta's second song was splendid indeed ! Nothing could be more perfect than her style of singing it, and the admirable management of her voice. This time, too, she recollected the concert-room :—Paisiello had never greater justice done to his beautiful music. "Envy," the Concerto, and "Avert these Omens," were, as usual, effectively performed, and Wilbye's Madrigal would have *told* (as the expression is) better, had the soprano voices been less shrill.—Fair ladies should recollect that in glee and madrigal singing, the tone should be so subdued as to mingle with, not overreach the other vocal parts, so that the *whole* may be in keeping.—The more mellow tones of a boy suit always best in glees. Miss Stephens might have thrown a little more animation in "Praise the Lord" without spoiling it ; it is not a song exactly calculated for her.

"Sing unto God" and "Avert these Omens" should have changed places and then this admirable selection (dull though the ancients proclaimed it) would have been complete.

ELEVENTH CONCERT.—*Under the direction of the Earl of Derby, Wednesday, May the 25th, 1825.*

ACT I.

Overture 7th, and March.		*Martini.*
Canzonet. Haste, my Nannette.		*Travers.*
Recit. acc. The good we wish for. }	(*Samson.*)	*Handel.*
Song. Thy glorious deeds. }		
Musette.	(*Concerto 6th, Grand.*)	*Handel.*
Song. Vado ben spesso.		*Salvator Rosa.*
Chorus. Lift up your heads.	(*Messiah.*)	*Handel.*
Recit. acc. Tranquillo. }	(*Romeo e Giulietta.*)	*Guglielmi.*
Song. Ombra adorata. }		
Portuguese Hymn. Adeste fideles.		
Song. O beauteous Queen.	(*Esther.*)	*Handel.*
Double Chorus. Immortal Lord.	(*Deborah.*)	*Handel.*

ACT II.

Overture.	(*Hercules.*)	*Handel.*
Duet and Chorus. Time has not thinn'd.		*Jackson.*
Recit. acc. Berenice ! ove sei ? }	(*Lucio Vero.*)	*Jomelli.*
Song. Ombra che pallida. }		
Quartet and Chorus. Saints and angels.		*Wolf.*
Concerto 2nd.		*Martini.*
Song. Pleasure, my former.	(*Time and Truth.*)	*Handel.*
Madrigal. Let me careless.		*Linley.*
Recit. acc. Ye verdant. }	(*Acis and Galatea.*)	*Handel.*
Song. Hush, ye pretty. }		
Verse and Chorus. God save the King.		

MARTINI'S fine Concerto did not well introduce "Haste my Nannette"—we were however right glad to see our old friend Bellamy again : there are some things, yet, in which his general good taste and experience give him the pre-eminence, and he has a just claim still to the notice and patronage of the directors of the ancient concerts, and the public in general. Phillips's arduous song from Samson had been better placed elsewhere, it looked a little like setting him, as it is termed, against his able competitor. We cannot say much in praise of Salvator Rosa's air; it was prettily sung by Miss Wilkinson, but nevertheless ineffective. "Lift up your heads" requires no comment as to the composition itself, but we got no relief from it. A worse song for Sapio than "O beauteous Queen" could not have been selected —it is altogether unfit for him:—what there is pretty in the song requires the most delicate singing to divest it of insipidity, and Vaughan is the only singer to give it the least effect. "Immortal Lord" we must not overlook, but we have nothing new to say about it.

The opening of the second act with the admirable overture in Hercules, did very little towards reconciling us to the absurdity that followed. Madame Pasta's "Berenice" was not what the actors say of a successful Drama, *a hit,*—she sang the softer parts well, and indeed, on all occasions, when this fine singer indulges us with her subdued tones, they are exquisitely beautiful. In the present difficult *scena* and *aria,* Madame Pasta appeared to sing without confidence in herself;—she wanted the stage and the appropriate action, and, to say the truth, this fine invocation, without these helps, must lose much of its effect, be the performer whom she may. Mr. Wolf's "Funeral Anthem" was a very *lackadaisical* affair, and we could wish to *bury* it in oblivion this time forth and for evermore!—We had a *nightcappy* thing of this worthy's last year, and hoped we had got quit of him.—Now really the composer must have had good nature at least in his composition who could sit down to set the following words.

> Saints and Angels joined in concert,
> Sing the praises of the Lamb :
> While the blissful seats of Heaven
> Sweetly echo *with* his *name.*

Name and *lamb* make the most ingenious rhyme that ever met our eyes or ears.—Poor Vaughan !—How glad he would be to be able to say, for the last time, "Thee, Pleasure, now *I leave*" —but we would rather hear him sing *that,* than not sing at all.

We wish Miss Travis would not think quite so much of her own sweet pipe the next time she favours us with "Let me careless"—she quite overwhelmed the other singers, and we know of no composition that requires more a distinct blending of the voices than the charming madrigal in question ; a composition which, in itself, is sufficient to rescue the English school from the reproach of want of genius.

There was such a sudden move (we trust for *loyalty's* sake not to hurry away from the concluding chorus) when Miss Stephens began her song, that she was scarcely audible. What can we say of "Hush, ye pretty warbling quire?"—we entertain too sincere a respect for the good old Earl, the director of the night, to say that we were dissatisfied with his selection—but we suspect that he would have given us a much better one, had he been left to judge and determine for himself.

TWELFTH CONCERT. — *Under the Direction of the Earl of Darnley, Wednesday, June the 1st, 1825.*

ACT I.

Overture.		
Recit. This day a solemn. }	(*Samson.*)	*Handel.*
Chorus. Awake the trumpet's }		
Duet. Dunque, mio ben.	(*Romeo e Giulietta.*)	*Zingarelli.*
Recit. acc. Foile è colui. }	*Ætius.*	*Handel.*
Song. Nasce al bosco. }		
Glee. Swiftly from the mountain's brow.		*Webbe.*
Chorus. Populous cities.	(*L'Allegro.*)	*Handel.*
Concerto 1st.		*Martini.*
Chorus. The depths have. }	*Israel in Egypt.*	*Handel.*
Double Chorus. Thy right hand. }		
Recit. acc. Grazie vi rendo. }		*Guglielmi.*
Song. A compir. }		
Coronation Anthem. The king shall.		*Handel.*

ACT II.

Music in Macbeth.		*M. Locke.*
Quartetto. Tacite ombre.	(*Il Cid.*)	*Sacchini.*
Madrigal. Will you know my mistress' face ?		*Lawes.*
Recit. Chi per pieta. }	(*Sacrificio d' Abramo.*)	*Cimarosa.*
Song. Deh parlate. }		
Luther's Hymn.		
Selection from Saul.		*Handel.*

WE would willingly say of the twelfth, and last, concert, though last not least, but our conscience forbids,—what the performance *might* have been is another affair, but more of that anon.

The opening of Samson will always be delightful to those who are fond of characteristic music, and "Awake the trumpet's lofty sound," is one of the few heathen chorusses which is sufficiently airy and pointed to stand by itself. The duet between Madame Pasta and Miss Wilkinson did not particularly strike us ;—Zingarelli has great sweetness and taste in his compositions, generally, but we do not discover in them much imagination. Phillips's "Nasce al bosco" was a rich treat—he sang it with spirit, feeling, and clearness ;—but it is impossible for a singer of any pretensions, and who has a nerve in his system, not to give something like interest to this incomparable air. Miss Travis sang better this evening in the glee—her voice mingled much sweeter with the others. The poet of "Swiftly," is greatly indebted to the musician for one of the most happy adaptations we ever heard ; the lovely landscape presented to our imaginations owes as much to the lyre of the one as to the pencil of the other. "Populous cities," formed a good contrast, certainly, but it is the least effective part of L'Allegro, which is, perhaps, altogether, the most delightful effort of Handel's genius. The first Concerto of Martini we must not pass over without comment :—It possesses great originality, and is conducted throughout in a most masterly manner: Cramer played with spirit and feeling, but he *will* get on.—He reminds us of Johnson's line,

> "Panting time toils after him in vain."

We have heard the chorus from Israel in Egypt better sung, but, truth to say, the latter part of it, where the voices and instruments clash together without any leading symphony, is almost an impossible performance; Rossini himself would own to a little difficulty in it. We cannot compliment Mad. Pasta very much in her song from Semiramide, yet we have

little doubt of her pleasing us in it on the Opera stage.—
She seems herself to feel her inefficiency in the orchestra, and
deprived of the assistance of action:—we, therefore, regret
that Italian scenas have not been given, that are not so familiar
to her, and less of a dramatic cast; she would perform them
much more to her own satisfaction, and, we doubt not, to that
of the public.

"The King shall rejoice," was all heaven till *Mr. Jenkinson*
burst upon us like Zamiel in the Freischütz!—We cannot
deny that Handel occasionally introduced these hateful *Tym-
panums* in his Anthems, but then the subject has been triumph
and victory!—In the most strikingly harmonious of his religious chorusses, he invariably avoids them,—so do we not at
the Ancient Concerts, unhappily.

The music in Macbeth, which opened the second act, was
performed in a very feeble, and even slovenly manner, and
who can wonder at it?—This *witchery* seems to *haunt* the
director of the evening more than any other of his noble colleagues, for we have observed that Lord Darnley never passes
over the season without it. Would to heaven he would grant
us a respite, if only for once! Sacchini's Quartetto would have
pleased more had Madame Pasta flourished less; her shake is
by no means perfect, and we would advise her by practice to
improve it; this is a beautiful composition, and was, altogether,
very sweetly sustained. A pretty old madrigal, (or rather
glee, for it does not belong to the madrigalian school) by
Henry Lawes, whom Milton has immortalized, pleased us
very much, though there is nothing particularly striking in it;
we recognised that pure English style which was afterwards
carried to such perfection by Boyce, Arne, Hayes, &c., but
which, alas! (so far at least as the public is concerned) has
sunk under the weight of the foreign schools,—" never," we
fear, " to rise again."—England is the only nation in Europe
that has trod her national music under foot, and if she continue to neglect and degrade it, the very names of the great
masters we have mentioned, nay, even of Purcell himself, will
in twenty years be forgotten! We think Madame Pasta sang
" Deh parlate" rather fast:—her recitative was by far the
most striking part of her performance. Luther's hymn, as it is
called, should have been sung by Vaughan—for Miss Wilkinson it was a most unfortunate choice:—we mean not to dis-
parage the young lady's talents; in tender and solemn airs she
is impressive in a great degree, but where every thing, as in
the present instance, depends upon force and animation, she is
very inadequate to the task. When the chorusses of Handel
come before us *once* during the season, we endeavour to give
them a notice that we have not precisely given before; but
really when they cross us a second time, we must perforce be
silent. " Gird on thy sword" had not, however, been performed before. The first part is magnificent—the winding up
in triple time we ever did, and always shall, think a sad falling
off; we were not sorry that it came in at the close.

And now, before we take our leave, we must be permitted
to remark upon a circumstance connected with the present
concert, which makes us almost entirely despair of any change
in the performances, generally, for the better. We were informed by an intelligent friend, a subscriber, a day or two
ago, that he attended this last concert, giving up a particular
engagement elsewhere, purposely to enjoy a *repetition* of two
pieces that had struck him with no less surprise than gratification at the rehearsal,—viz., the beautiful air from Semele,
" O sleep," to which Greatorex had, with a taste and skill
never more successfully displayed, added a Violoncello accompaniment for Lindley, and which produced a soothing and
delicious effect;—and a chorus of Marcello, beginning " Be
thou exalted," prepared for the orchestra by the same excellent
musician, of such variety of merit as to make it difficult where
to give a preference, but closing with a fugue that Handel
himself has rarely ever equalled!—" These delightful novelties,"
sighed my friend, " I went on purpose to hear again,—but, lo!
they had been cut out, as *heavy* and *stupid!!*"

We do not feel ourselves authorized to call in question the
fiat of the noble director in this matter; the ancient concert is
not exactly a public one, and we are well aware that it can
only be enjoyed through the medium of the most respectable

introduction; but this very circumstance should, we humbly
conceive, render some little attention to the subscribers' entertainment the more necessary on the part of the directors;
and make them consult their feelings generally, rather than
the will and pleasure of a *few*, because on the level of rank
with themselves. We can venture respectfully to assure them,
that eight subscribers at least out of ten would equally regret
with ourselves the omissions alluded to, and who equally
deplore the close of another season without a ray of hope
afforded them of change; and who sadly predict that the
spring of 1826 will bring with it the same *luckless Nannies*,
the same *Shepherds* and *Canzonet chorusses*, that cruellest of
all *cruel Tyrants*, Love, and—*finis coronat opus*—Mr. Jenkinson's double drums, with, we fear, new *Kettles*.
Clio.

PHILHARMONIC CONCERTS.

SEVENTH CONCERT, *Monday, May 23, 1825.*

ACT I.

Sinfonia, Eroica	Beethoven.
Aria, Madame Caradori Allan, " *Dammi un segnale.*"	Mosca.
Fantasia, Harp, Mr. La Barre	La Barre.
Aria, Madame Pasta, " *Ave Maria*," accompanied on the Corno Inglese, by M. Vogt	Cherubini.
Overture, Lodoïska	Cherubini.

ACT II.

Sinfonia, No. 9	Haydn.
Aria, Madame Pasta, " *Tu ch' accendi*," (*Tancredi*)	Rossini.
Quartetto, two Violins, Viola, and Violoncello, Messrs. Kiesewetter, Oury, Moralt, and Lindley, (by parti- cular desire)	Mayseder.
Duetto, Madame Caradori Allan and Mr. Phillips, " *Dunque io son*," (*Il Barbiere di Seviglia*)	Rossini.
Overture, Egmont	Beethoven.

Leader, Mr. Spagnoletti.—Conductor, Mr. Potter.

BEETHOVEN's Heroic Symphony, composed, he tells us, *per
celebrare la morte d' un' eroe*, is a very masterly work, though
much too long for public performance. The *Marcia Funèbre*,
in C minor, beginning—

is a very fine specimen of the genius of this highly-gifted musician, and is appreciated as it deserves by the frequenters of the
Philharmonic Concerts. It is just as suggestive—or imitative,
as the metaphysical writers express themselves—as music is capable of being, the dying conclusion particularly, which always
affects the audience powerfully. Haydn's symphony, in B flat,
the ninth of the set composed for Salomon's Concerts, has never
been so popular as most of the twelve, and is therefore something like a novelty when performed. But the true connoisseur
discovers in it abundant proofs of genius, and striking beauties
in every movement. What instrumental piece offers a more intelligible and charming melody than the adagio—a more original
subject than the minuetto—or a more brilliant motivo than the
finale?

Cherubini's Overture to Lodoïska is more scientific than that
to Anacreon, we admit, but it shews less of genius: nevertheless it is a very fine production, and sufficient in itself to establish the reputation of a composer. The *Egmont* of Beethoven
is a sublime work, which we have more than once mentioned in
these columns.

Madame Caradori's Aria was worthy of the place: she obtained great applause for her manner of singing it. Her duet,
by Rossini, was well executed, but badly chosen. Why perform
at a concert a piece that is in constant use at the theatre, where,

having all the advantages of scenic effect, it must be heard in a more perfect manner? The aria, *Ave Maria*, good as it is, and judiciously as it was sung by Madame Pasta, produced but little sensation. Why was this?—We were amongst those on whom it made no impression. Her *Tu ch' accendi* was, as usual, quite delightful; but—for we seem to be in an interrogative humour—does this style of singing it accord with the author's intention, and will it thus continue to please?

M. La Barre is the best harp-player now in England. He understands the character of his instrument, and brings out of it every good quality that it possesses, without straining it beyond its power, and converting all its sweetness and expression into hardness of twang and jarring noise. The quartetto of Mayseder is a mixture of good and evil; much bad, but prevailing taste, with a little of what will always be admired sprinkled here and there. We have known M. Kiesewetter more successful than in this piece.

EIGHTH CONCERT, *Monday, June 6, 1825.*

ACT I.

Sinfonia in A - - - - *Beethoven.*
Quartetto, " *Cielo il mio labbro ispira*," Madame Caradori
   Allan, Signora Garcia, Signor Garcia, and Signor De
   Begnis (*Bianca e Faliero*) - - - *Rossini.*
Concerto, Piano-forte, Mr. Moscheles - - *Moscheles.*
Aria, " *Gran' Dio,*" Madame Caradori Allan - *Guglielmi.*
Overture Der Freischütz - - - *Weber.*

ACT III.

Sinfonia, No. 6 - - - - *Mozart.*
Aria, " *Alma invitta*," Signora Garcia - - *Rossini.*
Concertante, Flute, Oboe, Horn, and Bassoon, Messrs.
   Nicholson, Vogt, Platt, and Mackintosh - *Tolou.*
Aria, Signor Garcia, " *Suoni la tromba*" - *Garcia.*
Overture, *Zauberflöte* - - - *Mozart.*

Leader, Mr. Mori.—Conductor Mr. Attwood.

THE merits of Beethoven's symphony in A we have before discussed in this work, and we repeat, that, except the movement from it published in a former number of the Harmonicon, it is a composition in which the author has indulged a great deal of disagreeable eccentricity. Often as we now have heard it performed, we cannot yet discover any design in it, neither can we trace any connexion in its parts. Altogether it seems to have been intended as a kind of enigma—we had almost said a hoax. Mozart's symphony in C, the sixth in the edition of Sperati and Cianchittini, is full of fire, and was written in the vigour of his health and genius. We know none of his instrumental compositions that show such a continued flow of animation as this: its beauties are all of the sparkling kind, and the hearer is as much exhilarated by it, as if he had swallowed copious draughts of champagne.

The Overtures to the *Freischütz* and the *Zauberflöte* have been too often eulogized here to require any further mention. The concerto by M. Moscheles was a surprising and most charming performance. The music, and the execution of it, were of the highest character, and equal to each other. The applause he received was great, but by no means unearned. The concertante by Tolou, much in the manner, but not possessing a tithe of the genius of Pleyel, was admirably executed, and this is all we can venture to say of it. The directors of these concerts are not now very scrupulous in their choice of pieces; witness the aria by M. Garcia, sung by him. The beautiful quartett by Rossini was half spoiled by giving the fourth part to Signor De Begnis, for whose voice it is altogether unfit. Madame Caradori sang an aria by Guglielmi most agreeably, and pleased every body by her performance. The composition of this air forms a remarkable contrast to the vocal productions of the present age; its comparative gentleness and tranquillity afford a great relief, and its reception at this concert convinces us that, in a few years, the rage for the " trumpet's loud clangor" will be abated, and a taste for the music of the olden times be revived: or rather that new composers will start up, who will seek to produce the effect of novelty, by imitating that which is nearly forgotten. Madlle. Garcia made, we believe, her first public appearance at this Concert. She has a rich contr' alto voice, and is apparently a good musician; but her manner, like

her father's, is too ornamental, and is not calculated to give her any lasting fame. Her aria was very unskilfully selected for the occasion.

This performance terminated the season—a season in which there has been much to censure and much to commend. With attention, this Concert may continue, as it has long been, a fine school of music, a counterbalance to the influence of feverish and fluctuating fashion, and a standard by which the taste of those who really desire to cultivate the art may be regulated. But if the managers of the society are carelessly chosen, and persons are elected to fill the office of directors who are likely to be influenced by their own personal views, then the Philharmonic Concerts will degenerate—as they have once or twice threatened to do—the lovers of good music will be left without any resource, and the art will, for a time, be under the guidance of the weakest of that part of the community which has leisure to affect the characters of cognoscenti and patrons.

THE DRAMA.

KING'S THEATRE.—On the 26th of last month, Madame Pasta had her benefit at this theatre, on which occasion Paisiello's *Nina* was performed, as reduced into one act, by M. Paer, and thus represented with great applause in Paris. To this was added the first act of *Tancredi*. The former was thus cast;—

Nina, beloved by *Lindor* - - Mad. PASTA.
Lindor, lover of *Nina*, - - Sig. CURIONI
The *Count*, father of *Nina* - Sig. PORTO.
Elisa, gouvernante of *Nina* - Mad. CASTELLI.
Georges, bailiff of the Count - Sig. RUBBI.

Nina is by many people considered as the best of Paisiello's serious operas; and some forty years ago, *La Pazza per amore* (the second title of *Nina*) was as much raved after by the *Pazze per la musica*, as *Most in Egitto* will shortly be. *Nina* is full of beauties of the gentle kind; its melodies are original, pure, and delightful, and every note in the opera is appropriate to the words. But it is not adapted to a theatre of large dimensions; composed for the palace of Versailles, it there succeeded, and even now succeeds at the *Louvois* in Paris—a room fitted up as a theatre—where none of its delicacies are lost in space, and where its mild, unobtrusive merits are perceived, and therefore felt.

The opera certainly did not now please, as it once did, in London, and only so great a favorite as Madame Pasta has been this season, would have gained for it a second audience of any extent as to numbers.

Madame de Begnis took for her benefit the second and third acts of *Romeo e Giulietta* by Zingarelli, in which, of course, Madame Pasta represented the lover. This drew two enormously full houses; indeed the charming singer and actress, who during a short month deserved and enjoyed so much public favour, proved much more useful to the treasury of the theatre than all the other performers put together; for Madame De Begnis had been continually disqualified by illness from appearing, and the chronic cough, rheum, &c. of Sig. Garcia, had frequently incapacitated him from singing. His absence, however, was never felt after the arrival of Signor Curioni.

The return of Madame Pasta to Paris, and the inability of the *prima donna* to resume her place, have thrown a damp on the performances of the Italian Opera up to the present period. Mademoiselle Garcia was suddenly engaged to fill up the vacancies, and made her first appearance on any stage, on the 7th of June, in the character of *Rosina*, in Rossini's *Barbiere de Siviglia*; but though possessing a good contr' alto voice, an ample knowledge of music, and a considerable share of vocal talent, has not assisted the finances of the establishment, by attracting to the theatre those useful persons who pay, though numbers have been drawn together to applaud. Before this present number of our work is published, *Il Crociato in Egitto*, the celebrated opera of Meyerbeer, will, in all probability, have been produced, and should Signor Velluti succeed, will doubtless restore the theatre to a flourishing condition, and afford the public the means of hearing one of the finest works that has ever been performed on the Italian stage.

IL CROCIATO IN EGITTO,

AN HEROIC OPERA IN TWO ACTS,

WRITTEN BY ROSSI,—COMPOSED BY GIACOMO MEYERBEER.

HIS opera was first produced in the *Grand Teatro la Fenice* in Venice, for the season of the Carnival of 1824. It has since been brought forward in most of the principal theatres of Italy, and is now rapidly making the tour of Europe.

The Dramatis Personæ are as follow, and are thus cast for representation:—

Aladin, *Sultan of Damietta* . . .	Signor Remorini.
Palmide, *his daughter*	Madame Caradori.
Osmin, *a Vizier*	Signor Crivelli.
Alma, *a confidante of Palmide* .	Madame Castelli.
Adrian de Montfort, *Grand Master of*	
the Order of the Knights of Rhodes	Signor Curioni.
Felicia, *a relative of Adrian, in male*	
attire	Signora Garcia.
Armand D'Orville, *an initiated Knight*	
of Rhodes, under the assumed name	
of Elmireno	Signor Velluti.

The argument prefixed to the opera, by the poet, Signor Rossi, is as follows:—

In an expedition on the coast of Egypt, which took place in the Sixth Crusade, in the neighbourhood of Damietta, a band of the Knights of Rhodes, commanded by Esmengarde de Beaumont, was surprised, betrayed, and after a most heroic resistance, overpowered by the superior numbers of the enemy.

Armando d'Orville, a young Knight of Provence, was one of this valiant band. Fainting from loss of blood, he lad remained among the slain. He returns to himself; night comes on, and he sees no other means of escaping from the disgrace of slavery, than by concealing himself in the spoils of an Egyptian warrior who had fallen on the field. He hopes, by mingling with the enemy, to discover their plans, and to find a favourable moment for escape.

Armando, under the assumed name of *Elmineno*, finds an opportunity of signalizing his valour, and of saving the life of *Aladino*, Sultan of Damietta.

The supposed young soldier of fortune, by means of his superior valour and gentle manners, wins the affections of the Sultan, who becomes his friend, and receives him into the bosom of his family. The Sultan has a daughter named *Palmide*, who is regarded as the flower of the

Egyptian maidens. She sees the supposed Elmireno, and a mutual passion is the consequence. Afar from his country, almost without a hope of ever returning to it again, young, and of an ardent mind, Armando forgets himself, his duties, the faith he had plighted to *Felicia*, a noble maiden of Provence, and yields to the love of Palmide. He has secretly instructed her in the mysteries of his faith; they are privately united, and the product of this union is a son. But the call of honour, the love of his country, and the sense of his dereliction of duty, are ever present to his mind, and throw a gloom over his happiness. Aladino observes their mutual attachment, and only waits the return of Elminero from a glorious campaign, in order to unite their hands. Meanwhile overtures are made to the Sultan by the Knights of Rhodes, for a purchase and exchange of prisoners: terms of peace are also offered, and an embassy from them arrives at Damietta.

The action commences at the arrival of this Embassy.

ACT THE FIRST.

The opening scene represents a spacious enclosure in the palace of the Sultan Aladin. To the right is seen the Residence of the European slaves destined to labour at the public works; to the left is part of the Palace and gardens of the Sultan.

The overture is expressive of the following *tableau*:—
All is hushed in the silence of night, which is beginning to give place to the dawn. The sound of the morning trumpet of call is heard; a general movement within the residence of the slaves. Keepers come and open the gates; the slaves come forth, who are recognised by their dress, as belonging to different European nations. They salute and embrace each other, and prepare for the labours of the day. The greater part are employed in the construction of a small temple. All is in action. A youth is seen supporting the chains of his aged father; a slave takes a portrait from his bosom, gazes on it affectionately, presses it to his lips, and hastily conceals it again, through fear of being discovered. Another reads a letter, which he kisses and presses to his heart. Other groups are variously employed, while a part give utter-

ance to the emotions of their hearts in the following chorus * :—

Patria amata ! oh, tu il primiero
De' miei fervidi desiri;
Fra catene, fra sospiri,
A te anela il mesto cor.
Fier destin ci rese schiavi,
Mare immenso ci separa ;
Ma tu ognor mi sei più cara,
Tu mi sei presente ognor..
Cari oggetti del mio core !
Più vedervi io non potrò ?
Fra i sospir di triste amore
Qui penar, morir dovrò ?
Sposa !—figli !—patria !—amici !—
Più vedervi io non potrò ?
Da voi lunge moriro ?
Cessi omai si acerba vita ;
Cangi omai si orribil sorte :
O pietosa tronchi morte
Il mio barbaro dolor !

In scene the second, slaves are seen coming from the palace, bearing baskets full of various presents ; shortly after appears *Palmide*, who is come to pay her morning visit to the slaves, and brings them various presents to comfort and console them ; we learn that these gifts are sent by the wish of her lover *Elmireno*. Rejoiced at the appearance of their benefactress, the European slaves change their notes of sorrow into grateful and more joyous accents †.

Ma già di Palmide gli schiavi avanzano,
La regal vergine a noi già recasi,
Brillante raggio in sua beltà.
Consolatrice de' nostri mali,
Benefattrice de' egri mortali,
Vieni, o bell' angela della pietà !

Palmide replies to their grateful salutations in the following cavatina ‡ :—

* Beloved country, oh, thou first,
Fond object of my fervent vows ;
Amidst our chains, our bitter sighs,
To thee the sorrowing heart aspires.
Fell destiny has made us slaves,
Between us boundless oceans roll,
But distance makes thee doubly dear,
And paints thee present to my thoughts.
Beloved objects of my heart ! .
And shall I ne'er behold you more ?
Amidst the sighs of love forlorn,
Here must I ever pine and die ?
Wife !—children !—country !—friends !—
And shall I never see ye more ?
And must I die from you afar ?
Soon may a life so wretched close ;
Soon may a fate so horrid change :
And ah ! may death in pity come
To free me from such bitter woes.

† But see Palmida's slaves advance,
The royal virgin hither comes,
A star in beauty's lustre bright.
Consoler of our bitter ills,
Thou benefactress in our needs,
Angel of pity, come this way !

‡ With gifts from Elmireno sent
I here present you, friends !
With him for the unhappy still
How fondly do I sympathize !
(E'en now perhaps is love
Whispering fond thoughts of me.)

I doni d' Elmireno
Io vi presento, amici;
Con lui per gli infelici
Divido la pietà !
(Or per me forse in seno
Amor gli parlera.)

(Soave immagine di quel momento,
A te sorridere il cor io sento !
Accenti e palpiti, sospiri e giubilo,
L' amor piu tenero confonderà !)

Scarcely have these accents of tenderness died away, when guards from the palace announce the approach of Aladin and his vizier Osmin. The Sultan announces to his daughter, that he has just received the news of the arrival of Elmireno, who has returned triumphant over the enemies of his kingdom ; he commands a triumph to be prepared for the conqueror, and requests Palmide to present him with the laurel crown, convinced that from her hand it will prove doubly acceptable. Palmide is all confusion and joy at the words of her father, while Osmin is scarcely able to restrain his rage. The ambitious vizier is secretly aiming at the throne, and has aspired to the hand of Palmide. At this moment, trumpets in different directions are heard. A signal from the tower of the port announces the arrival of a vessel in the bay ; at the same moment the banner of the Knights of Rhodes is recognised, and the Sultan makes known that the valiant warriors of Rhodes are come to sue for peace and friendship. The other signal announces, at the same moment, the arrival of the conqueror Elmireno. Palmide and Aladino express their mutual joy at this event in the following duet, and their sentiments are reiterated by the chorus §.

Vincitore a questo petto
Stringerò, } l'ero e diletto !
         } l'amato oggetto !
Ah ! maggiore di quel ch'io sento
Un contento non si dà.

Coro.
Concenti bellici all' aure echeggino,
L'ero e festeggino, il vincitor ;
E a'suon belligeri s'alternin teneri
Di pace i cantici, gli inni d'amor.

Aladin, in a transport of joy, declares that on so propitious a day all the wishes of his heart shall be fulfilled. " Thine too, oh daughter, he exclaims, shall be accomplished. Long have I observed the affection that thou hast cherished for Elmireno ; nay, blush not, I rejoice at it, and had already planned thy happy union on the return of the victor ; yes, the brave man who formerly saved my life, shall be thine." Alas ! what an announcement is this to Palmide ; what a dreadful veil is rent

Oh pictur'd bliss of that sweet hour,
I feel my bosom yearn for thee !
Soft words, and sighs and thrills of joy,
The tenderest love will mingle then.

§ How will I to this bosom press
The conqueror, { the hero loved !
              { my bosom's love !
Ah what greater happiness
Could be found on earth than mine.

Chorus.
What warlike strains of triumph swell the gale.
To hail the hero, the proud conqueror ;
And with these warlike sounds alternately
Arise soft songs of peace and hymns of love.

before her eyes. For five years has she been secretly united to Elmireno, and a son is the fruit of this union.— Aladin bids her go, and announce in person the joyful news to Elmireno. She retires in distraction. Aladin congratulates Osmin on the happy event, and bids him prepare the royal galley for the landing of the victor, and make all the due preparations at the palace, for, the reception of the knights who compose the embassy from Rhodes.

The following scene brings us to a retired spot in the gardens of the Sultan, contiguous to the apartments of Palmide, where her son *Mirva* is discovered asleep on a bank of flowers. Alma, the confidante of Palmide, guards the child in this retired spot, that he may be near his mother; she also obviates any suspicion that might arise, by giving out that it is her son. Palmide enters all agitation from the interview with her father, and, in the agony of her heart, reveals to Alma that she has renounced the faith of her father and embraced the religion of Elmireno. At this moment the sound of trumpets announces the landing of the conqueror. Alma exhorts her friend to take courage, and not ruin all by betraying herself.

The scene now changes to the Port of Damietta; the people are seen hastening to the landing of the royal vessel which is pompously adorned. A chorus of great beauty and effect, intermingled with gay dances, hails its approach to the strand*.

Coro alternato colé danza.

Vedi il legno, che in vaga sembianza
Mollemente sul Nilo s'avanza ;
   Ci porta la pace.
Spira un'aura leggiera, soave,
   E' l'aura di pace.
L'onda mormora placida e cheta,
Lieta bacia, accarrezza la nave
   Che porte la pace.

Il vascello approda.

Di nostre palme all'ombra amica,
Qui, sulla sponda del Nilo aprica,
Dolce catena di mirti e fior,
Nave propizia ! t' arresti ognor.
Mai t' allontana da' nostri lidi,
Tu che a noi guidi la bella pace,
Voto verace dei nostri cor.
Echeggi d' intorno di pace l' accento,
Di gioja conceuto festeggi tal dì,
E lieta la sponda risponda così.

* *Chorus, alternately with Dances.*

Behold the vessel which in stately pomp
Glides softly on the bosom of the Nile ;
   She brings us peace.
A sweet and gentle zephyr breathes around,
   It is the breath of peace.
The wavelets break in stilly murmurs round,
Caressing joyfully the happy bark
   That brings us peace.

The Vessel reaches the Strand.

Beneath the friendly shadow of our palms
Here on the banks of sunny Nile,
May bands of myrtle and of flowers,
Propitious vessel ! stay thy course.
Ne'er mayst thou quit our shores again,
Thou that fair peace has guided hither,
The object of our hearts' warm sighs.
Let the voice of peace be heard around,
Let songs of joy salute the day,
And echoing shores repeat the strain.

Armando is received on the strand by Aladin and his attendants ; Palmide too is there, but she keeps in the background. The hero receives the congratulations of the Sultan, and is introduced by him to his daughter, with the fervent wish that the hand of love may crown his valour and fidelity. Armando replies in the following air, which is interchanged with a chorus and dances*.

ARIA.

Cara mano dell' amore
   Io ti bacio, e son felice ;
   Se mercè sperar mi lice,
   Io la spero dall' amor.

CORO, *coll danza.*

Fortunato vincitore !
   Godi il premio del valore ;
   Porge allori a te la gloria,
   Mirti e rose ti offre Amor.

ARMANDO.

Regna all ombra degl' allori,
   È de' figli tuoi nel core ;
   A te sacro è il mio valore,
   Di mia fede il bel candore.

CORO, *come sopra.*

Fortunato vincitore !

ARMANDO.

Ah ! non v'è, non v'è trionfo
   Al mio cor piu lusinghiero,
   D'un ardor così sincero,
   Del sorriso dell' amore.

CORO.

Fortunato vincitore !

The scene now changes and introduces us to a retired spot on the shores of the Nile, where the Knights of Rhodes reside. Near this there is a temple, from which Adrian, the grand master, is seen to come forth, dressed in the habit of a simple knight. He wishes to pass unobserved, in order, if possible, to discover tidings of the fate of his favourite nephew Armando, whom he believes

* I kiss thee, thou dear hand of love !
   I kiss thee, and my joy is full ;
   If I may hope a recompense,
   I hope it all from love alone.

CHORUS, *with dance.*

Thrice happy conqueror !
   Enjoy proud valour's noble meed ;
   Glory presents her laurel wreath,
   And love his rose and myrtle crown.

ARMANDO.

Beneath the laurel's shade may he
   And in thy sons' brave bosoms reign ;
   Devoted is to thee this arm,
   And the pure feelings of this heart.

CHORUS, *as before.*

Thrice happy conqueror !

ARMANDO.

Ah ! no, there is no triumph, none
   So flattering to this heart of mine,
   As an affection thus sincere,
   As is this gentle smile of love.

CHORUS.

Thrice happy conqueror !

U 2

to have perished on these shores. On his way, he meets his relative Felicia, who has assumed the dress of a knight, intending to proceed on the same melancholy office of attempting to discover the spot where repose the ashes of her former lover, Armando, to whom she had been betrothed before his departure to join the Crusades.

Meantime, Armando having heard of the arrival of the Knights of Rhodes, is all anxiety to learn tidings of his relative. For this purpose he has quitted the palace, and now encounters Adriano; they recognise each other; the first moments are all transport, till the uncle surveying the saracen dress in which his nephew is attired, shrinks from him with horror and indignation; he demands from him his sword, and breaks it before his eyes. Then follows one of the master-pieces of the opera, a duet, admirably expressive of the indignation of the uncle, and the humiliation and repentance of the nephew *.

DUET.

```
        * Go, thou hast joined, apostate one!
           The standard of the infidel ;
           Abandoning thy faith, thou hast
           Betrayed thy country and thy honour.
         I leave thee to thy guilt and shame,
           With horror thou dost make me shudder.
Arm.     Ah ! by remorse o'erwhelmed,
           I shrink with horror from myself ;
           Pardon, oh heaven ! my errors past,
           Look on me with a pitying eye.
         The flame of honour and of faith
           Is still alive within my heart.
Adr.     And would'st thou merit pardon still ?
Arm.     Ah ! may I hope it still ?—command—
Adr.     Then lay aside those guilty spoils ;
           Let Aladin know who thou art ;
           Then must thou quit this land with me,—
Arm.     Quit !—(oh heavens !—and Palmide ?)
Adr.     Spouse of Felicia thou must—
Arm.     How ! I Felicia's spouse ?
Adr.     Why shrink'st thou at my words ? ah ! say—
           And can it be—tremble,—thy oaths !—
Arm.     Kill me at once—I have betrayed them all.
Adr.     Ah, traitor !—but declare, for whom ?—
Arm.     Then hear ?
Adr.     Withold   } this added horror!
Arm.    Thou know'st not by what spell my soul was bound,
           She who awaked the flame is more than mortal.
         Sweet unison of grace and innocence,
           'Twas in my heart she found their recompense.
         The wretched one will die,—and die for me !
Adr.     In grief and pain thy mother moaned,
           I wept with her, ungrateful one ! for thee.
         And thou, meanwhile upon the breast of love
           Dissolved, betray'dst honour, vows, and faith
         Thy mother dies the while—and dies for thee !
Adr.     Choose then—this senseless love of thine—
Arm.     I will o'ercome.   Adr. Virtue—fair honour—
Arm.     I will pursue.   Adr. Upon this sword—
           It was thy noble father's sword,
           Now swear.  Arm. Ah ! give it here, that I
         May kiss it.—Ah, beloved father !
         I do invoke thee—by thy memory swear
         That I will worthy of thy love return.
```

Both.

```
The father's matchless brand shall wake
   The flame of valour in  {my
                            {his  heart ;
O'er every danger, every foe
   With this his son shall triumph still.
```

DUETTO.

```
         Va ; gia varcasti, indegno !
           Delle perfidie il segno ;
           Traditi patria, onore,
           Scordasti la tua fe.
         Ti lascio al tuo rossore,
           Fremo d'orror per te.
Arm.     Ah ! dei rimorsi oppresso,
           Orror ho di me stesso ;
           Perdona, oh Dio ! l'errore,
           Abbi pieta di me.
         M'avvampa ancor nel core
           Fiamma d'onor, di fe.
Adr.     Vuoi meritar perdono ?—
Arm.     Posso aspirarvi ?—imponi—
Adr.     Le insegne ree deponi ;
           Sappia Aladin qual sei ;
           Meco partir poi dei.
Arm.     Partir ! (o cielo !—e Palmide !—).
Adr.     Sposo a Felicia omai—
Arm.     Io sposo di Felicia !
Adr.     Tu fremi ?—di, se mai—
           Trema—i tuoi giuri !—
Arm.     Svenami—io tradii tutto.
Adr.     Perfido !—e per chi mai ?
Arm.     Odi  }
Adr.     Taci } qual nuovo orror !
Arm.    Non sai quale incanto quest 'alma sorprese ;
           Colei che m'accese mortale non è.
         Di grazie e candore complesso celeste,
           Nel solo mio core trovava mercè :
           La misera or muore— e muore per me !
Adr.     Nel duolo, nel pianto, tua madre gemeva,
           Io seco piangeva, ingrato ! per te :
         E in seno all 'amore tu intanto languivi ;
           Tradivi l'onore, i voti, la fè.
         Tua madre si muore—e muore per te !
Adr.     Scegli dunque ; un cieco amore—
Arm.     Vincerò.   Adr. Virtude—onore—
Arm.     Seguirò.   Adr. Su questa spada—
           Fu la spada di tuo padre—
           Or lo giura.   Arm. Ah ! porgi, ch' io
           Or la baci.—Padre mio !
           Io te invoco—per te guiro—
           Di te degno io tornerò.
```

a. 2.

```
Il brando invitto del genitore
   Il valore  {mio
              {tuo accenderà ;
D' ogni nemico, d'ogni periglio,
   Con esso il figlio trionferà.
```

Meantime Felicia, in prosecuting her search, has wandered through the mazes of the garden to the spot which serves as a retreat for Alma and Mirva. She sees the lovely child, is struck with its features, and fancies she traces some resemblance to one she holds dear. Palmide enters, she is alarmed at the sight of a stranger in this secluded spot, and for the safety of Mirva. She calls the child to her ; Felicia apologizes for detaining him an instant longer. Palmide is surprised at the interest manifested by a stranger for her child. An explanation ensues. The name of Armando d'Orville is mentioned, which leads to a disclosure of the person of Felicia, and of the love of Armando and Palmide. The consequence is, a struggle between generosity and love. Felicia nobly declares that the child has dissolved the ties that bound her to Armando, and that severe as the effort is, she has determined to yield him up to Palmide. Memory awakens ; she recals the time when Armando, the youthful troubadour, first awakened her heart to love, she recals the song in which he painted his passion, and sings the following canzonette * :—

CANZONETTE.

Giovinetto cavalier,
  Di bel giorno al tramontar,
Colla Dea de' suoi pensier
  Sotto un salcio s'arrestar.

Tacque un po', su lei fissò
  Poi lo sguardo, e sospirò;
La sua man portò al cor,
  " E qui, disse, qui v'e amor."

Non fidarti, o giovin cor,
  Dell' accento dell amor !

Palmide recognises the air, which Armando had often sung to her, and thus resumes the song †.

Cloe d'eta nell' bell April,
  Era giglio di candor ;
Sorrideva al suo gentil
  In un tenero languor.

Ma balzar quel cor senti,
  E il suo tutto s' agitò ;
Un sospiro le sfuggi—
  Ei l' intese, e l'abbracciò.

Non fidarti, o giovin cor,
  Dei sospiri dell' amor !

Scarcely have the last sounds died away upon the lips of Palmide, when the voice of Armando from the neighbouring grove is heard to repeat the last verses. All is surprise and emotion. Palmide becomes greatly agitated. She imagines that the song of the knight is intended to express the farewell, which he is obliged to take of her. Felicia entreats her to be calm. The voice of Armando is again heard ; he terminates the song ‡.

CANZONET.

* At the gentle day's decline,
  Came the youthful cavalier,
And beneath the spreading vine
  Seated him beside his dear.

On her face he silent gazed,
  Then he sigh'd so tenderly,
To his heart her hand he raised,
  And here true love beats said he.

Unsuspecting heart of youth,
  Think not all love says is truth !

† Chloe show'd in youth's fair spring
  Charms, the lily's pride above,
With soft looks, how languishing
  Smiled she on her gentle love.

Soon she felt her heart oppress'd,
  Her bosom throb'd with soft alarms,
A sigh escaped her gentle breast,
  He heard—he caught her in his arms.

Trust not, youthful heart, the sigh
  Love will pour so fervently.

‡ Once he came in arms complete,
  And exclaim'd with many a sigh,
A Crusader, I afar
  From thy tender arms must fly,

A chilly coldness seized her frame,
  Half dead upon the earth she lay,
He kiss'd her cold hand—breath'd her name,
  Dropt one sad tear—and fled away.

Tutto armato a lei venir
  Vide un giorno il suo tesor ;
" Cara, addio !" con un sospir,
  " Son Crociato," ei disse allor.

Cloe gelarsi il cor senti.
  Quasi estinta al suol piombò :
Ei la fredda man baciò,
  Su lei pianse, e—disparì.

Armando appears, flies to Palmide's arms, and repeats§ ;

Mai provare, o giovin cor,
  I martiri dell' amor !

But a sense of duty, and of the solemn pledge he had given to Adrian, prevail over the delirium of the moment, and he tears himself from Palmide's embrace. Felicia, who has withdrawn, returns, and the situation of the three lovers is admirably painted in the following terzetto‖ :

ARMANDO.

Ma—il dover !—un sacro onor !—
  Ah ! che l'addio sul labbro muor,
  E mai partir da lei potrò.

PALMIDE.

S'ei la vede !—un di l' amò—
  Può amarla ancor !—che far allor !—
  Mi gela il cor crudo timor.

FELICIA.

D'avanzar ardir non ho—
  D'un altra in sen chi su di l'amò !—
  Questo e soffrir—questo e dolor !

a 3.

Mai provare, o giovin cor,
  I sospiri dell' amor !

The struggle of affection in the bosom of Armando is severe, but the sense of duty prevails ; he snatches a hasty embrace, and flies from the spot.

The scene changes, and we are ushered into a magnificent saloon of the palace, where all the preparations have been made for the nuptial ceremony. A grand march. Palmide is seen in the procession, accompanied by Alma, who leads Mirva by the hand, followed by slaves. Imans bear the nuptial veil. On the other side, the sultan's guards of honour precede the Knights of Rhodes ; after appears Adrian in his dress as grand master, followed by his pages, among whom is Felicia. Aladin is waiting to receive them, and at a sign from him, Adrian and the knights are seated. Mirva presents an olive crown to Adrian, and other children to the

§ Oh, may thy youthful heart ne'er prove
  The bitter pangs of hopeless love !

ARMANDO.

‖ But duty's call—fair honour's voice—
  Ah ! how th' adieu dies on my lip !—
  Nor can I tear myself away.

PALMIDE.

But she is there, he loved her once,
  May love her still,—then I'm undone,
  How cruel fears freeze all my heart !

FELICIA.

Ah ! to advance I've not the heart,—
  My lover in another's arms,
  What anguish this !

a 3.

Ah ! may the youthful heart ne'er prove,
  The bitter pangs of hopeless love.

knights. Adrian in receiving it, regards Mirva with interest, and caresses him. Palmide and Felicia anxiously watch the motions of Adrian. The sultan, after announcing to all his choice of Elmireno as the husband of his daughter, Palmide, and the successor to his throne, commands him to be called in. To the amazement of Aladin and his suite, he presents himself in the habit of a Knight of Rhodes, declares that he is no longer Elmireno, but the nephew of Adrian, before whom he prostrates himself.. The grand master announces that his nephew has awakened from the delirium of a blinded passion, and listened to the voice of duty and of honour; that he still finds him worthy of his love, and is prepared with him to quit the territories of Aladin. The indignation of the sultan is aroused at the insult offered to himself and his daughter; he sternly commands Armando to retract his resolution, but finding him inflexible, is wrought up to such a frenzy of passion, as to draw his dagger with the intention of plunging it in Armando's bosom. He is, however, prevented by Felicia, who darts forward, and throws herself between the sultan and Armando. All is tumult and confusion. Aladin commands the knights instantly to quit the city, and orders Armando to a dungeon, there to be reserved for his fury. The general feeling is admirably depicted in the following canon *.

CANONE.

Sogni ridenti
  Di pace e amor,
Furo i contenti
  Di questo cor!
Non v'è più } pace,
        } fede,
Non v'e più } amor.
        } onor.

All now is rage, fury, and defiance. Aladin commands the Imans to throw open the door of the Mosque, to sound the formidable gong, which is ever a signal of war, and to wave the banner of the crescent. Adrian, on his part, commands his knights to unfurl the standard of the cross. Open war is declared. Armando is surrounded by guards; a general movement takes place; the knights gather round Adriano, and Osmin and the Emirs round Aladin; a double march; Palmide and Felicia in anguish taking their farewell of Armando. Such are the materials that form the splendid

FINALE OF THE FIRST ACT.

THE SECOND ACT.

AT the opening of Act the Second, we learn that the ambitious Osmin has secretly fomented a sedition, and that he purposes taking advantage of the present troubled state of things, in order the better to carry his plans into execution. After his deliberation with the Emirs, he is sent by Alma, who anxiously inquires all particulars re-

CANON.

  * Mere smiling dreams
    Of peace and love,
  Were all the joys
    Of this poor heart!
Peace } is for ever fled,
Faith }
Love } is no more.
Honour }

lative to the knights, and particularly with respect to Armando. He informs her that the rage of Aladin knows no bounds, that Armando is confined in a deep dungeon, and there awaits his fate; that Palmide has employed all her entreaties in vain, that she is sunk in despair, and that even her life itself appears in danger. Struck by the evils that threaten on every side, Alma in an unguarded moment exclaims; Ah Palmide, what will become of thy son!—The secret is revealed; the child which she has so long contrived to pass off as her own, is discovered to be Palmide's, and Osmin is determined to take advantage of this discovery, in order the more to exasperate the mind of Aladin, and further his own designs, by urging him to acts of greater violence.

In the meantime, Felicia is seen wandering in grief and distraction, in the environs of Damietta. She laments the destiny of her beloved,—for she still loves Armando; and gives vent to her feelings in the following air†.

ARIA.

Pace ei recò, a' noi più grata
  Delle palme di vittoria;
  E la patria consolata,
Lieta omai per lui tornò:
Ma più cara della gloria
M' è la sua felicità.

Mentre il sacro dellà pace
  Ei ci porta amato pegno,
  Lo splendor, di questo regno
In fra i ceppi se ne sta.
Ah! se pena il caro bene,
  Per me pace or più non v' ha!

Ah! piu sorridere
  Labbro d'amore,
  Fra i dolci palpiti
  Non ti vedro,
Mai, cara imagine,
  Ti rivedro!
  Oh cielo! arrenditi
    Ai voti miei:
    Se vuoi dividermi
    Dal mio tesor,
Cambiami il tenero
Ardente cor!

We are next brought back to Palmide, who, sad and lost in thought, has wandered to the scenes of her former happiness; but these grateful shades can now afford no

AIR.

† He brought us peace, more grateful far
  Than glorious palms of victory;
Our country, all its troubles soothed,
  Through him breathes joyfully again.

Yet he who brought the much lov'd pledge
  Of sacred peace to bless this land,
Himself, this realm's best ornament,
  Pines in a dungeon's mournful gloom.

Ah! while my loved one suffers thus
  No peace can this poor bosom know.

  Ah! that smiling
    Lip of love
    No more shall I
    With rapture see!
Never, sweet image,
  Shall I behold thee more!
Oh heaven! propitious
  Hear my vows:
  If from my love
  Condemned to pine,
Ah, change this too,
  Too tender heart.

relief to her wounded bosom; all seems changed, sad and mute, and reminds her of him who is no longer there *.

ARIA.

Tutto qui parla ognor
Del mio felice amor;
L'imago del piacer
A me presenta.

Una sol volta ancor
Ch' ei torni a questo cor!
Lo sposo mio veder
Morrei contenta!

Alma enters with Mirva, and pointing to the child, replies, that there are other motives to attach her to life. She flies to embrace her child, exclaiming, Oh, my son! my son! at that moment Aladin and Osmin enter, and the former overhearing her words, is on the point of killing Mirva, when Palmide informs him, that she has anticipated his wishes, by uniting herself to Armando, and that this child is the fruit of their union. She pleads for him with all a mother's fervour, and the eloquence of her tears softens the heart of Aladin. This is admirably expressed in the following air and duet †.

ARIA.

Ah! miri l'angelo	Chiede clemenza
Dell' innocenza	Per l' infelice
A te sorridere	Sua genitrice,
Nel suo candor!	Perdono al misere
Le braccia stendeti	Suo genitor!

Ala. Come si può resistere?
　　Venite a questo seno!
Pal. Stringe il mio figlio, oh giubilo!
　　Ah, del affanno il palpito
　　Tutto in piacer cangiò!
　　E dov'è Elmireno?
Ala. Tosto Adriano invismi; 　　*(ad un Emir.*
　　Attendi Elmireno.
Coro. Come repente in giubili
　　La pena tua congiò!

AIR.

* Here every thing around
　Speaks of my happy love,
　And to my view presents
　The image of past joy.

Would he but once again
　Return to this fond heart!
To see my love again,
　Then should I die content.

AIR.

† Behold this angel	Imploring clemency
Of innocence,	For his unhappy
Smiling on thee	Desolate mother,
In gentleness!	And pardon father!
He spreads his hands	His wretched father!

Ala. Ah how resist appeal like this?
　　Oh come to this relenting breast!
Pal. He does embrace my son, oh joy!
　　How is the bitter pang of grief
　　Converted into joy!
　　And where—where is my Elmireno?
Ala. Quickly let Adrian hither come; *(To the Emir.)*
　　Let Elmireno wait me here.
Chorus. How quickly have thy sorrows been
　　Converted into joy!
Pal. Ah! with what joy will I unloose
　　The fetters of my best beloved;
　　Other more gentle bonds,
　　Embraces chaste, will I bestow.
　　To my bosom, oh what rapture!
　　Will I press my spouse, my son.
　　At a moment blest as this,
　　Sure with joy I shall expire!

Pal. Con qual gioja le catene
　　Altri lacci più soavi
　　Casti abbracci io recherò
　　Del mio bene io sciogherò!
　　Altri lacci più soavi
　　Casti abbracc io recherò
　　Al mio petto, qual diletto!
　　Sposo e filio stringerò.
　　A si caro bel momento
　　Di contento morirò!

Adrian appears; he comes prepared to meet some new outrage at the sultan's hands; what then is his surprise and joy to hear that Aladin has relented, and that his nephew is pardoned and set at liberty. The latter entreats Adrian to imitate his example, and pardon his nephew for all offences past. He declares that he has already pardoned him, an avowal that leads Aladin to suppose he is acquainted with all the particulars relative to the child. He therefore declares how much he was melted at the sight of Mirva at the festivity, and observes that he witnessed the emotions of Adrian, when he kissed and embraced the child on the same occasion, though then unconscious it was his nephew's child. At this moment Armando enters, and confesses the truth of the sultan's words. Adrian repulses him, declares him to be deprived of the honours of knighthood, disowns him as a relative, and indignatly quits the apartment.

Aladin is overwhelmed with anguish, and gives up all for lost. Aladin comforts him, and renews his promises of protection and friendship. Armando sinks into a profound reverie, a thought flashes across his mind—he entreats permission to conduct Palmide and her child to the presence of his uncle, and on obtaining permission flies to execute his purpose.

We are again conducted to the residence of the knights, at the side of which stands their ancient temple. Armando leads in Mirva and Palmide; he demands of her whether her heart is capable of a lofty exertion—prepared for a great sacrifice—no less than to reveal to Adrian their union and her new faith, and to quit the land of her fathers. A struggle ensues between her love to her father, and her affection for her husband and child, but the latter gains the victory. The gates of the temple unfold, and Adrian and Felicia are seen on the threshold. Palmide avows herself a believer, offers to ratify her belief by new vows, and consents to accompany her husband to his own land. Armando and Palmide kneel; Mirva is between them, Adrian is behind them, and with his eyes raised to heaven, and his hands placed on their heads, he implores the bounty of heaven in their favour; Felicia looks on with deep emotion, while the knights contemplate the effective scene. It is in this place that occurs one of the most effective pieces of the whole opera, the preghiera ‡

QUARTETT.

‡ O, clement Deity,
　Who readest in my heart,
　Receive and ratify
　This innocent vow:
Nature and love
　Implore, adore thee.

This union and these vows,
　Oh! do thou bless,
　Make happy now
　And consecrate, O Lord!
Nature and love
　Implore, adore thee.

QUARTETTO.

O Nume clemente!
Che in seno mi leggi,
Il voto innocente
Accogli, proteggi;
T' adora, t' implora
Natura ed amor.

Quel nodo, quei giuri
Deh! tu benedici;
Tu rendi felici,
Consacra, O signor!
T' adora, t' implora
Natura ed amor.

In the midst of this impressive scene, Aladin enters, attended by Osmin, Emirs, and guards. Astonished at the scene before him, he sternly inquires the cause. Adrian replies with dignity, that Palmide has offered up her vows to the divinity they adore, and has embraced the faith of her spouse. The fury of Aladin knows no bounds, and he condemns the whole of them to death. This scene gives occasion to a sestetto, which ranks among the most brilliant pieces of the opera* :—

SESTETTO.

Pal. Ah! questo è l'ultimo	*Arm.* Frena le lagrime,
Crudele addio:	Mio dolce amore!
Ti deggio perdere	Vivi a quel tenero
Dolce amor mio?	Pegno d' amore.
Ma teco Palmide	Cedi a una barbara
Morir saprà.	Fatalità ;
Così la vita	E consolarti
Orror mi fa.	Il ciel saprà.
Fel. Per me non palpito	*Adr.* Sfogati, o barbaro!
In tal momento ;	Appaga il core ;
Per lor quest' anima	Tutto poi struggere
Gemere io sento :	Nel tuo furore,
Piango a si barbara	Ma a te questa anima
Fatalità.	Mai cederà;
Per essi è vano	Il tuo furore
Sperar pietà.	Sfidar saprà.

ALADINO e OSMIRO.

Mirate esempio	Paga quest' anima
Del mio} furore! suo}	Aldin sarà,
	I traditori
Tremate, o perfidi,	Punir saprà.
Nel vostro core!	

---

* SESTETTO.

Pal. Alas! the last	*Arm.* Restrain those tears,
Sad farewell this!	My sweetest life !
And must I lose	Live for this tender
My best beloved ?	Pledge of love.
But with thee too	Yield to the rage
Shall thy Palmide die.	Of angry fate :
Without thee I	Heaven will at length
Should loath existence.	Console thy heart.
Fel. Not for myself	*Adr.* Barbarian, here
I tremble now ;	Glut thy fell rage !
It is for them	Thou may'st destroy
This bosom groans ;	All in thy fury,
I wail their sad	But ne'er to thee
And hapless fate.	This soul shall yield ;
All hopes of pity	Thy utmost fury
Now are vain.	I defy.

ALADIN AND OSMIN.

Behold an example	At length this soul
Of my } fury! his }	Shall be appeased,
	And wreak its vengeance
Tremble ye traitors	On the traitors.
To the inmost heart !	

Armando and the knights are led out guarded; Aladin takes Palmide with him, and Osmin retires rejoicing at the thought that the very rage of Aladin, which he has fostered, will prove the means of his advancement to the throne, by affording a pretext to the knights to rebel.

The next scene ushers us into the great square of Damietta. An Emir and guards lead in Armando. His firmness is scarcely proof against the agonizing reflection, that he has embraced Palmide and the other objects of his affection for the last time. While buried in these reflections, Adrian, Felicia, and the knights are also led in, guarded by Osmin and a band of Emirs. Adrian seizes the opportunity afforded him by this momentary meeting, and exhorts them all to firmness, faith, and constancy. At this instant, Osmin and the Emirs accost the knights with an air of mystery; they declare that they have an important secret to impart, which may prove the means of saving their lives; they tell them that an enterprise is on foot for their deliverance from the horrors of slavery and death; they place weapons in their hands, and exhort them to employ them in freeing themselves from their oppressors. Osmin boldly declares that he will be the first to fall upon the tyrant, and avenge his wrongs and their own in the blood of Aladin. Adrian, in receiving the weapons in his hands, declares in a marked and emphatic tone, that the arms intrusted to him shall be employed to punish the traitor.

Aladin enters, accompanied by Palmide; he is yet willing to extend his mercy to Adrian and his companions ; he bids them still choose.—Death and glory ! is the proud reply. Aladin's fury is again roused by this spirited defiance; he calls upon Osmin to lead them away to instant death. At this moment, Osmin placing himself at the head of the Emirs, rushes upon Aladin, exclaiming, No! thyself be the first to perish! Armando draws his sword, and flying to the side of Aladin, boldly takes his stand there, calling on his brother knights to succour a king who is betrayed, and to learn their duty from him. The traitors are disarmed and secured. The sultan is all astonishment, admiration, and gratitude. Learn, cries Adrian, from the example of Armando, our manner of avenging ourselves. Armando advances towards the sultan, and laying at his feet the sword that has saved his life and throne, exclaims,—I am again thy prisoner ! Aladin is overcome at the view of such unexampled heroism and virtue ; he embraces his heroic deliverers, and joins the hands of Armando and his daughter.

The whole of this scene allows scope for a very splendid and effective finale, and Meyerbeer has amply availed himself of the materials here afforded him. He has thus maintained the same vigour to the last, displaying to the concluding movement, the same copiousness of inocution, the same happy combination of new forms of melody with powerful and expressive harmony, the same fire and spirit, which animates all the other parts of this masterly composition.

THE
HARMONICON.

No. XXXII., August, 1825.

MEMOIR OF BENEDETTO MARCELLO.

BENEDETTO MARCELLO, a noble Venetian, whose family is mentioned by all the historians of Venice, was born in the month of July, 1686. His father, Agostino Marcello, was a senator ; his mother, Paolina, was of the honourable family of Capello, being the daughter of Girolamo Capello, and aunt of Pietro Andrea Capello, ambassador from the States of Venice to the courts of Spain, Vienna, and Rome, and who also was resident in England in that capacity about the year 1743.

His elder brother, Alessandro, had attained a great knowledge in natural philosophy and mathematics ; and Benedetto, after having been instructed in classical literature, and having gone through a regular course of education under proper masters, was committed to his tuition.

Alessandro lived at Venice, and had in his house a weekly musical meeting, in which his own compositions were frequently performed ; being a man of genius and rank, his house was the resort of most of the strangers that came to visit the city. The Princes of Brunswick, when at Venice, were invited to one of the musical performances ; and Benedetto, at that time very young, being present, they took particular notice of him. In the hearing of Alessandro, they asked him, among other questions, what were the studies that most engaged his attention ; "O," said his brother, "he is a very useful little fellow to me, he fetches my books and papers, and this is fittest employment for him." The boy was nettled at an answer which reflected as much upon his supposed want of genius as his youth. He, therefore, resolved to apply himself to some particular study, and soon fixed upon that of music. His principal instructors were Gasparini and Antonio Lotti.

In the year 1716, the birth of the first son of the Emperor Charles the Sixth was celebrated at Vienna with great magnificence ; and on this occasion a serenata composed by Benedetto Marcello was performed there with great applause.

Marcello's compositions are very numerous. Two of his cantatas, *Il Timeteo* and *La Cassandra*, have been much admired. He wrote also a *mass* which is highly celebrated. This was performed for the first time in the Church of Santa Maria della Celestia, on occasion of the daughter of his brother taking the veil in that monastery. He likewise set to music the *Lamentations of Jeremiah*, the *Miserere*, and the *Salve*. These, with many other sacred compositions, he gave to the Church of Santa Sophia, and was himself at the pains of instructing the singers in the manner in which they were to be performed.

In the year 1724, appeared the first four parts of a *Paraphrase of the Psalms*, in Italian, by Giustiniani, set to music for one, two, and three voices, by Marcello ; and in the course of the two following years four more parts, including in the whole the first fifty psalms, were published. In the prefatory address of the poet and composer, the nature of the work is explained. Of the paraphrase they state, that the original text is as closely followed as possible, and that the verse is of various metres and without rhyme. Of the music it is observed, that as the subject required the words and sentiments to be clearly and properly expressed, it is for the most part adapted to two voices only. The writer says, however, that it may and ought to be sung by a great number of voices, agreeably to the practice mentioned in the sacred writings, of psalms and hymns being sung by many companies and choruses. There are introduced into the work several of the most ancient and best known intonations of the Hebrews, which are still sung by the Jews, and are a species of music peculiar to that people. These, (which, for want of a better word, we must call *chants*) he says, he has sometimes accompanied according to the artificial practice of the moderns ; as he has also done by certain *cantilenas* of the ancient Greeks. The latter, he informs us, he has interpreted with the utmost diligence ; and by the help of Alypius and Gaudentius, has reduced them to modern practice.

To those mysterious and emphatic sentences, in which the royal prophet has denounced the terrors of divine justice, Marcello has adapted a peculiar kind of music, a modulation, as he calls it, in the *madrigalese* style, with a commixture of the diatonic and chromatic genera. In doing this, he compares his labours to those of a pilot, who, in a wide and tempestuous ocean, avails himself of every wind that may conduct him to his port, yet, in a long and dangerous voyage, is constrained to vary his course.

A few brief directions for the performance of the several compositions, and a modest apology for the defects of the work, conclude this preface ; which, though written under the influence of strong prejudices, contains an ingenious and learned dissertation on the subject of poetry and music.

X

For a character of the work we must refer to the numerous letters and testimonies of eminent musicians and others, which accompany it. In these it is stated, that some of the music had been adapted to German words, and performed, with great applause, in the Cathedral Church of Hamburgh; that the Russians had translated the paraphrase into their language, adapting it to the original music of Marcello; that, at Rome, the compositions were held in the highest estimation by all who professed to understand or to love music; and that at the palace of Cardinal Ottoboni, there was a musical assembly once a week, in which some of the works of Corelli and one of the psalms of Marcello made constantly a part of the entertainment.

When the news of Marcello's death arrived at Rome, the Pope, as a public testimony of respect for his memory, ordered a solemn musical service to be performed on a day appointed for the usual assembly. The room was hung with black, and the performers and all other persons present were in mourning.

Mr. Charles Avison, organist of Newcastle, has celebrated the above work of Marcello in a tract, entitled an Essay on Musical Expression; and he issued proposals for publishing, by subscription, an edition of it revised by himself. The execution of this design devolved, however, upon Mr. John Garth of Durham, who adapted to the music suitable words from our own prose translation of the psalms; and, by the assistance of a numerous subscription, the work was completed and published in eight folio volumes. Several specimens of his psalms are to be found in Stevens's Sacred Music; and parts of his fourth and seventh psalms, as arranged for keyed instruments, are inserted in Dr. Crotch's Selections.

From the extent of his studies, it might be supposed that Marcello devoted himself wholly to a life of ease and retirement. This, however, was not the case; for he held several honourable posts in the state, and, as a zealous and active magistrate, was ever ready to contribute his share of attention and labour towards the support of that government under which he lived. He was, for many years, a judge in one of the Councils of Forty; but from thence he was removed to the charge of proveditor of Pola, and afterwards was appointed to the office of chamberlain or treasurer of the city of Brescia. He died at this place in the year 1739, and was buried in the Church of the Minor Observants of St. Joseph's of Brescia.

Marcello left behind him, in manuscript, a *Treatise on Proportions*, another on the *Musical System*, and a third on the *Harmonical Concords*, with a great number of poetical compositions.

His printed works inserted in the Dutch catalogues were, " VI *Sonate à Violoncello solo e Basso continuo, Opera Prima;*" " XII *Sonate à Flauto solo e Basso continuo, Opera Seconda;*" and " VI *Sonate à tre, due Violoncelli, o due Viole da Gamba, e Violoncello o Basso continuo,*" called " *Opera Seconda.*"

Mr. Avison has asserted that the psalms of Marcello contain the most perfect assemblage of the grand, the beautiful, and the pathetic in music, that had ever been known; yet there have not been wanting men of sound judgment and great skill, who assert that their general levity renders them more adapted to private entertainment than the service of the church. That they abound in evidences of a fertile imagination, improved to a high degree by study, all persons must allow; but whoever will contemplate that style of music which, in the purest ages, has been thought best adapted to excite devout affections, and understands what is meant in music by the epithets sublime and pathetic, will be apt to entertain a doubt whether these epithets can, with greater propriety, be applied to them than to many less celebrated compositions.

OF THE MUSIC, DANCES, AND COSTUME OF THE SCOTCH.

ALTHOUGH, with the exception of some few districts, the inhabitants of the mountains of Scotland have long mingled with other nations, and though in the course of these latter years, many points of belief, of manners, and of traditions, which were peculiar to them, have disappeared in consequence of their extended intercourse; yet with respect to their music, dances, and costume, the Celts possess original monuments, and types of the olden time, which, according to all the chances of probability, will never lose their primitive character. Hence the national airs which they have been accustomed to sing, either on domestic occasions, or on their march against the foe, their dances which tend to give them their extreme agility, and their costume, so remarkable for its grace and convenience, will most likely survive when their language and their physiognomical structure shall have been either lost, or changed in their mixture with other people.

As long as the ear shall continue to be charmed, and the heart to be warmed, by the magic of melody, so long will the music of the Celts continue to claim its admirers. Added to which, it has this peculiarity, that it cannot be combined with the learned theories of our composers; its gamut being defective in the intervals of the major fourth and seventh, and not admitting of any harmonic accompaniment, stamps it with that character of simplicity which proves it to be the true music of nature, and, as such, the sure favourite of those who judge of music by their feelings, and not according to the rules of science. Another very remarkable character of this music, is its great ductibility, by means of which the performer can at pleasure communicate to his hearers the sentiment, the passion, by which he is animated. The mountaineer, whether he sadly follow the funeral of his friend, traverse the narrow defiles of his mountains, skim over the smooth surface of his lakes, or march proudly against the enemy, causes us to recognise, in the different airs which he sings on each occasion, something that partakes of the nature of the situation, something, according to his subject, powerfully expressive either of grief, of melancholy, or of resistless valour. Be it either graceful, complaining, playful, or warlike, the moment that it receives a peculiar character, no variation can give a new feature to it.

Between the *Reel*, the original dance of the Scotch, and the *Waltz*, a German dance, which may equally be considered as original, there exists nearly the same difference as between the two respective kinds of music. The Reel is light, gay, and energetic, and preserves its native character in spite of the strange innovations which have been attempted to be introduced into it: the Waltz is more voluptuous, full of art and contrivance, and has nothing of the vigour and simplicity of the Reel.

When we behold the Scotch giving a loose to the pleasure of this favourite dance, we are at once induced to believe that their very hearts and souls possess something of the liberty and freedom displayed in its movements; whilst those who take a pleasure in the multiplied gesture and soft evolutions of the Waltz, lead the spectator to conclude, from the very opposite reason, that their ideas and their conduct are in some measure in accordance with the same.

The other European dances are composed of figures and combinations taken from the Reel; the country dance, for instance, is but a modification of it, and much less ingenious than the original, since the majority of the dancers remain for the greater part inactive. The Waltz, it is true, has also served as the type of the national dances of some of the countries of Europe.

The Scotch costume does not possess less grace, elegance, and simplicity than their music and their dance. By this costume I do not mean that fantastical dress which the caprice of certain strangers has been pleased to designate by that name, but such as it is still seen in the families of the mountaineers, who have lost nothing of their ancient inheritance. The kilt, which has been unworthily mutilated in the service of the English army, bears scarcely any relation to the original tunic, harmoniously diversified by a variety of colours. It is the same with respect to the bonnet, some vestiges of which are still to be found among the Biscayans, and which has been so perverted in its form as to resemble the cap worn by the Prussian grenadiers; a medley scarcely less strange and discordant, than would be a simple Gaelic air interpolated by German harmony.

A FRENCH TRAVELLER.

HAYDN'S LAST APPEARANCE IN PUBLIC.

To the Editor of the HARMONICON.

SIR,

As the great object of your valuable journal is to afford the public correct details of the history of the art, and authenticated anecdotes of the great musicians who have raised it to its present importance in the scale of human attainments, you will oblige me by giving an early place to the following observations. In the extracts which you made in your number for June last, from Mr. Crosse's interesting account of the grand music meeting at York, is a statement that Haydn's last appearance in public, on occasion of the performance of his sublime oratorio of the *Creation*, took place in the year 1805. A mistake is here made in dates; it was on the 27th of March, 1809, that this interesting circumstance in the history of the art occurred, and which preceded Haydn's death by exactly two months. The following are the correct particulars of this fact, as I collected them from the German journals of that period, for the purposes of my Biographical work.

During the winter of 1809, numerous meetings had been held of all the principal amateurs in Vienna, who assembled every Sunday evening, to execute the works of the best masters. On these occasions more than 1500 persons met in the great hall of the city, all eager either to enjoy the best of music, or to take a part in its performance. As a worthy termination to this series of concerts, it was determined to give the *Creation* of Haydn.

Though the venerable composer had not quitted his retreat for nearly two years, yet some of his more intimate friends were fortunate enough to prevail upon him to attend on this occasion. When it was known that he had given his assent, there was not a lover of music in this most musical of towns who did not crowd anxiously to the spot, in order to obtain an entrance. This was the evening of the 27th of March, 1809. For several hours before the arrival of the illustrious man, the hall was crowded to excess. A triple row of elevated seats occupied the centre of the room, on which were seen the first artists of the place, waiting to receive their venerable master, among whom might be noticed a Salieri, a Girowetz, a Hummel, &c. A more elevated spot was left vacant to receive Haydn.

The moment the signal of his approach was given, one individual feeling, a kind of moral electricity, communicated itself to every soul present. The Princess Esterhazy, at the head of several ladies of distinction, went to the door to receive him. The illustrious old man was carried in an arm chair to the place destined for him, amidst a tumult of acclamation, intermingled by a salute of trumpets, and of the whole orchestra. The Princess Esterhazy was seated on his right, and on his left the author of *Les Danaides*.

Haydn, who had not anticipated such a triumphant scene, was quite overcome, and could express his feelings only in interrupted words:—"Never," said he, "did I experience such delight as this!—were I but permitted to breathe my last at this moment, then should I be sure of entering happy into another world!"

At this moment, the signal was given by Salieri, who directed the orchestra. At the piano was Kreutzer, Clementi was first violin, and Madam Fischer, and MM. Wainmuller, Radichi, and the very elect of the amateurs of Vienna, commenced the execution of the most beautiful work of Haydn's genius, with an enthusiasm and a force of expression caught from the presence of the master, and inspired by the occasion. Every virtuoso seemed to surpass himself; the audience participated in the enthusiasm of the moment, and experienced emotions which justly rank among the noblest of our nature; many a handkerchief was seen waving, but more were moist with the tear that had glistened in many a bright eye. Unable to give utterance to his feelings, Haydn could but bow, and raise his hands to heaven, in token of his gratitude.

The exquisite sensibility that had directed this fête had also foreseen that it might prove too great an effort for the weakness of age. The persons who were to carry him out, therefore, made their appearance at the end of the first act. The ladies and all around joined in entreating him to retire, and he was borne forth with the same triumphant acclamation that had greeted his entrance. There was, however, this difference of feeling in the latter case, that, at the moment he was seen to disappear at the end of the hall, it appeared to each spectator as if he had bade them the last farewell. This presentiment was too just. Haydn re-entered his retreat, and existed no longer for this world, on the 31st of May following.

I have the honour to be,

Sir, &c. &c. &c.

FAYOLLE.

THE PRESENT STATE OF MUSIC IN SPAIN.

As it but rarely happens that·we receive original communications from Spain, or even indirect information respecting the state of the fine arts in that ill-fated country at the present period, we trust that the following particulars, translated from a foreign journal, that pledges itself for their authenticity, will not prove unacceptable to our readers.·

Extract from a private letter, dated Madrid, Dec. 1824.

* * * * Allow me now to speak to you on *musical* subjects; and though the pupil here addresses his master, it may be fairly supposed, that the latter will be pleased to receive a perfectly *faithful* account of the state of the art in this country.

The·office I hold leaves me leisure enough to keep up an intercourse with the principal artists of this city, and to frequent the musical assemblies, but these take place very rarely. Though I am but an amateur, yet you will laugh, when I tell you, that I pass here for a performer (*virtuoso*) of the second rank, and for a musical judge of the first. I should never have dreamt that my exceedingly humble pretensions as a player on the flute, and particularly on the flageolet, would procure me the honour to play duets almost daily with the king, and sometimes with the Infant of Spain.—I have also been obliged to compose for these most high personages, as well as for other amateurs and friends, a great many Waltzes, Sonatas, Preludes, &c.

The taste of the Spanish public* requires, of all things, subjects that are merely pleasing, somewhat like those of the elder Pleyel. Upon the whole, instrumental music is much less liked than vocal music, and boleros.

The *native composers* are, generally speaking, extremely insignificant. Spain can boast of but *one* good composer—Carnicer. He at present directs the Opera of the capital, and has acquired considerable fame by several works written in the style of Rossini, without, however, attaining to the high genius of his prototype. The productions of the other composers do not often exceed the limits of waltzes, country-dances, variations, and the like; and whatever is produced as original in church music is very shallow, and deficient in knowledge of harmony.

Though the Spanish genius is not, or seems not, capable of giving birth to any musical works of importance, yet the old adage is illustrated here, that it is easier to find fault with what is done, than to do better: the Spaniard has a decided passion for criticism and satire; whether just or not is the same thing, so that he may vent his spleen.

Rossini is raised here into "the highest heaven of invention;" and his principal operas, to be candid, are tolerably performed in this city, as well as in Barcelona, both places having very respectable singers, both male and female, the orchestra consisting partly of natives, and partly of Italians. Rossini ranks in Spain far above Mozart, of whose works they know nothing but a few piano-forte pieces, and some quartetts. It would, indeed, be a desirable, but a very arduous undertaknig, to introduce into Spain the best works of this divine composer.

Among the *instrumental* performers of note resident here, I name to you, above all others, a first-rate piano-forte player, Madame Medeck, of Russian origin, and

* We have printed in Italics whatever is written so in the original.

brought up in the Conservatory of Music at Paris. Her husband, a native of Germany, is a good violoncellist, and possessed of profound acquirements in harmony. His compositions are, however, of too serious a character to please the taste of the "gay world" of Madrid.

This clever couple came here from Valencay, and were afterwards received in the King's chapel. But, a few months ago, both lost their places, and they now support themselves by giving instructions. A grand piano-forte of six octaves, which they had procured at a great expense from Vienna, passes for the very best in the kingdom. In their house one hears, from time to time, selections of German music by Mozart, Himmel, Dussek, Klengel, Cramer, Kalkbrenner, &c., which are here considered to be great rarities, since foreign printed compositions can, strictly speaking, be only obtained by being *smuggled* into the country.—A Portuguese pianoforte player, *Bomtempo*, is perhaps known to you by his compositions in the Portuguese taste. Besides him, we have some other good pianists, and particularly good organists, yet who would probably, in our country (Germany), pass only for artists of the second rank.

We have also three good *violin-players*, neither of whom, however, at all equals Kreutzer, Rode, and others of more modern reputation. We have likewise an excellent *violoncellist*, though considerably inferior to such men as Romberg and Duport; and, lastly, one solitary performer on the *hautboy*.—The harp is little played here, as there is much want of a well-qualified master for that instrument. To make up for these deficiencies, we have, however, a host of guitar-players of the very first excellence. The guitar is indeed the hobby of the Spaniards, in the learning of which they frequently employ much more time than would be requisite to make an excellent violin-player. It was here that I first heard difficulties executed on the guitar, that I had only been in the habit of hearing mastered on the piano-forte. But, notwithstanding, they excite in every one, save a Spaniard, but a very short-lived interest.

I was rather surprised to meet in this city with three very skilful *female* players on the *flute;* so skilful indeed, that one cannot hear their performance without pleasure. Yet to my taste, beautiful women were not created to be accomplished on an instrument so entirely masculine.

THE FITZWILLIAM MUSIC.

THE University of Cambridge, among other magnificent collections of works connected with the Fine Arts, possesses the rare and valuable manuscript music collected by the Earl Fitzwilliam during his residence in Italy. It consists of a numerous collection of the music, principally sacred, of Palestrina, Pergolesi, Carissimi, Durante, Leonardo Leo, Jomelli, Clari, Padre Martini, and other classical composers of the Italian school, and contains compositions which have never yet been published, and which, even in manuscript, are extremely rare. We learn that the University has most liberally granted to the well-known organist and composer, Mr. Vincent Novello, permission to publish such parts of this music as he may think will prove most gratifying to the admirers of the Ancient school. As the productions of the early masters are, for the most part, written for comparatively few instruments, it is Mr. Novello's intention to publish the full score of the pieces he selects, exactly as they were intended to be performed by the composers, with the important and useful addition, however, of an arranged accompaniment for the organ or piano-forte, for the accommodation of those not used to play from score. In this age when music seems rapidly sinking into triviality, it is highly gratifying to see this attention paid to the great pillars and founders of the art, of whose works it may be said, as of the works of another great master of the human passions, "they are not of an age, but for all time." We at the same time feel assured, that there is no person better qualified for so delicate and difficult a task as Mr. Novello, it being a department of the art to which he has long usefully devoted his attention; and as the work is to be brought forward under the immediate patronage of the Chancellor and University of Cambridge, we can have no doubt of the success of the undertaking.

THE AFFAIR OF THE HEART.

A WORK has just appeared at Paris, entitled, "Particulars relative to the Consecration of the Heart of Gretry, or an Historical Sketch of the Facts that transpired in the Action brought by the city of Liege against his Nephew, Flamand Gretry*;" which is followed by the arguments employed in justification, and which were laid at the feet of his Majesty Charles X. This sketch is embellished with different views by distinguished artists; a fine portrait of Gretry, after Isaby; of fac similes, &c.; with the following epigraph taken from Gresset:

La noirceur masque en vain le poison qu'elle verse;
Tout se sait, tôt ou tard, et la vérité perce;
Par eux-mêmes, souvent, les méchans sont trahis.

All the public prints have teemed of late with accounts of the trial relative to the heart of Gretry, and of the statements which M. Flamand has drawn up in justification of his conduct, which were intended to have been offered to the city of Liege, but of which M. Flamand seems to have changed the destination. Several of the Cours Souveraines have returned verdicts in favour of Gretry's townsmen, and the reason of these decrees not being carried into effect is, that M. Flamand has referred his cause to the Council of State, which has not yet pronounced a definitive sentence. So far, no censure attaches to the nephew of Gretry. He is anxious that the heart of his uncle should not be transported into a foreign land; and, under this view of the question, the whole of France cannot but offer up one united vow that his pious resistance may obtain a complete triumph. But there is another point, relative to which we cannot excuse him; and that is, the style of the documents which he has just published. The shade of Gretry will, on more than one occasion, have reason to feel indignant at the tone which he assumes, and above all at the kind of diatribe which he launches against the gentlemen professionally employed by his opponents. That he should refute the arguments of his adversaries, that he should oppose reason to sarcasm, nothing is more natural: but let him not transform himself into a gladiator; let not the tomb of Gretry be converted into an arena, where the worst passions of our nature are brought into sanguinary conflict. Genuine good feeling will never borrow the language of the bar to justify its pious sorrows; all it has

to do is to expose facts, in order to excite the sympathy of every generous mind.

The misguided zeal of M. Flamand Gretry sometimes hurries him into details, which are not without their pleasantry. Let us hear the words in which the writer describes his conduct after an audience at the Cour Royale, in which M. le President Seguier had ordered that the decrees of this court should be carried into execution, notwithstanding the opposition of M. le Préfet de Police.

"Figure to yourself, if possible," exclaims M. Flamand Gretry, "what were the feelings that overwhelmed my shuddering spirit, when I heard these two frightful decrees, which were hurled like a thunderbolt against me! Suddenly, leaving all my papers upon the bench before me, I dashed like one distracted through the double folding doors of the tribunal, and rushed to find the Prefect of Police, in order to give him instant notice of what had passed, and warn him of the danger that loured over his head. This magistrate, actuated by a laudable zeal for the powers of his office, and the respect due to its decrees, immediately gave me an order to carry to M. le Maire d'Enghien. Happy at being the bearer of such an order, but seized with a horrible fear of not arriving in time at the Hermitage, with bewildered brain and haggard eye, like some wretch who has escaped from the hands of justice, I rushed out upon the Place, I sprung into the first cabriolet that presented itself; the driver gazed at me in astonishment, not knowing what to do. All the words I could utter were: 'On, on!'—'Where, Sir?'—'I will tell you'—'But where am I to take you, Sir?'—'On, I say, on!'—'But good God, Sir, where?'—'I will tell you—it is an affair of the heart....'"

We will not extend our quotation farther; this will be quite sufficient to prove that M. Flamand Gretry is never more merry than when he is sad.

The author has swelled his volume with all verbal processes, pleadings, opinions, decrees, and ordinances to which his dispute with the city of Liege gave occasion. It is true that this is not the most amusing part of the work, but, by way of making some amends, he has embellished his memoir with several very pretty lithographic designs, a portrait of Gretry, which is a perfect likeness, and two fac similes of the celebrated composer's writing. These ornaments may serve to rescue for awhile M. Flamand's book from oblivion.

YORKSHIRE AMATEUR MEETING.

THE rapid progress of music in England may be inferred from the following account, which exhibits a taste and judgment in selection, that puts to the blush some of the most fashionable private concerts, performed by professors, that the metropolis has witnessed during the season now terminating.

The seventeenth annual meeting of the Yorkshire Amateurs of Music was held at Leeds, at the latter end of June last, and very numerously attended by gentlemen from all the principal towns of the county. These meetings deservedly excite great attention in the musical world. The first concert took place on Wednesday morning in the Music Hall, when about 560 tickets were disposed of, and the room was quite filled: the performances were ably led by Mr. White, assisted by Dr. Camidge. The band consisted of forty-seven persons,

* In the HARMONICON, Vol. II. page 88, will be found some particulars of this extraordinary trial.

of whom twenty-four performed on stringed, and twenty-three on wind instruments, &c. The selection combined much of excellence and novelty. The first piece was a Symphony of Haydn, No. 8 of Salomon's set, in E flat, in which the composer has endeavoured to depict the approach of a thunder storm, and the consequent dispersion of a family in the country, with the subsequent return of fine weather. This was followed by Webbe's Glee, composed for the Royal Society of Musicians, *Thy Voice, O Harmony*; Rossini's Song—*There's a Grief*, was prettily sung by Miss Scruton. This was followed by an Overture by Schmitt, a composer of whom we had not previously heard, but whose reputation cannot fail to be raised by it; a Glee, by J. S. Smith, *As on a Summer's Day*, remarkable for its happy expression of the words; and Arne's celebrated *Hymn of Eve*, beautifully sung by Miss Farrar. Wilbye's fine old Madrigal, five voices, *Flora gave me fairest flowers*, was deservedly encored. The first part was closed by Spontini's magnificent Overture, *Olympia*. The second part opened with Winter's Grand Battle Symphony and Chorus, which was most effectively performed. Webbe's difficult glee, *Discord*, was well executed. Handel's *Lascia amor*, the finest perhaps of his Italian songs in *Orlando*, which has this season been revived at the Concerts of Ancient Music, was sung with admirable spirit and effect by John Crosse, Esq. Spohr's Overture, *Faust*, was not particularly pleasing or effective. The Glee, *Oh! snatch me swift*, the first of Callcott's compositions, was well sung. Miss Farrar's powers appeared to much advantage in Cianchettini's *Se mai turbo*. Callcott's glee, *Hail, happy Albion*, was very fine. The day was appropriately concluded by Weber's Grand Jubilee Overture, composed for the King of Saxony, when he entered on the 50th year of his reign, and concluding with *God save the King*, which we are informed by Mr. Russell, in his recent tour in Germany, is adopted as the national song of the Saxons, Prussians, and Weimarese, as well as of the English. The air is taken by the wind instruments, with a rapid violin accompaniment; and it was extremely well performed.

In the afternoon of this day, at half-past six o'clock, a hundred and forty-eight gentlemen sat down to a sumptuous dinner, Darcy Lever, Esq. in the chair, who presided with his usual taste, wit, and spirit over a delighted company.

After *Non Nobis Domine* had been sung, the chairman thus addressed the meeting:—

GENTLEMEN,—In rising to express my thanks, for the honour you have done me, by placing me a second time in this chair, but, at the same time, considering myself the representative of one, whose high talent and attainments would have done ample justice to the station; and, conscious too of the insufficiency of my own resources, adequately to supply his place, I confess I labour under no little embarrassment: more especially, as I am in the presence of a number of gentlemen, all of whom I will presume have more unequivocal claims than I can possibly pretend to, to so gratifying a compliment. As we are assembled here, not only to celebrate the anniversary of the Amateur Concerts, but also to acknowledge our high opinion of the art and of the science of music, our attention is particularly attracted to the Universities of Oxford and Cambridge. In these seats of learning, when music received little or no encouragement from the community at large, its consequence was always recognised; and they conferred the degrees of *Bachelor* and *Doctor* on its students—degrees which elevate them to a rank in society so justly claimed by the professors of the liberal arts. Lightly as this delightful art was esteemed some years ago, it

has required, for its development, the labours of profound mathematical skill; without the aid of which, the minute and accurate division of sounds could never have been demonstrated. It was through this medium that the immortal Newton discovered the *major key* in music to have its foundation in *nature*; from the affinity between musical notes and the refrangibility of light. Walker, in his optics, says, the "analogy is double, there are only seven notes in music, exclusive of interposing semi-tones, and there are only, what are called, seven primary colours in nature, and these colours suffer a refraction through the prism, which marks proportionably the distances at which a performer would place his fingers on the finger board of his violin." That is, in the *diatonic* scale. Here, then, it is decidedly proved, that music is a *divine* art, and that the Almighty Being regulated its scale, in similar divisions with the good light which he gave to the universe! *(applause)*—and as the organ of sight is cheered by that great blessing, so is the ear delighted, and the mind soothed, by the delicious combination of musical sounds. From this proof alone, then, music can hold no *second* place in the arts. It must stand before all *human* and *mechanical* inventions: and greatly, indeed, are we, as Amateurs, indebted to those ancient nurseries of science, which had the *liberality*, at a time when music was nearly decried in this country, to rank it as worthy of a station in the four faculties, which are there taught, for the benefit of the human race.

The health of His Majesty was then drank, with four times four.

After this the chairman gave, THE LADIES. His third toast he thus prefaced:—

The military men, of all nations, have ever been attended to the field by music—nay, it is said, that even the effeminate Sybarites marched to the soft breathings of their flutes: and, that the Lacedæmonians "rushed like a torrent" on their foes to "the shrill screaming of the wry-neck'd fife."—Now, if these single instruments could so arouse and keep alive the energies of the soldiers, what effect must the more numerous, as well as the higher order of instruments produce, which compose the bands of the *British* army! an army which has so many claims on us, for the wonders it has achieved, the peace it was so instrumental in restoring to us, and the sacrifices and privations it has suffered for our sakes. Gratitude alone, independent of any other feeling, will prompt us to drink

The Duke of York and the Army.

After which, the DUKE of CLARENCE and the Navy was introduced in the following words:—

I must now launch into the stream of gratitude the generous navy of our country; and, as it is always customary to *crack a bottle*, whenever an individual ship is borne from her cradle to the fair bosom of the deep, we may very well afford a single glass to the numerous and stately progeny of Albion. Notwithstanding the refinement of our taste in music, Jack will always be a passionate admirer of the old song of "*Hearts of Oak*," and poor fellow! he has but too much experience, that "*a light heart, and a thin pair of breeches, go through the world my brave boys.*" A real British seamen is the pride, and however uncouth his carriage, the ornament of his country: to us of this institution, he comes particularly recommended; for, he is notorious for his attachment to a *fiddle*; and I have often heard by moonlight on the forecastle, in the midst of an unruffled sea, and under the steady breeze of a trade-wind, voices, natural taste, and pathos, that would have been no bad study for some of the more cultivated singers in an English orchestra. A British seamen is manly in his character; and I have ever observed, amidst the wildest traits of his eccentricities, that he has an unbounded reliance on an over-ruling Providence, and ever bears in mind, "the sweet little cherub that sits up aloft, to keep watch for the life of poor Jack!" Undaunted men of this cast were they then, and with officers so educated as the system of the new school has turned out, we may fairly rest in the assurance, that, "Britannia" will always "rule the waves!" and that

"Nought shall make our country rue,
If Britain to herself be true."

The greatest of Musicians,—he whose sublime, intellectual works are now despised by the *fashionable world*,—was thus remembered :—

We must now turn our pleasing attention to those who laid the foundation, on which the structure of our musical taste was erected. Our grateful recollection will point to the names of Corelli, Purcell, Matt. Lock, Pepusch, Boyce, Arne, and many others ; but above all, the name of him who stood so proudly pre-eminent, and who devoted his fine talents, to the praises of the *Source of all good*. Handel was truly the father of that sacred composition, entitled the Oratorio,—this mass of excellence burst on the astonished ear, at a time when instruments were very imperfectly known, their numbers extremely limited, and when the performers, in comparison with those of the present day, were scarcely versed with the mysteries of their art. And yet even at that time, who, that heard the combination of his chords, and the various modulations by which he enraptured the senses, but was fit to exclaim with the poet

" When the loud organ joins the tuneful choir,
Immortal powers incline their ear ;
While solemn sounds improve the sacred fire,
Borne on the swelling notes our souls aspire,
And Angels lean from Heaven to hear."

With such perceptions of this his wondrous power, I am sure we shall all celebrate with delight,

The memory, the immortal memory of Handel.

The name of a British genius, to whom the high title of BARD so peculiarly belongs, was not forgotten,—said the Chairman,—

—If ever individual equalled the boasted powers of the ancients, in the combination of poetry and music, and in its influence over the minds of men, it was certainly Charles Dibdin. If we look over the volumes of his productions, what a record do we see of the versatility of his talent, and of the strength of his muse, which never wearied. Where can we find a more powerful appeal to the feelings of humanity, than in his pathetic description of the death of the race-horse; and where a more affecting display of religious resignation, than in the "sheer hulk of poor Tom Bowling." His simple melodies, and easy rhymes held a dominion over the mind of the British seaman, which swelled the high tone of his manly daring into an enthusiasm, which rendered our national bulwark impregnable to the associated exertions of the whole world. When he descended from the station of high feeling, to the lower walk of satire, or of ridicule, his wit was too genuine to be debased by obscenity or atheism : and if his muse were indeed humble, she has at least this proud boast, that she retired from her labours, innocent, and untainted.

The memory of the modern Thales, Charles Dibdin.

A multitude of other toasts were drank, each accompanied by an appropriate speech from the inexhaustible chairman, who did not quit his seat till one in the morning.

Thursday's Concert, which was almost as numerously attended as that of the preceding day, opened with André's Grand Symphony, a very beautiful piece, the repetition of which was much desired, notwithstanding its great length. Webbe's Glee—*Hence! all ye vain Delights*, six voices, was well executed ; the two trebles by Miss Farrar, and Master Bridgewater, from York, Bishop's Song, *I give thee all*, by Miss F., was light and pretty. Stevenson's Glee, *Oh! Stranger, lend thy gentle Bark*, was also very pleasing. Weber's Overture, *La Preciosa*, though not one of his best, was well performed. In Bishop's Round, four voices, *Hark! 'tis the Indian Drum*, we were glad to see a Leeds amateur take part. Mr. Chadwick sang Pergolesi's well known song, " O Lord, have mercy upon me," with great taste and energy. Arne and Jackson's Glee—*Where the Bee sucks*, is a

specimen of genuine English music, and would. alone vindicate the claim of this country, to have produced eminent composers. The overtures of Romberg (Op. 60) and Beethoven, *Egmont*, were rendered highly effective. Horsley's charming glee, *By Celia's Arbour*, was performed with all the pathos, delicacy, and feeling which it so eminently requires. Mozart's Overture, *Idomeneo*, was perhaps never more finely performed ; Callcott's Glee, *Queen of the Valley*, followed, and was succeeded by Pacini's Scena e Rondo—*E chi sa mai*, which exhibited Miss Farrar's talents in a very favourable light. The vocal part closed with another of Callcott's glorious glees, from Ossian—*Father of Heroes*, which was sung with precision and powerful effect. The Finale was Rossini's striking overture—*La Gazza Ladra*, in which the military drums and fife are prominently introduced : it is unquestionably one of the best and most characteristic of his compositions, and was loudly encored, though the performance had already been prolonged till past three o'clock. On the whole, this musical meeting has gone off in an admirable manner, and with universal satisfaction both to the amateurs, and all whoat tended the concerts ; and the public of Leeds will look forward with pleasure to the next triennial meeting in that town.

HULL CHORAL SOCIETY.

On Friday, July 8th, the new organ built by Mr. Ward, of York, for the Hull Choral Society, was opened at their room, in Myton-gate, late the Rodney Lodge, by Dr. Camidge, who came over from York for the purpose. This instrument, which has given the most entire satisfaction to all who have heard it, contains eight stops and five octaves of keys, with an octave and a half of pedals, and has been acquired by the Society at a cost of 200l. A pair of fine kettle drums, recently purchased from Mr. Jenkinson, were also made use of on this occasion. Each subscribing member was furnished with two tickets of introduction, and the room was quite filled with a highly respectable audience. The performance was divided into two parts ; each of which was introduced by a voluntary by Dr. C., whose masterly finger commanded the most profound attention, and elicited strong testimonies of approbation. The first part consisted of the chorus ' Join voices,' by Dr. Cooke ; part of a service by Pergolesi and Mozart ; the 100th Psalm, as arranged by Dr. Hayes ; the chorus ' When his loud Voice,' from Handel's *Jephthah*, concluding with the *Hailstone* double chorus, from *Israel in Egypt*. The second part was composed of Haydn's Austrian National Hymn, and five choruses, from the *Messiah*—' Glory to God,' ' Behold the Lamb,' ' All we like Sheep,' ' Their Sound is gone out,' and ' Worthy is the Lamb.' The whole concluded with ' God save the King.' All the pieces were exceedingly well performed, particularly the chorus from *Jephthah*, and the last from the *Messiah*. The orchestra was under the direction of John Crosse, Esq., and consisted altogether of about 100 performers.

To the Editor of the HARMONICON.

SIR,—Amongst the various interesting subjects with which your excellent Miscellany abounds, I do not recollect to have seen any article upon that species of vocal music denominated *Madrigals*—nor any notice of the society whose name is derived from these compositions. Perhaps, therefore, the following sketch may not prove either unacceptable to you, or uninteresting to your numerous readers, and by giving it insertion you will oblige,

Sir, your obedient humble Servant,

G. N.

MADRIGAL SOCIETY.

Of the word *Madrigal*, it would be difficult to give a definition; etymologists are not agreed upon its meaning; the Italians of the sixteenth and seventeenth centuries first applied the term to music adapted to words on pastoral subjects, or the tender passion, and composed for four, five, and six voices [*].

In the time of Queen Elizabeth, it was the fashion for certain poetasters, whose names are now lost, to lavish adulation on her under the title of *Oriana*, and even to the close of her reign, many a hyperbolical lay was manufactured in praise of her beauty. No sooner had the verse appeared, than up rose the musician to set it to notes, and the joint emulation of writer and composer was incense most agreeable to the royal and antiquated virgin. These musical productions were styled *madrigals*, a name long before given in Italy to similar works.

These compositions, beautiful as they are, remained for a period neglected; a fate, let it be remembered, that also attended the dramas of our great bard. We have no record of any performance of madrigals until the early part of last century, when an association, consisting of a few individuals, met at a tavern for the purpose of practising, not only madrigals, but also the best specimens of music on sacred subjects, both of Italian and English masters, and they designated themselves by the title of the "*Madrigal Society* [†]."

An ancestor of the present city solicitor, Mr. Newman, was an early member of this Society, which met once a week at the Twelve Bells, in Bride-lane. In 1745 it was removed to the Founders' Arms, Lothbury, where by reason of many candidates seeking admission, it was found necessary to frame new laws and regulations to meet the exigences of their increased number; laws that, with a few alterations, form the code by which the society is now governed.

Rather beyond the middle of the last century, the following well known names appear on the list of members; viz., Dr. Worgan, Signor Barsanti, Dr. Arne, and his son Michael; and at a later period, Sir John Hawkins, the learned historian of music, E. T. Warren, the well known Secretary to the Catch Club, and Editor of that most invaluable work, *A Collection of Catches, Canons, and Glees for three, four, and five voices*; Alderman Clarke the present city chamberlain, G. Berg, the late philanthropic Granville Sharp, Drs. Cooke and Callcott, and some of the most eminent musicians of the present day.

The society, like all other human institutions, has suf-

fered the vicissitudes of prosperity and adversity: a living member can recollect the time when the attendance was insufficient for the performance of a madrigal. Though weak in numbers, the madrigalists were strong in zeal; they rallied, and the society became as efficient as ever.

The number of members is now limited to thirty; they dine together once a month at the Crown and Anchor Tavern, except in August and September, when there are no meetings; and the members take the presidency in rotation.

Their last meeting was on the 30th ult., Sir John Rogers, Bart., in the chair, and as a proof of the estimation in which that style of music, preserved by the Society, is held, the following distinguished list of amateurs, and professional visitors, united their talents with the members in the performances of the day, namely—

Of Amateurs,—Messrs. Blunt, Timothy Bramah, Cooper, Ferguson, Leslie, Luttrell, Nugent, Captain Rogers, Dr. Sainsbury, Sandford, Wentworth, Temple West, and Windus.

Of Professors,—Messrs. Attwood, Beale, Bellamy, Blackbourn, Braham, Dr. Carnaby, Clarke, Cole, T. Cooke, J. Elliott, C. S. Evans, Gore, Goss, Goulden, Horncastle, Horsley, Jolley, John Jolly, Nicks, Nield (Sen. and Jun.), Phillips, Sale (Sen. and Jun.), Smith, Terrail, Turle, and Vaughan; aided by the Choristers of St. Paul's and Westminster Abbey.

The pieces selected, for performance were the best specimens of the English and Italian schools of the seventeenth and eighteenth centuries, periods as rich in vocal composition as in literature.

Of the English school, the following masters are familiar to the amateur; viz., Morley, Ward, Wilbye, Bateson, Orlando Gibbons, and others of the *Elizabethan era*. Of the *Italian*, Palestrina, Steffani, Rossi, Stradella, Ferretti, Luca Marenzio, and other composers of about the same periods.

Immediately after dinner, "Non Nobis," and Dr. Cooke's "Amen," were sung; the voices of nearly seventy persons, in perfect harmony, produced a thrilling effect.

The performance commenced with "We have heard," the music by Palestrina, adapted to English words by Dr. Aldrich: followed by "Draw on, sweet Night," by Wilbye; "Laudate Dominum," by Rossi; "There's not a grove," by Ward; "Clori son fido Amanti," by Stradella, &c. &c. The following appeared to be favourites, and were sung twice; "I love, alas! I love thee," by Morley; "Singing alone," by the same author; "Gettano il Re," by Steffani; "Sister awake," by Bateson; "Stay, Corydon," by Wilbye.

"I will arise," by the Rev. Dr. Creyghton, was sung verse and chorus; the former by Master Lloyd, Messrs. Terrail, Vaughan, and J. B. Sale; the repetition in chorus had a fine effect.

The bass solo in "Qui diligit" was given by Mr. Bellamy with considerable energy; and the duet, by Masters Marquet and Mackellar, of the Westminster Choir, was sung very sweetly.

Mr. Greatorex, who is a member of the society, conducted the whole, which consisted of above twenty compositions, and the precision with which every performance was executed, gave evidence of the talent which he possesses.

The meeting broke up at eleven o'clock, every person present having been highly pleased with the entertainment. Probably so numerous and efficient a body of vocal talent has never been collected together by this Society since its first establishment.

---

[*] The word madrigal is derived by Menage from *mandra*, a sheepfold, for he supposed it to have been a pastoral song: hence *madrigale* in Italian. Bishop Huet considers it as a corruption of *Martegaux*, a name given to the inhabitants of a district of Provence, who, according to a learned French writer, excelled in this species of composition. (See *Revolutions de la langue Françoise, par M. l'Evêque de la Ravaliere.*) The latter seems the most reasonable etymology; though Dr. Burney is inclined to derive the word from *Olla Madra*, the commencement of certain short hymns addressed to the Virgin.—ED.

[†] The Madrigal Society was founded in 1741, by Mr. John Immyns, an attorney: the subscription was five shillings and sixpence a quarter, which defrayed all expences. They met on every Wednesday evening.—ED.

REVIEW OF MUSIC.

EIGHTH GRAND CONCERTO *for the* PIANO-FORTE, *with* ACCOMPANIMENTS *of a full Orchestra; composed, and dedicated to the Duchess of Hamilton, by* J. B. CRAMER. Op. 70, (Boosey and Co.) *Holles-street.*

It is the lot of most fine musical compositions to be heard while new with admiration, to be applauded with enthusiasm, to be performed everywhere and by every body for a certain time; then to be slighted, and though, perhaps, not "clean forgotten," to be at length discarded by those who at first hailed them with rapture, and ultimately to be almost utterly unknown, except by name, to the very next generation.

In proof of this assertion, so far as it regards music written for keyed instruments, we ask, where is the amateur to be found who knows anything of Scarlatti's or of Handel's lessons, once most deservedly the delight of their age? Doubtless, some few persons exist who have explored these rich mines of harmonic wealth, but we should be exceedingly perplexed if called upon to point out the individuals; it being understood that we speak not of professors, though we fear that a vast number of even these would shrink from such a question. Where now are any of Schobert's, Edelmann's, Koželuch's, or Pleyel's sonatas to be heard, though formerly so highly valued? But let us cast a view to the works of our own times, and inquire how many there are among the present youthful host of good performers that are acquainted with the compositions of Clementi and Dussek,—compositions so replete with every thing that genius, science, and strong feeling could impart? Alas! we fear that they are wretchedly small in number, and that the inordinate love of novelty will encourage the circulation of too many weak and evanescent productions, and thus check the progress of the musical art.

We are led to these remarks by reflecting on the neglect which Cramer's Concertos at present suffer, for we never now hear them publicly performed, and very rarely privately. Yet they are beautiful, and composed of materials that promised greater longevity; particularly Op. 10, in E flat, dedicated to Miss Jervis; Op. 16, in D minor, his *chef d'œuvre*, dedicated to Miss Scott; Op. 48, in C minor, dedicated to the Marchioness of Douglas, now Duchess of Hamilton; and Op. 51, in E flat, dedicated to Mrs. F. G. Smyth. If these are falling into disuse, while the author is living and floating on the full tide of popularity, must we be surprised that other works, not enjoying similar advantages, should be rejected and forgotten?

But Mr. Cramer is too active and well-judging, not to regulate himself in some degree by the prevailing wants of the day; novelty is demanded, and he wisely obeys the call; hence he has published the work now under notice, which we hope will satisfy for awhile the cravings of those who cannot relish anything that time has sanctioned. We may add, that we should not complain of the impatience for new compositions, if only such as the present were produced.

This Concerto is, according to the usual practice, divided into three movements; the first, in D minor, commences with a charming, though rather a lengthened, *tutti* of three pages, in a small character; the *solo* begins most splendidly, and proceeds, without any interruption from the orchestra, through a variety of brilliant passages, till it comes to a pause on the leading note of the key, when it passes into the second movement, a *larghetto* on the annexed elegant motivo:—

Melodious as this subject is, we do not think that in expanding it Mr. C. has wrought so much out of his material as he might have done; and the long *cadenza* of four closely-printed pages by which it concludes, though it will answer the purpose of a good exercise, is not in the author's happiest style. The Rondo, *à l'Espagnola*, atones amply for any deficiency in the middle movement. It is written on the following characteristic theme:—

This subject is worked with great ingenuity and spirit through fourteen pages, in which are many very remarkable passages, particularly for the left hand, and some striking modulations. The *tutti* of this Rondo contain a few bars of excellent imitation, in the good old style, which we regret not having room to insert, but recommend them to the especial notice of our readers. Of the *time*, by which term we mean the degree of quickness, of this last part of the Concerto, no indication appears; not even a solitary syllable is given to direct the performer, who is left to guess at the author's intention. We lament that Mr. Cramer does not fall into the laudable, and now almost universal custom, of denoting the time by Maelzel's metronome. During much more than a century, men of judgment and acknowledged ability have been struggling to introduce the pendulum in music, for the purpose of determining the exact measure of the first bar, though not to reduce the whole of a composition to mechanical precision; we cannot, therefore, but regret that, at a moment when so desirable an object is nearly accomplished, an artist of so much influence as Mr. Cramer possesses, should not give his countenance to a practice of such vast utility.

BEETHOVEN'S GRAND SYMPHONIES, *arranged for the* PIANO-FORTE, *with* ACCOMPANIMENTS *of* FLUTE, VIOLIN, *and* VIOLONCELLO, *by* J. N. HUMMEL, *Maitre de Chapelle to the Duke of Saxe Weimar.* No. 1. (*For the Proprietor, by* Chappell and Co., 50, *New Bond Street.*)

THIS is the first number of a work which the spirited proprietor of the edition of *Mozart's Symphonies, arranged by Hummel,* has just commenced publishing. We hope that his present undertaking may, in every way, prove as successful as that which he has recently completed. The Symphony in C, now printed, is No. 1 of the quarto edition in score, and as it is amongst the earliest, so it is one of the most popular of Beethoven's grand orchestral compositions. In all the arrangements by Hummel that have passed under our notice, it has appeared to us that he might have rendered them more practicable to the great majority of amateurs, by thinning some of the passages where a multiplicity of notes demand a larger and more powerful hand than most female performers possess. In the present symphony, we do not perceive so much of this disposition to retain the less essential notes—octaves, for instance—as we observed formerly; yet the zeal of the editor to do justice to the composer has induced him to adapt several passages in a manner that will call the whole means of many performers into very active service. But, at the same time, it must be acknowledged, that what is lost in facility is gained in effect.

We regret not having given the first two or three bars of all Mozart's Symphonies that have been reviewed in this work; a *catalogue thématique* of them might thus have been formed, of a very useful kind. In some early number we will supply the deficiency. The *allegro* of the first movement of the present symphony begins thus:—

Amusemens de l'opera, *a Selection of the most admired* PIECES *from the latest foreign* OPERAS *and* BALLETS, *arranged for the* PIANO-FORTE, *without the words.* No. 7. (Boosey and Co., *Holles Street.*)

Terpsichore, *choix des* PIECES *tirées des* OPERAS *et* BALLETS, *par* Rossini, Weber, Gallenberg, Mozart, Beethoven, &c., *et mises pour le* PIANO-FORTE. No. 12. (Wessel and Stodart, 1, *Soho Square.*)

THE former numbers of the *Amusemens de l'opera* have been noticed in this work. The present consists of four pieces from Spohr's opera, *Jessonda*, which are well selected and arranged for the piano-forte.

No. 2, is a Rondo *alla polacca*, from the same opera, arranged by M. Mollwo.

---

favourite CONCERTO *for the* PIANO-FORTE, *composed by* MOZART, *newly arranged for Additional Keys, as performed in public by* J. B. CRAMER. (J. B. Cramer and Co., 201, *Regent Street.*)

THE comparative simplicity of this Concerto renders it one of the best, for the generality of performers, of the many composed by Mozart; full of a very intelligible melody, and abounding less in those passages of elaborate modulation and difficult execution than most of his other works of the same class, it will invite a greater number of practitioners, and obtain a much wider circulation, than can ever be expected for those of the more scientific kind. But while we admit that this composition has many admirers, and amongst these some of the first professors of the age, we must avow that it has never appeared to us as one of Mozart's happiest productions. There is, judging by the impression it makes on our sense, a commonness in its subjects and cadences that does not announce the name of its illustrious author. It was written, according to the composer's own *catalogue thématique* of his works, in 1784, and before any of the most astonishing proofs of his genius had been given to the world. This concerto is composed for a full orchestra, but the piano-forte part only is published in the present edition. It opens thus :—

The second movement is an andantino in B flat, two-four time. The last movement, an *allegro* in F, is in the same time as the second.

We are decidedly of opinion that Mr. Cramer has acted with judgment in the occasional use which he has made in this edition of those additional notes that were unknown in Mozart's time. He has introduced them with great caution, and very sparingly, and has, we are quite persuaded, employed them only where the author would have used them, had they been invented during his life. The work is remarkably well brought out, and, considering all things, at a reasonable price.

---

1. The Huntsman's Chorus, LA CHASSE, *for the* PIANO-FORTE, *composed by* AUG. MEVES. (Clementi and Co., *Cheapside.*)

2. The Laughing Chorus, a DIVERTIMENTO, *for the* PIANO-FORTE. *Composed and published by the same.*

3. A DIVERTIMENTO *for the* PIANO-FORTE *and* FLUTE, *in which are introduced admired airs from Der Freischütz, arranged by* JAMES CLARK. (Eavestaff, 66, *Great Russell Street.*)

4. Aufforderung zum Tanze, *or the Invitation to Dance,* BRILLIANT RONDO, *for the* PIANO-FORTE, *composed by* CARL MARIA VON WEBER. Op. 65. (Paine and Hopkins, 69, *Cornhill.*)

Nos. 1 and 2 of the above, are divertimentos made up of airs from the *Freischutz*. Mr. Meves has combined and enlarged the subjects, with a great deal of taste, in a popular manner, and adapted them exceedingly well to the piano-forte, avoiding the extremes of difficulty and ease; so that they will suit a large class of performers.

No. 3, by Mr. Clarke, is also a selection of some of the most charming airs from the same admirable opera, which are united very skilfully, so as to produce a charming piece of music, and one that we recommend without any hesitation to our readers.

The last of these pieces, No. 4, is very pretty, very easy to execute, and has other recommendations of a minor kind; but we should not have named the original, the romantic Weber, as its author, had we been desired to guess the writer: we should rather have ascribed it to some of our own countrymen, who often assume the title of composer, in consequence of having succeeded in imitating something by somebody else, and then proved equally successful in passing it off amongst the unwary as their own. After a page of very good introduction, the rest of this piece is an extended waltz, full of suavity, and too genteel in its manner, to possess any thing that is striking or new, but very likely to find its way into a great deal of extremely good company.

---

1. Aure Felici, *composed by* CARAFA, *and arranged, with* VARIATIONS *for the* PIANO-FORTE, *by* LOUIS JANSEN. (Bedford Musical Repository, *Southampton-Row*).

2. Fra Tante Angoscie, *with* VARIATIONS *for the* PIANO-FORTE, *composed by* RICHARD PLATT. (Balls, 408, *Oxford Street.*)

3. INTRODUCTION *and* AIR, Adeline, *composed and arranged with* VARIATIONS, *by* WILLIAM KNOWLES. (Monro and May, 11, *Holborn Bars.*)

4. *The Admired* SICILIAN MELODY, *known as* "Home! sweet home!" *arranged with* VARIATIONS *for the* PIANO-FORTE, *with an* ACCOMPANIMENT *for the* FLUTE, *by* G. B. STANLEY. (Bedford Musical Repository.)

MR. JANSEN has given the charming air of Carafa without very highly illustrating its beauties, but he has treated it like a musician, and it passes out of his hands undamaged. Mr. Platt has altered the original base of the same air as the preceding, by the introduction of an F sharp, and robbed it of a peculiarity that added much to the beauty of its effect. In variation the second there is a clash of discords, arising out of a carelessness in the manner of treating the passing notes, that assailed our ears most uncivilly. Mr. Platt mistakes the name of the air he has arranged; *Fra Tante Angoscie* are the words of the first movement; he has chosen *Aure Felici*, the second movement.

No. 3 is rather trite in its manner, and has nothing very remarkable in its fabric. No. 4 may be designated much in the same language; though we admire Mr. Stanley's spirit, manifested in his title-page, in boldly reminding the world that "Home! sweet home!" is a Sicilian, and not an English air.

---

1. *The Celebrated Tyrolienne,* "Celui qui sut toucher mon cœur," *arranged with* VARIATIONS *for the* PIANO-FORTE, *by* E. BERLOT. (Bedford Musical Repository, *Southampton Row, Russell Square.*)

2. *The Scottish Melody,* "Coming through the rye," *arranged with* VARIATIONS *and embellishments for the* PIANO-FORTE, *with a* FLUTE *Accompaniment,* ad lib. *by* CHARLES ARNOLD. (*Published by the same.*)

3. *The Popular Air introduced in the Opera of* The Barber of Seville, *arranged as a* RONDO *for the* PIANO-FORTE, *by* M. HOLST. (*Published by the same.*)

4. *The Imperial* GRAND MARCH, *and Quick-step, with* ACCOMPANIMENTS *for the* FLUTE *and* VIOLONCELLO, *by* T. B. PHIPPS. (*Published by the same.*)

5. THE PRECIOSA RONDO, *from* WEBER'S Preciosa, *arranged as a* DIVERTIMENTO *for the* PIANO-FORTE, *by* T. B. PHIPPS. (*Published by the same.*)

THE whole of these are very much in the ordinary style of airs with variations. There is a certain share of prettiness in most of them, and they are all divested of every kind of difficulty that might operate in deterring general purchasers.

---

1. RONDOLETTO BRILLANTE, *on a Cavatina introduced in* L'Italiana in Algieri, *composed for the* PIANO FORTE, *by* CHARLES CZERNEY. Op. 74. (Boosey and Co., *Holles Street.*)

2. BAVARIAN AIR, *composed by* SPONTINI, *arranged with an* Introduction and Variations *for the* PIANO-FORTE, *by* C. CZERNEY. Op. 86. (J. B. Cramer, Addison, and Beale, 201, *Regent Street.*)

3. A FIRST RONDINO, *on the Cavatina,* "Cara deh attendimi," *from* Rossini's Zelmira, *for the* PIANO-FORTE, *by* C. CZERNEY. (Cocks and Co., Princes Street, *Hanover Square.*)

THE termination *etto* is, as probably every one of our readers knows, diminutive in the Italian language; rondoletto is, therefore, a little rondo; but whether little in

length, or little in difficulty, the term does not actually imply. As this rondoletto extends to thirteen pages, shortness in duration cannot be meant. On the other hand, since the author, by means of extraneous modulations, or sudden transitions into keys rarely frequented, has rendered his present work anything rather than easy, he cannot mean to indicate facility by his title; we are, consequently, driven to conclude that it signifies nothing, an inference by no means hazardous in whatever concerns musical language. What the air is, we know, not, but take it for granted that it is an interpolation of Viennese origin. It was never, we believe, introduced into the opera in London, and has so small a claim to our notice, that it is not worth while to inquire into its history. M. Czerney certainly has not studied how to make it engaging to English performers generally: but possibly it may have charms for Germany, for which region he composed it, and he is not answerable for its migration to a country for the latitude whereof it is not calculated.

No. 2 having no diminutive title, is, by the rule of contrary, perhaps, less difficult than the former piece, but not possessed of more attractive qualities. The air itself has no feature, and the variations are all of the true manufactured kind,—composed at so much per page, and produced as a carpenter produces a packing case, or a smith a kitchen poker: except, however, the third, which is expressive, and shews that the composer is equal to better things when he is in the right humour.

The third of these has a received a diminutive title, as well as the first; but as it possesses merit, we are not inclined to dispute the propriety of its name. The *rondino* is not half so difficult as the *rondoletto*, and the subject of it * is one of Rossini's best airs. M. Czerney has treated it with discretion, and introduced into it no passages that a tolerable proficient on the instrument may not perform; and though he has spun it out to the unreasonable length of thirteen pages, yet it is not tedious. But the English price of it, three shillings and six pence, there having been no copyright to purchase, is most extravagant.

Qu'en pensez-vous? *a fifteenth* DIVERTIMENTO *for the* PIANO-FORTE, *composed by* J. B. CRAMER. (Paine and Hopkins, 69, *Cornhill.*)

THIS is but a bagatelle, and is, it must be acknowledged, very slight in texture; but nevertheless there is in it some air—it is therefore very reviving after the dry labours of M. Czerney, which we have just toiled through. We know not if our answer to the composer's question will be satisfactory; but we like candour on all occasions, critical ones particularly. This divertimento, we will add, is easy in point of execution, and a good deal of melody flows through it.

---

1. Il Sollievo, RONDO SCHERZANDO, *on a favourite* Scotch Air, *for the* PIANO FORTE, *composed by* CIPRIANI POTTER. *No.* 10 *of Airs.* (Clementi and Co., *Cheapside.*)

2. La Primavera, DIVERTIMENTO *for the* PIANO FORTE, *with* ACCOMPANIMENT *for the* FLUTE (*ad libitum,*) *introducing two favourite Airs, composed by* T. A. RAWLINGS. (Goulding and Co., *Soho Square.*)

THE first of these is formed of the beautiful Jacobite air, "Will ye go to Inverness??" and is arranged with

---

* Published in No. 12, p. 212 of the HARMONICON.
† Published in No. 7, p. 126 of the HARMONICON.

a studied attention to the ease of the performer. The author has not thrown much of his force into the present publication; and, indeed, a simple air is best treated in a simple manner.

Mr. Rawlings's divertimento is one of the most elegant trifles that we have met with for some time past: easy, but not beneath the notice of good performers; and though very simple, likely to gratify the best tastes, because these are always unsophisticated, and not confined to one species, or one age, of music. The two airs on which it is composed, are, "Since first I saw your face," Ford's beautiful madrigal, and Dr. Arne's charming song, "When daisies pied *," which are preceded by a good, and rather a shewy, introduction of three pages. The first of the airs is given almost note for note from the original; the slight deviations, upon the repeat of the parts, are modest and judicious. The second has some few additions made to it, but they are entitled to the same praise that we have bestowed on the alterations of the first.

THREE GRAND SONATAS for the PIANO-FORTE, composed by CHARLES AMBROSE. Nos. 1, 2, and 3. (Royal Harmonic Institution, 246, Regent Street.)

THE term Sonata is become rare, and its style is now rather uncommon. Mr. Ambrose has made a very respectable effort to revive the title and manner of this once esteemed species of composition, and has given us three Sonatas, published separately, that, thirty years ago, would have been in great request. They are after (in the language of painters) Dussek, in whose school the author seems to have studied much, and not unsuccessfully, with a little mixture of Kozeluch. The first and third are in E major, and the second in F flat. In the latter is introduced the sweet Scottish air, "Oh! my love's like the red red rose," with some variations, that would be deserving of much commendation, did they not depart too widely from the character of the air. We fear that these sonatas are too long, and in a form too unfashionable to repay Mr. Ambrose for his labour and ingenuity: but he is nevertheless entitled to praise from those who are not influenced in their opinions by the prevailing taste of the moment.

---

1. Pot-Pourri of FAVOURITE AIRS, from LOUIS SPOHR's Opera, Jessonda, arranged for the PIANO-FORTE by MOCKWITZ. (Ewer and Co., Bow Church Yard, and 263, Regent Street.)

SPOHR's Jessonda is a fine, scientific composition, but it is said to be too grave and learned for theatrical performance. This we can easily believe, judging from an examination of the adapted score; but there is much in it that is well calculated for the purpose to which it is applied in the present publication, which consists of many of the best pieces in the opera, exceedingly well arranged for the piano-forte, and published at a price that is marvellously moderate,—nineteen pages for three shillings—and ought to meet with public encouragement.

---

1. "La dolce Speranza," a favourite RONDO, composed by CARL MARIA von WEBER, with accompaniment of PIANO-FORTE. (Ewer and Co., 263, Regent Street.)

* For the latter air, see No. 25 of HARMONICON.

2. DUETTO, "Mentre Francisco faceva il brodo," in the Opera of Carlotta e Werter, composed by SIGNOR COCCIA. (Birchall and Co., New Bond Street.)

3. CAVATINA alla Polacca, "De sdegni tuoi mi rido," in the Opera of Adele de Lusignano, composed by SIGNOR CARAFA. (Birchall and Co.)

4. A Collection of select GERMAN NATIONAL MELODIES, arranged with ACCOMPANIMENT of PIANO FORTE, or GUITAR, by Mollwo and Derwort, Nos. 1 to 7. (Ewer and Co., Bow Church Yard, and 268, Regent Street.)

THE rondo by Weber is very airy and agreeable, but has none of those original traits that distinguish his music when he gives any force to his compositions.

Signor Coccia's duet is written entirely for scenic effect, and must lose much when deprived of action. It is exceedingly gay, and the words are set with a due regard to their meaning; praise that cannot always be bestowed on Italian dramatic music. There is a passage at the beginning of this composition, which shews that the author has formed his taste in the right school. Ex pede Herculem.

No. 3 is in Caraffa's usual style. He has gained a name from one composition, which is an excellent one undoubtedly; but he never exhibited much vigour before that appeared, nor has manifested much since. The present is tasteful, not new in any one passage, but unobjectionable as to construction.

The three first of the German melodies, are rather pretty, but possess no feature of nationality. In cases of this kind, either the names of the composers, or the original titles of the airs, should be affixed; or else they should be declared to be unknown. This would avoid any suspicion of their not being genuine. The fourth number, by Himmel, has more of character in it, but the English words are wretchedly set to it; doubtless by some stranger to the language. The fifth, by Weigl, is a graceful duettino. The sixth, by the same, is very common. The seventh, by Beethoven, a melody of sixteen bars, is exceedingly simple, but not devoid of a certain kind of beauty.

---

1. RECIT. and AIR, "Man to Man," the words from TASSO, composed by J. C. NIGHTINGALE. (Monro and May, Holborn.)

2. SONG, The lullaby of the Dove, composed by J. F. DANNELLY. (Preston, 71, Dean Street, Soho.)

3. SONG, "Grief's a Folly," in Der Freischütz, words by W. T. COLLARD, composed by WEBER. (Clementi and Co., Cheapside.)

4. SCOTTISH SONGS,—
    1. O say, bonny lass;
    2. The birks of Invermay;
    3. Auld Robin Gray;
    4. Donald;
    5. Tak' your auld cloak;
Sung by MISS PATON, as expressly arranged for her by S. WEBBE. (Eavestaff, 66, Great Russell Street, Bloomsbury.)

5. BALLAD, "There was a time," written by H. NOBLETTE, Esq., composed by ALEX. D. ROCHE. (Clementi and Co., Cheapside.)

6. SONG, "There is a sweet and pleasing hour," *written by* THOMAS BLAKE, *the music by* AUG. MEVES. (*By the Same.*)

7. BALLAD, "My ain sweet Annie," *in the Scottish style, composed by* JOHN WHITAKER. (Eavestaff, 6s, *Great Russell Street.*)

No. 1 is in the unmixed English style, with plenty of trumpets and drums; but there is some talent in it: the pastoral opening is pleasing, though not abounding in novelty of thought. In the third vocal staff, page 6, is a passage, containing false fifths, that are very painful, notwithstanding the covering of the accompaniment, which will perhaps be pleaded in abatement.

No. 2 will not circulate much beyond the composer's own friends.

We insert No. 3, merely to praise the manner in which the English words are written and adapted to the fine and celebrated Bacchanalian Song of Weber.

Under the fourth of these heads are five popular Scottish airs, with an accompaniment for Harp, or Piano-Forte, which are arranged in a very simple, modest manner, and form a striking contrast to some that have been published under great foreign names.

No. 5 has nothing uncommon in it, and the same remark will apply to No. 6.

No. 7 is a pretty Scottish song, but like so many of the Caledonian airs, that it seems to us more to resemble a republication than an original work.

FOREIGN MUSICAL REPORT.

VENICE.—(*Teatro alla Fenice.*) The new opera of *Alcibiade*, by Cordela, made a *fiasco*; as did also the Fabbrica, (*primo musico*,) and the tenor Falchinioni. The Borgondio (also *musico*) with her powerless voice, and want of method, made, as the Italians say, *nè freddo nè caldo*, (neither hot nor cold.) The *prima donna* Lalande, and the bass, Tamborini, pleased much. After the second representation, the theatre was closed, and opened again after a short interval with the *Mosè* of Rossini, which made a *furore*, and afforded an admirable opportunity for the display of the voice and action of David. An Englishman of the name of John Kellner gave the character of *Mosè*. The third opera of the season was Meyerbeer's *Crociato in Egitto*, which was received with the most unbounded applause; but unfortunately as the performer who sustained the principal character was unequal to the task, and did not please, it was suspended.

———(*Teatro San Luca.*)—Principal singers: Fanny Ayton, (an English lady,) *prima donna;* Favino Monelli, *prima tenora;* Ferdinando Lauretti, and Pietro Cappini, *buffi.* The operas last given here were *Clotilde*, by Coccia; *Chiara di Rosenburg*, by Generali; and *Elisa e Claudio*, by Mercadante. Fanny Ayton has a voice of no great power, but of a very pleasing kind, and she shows an excellent school.

MILAN.—The feast of St. Stephen, which is held in so much awe both by artists and composers, and so productive in *fiascos*, has passed, and we will give a short sketch of its products. Our theatre on this day, was filled to overflowing by more than 4000 persons, whose countenances beam with the liveliest satisfaction. But a singular fate seems to hang over new pieces; they all fail, and the disappointed multitude issue forth with altered brow, and changed demeanour; they repair to the *cafés*, where they launch forth with unsparing severity against all, both impressarj and singers, ballet-masters and dancers, which is as frequently retorted upon them by the indigent composers and artists, who accuse them of a want of all good taste, judgment, and discrimination. Means must,

however, be found to counteract the evil impression, and some other composition is resorted to, as unsuccessful, perhaps, as the former, when the only remedy is to retreat upon their body of reserve, and bring forward something of Rossini, beginning generally with that universal stopper of gaps, the *Barbiere*.

This year, however, did not commence with anything new. The opening opera was the *Vestale* of Spontini, with the grand ballet of *Tippoo Saib* by Taglioni. The company was the same as last season, with the exception of the substitution of the very mediocre tenor, Winter, and a bass of the name of Guglielmo Guglielmi, in place of Signori Verger and Reina. Signora Elisabetta Feron, the wife of our present impressario, without any regular engagement, gave the *Vestale*. Owing to indisposition, she was not in the best voice, but her style of singing is chaste, and without any superfluous ornaments, which in the performance of this character is an instance of self-denial, entitled to our warmest praise. But it is more than probable that *La Vestale* would have produced no impression with the best of orchestras, and the first of singers; so much for the taste of this place. On the fourth representation, recourse was had to Rossini, the *refugium peccatorum* of all theatres of the present day, and his *Semiramide* was produced. This was followed by *I Bacchanali di Roma* of Generali, after which came the *Il Don Giovanni*. Two new *Farci* are expected, one of which is from the pen of Carulli; then is to be produced a new opera by Sapienza, which is to be followed by the *Mosè* of Rossini, and heaven knows what besides. Our orchestra this season was augmented by two additional violins, and two violoncellos, which were a great improvement to it. The wind-instruments, and those of percussion are arranged in a single row next to the stage; the following is the distribution of the whole orchestra:—

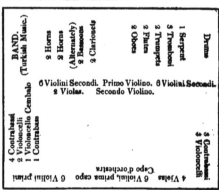

| | | | | Drums | 1 Serpent | 3 Tromboni | 2 Trumpets | 2 Flute | 2 Oboe | |
| BAND. (Turkish Music.) | 2 Horns | 2 Horns | (Alternately) 2 Bassoons | 2 Clarionets | | | | | | |

6 Violini Secondi. Primo Violino. 6 Violini Secondi.
2 Violas. Secondo Violino.

4 Contrabassi
Violoncelli
Violoncello Cembalo
Contrabass

Capo d'orchestra.

6 Violini primi, prima capo 6 Violini primi

4 Violas

Contrabassi Violoncelli

The administration of our theatre has recently received the important addition of 240,000 francs to the annual salary, besides perquisites to the amount of 70,000 of Milanese livres, and therefore upwards of 300,000 francs. Under the French government, it was quite the reverse; the administration was made to pay an enormous annual sum, by the way of tax, but for this purpose permission was granted to keep hazard tables in the saloons!—a system which happily has been abolished.

MILAN.—Among our Concerts, was one which I must not pass over without giving you some account of it. It was given by a Signor Angelo Casirola, of Tortona, and entitled in the bills *Academia Strordinaria*, an appellation to which it was justly entitled. He played a concerto of Zamboni with *arco fisso*, that is, with a fixed bow; a larghetto and rondo, composed by himself; and a Rossinian theme with variations on the G string, in which he imitated, at least so he announced, various stringed and wind-instruments; variations by Madame Catalani, again with fixed bow; and lastly, for the *first time,* a *sonata scherzosa* with two violins and two bows!! This is really murdering precious time, in order to attempt effects, which after all were not produced. Signor C. fastens the bow in an upright position upon a table, and plays upon it with a violin in the best manner he can. That in this awkward manner of performance, harsh and piercing tones should frequently be produced is not to be wondered at, since the heavy end of the violin comes in the right hand, and the upper and lighter part in the left; hence the greatest pressure will be on one side, and the play must be uncertain even to the most practised performer. The whole, together with the attitude of the player, is by no means pleasing to the eye. The larghetto and rondo were given in the usual way, but with little taste and bad bowing. In the variations upon the G string, he imitated the tones of the trumpet and flageolet, but the effect was not extraordinary, and those were the stringed and wind-instruments mentioned in the announcement. In giving the *sonata scherzosa*, he had two violins fixed with the heads screwed on a table, upon which Signor C. worked away right and left with a bow in each hand, accompanied by a full orchestra; but the merit of this contrivance we were unable to discover. However, the company present seemed very much delighted with the performance, and applauded to the very echo.

NAPLES.—*(Teatro San Carlo.)*—The new opera by Pacini, *Alessandro nelle Indie*, found but a cool reception; but, however, had a long run, because the Tosi pleased in her character, which is a proof how much the success of a piece will frequently depend upon the performers. Raimondi's opera of *Berenice* was also unsuccessful; and *Tamerlane*, a new operetta by Sapienza, shared the same fate.

——— *(Teatro Nuovo.)*—A new opera was produced here from the pen of Donizetti, entitled *Emilia*, which was but coldly received in the first representations, but afterwards became rather a favourite. It is quite decided that Sig. Barbaja is again to undertake the direction of the two royal theatres. The court has lost its two *Maestri di Capella*, Giacomo Tritto and Luigi Mosca. The first was born at Altamura, in the province of Bari, in 1734, and since the year 1780 has been the professor of composition in the Conservatorio of this place.

ROME.—*(Teatro Valle.)*—Principal singers: Clelia Pastori, prima donna; Luigi Sirletti, tenors; Antonio Tambarini, and Nicola Tacci, basses. The operas recently given have been Rossini's *Cenerentola* and *Barbiere di Siviglia*, as well as Mercadante's *Elisa e Claudio*.

——— Pastori is the great favourite here, her bust has been taken by a celebrated sculptor, and in all respects she is the reigning attraction of the day.

TURIN.—During this season, this place was visited by Signor Mercadante, who brought out with him his finished opera of *Nitocri*; the poem by Count Piossasco. A man of consideration and of wit, thus wrote from Turin to a friend. "The music is made up; the only good thing in it was, that it afforded me constant opportunities of recognising my old acquaintances. The director caused chocolate to be served up; the Maestro Ottain (who presided at the piano, and who is above seventy years of age) declared that all went well, because it was exactly in this way that things went in the days of Padre Martini; the scene-painter has made a great deal of money; the subscription list is full. I proclaimed aloud through all the town that the opera was a chef d'œuvre; it was believed with the same implicit faith that is placed in the Eleusinian mysteries, respecting which it is equally forbidden to say either that a thing is good or that it is bad." Certain it is, that as the Count was present at the first representations, and as all marks either of approbation or displeasure are strictly forbidden on these occasions, it is impossible to form a correct judgment of the public opinion. But if we may believe the common town talk, it is impossible for a piece not to make a *fiasco* on St. Stephen's day. The music had but little that could boast of originality, but there were many pleasing things, and among others a quartett in the second

act was particularly distinguished. Tachinardi, Lanusgeoui, and Congei pleased much, and tended very materially to save the piece from utter destruction.

TURIN.—*(Teatro Cariguano.)*—Principal singers: Santina Ferlotti, prima donna; Domenico Bertozzi, besides the two celebrated buffi, Nicolo de Grecis, and Domenico Vaccani. G. Mosca's opera, *La Sciocca per Astuzia*, which was revived, made a *fiasco*. The new opera *La Pastorella Feudataria*, (taken from the French melodrama *A la Bergère Chatelaine*,) the music by Nicolo Vaccai, was received with much applause; afterwards Paer's *Griselda* was given, but, strange to say, was received very coldly.

TRIESTE.—The first opera of the season was *L' Equivoco Estravagante*, originally a Rossinian farsa, and, properly speaking, is only Carinso's opera *L' Avviso a' Maritati*, first produced in 1814, in another form. Rossini had but little hand in the piece; the greater portion was by Carinso, and parts by Bassi and Bulgarelli, a violinist; the overture was by another hand, a dilettante of Udine. The whole pasticcio was very properly hissed from the stage. The only applause obtained, was by Signora Melas, in the cavatina which she sung on her entrance. The tenor, Sirletti, fell very opportunely ill, and the insignificant soprano Viller, and the two buffi Coppini and Lauretti, shared the fate of the opera. The vacuum was as usual filled up by the *Barbiere di Seviglia*.

MODENA.—The same operas were given here as at Bologna, and by the same singers. On the *Teatro Reale*, the entrance to which is by favour, and where no money is received, was given a new opera seria, entitled *Antigone*; the text by her Imperial Highness, (who is already known by several excellent productions of the same kind;) the music by Antonio Gaudini, music-director, and *Guardia Nobile* to his Imperial Highness the Duke of Modena.

BOLOGNA.—*(Teatro Communale.)*—Meyerbeer's opera *Margherita d'Anjou* has been the great attraction here; the second act in particular always created a great sensation. Afterwards a new *Farsa* was produced, entitled *La Capanna Moscovita*, the music by Capeletti, which obtained considerable applause. Among the singers, the principal were Fanny Corri Paltoni, and Francesca Grassi. According to report, Capeletti is a composer of only mediocre talents.

GENOA.—The opera of *Evandro di Pergamo*, by Signor Mirecki, which, as we before had occasion to mention, was retarded in its representation last season, was produced here, but did not succeed, and with it too fell the new singer, Signor Ersilia Mattei. Signora Bassi pleased, and the tenor Binaghi, though not equally with the former. The second opera was Meyer's opera *La Rosa Bianca e la Rosa Rossa*, which was followed by Meyerbeer's *Crociato in Egitto*.

CORFU.—The theatre of this place has gained much by the recent measures taken by the government, which has appointed three commissioners to superintend its administration. The company consists of the following artists: Cristina Casotti, *prima donna assoluta in soprano*; Maria Marchesini, *primo musico, e prima donna in contralto*; G. Fusconi, *primo tenore*; Gerolamo Donati Candetta, *primo buffo comico*; Giuseppe Ferlini, *primo buffo cantante*; Angiola Martinelli, *supplemento al contralto*; Barbara Voitaceski, Candida Pagnini, *seconde donne*; Giovanni Como, *secondo tenore*; Giacomo Franchi, *secondo buffo*. The operas given were, the *Odoardo e Cristina* and the *Cenerentola*, of Rossini; and afterwards, *Giannina e Bernardone*, by Cimarosa, with new pieces introduced. The whole of these operas were well sustained, and enjoyed their share of favour.

LISBON.—The politics of this part of the world have had a very unfavourable influence upon the lyric theatre of this city; and on account of the long absence of the court, the interruptions have been numerous, and sometimes of long continuance. Towards the close of last year, the performances became more regular, and the company was better organized than for some time past. The first opera given on the opening of the house was the *Edoardo e Cristina* of Rossini. The *prima donna* was Adelaide Varese, a singer who is a great favourite here. Her voice and manner are both entitled to great praise; and she has the additional advantage of grace and beauty on her side; but her taste and ornaments are of a questionable kind : she is too fond of conforming to the predominant taste of the time, which is bad, and has evidently sacrificed a good school to this temporizing spirit. Another defect is her lisping, indistinct pronunciation; but this is a defect in which, unfortunately, she is by no means singular, as this is the besetting sin of the time, and cries loudly for a remedy. The next female singer is Adelaide Cresaotti, a mezza soprano of great compass of voice, particularly in the lower parts. The tenorist, Lombardi, is but a second-rate singer, but his action is better than his voice. The *buffo cantante*, Paolo Lembi, has a beautiful bass voice, but too feeble for the theatre, and but little energy in his performance. The rest of the company consists of Italians, who have long been attached to this theatre, among whom Martinelli still enjoys his former reputation.

Besides the opera already named, the company gave several other productions of the same composer. During Lent was performed the oratorio of *Mosè*; and on occasion of the birth-day of the king, the *Zelmira*. Besides these operas, we have had the *Emma* of Meyerbeer, Meyer's *Genevra di Scozia*, Paer's *Agnese*, and Pacini's *Adelaide e Comingeo*.

LISBON. The agitated state of this city has been unfavourable to all other artists except the bull-fighters, who have met with abundant patronage; but St. Carlos was left empty. An exception to this, however, was the birth-day of the king, which this year was solemnized with more than wonted splendour. On this occasion was given a new opera seria by Coccia, entitled *Fayello*, together with a grand allegorical ballet, called *O Heroe entre os Filhos* (the Hero amidst his Children); in which recent political occurrences were depicted in a striking manner. Though the theatre St. Carlos is under the protection of the government, and has its expenses in part paid thereby, yet the artists were unable to obtain the whole of their salaries. The cause of this is attributed to the *impressaria*, Madame Bruni, who, like others of the same stamp, paid herself, but left the rest in the lurch; and the company broke up in consequence. The principal singers engaged themselves at the theatre at Oporto, where they still continue. In consequence, an agent was despatched from Lisbon to Italy to engage a new company; but the task was not found very practicable, as a report had gone forth to distant lands that credit was not sound, and payments tardy. The theatre, therefore, remained closed for several months, till at length came a new reinforcement of thirty-eight personages, the greater part of which were for the ballet; among these artists was Jacomo Piglia. A rich individual, Senor Falcao, made the necessary advances, to enable the establishment to get into action. For the opera, there were among the new members, Louisa Valsovani Spada, Josefa Julien, Maddelena and Catarina Pereno, and Maria Mori: Signor Felippo Spada, a good buffo cautante; Alex. Mombelli, tenorist; Ant. Colla, Bassist, Luis Canpiteli, and J. Rioboli. The operas given were *Bianca e Faliero*, with moderate applause; afterwards *L'Inganno Felice*, with but little success; afterwards *Il Turco in Italia*, but not so well got up as on a former occasion ; *Il Barbiere di Seviglia*, and a few others of the more popular operas of Rossini. Besides these, we had the *Elisa e Claudio* of Mercadante, and lastly Morlacchi's *Teobaldo e Isolina*. The latter pleased extremely, and had a run of ten nights; but the critics here complained that the music was too German, a complaint which others, perhaps, might construe into a compliment. Signora Valsovani Spada is an excellent performer, and possesses merits of a superior kind; the only thing to be regretted is, that her voice has lost its youthful freshness, and shews only the relics of its former beauty. The part of Isolina is too high for her; but the part of Teobaldo was admirably performed by J. Julien. The young Mombelli has a charming tenor voice, and sings with great taste; he is the son of the

veteran Mombelli, who was formerly so great a favourite in this city, and the whole of whose family is so renowned in music.

—— In church music we have had but little that was new. On the 22d of November a new mass by Rego was given in the church of *Dos Martires*, on occasion of the feast of St. Cecilia. The composer himself was at the time labouring under severe illness, but he summoned forth his energies for the occasion, was brought to the church and directed his own music, which was very generally admired, particularly the *Et incarnatus est*, which was spoken of as a masterpiece of the pathetic kind. On the 29th of the same month, was given the Grand Requiem of Jomelli, and the famous Responsorios of David Perez, which were performed with great correctness and effect, as all the musicians of the town take a part on this solemn occasion. Mozart's *Requiem* was given on the same fête last year, but the singers of this place do not like the music of Mozart; the most probable reason for which is, that it will not allow them to show off their protracted trills and *gorgheggi*. There was also given, for the first time, a grand MS. mass by the late composer Leal, which created a great sensation. Another mass by the able composer Joao Giordani, was also lately produced, and is highly celebrated. But the misfortune is, that nothing now goes down in church music but compositions cast in the Rossinian mould; almost every church festivity commences with one of Rossini's overtures, that to *La Gazza Ladra*, especially, is often heard on these occasions. The concerts of the greatest note have been those given by the composer and pianist, Bomtempo; which, however, were complained of as presenting too little variety. The symphonies of Haydn were, however, given on these occasions with considerable spirit and correctness. In song, the performer who pleased the most was a sister of the composer, who made a debut at these concerts. The following programme of the pieces, vocal and instrumental, (performed in the course of these concerts,) may serve to convey an idea of the musical taste of this city. A trio from Coccia's *Festa della Rosa*; scene and air from the *Elena e Constantino* of the same; a cavatina by Marco Antonio Portogallo; a selection of the airs, duets, torzettos, quartettos, and a quintett of Rossini; a duet from *Il Matrimonio Secreto* of Cimarosa; an air of Pucitta, and a terzetto with chorus by the same ; terzetto by Paer, and a duet by Generali, in instrumental music; a selection of the symphonies of Haydn; Mozart's symphony in o flat, together with his overture to the *Zauberflöte*; an overture by Romberg, Mehul's overture to *Stratonice*, and Rossini's overture to *La Gazza Ladra*. Each evening M. Bomtempo played a piano-forte concerto of his own composition, with great power and taste. M. Brelas and his son, both dilettanti, played a concerto for two flutes by Gianella, which met with great success. M. Martino played a solo on the bassoon, and a concerto by Ozi with M. Thiago, on the same instrument. M. J. P. Scola gave a concerto with variations on the keyed bugle, which for a dilettanti was excellent; and M. Thiago played Rode's variations in o major on the clarionet. But politics, that foe to all harmony, interfered with this artist's concerts, and though it was impossible they could have any connexion with political affairs, being entirely public, they were for a time interrupted. At length, through the interference of the Marquis de Castello Melhor, permission was given to him to continue them in the grand saloon of the palace of the Duke of Cataval, in the Roscio. This is built in the octagon form, and opens into several large side rooms, which altogether are capable of containing some hundreds of auditors. The orchestra on this occasion was not so large as formerly, but was far more select, being composed of most of the dilettanti of the place. M. Bomtempo presided at the piano, and the two brothers, Giordani, were the leaders. The private theatre of the Baron Quintella, at Laureujeiras, near Lisbon, was lately finished, and is lighted by gas by the English company that is speculating here. It is of very good dimensions for a private theatre, and the ornamental parts are very rich and massive. Attached to the establishment of the Baron Quintella, is the celebrated clarionet player, M. Conongis, and it is expected that the Baron's musical soirées are to be more splendid than in old times.

LISBON.—Lately has died here, the excellent composer and patron of composers, Joze Dias Pereira Chaves, at the advanced age of 74. In his youth he had travelled much, and had opportunities of forming an acquaintance with almost all musicians of eminence, besides being honoured by the notice of more exalted personages; for while at Rome, he was the intimate friend of the celebrated Pope, Ganganelli, as well as of Don Pedro of Portugal, and Donna Maria, the mother of the present King. In him, the young artist has lost a generous patron and support; it may with truth be said, that the best among the virtuosi of this city are indebted to him for their advancement in the art, for his house was always open to them, and where they had opportunities of hearing his personal instructions, of enjoying some of the finest masterpieces of the art, and of being introduced to the first professors of the day. Nor was this all, he provided means for many a meritorious young artist, and supplied him with the best instruments suited to his particular taste or capacity.

PARIS.—(*Theatre Italien.*)—The additional night given here in order to afford Madame Sessi an opportunity of appearing in the *Orazzj* of Cimarosa, by no means attracted in the degree that had been anticipated. This opera, the success of which was so prodigious, when it first appeared here some fifteen years since, seems now perfectly to have fallen in public estimation. Certain it is that the music of it is any thing but grand, and if is difficult to conceive how it could obtain any success in France, where this subject has been treated with so much severity, and in so masterly a manner by the great Corneille. If there be any subject less adapted to roulades and warblings, ad infinitum, it must be this. The admirable talents of Madame Pasta having been found inadequate to the task of resuscitating this opera, it was not likely that any other person would operate such a miracle. Madame Sessi has nevertheless ventured upon the trial, but her attempt has not been successful. The coldness with which she was heard till the very dropping of the curtain, must have tended to convince her, that what is impossible for a Pasta, has no very great chance of success in other hands.—The production of *Il Pretendente Burlato*, an opera buffa of the younger Guglielmi, put the public in good humour again, after the infliction of the *Orazzj*. It is full of spirit, and the music is of a nature better calculated to stand the test of criticism than most of the productions of the same school. It was extremely well executed by Bordogni, Pelegrini, and Madlle. Cinti, who was several times interrupted in her songs by the applause of a very crowded house.

——— M. Sigismond, who last Wednesday gave a musical entertainment, is a young German, travelling for instruction, and to perfect himself in the art of Baillot and Lafont. This young man, who is only thirteen years and a half old, has already obtained the great gold academic medal of the university of Rome, and is a member of all the musical institutions of Austria and Italy. He is now about to travel over France, where the precoseness of his talents, as a performer upon the violin, has already excited the enthusiasm, and even the poetic vein of some of the provincial amateurs. But, finally to establish the reputation of an artist, these triumphs must be confirmed by the public of the capital of the arts; and Sigismond has thrown himself upon their judgment. If he has not completely succeeded, it is at least very honourable to him, to have obtained, and merited, the encouragement of the connoisseurs of Paris. M. Sigismond displays vigour, and often grace, but unhappily he does not always play in tune. We point out these rocks to him, because we think, that with care he may avoid them. The music which he executed, did not appear to us well chosen; the first air, which was rather varied, terminated in a polonaise, of which the motivo is common and hacknied. As to Polledro's variations upon the air *Nil cor più non mi sento*, they are difficult, but without any beauty.

——— M. *Mondonville* has made his debut at *L'Opera Comique*, in *Euphrosine et Coradin*, and *La Fête Village voisin*. As a singer, M. Mondonville has already obtained decided success. His voice is a very fine bass; he easily passes from the lowest to the highest notes, and has often been deservedly applauded. His diction, as a comedian, wants firmness and strength; but he has no very essential fault, and we hope that by practice and application, he will distinguish himself, and become useful to the theatre which will form his talents.

——— *La Niege* is about to be reduced to three acts, and produced at court. Many new operas have been performed at the *Feydeau*. The public will, perhaps, say with Lafontaine:—

N'en ayons qu'un mais qu il soit bon.

——— M. Chérubini, as a recompense for the services he has rendered *L'Ecole Royale de Musique*, which he has for some years directed with so much zeal and success, is about to be made an officer of the Legion of Honour. All the friends applaud this just distinction. This great composer will add to his fame, by a mass which he has composed on the occasion of the coronation, and which all the connoisseurs admire.

——— *Le Petit Ramoneur*, a drama in three acts, represented at the theatre *De la Porto St. Martin*, was favourably received. The few who were in the green room, attributed the words to *M. Sauvage*, and the music to *M. Alexandre*.

THE DRAMA.

KING'S THEATRE.

On Thursday the 23rd of last month *Il Crociato in Egitto*, the new grand opera of a composer whose name was completely unknown in this country only a few months ago, was brought out at this theatre. For the *dramatis personæ*, &c., we refer our readers to the last number of this work; and some account of M. Meyerbeer the composer, as well as of the manner in which this masterly production has been performed and received in Italy, will be found in the former pages of the HARMONICON. The opera itself will be reviewed in our next, so that we have now only to speak of its performance and reception in London.

The theatre was crowded to excess in all parts, for the public were not only attracted by the first representation of a work concerning which fame had spoken so loudly, but also to witness the debut of Signor Velluti, whose peculiar voice excited much curiosity, a male *mezzo-soprano* not having been heard on the stage of the King's Theatre during the last thirty years. Besides which, it was expected that his appearance would be strongly opposed, and numbers were drawn together to support him; while many attended to witness, if not to assist, in any contest that might take place.

The opera was received with the most unanimous and enthusiastic applause; its numerous beauties were recognised even at its first hearing, a result which, the scientific nature of the music considered, was hardly expected in so great a degree. The performers exerted themselves to the utmost of their abilities in support of the piece, though they did not anticipate a success so decided and extraordinary as that which crowned their efforts. Even Sig. Velluti himself wished, as is well known, to be first heard in an opera of Morlacchi, and used all his influence with the director for this purpose; fortunately for the singer, in vain. The opening chorus of the opera was encored, a circumstance we believe unprecedented, and tended to prove that the house contained a discerning audience. When Sig. Velluti appeared, about twenty, or at the utmost thirty, persons shewed the usual symptoms of disapproval; but all opposition was instantly overwhelmed by the thundering plaudits that it produced. In fact, no small share of the debutant's triumph must be ascribed to the fierceness of an attack made on him, previously to his appearance, in a leading daily paper, which brought to his support all the friends that his letters had procured him, persons who otherwise would not have exhibited the same activity and energy. Signor Velluti's voice has a compass of full two octaves, from the G above the treble clef, to the G above the bass. It is powerful, and in its softer tones is sweet; but when strained is harsh and painful. His style of singing is of the best school;

expression is its characteristic ; *roulades,* and such vulgar finery, such " Brummagem ware," he appears to despise, and though he decorates much, yet his ornaments are new, and in fine taste. In our next we shall renew this subject; for the present, our space warns us that we must compress the rest of our matter.

Signor Curioni, as *Adrian de Montford,* has proved a tower of strength to this opera: his clear, rich voice, his perfect intonation, his pure style, free from all gewgaw ; his manly, well-formed person, dignified deportment, and admirable conception of the part, have gained every suffrage in his favour. Madlle. Garcia, disguised in male attire, performed the part of *Felicia* with great ability, both as a singer and actress. Signor Remorini as *Aladino* was every thing that the lover of the musical drama could wish ; and Mad. Caradori exhibited powers that, till now, few people knew were in her possession. Her last duet * with Veluti produces an effect which we have very rarely witnessed before ; it is listened to with unfeigned delight, and regularly encored from all quarters of the house, without the aid of a single *claqueur* sent in for the purpose.

HAYMARKET THEATRE.

THE burletta of *Midas* has been got up at this house ; Madam Vestris as *Apollo,* in which character she has captivated every heart that she had not previously enslaved. Liston's *Midas* is, perhaps, a little over coloured, but it is highly entertaining, and keeps the house in a constant roar of laughter while he is on the stage.

ENGLISH OPERA HOUSE.

A NEW " balled opera," under the title of BROKEN PROMISES, or *The Colonel, the Captain, and the Corporal,* was brought out at this theatre, on Tuesday, July 5th.

---

* Page 179 of our present Number.

The following are the characters, and their representatives :

Mr. Fairfield, ...	Mr. BARTLEY.
Charles, ... } *(his Sons)* .	Mr. BROADHURST.
Captain Edward Fairfield, }	Mr. THORNE.
Colonel Coolard, ...	Mr. WRENCH.
Bagwell, *(Mrs. Woodland's Steward)* . . .	Mr. W. BENNETT.
Corporal Balance O'Conner, ...	Mr. POWER.
Louisa, } *(Adopted Daughters of Mr. Fairfield)*	Miss NOEL.
Emma, }	Miss STEPHENS.
Mrs. Woodland, ...	Miss GRAY.
Susan Roseby, ...	Miss KELLY.
Margery, ...	Mrs. GROVE.
Betty, ...	Mrs. WEIPPERT.

Servants, Villagers, &c. &c.

Broken Promises is from the French, the source of most of our best modern short dramas. The music is compiled, chiefly from the Scotch and Irish melodies, with some pieces by Weber, Mayer, Cherubini, Berton, Himmel, and Meyerbeer, the whole of which is arranged by Mr. Hawes.

The dramatic part of this opera is lively, without possessing much claim to wit, and interests the audience, though it leaves no impression in them. The music contains two or three good Scottish airs, one of which, "Here 's a health to those far awa'," * beautifully sung by Miss Stephens, is always encored. Another " Here awa', there awa'," produces no effect, because, we rather think, it is performed too quick, and thereby loses much of its pathos.

The airs from Weber and Himmel are not well chosen, and fail altogether. The *Giovinetto Cavalier,* from Meyerbeer's *Crociato in Egitto,* with English words, excites here so little attention, that latterly it has been omitted entirely. The short chorusses by Berton have great merit, and the *Dusty Miller,* as sung with delightful naiveté by Miss Kelly, is more applauded then any thing in the opera. This piece is successful, and draws a most respectable company whenever performed.

---

* Published with a new Accompaniment in the first Number of the HARMONICON.

THE
HARMONICON.

No. XXXIII., September, 1825.

MEMOIR OF FRANCESCO GEMINIANI.

FRANCESCO GEMINIANI, a native of Lucca, was born about the year 1680. He received his first instructions in music from Alessandro Scarlatti, and afterwards became a pupil of Carlo Ambrosio Lunati, surnamed *Il Gobbo*, a celebrated performer on the violin. His studies were completed under Corelli.

In the year 1714, he arrived in England, where, in a short time, his exquisite performance rendered him celebrated; and, amongst the nobility, several laid claim to the honour of being his patrons. The person, however, to whom he was most attached was the Baron Kilmansegge, chamberlain to King George the First, as Elector of Hanover.

In 1716, Geminiani published and dedicated to this nobleman, " *Twelve Sonatas, à Violino, Violone, e Cembalo.*" These had such an effect, that the public were at a loss to determine whether Geminiani's greater excellence lay in his performance, or in his skill in composition. The Baron had ventured to speak of this work to the king in such terms of approbation, as induced him to direct that some of the compositions contained in it should be performed in his presence by the author. Handel was desired to accompany him on the harpsichord, and Geminiani acquitted himself in a manner worthy of the expectations that had been formed of him.

Geminiani was an enthusiast in painting; and, to gratify this propensity, he not only suspended his studies, and neglected his profession, but often involved himself in pecuniary embarrassments, which a little prudence and foresight would have enabled him to avoid. To gratify his taste he bought pictures, and to supply his wants he sold them. The consequence of this kind of traffic was loss, and its concomitant, necessity.

In the distress which, by such imprudent conduct, he had drawn upon himself, he was compelled, for the security of his person, to avail himself of that protection from arrest which the English nobility had then the power of extending to their servants. The Earl of Essex was prevailed upon, for this purpose, to enrol Geminiani's name in the list of his domestics.

The place of master and composer of the state music in Ireland became vacant in the year 1727, and the Earl obtained from Sir Robert Walpole, a promise of it. He then told Geminiani that his difficulties were at an end, as he had provided him a place suited to his profession, which would afford him an ample provision for life. On inquiry into the conditions of the office, Geminiani found that it was not tenable by a member of the Romish communion. He therefore declined accepting it, assigning this as a reason, and at the same time observing, that, although he had never made any great pretensions to religion, yet to renounce for the sake of temporal advantages, that faith in which he had been first baptized, he could not answer to his conscience. The place was given to Mr. Matthew Dubourg, a young man of great merit, who had been his pupil.

Some years having elapsed after the publication of his *solos*, Geminiani resolved to turn into *concertos* the first six *solos* of Corelli. These he completed, and published, in 1726, by subscription. Their success was fully answerable to his expectations, and, a short time afterwards, he altered in the same manner the remaining six. These, however, having no fugues, and consisting altogether of airs, afforded but little scope for the exercise of his abilities, and met with an indifferent reception.

He likewise arranged as *concertos* six of Corelli's *sonatas*, that is, the ninth in the First Opera, and the first, third, fourth, ninth, and tenth of the Third. This seems to have been a hasty production, and is now scarcely remembered. In the year 1732, he printed what he called his *Opera Seconda*; or, *VI. Concerti grossi con due Violini, Violoncello, e Viola di Concertino obligati, e due altri Violini, e Basso di Concerto grosso ad arbitrio*. The first of these is celebrated for the fine minuet with which it closes. The publication of this work was soon followed by another of the same kind, his *Opera Terza*, consisting of *six concertos for violins*, the last of which is esteemed one of the finest compositions of the kind in the world.

Geminiani now enjoyed a high degree of reputation as a composer for instruments; yet his circumstances were not much improved by the profits resulting from his publications. The manuscript of his *Opera Seconda* had been surreptitiously obtained by Walsh, who was about to print it; but thinking it would be benefited by the corrections of the author, he gave him the alternative, either of correcting it, or submitting it to appear with its faults before the world. Geminiani rejected the insulting offer with the contempt it deserved, and instituted a process in Chancery for an injunction against the sale of the book. Walsh compounded the matter with him, and the work was published under the inspection of the author,

The *Opera Terza* he sold to Walsh, who in his advertisements gave the public to understand that he came honestly by the copy. In the year 1739, he published the *Opera Quarta*, consisting of *Twelve Sonatas for a Violin and Bass;* and also a new edition of the *Opera Prima*, with considerable additions and improvements. Soon afterwards appeared a tract by Geminiani, entitled, *A Treatise on Good Taste;* and another, denominated, *Rules for Playing in Taste*. These two publications contained, besides examples of such graces as Geminiani had adopted himself on the violin, variations on several well-known airs and some select Scotch tunes. About this time also he printed *The Art of Playing on the Violin*, a work which contains the most minute directions for holding the instrument, and for the use of the bow; as well as the graces, the various shifts of the hand, and a great number of examples adapted to the rules.

About the year 1740, he published, and dedicated to the Academy of Ancient Music, his *Opera Settima*, consisting of six *concertos* for violins; and, in the month of April, 1742, came forth his long-expected work, *Guida Armonica, o Dizionario Armonico*. In this work, after giving due commendation to Lully, Corelli, and Bononcini, as the first improvers of instrumental music, he successfully controverts an opinion that the vast foundations of universal harmony can be established upon the narrow and confined modulation of these authors; and makes many remarks on the uniformity of modulation apparent in the compositions that had appeared in different parts of Europe for several years back.

The publication of the Guida was attended with circumstances that seemed to promise but little success. The old musicians stood aghast at the licenses which it allowed, and declared that, if well received, it would tend to the entire destruction of the science of music. They consequently determined to prejudice the public against it. Many persons believed it to be only an attempt to get money, from the novelty of its contents, and these, on all occasions, ridiculed it. There were, indeed, very few who were able to comprehend either the motives of the writer, or the tendency of his work. In one of those excursions which after Geminiani had settled in England, he made to Italy, France, and other parts of the Continent, he visited at Paris Père Castel, a learned and ingenious Jesuit, and a man well skilled in music. To this person he shewed his manuscript, and explained its nature and design. Castel, with a view to remove the prejudices that had been entertained against it, printed, in the *Journal des Sçavans*, a dissertation on the *Guida*, and a strong recommendation of it, which Geminiani, on his return to London, got translated into English, and published in a small pamphlet of about thirty pages.

In a life so unsteady as that of Geminiani, spent in different countries, and employed in pursuits that had no connexion with his art, and only served to divert his attention from it, we must suppose, in order to account for the means of his support, that he received very considerable pecuniary assistance from his patrons and friends. The emoluments arising from his publications were not, in general, such as in any degree to compensate for the many years of study and labour which they had occupied. Towards the conclusion of his life, he had recourse to an expedient for raising money which had never before been attempted: in the year 1748, he issued advertisements announcing that a *concerto spirituale*

would be performed for his benefit at Drury Lane Theatre, to consist chiefly of the music of Italian masters of eminence, but whose names were scarcely known in England. Geminiani, an entire stranger to the business of an orchestra, had no idea of the trouble and labour that were required to prepare singers for the performance of music which they had not before seen, or of the frequent rehearsals that were necessary for all the parties engaged. The consequence was, that the vocal department, not being perfect, the performance miscarried. The audience were sufficiently numerous to constitute what is called a good house, and the performance commenced with one of Geminiani's *concertos*, which was succeeded by a grand chorus. Both these pieces had justice done them; but the first of the women, to whom a solo air had been given, was unable to execute it, and the whole band, after playing a few bars, were compelled to stop. The audience, instead of expressing resentment, seemed to pity the distress into which Geminiani was thrown. An apology was received by them; and they sat silent till the books were changed for those which contained Geminiani's own compositions.

The profits arising from this entertainment enabled him once more to gratify that inclination for rambling which was so inherent in his disposition. He went to France, and took up his residence for some time at Paris. As the engraving of music was then much more neatly executed in that city than in any other part of the world, and as his *concertos* had never been printed in such a manner as he wished, he was now determined to publish them himself in score. Accordingly he revised, for this purpose, his Second and Third Operas; but such were his desire for making improvements, and his passion for refinement, that he not only betrayed himself into numerous errors, but likewise was led to the insertion of many new and ill-constructed passages.

He staid long enough in Paris to get engraved the plates both for the score and the parts of the above-mentioned two sets of *concertos;* and about the year 1755, he returned to England, and advertised them for sale. About the same time he published what he called *The Enchanted Forest*, an instrumental composition, grounded on a singular notion which he had long entertained, that betwixt music and conversation there is a very near and natural resemblance. This he used to illustrate, in conversation, by a comparison between those musical compositions in which a certain point is assumed in one part, and answered in the other with frequent repetitions, and the form and manner of conversation. With the design of reducing this notion to practice, Geminiani endeavoured to represent to the imagination of his hearers the succession of events in that beautiful episode contained in the 13th Canto of Tasso's Jerusalem, where, by the order of Ismeno, a pagan magician, a forest is enchanted, and each tree informed with a living spirit, to prevent its being cut down for the purpose of making battering rams and other military engines for carrying on the siege of Jerusalem.

The *Enchanted Forest* was succeeded by the publication of two numbers of a work entitled, *The Harmonical Miscellany, containing sundry Modulations on a Bass, calculated for the Improvement of Students in Music, and the Practice of the Violin and Harpsichord*. Geminiani intended to continue this work by periodical publication; but as it did not receive much encouragement, he desisted from his intention.

In the year 1761, he went over to Ireland, where he was kindly received and entertained by Dubourg, at that time master of the king's band there. Geminiani had spent many years in compiling an elaborate treatise on music, which he intended for publication; but soon after his arrival in Dublin, by the treachery of a female servant (who, it has been said, was recommended to him for no other purpose than that she might steal it), the manuscript was purloined out of his chamber, and could never afterwards be recovered. The magnitude of this loss, and his inability to repair it, made a deep impression on his mind, and had such an effect upon his spirits as to hasten fast his dissolution. He died at Dublin on the 17th of September, 1762, in the eighty-third year of his age [*].

It is observable from the works of Geminiani, not only that his modulations are original, but that his harmonies consist of such combinations as were never introduced into music till his time. His melodies are in the highest degree elegant; and, in their general cast, most of his compositions are exquisitely tender and pathetic. Of his execution on the violin, it may be stated, that he had none of the fire and spirit of modern performers; but he possessed an abundance of grace and feeling: nearly all the powers that engage the attention of the hearer, and render it subservient to the will of the artist, were united in him.

The following is a list of the whole of Geminiani's productions, except two or three articles that are considered of little value:—

Twelve *Solos* for a Violin, Opera 1.
Six *Concertos* in Seven Parts, Opera 2.
The same in Score.
Six *Concertos* in seven Parts, Opera 3.
The same in Score.
Twelve *Solos* for a Violin, Opera 4.
Six *Solos* for the Violoncello, Opera 5.
The same made into *Solos* for a Violin.
Six *Concertos* from the *Solos* of Opera 4.
Six *Concertos* in eight Parts, Opera 7.
Twelve *Trios* in two Sets.
Six *Trios* from Opera 1.
Rules for playing in true Taste.
A Treatise on Good Music.
The Art of playing the Violin.
Twelve *Sonatas* from his first *Solos*, Opera 11.
Harpsichord Pieces, two Books.
Guida Armonica.
Supplement to *Guida Armonica.*
The Art of Accompaniment, two Books.
The Enchanted Forest.

NOTES TO ASSIST THE MEMORY.

UNDER this very modest and unassuming title [†], a small volume has lately appeared, consisting of short memoranda in various sciences, arranged under their respective heads, from which we extract the following notices, relative to music. Familiar as some of the facts may be to a great proportion of our readers, we consider them worthy of the space they occupy in our columns, for the benefit of those who may either not have seen, or may have forgotten them.

The Musical Signs.—The seven musical signs, ut, re, mi, fa, sol, la, sa, invented by the Benedictine monk Guido Aretine, are the first syllables of some words contained in the first strophe of a Latin hymn, composed in honour of St. John the Baptist, which runs thus—

Ut queant laxis, Resonare fibris
Mira gestorum, Famuli tuorum;
Solve polluti, Labii reatum,
Sancte Joannes.

Octaves and Concord.—When two strings, whose length is as one to two, vibrate together, it is obvious that the one vibrates twice, while the other only vibrates once; they will coincide at the beginning of every alternate vibration, and their sounds will then accord. When the strings are in this proportion, their coincidences are more frequent than when their lengths are in any other ratio, and hence it is that the octave is the most perfect concord. If the lengths be two to three, which is the ratio of the fifth, every third vibration of the one coincides with every second of the other; the coincidences are consequently not so frequent as in the octaves, on which account the concord is not so frequent.

Discord.—If their lengths be such that they never describe the arcs of vibration together, but perpetually cross each other in their oscillations, then their sounds are jarring and unconcentaneous, and thus discord is produced.

Scottish Music.—The Scottish airs of genuine character are composed on a scale which does not contain the fourth and seventh of the diatonic scale of music. From this is derived the peculiarity by which they are immediately recognised.

Beating Time.—An attentive person can beat time pretty accurately for one minute, but it is very difficult to be correct for a greater length of time.

Stammering.—A drunken man, or a person afflicted with St. Vitus's dance, can run, although he cannot walk or stand still. In the same manner a stammerer can sing, which is *continuous* motion, although he cannot speak, which is *interrupted* motion.

Sound.—All sound travels at the same rate (1142 feet per second, or thirteen miles per minute), a whisper, as far as it goes, as fast as the report of a cannon. It also describes equal spaces in equal times. The strength of sound is greatest in cold and dense air, and least in that which is warm and rarefied. During Captain Parry's first voyage, in lat. 74° 30′ N., people might often be heard conversing distinctly, in a common tone of voice, at the distance of one mile.

Musical Figures resulting from Sounds.—Cover the mouth of a wide glass, having a foot-stalk, with a thin sheet of membrane or vegetable paper, over which scatter a layer of fine sand. The vibrations, excited in the air by the sound of a musical instrument held within a few inches of the membrane, will cause the sand on its surface to form regular lines and figures with astonishing celerity, which vary with the sound produced, affecting a particular mode of division according to the number of vibrations.

Musical Flame.—Musical tones are produced by the combustion of hydrogen gas in tubes of different diameters,

Uncertainty of Sound.—In listening to sounds, we are

[*] Dr. Burney dates the birth of Geminiani in 1666, and consequently makes his age ninety-six. Our account is from Sir John Hawkins, who, being acquainted with the subject of this memoir, is probably the more correct in his history.

[†] Notes to assist the Memory in Various Sciences. One vol. small 8vo. Murray, 1825.

deceived as to the quarter from whence they proceed, by the change produced in the direction of the sonorous waves by intervening obstacles, so that we mistake the reflected for the radiated vibrations, echo for direct sound.

Singing Birds[*].—The following table, formed by the Honourable Daines Barrington, is designed to exhibit the comparative merit of the British singing birds. In this scale, *twenty* is supposed to be the point of absolute perfection.

	Mellowness of Tone.	Sprightly Notes.	Plaintive Note.	Compass.	Execution.
Nightingale	19	14	19	19	19
Skylark	4	19	4	18	18
Woodlark	18	4	17	12	8
Titlark	12	12	12	12	12
Linnet	12	16	12	16	18
Goldfinch	4	19	4	12	12
Chaffinch	4	12	4	8	8
Greenfinch	4	4	4	4	6
Hedgesparrow . . .	6	0	6	4	4
Aberdavine, or Fiskin . .	2	4	0	4	4
Redpoll	0	4	0	4	4
Thrush †	4	4	4	4	2
Blackbird	4	4	0	2	4
Robin	6	16	12	12	12
Wren	0	12	0	4	2
Red-sparrow	0	4	0	2	4
Blackcap, or Norfolk Mock Nightingale . . . }	14	12	12	14	14

ON THE ORIGIN AND HISTORY OF THE ORGAN.

From the *Account of the Musical Festival at York*, in 1823. By JOHN CROSSE, Esq., F.S.A., &c. &c.

OF this noblest of all instruments, as its name denotes, οργανον, "the instrument," by way of excellence, a few historical notices may probably afford some amusement to the reader. Notwithstanding many laborious researches, its origin is still enveloped in much obscurity, chiefly arising from the various senses in which the general term *organum* was used. Some of the instruments so called were acted upon by the force of water, whilst in others the application of bellows is mentioned; the only difference between them, however, was in the mode of introducing the air into the pipes, and their common origin may probably be referred to the ancient Syrinx or Pan's pipe, made of reeds. Although the earliest descriptions appear to belong to the *hydraulicon*, of which Ctesibius of Alexandria was the discoverer about A.C. 220, yet it seems natural to suppose, that the

pneumatic organ was the prior invention; and its antiquity seems to be confirmed by the discovery of a monument at Rome, mentioned by Mersennus, and engraved in the first volume of Hawkins's *History of Music*, p. 403. The first account of any instrument of the kind occurs in the tenth book of Vitruvius, who flourished above a century before the Christian era: this was an hydraulicon. An empigram by the Emperor Julian, about the year A.D. 360, first quoted by Du Cange from the *Anthology*[*], describes one, which greatly resembles the present pneumatic organ. St. Jerome mentions one which had twelve pairs of bellows, and fifteen pipes, and was heard at the distance of a mile; and another at Jerusalem, which was heard at the Mount of Olives. Mersennus, however, doubts the genuineness of the piece ascribed to Jerome, and Mason, in his *Essay* on instrumental church music, has questioned that of the monument above named.

The date of the introduction of the organ into the churches of Western Europe is uncertain. The use of musical instruments therein is unquestionably as old as the time of St. Ambrose, if not of Justin Martyr, two centuries before him; but Pope Vitalian is generally allowed to have been the first who introduced the organ into the service of the Romish church about the year 670, and the enemies of church music have ingeniously contrived to fix upon the exact year 666, as corresponding with the mystical number of the apocalyptic beast. Be this as it may, the first tolerably *certain* account of an *organ*, properly so called, in the West, is about the year 755, when the Greek Emperor Constantine Copronymus sent one as a present to Pepin, King of France; though doubts have been raised even on this point, which most writers have taken for proved. In the time of Charlemagne, however, organs were brought from Greece into Western Europe, and soon became common. The artists of that Prince built one at Aix-la-Chapelle in 812, on the Greek model, which the learned Benedictine, D. Bedos de Celles, in his *L'Art du facteur des orgues*, 1766, thinks was the first that was furnished with bellows, and in which water was not employed. In 826, a Venetian presbyter, named Georgius, visited the Court of Louis le Debonnaire, and built another organ, at Aix, on the hydraulic principle; he is supposed to have been the father of the art of organ-building in Germany, from whence we soon after this time hear of artists in that line being sent into other countries.

Our historian, Bede, does not mention organs in his account of church ceremonies, but before the tenth century they not only became common in England, but seem to have surpassed those of the continent in size and compass. Dunstan is recorded to have given one to the Abbey of Malmesbury in the reign of Edgar; he is also said to have introduced singing in parts; and if, as some suppose, organs were then built with fifths and octaves, (it having been discovered from the vibrations of a bell, that the fulness of tone would be thereby increased,) that circumstance may have led to the invention of harmony, consecutive fifths not being, of course, regarded as forbidden in the then state of musical science. In this way, therefore, to the organ may be traced the first dawn of harmony, of which the ancients appear, from all that we can discover, to have been unaccountably

---

* Mr. Blackwall, in opposition to the Honourable Daines Barrington, considers the notes of birds to be instinctive, and not depending on the master under whom they are bred.

† The thrush does not appear to have his proper rank in this scale.

* Lib. i. cap. 86.

ignorant, unless octaves, intended probably for unisons, be considered as such. Elfeg, Bishop of Winchester, procured an organ for his Cathedral in 951, which was the largest then known, having twenty-six pairs of bellows, and requiring seventy men to fill it with wind; it had, however, but ten keys, with forty pipes for each key: a description of it by Wolstan, in barbarous Latin verse, is given in Mason's *Essay*, where it is erroneously said to have been at *Westminster*. Oswald, Archbishop of York, consecrated the church at Ramsey, where Count Elvin had placed an organ, with pipes of brass, that cost thirty pounds sterling; there was also one previous to the year 1174 in Canterbury Cathedral; where choral service, which took its rise at Antioch, appears to have been first introduced into this country.

Notwithstanding these early attempts, the organ long remained rude in its construction; the keys were from four to five or even six inches broad, and must have been pressed down by the fist; the pipes were of brass, loud and harsh in their sound, and the compass did not exceed two octaves in the twelfth century, about which time half-notes appear to have been introduced at Venice; and it was not until the fifteenth century that both hands were made use of in playing on it. At Venice also, the important addition of pedals was first made by Bernhard, a German, to whose countrymen we owe most of the other improvements of the instrument, in bellows, stops, &c., and among whom its construction has always been a work of great repute, though in excellence of finish they have been surpassed by our English builders. Several elaborate French and German works, on the subject of organs, are in existence, which are scarcely known even by name in this country; but some idea may be formed of the great importance attached to the possession of a good organ, from the fact that one Beck having contracted with the magistrates of Gröningen in 1592, to build one for the castle church, no less than fifty-three organists certified, in 1596, that he had fulfilled his contract. The names of the early builders, also, are still remembered with honour; among which may be mentioned those of Smid of Peyssenberg, in 1433; André of Brunswick, in 1456; Castendorfer of Breslaw, in 1466; and Rosenburger of Nuremberg, who built the great organ of the Cathedral of Bamberg about 1470. In the south of Germany organs were not known so early as in the north; since it appears that Nuremberg first became possessed of one in 1443, and Augsburg in 1490.

We find scarcely any particulars recorded respecting the organs of this country from the period of the reformation down to the time of Charles the First. Camden mentions one at Wrexham; and Fuller has been strangely misquoted as describing it to have possessed pipes of gold: it shared the general fate of organs in 1641; and probably the York organ is nearly the only one in the kingdom which escaped the destruction of those times, (owing, no doubt, to the protecting care of Lord Fairfax, who saved the painted windows of the Cathedral,) the old work of which, though greatly improved and enlarged, still exists. During the wars of that unfortunate reign, the organs throughout the kingdom were, it is well known, either sold or destroyed; the service books perished in the flames, and the professors of the art of music were driven to other resources for their support, by the furious haters of episcopacy and cathedrals; so that on the restoration of choral service, instruments, performers, books, and singers were equally difficult to be procured.

Yet Cromwell himself was partial to the organ, and caused the one belonging to Magdalen College, Oxford, to be removed to Hampton Court, where he often entertained himself by listening to it: it was restored afterwards to the college, and remained there until about the middle of the last century. He also connived at Dr. Busby having choral service with an organ, in his house, at Westminster, when it was forbidden throughout the kingdom. In 1660 it was found, that there were only four organ builders of repute surviving.—Preston, of York; Loosemore, of Exeter; Thamar, of Peterborough, and Ralph Dallans*. This led to the introduction of foreign artists, the celebrated Bernard Schmidt, commonly called Father Smith, and his two nephews, with the elder Harris, and his son Renatus. The well-known bitter dispute between these rival builders may be found in amusing detail in Burney's vol. ii. p. 437. Each had erected an organ in the Temple church for trial; Blow and Purcell performed on Smith's, and Lully upon Harris's, and several new-invented stops were introduced; when Lord Chancellor Jefferies at length decided in favour of Smith's, the bellows of which were cut open by the friends of Harris on the night previous to the final trial of the reed stops. Smith's principal organs are those in the Temple church, Christ church, and St. Mary's Oxford; Trinity College, Cambridge; St. Margaret's, Westminster; St. Clement Danes; Southwell Minster; and Trinity Church, Hull; which last has 20 stops, and was originally intended for St. Paul's Cathedral; besides the fine one which is now placed there, " in every respect worthy of that beautiful and stupendous structure," and " which is generally allowed to have the sweetest tone (except that at the Temple,) the most noble chorus, and a swell which produces the finest effects, of any in the kingdom." The Temple organ is further remarkable for the division of two of the five short keys, by which G sharp, and A flat, D sharp, and E flat, are made different notes. Harris's organ, after rejection at the Temple, was divided; part of it was erected at St. Andrew's, Holborn, and part in Christchurch, Dublin, which was afterwards removed to Wolverhampton. His other principal instruments, are those at St. Mary Axe, St. Bride's, St. Lawrence's, &c.; and one at Doncaster, erected in 1739, which did him great credit, and which contains two trumpets and a clarion stop throughout the whole compass of the great organ, so excellent, that the celebrated Mr. Stanley told Dr. Miller, that each pipe was worth its weight in silver. It was repaired by Donaldson, of York, about 1798. Harris appears to have been very ambitious of building an instrument for St. Paul's Cathedral, which should transcend every former work of the kind†. To these celebrated artists succeeded Schreider, Smith's-son-in law, who built the organ at St. Martin's-in-the-Fields, a present from King George I. as churchwarden; Byfield, Bridge, and Jordan, who united in partnership; Snetzler, &c., and at a later period, Green, Gray, Avery, Elliot, England, Flight, Nicholls, &c.

* Sir J. Hawkins informs us, that *Ralph* Dallans died whilst building an organ at Greenwich, in 1672-3. It therefore appears that the supposition (at p. 134) of his being the same person with *Robert* Dallam or Dallom, cannot be correct.

† *Spectator*, No. 552, Dec. 3d, 1712; by Steele.

M. HUMMEL.

[*From a Paris Journal.*]

THE concert of M. Hummel, on the 23d of May, in *La salle des menus-Plaisirs*, ought really to be considered as a musical solemnity, for we heard for the last time, that celebrated virtuoso, whom all Europe, long since, has proclaimed the modern Mozart of Germany.

During the short stay that M. Hummel has made in Paris, the amateurs and performers, full of admiration of his talents, have struck a bronze medal in his honour, bearing his portrait, which is very like, and has the marks of that genius which animates the original. This medal will add to the just reputation which the young man who cut it has already obtained by other works of a similar nature. The subscribers inserted their names in a book, which was given at his departure to this celebrated composer, who will live in our memory as well as upon bronze, and has found as many admirers and friends in the capital of the arts, as in his own country.

Previously to M. Hummel's departure from Paris, he addressed the following letter to the editors of the French journals.

Gentlemen,

Allow me, through the medium of your journal, to express the lively gratitude which I feel towards the French public, for the flattering reception they have deigned to give me. I also beg to return my most sincere thanks to those celebrated performers, the ornament of this city, of the arts, and the admiration of Europe, who have kindly embellished my concerts by their talents. It is also particularly my duty to give well-deserved praise to the Messieurs Erard, for the clear and beautiful sound of their instruments, which has obtained them a most distinguished reputation for more than forty years.

I carry away with me the most tender remembrances, and regret that I cannot more strongly express my gratitude, for the proofs of good-will that I have received in Paris, and which will for ever remain engraved on my heart.

Accept, Gentlemen, the assurance of the distinguished consideration, with which

I have the honour to be, &c.

HUMMEL.

Paris, May 31, 1825.

THE MOUNTAIN-SPIRIT,

(DER BERG-GEIST.)

A NEW OPERA BY LOUIS SPOHR.

THIS opera was produced in Cassel, to celebrate the nuptials of the Duke of Saxe-Meiningen with the daughter of the Elector of Hesse Cassel. The poem is by the well-known G. Döring, and possesses great merit; it abounds with those situations, which are well calculated to animate the genius of a composer. As the poem describes the world of spirits, Spohr has endeavoured, and we think successfully, to impart to his music that mysterious character which is in unison with the sentiments of the piece. He appears throughout the whole to have wisely borne in mind that the love of men, and

the love of spiritual beings, require a very different character and tone of music; and accordingly the feelings of these unearthly beings are expressed in sounds which, though impassioned have a certain definite character, and leave much to the imagination to supply. This composer in the powerful music of his *Faustus*, in the tender strains of his *Zemire*, and the deep feeling of his *Jessonda*, has already displayed the variety of his talent; the present opera will shew him in another, but not less praiseworthy, point of view. The design is well conceived, and full of invention; the contrasts of the tender and the terrible are in the highest degree striking, and yet the unity of the whole is sustained in a masterly manner throughout. The recitative is admirable, but particularly in those places where the *cantabile* is required. In this, as in his former operas, Spohr has proved how great a command he possesses of instrumentation and the powers of harmony; but in no other opera has he shewn so wise an economy of accompaniments, so that the song is nowhere oppressed, but admirably supported, and allowed freely to develope all its beauties.

In the overture, which begins with a novel subject, characteristic of a march, and advances with a copiousness of rich ideas, the most important features of the opera are portrayed, without being distorted and exaggerated, as is the case in so many compositions of this kind. The contrasts of opposing feelings are powerfully depicted, till at the conclusion, the bursting sounds of jubilee announce the victory which forms the catastrophe of the piece. This is followed by an opening chorus of spirits, of a highly original character; a subterranean scene, lighted by a fire in the centre, displays them ranged in groups around. *Trall*, one of the spirits of the earth, appears; he is the favourite of the great Mountain-Spirit, but is dissatisfied at the eternal toil and labours endured in the bowels of the earth, and speaks in praise of the destiny of men who are permitted to enjoy the light of heaven and walk the airy surface, and to whom in days of old it was permitted them to pay a visit. The recitative of Trall and of the others is here admirably managed. The inquiries of the spirits, their anxious curiosity to learn something of the unknown upper world, are marked with great genius and character. An air of Trall which follows, is full of beauty, and mingled with a certain humour, that distinguishes all the songs of this spirit. When Trall pronounces the word "love," the Mountain-Spirit, who has till now set in a gloomy and abstracted attitude, starts from his throne. This moment of the piece is expressed by the music with great strength and truth. Every one feels and acknowledges, that at this instant the life-spark of the whole action is kindled, and will soon burst into a flame. This is still more strongly expressed in the duet between the Mountain-Spirit and Trall, which is taken up by a chorus, and by the life and freshness which it breathes, is truly admirable, concluding the first scene with great effect.

The scene changes, and a rustic chorus follows of the female attendants of Alma, the bridegroom of Prince Oscar, who has just returned triumphant from the wars. The recitative of *Alma*, which succeeds, is full of passion, tenderness, and the consciousness of a love that meets return. This is followed by a duet between Alma and Oscar, graceful and rich in melody. This leads to a very effective terzetto between the lovers and the father, who now first makes his appearance. It is in part without accompaniment, and independently of its merits, in a melodial point of view, it distinguished by a peculiar management of the voices. After this comes a situation of the highest dramatic effect, in which the composer appears in his native worth, as a great and original artist. Alma is seen alone, meditating on her approaching happiness; but is suddenly aroused from this reverie of delight, by a shuddering which seizes her whole frame, caused by the approach of the spirits. She struggles against the feeling, but in vain; she attempts to quit the place, but remains fixed, as if spell-bound, to the spot. The intrinsic value of the melodies in the air which she sings in this situation, the horror excited by the gradual approach of the spirits, and at last the burst of terror at the appearance of the Spirit of the Mountain, produce an effect which it would not be easy to describe. An increasing energy of feeling, a deepening interest in the scene, a continually progressive beauty of the harmonies and melodies, and great truth of expression, reign in the subsequent finale, in which Alma is transported by the Mountain-Spirit to his subterranean abode, while the bridegroom, her father, and friends, are seen bewailing her fate in fruitless grief, and venting in their fruitless rage on the malignity of the Mountain-spirits.

In the second act we find Alma, in the subterranean empire, in the power of the Mountain-Spirit. On her returning to herself, he attempts with soft words to soothe the terrors of the maiden; he avows his passion, and entreats her to yield him her heart in return. But his gentle expressions cannot hide the malignity of his nature; Alma is at first all terror; but at length she acquires confidence, aware that her only means of gaining time, is to pretend to be moved by the tenderness of his professions. The composer has in the first duet of this act, admirably expressed the contrasted feelings of the two characters; the situation is new, but Spohr has evinced the versatility of his genius. For depth of sentiment, and happy discrimination of character, we consider this duet as one of the most original compositions of the whole opera. Alma expresses a wish to see her friends who are upon earth, and asks as an only boon that she may be allowed to have them occasionally near her. The Mountain-Spirit gives her the power to call up the forms of men by means of certain magical flowers, which Trall is commissioned to procure. Alma dares not venture to summon before her the forms of her bridegroom or her father, but she commands her friend and companion Ludmille to appear, that from her she may learn tidings of those she holds dear. In the following scene between Alma and the shade of Ludmille, the composer has again shewn himself a master who has the command of the brightest and most original fancies. The colourless song of the shade, comprised of a few simple chords, opposed to Alma's deep-felt and glowing sensibility, is productive of an effect, more easily imagined than described. Afterwards Alma calls up other forms, and a recitative and chorus which follow, are of the same extraordinary and mysterious character. A duet succeeds between Trall and the shade of Ludmille, in which he declares to her his love. The amorous professions of the whimsical spirit, blended as they are with his characteristic gaiety, his anger at the indifference shewn by the shade, afford the composer an ample field for the display of his versatile talent, and he has not failed to profit by it accordingly. The melodic beauties and harmonic conduct of this part of the opera is altogether worthy of the master.

After the duet, the scene changes; Oscar the un-

happy bridegroom, is discovered wandering in a mountain scene, in search of his lost love, and calling in rage on the daring ravisher to restore his victim. The air which he sings on this occasion, is of the most impassioned kind, and highly expressive of the stormy feelings that rend his soul. Of the duet that follows between Oscar and Damaslav, though it contains many beauties, yet it cannot be denied that it is too long, and might have been concentrated with advantage. The second act concludes with a festivity given by the Mountain-Spirit, in honour of the beauteous daughter of earth, who graces his subterranean abode, and affords the composer an occasion for a display of a truly dramatic character, in which the music of the dances is of the most enlivening and characteristic kind; while, at the same time, the wild and savage character of the scene is not forgotten, but breaks through the sweeter melodies.

The third act opens with a recitative and air of Alma, full of spirit and feeling; a terzetto follows between Alma, Trall, and the Mountain-Spirit, which terminates in a chorus of great effect. Meantime Trall, dissatisfied with the mere shade of his beloved Ludmille, makes a journey by stealth to earth, and brings back with him the real female friend of Alma. The joy of these two friends on their meeting is charmingly expressed in a duet of great tenderness. The two females are now together, and they contrive to obtain the spell by which Trall effected his passage to the upper regions of earth. The Mountain-Spirit gains intelligence of their flight, and pursues them amid thunders and lightnings. He arrives; terrible appearances precede him; an earthquake shakes the ground, and the rocks are rent asunder. In depicting all this in tones, the genius of Spohr soars into the true sublime, and the author of *Faustus, Zemire,* and *Jessonda,* adds fresh laurels to his wreath. At this moment, the Mountain-Spirit receives an admonition from a superior power, and becoming sensible of having degraded his superior nature by an attachment to a daughter of earth, yields Alma to the arms of her lover. The whole of this conclusion is of the same lofty tone and character as the rest of the piece, full of sweet melodies, combined with harmonies of great power and effect. We feel assured, that great as is the fame of M. Spohr, this composition will tend to augment it. It is delightful to see how rapidly many of the later compositions of the German-school are making their way through Europe, and dividing that attention which was before too exclusively directed to the lighter compositions of the Italian school; and we do not hesitate to say, that the present opera is as worthy of distinction as several of its rivals of the same school.

Cassel, June, 1825. J. T. R.

ON A SCARCE WORK OF BENEDETTO MARCELLO.

To the Editor of the HARMONICON.

SIR,

IN the Memoir of Benedetto Marcello, which appeared in your last, no mention was made of a satirical tract of this master, entitled *Il Teatro alla Moda,* which is extremely rare, but of which I am so fortunate as to possess a copy. Disgusted at beholding the musicians of his time studious rather to flatter the ear, than to speak to the imagination and inform the heart, this great composer conceived the idea of offering some corrective to the evil in the tract in question. I will proceed to give an outline of the satire, and concentrate the more striking parts of it, convinced that in so doing, I shall not only succeed in interesting your readers by some account of a rare work, but also in exciting their curiosity at the perusal of sentiments, which are not less just and piquant, than applicable to the poets and musicians of our times.

The author has divided his tract into two parts ; in the first he addresses himself to the poet, and in the second to the composer.

FIRST PART.

The modern poet should completely abstain from reading the ancient writers, and for this very reason, that the ancient writers never read the moderns.

Before entering upon his task, he will take an exact note of the quantity and quality of the scenes which the manager is desirous of introducing into his drama. It will be requisite that the poet should come to a good understanding with the mechanist of the theatre, in order that he may learn by what exact number of ariettas he ought to prolong his scenes, for the purpose of affording the workmen time to arrange all things behind the curtain. He will compose his poem verse by verse, without giving himself any trouble as to the action, in order that it may be impossible for the spectator to comprehend the plot, and that by this very circumstance, curiosity may be kept alive to the end of the piece. By the way, he will not forget to introduce a brilliant and magnificent scene at the close of his piece, terminating in a chorus in honour either of the sun, the moon, or even of the *impresario*.

He will place at the head of his poem a long discourse upon the art of poetry. He will take care to interlard it with abundant quotations from Sophocles, Euripides, Aristotle, Horace, Longinus, &c., but he will conclude by declaring that a fashionable poet ought boldly to swerve from the rules which they have laid down, in order to conform to the genius of his age, to the corruption of the theatre, to the caprices of the composers, to the whims of the singer, to the delicacy of the *great bear (del grand' urso,)* [query, *Impresario*], &c. &c. He will have recourse as frequently as possible, to the dagger, to poison, to earthquakes, to spectres, to incantations, &c. All these means are admirable ; they cost but little, and produce a prodigious effect on the people.

He will always take care to have a copious store of airs, &c., in reserve in his portfolio, in order to be able to change them at the will of the manager or singer.

Even should the virtuosi pronounce an unfavourable judgment, still the poet will do wisely not to complain ; he should bear in mind, that if the text were pronounced distinctly, the sale of the *Libretti* would suffer considerably.

He will not neglect a regular and orthodox explanation of the three important points of a drama, time—place—and action. Such and such a theatre—so much for the *place ;* from eight o'clock in the evening till midnight—so much for the *time;* the ruin of the manager—so much for the *action.*

SECOND PART.

The modern composer will have no occasion for a knowledge of the rules of composition. Practice, and some few general principles, will be abundantly sufficient.

Nor will he feel any more occasion for an acquaintance with poetry ; it will not even be necessary for him to distinguish the long syllables from the short ones.

He will do well not to read the entire poem before setting it to music, for fear of overloading his imagination and oppressing his genius. He will compose it verse by verse, and will not fail to adjust to the words such airs as he has composed during the course of the year, even though the metre and the quantity should be at perfect variance with his ideas.

He will produce no airs but such as are accompanied by the whole orchestra ; for in order to compose in the modern taste, it is indispensable above all to make plenty of noise.

Should it be found absolutely necessary to shorten the drama, the composer will take care to insist that whole scenes should be suppressed, rather than permit a single note of any of his airs or ritornellos to be retrenched.

If any air should displease, he will answer, that in order to form a right judgment of it, it should be heard upon the stage with full orchestra, dresses, decorations, and lights.

As to the singers, they should never by any chance practise solfaing, for fear of falling into the old-fashioned practice of singing in tune and time ; both which things are at absolute variance with the taste of the day. And not only will they begin by changing the *time* of the airs, but they will also alter the airs themselves, by adapting them to their manner, although their variations are in direct opposition to the bass, and the whole of the instruments. I have the honour to be,

&c. &c., FAYOLLE.

London, August 10th, 1825.

ADVICE TO THE YOUNG COMPOSER,

ON THE AUTHORITY OF MOZART.

[From the German.]

" ADVICE from Mozart!" methinks I hear the reader Exclaim,—even so. "And now first brought to light ?"— Exactly so. " Yet, surely, Mozart was not one of those who were fond of giving advice."—That indeed is true. He was content with doing things as they ought to be done, and left it to others to imitate his example. This is precisely what he did in the instance before us, and the instruction which he afforded by his example, I shall endeavour to translate into language, in order that it may serve for the imitation of others. " But will artists like to hear it ?"—I hope I shall succeed in awakening attention. " How will you contrive to do so ?"—By beginning with some particulars relative to this glorious master.

The observation was made during Mozart's lifetime, and cited rather as a subject of praise, than of censure, that he wrote even his best and most finished works with amazing rapidity, and, according to the common German proverb, " shook them from his sleeve." Having had the happiness of a personal acquaintance with this extraordinary man, and the best opportunities of studying his character, I trust that the following particulars will afford some explanation of a fact that has excited so much wonder.

The truth is, Mozart was not fond of writing, I mean as far as regards the mechanical part of it, and the sedentary posture which it requires. In order to induce him to sit down to his desk in good earnest, some strong motive was necessary ; he never would do so, except from necessity. But when such an impulse was given, and he began to kindle with his subject, it was finished with a despatch that was really astonishing. And yet, at least in his latter years, such was the concentration of his mental powers, that he had very rarely any thing considerable to correct in what he wrote. But, nevertheless, Mozart did not create so quickly as might be supposed; when he sat down to commit any thing important to paper, it was rarely an invention of the moment, dropping, if I may so express myself, from heaven by chance. Much less was this the case with the arrangement and completion of any work of his. No, Mozart's method was this. When alone, or with his wife, or in company with those with whom he stood upon no ceremonies, as well as during his frequent journeys in a carriage, he had the habit not only of keeping his fancy upon the stretch in search of new melodies, but also of working up and arranging the ideas floating in his mind. Without appearing to be conscious of what he was doing, he would hum over, or sing aloud the elements of his embryo work, and when warmed with his subject, would suffer no one to interrupt him. In this manner he completed whole pieces of music in his mind, without committing them to paper, till a convenient opportunity presented itself for so doing *.

When, however, such an occasion occurred, the subject being fully arranged in his mind, he committed it to paper with a rapidity that appeared to the casual observer almost miraculous. He was even fond of writing while others were engaged in conversation around him, and would every now and then throw in a remark, chiefly in a jocular strain, which shewed that he was not so absorbed, but that he followed the general drift of the topic in discussion. So extraordinarily tenacious was his musical memory, and so abundantly was his mind stored with all the means and resources of his art, that in order not to confuse and forget the casual labours of his mind, a few short notes only were necessary. For this purpose, he always took with him, a number of slips of ruled paper, to which he committed his passing thoughts; and these little slips, carefully preserved in a box, constituted the singular diary of his journeys.

Let us now proceed to the moral application. If we review the works of the best German composers of the last fifteen or twenty years, we must be at least prejudiced and uncandid, if not unjust, to deny that a rich and highly-finished style of composition has been eminently advanced by zeal and perseverance; that the art of a skilful management of forms, of a well-adapted instrumentation, and of all that can be obtained by unceasing practice and persevering industry, has been accomplished, and that the means of art which were formerly known only to the first masters and their more favoured disciples, have now become generally diffused. So entirely is this the case, that if an artist of our times should show himself weak, defective, or negligent in these respects, he cannot hope to rise in the estimation of the public. Nay, so far do we carry this feeling, as to treat with contempt and ridicule foreigners of great natural talents, who show themselves deficient of these advantages, and who if they succeed in producing brilliant effects, do so rather through a natural impulse, than a profound knowledge of

the art. So much for the balance in favour of our composers.

But on the other side, in *invention*, and above all in melodial invention, by far the greater part of our musicians, even those of the more distinguished order, will, if compared with those of an early period, appear tame and jejune. In truth, it cannot be denied that they are far from original, abound much less in feeling and expression, and therefore are much less diversified and interesting. Their works, it is true, may have little or nothing to blame, but they have still less wherewith to fire and fill us with enthusiasm. Though on the whole not defective in individual character, they still betray a certain monotony, between which and absolute dryness the difference is but trifling. This is secretly and sensibly felt, and in order to disguise their paucity of invention, they take refuge in violent and glaring resources, which are either purely mechanical or artificial, and sometimes even hyper-artificial; thus in either case having recourse to means which may be acquired by study and labour, and which consist in modulations that confuse the unlearned in music; in the noisy effects of parts, whereby the unity and consistency of the whole is destroyed; in accumulated instrumental effects, and the deafening noise that naturally results; in figures of the most difficult, and from their very difficulty, of the most astonishing kind; in a word, by carrying the external means of the art to extremes. But such is the nature of things, that every extreme, when habitually employed, does not produce the effect of an extreme, but that of an ordinary means; what is external soon satisfies the senses, and the senses thus satisfied demand a more violent stimulus; at length these can no longer be obtained, for nature can go only to a certain point; it is only the mind, the sentiment, that is infinite. A degree of interest may be excited in the hearer, when these resources have been employed with spirit and effect, but he will still fancy that he has heard the work before, and indifference will be the natural result; the music will only pass through the ear, and die away with the last sounds, without possessing either the judgment, the fancy, or the memory with one substantial idea, one strain that roots itself in the mind, one sound that we love to reflect upon, desire to hear again, and to retain the recollection of for ever

Whence arises this decay of invention? The Italian is at once ready with his answer. "Invention, (says he,) pure and original invention, is the gift of genius alone. The Germans," he adds, "are, with some brilliant exceptions, a people without any real genius for the art; but, as a compensation for this, they possess great solidity of judgment, profound knowledge, and unwearied industry and perseverance." Upon this answer the Italian prides himself not a little, and why? Because it is but saying in other words: "We ourselves possess a vast deal of genius, and as much talent, though we employ it otherwise. It is true we do not possess equal industry and perseverance; but, why should we lay claim to that of which we do not stand in need?" The German will do well to adhere to his wonted justice and modesty; to leave to the Italians their just meed of praise, and to oppose to such reasoning the only real answer—the matter of fact. Oppose to them our works of genius, the great masterpieces of the art.

But to complain of the decline of invention, yet still to demand new works of genius, may appear a contra-

* We shall have occasion in our next, of laying before the reader some extraordinary instances of the power of Mozart's memory.

VOL. III.

2 B

diction, and be saying in earnest what Jean Paul says in jest: "My dear sirs, let us but have a good stock of genius, and the rest will follow of itself." We do not, however, think that there is any want of genius amongst us, but that a wrong method of employing, or rather of squandering it away, is prevalent. The divine gift of genius cannot be forcibly obtained, either by human exertions, or by magical means; it is either given or denied; it either exists, or does not exist; but when it does exist, like the rocky spring in the bosom of the earth, it may be dug out and a free course be made for it: but it may also be neglected, it may be left to stagnate and corrupt, it may be mixed with loathsome elements, and become noxious instead of useful. In plain truth, the decay of invention in many of our modern musical composers, chiefly as regards melody, does not in general proceed so much from a want of genius, as from careless-ness on the part of those who really possess this divine gift. The evil arises from an improper method of em-ploying their time, of squandering their resources, and losing the happy moment of inspiration; as well as, in a great measure, by over-rating the efforts of mechanical labour, practice, and industry. Both the one and the other of these evils proceed, we think, from the manner in which the greater part of composers have been taught and continue to practise the art of music, and perhaps still more from the manner in which they are accustomed to write down their compositions.

Let us briefly discuss these two last points, more particu-larly the latter, as being the real object of the present Essay.

In our days, pupils, and particularly those who from their precocious talents are early destined to the study of the art, are made acquainted with such compositions only as are adapted to a correct, flowing, and finished mecha-nism in the execution. As far as regards practice, this may be an excellent method for the future ripieno-player; it may be deemed indispensable, considering what is ex-pected from him. Yet it cannot be denied that this me-thod gives the mind a decided bias to the mechanical part of the art, and habituates it to the same. It is a practice that cannot, in my opinion, but prove disad-vantageous to the solo-player, in as far as regards ex-pression and sentiment; how much more so then in respect to composition, and, above all, to invention.

Again, the endless reading of notes which follows the pupil's first progress; the immense value attached to a rapid, though correctly cold, playing, a prima vista: the running through an immense mass of the ever-renewed and renewing labours of others; and the consequent neg-lect of the powers of fancy and of extemporaneous execu-tion, of original thinking and feeling when at the in-strument—all which tends to choke up the sources of in-vention, or at least to prevent original ideas from flowing so copiously and freshly as they might otherwise do.

I have pointed out these among many other causes of a similar nature, which strike me as having a tendency to produce the evil in question; an evil which is seen to abound nowhere so strongly as among the Germans. It is true that men of extraordinary genius, such as Haydn, Mozart, and Beethoven, even though educated somewhat in the manner here described, have, by the native force of their genius, triumphed over the obstacles presented by this mode of education. But these are exceptions of the rarest kind, and when the question is one of general rule, it is folly to refer to exceptions. Nay, perhaps, those very master-spirits may at certain

periods have been betrayed, by a recollection, and, as it were, distant re-action of these early impressions, into extremes which they had better have avoided; as, for in-stance, Haydn in some of his sportive passages, which almost border on buffoonery, and Beethoven in some of his more wild and grotesque caprices.

From their extensive and multifarious reading, the young composers of the present day have formed within them-selves certain models, as it were, of the styles of different masters. Possessing all the external means of the art, a correct taste, a good knowledge of instrumentation, and of the best means of grouping their ideas, and a general acquaintance with the symmetry of parts, &c., they seat themselves at the desk without waiting for any interior impulse or direction of the mind to a given object, ar-range their music-paper, and confidently commence the task of composition, trusting to experience, and the hope that life and inspiration may come in the course of their writing; or if not, that they shall, at least, produce something tolerably clever, and not unpleasing. Stored as they are with the means of art, they may chance to succeed in producing a work of respectable mediocrity; or should it happen to turn out more spirited and impor-tant, it may owe its merits either to the correctness of the finish, to certain surprising effects; to the charm of instrumentation, &c., but rarely, if ever, to inven-tion, to fresh and original ideas. The other produc-tion, however faultless, decent, or well-adapted to the end proposed, will still possess nothing truly new; truly characteristic and impressive, and therefore nothing that can excite any lasting interest. Nor indeed can this be otherwise, except on the supposition that an artist during such a writing-lesson should all at once be wrapt into inspiration, and that the fervour should last till his task be finished; an event which may perhaps occur but once during the life of the greatest genius—a wonder, a real miracle! and consequently an event upon which no one should calculate, and to the chance of which no rea-sonable man would trust. The most distinguished mas-ters of the art, men gifted with the greatest inventive powers, have never been so presumptuous as to reckon upon such chances. Though conscious of their own powers, they had learned to be more humble; they hailed with joy and gratitude the moments of pure inspiration, as direct gifts from heaven; carefully distinguishing such moments from those beneficially devoted to the working up and final disposition and completion of their conceptions. Those favoured moments of inspiration are of such short duration, and the ethereal gifts which they bring so easily evaporate, that such masters have wisely had recourse to means to grasp them instantly, and give them a "local habitation and a name," in order that they may profit by them afterwards in the hours of labour. Their method, with but slight deviation, was that pursued by the great Mozart, as already described: it is known to have been the practice of Gluck, and Haydn, and there can be no doubt but Beethoven and others have nearly a similar method. Unfortunately as we have before observed, the young composers of our day act in another way. They have not learned the wisdom of duly estimating the "gift of the moment," as Schiller happily calls it, and they do not bear in mind what this poet adds, that the moment is "the mightiest of all the gods." Trusting to the self-elected hour and to themselves, they neglect these nobler re-sources, or omit to profit by their practical application.

REVIEW OF MUSIC.

IL CROCIATO IN EGITTO, Melo-Dramma Eroico, *in due Atti: Poesia del* Signor Gaetano Rossi; *Musica del* SIGNOR Maestro GIACOMO MEYERBEER.

FOR many years past the Italian opera may be said to have been shared, in most of the great lyric theatres, between Mozart and Rossini. A few works by inferior composers, or, rather, by servile imitators of those great masters, have been occasionally heard, and even applauded, by audiences for whom a new name possesses a charm; but they have not been able to maintain their ground, and have passed into oblivion after a short season or two.—Such are the productions of Nicolini, Morlacchi, Mercadante, Soliva, Pavesi, and *id genus omne.* It is true that the operas of Winter and Paër are now and then brought forward, but this is chiefly, if not entirely, in the north of Germany, where a better taste for music —because an unprejudiced one—prevails, than in any other part of Europe; and Zingarelli's *Romeo e Giulietta* has gained a popularity in Paris and in London, from the pathetic acting of Madame Pasta. In examining the lists of performances at the *Scala,* the *Santo Carlo,* the *Fenice,* the *Louvois,* and the King's Theatre, it will be found that, with the admitted exceptions, what we have stated is supported by unquestionable acts.

Such being the case, the appearance above the musical horizon of a fresh composer, possessed of brilliant talent, is really a subject of general gratulation, in an age when the public amusement so much depends on the harmonic art; for a little change, or at least some variety, is as necessary to the auditory as to any other sense, if we would avoid that satiety which a few things reiterated year after year is sure to produce. We hail, therefore, with no ordinary satisfaction, the rising up of such a genius as M. Meyerbeer* has proved himself, if we may be allowed to judge by a single opera. He comes very opportunely, for nothing by the "divine Mozart" is left unknown; Rossini seems exhausted, or, at least, is become wealthy, and indulges in repose; and Weber has hitherto confined himself to dramas in the German language.

Concerning the dramatic part of the opera now before us, we have only to say, that the composer has not depended upon the materials furnished by the poet for much assistance, except as to situations. We have given so copious an analysis of the poem in our thirty-

* For some account of M. Meyerbeer, see the present Volume of the Harmonicon.

first number, that it is unnecessary to enter any further into it now.

Il Crociato in Egitto is the offspring of real genius, because it abounds in invention: it is no less the work of an excellent musician and man of taste, for it is full of those effects that none but an able harmonist can produce, and of numerous beauties that only proceed from a fertile and refined imagination. The words, so far as the sense is concerned, are carefully and judiciously set: the composer very rarely mistakes the nature of the passion to be expressed, and is in most cases scrupulously true to the sentiments of the poet, so long as the poet is true to his own meaning. But M. Meyerbeer does not always shew that he is intimately acquainted with the prosody of the Italian language; at the same time it should be borne in mind, that he is a German, and this being considered, his occasional errors in accent are neither surprising nor inexcusable. The orchestral accompaniments are not elaborately composed, nevertheless they shew the great master, by admirably supporting and illustrating the principal design. Those on the stage are written *ad captandum;* but military bands in operas are the fashion, and fashion must not be too stubbornly opposed by those who wish to conciliate public favour.

Having thus given our opinion generally of this opera, we shall next speak of some of its parts. As, however, much of the work has been published in the Harmonicon, and our readers therefore have been enabled to judge of a considerable portion of it for themselves, we will not put their patience to a trial by any minute and lengthened detail. The first act comprises ten pieces, the second eight. The *Pantomimic Overture* [page 144 of Harmonicon,] terminates in a fine chorus of slaves, "*Patria amata!*" No. 2 is a cavatina for *Palmide,* which passes into a duet, "*Soave immagine,*" for the same and *Aladino,* on the following motivo:—

Allegretto.

The chorus then announces the arrival of vessels in the harbour, and the duet is continued in a second charming subject, which however is a little à la Rossini. After this occurs, in the original score, the duet "Non v'è per noi", [page 170,] a beautiful morceau that was omitted at Florence, and also in London, having being thought to resemble too closely the duettino at the end of the opera. The Chorus, " Vedi il legno", in A minor, introducing Armando, is one of the cleverest things in the opera; the change into the major key, when the military band enters and joins the orchestra, produces a new and remarkably imposing effect. Armando then sings the Cavatina, " Caro mano", [page 184,] which, it has been suspected, is not the composition of Meyerbeer, though no evidence of the fact has been adduced. It was certainly performed with his sanction at Florence: but a considerable alteration was made in this part of the opera, when produced in the latter place, on account of the insufficiency of the tenor there engaged, and it was represented in London nearly according to the arrangement made at Florence. A very fine accompanied recitative, " L'angustia mia," and the grand duet, " Va! già varcasti, indegno!" occur in this part of the opera. The composer has exerted all his strength in the latter, and given to the world an example of dramatic music that has rarely been equalled on the Italian stage: the bursts of vehement passion, the subsidence of these into pity and tenderness, the struggle of conflicting feelings, meekness, contrition, all find corresponding notes in this duet, and if measured sounds have any power to express natural emotion, they have been successfully employed for the purpose in the present instance *

The Terzetto, " Giovinetto Cavalier," follows the above duet. [Harm. page 153.] The undivided opinion in London has been loudly declared in favour of this composition ; yet at Florence it produced so little effect, that after the second performance, it was cut out of the opera! It has been remarked that the opening of this is borrowed from a chorus in Mozart's Figaro, beginning thus,—

Ri - ce - ve-te, o Pad-ron - ci - na

The above bars, compared with Meyerbeer's, will shew the similarity, to the extent of four notes, and no more. The coincidence was, most likely, accidental; but if not, the trifling plagiarism is turned to so good an account, that it is amply atoned for. The chorus of Priests and Knights [page 174] is well contrived for stage effect, and good in any form. The commencement is so perfectly Handelian, that the imitation, in all probability, was intentional. The Finale opens with great solemnity: the whole of this long and important portion of the opera displays the richness of M. Meyerbeer's fancy, and the justness of his conception. By referring to our analysis of this drama, [page 125,] the reader will perceive how large a demand is made on the composer by the various feelings to be depicted, and how difficult his task, amidst so many sudden changes, to preserve a due musical relation in all the parts, and to combine them as a consistent

whole. Yet he has effected his purpose, and in a manner that may challange competition with any composer, Mozart alone excepted *. The Canone which forms a part of this Finale, is a very happy effort of genius; it is scientific, but not dry, and though quite new, immediately felt. The following enharmonic modulation in it, is beautiful in effect:—

The annexed, in the same, for five voices, is a singular vocal passage:—

Sog - ni ri-den-ti di pa-ce e a-me-re.

The winding up of this Finale we must still view as a very masterly climax ; though it has been censured as too gay, the warlike designs of the various persons being considered. But, whatever soldiers may really feel, they never wish to appear sad on the eve of a battle; therefore a brilliant chorus in a major key may well express the state of mind that warriors at such a moment would at least affect.

The second act begins with a pleasing elegant Rondo, [page 161] which was excluded from the King's Theatre in order to make way for a wretched air, the composition of Signor Garcia. The grand Scena ed Aria for the prima donna follows, and is not the most successful of the composer's efforts, though he doubtless spared no pains to render it so. The most agreeable part of it we have published in this work. [page 164.] The chorus of conspirators that succeeds this, is exceedingly original, characteristic, and efficient: the talent of the author shines conspicuously in this fine composition. The subjoined

* For a large extract from this duet, see No. XXXI, page 199, of the Harmonicon.

* In this finale are, the March and Chorus printed at page 158, the Canone, page 167, and the Solo, page 194, of Numbers XXXI. and XXXII. of the Harmonicon.

harmony, which is the commencement of the symphony, is very impressive:—

As we intend in a future number to print the whole of this chorus, arranged for the piano-forte, we refrain from indulging in any further extracts from it here. The Canone, " *O Cielo clemente!*" comes next in order, the whole of which has appeared in this work, [page 188.] But we could not make room for the quartett and quintett

that follow. The former is a beautiful *coda* to the Canone: the latter two quick movements, in dialogue; the first built on the following elegant melody:—

Pal - mi-de, u - ni - ta al fi - - - - glio, al

Nu - me del suo - spo - so i lo - ro vo-ti han

por - - to, già n'ab-brac - ci - - ar la fè.

The second melody is equally charming, *quoad* melody, but too lively for the scene, which threatens nothing less than "dire despair and death." The whole of this is worked up in a manner that demonstrates the scientific knowledge of M. Meyerbeer, and his skill in rendering science conducive to effect; and extended as the present article already is, we must lengthen it, to give one passage from this quintett that will be acceptable to all who enjoy harmony that never fades.

The *Inno di morte* is next in succession in the original score, but was rejected at the King's Theatre, on account of the length of the opera, which is seldom allowed to exceed three hours in London. This *Hymn of Death* is cal-

culated for stage effect, and most ably written; but would be extremely deteriorated if performed without the necessary action and the scenic adjuncts.

We have now nearly concluded this subject, and have

only to mention the animated conversation-chorus, published in our last, [page 196,] and the delicious duet, "Il tenero affetto," the most popular piece in the opera, which also appeared in the same number. [Page 179.] Of these there is but one opinion: the latter was never performed in public without an immediate encore, and its reception in private has not been less decisive of its merit.

By this opera M. Meyerbeer has already established his fame: should his love of the art—for he pursues it with no interested views—prompt him to continue so elegant a pursuit, it is more than probable that he will gain a celebrity which will transmit his name to posterity as one of the benefactors of mankind.

1. The MARCH from the Opera of Cendrillon, with varia-·tions for the PIANO-FORTE, by J. N. HUMMEL, Maître de Chapelle to the Duke of Saxe Weimar. (Cocks and Co., Princes Street, Hanover Square.)

2. Two favourite RONDOLETTOS, in the form of Waltzes, composed by the same. (Published by the same.)

3. "O Pescator dell' onda," VENETIAN AIR, varied for the PIANO-FORTE, by CHARLES CZERNY. (Published by the same).

WE have been uncommonly gratified by M. Hummel's variations to the fine march in Cendrillon; the great master appears in every line, and the difficulties presented throughout are worth overcoming, because the passages involved cannot be rendered more easy without a loss, and a considerable one, of effect. The variations are eight in number; the last, which alone occupies seven pages, is the least meritorious of the whole, but calls for a greater power of hand, and more rapid execution than all the rest. In a piece of seventeen pages, it is generally prudent to curtail, and we advise most players to retrench this eighth variation, the performance whereof would surprise more than please. The first, third, and sixth variations must delight the lovers of fine harmony; the second is excellent practice for the left hand, and the fifth is a good exercise in the interweaving of the fingers, while it produces an agreeable and novel effect.

The Rondolettos can neither of them substantiate any claim to originality, if they are recent compositions. The first is a glaring imitation of the waltz in the Freischütz, as the annexed four bars will shew:—

The second is much like a composition of the same species that we know by heart, but cannot recal the author. Hummel is not thought fastidious in the use he makes of other people's ideas, but he very often improves them we willingly allow. These Rondolettos are very brilliant and lively; the last of them has some troublesome skips, but both are in a popular style, short, and simple in construction.

The universally admired air, "O Pescator dell' onda," has met with cruel usage. Were the ingenious composer of it, Madame Gail, now living, she would speedily complain, and bitterly too, of the treatment which her delightfully simple melody has received in Germany, where it has been made to skip and jump, to scream and grumble; has been whipped about in all directions, tortured above and below, and split into ten thousand notes; M. Charles

Czerny, the slight-of-hand man, officiating as executioner. Is it possible that in Vienna, where such honours were paid to Haydn, a piece like this should be considered as music?—Is it possible that in London, where in despite of the pedantry of a few masters, and the folly of fashion, good taste in the art prevails, such a republication as this should remunerate the dealer?—But let us be just; part of the third variation is very good: all the rest is downright absurdity, and there are thirteen pages of it.

1. Melange on Favourite Airs from Meyerbeer's Opera, Il Crociato in Egitto, arranged for the PIANO-FORTE, by J. B. CRAMER. (Cramer, Addison, and Beale, 201, Regent Street.)

2. Melange on Favourite Airs from Meyerbeer's Opera, Il Crociato in Egitto, composed for the PIANO-FORTE, by CAMILLE PLEYEL. (Cocks and Co., Princes-st., Hanover Square; and Messrs. Pleyel, Paris).

3. Impromptu on Meyerbeer's Favourite Air, Giovinetto Cavalier, for the PIANO-FORTE; arranged by J. B. CRAMER. (J. B. Cramer and Co.)

ONE of the certain consequences now of an opera becoming popular is, an arrangement of its most favourite airs for the Piano-Forte. Where one vocal piece with Italian words is sold, a dozen of the same melody in the form of an instrumental rondo obtain circulation; for players compared to singers of music set to that language, are in about the proportion, we should estimate, of twelve to one in England. Besides, at the present period there seems to be a dislike, rather general, to any thing bearing the name of sonata; nay, even its successor, the divertimento, begins to be looked upon with a sour countenance, and nothing but airs or marches from operas and ballets suit the reigning taste. Composers, therefore, discreetly adapt themselves to the prevailing rage, and then adapt melodies; thus saving an infinite deal of trouble; for to arrange demands no extraordinary quantity of thought, to invent requires genius.

Mr. Cramer and M. Camille Pleyel have both fixed their attention at the same moment on the favourite work of the day, and to the produce of their labours have, singularly enough, given nearly a similar title; but they have selected different parts of the opera, therefore in no way clash with each other. M. Pleyel has been most fortunate in the choice of subjects, and Mr. Cramer most successful in his mode of treating them. The former has introduced passages that call for a little more execution than the nature of the publication warrants; the latter has studied to impart a reasonable degree of facility to his pages. But both these Melanges shew much excellent taste, and will make their way in the musical world.

No. 3. is the Romance, or Terzetto, published in our Thirty-first Number. Mr. Cramer has given it very faithfully from the original, adding a few passages, and modulating it into C major, for the purpose of extending it to the usual length of a Piano-Forte piece. He has also prefixed a short introduction, and the whole is contained in seven pages.

1. SACRED MUSIC, being a large and valuable selection of the best PSALM TUNES, both ancient and modern, arranged for Four Voices, or a Single Voice, with an Accompaniment for the Organ or Piano-Forte, by ROBERT JAMES EDWARDS, Organist of Banbury, Oxon. (Preston, 71, Dean Street, Soho.)

9. *A General Collection of* PSALMS *and* HYMN TUNES, *with New* INTERLUDES, &c. *Selected by* JAMES PECK. *The Interludes by Mr.* NIGHTINGALE. (James Peck, 52, *Paternoster Row.*)

WE have such an abundant supply of the orthodox Psalm tunes in every possible shape, that it would seem to be almost unnecessary to multiply editions, without some distinct public advantage. Mr. Edwards has here given us a collection of between sixty and seventy tunes, amongst which we find one—new we conclude—composed by himself; all the rest, to the best of our belief, have been in print before; most of them for nearly a century, and many much longer. Had he thrown any fresh light on them, by means of accompaniments, or of some improved version, his work would have been received with thanks, perhaps with general encouragement: but he has left the matter exactly where he found it, and only given us a new title-page.

In reading over some of the sacred poetry in this volume, it struck us that the version in a few instances, might have been amended. In the very first page we find this stanza:

"Come, let us break his bands," say they,
"This man shall never give us laws:"
And thus they cast his yoke away,
And nail'd the Saviour to the cross.

The work is published by subscription, and the list shews that the compiler is much respected in his neighbourhood.

Mr. Peck's collection amounts to nearly one hundred and thirty tunes, in a pocket volume, and at the economical price of three shillings and sixpence. "The new Interludes," says the editor, "will be found suitable to either of the tunes which follow them, and it is hoped will be considered as a feature of originality and usefulness peculiar to this work, which has for a considerable time past occupied the incessant attention of the publisher."

1. THREE ROUNDS, *with an accompaniment for the Piano-Forte; the music by* GEORGE B. HERBERT: *the Poetry by* J. R. PLANCHE. Book 1. (Goulding, D'Almaine, and Co. *Soho Square.*)

2. "O! say not Woman's Heart is bought," *song by* John Whitaker, *Harmonized for* THREE VOICES, *by* SAMUEL WEBBE. (Mayhew and Co., 17, Old Bond Street.)

3. The Huntsman's Chorus *from* Der Freischütz, *translated by* I. W. Bowden, Esq. *arranged for Two Voices, with an accompaniment for the Piano-Forte, or Guitar, by* C. M. SOLA. (Clementi and Co., 26, *Cheapside.*)

THOUGH the Rounds by Mr. Herbert have been in our possession some time, we have never been able to notice them till the present moment, which we much regret, for before we had devoted many minutes to them, we found that they possess a very superior degree of merit, and ought to have had the advantage of what little service our recommendation might have afforded them, long ago. Their design is thus stated in a preface; "—there is scarcely one concerted piece in twenty, the subject of which is calculated for ladies to sing; they being generally the sentiments of soldiery, seamen, hunters, banditti, smugglers, &c. The natural consequences of these circumstances are the utter banishment of part-music from school and drawing-room." We hardly need tell our readers that a Round is a kind of Canon in the unison, each part singing the same air, the first part beginning, and others following in succession. These Rounds are for three voices, equal ones they should be, namely, three sopranos, or tenors. The melodies have nothing common or vulgar about them; the harmony is smooth and agreeable, more so than is usual in music of this description, and the composer has read the words with care and judgment, thus doing that justice by the poet which he seldom receives at the hands of the musician. The former had a right to expect thus much from his coadjutor, for he supplied him with some very pretty verses,—verses which deserved the notes that have been joined to them. We extract the words of the second Round, entitled "THE WILLOW'S WARNING," from the German."

Rest ye, rest ye, rapid streams!
How like heedless youth ye go,
Kissing ev'ry flow'r that beams
On the bank through which ye flow.
Pure and sparkling was your spring;
Sweet and stainless still ye be;
Why thus haste yourselves to fling
In a salt and stormy sea?
Rest ye, rest ye, &c.

Book the second, which is published, we shall notice in our next.

No. 2, Mr. Whitaker's deservedly popular air, is well harmonized by Mr. Webbe, and converted into a very pleasant trio, or glee. He should have pointed out that the second voice is to be sung an octave lower.

Mr. Sola would have rendered a service to many vocal ladies, by altering the Huntsman's Chorus of Weber into a duet, had he been cautious in the management of the harmony, which he has very much neglected in the present arrangement.

---

1. BALLAD, "To welcome Jamie hame again," *written by* H. S. VAN DYK, ESQ., *composed by* T. A. RAWLINGS, *and sung by* Miss Stephens. (J. B. Cramer & Co., 201, *Regent Street.*)

2. BALLAD, "My own dear Maid," *written and composed by the same, and sung by* Mr. Sapio. (*Published by the same.*)

3. "Let the shrill Trumpet's warlike Voice," *composed by* W H. CUTLER, *Mus. Bac. Oxon., Sung by* Mr. Atkins. (Lindsay, 217, *Regent Street.*)

4. BALLAD, "The Rose," *written by the late* Rt. Hon. C. J. Fox, *composed by* W. H. CUTLER, *M. B.,* (*Published by the same.*)

5. BALLAD, "The Farewell," *the Poetry by* SAMUEL ROGERS, ESQ., *the music by* W. H. CALLCOTT. (Birchall & Co., 140, *New Bond Street.*)

6. "The Merry Mariners," *by* CHARLES M. KING. (Dover, 68, *Chancery Lane.*)

7. "O lull me!" *by the same.* (*Published by the same.*)

8. "Oh! it is not while Riches," *an original Irish Melody, the words by* W. H. BELLAMY, ESQ., *with an accompaniment for the* PIANO-FORTE, *by* W. EAVESTAFF. (W. Eavestaff, 66, *Great Russell Street; Bloomsbury.*)

9. BALLAD, *written by* H. PARKER, ESQ., *composed by* W. A. WORDSWORTH. (Monro and May, 11, *Holborn Bars.*)

To find a new melody now, is almost as fortunate, and

quite as rare, as to get the ticket that is to gain the great prize; we therefore do not blame those who fail in their search after so scarce and valuable a commodity; neither do we encourage them to continue their pursuit, for no labour will discover it,—it sets all industry at defiance, and comes of its own accord, unsought, un-solicited. We do not perceive that it has fallen in the way of any of the above composers; the chances, indeed, in only nine songs were much against such luck. Mr. Rawlings's two ballads possess a large portion of elegance, and but a small one of originality. The first is very like what a compound of Shield's excellent sea-song, "The heaving of the lead," and the Scotish air, "Down the burn davy, love," would produce. The second has the same easy, genteel manner, but without any prominent feature. The accompaniment of this is too much crowded with notes, the last bar in the bass, page 3, particularly, and the words are too often repeated. In both there is too great a display of Italian, in the shape of directions; nevertheless, they are much superior to the generality of modern compositions of this class.

Mr. Cutler's two songs must abound in engraver's errors; should they ever come again into our hands in a corrected form, we shall be happy to re-consider them.

Mr. W. Callcott's ballad is full of taste and tenderness; the words are correctly and feelingly set, the accompa-niment is judicious, the compass is adapted to any voice, and it presents no difficulty to the singer. The melody reminds us of a pathetic song, "Too plain, dear Youth," by Dr. Howard, a composition of which Mr. C. probably never heard.

Mr. C. King's two songs lead us to believe that he inherits his father's talent. No. 7, is an uncommonly animated sea-song, and shews an inventive faculty. No. 8, is in another style, more gentle and expressive; but it was a bold attempt to set such words, and almost rash to make even a slight alteration in them. In two instances Mr. K. has mistaken the accent, and has not read this beautiful little poem,—written two hundred years ago by Strode,—with due attention. His general conception, however, of the author's meaning is correct, and his melody is pleasing.

Mr. Eavestaff's Irish melody is decidedly an imitation, and a very good one, producing an agreeable well set song. The words are not less deserving of praise, but the author has had the great lyric poet of our day, Moore, in his view while writing them.

The last of this list, No. 9, is free from any of those faults which we too often have to expose, and in its accompaniment, proves the composer to have a good taste for harmony; but we must not deceive him by saying that it has any pretensions to novelty.

1. Havering Bower, a *Second* SERENADE *for the* HARP *and* PIANO-FORTE, *with* FLUTE *Accompaniment,* ad lib., *by* T. A. RAWLINGS. (J. B. Cramer & Co., 201, Regent Street.)

2. The Incantation Scene *in* Der Freischütz, *arranged for the* HARP *and* PIANO-FORTE, *with* FLUTE *and* VIOLONCELLO *Accompaniments,* ad lib., *by* N. C. BOCHSA. (Boosey and Co., 28, Holles Street.).

3. A Selection of *Airs from* C. M. VON WEBER's *cele-brated Opera,* Der Freischütz, *arranged for the* HARP *and* PIANO-FORTE, *by* W. H. STEIL. (Goulding, D'Almaine, and Co., Soho Square.)

4. The favourite French Romance, Le Petit Troubadour, *arranged with* Variations, *as a* DUET *for the* HARP *and* PIANO-FORTE, *by* J. T. CRAVEN. (Paine and Hopkins, 69, Cornhill.)

5. "Amor, possente nume," *from* ROSSINI's Opera; ARMIDA, *as a* DUET *for the* HARP *and* PIANO-FORTE, *by* GUSTAVUS HOLST. (Cocks and Co., Princes Street, Hanover Square.)

Havering Bower is a pretty, easy duet, in which the beau-tiful air "Donald" is introduced with propriety, and aug-mented with judgment. There are in it arpeggios of demisemiquavers, it is true, but the movement is *larghetto,* and they are meant to be swept with the utmost delicacy and lightness, producing the soft, celestial, effect of an Æolian harp. "Cease your funning"—very properly marked *andantino*—follows; and the last movement is the popular song in The Antiquary.

The Incantation Scene is remarkably well arranged by M. Bochsa, all the extraordinary effects rendered by the orchestra being concentrated in the Harp and Piano-Forte parts, but in such a manner as to avoid any repul-sive difficulties for either instrument. M. Bochsa really seems quite at home in this scene.

No. 3 is. like many other arrangements, German, French, and English, for Harp and Piano-Forte, that have fallen under our view since the birth of the Frei-schütz. Indeed, it would be next to a miracle to give any thing like an air of novelty to the popular pieces chosen from this opera by Mr. Steil, therefore we cannot help wishing that he, amongst many others, had turned his attention to some other.

In Numbers 4 and 5, ease has been the prime object of Mr. Craven and Mr. Holst, and they have accom-plished their purpose. We are glad to see the gay French air, and the magnificent duet of Rossini, in such prac-ticable instrumental shapes.

1. "La Jeune et sensible Isabelle," Introduction *and* Air *with Variations for the* HARP, *by* F. DIZI. (J. B. Cramer and Co., 201, Regent Street.)

2. The Huntsman's Chorus, *arranged for the* HARP, *with an* Introduction, *by* T. H. WRIGHT, Jun. (By the same.)

3. "Auld Lang Syne," *a favourite* Scotch Air, *with* Variations, *for the* HARP, *by* W. ETHERINGTON. (Skillern and Challoner, Regent Street.)

THE French Air, No. 1, is unknown to us: with the words and the melody in its simple state, it may, very likely, be interesting; but in its present form it so much resem-bles a thousand other things, that it does not appear to have any claim as an original composition. Mr. Dizi has not given any colouring to this melody of his adoption that affords a new feature to it; the whole, including the Introduction, is monotonous, though perfectly faultless as to grammatical rule.

The Huntsman's Chorus follows the copy arranged by M. Weber for the Piano-Forte, allowing for the changes necessary to adapt it for the Harp. The two last pages of this publication, which we suppose are meant as something like an amplification of the chief subject, are more in the style of an interlude, and remaining most obstinately in the same key as the Chorus—which is here transposed into E flat—afford no 'relief to it whatever. The Introduction has the same fault; we do, it is true, find an A natural, once or twice, but this can hardly be considered as even an apology for modulation.

The fine Scotish Air, *Auld lang syne*, has been sadly tortured and twisted within the last dozen years. Had Mr. Etherington given it us once in a simple form, we might have compounded for all the tricksy variations that follow: but he sets out with a fidgetty bass of semiquavers, and will not once allow it to be heard in its mother tongue. The very first variation is marked *scherzo*, (*scherzoso*, we presume, is meant.) But in what can this pathetic tune have offended, that it should be punished by so unnatural a disguise? Then we have a *con spirito*, and double demisemiquavers. Spirits of ancient song! protect your Scotish airs from double demisemiquavers, played *con spirito!*

1. FANTASIA BRILLANTE, *introducing* The cries of Paris, *for the* FLUTE, *with a* Piano-Forte accompaniment, *by* TOULOU. *Op.* 30. (Lindsay, 217, *Regent Street.*)

2. INTRODUCTIONS *and* VARIATIONS *on a* Theme *by* CIMAROSA, *for the* FLUTE *and* PIANO-FORTE, *composed by* MAURO GIULIANI, *of Vienna. Op.* 84. (Wessel and Stodart, 1, *Soho Square.*)

3. AIR, " *Sul margine d'un rio,*" *with* Variations *for the* PIANO-FORTE *and* FLUTE *obbligato, composed by* CHARLES SAUST. (Cocks and Co., *Princes Street, Hanover Square.*)

4. THREE THEMES *from the Operas of* Hummel *and* Spohr, *arranged for* TWO FLUTES *and* PIANO-FORTE, *by* WILLIAM FORDE. (*by the same.*)

5. INTRODUCTION *and* AIR, *with* Variations *for the* FLUTE *and an* Accompaniment *for the* PIANO-FORTE, *by* J. N. HUMMEL. *Op.* 102. (Paine and Hopkins, 69, *Cornhill.*)

6. *A Selection of original* IRISH AIRS *set for the* FLUTE, *by* CHARLES SAUST. (Cocks and Co.)

7. *The Beauties of* Weber's Preciosa, *set for the* FLUTE, *by* CHARLES SAUST. (Cocks and Co.)

THE practice of the Flute is making rapid strides in England, if we may judge by the quantity and quality of the music published for it. We have before us pieces that twenty-years ago would have been thought fit only for the professional player, but now are addressed to the amateur. The first of them is founded on the popular French air, " Voila le plaisir, mes dames," with an extremely easy accompaniment, consisting only of chords. The second is an elegant melody in the *Matrimonio Segreto*, and the third Millico's sweet arietta; these two requiring rather a better piano-forte player as accompanist than the former. No. 4 consists of two subjects, a Romance and a Terzetto, from the new opera by Hummel, *Mathilde von Guise*, and an aria from Spohr's *Faust*; the accompaniment simple. No. 5, Hummel's Introduction and Air, opens with an adagio in F. minor, that looks formidable, but proves very manageable. The credit of playing the music of this generally elaborate composer, may be acquired without much labour for the Flutist, and with scarcely any for the Pianist.

Numbers 6 and 7 are small books of tunes for beginners; the respectable name under which they are published ought to be a sufficient recommendation of them.

1. *Boosey's Selection of Airs, &c., for* PIANO *and* VIOLONCELLO, *by the most admired* Foreign Composers. Book 3. (Boosey and Co., *Holles Street.*)

2. B. ROMBERG'S ARIA, " Bel piacer," *adapted as a Solo for the* VIOLONCELLO, *with* PIANO-FORTE Accompaniment, *by* W. H. HAGART. (Wessel and Stodart, 1, *Soho Square.*)

3. TWELVE EXERCISES *for the* VIOLONCELLO SOLO, *composed by* J. J. F. DOTZAUER, (Banister, 109, *Goswell Street.*)

4. *A Set of* EXERCISES *for the* VIOLONCELLO, *selected from the works of* Corelli, Haydn, and Kreutzer. *Edited by* H. J. Banister. (*Published by the same.*)

5. *Cock's Collection of Choice* PIECES *for the* VIOLONCELLO *and* PIANO-FORTE, selected from the best foreign Composers, *by* W. H. HAGART. Books 2 and 3. (Cocks and Co., *Princes Street, Hanover Square.*)

6. *A Selection of* Melodies *from* Der Freischütz, *arranged for the* VIOLONCELLO *and* PIANO-FORTE, *by* H. J. BANISTER. (*The Editor*, 109, *Goswell Street.*)

7. *Twenty-four* Scotch *and* Irish AIRS, *set for the* VIOLONCELLO, *by* W. H. HAGART. (Cocks and Co.)

THE first in this list is certainly not a foreign composer, as the publisher announces, being a divertimento by Mr. Cipriani Potter. It is written in rather a grave style, and wants the animation which a more strongly-marked character and a freer melody would have given to it. The Violoncello part is very easy, and that for the Piano-Forte requires no great powers of execution.

No. 2 differs very little from the Violoncello Solos that we have heard all our lives. But comes out as new, and is well arranged for the instrument. The accompaniment is perfectly simple.

The two books of Exercises are extremely well worth the notice of students. In No. 3 are some good exercises in bowing; and No. 4, selected from such masters, cannot fail to give or to improve a taste.

Book 2 of No. 5, is from the *Freischütz*; and Book 3 is from Mayseder's divertimento. Both are well arranged, with an easy accompaniment.

No. 6 is also from the eternal opera by M. von Weber, and consists of five of the most favourite pieces. In this the piano-forte has quite as much, if not more, to do than the violoncello, which assumes rather the form of an accompaniment.

No. 7 is a pretty set of national airs, in a very cheap form, and calculated to amuse as well as to instruct beginners.

We rejoice to observe the vast progress which the violoncello, a rich, manly instrument, is making in England, as well as abroad. The intercourse with the continent by means of our army during the war, and encouraged since to so great an extent by all classes of our countrymen, has contributed much to the cultivation of this branch of music, as well as every other amongst amateurs, in a degree that cannot have escaped the notice of all who observe the present state of society.

FOREIGN MUSICAL REPORT.

VIENNA.—We mentioned in our last report from this place, that *Il Turco in Italia* had been produced with great effect, and with all the power of the Italian company here; it still continues a great favourite, as well as Paer's masterpiece, the *Agnese*, in which Madame Fodor continues to delight the public. The season is shortly to close, and we have the following announcements in colossal letters; for the last time *Figaro!* a few days afterwards, for the last time, *Il Turco in Italia!* again, for the last time, *Il Barbiere di Siviglia! La Gazza Ladra*, the same; *Il Matrimonio Secreto*, the same; after this we have a repetition of the self-same names with the announcement changed into rubric letters, " for the very last time." The managers find their account in all this, for it is the fashion here to be present at all these farewell representations, and therefore the thicker the farewells, and the oftener and more tenderly repeated, the better for the treasury of the house: so much for fashion, and the magic of a name!

The season has been rich in concerts, and among them there have been several remarkable for the good taste shown in the selection, and the laudable resolution manifested to rise above the trivial, and produce something worthy of the approbation of the public. Of this kind was the concert given by the Musical Society, for the benefit of the public charities, when the following was the admirable bill of fare :—1. Symphony in E flat, by Mozart; 2. Hymn from Cherubini, (Chorus of the Sacrifice in *Medea*) ; 3. *An die Nymphen der Bacchus-quelle*, (To the Nymphs of Bacchus's-fount) a Double Chorus by J. F. von Mosel; 4. Overture to *Anacreon*, by Cherubini; 5. Warlike Chorus from Haydn; 6. Overture, and 7. Finale of the first act of *Ahasuerus*, from Mozart, by J. G. R. von Seyfreid. Were the same taste displayed in all the numerous concerts given in this place, we feel persuaded that the true friends of music would blush to be backwards in bestowing their patronage. Let then such an example have its due weight with those to whom is intrusted the task of selection.

BERLIN.—Since our last report, there has been nothing new in the theatre of this place. Repetitions are the order of the day; Gluck's *Armida*, and *Iphigenia in Aulis*, Rossini's *Tancredi*, the *Ferdinand Cortez* of Spontini, and the *Œdipe de Colonne* of Sacchini.

The concert of the greatest attraction has been that of the celebrated Madame Milder, on which occasion she sung, with great effect, the *Troubadour*, a new song, composed expressly for her by Carl Blum, accompanied by him on the guitar. The remainder of the pieces were cast as follows, and may serve to give an idea of the reigning taste of the town: Scene from Haydn, *Berenice, che fai*; Schubart's favourite song, *Die Forelle*; a favourite duet from Meyerbeer the well-known duet from Zingarelli's *Romeo e Giulietta*; and, lastly, a terzetto from Beethoven.

An attempt has recently been made here to alarm the lovers of theatricals, by a Tract, of 46 pages, 8vo., from the pen of M. Tholuck, the professor *extraordinary* of theology. It is entitled " A Warning Voice to the Lovers of Theatricals; accompanied by the evidence of the two dear men of God, the late Philip Spener, and A. H. Franke. " Among other specimens of the sublime eloquence of this piece, we may select the following : " Theatricals is the only art with which the Christian has nothing to do; it is not in his line. It is the art of the loose and abandoned, whether we regard it on the side of the artists or of the spectators; for there is not a straw to choose between them," &c. &c. We have not as yet heard of any converts to the warning voice.

LEIPSIG.—The critics of this place are loud in their praises of a Grand Mass for four voices, with choruses, by the Chevalier von Seyfried, which has just appeared here. The *Agnus Dei* is particularly spoken of as a piece of very lovely and effective music. A Journal of this place has the following pertinent remarks: " We are very much delighted with this native production of our esteemed artist, for which we owe

him our gratitude, and hope, before long, to have occasion to hear other productions of the same kind. We acknowledge how infinitely more we are gratified with hearing the creations of his own fancy, than in seeing the artist employed in working up the instrumental music of Haydn and Mozart into song; works like these require no such process, neither do they want our eternal *Ahasuerus* to render them immortal * ."

DRESDEN.—On occasion of the birth-day of His Majesty the King of Saxony, was produced here for the first time, the opera of Morlacchi, *Teobaldo ed Isolina*. The other operas given at intervals have been Mehul's *Joseph et ses Freres*, which afforded real pleasure to all the friends of simple and effective music; and Schmidt's pleasing opera *Ein Abend in Madrid*, the charming Cavatina in the third act of which, delightfully sung by Mlle. Veltheim, is always sure of a hearty encore.

PRAGUE.—The only novelty of the theatre of this place has been one of those fairy operas which are so much in favour with the people of this part of the world. It is entitled *Rübezahl*, or the Benevolent Spirit, the music by Würfel, who is a popular composer here, and piano player. It was followed by Cherubini's masterly opera of *Faniska*, and Paer's *Sargine*, both of which are deservedly favourites here.

WEIMAR.—There are few places where the greater part of the masterpieces of the new, as well as the old, school are given in a more effective manner, than in the Grand Ducal Chapel of this city, under the direction of the indefatigable Kapellmeister Kranz. The fame of the music here gains daily on the public ; crowds are seen flocking from the neighbouring towns and villages to enjoy the treat, and gratify that inborn love for the art, that hunger and thirst for music, which distinguish the inhabitants of Germany. The Opera too continues with its wonted vigour ; the pieces given since our last notice are the following: Rossini's *Cenerentola*, *Il Flauto Magico*, *Nozze di Figaro*, *Sonntagskind*, *Camilla*, *Richard Cœur de Lion*, *Fanchon*, *La Folie*, *Jean de Paris*, *Graf von Gleichen*, *Euryanthe*, and *Ferdinand Cortez*.

CASSEL.—The lovers of music of this town have recently enjoyed a great treat in the production of Spohr's new and romantic opera, entitled *Berggeist*, (the *Mountain Spirit*). Even before its appearance, many favourable reports were spread by those who had been present at the rehearsals, or had caught a glance at parts of the score, and curiosity was raised to the highest pitch. This, when carried to excess, is frequently injurious, not to say unfair; but in the present instance, the curiosity thus excited was amply gratified. Suffice it for the present to say, that a copiousness of song and instrumental melodies, a rich and ever-clear harmony, an expressive, powerful, and yet by no means overcharged, orchestra, are excellencies of which this opera can justly boast †. The opera was given with particular splendour and effect, as it was produced on occasion of the marriage of the Princess Maria with the Duke of Meiningen. As these illustrious personages were present on the first representation, etiquette demanded that no applause should be given ; but on the second representation, the approbation, thus accidentally suspended, was bestowed with redoubled enthusiasm.

BREMEN.—The principal musical novelty of the theatre of this place, has been the reproduction of Catel's *Semiramis*, a grand Opera in three acts. The excellencies of this work are such, that it is to be regretted it should have been suffered to lie so long upon the shelf; and the zeal of those to whom we are indebted for its reproduction is deserving of all praise. It abounds with just declamation, a flowing song, an artful but praiseworthy texture of harmonies, and a well-sustained keeping throughout. One must be sadly blinded by party spirit,

* The allusion here is to the Oratorio of *Ahasuerus*, which Seyfried has composed from various portions of the instrumental works of Mozart, to which he adapted words.

† We have had occasion to give a more detailed account of this opera in another part of our present number.

not to acknowledge these excellencies; indeed, such is the merit and character of this composer, that we do not hesitate to compare him to our great Mayer, whom he resembles in many important points. The same flowing character in his melody, the same vigorous and judicious management of his bass; the only difference is, that our composer evinces greater powers of fancy, which will always triumph over learned harmonies. If there is any drawback to the merit of *Semiramis* it is that the recitative is sometimes monotonous; but this is more than compensated for by the beauty and expression of the airs. Among others, that of Assur in the second act, with a violoncello accompaniment, is a masterpiece of its kind; the duet between Semiramis and Assur, and the concluding chorus of the second act, are also compositions which it is vain to praise, as they rank among the first compositions extant in the province of declamatory music. We may add, that every praise is due to the management for the splendid and effective manner in which the piece was brought out, and which was worthy of the subject which it had to decorate. Its success was decided; indeed, where such liberality is shewn in the productions of the masterpieces of art, the public will always be found ready to give their zealous and effective support.

HAMBURG.—Hamburg has to boast of its progress in instrumental music, and the musical association called *Der Apollo Verein*, cultivate this branch of art with zeal and assiduity. The academy for song, conducted by Messrs. Steinfield and Berens, also continues to answer the expectations of the lovers of the art; some judgment may be formed of the progress made, when we inform you that Handel's Oratorio of *Joshua* was given entire and with great spirit and correctness. B. Romberg, the brother of the late celebrated Andreas Romberg, and who himself treads close in the footsteps of his fame, is living among us.

MAINTZ.—The only novelty, in a musical point of view, in this place, is the appearance of a publication entitled, *Vollständige Singschule, &c.* (The Complete School for Song), with preliminary observations in Italian, German, and French, by Kapellmeister Peter von Winter.

HARRLEM.—A keyed trumpet of wood, intended as a substitute for copper trumpets, is about to be sent to the approaching exhibition at this town. It has been examined and approved of by a society of musicians, who have named it the Tuba-Dupré, in honour of its inventor. A similar attempt was made some years ago at Paris, by M. Boileau, a musical instrument maker, who constructed horns and trumpets entirely of wood, excepting the mouth-piece and rim, which were of copper. These instruments were also tried and approved of by several musicians, but were never adopted, as their only advantage over the old trumpets was cheapness, and they were inferior to them in tone.

COPENHAGEN.—There has recently appeared here a work entitled, " Music to the Tragedy of Macbeth, by C. E. Weyse." The critics speak of this composition, and particularly the scene with the witches, as of a very superior and characteristic kind.

PARIS.—The opera of *Il Viaggio à Reims* (the Journey to Rheims,) was performed, for the first time in public, at the Théâtre Italien, on Thursday, the 23d of June. This representation drew together a great number of spectators. The heat was excessive, but the amateurs of good music were recompensed by the pleasure they received, for the punishment they endured: like the inhabitants of the infernal regions, their pains were relieved by the song of Orpheus.

It is difficult to pronounce a decided opinion on a great musical composition the first time of hearing it. We will therefore defer our observations on this opera till, having had time to study it, we shall be able to speak with some degree of certainty. In the mean time we do not hesitate to point out the duet, *Nel suo divin sembiante*, as a piece full of spirit and grace; and the banquet-scene, which is the finale, as one of the most original compositions that ever was conceived and executed by any composer whatever.

In this banquet, where, as in a congress, each nation in Europe has its representative, every person sings, to one of his own national airs, the praises of the grandson of Henry the Fourth, and a sketch of each of these airs is in the overture, which serves as an accompaniment to all of them. There is equal beauty in the *gran pezzo concertato*, for four voices, in the same opera; an ordinary head would have been lost in combinations so multiplied: but a great general can manœuvre an army as easily as a battalion. Such power is peculiar to genius.

We must allow that the poetry of *Il Viaggio à Reims* is as good as circumstances would permit. The idea is ingenious, the style easy, and the plan is combined in such a way as to give room to the musician to display his powers in the happy manner he has. These things constitute the merit of such a piece. Let us then bestow on M. Balocchi the praise which he deserves.

The principal characters in this piece were, as they always appear to be at the *Théâtre Italien*, distributed with great discernment. *Zuchelli*, born in London, played the Englishman; *Graziani*, the German; grave *Levasseur*, the Spaniard; the ardent *Donzelli*, the Frenchman; and *Bordogni*, in a Russian uniform, represented this people of the hyperborean region. Mesdemoiselles *Cinti* and *Schiassetti* were charming; the former as a Parisian, the other as a Polonaise. Madame *Pasta*, as an *improvvisatrice Romaine*, recalled at once, by her accent in declaiming, and the expression of her countenance, the *Corinna* of Madame de Staël, and the not less beautiful *Corinna* of Gérard.

—— A new piece is about to be brought out at the *Opéra Italien*, in which Galli will appear. While this is preparing, Galli will perform some of the parts of *Pellegrini*. The former will appear in August, as *Figaro* in *Il Barbiere di Siviglia*, and will afterwards perform the part of *Dandini* in *La Cenerentola*.

The *Otello* of M. Castil-Blaze has only been performed twice. At the second representation there was much less discordance between the singers, and much more among the public.

The Frankfort Journal announces that Rossini's opera, called *Bianco e Faliero*, has turned out quite disastrously for the theatre of St. Carlos, at Naples.

—— The *Opera jury* have approved of the musical part of young Liszt's opera, but have required some alterations in the poetry; alterations which are vulgarly called corrections.

The health of Signor Rossini is continually giving some inquietude to his friends: it is hoped that the repose and air of the country will hasten his recovery. He now inhabits one of prettiest houses at Sabonville, near Paris.

M. Spontini, director of the grand Theatre at Berlin, has obtained a *congé* for eight months from the King of Prussia, which time he will pass in Paris. M. Spontini is expected to arrive here in a few days, and will himself bring forward, at the *Académie Royale de Musique*, the opera of *Alcidor*, which has succeeded at Berlin.

THE CONCERTS OF THE SEASON, 1825.

THE only regular Subscription Concerts now supported in London, are the Ancient and the Philharmonic. Of these we have periodically endeavoured to make a full and clear report. It remains now to give a brief sketch of the single concerts, chiefly benefits, that took place during the season just terminated: but amongst them we shall include four private ones of the most fashionable description, in order that such of our readers as were not enabled to partake of the amusement afforded by them, may judge of the taste of the highest classes in music; and also as a record that hereafter will prove useful in tracing the progress of the art. With these we commence our list, and at the head of them we place a concert given by His Majesty, at Carlton Palace, on

WEDNESDAY, JUNE 15.

FIRST PART.

Quintetto, " *Sento oh Dio !*" Madame Casadori, Mlle. Garcia, Signors Garcia, Remorini and De Begnis, (*Cosi fan tutte*) . . . . . *Mozart.*

2 C 2

Terzetto, " *Giovinetto Cavalier*," Madame Caradori, Mlle.
  Garcia, and Signor Velluti, *(Il Crociato in Egitto)* *Meyerbeer.*
Duetto, " *Per piacere*," Madame Caradori, and Signor De
  Begnis, *(Il Turco in Italia)* . . . *Rossini.*
Romanza, " *Notte tremenda*," Signor Velluti ; Harp, Mons.
  Labarre, and Flute, Mr. Nicholson, *(Teobaldo e
  Isolina)* . . . . *Morlacchi.*
Terzetto, " *Qual Silenzio*," Signors Begrez, Garcia, and
  De Begnis . . . . *Attwood.*
Romance " *Ca m'est egal*," Madame Caradori . . *Jardin.*
Finale, Madame Caradori, Mlle. Garcia, Signors Velluti,
  Curioni, Remorini, and Crivelli, with chorus, *(First
  Act of Il Tancredi)* . . . *Rossini.*

SECOND PART.

Quintetto, " *Oh guardate*," Mad. Caradori, Mlle. Garcia,
  Signors Begrez, Remorini, and De Begnis, *(Il Turco
  in Italia)* . . . . *Rossini.*
Duetto, " *La dolce immagine*," Signors Velluti and Cu-
  rioni, *(Teobaldo e Isolina)* . . . *Morlacchi.*
Duetto, " *Ah se puoi*," Madame Caradori, and Signor
  Curioni, *(Mosè in Egitto)* . . . *Rossini.*
Barcarolle, " *La notte si bella*," Signor Velluti . *Perruchini.*
Spanish Air, " *St. Anton.*" Mlle. Garcia . . *Garcia.*
Duetto, " *Questo acciara*," Signors Velluti and Curioni,
  (Teobaldo e Isolina) . . . *Morlacchi.*
Preghiera, Madame Caradori, Signors Begrez, and De Be-
  gnis. *(Mosè in Egitto)* . . . *Rossini.*
Finale, " *Buona sera*," with a chorus, *(Barbiere di Sivi-
  glia)* . . . . . *Rossini.*

This concert was conducted by Mr. Attwood, Sir G. Smart,
and Signor Scappa. The instrumental accompaniments were
harp (Labarre), flute (Nicholson), violoncello (Lindley), and
contra-basso (Dragonetti). The King's taste in music is, as is
well known, excellent, and decidedly in favour of the classical
masters. Handel, Haydn, Mozart, Cherubini, and Beethoven,
are his favourite composers : the fine English church-music he
greatly admires, and in his domestic parties takes great delight
in listening to our best glees : but he does not suffer himself
to be influenced by prejudices ; and, though not an absolute
pazzo for the newest productions of the day, enjoys many things
of Rossini, and tolerates at his large assemblies works recommended by his friends, though not much calculated to please
himself. Of the latter description some few will be found in
the above programme. It ought to be known that the performers at this concert were liberally paid half as much again
as they usually receive. His Majesty's rule was, till lately, to
pay them double, but the demands of the *singers* are now
become so extravagant, that it is impossible for even royalty
itself to indulge its generous wishes in the same proportion as
formerly.

The next, not in the order of dates, but according to the rank
of the giver, was performed at Prince Leopold's. Of the card
distributed on this occasion, the following is a *literal* copy.

MARLBOROUGH HOUSE,

JUNE, 2d.

1. Trio—" *Proteggi*" S^a. Caradori, Mlle. Garcia, S^r.
   Garcia . . . . . *Mozart.*
2. Duetto—" *Ricciardo que veggo*" S^a. Caradori, S^r.
   Curioni . . . . . *Rossini.*
3. Aria . . . . . . *Rossini.*
4. Quartetto—" *Del crociato*" Mad^m. Pasta, S^a. Caradori, Mlle. Garcia, e S^r. Curioni . *Mayerbeer.*
5. Duetto—" *Parlar Spiegar*" S^{rs}. Curioni, e Remorini . . . . . *Rossini.*
6. Finale—" *Il Barbiere de Siviglia*" . . *Rossini.*

1. Trio—" *Con rispetto*" S^{rs}. Curioni, Garcia, e Remorini . . . . . *Mosca.*
2. Aria . . . . . . *Zingarelli.*
3. Duetto—" *Ah Vieni*" S^{rs}. Curioni, e Garcia . *Rossini.*
4. Duetto—" *Eben a te fevisci*" Mad^m. Pasta, e Mlle.
   Garcia . . . . . *Rossini.*
5. Quartetto—" *De Nina*" Mad^m. Pasta, S^r. Caradori,
   S^r. Garcia e S^r. Remorini . . *Paesiello.*
6. Terzetto—" *Incerta l' anima*" Mad^m. Pasta, S^{rs}.
   Garcia e Remorini . . . *Rossini.*
7. Coro—" *L' Asia in Faville*" Tutti . . *Rossini.*

On Friday, May 6th, the Duke of Devonshire made a most
laudable attempt, at his magnificent mansion, to please the
fashionable world by a concert in which some of the best
music by the ancient masters, and by English composers, was
introduced ; but the majority of the visitors declared it to be
very dull ; his Grace therefore, in the following week, endeavoured to adapt his entertainment more to the taste of his
company ; and the annexed is a list of the selections made for
the purpose.

FRIDAY, MAY 13.

PART I.

Sonata, Corno, Signor Puzzi . . .
Terzetto, " *O Nume benefico*," *(La Gazza Ladra)* . *Rossini.*
Duetto, " *Mille sospiri*," *(L' Aureliano in Palmira)* . *Rossini.*
Terzettino, " *L' usato ardir*," *(Semiramide)* . *Rossini*
Romanza, " *Notte tremenda*," *(Teobaldo e Isolina)* *Morlacchi.*
Finale, *(Semiramide)* . . . *Rossini]*

PART II.

Sonata, Piano-forte, Madame Szymanowska . .
Duetto, " *Bella Imago*," *(Semiramide)* . . *Rossini*
Aria, " *Che farò senza Euridice*," *(Orfeo)* . . *Gluck.*
Duetto, " *Ricciardo, che veggo*," *(Ricciardo e Zoraide)* *Rossini.*.
Quintetto, " *Sento, O Dio!*" *(Cosi fan tutte)* . *Mozart.*
Duetto, " *Per pietà*," *(Ginevra di Scozia)* . *Mayer.*
Finale, *(Tancredi)* . . . . *Rossini.*

Among the singers were Madame Pasta and Signor Velluti.
The noble Duke, with great spirit, and purely out of consideration to those that give parties, but who are not so
wealthy as himself, declined, during the whole of the late season, to comply with the unreasonable demands of many of the
foreign vocal corps, and therefore dispensed with their services
at his concerts. We trust that this example will be followed,
and then we may hope that two or three of these people, whose
pride and insolence are becoming intolerable, will be brought
to their senses.

The Marquess of Hertford, whose entertainments of all
kinds are splendid, and *recherchés*, gave a concert in his grand
saloon on the 29th of March. The music was chiefly selected
from Mozart's *Serraglio*, an opera little known,—or, at least, not
hacknied,—in this country, and from Weber's *Freischütz*.
The ultra-fashionables thought the selection very tiresome, and
we have heard it hinted that one, at least, of the performers
strove hard to ridicule it, in order to discourage the introduction of compositions that, not being sung almost every night in
parties, cost some little trouble in getting up. The Marquess,
on the 1st of June, gave another grand musical entertainment,
consisting of the pieces in the subjoined programme, which
were sung on a stage erected in the fine saloon of his new
mansion in Piccadilly. These connected together in a dramatic
form by means of a dialogue in French, written by M. Steffano
Vestris, and carried on by Messrs. Pelissié and Sarthé, of the
Theatre in Tottenham-street, in the characters of an *Impresario* and his assistant. The opera of *Il Crociato in Egitto* had
not then been performed in London, and the noble Lord
wished to afford his friends an opportunity of hearing parts of
it before it was publicly produced. The chief performers of the
Italian Opera-house, both vocal and instrumental, were engaged upon most liberal terms ; but the indisposition of Mad.
De Begnis and Signor Velluti, and the tuning of the accompanying instruments considerably below the usual pitch, at the
request of the latter, threw a damp on the performance. This
entertainment was entitled a

DRAMATIC CONCERT.

PART I.

Sinfonia, *(Calypso)* . . . . *Winter.*
Terzetto, " *Il pietra di paragone*," Signori Curioni, De
  Begnis, and Remorini . . . *Rossini.*
Duetto, Madame Pasta, and Signor Velluti, *(Aureliano in
  Palmira)* . . . . *Rossini.*
Duetto, Signor and Madame De Begnis . . *Mercadante.*
Romanza, Signor Velluti, *(Teobaldo e Isolina)* . *Morlacchi.*
Coro, *(Il franco Arciero*,) . . . *Weber.*

PART II.

Quartetto, Madame Pasta, Signora Marinoni, Signori Velluti, and Curioni, (*Il Crociato in Egitto*) . *Meyerbeer.*
Scena ed Aria, Madame Pasta, (*Romeo e Giulietta*) . *Zingarelli.*
Terzetto, Madame De Begnis, Signora Marinoni, and Signor Velluti, (*Il Crociato*) . . . *Meyerbeer.*
Duetto, Mesdames De Begnis and Pasta, (*Romeo e Giulietta*) . . . . *Zingarelli.*
Canone, Madame De Begnis, Signora Marinoni, Signori Velluti, Curioni, and Remorini, (*Il Crociato*) . *Meyerbeer.*
Coro, *Tutti* . . . . . *Rossini.*

Mr. GREATOREX had his annual concert on Monday, April 18th, at the Hanover-square Rooms, at which all the performers of the Ancient Concert assisted; and many of the subscribers, together with other lovers of classical music, attended.

Mr. VAUGHAN's was given in the above rooms, on Friday, May 6th, by nearly the same performers, with the addition of Signor and Madame De Begnis. The selection rather wanted novelty,—we do not mean music newly composed, but the revival of good compositions now forgotten, therefore virtually new.

Mr W. KNYVETT's farewell concert took place in the same rooms, on Friday, the 13th of May. It was not so fully attended as we expected, but the company was highly respectable. This gentleman retires from his profession immediately after the York Festival; he will carry with him into private life the well-earned esteem of the public, and the unfeigned friendship of his brethren.

Mr T. ROVEDINO collected his friends together on the 16th of May, in private, at Mr. Maude's, in Great George-street, Westminster. Tickets one guinea each; but as Madame Pasta, who was newly arrived, sung for Mr. R., the house was crowded to excess.

On Tuesday, May 24th, the Messrs. CRAMER had their annual Morning Concert at Willis's Rooms. We conjecture that not less than a thousand persons were assembled on this occasion, many of whom could gain no admittance into the great room, which was filled at an early hour. As we were amongst this number, we can only say, from report, that Mr. Cramer never played in a more finished manner than on this occasion; and as it was announced as his last public performance, an extraordinary interest was excited to hear the final notes of an artist who does not leave an equal to supply his place. The subjoined will show that the Messrs. CRAMER are not forgetful of music which, though not new, being founded on an immutable basis, will never cease to gratify real lovers of the art.

ACT I.

Grand Symphony . . . . *Haydn.*
Recit. and Air, Mr. Vaughan, "*Gentle Lyre,*" . *Horsley.*
Eighth Concerto, Piano-forte, Mr. Cramer, (*By desire*) . *Cramer.*
Scena, "*Gran Dio! che del mio core,*" Madame Caradori *Guglielmi.*
Duet, Piano-forte and Harp, Mr. Cramer, and Mr. T. Wright . . . *Dussek and Cramer.*
Recit. and Air, "*Softly sighs the voice of evening,*" Miss Stephens . . . . *Weber.*

ACT II.

Grand Overture, (*Idomeneo*) . . . *Mozart.*
Trio, for Violin, Violoncello, and Contra Basso, Messrs. F. Cramer, Lindley, and Dragonetti . *Handel and Martini.*
Ballad, Miss Stephens, (accompanied on the Harp by Mr. T. H. Wright) . . . . *Chipp.*
Concerto, Piano-forte, Mr. Cramer, (*never performed in this Country*) . . . *Mozart.*
Duet, "*Together let us range the fields,*" Miss Stephens and Mr. Sapio . . . *Dr. Boyce.*

Mr. SPAGNOLETTI's annual Benefit Concert took place at the Argyll Rooms, on Friday, May 27. All the performers attached to the King's Theatre, both vocal and instrumental, attended, together with others from the band of the Philharmonic Society, and gave an excellent selection of sterling music.

Signor PUZZI had his private concert at Mrs. Cox's house in Grosvenor Place on the 3d of June. Tickets one guinea each! Mr. Pio CIANCHETTINI's was given in Willis's small room on the 4th; and on the 7th the Young LISZT had a morning performance at the Argyll Rooms, in which he displayed his wonderful powers of execution. We hope that he will now begin to turn his attention to expression, without which he may for a while astonish, but will rarely please.

Madame SZYMANOWSKA gave a morning concert at the Hanover Square Rooms, on Saturday the 11th of June, and delighted a remarkably select audience, by her elegant and expressive style of performing on the piano-forte. Signor Velluti sung for the first time in public. Many of the Royal Family were present, but the company was not very numerous, though of a high class, for guinea admissions rather deter visitors.

Mr. KIESEWETTER's private concert was performed at the house of William Curtis, Esq., in Portland Place, on Monday, June 13th.; and Mr. BEGREZ's was on the 15th, at the Argyll Rooms. Both of these were guinea concerts, and a good deal of talent was exhibited at each.

The LONDON ORPHAN ASYLUM at Clapton, was opened on the 16th of June, with a public breakfast and concert. The efficient patrons of the institution are wealthy merchants, &c., and we always observe, that where such gentlemen direct a musical performance, the selection shews good sense and a refined taste.

The Young MINASI, a prodigy on the flute, had a concert at the Argyll Rooms on June 17th. The Master SCHULTZ's gave a morning concert at the same place on the 22d, and on the same day, Madame CASTELLI had her private concert at Mrs. Otway Cave's, South-street. On the 25th, at the Argyll Rooms, Messrs. VOGT and LABARRE jointly took a benefit. The former is the principal oboe at the *Académie Royale de Musique*, or Grand Opera, at Paris; and the latter is a performer on the harp, who has not long been known. M. Vogt has astonishing execution, with an indifferent tone. As steady in the orchestra as knowledge and great experience can make him, but forces his instrument, and makes it resemble too much the "scrannel pipe." M. Labarre is admirable on the harp; he is beyond compare, the best player now in England.

M. MOSCHELES, who returned to us with the spring, gave the public an opportunity of hearing him again, after his long absence, at the Argyll Rooms, on the 27th of June. He played his fine concerto in G minor, and a new concertante, accompanied by Kiesewetter. His performance was masterly and delightful; full of energy and meaning; and, though abounding in extraordinary instances of rapidity and strength, was not less remarkable for taste and feeling. The great room was crowded to hear him. Madame Cornega, the contr'alto, made her first appearance at this concert.

The pupils of the ROYAL ACADEMY of MUSIC, performed a concert at the Hanover Square Rooms, on the morning of June the 30th. After which the prizes were distributed by the Princess Augusta. Much talent was exhibited, and the dawn of future excellence was seen in many of the youthful candidates for fame. The scene was an interesting one; but why was it clouded by the presence of a man who should never be allowed to appear before the public, and whose only proper place now is, the gallies at Marseilles, to which he was a few years ago condemned.

On the 11th of July, a concert was performed at the Argyll Rooms, for the benefit of Signor PLACCI, well known as the Italian Opera as a very useful artist, who had been, for many months, suffering under one of the heaviest afflictions of Providence. The list of vocal and instrumental talent was exceedingly strong, and a tolerably good bill of fare was made out; but the undertaking was ill managed, and we fear that the result was not by any means so beneficial as it might have proved.

The last concert of the season was given by Madame Cornega, on Wednesday morning, July 13th, at the Argyll Rooms. Madame Cornega is certainly the finest singer with a contralto voice that we at present have in England, and we venture to predict, will become very popular next season. She arrived too late this year to be much known, except in that circle to which the Duke and Duchess of Cambridge introduced her.

THE DRAMA.

KING'S THEATRE.

THE Italian Opera did not close till the 13th of August, having been opened only on Saturdays for the last three weeks. _Il Crociato in Egitto_ kept exclusive possession of the stage to the end, and proved more and more attractive; every piece in it told,—for the trumpetty Air foisted into it, and condemned by all save the _claqueurs_, forms no part of the work,—and the admiration of Meyerbeer's talents increased at every fresh hearing of his new production. The management is infinitely indebted to his opera, for it restored the finances of the theatre, and saved it just at the moment when the termination of Madame Pasta's engagement, and the absence of Madame De Begnis, had plunged it into most alarming difficulties. It is true that Signor Velluti brought many to the house, particularly at first, when several were drawn out of mere curiosity; but his personal attraction soon abated, the opposition to him ceased, and the interest excited in his favour died away. With all the merit that he possesses, he is not a singer that now can long keep hold of the public. Independently of moral considerations, his voice is not in its prime, and his intonation is defective. When we first heard him, many years ago, his middle tones were good; they are now imperfect, if not actually disagreeable, and he is no longer young. His taste however remains, and though in the repetition of the final duet, _Il tenero affetto_, we witnessed some symptoms, the last few nights, of an erroneous judgment and a neglect of the harmony in the variations he introduced, yet we must hope that such aberrations from his usual habits were accidental.

ENGLISH OPERA HOUSE.

ON Monday, the 15th of last month, an opéra, under the name of _Tarrare, the Tartar Chief_, was produced at this theatre; the characters as follows:—

Atar, (_Sultan of Persia_)	Mr. H. PHILLIPS.
Artenio, (_High Priest of Brahma_)	Mr. J. O. ATKINS.
Altamore, (_Son of the High Priest_)	Mr. PERKINS.
Tarrare, (_A Tartar Chief in the service of the Sultan_)	Mr. BRAHAM.
Calpigi, (_An Italian Slave, Chief of the Sultan's Household_)	Mr. THORNE.
Astasia, (_Wife of Tarrare_)	Miss HAMILTON.
Ninetta, (_An Italian Slave, Wife of Calpigi_)	Miss PATON.

This drama is abridged from the _Tarare_ of Beaumarchais, an opera in five acts, written with the political design that most of this author's works manifest. _Tarare_, a whimsical title, is a French interjection, signifying _fiddlestick!_ a term of contempt, and M. Beaumarchais thus explains the object of his work :— " _Tarare_ is the name, but not the aim, of my opera. The following maxim, at once consoling and severe, is the subject of my drama :—

"Homme! ta grandeur sur la terre
N'appartient point à ton état;
Elle est toute à ton caractère.

"The dignity of man, therefore, is the moral point that I would exemplify, the theme that I have taken. To put into action this precept of the poet, I have supposed, in Ormus, two men in the most opposite conditions; one all-powerful, but an absolute Asiatic despot, but a most vicious character. 'He was born wicked,' I have said, 'let us see if he will be unhappy?' The other drawn from the lowest ranks, deprived of all, a poor soldier, has received from heaven but one blessing, a virtuous soul. 'Can he be happy here below ?'—"

The following is the plot, as it appears in the English version Atar, hating _Tarrare_ for his virtues, and enamoured of his wife, has her seized and conveyed to his seraglio. _Tarrare_ repairs to the Palace of the Sultan, where he learns, to his surprise, that his wife is a captive. But though he had once the good fortune to save his monarch's life, who has now robbed him of his wife in return, poor _Tarrare_ is so unlike a Tartar in ferocity, that he lingers about the seraglio in the most deplorable state, hoping to obtain that relief from chance which others of his tribe would have sought from the sword. The Sultan, however, is not much more fortunate. _Astasia_ resists all his solicitations, and at length he resolves, in a fit of rage, to punish her perverseness, by compelling her to marry an African slave belonging to the seraglio in which she is confined. It so turns out, accidentally, that _Tarrare_ himself, in the disguise of a slave, is the person fixed upon, but _Astasia_ being ignorant of the person on whom the Sultan intended to bestow her, permits _Ninetta_ to appear as her substitute, and thus the happy meeting is prevented. This _Ninetta_ is a cunning chambermaid, whose disposition it is not easy to unravel, for her conduct does not appear quite intelligible, as relates either to the hero or the heroine of the piece. After matters have proceeded thus far, _Tarrare_ is by some sort of legerdemain created General of the army, and just as the Sultan is about to despatch him and his wife together, the soldiers rush in to despatch the Sultan. This rouses the loyal spirit of the Tartar, who turns round upon the troops, abuses them for having dared to meditate the death of the Sultan, and reads them such a lecture on the doctrine of "divine right," that the tragedy is turned into a comedy all at once, and the Sultan, embracing his deliverer, becomes one of the best of Kings.

This must be considered solely as a vehicle for music; as a drama it will not bear the test of a rigorous examination.

Tarare was composed by Salieri for the _Académie Royale de Musique_, where it was first performed in 1787[*]. It was soon afterwards translated into Italian, and produced at Vienna under the title of _Axur_, (or _Assur?_) _Re d'Ormus_, and such was then the effeminate taste of the Viennese, that they preferred it to the fine works of Mozart, at that time performing at the secondary theatres of the German capital. The characteristics of this opera, are smoothness and prettiness : at the time it was first brought out, its accompaniments, compared to those of Piccini and Paisiello, were new and vigorous; but heard after Mozart's and Rossini's, they are meagre and _passé_. Salieri had neither the beautiful melody of the earlier Italian composers, nor the rich orchestral effects of the German masters; his reputation was chiefly made by the patronage of Gluck, and he has been much over-rated, both in the capitals of France and Austria. Our own journals have made mention of this opera in terms that shew how very backward the state of musical criticism is even yet in England: by their epithets it would seem that they place it on a level with the greatest works the age has produced. Some parts of it certainly are very pleasing, but we cannot point out a single passage that shews a first-rate genius. The popular pieces in it abroad are, the _Canone_ and _Romance_, published in our present number : the first is always encored here, but the last is sung so much too quick, that it produces no effect on our stage. The song, "Revenge!" made out of a march, and given with great spirit by Braham, is original and animated; and there are two chorusses—which Mr. Kelly introduced in, we think, Blue-Beard—of considerable merit, that are much applauded. The opera is altogether very successful; Mr. Braham sings gently in it, and pleases everybody thereby. Miss Paton sustains her part exceedingly well, though it were to be wished that she would reform her shake, and abolish the eternal sameness of its terminating _appoggiatura_. Mr. Phillips, both as actor and singer, is a very superior person. Miss Hamilton, a debutante on the present occasion, does not yet produce much effect; but she has time in plenty before her, and seems to have some of the requisites of a singer. Mr. Arnold has brought out the piece in a very liberal manner, to which much of its success may be ascribed.

---

[*] See Harmonicon, Vol. I, page 158, for some account of Salieri, and his works.

THE

HARMONICON.

No. XXXIV., OCTOBER, 1825.

MEMOIR OF CHERUBINI.

MARIA-LUIGI-CARLO-ZENOBI-SALVADOR CHE-RUBINI was born in Florence, the 8th of September, 1760. At nine years of age he commenced the study of composition under Bartolomeo Felici, and his son, Alessandro Felici. They were able masters, and under their care he made considerable advancement in an art in which he was already an enthusiast. But he had the misfortune to lose both his instructors, who died one shortly after the other, when he passed under the care of Pietro Bizzari, and Giuseppe Castrucci. In 1773, that is before he had completed his thirteenth year, he produced a mass and an anthem, which were executed at Florence, and excited a great sensation. In the space of four or five years from this period, he laid before the public a great number of works, as well for the church as for the theatre, which were received with applause. These successes attracted the notice of the Grand Duke, Leopold II., of Tuscany, a zealous friend and patron of the arts, who, in 1778, granted him a pension, in order to enable him to continue his studies, and perfect his talents under the celebrated Sarti, who was at that time residing at Bologna.

Cherubini passed nearly four years under this admirable master, and doubtless it is to his talents and instructions, that the former stands indebted for the profound knowledge which he acquired in counterpoint, and in the ideal style, as well as for that perfection of talent, which has raised him to such eminence in the art, and entitled him to rank among the most learned and able composers. So devoted was Sarti to the improvement of his favourite pupil, that though overwhelmed with occupations, he always contrived to find time for the exercise of his talents; and so rapid was his progress, and so well did he correspond to his master's care, that he was intrusted with the composition of the secondary parts of his operas. Hence the scores of Sarti contain a great number of pieces which were thus composed for him by Cherubini.

In 1784, he quitted Italy and paid a visit to London, where he resided nearly two years, and produced his two operas La Finta Principessa, and Giulio Sabino, in the latter of which the celebrated Marchesi made his debût in the British capital, and formed a new era in the musical annals of our country. This singer was not only inexhaustible in fancy and embellishments, but possessed the more rare and, perhaps, important talent of giving to the recitative all its power, expression, and varied energy. Independently, too, of his vocal powers, his performance was highly set off by the beauty of his person, and the grace and propriety of his gestures.

In 1786, Cherubini quitted this city, and repaired to Paris, where he came to a determination of taking up his residence, and where he has since reaped so abundant a harvest of fame. He, however, occasionally visited Italy, and in 1788, produced, at Turin, his opera of Ifigenia in Aulide, which tended very considerably to raise his reputation in his native country. On his return to Paris, he produced on the third of December of the same year, at the Academie Imperiale de Musique, his opera of Demophoon, the first work with which he enriched the French lyric theatre. He afterwards composed a great number of detached pieces, which were introduced in the Italian opera executed in 1790, and the following years, by the admirable Italian company which Paris at that time possessed. Among many other masterpieces of this kind, still continues to be sung with increasing delight, the magnificent quartett, Cara da voi dipende, which was introduced in the opera Dei Viaggiatori felici, and was received at the time of its production with an enthusiasm which is not yet forgotten. Cherubini always presided at the execution of his works, and immense were the advantages which both the singers and instrumental performers derived from his zeal and talents. Added to this, he had the happy art of gaining over the singers to his views, by a suavity of manners, and a conciliatory mode of address, not always possessed by persons of his talent and profession. Suffice it to say, that he raised the lyric stage to a degree of eminence to which it had never before attained, and of which later periods convey but a very imperfect idea.

The opera of Lodoiska was produced in 1791, at the Theatre Feydeau. This production forms an epoch in the annals of the comic opera. It was the first time that a composition had been heard at this theatre, in which the song was sustained by all the power and all the richness of the symphony. It was now that Cherubini was seen to tread, and to tread not unworthily, in the footsteps of Haydn and Mozart.

To Lodoiska succeeded Elisa, Medée, Les deux Journées, and L'Hotellerie Portugaise. These compositions were not unworthy of the great masterpiece to which they succeeded, and gave Cherubini a just title to rank among the first of living composers. It was at this period, that the

French lyric drama attained to its greatest eminence, for while the subject of this memoir was operating these wonders at the *Theatre Feydeau*, Mehul was effecting a similar revolution at the *Theatre Favart*, by his admirable productions *Euphrosine et Coradin, Stratonice, Phrosine et Malidor*, &c. Nothing can be more delightful than to see the mutual esteem of two great artists, increasing with their success, and interweaving the garland of friendship with the laurels of glory. Some ill disposed persons having spread a report, that Mehul was jealous of Cherubini, the former wrote a letter, which appeared in the public journals, stating that he considered Cherubini as the greatest composer in Europe. This was in 1810, a year after the death of Haydn.

In 1805, Cherubini visited Vienna, where his reputation had preceded him. It was in this city that he brought out his *Faniska* on the imperial theatre. Previous to his return to Paris, in March, 1806, he went to bid adieu to the illustrious Haydn, and entreated as a parting favour, that he would give him the original MS. of one of his scores. Haydn presented him with an unpublished symphony, and said to him, while he affectionately pressed his hands; " Allow me to call myself your musical father, and to greet you by the title of my son." —Nor must we omit to mention in this place, that in 1801, Cherubini was commissioned by the *Academie de Musique* to repair to Vienna, in order to present to the immortal symphonist the medal which they had caused to be struck in his honour, after the execution of his sublime oratorio of *The Creation*, the 12th of December, 1800. This was in all respects a remarkable day, for it was on his way to the *Academie de Musique*, to hear this very oratorio, that Napoleon had so nearly fallen a victim to what was called the infernal machine. It is no mean proof of this extraordinary man's presence of mind, and intrepidity of character, that even after the danger that had threatened his life, he was determined to attend at the performance of the music, into the whole spirit of which he seemed to enter.

In 1815 Sig. Cherubini was invited to London by the Philharmonic Society, for which he composed an Overture, a Symphony, and a grand concerted vocal piece, all of which were performed at the concerts of this distinguished body of professors, under his own immediate direction. He remained in England during a great part of the spring season, and received a liberal remuneration for his labours. When he returned to the metropolis of the French nation, he found his interests considerably involved in the changes making by the restored dynasty in the musical as well as other establishments of that country. He even retired from some of his situations for a time in disgust, but was soon recalled to them by the government, and now fills some of the most respectable offices that the members of his profession can occupy: he is one of the composers of the *Chapelle du Roi*, professor of composition at the *Ecole Royale*, a Member of the *Academie Royale des Beaux-Arts*, and also of the Legion of Honour.

In his *Dissertation on the State of Music in Italy*, Perotti makes the following reflection on certain living composers, such as Asioli, Paer, Mayer, and Cherubini. " The desire," says he, " of improving and refining the art, has frequently led them to seek for éclat in the pomp of instrumentation ; even without being able to plead the plausible excuse of incapacity in the singers ; though even this apology could not avail them, upon the principle of the received axiom, that one fault cannot justify another."

But if in his vocal compositions Cherubini has laid himself open to some reproach, his instrumental music is beyond the reach of criticism, as is his sacred music beyond all praise.

We may remark, that when a musical education has been perfect, when the fundamental principles of the art have been thoroughly imbibed, the powers of the man of genius acquire strength with age ; as in the instances of Handel, Haydn, Gluck, Beethoven, and Cherubini. On the contrary, when precocious composers, who have neglected early to draw from the profound sources of counterpoint, arrive at maturity, they feel the need of making good the deficiencies of their early education : but it is too late ; the happy moment is past ; science is now a fetter to them, and they fall oppressed beneath its galling load. We will not be invidious in particularizing individuals ; there are few of our readers who will not be able to fill up the list which we leave vacant. It is with reason, that the able theorist Koch has laid such stress upon the study of counterpoint, and so strongly recommended it to every young artist, who aspires to a renown beyond the empty honours of the moment, and feels nobly ambitious of solid glory. As the question is so immediately connected with the subject of our Memoir, we shall be excused for citing a short passage from an author whose authority is allowed to possess so much weight. "Through the study of counterpoint, the composer reaps the advantage of learning to combine a variety of parts with facility, and of being able to view at a glance their whole harmonic connexion ; he is thus enabled fully to develope the melodies best adapted to the expression of his ideas, and among all the variations, all the harmonic combinations of which they are capable, of selecting those which best answer his purpose. In a word, by the study of counterpoint, he acquires a tact or dexterity in the employment of harmony, without which he is unable fully to embody the ideas of sound conceived in his fancy, and, without which, he cannot arrange and complete them to advantage in their harmonic extent."

In instrumental music, Cherubini enjoys a reputation truly European. In Paris, in Berlin, in Vienna, in London, his overtures are hailed with undiminished applause, particularly that of *Les Abencerages*, of *Anacreon*, and *Les Deux Journées*. That of *Anacreon* is the most known among us [*] ; it is less learned than the overture of *Les Deux Journées*, but it offers the powerful contrast of solo passages for various instruments, finely blended with the more massy parts, to which they impart lightness and effect. With respect to the overture of *Les Abencerages*, it is obscure in several of its parts, and has been compared to the sun disengaging himself with difficulty from the clouds by which he is enveloped.

It is in the opera of *Les Deux Journées*, that we find the admirable finale, which has been so justly admired, and of which Castil-Blaze has given so picturesque an analysis in his work on the French opera.

But it is in the field of sacred music, that the genius of Cherubini has most distinguished itself. His masses, psalms, motets, and oratorios, unite, to the most learned structure, all the charms of the sweetest melody. In this respect he is justly entitled to the appellation of the Jomelli of the present day. His mass *à trois voix*, is regarded as a masterpiece of the kind, and which would of it-

[*] It has recently become very familiar to the English public, by the admirable manner in which it has been arranged on the Apollonicon of Mr. Flight.

self have been sufficient [to insure the composer a place in the temple of immortality.

At the epoch of the organization of the *Conservatoire de Musique*, he was named one of the five inspectors, and afterwards he was chosen to fill the post of director. He has co-operated in several practical works published by this establishment; among others, in *Les Méthodes d. Violon et de Violoncelle*, edited by Baillot; to the various musical examples employed in these, he has added basses, which are admirable studies for the young virtuosi on these instruments.

The following is, we believe, a correct list of this composer's works.

From 1773 to 1779, various Masses, Psalms, Motets, Cantatas, Arias, Interludes, &c.; during his residence at Florence.

In 1780, *Quinto Fabio*, an opera in 3 acts, produced at Alessandria.

In 1782, *Armida*, and *Messenzio*, both in two acts, and at Florence: *Adriano in Siria*, at Leghorn.

In 1783, *Quinto Fabio*, at Rome; together with *Lo Sposo di tre femine*.

In 1784, *L'Idatide*, an opera in two acts, at Florence; *Alessandro nell' India*, at Mantua.

In 1785, *La Finta Principessa*, produced in London.

In 1786, *Giulio Sabino*; together with a great number of new pieces acted in *Il Marchese di Tulipano*, also in London.

In 1786, *Ifigenia in Aulide*, at Turin; and *Demophoon*, at Paris.

In 1790, Additions to the *Italiena in Londra*, of Cimarosa, at Paris.

In 1791, *Lodoïska*, at the *Theatre Feydeau*.

In 1794, *Elisa*; in 1797, *Medée*; in 1798, *L'Hotellerie Portugaise*.

In 1799, *La Punition*, and *La Prisonneire*.

In 1800, *Les Deux Journées*.

In 1803, *Anacreon*: all at Paris.

In 1804, *Achille à Syros*, a ballet, at Paris.

In 1806, *Faniska*, at Vienna.

In 1809, *Pygmalione*, produced at the *Theatre des Tuileries*.

1810, *Le Crescendo*, a comic opera.

—— *Les Courtes des Newmarket*, ditto.

In 1813, *Les Abencerages*, an opera in three acts, the poetry by Jouy.

In 1814, *Bayard à Mezières*, conjointly with Boieldieu, Catel, and Nicolo.

In 1821, *Blanche de Provence*, *ou La Cour des Fees*, an allegorical opera, conjointly with Berton, Boieldieu, Kreutzer, and Paër.

To this list we may add the following pieces:

1st, A Sonata for two organs.

2d, A *Hymn to the Memory of Haydn*, executed at the Conservatoire, in 1809, and in every respect worthy of the great genius to whom it was consecrated.

3rd, Overture composed for the Philharmonic Society of London.

4th, Grand Sinfonia for Ditto.

5th, *Cantata Pastorale*, with full orchestral accompaniments, for Ditto.

6thly, *Missa pro Defunctis*, or *Requiem*, executed at the Abbaye de St. Denis, in 1818. This composition breathes the true sublime of the high and pathetic order.

7thly, Ten Canons, published by Clementi in 1821, not less remarkable for their learning than their beauty and expression, and which are deserving of being better known than they appear to be.

8thly, All the world is acquainted with *Perfida Chlori*, a canon which is the very perfection of the art, and proves with what dexterity a difficult musical problem may be solved by a man of genius.

9th, A *Requiem*, executed at the obsequies of Louis XVIII., of which amateurs have spoken in very flattering terms.

10th, Lastly, a *Mass*, performed on occasion of the coronation of Charles X., which is said to be a masterpiece.

CURIOUS EXPERIMENT RELATIVE TO SOUND.

To the Editor of the HARMONICON.

SIR,—Among the extracts which you gave in your last Number, from the ingenious little work, entitled, " *Notes to assist the Memory*," there is a very brief notice of an experiment made in Germany, relative to the properties of sound. As the subject is curious, and calculated to lead to important results, a more detailed account of the way in which the experiment may be tried, will not, perhaps, prove unsatisfactory to your readers.

Among other properties of sonorous bodies, it was discovered that they possess that of acting upon light substances, under particular circumstances, and of disposing them in certain directions according to the various proportions of the vibrations; or, in other words, of arranging them into various figures corresponding to the proportions of musical tones.

For example:—if we take a piece of glass of exactly equal thickness, eight inches in length, and one in breadth, cover it with a thin layer of fine sand, and either holding it in a particular position between the finger and thumb, or having it fastened in that position to some other body, play on its side with a violin bow *, not only will tones be produced, but the different vibrations caused by these tones, will have the effect of distributing the sand in certain directions, corresponding to the proportions of the tones so produced. The method in which this is effected, will be more clearly shewn by a few figures.

Take a piece of glass, as in Fig. I. covered with a slight layer of fine sand, and holding it between the finger and thumb at *a*, vibrate it with a violin-bow at *b* or *c*, the glass will give its fundamental tone *ut* †; and the vibrations will throw the sand into one horizontal, and one transverse line, as in Fig. II., where the lines are represented by dots.

Fig. I.

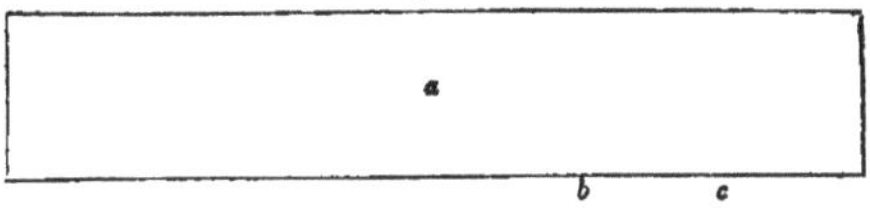

a

b   *c*

Fig. II.

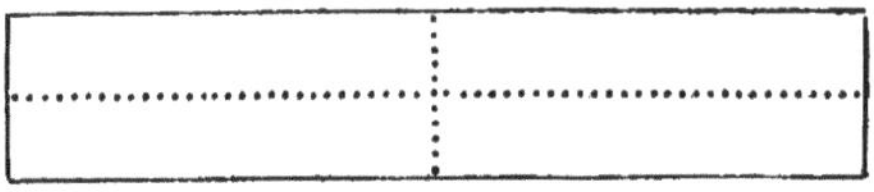

If the piece of glass Fig. III. be held at *a*, and be vibrated by the bow at *b*, the octave *ut* above gamut is heard, and the vibrations throw the sand into the longitudinal line, and *two* transverse ones, as in

---

* Care should be previously taken to smooth down the rough edges of the glass on a grind-stone, in order that their sharpness may not injure the bow, but more particularly that the horse-hair may be enabled to act so delicately upon the glass, that no violent friction may ensue.

† It is self-evident that this *ut* will differ more or less from the *ut* of common concert pitch, according as the piece of glass varies in thickness. For the rest, it may be observed, that in the text, the appellation of fundamental tone is given to this *ut*, as being the lowest tone that can be produced from the piece of glass.

2 D 2

Fig. III.

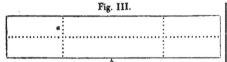

If the piece of glass in Fig. IV. is held at *a*, and vibrated by the bow at *b*, then it gives the tone *sol* above gamut, or the fifth of its fundamental tone, and the sand is thrown in one longitudinal line, and *three* transverse ones, as in

Fig. IV.

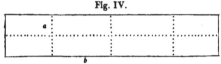

In the same manner arise the tone *fa* above gamut as fourth, the tone *mi* above gamut, as third of the fundamental tone, &c.; according as the piece of glass is held nearer its end, and intoned with the bow. By the Fourth the sand is thrown into four, by the Third into five, transverse lines, &c.

The results obtained from this experiment are as follow:
1st. That the lines which thus form themselves, correspond to the proportions of the intervals produced; and
2dly. That two distinct kinds of vibrations take place, *viz.*, one by which the sand is thrown into a longitudinal line, and which are therefore called *horizontal vibrations;* the other, that throw the sand into transverse lines, and are therefore termed *transverse vibrations.*

These particulars are collected from a minutely detailed account in a work of the celebrated E. F. F. Chladni, entitled, *Entdeckungen über die Theorie des Klanges,* (Discoveries relative to the Theory of Sounds,) Leipsic, 1820. This subject has also been investigated in a Dissertation by Panzer, entitled, *Dissertatio Physica Sistens Investigationem motuum et Sonorum, quibus laminæ elasticæ contremiscunt.* Jena, 1801.—I remain, &c. &c.
W. J. W.

ACCOUNT OF THE MOST CELEBRATED ORGANS.

From the *Account of the Musical Festival at York,* in 1823. By JOHN CROSSE, Esq., F. S. A., *&c. &c.*

As very much has been said and written respecting the great organ at Haarlem, the following list of celebrated instruments, arranged according to the number of their stops, may not be uninteresting. It has been collected from various sources, and enriched with some additions by the kind communication of the Rev. C. I. Latrobe; to which it may be added, that no similar list has ever fallen under our notice. It includes the largest organ existing in England; to which we are enabled to add a notice of the largest one in the United States, from the *Harmonicon* for December, 1824. It may be rendered more intelligible to the general reader by stating, that an 8-feet open pipe produces a sound equal to the lowest C upon the violoncello, therefore a 16-feet pipe is equal to the octave below, and a 32-feet pipe to two octaves below that note, or four octaves below the middle C of the piano-forte.

SEVILLE.—The Cathedral organ has 100 stops, 5300 pipes, and 7 pairs of bellows, of very peculiar construction, which fill it with wind in 15 seconds.

GOERLITZ, in Upper Lusatia.—The organ in the church of St. Peter and St. Paul, was built by Eugenius Casparini, and his son Adam Horatius, in six years, and was consecrated by a solemn service, August 19th, 1703. It has 82 stops, 57 of which are whole stops; and 3270 pipes, 522 of which·are of metal. The towers in front shew above 280 polished metal pipes, the largest of which, F in the pedals, is 24 feet long, and contains 31,971 cubic inches; there are two octaves of pedals, the lowest note of which, C, is from a pipe 32 feet in length, and there are also 7 others of 16 feet; it has 3 rows of keys, and 12 pairs of bellows.

MERSEBURG, in Saxony.—The Cathedral organ has 75 stops, 64 of which are whole ones, containing 8 pipes of 16 feet, and 2 of 32 feet; 4 rows of keys and pedals, 10 sound-boards, and 6 large pairs of bellows.

HAMBURG.—St. Michael's organ has 67 stops, (Burney's *Musical Tour* says 64:) containing 9 pipes of 16 feet, and 3 of 32 feet; 4 rows of keys, and 10 pairs of bellows, with the pedals, extending from double double C to F in altissimo. The flute stop is composed of as many real flutes as there are notes. It was built by Hildebrand, at an expense of above 4000*l.*, agreeably to the will of Mr. Mattheson, and is probably the most complete, if not the largest, in Europe. There are four other large organs in Hamburg, one of them as old as the 15th century; the other three built by Splitger before the year 1700.

AMSTERDAM.—The old church organ has 64 stops, and requires nearly the weight of 2lbs. to put down the keys; it is better toned than that of Haarlem, and was finished by Batti, of Utrecht, in 1760.

LISLE.—St. Peter's church has an organ of 64 stops, and 4 rows of keys, with a front containing 13 columns of pipes: it was built about 1710.

WEINGARTEN.—A Benedictine monastery in Suabia, possesses an instrument of great celebrity. The great organ contains 11 stops and 2176 pipes; the choir organ 10 stops and 1176 pipes; the third manual 12 stops and 1274 pipes; the echo 11 stops and 1225 pipes, and the pedals 16 stops and 815 pipes. The whole number of stops is 60, (Sir J. Hawkins says 66,) and of pipes 6666; 7 of which are of 16 feet, and 3 of 32 feet. The builder, Gabelaar, of Ulm, gave such satisfaction, that the monks, who were immensely rich, are said to have presented him with 6666 florins above his charge. There is a drawing and a description of it in the *Facteur d'Orgues.*

TOURS.—The Cathedral organ has 60 stops, and possesses immense power. It has 5 rows of keys, and 13 pairs of bellows; 5 pipes of 16 feet, and 3 of 32 feet, and was built by J. B. N. Le Fevre, of Rouen.

HAARLEM.—The celebrated organ of this place, so generally, though erroneously, said to be the largest in the world, was built by Christian Müller, of Amsterdam, in 1738, at the cost of more than 10,000*l.* It has 60 stops, and 12 pairs of bellows, each 9 feet by 5, and contains nearly 5000 pipes; 8 of which are 16 feet, and 2 of 32 feet; the greatest diameter being 15 inches. It is 108 feet high, and 50 feet broad. The present organist is M. Schumann, and the fee for hearing him display the powers of his instrument for an hour, is 11 guilders, or 18*s.* 4*d.* sterling, with a further charge of 3 guilders, or 5*s.*, to the bellows-blower. A list of the stops is given in Burney's *Musical Tour,* vol. ii., p. 305, and in Rees's *Cyclopædia*, art. *Organ*, which contains much information as to the construction of organs, and the recent improvements by Messrs. Flight, Liston, Loeschman, and others.

GRÖNINGEN.—St. Martin's church organ has 54 stops, and 4 rows of keys; the principal pipes of the pedals are 32 feet long: it was originally built by Rudolph Agricola, in the 15th century, and is one of the sweetest in existence; but the modern additions to it, according to Sir J. Hawkins, do not equal the old work.

ALOST.—St. Martin's church organ has 53 stops, and was built by Van Petigham, of Ghent, in 1767; it has but little variety, there being frequently more solo stops in an English organ of half the size.

AMSTERDAM.—The new church organ has 52 stops, besides half stops, 3 rows of keys, and 2 rows of pedals.

YORK.—The Cathedral organ has 52 stops, 3254 pipes, and 3 rows of keys; 60 notes in compass, with two octaves of pedals; its greatest pipe is 24 feet long, and it is the largest instrument in the United Kingdom.

BERLIN.—St. Peter's church organ had, in 1773, 50 stops. It was intended to have been the largest in the world, consisting of 150 stops, and 6 rows of keys, besides pedals, but remains unfinished.—The Garrison church organ has 3220 pipes, and 50 keys in compass.

ULM.—The Cathedral organ has 45 stops and 3442 pipes; the largest are 13 inches in diameter: it was built by Schmahl, in 1734, and is much esteemed. The gallery and ornaments are 150 feet in height.

VIENNA.—St. Michael's church organ has 40 stops. The disposition of its keys attracted the notice of Snetzler.

ROME.—The church of St. John Lateran has an organ of 36 stops: it was first built in 1549, and is the largest in Rome.

BALTIMORE.—The organ of the Cathedral is the largest in the United States, and was built by Mr. Thomas Hall, of that city. It contains 36 stops, and 2213 pipes; the largest, 32 feet long, has two octaves of pedals, and is 33 feet in height. An instrument of 13 stops was also lately built by Hall and Erben, of New York, for the Presbyterian Church in Charleston, so that the use of this noble instrument appears to be spreading among our Trans-atlantic brethren of various religious denominations.

STRASBURG.—This city has been famous for its bell-founders, clock-makers, and organ-builders, as well as its free-masons. So early as the end of the 13th century, there were several organs in its Cathedral, very curious in their structure, and sonorous in their notes. The present instrument, on the north-side of the *nave*, was built by Silbermann, nearly a century ago, and is placed about 50 feet above the pavement—it has 6 pairs of bellows, each 12 feet by 6, and contains 2242 pipes. "The tone," says Mr. Dibdin, in his *Bibliographical Tour*, " is so tremendous, though mellow and pleasing, that it almost overwhelms the voices of the musicians in the *choir*, at the distance of nearly 300 feet." Mr. D. also mentions the immense organs of the Cathedral and of the Abbey of St. Ouen, at Rouen, the latter of which he found, by pacing the ground, to be 40 feet in length.

Besides the above, St. Anthony's, at Padua, has four immense organs, and that at St. Roque's, at Paris, is a very large one, with 4 rows of keys. Notwithstanding the imposing enumeration of so many stops, the large organs of the continent are inferior in the choice and variety of them to the best English instruments, a great part being merely duplicates of unisons and octaves, and some of them performing other services, such as turning

wheels with bells, &c.; so that, though 70 or 80 may be in sight, only 50 or 60 of them are actually used. Pedals are the invention of Bernhard, a German, about the year 1470. It is to be wished that there was some rule for their uniform construction; the best plan probably is, to make one octave equal in compass to two in the manuals, C corresponding with C. Two full octaves are required to play them in the foreign style, which produces a wonderful effect under a skilful performer. The swell is certainly an English invention: Dr. Burney, in his tour, found only one, and that a bad one, in the whole of Germany in 1772, and none in France and Italy. Handel is said to have sent a model of the swell-box over to his native country; but it evidently was not imitated until long after his death. A recent writer has attributed much of the excellence of the Germans in the art of music to the great use which they make of the organ; whilst the cheapness of materials and of labour enables them to multiply large instruments at a small expense. We are informed by Mr. Latrobe that an organ was lately built by Gruneburg, of Brandenburg, for the church of St. Catherine, at Magdeburg, containing 29 stops, and 7 pipes of 16 feet, which cost no more than 450l. sterling.

Of English organs it is not easy to procure any account so as to compare their respective size and merits; but, in addition to those by Smith and Harris already mentioned, notices of the following may be acceptable. The famous one in Exeter Cathedral was built by John Loosemore, in 1666, and its largest pipes are 15 inches in diameter. It was thoroughly cleansed and repaired about 1805 by Micheau. Snetzler built one for St. Margaret's church, at Lynn, under Dr Burney's direction, with 30 stops, in which he first introduced the *dulciana* stop, which fixed his reputation; it cost 700l. He also erected a very fine one in Beverley Minster, containing 26 stops, which was opened with the performance of two oratorios, September 20 and 21, 1769. The noble instrument at Yarmouth, built by Jordan and Co., in 1740, has 29 stops. The one in Canterbury Cathedral, by Green, was, by permission, first used at the *Commemoration* in 1784; it cost 1500l. Green also built those at Windsor, Litchfield, and Salisbury, which last was presented to the Cathedral by his late Majesty in 1792. That in the Theatre at Oxford was built by Byfield and Green, the former of whom was likewise the maker of the one in Greenwich Hospital. The noble organ in Spitalfields church was built by Bridge, for the small sum of 600l. The very fine one at King's College, Cambridge, was erected by Avery, in 1803. One at Hinckley, built by G. P. England, which cost 525l., has 21 stops, 1370 pipes, and three rows of keys. It was opened with a performance by a band of 100 musicians, Oct. 19, 1808. St. Peter's, at Leeds, has an organ of 29 stops, and three entire rows of keys, besides the swell, built by T. Greenwood and Sons of that place, in 1815, which cost 1200 guineas; and a very noble one was built for Waterford Cathedral about the same time, by Elliot. The new church of St. Luke's, Chelsea, has been provided with an instrument, built by Nicholls, which contains 33 stops, and 1876 pipes, and is said to be the most powerful one in London. That in St. Paul's Cathedral, which is much too small for the building, contains 1976 pipes, of which the largest is only 16 feet long. An organ, recently erected in St. Nicholas's church, Bristol, possesses the novelty of a set of *iron pedals*. The large instrument in St. Patrick's Cathedral, Dublin, was taken in one of the ships that composed the Spanish Armada, and presented to it by Queen Elizabeth.

We cannot conclude these notices upon the subject of organs, without mentioning the evident change of opinion which has taken place among several Christian communities, with regard to the employment of them in the celebration of Divine Worship. The Wesleyan Methodists have instruments in several of their chapels, as at Wakefield, Halifax, Huddersfield, &c.; one at the latter place contains 19 stops, and cost 500 guineas. The Independents, and the Unitarians also, in several places with which we are acquainted, have organs in their chapels; one belonging to the former body at Manchester cost 850 guineas; and even in Scotland, where the prejudice against this noble instrument has long ran high, there is now a very prevalent feeling in its favour; and the question, of its admissibility into the service of the kirk, has, if we are not misinformed, lately become a subject of discussion in that country.

ON THE JOINING POETRY WITH MUSIC.

To the Editor of the HARMONICON.

SIR,—In reading lately William Jackson's ingenious Essays, *The Four Ages,* I met with some observations which I consider as valuable; and as the work is extremely scarce, and there appears to be an increasing appetite for musical criticism in the reading part of the public, I have extracted the Essay for your use, if you think with me that it is worth reprinting. I am, &c.
                                                        CLERICUS.

IN some late remarks on a musical publication, a wish is expressed, that the alliance of music and poetry were dissolved. If by this is meant, that they are two distinct things, and exist independently of each other, it cannot be doubted; but if it means, that they ought always to be kept asunder, or that they are not the stronger from being properly united; the assertion, at least, may be questioned.

When we read the *Faery-Queene* or *Paradise Lost,* it is without the intrusion of any musical idea; the poems might have been written if music had never existed, for the measure of the verse, which is all the analogy that can be pretended, bears no relation to *musical* measure. Nay, those pieces which have lines of such a length as easily coincide with equal bars, are written and read without any reference to music.

In like manner, when we hear a symphony, or any composition merely instrumental, it is unaccompanied by poetical ideas; the composer thought of nothing but his subject, and the audience do not associate with it either verse or prose—in this sense, then, there is no natural union between poetry and music: but an artificial union may be formed, and with increased effect. After we have been accustomed to hear the same words sung to a particular air, the latter, if heard alone, will weakly excite the same kind of passion as when performed together: —but if the tune had never been applied to the words, no such passion would have been excited, for music receives a determinate meaning from the words, which, alone, it can never attain[*]. The song and chorus of "Return, O

[*] It is true that we find the terms *summer* and *winter, noon* and *night, battle* and *chase,* given to pieces from some fancied resemblance between them. The proving that summer and winter, &c., have no connexion with musical expression, I suppose will not be expected. As marches are performed by military bands, they induce the idea of soldiers—when we hear *one* we think of the *other*; and as French-horns make part of the paraphernalia of hunting, in pieces where we find a frequent interchange of fifths, sixths, and octaves, we join with it the idea of a chase—but all this is association.

God of Hosts," in the Oratorio of *Samson,* is undoubtedly a fine piece of devotional music, but it might with equal ease have been adapted to the complaints of a lover for the loss of his mistress. The old psalm-tunes, so expressive of religious solemnity, were formerly in the French court applied to licentious songs; and that peculiarly fine melody appropriated to the hundredth psalm, was sung to a popular love-ditty. At present we may observe the reverse—many of our favourite song-tunes, are, by some religious establishments, applied to their hymns; which, as one of their teachers observed, is rescuing a good thing out of the clutches of Satan. These conversions could never have succeeded, if poetry had not the power to determine what idea the music should express. Take a yet stronger instance. Let us imagine ourselves unacquainted with the well-known chorus of "For unto us," &c., and that we heard the instrumental parts only—we should think it a fugue upon a pleasing subject, without applying it to any particular meaning, sacred or profane. Conceive it part of a comic opera—nothing is more easy than preserving the same form of words in a parody, to suit the purpose—suppose it done, and that there were common names in place of the sublime appellations of the original—they would be equally well expressed; perhaps in one part, better; for the space between "called," and the name, is so filled up in the violin parts, as would more properly introduce the names we have imagined to be substituted, than those terms which really follow.

Let us next suppose the composer of an oratorio applying the same music to the passage in the prophet, as at present, and the chorus is heard with its proper words. We have now a sublime and religious idea impressed, to which we think the music admirably adapted, and where our sensation is in unison. Religion and ridicule differing in the extreme, no other subjects could be found so proper for proving the point to be established.

By all these instances, it is plain, that the same music may be applied for opposite purposes, and equally well; and although they also evidently shew that music alone expresses no *determinate* sentiment, yet that it increases the expression, and even meaning of the words, whenever they are judiciously conjoined; for whether the music had been *only* applied to the psalms or songs—to the chorusses either for a serious or comic effect, yet it is most certain that the words and the music are the more expressive for each other.

Let music and poetry then be kept distinct, when it is for their mutual advantage to be so; they have each their particular and sufficient consequence, to subsist, without collateral support; but all the world has felt that they may be combined, and receive so much additional effect, that we must oppose the slightest wish to dissolve an union productive of such exquisite pleasure.

UNPUBLISHED LETTER OF DIDEROT, ON THE MUSICAL DRAMA.

[From an original MS. in the possession of M. Fayolle.]

THE great question between the Chevalier Chastellux [*] and his antagonist, (the anonymous author of the *Traité*

[*] Author of *L'Essai sur l'union de la Poesie et de la Musique.* This work was the fruit of a journey which the writer made to Italy, in 1750. At this period but little had been written relative to the nature and essence of the art, which was left to professors and

du Melodrame, published in 1772,) is, whether the poem ought to be composed for the music, or the music for the poem ; whether the poet is to be allowed the privilege of following the free course of his fancy, or is to be constrained servilely to follow the musician as his train-bearer. The latter is the opinion of the author of the *Treatise*, who can discover no real difference between the tragedy and the opera. Now, if the lyric tragedy is nothing more than the common tragedy, it will follow that they are both equally proper for music ; if so, will he oblige the curious by setting good and appropriate music to one of the tragedies of Racine ?

I cannot, however, conceal my surprise, that the author in question was not stopped short in his arguments by a well-known fact ;—that though the poems of Quinault are delightful to be read, nothing can be more flat than the music to which Lully has set them ; and yet, that this flat music having been composed for these poems, and these poems for this flat music, all those who, up to the present period, (1772,) have attempted to set a different music to *Armide*, from that of Lully, have produced a music still more flat than that of this composer*.

It always struck me that nothing could be more absurd than to abandon the ancient music, and yet retain the form of the ancient tragedy; and it also appears to me to be necessary that the style of the poet should be in accordance with the style of the musician.

The ridiculous contrast of our poetry with the music of Italy, which is continually gaining ground amongst us, the discordance of these two arts, led the Chevalier to examine the question somewhat more profoundly, and he discovered, that if music is essentially song, this song must necessarily have a real period †.

He pursued this idea till it led him to that result which at once excited the anger and the jealousy of Marmontel; namely, that verses intended to be set to music, ought, in their march and their form, to be subservient to the song. It appears to me that nothing could be more sensible or reasonable than this. And yet up springs an author, who exclaims that taste is trampled under foot, that the age of barbarism is returned, that all is ruined by our rendering the substance subservient to the form, the orator to the interpreter. Good heavens ! all this is surely very alarming. But let the good man who mounts the pulpit of science, and bawls aloud to us that we are lost, tell us, in mercy, what we are to do to find ourselves again.—What you are to do ? why it is this: pursue the beaten track of theatrical expression ; presume not to deviate from its maxims, though they pre-suppose the sacrifice of connexion, order, method, and consistency.

Happy in his ignorance, the good man is not aware to what a pass he is bringing the musical art ; fertile as it is in wonders, powerful as it is in extraordinary effects, he is reducing it to a nothing, a frivolous recreation, an irksome restraint, calculated to destroy the action of the singer, whether of the comic or tragic order.

Now what is the advice of the author of the *Treatise* ? "You have nothing further to do," says he, "than to enforce the expression by all the means of the musical art." But, my good man of maxims, if the poet has not afforded these means, if he has brought no powers into action, what has the poor musician to do but to cut the strings of his instrument !

But it cannot be denied that in his answer to the author of the *Treatise*, the Chevalier attempts to restrain within too narrow limits the principle of the fine arts, by confining it too closely to the imitation of nature. His reflections are very refined : he pretends that there is something inexplicable in the pleasure of our sensations, as being purely organic ; and in this respect he is right. A series of beautiful chords delights my ear, abstractedly considered from any sentiment of my soul, from any idea of my mind ; though, to say the truth, it would be impossible to listen for any long time together to music that possesses no other merit than this. I never heard a good symphony, above all an *Adagio* or an *Andante*, without being able readily to interpret it, and sometimes so happily, that I caught the precise sentiments which the master had proposed to himself to express *. I shall, therefore, never depart from the advice which I once gave to a clever master of the harpsichord: "Would you wish to produce good instrumental music, and that your instrument should never cease to discourse to me intelligibly ? Place Metastasio upon your desk ; read one of his *arias*, and then give the free rein to your fancy."

The author of the *Treatise* allows, that the Italian music possesses the divine power of shaking the inmost soul, of transporting us beyond ourselves, of filling our ear with every varied accent of passion, of conjuring up within us phantoms of every kind, of calling forth the tender tear, and of provoking the mirthful laugh. Rendered still more confident by concessions like these, the Chevalier presses him thus closely.—What more then would you require? What would you have us do with that music, the wonderful effects of which you are obliged to acknowledge ?—Do with it ? replies the author of the *Treatise*, why make a concert of it ; but never think of bringing it to the theatre.—And why ? Because it will be the death of the poor poet.—Granted, if his poem belong to the wretched and the poor in spirit.— Can we pretend to produce lyric poems better than those of Metastasio.—And why not ? There is music in *Sylvain*, and in *Lucile* † ; is this music in any way hurtful to the poems? Do you think that they could do without it ? And had Philidor been blessed with any other bard than Poinsinet, might we not have been allowed to conclude from the success of *Ernelinde*, that it is possible for a lyric tragedy to be heard with interest from one end to the other ? I should have no hesitation in swearing, that the man who advances the principles of the author of the *Treatise*, is either a Lullyist in disguise, or that he advocates the doctrines, is the dupe of his own delusions.

---

pedants, who did every thing but reason justly respecting it. Hence the reflections which M. Chastellux offered were not without their value at the time he wrote.

* It will be remembered that Gluck had not yet appeared ; his *Armide* was produced in 1776. The operas of Quinault, set to music by Piccini, are posterior to this epoch.—*Translator.*

† The Chevalier de Chastellux was the first writer who said anything respecting the musical period. The Abbé Arnaud promised to throw farther light upon this subject ; but it was reserved for M. Reicha to give a complete analysis of all its parts. See his excellent work entitled *Le Traité de Melodie*, which appeared in 1813.

* This opinion of Diderot offers a formal contradiction to that which Gretry represents him as entertaining in an address which he is supposed to make to Haydn, in order to induce him to renounce instrumental music, and devote himself wholly to that of the vocal kind, which *will render him immortal*. Such is the very expression of Gretry. (See his *Essais, vol. III.*) However, it so happens, that the reputation of this exclusive cultivator of vocal music declines in proportion as that of Haydn increases.—*Editor.*

† Two charming operas of Gretry.

SECOND YORKSHIRE MUSICAL FESTIVAL,

FOR THE BENEFIT OF THE YORK COUNTY HOSPITAL, AND OF THE GENERAL INFIRMARIES OF LEEDS, SHEFFIELD, AND HULL.

FOR this truly grand Musical Festival, our readers have been prepared by more than one announcement in this Work; and the important preparative to it, the erection of the new concert-room, has already been noticed, and some of the particulars given, in our columns.

The splendid success of the former meeting, held in York Minster, in September, 1823, naturally led its supporters to look forward to a repetition, at no very distant period of time; and, indeed, some distinguished patrons of music wished that another festival should take place in the September following;—but this was judged unadvisable, as the interval would be too short to insure success, if it embraced arrangements as extensive as those adopted on the former occasion.

The Committee who had so successfully conducted the Festival of 1823 was never dissolved, the members had frequent meetings to close up the accounts, and finally to arrange the affairs connected with it; in the course of which, the inconvenience experienced at the last festival, from the inadequate dimensions of the assembly-room, was often adverted to, and the question discussed, of how it was to be avoided in future?—There appeared no means of remedying the evil, but by building a new music-hall, or concert-room; and circumstances afforded an unexpected facility for carrying the wishes of the Committee and of the public into execution.

On the third of July, 1824, the first official announcement of the Festival appeared, together with a statement of the plan which had been resolved upon with respect to the new concert-room. Mr. Greatorex visited York, in the following January, to assist in forming the arrangements; and in March an application was made to the King, through his Grace the Archbishop, to accept the office of patron. This request was graciously acceded to; and by Sir Wm. Knighton, his Majesty conveyed his consent to the Archbishop, in the most condescending terms, expressing the great pleasure he had in complying with the wishes of the Committee.

On the 23d of April, His Majesty held a levee, previously to which he was pleased to grant a private audience to the Archbishop of York, and his Grace had the honour of presenting to the King, on behalf of the Committee of Management, the History of the Yorkshire Musical Festival in 1823. His Majesty received it most graciously, and expressed his satisfaction in becoming the patron of the next Festival.

The Committee, anxious to secure the aid of the highest talent in every department, entered into a correspondence with Madame Catalani, or rather with Monsieur Vallebreque; who, much to that lady's disadvantage, conducts all her professional negotiations.

This treaty failed, after pecuniary terms had been arranged, in consequence of a stipulation on her part having been insisted upon, of interfering in the transposition of several songs into a lower key, to suit her voice—a condition, which though conceded by the Committee with respect to detached airs, was firmly opposed in the instance of those which are connected with chorusses.

The Committee now endeavoured to procure the aid of Madame Pasta, and through the medium of his Grace the Archbishop, made an application to Lord Granville, His Majesty's ambassador at the Court of France, to endeavour to obtain permission for her to come over to York, the lady having consented, if the necessary permission could be secured. Lord G. entered into correspondence with M. le Vicomte de la Rochefoucault on the subject, which was closed by the receipt of the following letter from that nobleman, on the 21st of July.

My Lord,

I received your letter asking permission for Madame Pasta to go to London, some days in the month of September. You cannot have a doubt, my lord, of the great value I should attach to the being able to give you some proof of my lively wish to be agreeable to you, and on this account I feel the greater regret that it will not be possible for me to grant your request. The very recent absence of Madame Pasta will not allow me to give a second permission without materially compromising the interests of the Italian Theatre-Royal, and without making myself liable to the just complaints of the French public, which so well appreciates the admirable talents of this performer.

Thus disappointed in obtaining the aid of Madame Pasta, the Committee entered into negotiations with Mr. Braham, and several other eminent performers; and finally succeeded in obtaining the following assemblage of talent.

Mr. GREATOREX, Conductor.
Dr. CAMIDGE, Assistant Conductor.

Principal Vocalists.

Miss Stephens,	Mr. Braham,
Madame Caradori,	Mr. Vaughan,
Mademoiselle Garcia,	Mr. Sapio,
Miss Travis,	Mr. W. Knyvett,
Miss Wilkinson,	Mr. Terrail,
Miss Goodall,	Mr. Bellamy,
and	Mr. Phillips, and
Miss Farrar.	Signor de Begnis.

A Grand Chorus of

90 Cantos,	90 Tenors,
70 Altos,	100 Basses.

350

And in the Instrumental department,

Mr. Cramer,	Leader, Morning,		
Mr. Mori, do.	1st Evening,		Violins.
Mr. Kiesewetter, do.	2d. do.		
Mr. Loder, do.	3d. do.		

Violins	-	-	92	Serpents and Bass Horns	8
Violas	-	-	32	Trumpets	-	6
Violoncellos	-	24	Horns	-	12
Double Basses	-	16	Trombone Bass	-	3
Flutes	-	-	6	—— Tenor	-	3
Hautboys	-	-	12	—— Alto	-	3
Clarionets	-	6	Double Drums	-	2
Bassoons	-	-	12	Harp	-	1
			210		38

Conductors and Leaders	-	-	6
Principal Vocal	-	-	15
Chorus	-	-	350
Instrumental	-	-	248
			619

Madame Ronzi de Begnis and Mrs. Salmon, who had been also announced, were compelled to give up their engagements on account of ill health.

On Tuesday, the 5th of July, his Grace the Archbishop held a confirmation in the Minster; and on the following day, the preparations for the Festival commenced in that building. Messrs. Allison and Sharp were the architects under whose able direction these arrangements were carried into execution.

The concert-room was finished at the end of August; and the preparations in the Minster being completed, both were thrown open on the Tuesday, Wednesday, and Thursday previous to the Festival, to visitors, each of whom left some donation for the charities. The orchestra was erected as before, under the great tower; but it projected about fifteen feet further into the nave than on the former occasion, by which means the principal vocalists were carried beyond the area of that vast absorbent of sound. A wing was carried up from each side of the orchestra into the side aisles, under part of the first arch, in which the choristers were arranged. Under the able management of Mr. Ward,—whose contrivance for that purpose was as at once simple as efficacious,—the organ was made available at a much greater distance from the instrument than before. Fronting the orchestra, under the great west window, was the patron's gallery, the space between being filled with seats. Galleries were erected in the side aisles, with octagon fronts coming between the massy columns, and in a line with them: and seats were also placed under the galleries. The seats were covered with crimson cloth; and the whole had a rich appearance. The north transept was fitted up with seats, as it was thought many persons would like to avail themselves of the superior facility for hearing which that situation would afford.

There were six entrances; one at the great west door for the guinea tickets; the company with fifteen-shilling tickets were admitted at the south door, and the door under the north-west tower; the company with seven-shilling tickets were admitted at the door under the south-west tower, and at one on the north side of the Cathedral; and those with five-shilling tickets at a door near the Chapter-house.

The concert-room is a magnificent building, 85 feet long by 60 broad, within the walls, and 45 feet high. The orchestra, which is built to imitate rose-wood, will hold from 140 to 150 performers; and opposite the orchestra is a spacious gallery. The music-stands in the orchestra are very elegant and appropriate. Moveable seats, covered with crimson, and with railed backs, occupy the area, and the whole affords accommodation for 1600 persons. The walls are painted of a very pale straw colour, and the pilasters, of the Ionic order, are in imitation of yellow marble: the cieling is also painted in compartments to imitate marble; and a magnificent frieze, moulded from designs by C. Rossi, Esq.. R.A., and three feet beyond, adds to the beauty and richness of the whole. A lofty door, the height of the columns in the assembly-room, opens a communication with that apartment; and directly opposite is a spacious stair-case, which leads to the gallery, and in a niche on the landing, a statue of Apollo forms a prominent ornament. The room is lighted, for the evening performances, by two rich chandeliers, depending from the glazed domes, each containing 80 lights; and clusters of gas lights are ranged along the sides of the rooms. The tout ensemble of this splendid apartment is exceedingly striking.

On Saturday morning, the 10th, a rehearsal of the chorus-singers took place in the Cathedral, accompanied by the organ and a few instruments; the effect was very powerful, although upwards of one hundred of the choral performers had not then arrived.

At a very early hour on Sunday morning, Sept. 11th, numbers of persons were seen thronging to the Minster, and the streets in the vicinity presented the appearance of a moving mass. The sacred place was crowded, and the spectacle was very interesting. The musical parts of the service were admirably performed.

The sermon was preached by the Rev. John Eyre, Archdeacon of Nottingham, and one of the Canons Residentiary of the Cathedral. He concluded his address by an appropriate and eloquent peroration, of which the following is the substance:—

"At the eve of a grand festival, it would not be proper to pass it over in silence. In the early ages of Christianity, solemn festivals were observed, which soon sadly degenerated; profane ceremonies were intermixed with them, and they were associated with mummery and buffoonery. At the Reformation, these ceremonies were purified only—for the abuse of a practice was no reason for its discontinuance. During the gloomy reign of fanaticism, however, they were totally abolished. It is the glory of the Church of England, to walk in the more sober path; and neither to deck herself with the meretricious garments of the Church of Rome, nor the gloomy cloak of fanaticism; and she does not object to worshipping God with a cheerful countenance. Let us not, however, in the contemplation of the means, forget the end. All this splendour of preparation would indeed be indefensible, if the end was merely to procure an innocent amusement. It would scarcely be justified, even if no higher aim were to be served than the advancement of a beneficial charity. No—God forbid that any sounds should be heard beneath that roof, but those of praise to the God of Heaven. And cold indeed must be that heart, who, when thousands of voices were raised, and thousands of instruments heard, hymning loud Hosannahs, and ascribing 'Blessing, and honour, and glory, and power, to him who sitteth on the throne, and to the Lamb, for ever and ever,'—and when they are enjoying,—I speak it with great humility,—a foretaste of heaven—cold indeed must be that heart, which remained unmoved by such a scene; desperate must be that profligacy on which no amendment was produced—by the impressions of such a moment. Be it ours to pray God to give his blessing, that the hearts of the disobedient may be turned to the wisdom of the just."

The afternoon service was as numerously attended as that of the morning; and the anthem, "Ascribe unto the Lord," by Travers, was sung in a style which excited the admiration of the professors present.

On Monday, a second rehearsal took place in the Minster. This was a general muster of both vocalists and instrumentalists; and most of the pieces that were not familiar to the performers were rehearsed.

It is quite impossible to describe the bustle which the town was in all day, from the constant arrival of carriages in every direction. Every description of vehicle was put in requisition, and the poor horses had no easy day's work to perform. Many families were delayed on the road from not being able to procure relays; and those who arrived, and had not been fortunate enough to secure lodgings beforehand, had great difficulty in procuring accommodation.

The sale of Tickets continued this day at the Guildhall; and 5649l. 15s. 6d. were taken.

The amusements of the Festival commenced with a Ball in the Assembly-Rooms, which was attended by 434 persons, many of them of the first distinction. The dancing consisted of quadrilles and waltzes, and the excellent band of Collinet and Michaud attended.

TUESDAY, September 13, 1825.

FIRST GRAND SELECTION.

Leader, Mr. F. Cramer.

PART I.

Chorus, " Gloria Patri,"	HANDEL.
Duet, Messrs. Vaughan and Phillips, " Here shall soft Charity,"	BOYCE.
Chorus, " See the proud Chief," (Deborah)	HANDEL.
Song, Miss Travis, " Agnus Dei,"	MOZART.
Recit. and Air, Mr. Sapio, " O thou bright Orb," (Joshua)	HANDEL.
Chorus, " Behold the listening Sun," (Joshua)	HANDEL.
Motett, " Lord, have mercy,"	MOZART.
Recit. and Air, Miss Farrar, " O had I," (Joshua)	HANDEL.
Anthem, " O give thanks,"	PURCELL.

[The verses by Miss Travis, Miss Goodall, Messrs. Vaughan, Knyvett, Sapio, Terrail, Phillips, and Bellamy.]

Song, Miss Stephens, " Pious Orgies," (J. Maccabeus)	HANDEL.
Air, Mr. Knyvett, and Chorus, " Lord, in thee," (Dettingen Te Deum)	HANDEL.

PART II.

First Concerto (Grand)	HANDEL.

Recit. and Song, Mr. Braham, " Total Eclipse,"
Chorus, " O first-created Beam,"
Recit. and Song, Miss Wilkinson, " Return, O God of hosts,"
Chorus, " Fix'd in his everlasting seat,"
Recit. and Song, Mr. Vaughan, " Why does the God of Israel,"
Chorus, " Then shall they know,"
Song, Mr. Bellamy, " How willing my paternal,"
Symphony,
Recit., Mr. Bellamy, " Heav'n! what noise!"
Chorus, " Hear us, our God,"
Recit. and Song, Mlle. Garcia, " Let the bright Seraphim,"
Chorus, " Let their celestial Concerts," } Samson } HANDEL.

PART III.

Sanctus and Gloria	CAMIDGE.
Recit. and Song, Madame Caradori, " Ah! parlate," (Il sacrifizio d'Abramo)	CIMAROSA.
National Austrian Hymn, " Lord of Heaven,"	HAYDN.
Recit. and Song, Mr. Sapio, " O Liberty!" (Judas Maccabeus)	HANDEL.
Chorus, " Hark! the grave,"	HIMMEL.
Song, Miss Farrar, " If guiltless blood," (Susannah)	HANDEL.
Chorus, " Glory to God," (introduced in the Oratorio of Judah, by W. Gardiner)	BEETHOVEN.
Song, Miss Goodall, The prediction of the Messiah	BOCHSA.
March and Chorus, " Behold him !"	
Recit, Mr. Vaughan, " Over sin and death } (Mount of Olives)	BEETHOVEN.
Chorus, " Hallelujah,"	

THE Gloria Patri was selected for the opening of the Festival, in order that the whole mass of vocal and instrumental sound should burst at once on the ear, without any gradual preparation. The effect exceeded expectation, and was so powerful as to make a part of the audience start suddenly on their feet. This is the only Gloria Patri that Handel ever composed, and magnificent as the effect was, it would have been still greater had the singers possessed sufficient confidence in their strength.

The duet of Boyce was beautifully sung; and the following chorus was executed with the greatest precision; but did not prove a very remarkable feature. It is, in fact, "caviare to the general." The Agnus Dei was admirably performed, though never before sung by Miss Travis.

The chorus, " Behold the listening Sun!" was attended by some confusion. Mr. Sapio had been apprized of the short Recitative the preceding day. He did not attend the rehearsal, and on the morning refused to sing it, " as he did not know it." The other tenors did not

take it, because, according to their notion of etiquette, it would have been robbing another person of his part! The committee were highly, and justly, offended, and meant to mark their displeasure to Mr. S., but he quitted York on the Friday, indisposed. It was diverting to read in the Morning Chronicle of September 15th., " Mr. Sapio sung ' O thou bright orb,' with his usual correctness; his recitative in particular was exquisitely chaste, and could not be surpassed."

Mozart's Motett is a glorious specimen of the modern school, and being well rehearsed by the choral societies, was most effectively performed. The concluding fugue consists of a bold subject of nine bars, led off by the bases, followed by the tenors in the fifth above, by the altos in the octave, &c., and extends to 181 bars. Miss Farrar sung her air in a very respectable manner; but she ought to be placed for three years under the best masters. We would suggest to the Committee and the Yorkshire amateurs to be at the expense of her instruction, and she will amply repay their care. The anthem by Purcell, " O give thanks," produced a very fine effect.

In the grand concerto of Handel, the pianos were the most delicious that the mind can conceive. A very good judge said that he had never heard them so delicately executed: " he had not supposed that such a band could whisper so quietly," he remarked. There never was a finer—probably never so fine—a vocal performance heard as Braham's " Total eclipse !" He perhaps gave a little too much force to one note, on the word " sun"; the rest was perfection: the pathos most deeply affecting,—it was a master-piece; and such is the opinion of nearly all who are competent to form an opinion. Miss Wilkinson's voice was found quite unequal to the building: she sung her song well, however, had it been in a room. The chorus " Fix'd in his everlasting seat," was among the best performed, for all knew it by heart. " Why does the God of Israel sleep ?" was well sung upon the whole, though it is not in Mr. Vaughan's exact line. It is a difficult, but after all an ineffective piece; and, in our judgment, was done a little too quick.

" Let the bright Seraphim," was sung by Miss Stephens, in her best style ; Madlle. Garcia wisely giving it up. Who could have advised her to think of attempting it ?—the trumpet, by Harper, more wonderful than ever. We are decidedly of opinion that this song is sung too quick. The slackening of the time when the trumpet answers to the words " their loud," and again at " uplifted," may be tolerated, but the starting off again at " Angel-trumpets blow," is quite ludicrous. The double cadence was a fine performance, but a gross absurdity.

The Sanctus and Gloria of Dr. Camidge, by which the third act commenced, is full of eminent beauties. We have reason to know, that it met with the warmest approbation of the directors, as well as of the audience generally. The York Journals, with reason, proclaim loudly, the triumph of their ingenious townsman. Madame Caradori's " Deh! parlate," by Cimarosa, awakened no less surprise than delight. It was feared that this lady's voice would prove too feeble for so vast a space; but the result shewed all doubts to have been groundless. A murmur of approbation arose at the conclusion, which some of the reporters for the press have ridiculously called, " a burst of applause." This is only one of the many blunders of which they have been guilty, concerning the late Festival.

The *National Hymn*, by Haydn, has been better known by the words " God preserve the Emperor Francis." The score of this was now for the first time produced and employed in this country. This elegant and simple composition of a great master was performed by the principal singers in double choir, without any accompaniment whatever, both 1st and 2nd verses to sixth line inclusive; and then the whole band and chorus came in as one man, on the chord of the 6th, in a manner quite electrical. The third verse was, to produce a change, accompanied by the band *pianissimo*. It is not easy to say which of the modes proved most effective. This was the most generally attractive of any piece in this day's selection. The words adapted to this composition, and sung on the present occasion, were written by John Crosse, Esq., a member of the Committee of management*.

Mr. Sapio's song shewed, to the surprise of many, that he was in excellent voice, though he could not sing the first piece " set down for him." Then followed Himmel's sublime chorus, " Hark ! the Grave ! " This gigantic composition, of the German school, was written on occasion of the death of Frederic II. of Prussia. On the first performance of this extraordinary production, recourse was had to an agency not common in music—no less than the discharge of artillery at the word " Hark !" Divested of this tremendous accompaniment, it now produced an effect sufficiently appalling and grand.

Miss Stephens's song from *Susanna* is little known even at the Ancient Concert, but was greatly admired. The first part was unquestionably much too quick, but the last two lines in D major were deliciously executed. This furnishes a curious, and almost a unique, instance of an air ending in the 5th of the key.

Beethoven's chorus was admirably performed ; it is, in the opinion of a good critic, the finest thing he ever wrote. Bochsa's song had been studied by Miss Goodall, and was well sung. It has little merit, but that of shewing off the wind instruments, which the composer understands, having been for many years in a French Regimental band. The selection from the *Mount of Olives*, by which this day's performance concluded, was well performed, though the rehearsal threatened a failure.

FIRST CONCERT.
TUESDAY, September 13, 1825.

Leader, Mr. Mori.

PART I.

Grand Symphony (in D. Op. 36) . . .	BEETHOVEN.
Terzetto, " Soave sia il vento," Madame Caradori, Mlle. Garcia, and Mr. Sapio, (*Cosi fan tutti*)	MOZART.
Song, Madame Caradori, " Should he upbraid .	BISHOP.
Military Concerto, Harp, Mr. Bochsa .	BOCHSA.
Aria Buffa, Signor De Begnis, " Largo al factotum," (*Il Barbiere di Siviglia*) .	ROSSINI.
Duetto, Mlle. Garcia, and Mr. Sapio, " M'abbraccia Argirie," (*Il Tancredi*) .	ROSSINI.
Scotch Ballad, Miss Stephens, " Jock of Hazeldean," words by Sir Walter Scott	
Concerto Violin, (in D. No. 3) Mr. Mori .	MAYSEDER.
Aria, Mlle. Garcia, " Una voce poco fa," (*Il Barbiere di Siviglia*) .	ROSSINI.
Grand Finale, " Ciel che feci," (*Tancredi*) .	ROSSINI.

*　.* We are particularly happy in having obtained Mr. Crosse's permission to print this, in score, in our present number.

PART II.

Overture, (*Euryanthe*)	WEBER.
Song, Mr. Phillips, " When forced from dear Hebe to go," . .	ARNE.
Glee, " By Celia's arbour," Messrs. Knyvett, Vaughan, Terrail, and Bellamy . .	HORSLEY.
Cantata, Mr. Braham, " Alexis," (with Violoncello accompaniment obligato, Mr. Lindley) .	PEPUSCH.
Concertante for Flute, Clarionet, Horn, and Bassoon ; Messrs. Nicholson, Willman, Platt, and Mackintosh . . .	TULOU.
Aria, Miss Wilkinson, " Vengo a voi," con Coro.	GUGLIELMI.
Duetto, Madame Caradori, and Sig. De Begnis, " Con pazienza," (*Il Fanatico per la Musica*) .	FIORAVANTI.
Rondo, Mademoiselle Garcia, " Non piu mesta," (*La Cenerentola*) . . .	ROSSINI.
Overture, (*Olimpia*)	SPONTINI.

THE opening of the new concert-room excited great interest, and induced the attendance of a large number of persons, who filled every part except the gallery. The effect of the spectacle was beautiful ; and exclamations of approval and delight were heard from all sides.

The orchestra, however, in the opinion of all the musical men with whom we have conversed, is badly contrived. The basses, in particular, are cut off from all communication with, or sight of, the leader ; and it appears essentially necessary that it should undergo some alteration. The concert which ought to have commenced at eight o'clock was delayed, from a considerable degree of confusion created by there being no arrangements whatever made for the stations of the performers, and by other preparatory operations.

Beethoven's grand symphony had not justice done to it, from the circumstances to which we have already adverted. A small portion of the violins and basses were called into action ; a necessary consequence of the confusion which reigned around.* Mozart's Terzetto was charmingly performed. Mr. Phillips was loudly encored in Dr. Arne's simple and elegant ballad ; but such is the growing taste for instrumental accompaniment, that the audience were rather dissatisfied with that of the mere piano-forte. In the duet for flute and harp, Mr. Nicholson shewed all his wonderful powers of execution, and M. Bochsa did little more than accompany. " *Largo al factotum*" was well sung, and encored. The duet from *Tancredi* also was performed with great ability. Miss Stephens was much applauded in Bishop's air ; but an attempt at an encore failed. The applause was more for the singer than the song. " What can drums and trumpets," very shrewdly asks a York critic, " have to do with the *gentle lark* ?" Mayseder's concerto is a brilliant composition, and was skilfully executed, but the music is for the reigning fashion, not for the reign of taste. Of the performance of " *Una voce poco fa*," we quite agree that Madlle. Garcia, in attempting to do much, failed.

Owing to some misunderstanding, and a want of arrangement which increased experience will, it is to be hoped, prevent in future, the fine *finale* to *Tancredi* was executed without a chorus or a bass singer. Time was hastening on, and four out of six performers whom it requires, proceeded ; so that it was actually sung with the omission of the basses, or rather with such a substitution for them as the tenors could supply. This is a

---

* We learn that much of this confusion arose from the want of experience in the porters, who did not convey the instruments from the Minster in time for the evening performance.—(ED.)

painful thing to relate, but it can excite no wonder that the audience expressed their displeasure.

The bold and original overture to *Euryanthe*, was not executed in such a way as to shew its beauties in this concert. " Should he upbraid," was beautifully sung, in A flat, by Mad. Caradori, and vehemently encored. Horsley's glee is his best composition ; it was admirably performed. *Alexis*—which as generally performed, is an instrumental piece, accompanied by a tenor voice,—pleased every body, because what is intrinsically good, and full of melody, always gratifies an audience. But Lindley, in one of his eternal, though surprising, cadences, actually introduced " Over the hills and far away," and by this *mauvaise plaisanterie* excited the risible muscles of the company in no slight degree. There are times when we must either laugh or scold : it was well for the excellent violoncellist that the thing took a favourable turn.

The concertante by Toulou was performed last season at the Philharmonic concerts, and much disapproved. Such talent as the persons engaged in it possess, is thrown away on a composition of this inferior kind. Miss Wilkinson proved in Guglielmi's air, how much better calculated her voice is for a room than for a cathedral. Madame Caradori's archness in " *Con pazienza*," rather took us by surprise ; the whole went off *con spirito*. Madlle. Garcia's rondo came too late to be heard to advantage ; the company were all moving away, and this young performer had not influence enough to detain the audience.

The overture to *Olimpia* has no great merit, and as it was past midnight when it commenced, it had but few hearers.

WEDNESDAY, SEPTEMBER 14, 1825,

THE MESSIAH.

Leader, Mr. F. CRAMER.

THE oratorio of " The Messiah" was appointed for this morning's performance, and although perhaps no composition is more familiar to those who feel the least interested in sacred music, yet there is not its rival in general attraction. A strong proof of this was manifested on the present occasion. At half past eight o'clock in the morning, many who were anxious to hear this sublime production of the immortal Handel, had congregated at the several doors of admission into the cathedral—every minute brought fresh accessions to the throng, and hundreds endured the purgatory of being pent up in the avenues to the entrances for nearly the space of two hours, that they might have the first choice of a place in the opening Paradise of enjoyment. Before eleven o'clock, which is one hour before the performance commenced, every ticket was disposed of at the Guildhall, and numbers were obliged to submit to disappointment for the present, and delay their treat until the following day, in order to secure which, numbers of tickets were then taken. The throng in the cathedral was extreme, and every place, even the most disadvantageous for either hearing or seeing, was speedily occupied ; and long after the commencement of the performance, the workmen were busily engaged in procuring temporary seats for the numbers who could not otherwise be accom-modated. The immense concourse unavoidably occasioned some little confusion, and the casual breaking down of some of the benches, from their extreme pressure, disturbed at intervals the attention of the audience.

At a quarter before twelve His Grace the Archbishop of the Province, the President of the Festival, took his seat in the projecting front of the Western Gallery, and at twelve o'clock gave the signal to the Conductor, which was immediately answered by the commencement of the Overture.

Mr. Vaughan's opening, " Comfort ye," was decidedly one of his happiest efforts, and drew forth the warmest encomiums. The idle stories in circulation of Mr. Braham having felt mortified at not being selected for this duty, are scarcely worth contradicting. The fact is, that the committee in 1823, being obliged either to yield to Madame Catalani the commencement of the oratorio *, or lose the attraction of her name after they were pledged to the public, guaranteed to Mr. Vaughan this post of honour at the present Festival, of course long before Mr. Braham was engaged, who did not hesitate to concede the point in the handsomest manner ; a point, however, which, under any circumstances, the managers could not have yielded.

The first chorus burst on those who were not present on the former day, with astonishing effect. Bellamy's " Thus saith the Lord," was very animated, and it was generally allowed that he sung it with an effect that he never before produced in so eminent a degree. Miss Wilkinson's " O thou that tellest," was chaste, but her lower notes scarcely audible. The accompaniments of Mozart were used in this, and in the duet, " O Death, where is thy sting ?" but in no other part. They produced a most magical effect, and even the opponents of their introduction generally seemed to feel their power in these instances. It is much to be regretted that any prejudices should prevent their adoption every where, for they were added by a most sincere admirer of Handel, and a consummate judge of effect ; not in the spirit of innovation, but simply to fill up a vacancy which the great composer of this sublime work had not the means of supplying at a time when wind instruments were in a state so comparatively imperfect. The chorus, " For unto us," was the most perfectly-performed piece of the whole Messiah: the bursts were awfully grand. The brilliant and effective song, " Rejoice greatly," which used to be so splendidly sung by Mrs. Salmon, was given to Mademoiselle Garcia, who evidently has not studied Handel; and we, in common with all present, much regretted that the air had not been allotted to some one better acquainted with this high, intellectual, and difficult school of music. The second part of the air, " Come unto me," was omitted. Madame Caradori had, through some inadvertence, never been informed of it. This was much lamented, as those who attended only at the performance of this oratorio, had no opportunity of hearing the lady for whom it was intended. The conductor asked Miss Stephens to take it, but professional etiquette, and the fear of being misrepresented by the gentlemen of the press,—who have committed so many surprising blunders, and described in glowing terms pieces which were never

* Madame C. not only insisted upon having this piece, in opposition to the earnest entreaties of the committee, but obstinately persevered in singing it in D, and completely sacrificed it, as well as the succeeding chorus, which, necessarily was performed in G.

THE HARMONICON.

performed—prevented that lady from complying; though she, perhaps, ought to have considered the integrity of the *Messiah* of more importance than either of the other results. Such we suspect to have been the opinion in the patrons' gallery.

In the second part, the chorusses, "Lift up your heads," and "Their sound is gone out," (sung first as a quartett) were beautifully executed. "The Lord gave the word," which of late years has been left out, was restored. The committee also had determined to introduce the duet and chorus, "Break forth into joy," which was encored by his late Majesty at the Abbey, in 1787; but to the great mortification of many amateurs who expected it, the orchestral parts, through a neglect in some quarter, were not prepared. Mr. W. Knyvett's "He was despised" was even more excellent than usual: insensible must have been the heart that did not feel its effect. But how can we describe Mr. Braham's "Thy rebuke hath broken his heart?"—Language is unequal to the task: the style so pure, the pathos so deep, so unaffected, so opposite to any thing of a theatrical tendency!—the words, "But there was no man," went to the soul of all.

Notwithstanding the deep impression left by this, the next, "But thou didst not leave," was little less effective: it has usually been considered a third-rate song, but has been raised by Miss Travis to as high a rank as "From mighty Kings" was by Mrs. Salmon. Mr. Phillips, in the terrifically expressive composition, "Why do the nations," manifested vast energy, much dignity, and a full knowledge of the true character of this most masterly production. Miss Goodall's "How beautiful" was much admired; and Mr. Sapio's "Thou shalt break them in pieces" was an excellent performance.

The "Hallelujah Chorus," the most simple, but the grandest of Handel's compositions, produced an effect that we cannot convey any notion of in words, and therefore will not attempt so hopeless a task. In this was introduced, for the first time, we believe, a third drum, on the sub-dominant G. The great utility of this was particularly felt in the penultimate bar of the chorus, where, from necessity, a D drum has hitherto been employed, to the manifest subversion of that effect which the harmony demands. Our readers will find this important improvement suggested in the last page of *The Account of the Festival of* 1823, to the author of which (John Crosse, Esq.) the musical world are indebted for it.

"I know that my Redeemer liveth" was sung in Miss Stephens' best manner: more cannot be said. This charming performer may want dignity of voice and grandeur of style for such an air; but the place aided her much, and she delighted almost every body. Bellamy, in "The trumpet shall sound," went quite-beyond himself; the accompaniment of Harper was wonderful. The Duet, "O Death, where is thy sting?" shewed Terrail off to advantage: the divine accompaniments of Mozart were added to it. Miss Goodall gave a new character to "If God be for us:" and shewed evidently that she had been studying it with the utmost assiduity. The effect of this was very generally felt.

Then the sublime closing chorus, "Worthy is the Lamb," broke on the astonished ear in all the harmonious thunders of the host of musicians. The fine fugue on the "Amen" formed a climax to this, which left even professional judges immersed in wonder.

SECOND CONCERT.

WEDNESDAY, September 14, 1825.

Leader, Mr. Kiesewetter.

PART I.

Grand Symphony, (*Jupiter*)	Mozart.
Song, Miss Travis, "'Mid silent shades,"	Bach.
Coro, "Placido e il mar," (*Idomeneo*)	Mozart.
Aria Buffa, Signor De Begnis, "Amor perche," (*Il Turco in Italia*)	Rossini.
Concerto, Harp, &c., Mr. Bochsa	
Aria, Madlle. Garcia, "Alma invitta, (*Sigismondo*)	Rossini.
Concerto Violoncello, Mr. Lindley	Lindley.
Scena, Madame Caradori, "Gran Dio,"	Guglielmi.
Echo Duet, Miss Stephens and Mr. Braham, "Ah, whither is he straying,"	Braham.
Grand Finale, "Alla bella Despinetta," (*Cosi fan tutti*) Mozart.	

PART II.

Overture, (*Leonora*)	Beethoven.
Song, Mr. Sapio, "The triumph of freedom," (with trumpet accompaniment obligato, Mr. Harper.)	
Duetto Buffo, "Nella Casa," Madame Caradori and Signor De Begnis, (*La Pietra di Paragone*)	Rossini.
Madrigal, "Let me careless," Miss Travis, and Messrs. Knyvett, Vaughan, Phillips, and Bellamy	Linley.
Scotch Ballad, Miss Stephens, "Gin living worth."	
Concerto Flute, Mr Nicholson.	
Scena, Mr. Braham, "What blissful visions open," (*Tarrare*)	Salieri.
Romanza e Terzetto, "Giovinetto Cavalier," Madame Caradori, Miss Wilkinson, and Madlle. Garcia, (*Il Crociato in Egitto*)	Meyerbeer.
Overture, (*Der Freischütz*)	Weber.

This evening the room was crowded to excess, and great inconvenience was endured. It now appeared that the architects had not made a very accurate calculation of the numbers which the place would accommodate, and consequently more tickets were sold than could be well seated. The orchestra was much better arranged and managed than before; Keisewetter was the leader, and he was supported by Cramer, Mori, Loder, White, with many others of eminence in their profession.

Mozart's grand symphony was performed in a most magnificent manner. "'Mid silent shades" is not exactly calculated for Miss Travis. "Placido e il mar" was exquisitely sung, and charmed every body. No opera music will bear a comparison, either in sterling merit, or in the power of pleasing both amateurs and connoisseurs, with that of Mozart. The comic air by Signor De Begnis produced an encore. We suspect that this kind of music is frequently applauded in order to instil a belief that the Italian words are understood. The harp pleased somewhat more in the present concert than in the last; nevertheless it proved inefficient. "Alma invitta" was Madlle. Garcia's best effort at this festival. After which Mr. Braham introduced a song of his own, "Winter is past," which lost much of its effect from not being printed in the books. These intrusions are injudicious things, and should never be allowed by those who are in the management. Lindley always pleases by his beautiful tones and brilliant execution; but his music on the present occasion was almost as old as his instrument; or if new to the paper, was old to the ear. Guglielmi's *scena* was decidedly Madame Caradori's most successful performance, up to the present concert. The composer of this was a great musician, and must not be confounded with his son, whose vapid music has been within the last few years attempted to be forced down in Italy, and has been tried, without success, in this country. The *Echo Duet* has not *calibre* sufficient to please northern judges. Singers should remember that such an audience is not composed of the same materials as the company at a benefit in London. The *finale* from *Cosi fan tutti* was admirably performed; Miss Travis as *Despina* was peculiarly happy.

The second act commenced with the overture to *Freischütz*, the books for the wind instruments to the *Leonora* not being forthcoming. It was performed with prodigious effect, and encored. Sapio's song was scarcely heard, for dancing had commenced in the adjoining saloon, by those who could not get places in the concert-room, and the quadrille-band did not blend harmoniously with the grand orchestra. The doors at length were shut, and the air was continued; but had it all been drowned by Messrs. Collinet and Michaud, no loss could have been sustained, none would have grieved, for the singer made a woful choice. The delightful madrigal, "Let me careless," by the father of Mr. Sheridan, was most chastely and beautifully sung. This is a composition which, alone, is enough to prove of what the English school has been capable, and might be again, were the professors of it true to themselves.

The Scotch air was not very effective: the flute concerto all that could be wished. The song from *Tarrare* came too late, and Braham was not in good voice this evening; it was the only time during the festival that he seemed to flag. The terzetto from *Il Crociato in Egitto*, which is full of beauties, was executed in such a manner as to deprive it of every recommendation to the notice of the audience assembled at this concert: the harp accompaniment by some strange chance was omitted.

The band were now about to leave the room, but some gentlemen called for the overture to *Leonora*, which should have commenced the second part. At this time, nearly two-thirds of the performers, including most of the principals, had left the orchestra; and of course it was miserably performed. We really must censure this proceeding, as extremely disrespectful to the audience.

THURSDAY, September 15, 1825.

SECOND GRAND SELECTION.

Leader, Mr. F. Cramer.

PART I.

Overture, (*Saul*) — HANDEL.
Chorus, "Mourn ye afflicted,"
Duet, Miss Goodall and Miss Travis, "From this dread scene,"
Recit. and Song, Mr. Braham, "Sound an alarm,"
Chorus, "We hear, we hear,"
Song, Miss Goodall, "Come, ever-smiling Liberty,"
Recit. Mr. Sapio, "So will'd my Father,"
Trio and Chorus, "Disdainful of danger," Messrs. Knyvett, Terrail, Vaughan, Sapio, Phillips, and Bellamy
Song, Miss Wilkinson, "Father of Heaven," — HANDEL. (*Judas Maccabæus*)
Chorus, "Fall'n is the foe,"
Recit. and Song, Mr. Phillips, "The Lord worketh wonders,"
Song, Miss Stephens, "Wise men flattering"
Duet and Chorus, Miss Travis and Miss Farrar, "Sion now,"
Recit. and Song, Mad. Caradori, "So shall the lute,"
Song, Mr. Bellamy, "Rejoice, O Judah,"
Chorus, "Hallelujah,"

PART II.

Overture, (*Chaos*,)
Recit., Mr. Phillips, "In the beginning,"
Chorus, "And the Spirit,"
Recit. and Song, Mr. Vaughan, "Now vanish,"
Chorus, "Despairing,"
Recit. and Air, Mr. Phillips, "The dreadful tempest,"
Air and Chorus, Miss Travis, "The glorious hierarchy."
Recit. and Song, Mr. Bellamy, "Rolling in foaming billows,"
Recit. and Song, Madame Caradori, "With verdure clad,"
Recit., Mr. Sapio, "And the heavenly host,"
Chorus, "Awake the Harp,"
Recit. and Air, Mr. Braham, "In splendour bright,"
Chorus, "The heavens are telling," — (*Creation*) HAYDN.

PART III.

Recit. and Air, Mlle. Garcia, "On mighty plumes,"
Trio, Miss Goodall, Messrs. Sapio and Bellamy, "How beautiful!"
Chorus, "Jehovah reigns," (*Solos doubled*)
Song, Mr. Phillips, "Heaven now in fullest"
Recit. and Air, Mr. Braham, "In native grace,"
Hymn (doubled), "By thee with bliss,"
Chorus, "For ever blessed,"
Duet, Miss Stephens and Mr. Bellamy, "Graceful Consort,"
Chorus, "Accomplished is the glorious work," — (*Creation*) HAYDN.

THE disappointment sustained by many persons on the 14th, seemed to have had its influence on those desirous of witnessing the present performance. People began to congregate in the Minster-yard at an early hour, and between nine and ten o'clock, the addition to the throng was in two-fold proportion. Long before the period for opening the doors, they were surrounded by a suffocating press of persons continually increasing in force and density. When the period of admission arrived, the rush was tremendous, and the angry remonstrance, the earnest expostulation, mingling with the shrieks of females, rendered the scene, at certain periods, alarming in the extreme. We are glad to learn that nothing more serious than temporary inconvenience was sustained. A very few minutes after the opening of the doors, every seat was occupied, and before the period for commencing the performances, even the stairs, and every part where room for standing could be found, were appropriated: and, nevertheless, hundreds who would willingly have been present, were obliged to submit to a disappointment, not a ticket being procurable.

The first part opened with the overture to *Saul*; this was succeeded by a selection from *Judas Maccabæus*, commencing with the chorus "Mourn, ye afflicted," which was performed with great accuracy and feeling. "Sound an alarm," was another of Braham's happy efforts; he gave the requisite energy to it, without forcing his voice into harshness. We wish that the performers of this air would not dwell on the word *Sound*, but on the syllable *larm*: emphasis thus placed would greatly improve the effect. Miss Wilkinson's "Father of Heaven!" was certainly rather heavy, she wants that pathos, and indeed skill, which such music absolutely requires *.

---

* With every disposition to render this young lady justice, and to encourage her, it is impossible to conceal, that her ill-judging friends have done her injury by urging her engagement, and pressing it against the opinion, as we are informed, of the more musical portion of the Committee; who would, however, have conceded the point, and given her every fair and even favourable chance, at a rate of remuneration suitable to the attractions of a singer of a few months' standing. Miss W.'s demands were 210l., which were, as might

The chorus "Fall'n is the foe," a most elaborate composition, and exceedingly difficult to execute, was given with great energy and due attention to the pianos and fortes, the *chiar' oscuro* of music. Phillips, in "The Lord worketh wonders" was excellent; Miss Stephens sung "Wise men flattering" with delicious sweetness and simplicity; and "So shall the lute and harp awake" appeared more than respectable, all circumstances considered.

The instrumental opening of the CREATION, *Chaos*, and the succeeding Recitative and Chorus, were performed in a style of surpassing excellence, exceeding any thing we ever before heard.

One of the principal features in this part is, the air "With verdure clad;" Haydn reset it no less than three times; finally leaving it as we now possess it, replete with originality and elegance, and every way worthy of its author.—Madame Caradori was an admirable agent to convey to us Haydn's ideas. The recitative, by Mr. Sapio, "And the heavenly host," introduced the full chorus of "Awake the harp," which is a fine scientific production, replete with fire and spirit; and more of the latter quality was never, we imagine, evinced in its performance, than on the present occasion. It is succeeded by the celebrated scene, (the subject of much conflicting criticism), descriptive of the creation of the heavenly bodies, in which the song by Mr. Braham " In splendour bright," stands pre-eminent. It was given with his usual force, and with all those peculiar features of power and delicacy, which alternately mark this performer's efforts, and was acknowledged to be a most extraordinary display of fine, intellectual singing. "The heavens are telling," the most original, scientific, and magnificent of Haydn's chorusses, produced a stupendous effect; the beauty of its melody, and the prodigious power of the winding-up, shew the composer's genius to have been as fertile as sublime.

The second part of this oratorio opens with an air, describing the creation of the birds, which has often and

have been expected from men of taste and judgment, rejected. But after two counter-tenors, Messrs. Knyvett and Terrail, had been engaged, and after the lady's friends had declined the advice given from a high quarter, that she should offer her services for nothing, and be content with the eclat of singing on such an occasion, her terms we hear were suddenly, and without any abatement, acceded to! If these facts be correct, Miss W. has been much more injured than benefitted, and the charities have not been the gainers. Yet she is well taught, and will, no doubt, in time, prove a valuable acquisition to the Hanover Square Rooms. But York Minster is not the place for such hazardous experiments; in London there is enough of apathy, or urbanity as some call it, for any possible purpose of this nature.

We know not what Miss Travis or Miss Goodall receives, but report says that these two deserving singers do not exceed, if they reach half the sum, that we have mentioned. Miss Stephens is understood to have the same as Miss Wilkinson. There is a wanton absurdity in this. True it is, that pressing circumstances often compel managers to yield to some exorbitant demand, as in the case of Madame Catalani at the last Festival, for the sake of attraction; but that cannot be pleaded in this case. In the present instance of Mademoiselle Garcia, something may be said in extenuation of the extravagant, the ridiculous sum said to be given to her, when it was found that Madame Pasta could not be obtained, and that neither Madame De Begnis nor Mrs. Salmon could perform. If the remuneration be between 3 and 400 guineas as stated, we can only say that we know it to be about twice as much as Mad. Caradori obtains. We do not wonder at our English vocalists, Misses Stephens, Travis, and Goodall, and Mr. Vaughan, feeling hurt at such statements as we have adverted to, which though partially incorrect, are near enough the truth to excite remark, and to provoke angry feelings.

justly been criticised, as attempting more than music is capable of performing. The trio, song, and chorus which followed, pleased everybody; and were succeeded by that noble piece, " In native grace," in which the declamatory powers of Mr. Braham were finely exhibited.

The selection, and the morning's performance concluded with a highly appropriate chorus, "Accomplished is the glorious work," which we consider as one of the finest and most elaborate pieces in the work.

THIRD CONCERT.

THURSDAY, SEPTEMBER 15, 1825.

Leader, Mr. LODER.

PART I.

Grand Symphony (in C)	BEETHOVEN.
Song, Mr. Bellamy, "The Tempest"	HORSLEY.
Terzetto, "Ah taci," Mad. Caradori, Mr. Sapio, and Signor De Begnis, (*Il Don Giovanni*)	MOZART.
Song, Miss Goodall, "The Skylark calls,"	ATTWOOD.
Concerto Violin, Mr. Kiesewetter	
Song, Mr. Vaughan, "In life's gay scenes,"	CALLCOTT.
Duetto, Miss Stephens and Mr. Braham, "Amor, possente nome," (*Armida*)	ROSSINI.
Song, Miss Wilkinson, "The mansion of peace,"	WEBBE.
Grand Finale, "Ehi! di casa," (*Il Barbiere di Siviglia*)	ROSSINI.

PART II.

Overture, (*La Gazza Ladra*)	ROSSINI.
Song, Mr. Phillips, "Lascia Amor," (*Orlando*) (with Hautboy and Bassoon accompaniments obbligati, Messrs. Erskine, Sharp, and Mackintosh)	HANDEL.
Aria, Madame Caradori, "Dammi un segnale,"	MOSCA.
Quintetto, "Oh guardate," Madlle. Garcia, Mad. Caradori, Mr. Braham, Mr. Sapio, and Sig. De Begnis, (*Il Turco in Italia*)	ROSSINI.
Song, Mr. Braham, "Revenge," (*Tarrare*)	SALIERI.
Duetto, Flute and Harp, Messrs. Nicholson and Bochsa.	
Song, Miss Stephens, "Auld Robin Gray."	
Scena, Mlle. Garcia, "Oh patria," (*Il Tancredi*)	ROSSINI.
Duetto, Madame Caradori and Mademoiselle Garcia, "Fiero incontro," (*Il Tancredi*)	ROSSINI.
Aria Buffa, Sig. De Begnis, "I violini tutti," (*Il Fanatico per la Musica*)	SACCHINI.
Finale, "God save the King."	

THE band and arrangements were still not so perfect as could have been wished, though far better than before; and we add with regret that some of the performers did not shew much zeal in remedying the evils which the inexperience of the music-porters occasioned.

The symphony requires no eulogy; it was most brilliantly executed. "The Tempest" was Bellamy's best performance at this meeting; the poetry is by Dr. N. Drake, a native of York. It is a fine song, in the style of Callcott's "Angel of life!" The terzetto from the incomparable *Don Giovanni*, did amazing credit to the judgment of the singers. Attwood's song, which evinces great ability in the judicious adaptation of the sound to the sentiment, Miss Goodall sung very delightfully. We were very much surprised to find that Mr. Kiesewetter had chosen the same concerto which Mr. Mori played on a previous evening; but it is therefore just to conclude, that it was a preconcerted trial of power. Without wishing to provoke an invidious comparison, we must grant to this artist a fine, brilliant tone, wonderful execution, much occasional delicacy, and a complete command of the instrument. His cadenza to the first movement was perfectly astonishing; it is impossible to convey an idea of it in adequate terms. He is an ungraceful performer, and the extraordinary applause which he elicits,—which, this evening, was immense,—is the sole result of his wonderful powers, for the music selected by him is rather fashionable than good. Vaughan's song seemed a little tame after the concerto; it is quite in the style of that by the same composer mentioned above. The duet was finely sung, though never before attempted by these two performers together; not even in a rehearsal.

The celebrated ball-room scene from Don Giovanni was substituted for the finale announced; of which change no explanation whatever was given. Though beautifully performed, the effect was, of course, much diminished, as the audience were not in possession of the necessary verbal explanation.

The overture to *La Gazza Ladra* was, perhaps, never more finely executed. Mr. Phillips sang "*Lascia Amor*" charmingly. This is the air which in Handel's time made Signor Montagnana so popular: it has long been forgotten, and is one of the excellent revivals lately made in the Ancient Concerts. Instead of "*Dammi un segnale*," Madame Caradori sung Mozart's "*Voi che sapete*," pleasingly certainly, but a little too much decorated. The quintett delighted everybody, and was repeated by unanimous wish. Braham's song from *Tarrare* was far better than the piece from the same opera on a former evening. The duet for harp and horn did not please in any way. *Auld Robin Gray* proved as *auld* as ever; but charmingly sung. "*Oh patria*," excited much attention; but all who had heard Madame Pasta's performance of this, confessed the present to be an imitation. The duet from *Il Crociato in Egitto* gratified the audience very generally: and the *Aria Buffa* produced an encore, even at midnight, for all understand comic gesticulation. "God save the King" was sung by the whole choir: Miss Stephens very kindly relinquished the first verse to Madame Caradori, who, most likely, knew no other. The second was sung by the whole of the vocal corps, *sotto voce*, and the third in duet, by Miss Stephens and Braham, the chorus repeating each stanza: and thus terminated the last of the evening performances at half-past twelve o'clock.

FRIDAY, SEPTEMBER 16, 1825.

THIRD GRAND SELECTION.

Leader, Mr. F. CRAMER.

PART I.

First and fourth movements of the Dettingen Te Deum *HANDEL*.
Song, Miss Travis, "What tho' I trace," (*Solomon*) *HANDEL*.
Chorus, "Let none despair," . . . *HANDEL*.
Song, Mr. Phillips, "Tears such as tender Fathers shed," (*Deborah*) . . . *HANDEL*.
Dead March, (*Saul*) . . . . *HANDEL*.
Quartett, Miss Goodall, Miss Travis, Messrs. Knyvett, Terrail, Vaughan, Sapio, Phillips, and Bellamy, "When the ear heard him," (*Funeral Anthem*) *HANDEL*.
Chorus, "He delivered the poor," (*Funeral Anthem*) *HANDEL*.
Song, Miss Stephens, "Praise the Lord," (*Esther*) *HANDEL*.
Grand Chaunt, "Venite exultemus," and "Jubilate Deo" . . . . *HUMPHREYS*.
Recit. and Song, Mr. Vaughan, "Gentle airs," (*Athalia*) . . . *HANDEL*.
St. Matthew's Tune, as arranged for the Ancient Concert by Mr. Greatorex. Miss Travis, Messrs. Knyvett, Vaughan, and Bellamy . . *CROFT*.
Motett, "The arm of the Lord," (introduced in the Oratorio of Judah, by W. Gardiner) *HAYDN*.
Recit. and Air, Miss Stephens, "As from the power," *HANDEL*.
Chorus, "The dead shall live," (*Dryden's Ode*) *HANDEL*.

PART II.

Fourth Concerto, Oboe . . . *HANDEL*.
Luther's Hymn, Mr. Braham . . . *LUTHER*.
Chorus, "He gave them hailstones,"
Chorus, "He sent a thick darkness,"
Chorus, "He smote all the first-born," (*Israel in Egypt*) *HANDEL*.
Chorus, "But as for his people,"
Song, Madlle. Garcia, "Gratias agimus" . *GUGLIELMI*.
Chorus, "He rebuked the Red Sea," (*Israel in Egypt*) *HANDEL*.
Duet, Messrs. Bellamy and Phillips, "The Lord is a man of war," (*Israel in Egypt*) . *HANDEL*.
Song, Miss Wilkinson, "Lord to thee," (*Theodora*) *HANDEL*.
Recit., Solos, and Double Chorus, Miss Stephens and Mr. Braham, "The Lord shall reign," (*Israel in Egypt*) . . . *HANDEL*.

PART III.

Recit., March, Air, and Chorus, Mr. Sapio, "Glory to God," (*Joshua*) . . *HANDEL*.
Recit. accompanied, Mr. Braham, "Deeper and deeper still," (*Jephthah*) . . *HANDEL*.
Song, "Waft her angels," (*Jephthah*) . *HANDEL*.
Chorus, "O God, who in thy heavenly hand," (*Joseph*) *HANDEL*.
Duet, Miss Goodall and Miss Wilkinson, "Te ergo quæsumus," . . . *GRAUN*.
Hymn, "Glory, praise," . . . *MOZART*.
Song, Mr, Bellamy, "The Seasons," . *CALLCOTT*.
Chorus, "Rex tremendæ," . . . *MOZART*.
Quartett, Madlle. Garcia, Mad. Caradori, Miss Wilkinson, Messrs. Knyvett, Vaughan, Sapio, Phillips, and Bellamy, "Benedictus," (*Requiem*) *MOZART*.
Song, Mad. Caradori, "Holy, Holy," (*Redemption*) *HANDEL*.
Coronation Anthem, "Zadok the Priest," . *HANDEL*.

THOUGH the company was not so numerous on this fourth day as before, yet the crush at the doors was greater, and attended by more personal inconvenience. This selection was generally considered as the best. The Dettingen Te Deum made a magnificent opening. The trumpets,—important instruments in this—were both perfect, for Harper had Napier of Edinburgh as his second. Miss Travis's "What tho' I trace" was the very *beau idéal* of chaste singing: it is difficult to convey an idea of the perfect intonation, the correct taste, and graceful simplicity which she displayed in its performance. How is it that this lady should be engaged at less than half the sum given to her juniors, who are not her superiors? Does modesty in asking moderate terms meet no other reward than this? We speak the sentiments of nine-tenths of the company at the York Festival in saying, "these things ought not to be." The chorus, "Let none despair," being taken from *Hercules*, and not from a sacred oratorio, was, very properly, inserted in the books without any further indication. It was charmingly performed. "Tears such as tender Fathers shed," received ample justice from Phillips; though a serious undertaking for him. The Dead March was never heard with a more impressive effect, and the Anthem after it was delicious.

"Praise the Lord," could not be played on the organ at 125 feet distance with sufficient precision, therefore Mr. Bochsa was desired to accompany it on the harp. Much difference of opinion prevailed on this subject; but *quoad* harp, there could be no impropriety in it, for this instrument is continually mentioned in the scripture; but *quoad* the individual who performed on it, is quite a different thing.

The chaunt had an organ accompaniment only; the effect of it was grand and devotional. Instead however the whole choir singing it, it should have been performed *Decanis* and *Cantoris*, in the true ecclesiastical mode; giving the *Gloria Patri* in full chorus. "Gentle airs" was immediately followed by a great buzz of conversational applause. Dr. Croft's psalm-tune produced a sublimely religious effect.

Of the Motett it is perhaps not too much to say, that it proved the finest piece in this morning's selection. Looks of delight pervaded the whole of the audience during its performance. In the Solo, "As from the power of sacred lays," Miss Stephens, in our opinion, shone even more than in her songs: it is in pieces of this kind, that she rises higher than in those favourite airs which singers, naturally enough, are so anxious to introduce.

Luther's Hymn was the grand attraction of the day. Finely as it was done on the whole, there is something in a female voice which commends it more to our ears than when sung by a tenor, and it was the only piece in which we at all wished for Catalani. Mr. Braham's performance was, however, on the whole, admirable, with one solitary exception, which with every allowance for difference of opinion, we must express. This exception is, the ascent up to the key-note on the word " soul," which we can by no means be brought to approve, even if reached perfectly in tune. Contrary to his usual custom, Mr. Braham had the trumpet accompaniment introduced at the end of each line in the verse, which he used to allow only in the chorus. On the merit or demerit of this addition of Baumgarten, we shall not now dilate; its effect under the tower of York Minster almost subdues criticism. We must, however, observe, that we did not now feel all the emotion which we experienced in 1823, and we attribute it, on deliberate consideration, to Mr. Harper's having too much attenuated the sound of his trumpet in the third sounding of it, so as to give the effect of an echo himself, instead of producing tone enough to be followed by a slight echo from the tower, as he did at the last festival. The pause after the solo, before the repetition in chorus was most solemn and affecting. Though almost out of place, we must not omit to give the due meed of praise to the organ prelude by Dr. Camidge, who, we perceive, has provoked the anger of a disappointed violinist in a provincial paper, and who, it has been said by another writer, may have played the organ " well, or ill, or not at all, for any thing that could be heard," forgetting that the non-predominance of it over the other instruments is the player's best eulogium.

The Hailstone chorus was indeed grand: the tenors in " He sent a thick darkness" were rather faulty. This is the choral recitative which required so many rehearsals before it could be ventured at the commemoration of Handel: the perseverance of Mr. Joah Bates alone carried it through, and the effect justified the expense of time and labour bestowed upon it. " Gratias agimus tibi" was sung with much finish by Madlle. Garcia, who gave great satisfaction in it. Willman, in the clarionet accompaniment, was, as usual, excellent. " The Lord is a man of war," seemed to be a trial of strength between the singers, who performed it admirably. In the Recitatives mingled with the chorus "The Lord shall reign," Mr. Braham and Miss Stephens shone forth gloriously : the latter gave "Sing ye to the Lord," with a force and dignity worthy of Mara: she excited looks of delight and astonishment. The double chorus was the sublimity of music.

Mr. Sapio being unwell, Mr. Vaughan took the previous air to " Glory to God." There is an effect in this chorus, produced by the trumpets, at the words, " Dread-

ful sound," which is indiscribably agitating. It was this that created so much wonder and delight in the mind of Haydn, when he heard it in Westminster Abbey. Handel's anthem, " O magnify the Lord," was now introduced, it having been thought that Miss Travis was not so much engaged in this morning's performance as the public might wish. She sang it charmingly. The celebrated scene from Jephthah followed ; and here words absolutely fail in the power of conveying any notion of Braham's efforts to excel, and to abstain from any thing that might not conciliate the severest tastes. The recitative, in the opinion of all, was never surpassed, if ever equalled. In the air he closed the first part with a few descending chromatic notes and a shake: in the second part he was animated but chaste, though we thought the cadence overdone. But in the return to the first strain, his fine taste was again fully displayed, and the conclusion left us in the highest admiration.

Graun's Duet was sweetly sung. After this Miss Stephens introduced " Angels, ever bright and 'fair!'" which had, at her urgent request, been allowed. She sang it deliciously. Mozart's Hymn in D, (No. 3) is a glorious production, the chorus especially, which had been well got up. Dr. Callcott's song came too late to have justice done it, and the band appeared fatigued. Rex tremendæ ! was infinitely superior in effect at the present Festival to what it was at the last. The Benedictus, in which Braham took Sapio's part, was divinely sung. Mad. Caradori's " Holy, Holy !" kept the company to hear it, though it was by this time five o'clock, and every body nearly exhausted. She delivered it with great simplicity and devotion.

At this time the doors were thrown open, by order of the Dean, and the transepts were filled by the crowd ; and we must indulge our feelings by declaring how deeply we were impressed by this kind act of the Chief Dignitary of the Cathedral. His wish to gratify, for the reasonable space of a few minutes, that humbler class who had no means of obtaining even a taste of the innocent pleasures which those within the walls were enjoying, shewed a feeling heart and a liberal mind ; and his courage—for so we must view it—in admitting, without any precedent to lead or sanction him, those who contumeliously are called the mob, entitles him to the respect and praise of all who are governed by the genuine dictates of christianity.

And now we arrive at the close of this truly GRAND FESTIVAL, which was, with great propriety, terminated by the Coronation Anthem, at the commencement of which all the audience stood up, and presented a most extraordinary and imposing spectacle. When the voices burst simultaneously on the ear, in the words, " God save the King !" the force and effect produced admit of no description, — the imagination of our readers must supply the deficiency of language.

COMPARATIVE STATEMENT.

FINANCIAL ACCOUNT in 1825.

THE following statement is founded upon accurate calculations, by persons officially engaged; but as the accounts cannot be made up so soon, some trifling and unimportant difference in the figures may ultimately be found.

The Receipts of 1825	£20,550
Expenditure	18,000

The band cost more than that in 1823, by 2500*l.* This of course is included in the latter sum, and it also includes 6000*l.*, expended in the site and erection of the New Music Hall. It, however, should be understood, that there are two distinct funds—one formed by the receipts at the rooms, the other by those at the Minster. The music hall was to be paid for out of the former—but the receipts there being deficient for that purpose, and the hall having been devoted for ever to the public charities, it is more than probable, that the two funds will be joined in one, for the purpose of liquidating the debt.

CASH ACCOUNT IN 1823.

Receipts	. . . . .	£16,174
Expenditure	. . . .	8,809

The sum of 1800*l.* was immediately paid to the York County Hospital, and the same sum to each of the Infirmaries of Leeds, Hull, and Sheffield ; leaving a small balance in the hands of the committee.

We have been thus particular in giving a statement of the cash accounts of the two festivals, in order that our readers may form a pretty correct idea, as to the general bearing of each, though we cannot pretend to give exact particulars, until the removal of the erections, the sale of cloth, &c. &c. When those shall have been effected, there is no doubt but the receipts, including several liberal donations already received, will be very considerable ; as the total amount paid into the bank, is 20,550*l.*

Amongst the donations already received are the following :—

The Duke of Devonshire, 100*l.*; Earl of Carlisle, 50*l.*; Marquis of Ailesbury, 50*l.*; Earl of Scarborough, 50*l.*; Lord Macdonald, 10*l.* 10*s.*; Dean of Ripon, 5*l.*; Timothy Hutton, Esq., 5*l.*; Lord Tyrconnel, 25*l.*; Robert Cracroft, Esq., 10*l.*

A CORRECT STATEMENT OF THE

NUMBERS OF TICKETS ISSUED

For the Various Performances during the Festival of 1825.

	Tuesday.	Wednesday.	Thursday.	Friday.
One Guinea . . .	1155	1207	1449	1199
Fifteen Shillings .	1614	2500	2599	2372
Seven Shillings . .	604	1990	1900	1509
Five Shillings . . .	18	39	154	27
	3389	5736	6102	5107

CONCERTS.

Tuesday's 1179	Wednesday's 1894	Thursday's 1353

BALLS.

Monday's Ball.	Friday's (Fancy) Ball.
Seven Shillings 734	Fifteen Shillings 2262

NUMBERS PRESENT IN 1823.

First Morning . .	3050	First Concert . .	1355
Second Morning .	4685	Second Concert .	1525
Third Morning . .	4840	First Ball . . .	1450
Fourth Morning . .	4145	Second Ball . . .	930

The books of the several performances were neatly printed in small quarto, under the direction of the Committee of Management, and *fac-similes* of the autographs of Handel, Haydn, Mozart, Beethoven, and Weber were introduced as tail-pieces ; the autographs were also used as counter-checks to the admission tickets. By the kind permission of a member of the Committee, we are enabled to close the present account with the introduction of the engraved blocks used on this memorable occasion.

SUMMARY OBSERVATIONS ON THE YORK FESTIVAL.

WE could not resist the temptation of attending this truly magnificent spectacle,—this great congregation of musical talent in all its several branches of perfection;—and we have no hesitation in saying, that greatly as our expectations were excited, they have been gratified to their fullest extent. Indeed, whether we consider the awful and majestic splendour of the Minster itself, (unquestionably the noblest cathedral that the Christian zeal of our ancestors ever erected, and dedicated to the great cause of our holy religion) or whether we contemplate the assemblage of rank and talent of both sexes, amounting to nearly *eight thousand* persons, that filled and adorned every part of it,—filled it in anxious and almost breathless expectation of that burst of sublime harmony which an orchestra of six hundred performers was preparing to pour upon their ear,—we are lost in admiration !—the various solemn and affecting associations which took possession of our best feelings, conveyed us beyond this world, and we could only turn our attention from such a scene, to our Creator !

Such indeed were our sensations, when Handel's " Gloria patri," without any introductory symphony, and with instruments and voices combined, burst at once upon us, the vast concourse of auditors rising simultaneously to do homage to the theme;—It was a proof, amounting almost to demonstration of the soul's immortality; for could the soul be annihilated which imagined the heavenly strain ?—could that spirit " be brought to nought" which projected and reared the magnificent structure in which the strain was poured forth ?

So full and so satisfactory a detail of the performances, from our able York correspondent, will appear in the present number, that we shall confine ourselves to a few remarks only touching the performers. The most prominent feature of this wonderful festival was the choir: the chorus singers, male and female, were selected from the different towns and villages in the counties of Yorkshire, Lancashire, and, if we mistake not, Derbyshire and Nottinghamshire. (We believe we may safely aver that on these occasions, not a single chorus singer from London is engaged), and whether belonging to their several churches, or different musical societies, they are sure to be conversant with choral music of every description, and when united, sing with a feeling and precision which we must in vain look for in the metropolis, or any part of the west or south of England. To what cause to attribute this vast superiority among our northern countrymen, we know not; but true it is, that superior they certainly are, and, in an eminent degree, and it is not the mere accuracy with which so many to a part are sure to lead off the most intricate points of fugue, whether the composer be Handel, Mozart, Haydn, or even Beethoven; but there is a corresponding spirit; they are not the cold mechanical drudges that are paid for doing a reluctant task, but energetic musicians anxious to execute well and satisfactorily, a delightful duty.

In regard to the instrumental band, so much has been already, and justly said in its praise, that we shall confine our present panegyric to Dr. Camidge, who presided at the organ, and feel gratified in being able, most conscientiously, to acknowledge his very superior powers upon that noble instrument :—his management of the pedals was really surprising, and nothing short of the most constant and severe practice could have enabled him to manage them in the chorusses as he did, to the production of very sublime effects, preserving at the same time, the steadiest correspondence with the voices, and leading off the points of the chorusses with admirable precision. Thus much for the doctor's excellence as a practical musician, with which indeed we are so well satisfied, that we would rather remain silent altogether upon his merits as a composer:—After all, much finer music than our worthy organist's might have been eclipsed amidst such a splendid variety from the best productions of the greatest masters. We were however, much pleased with the style of Dr. Camidge's introductory voluntary to Luther's Hymn, but he lengthened it out past all endurance. There was a very striking and effective Motett of Haydn intro-

duced in the last day's performance, and certainly far better adapted to a cathedral than the music of the Creation, which, we fairly confess, could other words be substituted, we would much rather hear at the *Opera House*. As to Beethoven, we know what to say;—we must not venture to object to so mighty a genius, as he is universally considered to be, we must therefore honestly exclaim, like the poor Italian singer in the Critic—" me no understand." To return to Haydn, we feel regret that the British public at least is unacquainted with the *only* church music of this great master. His masses have never been excelled, and very rarely equalled, by the best of his contemporaries.

In the principal vocal department we must place first and foremost, Madame Caradori, whose performance of "Holy, holy," was perfection both in regard to feeling and execution :—it was *piously* sung, and greater praise we cannot award it. Braham's "Total Eclipse" differed a little from our notions of what it ought always to be: he made, however, ample amends by his " Deeper and deeper still ;" indeed all the other songs allotted to him, he executed with a force and animation never better displayed. Sapio *ought* to have introduced, in a beautiful and highly characteristic recitative, the fine chorus in Joshua, "The listening sun"—why he did not, remains to be explained. The consequence of this omission, was, a momentary confusion in the band, both vocal and instrumental, which with an orchestra less excellent, would have been distressingly perceptible to everybody. Of the other performers, we have nothing new to remark : their merits are well known, and have been duly panegyrized ; but, if we were called upon to decide as to any peculiar excellence in their respective powers, we should not choose the York Minster as the place of probation. Our friend Vaughan, for the first time, did *not quite* please us in " Comfort ye." We would advise him, in future, to recollect an old, but no less good adage— *" let well alone*,"—he will know what we mean. Bellamy " did his duty manfully" as the nautical poet has it, and we were agreeably surprised by all the renovated force and pathos of W. Knyvett in " He was despised." He never sang it in finer style. Phillips's " The Lord worketh wonders" was also exceedingly well sustained.

We shall now close our observations by respectfully suggesting to the Committee of Management, that if, on any future occasion, the orchestra and the patron's gallery were to change places, the general musical effect, though the *exhibition* may be less striking, would be wonderfully improved ; and we would also recommend that the chorus singers, instead of being placed opposite each other, should, with the principals, front the audience. The chorusses would be heard unquestionably better, and the singers find greater facility in their joint co-operation.

CLIO.

REVIEW OF MUSIC.

SACRED MELODIES *from* Haydn, Mozart, *and* Beethoven, *adapted to the best* English *Poets, and appropriated to the use of the British Church, by* WILLIAM GARDINER. Vol. 3. (Clementi and Co., *Cheapside*, and Birchall, *New Bond Street.*)

UPON taking up the pen for the purpose of giving some account of the present publication, we found ourselves stopped *in limine*, arrested in our progress by the very title-page, which ascribes the contents of the volume to the three great German musicians, and to the best poets of our own country; though it comprises but one movement by Haydn, and two pages by Mozart, and exhibits not a note by Beethoven, or a verse by any English bard, from Geoffrey Chaucer to Thomas Moore :—while the names of the actual composers of the music, and of the authors of the words, are, with the above exceptions, altogether suppressed.

We knew not, therefore, how to proceed in our review ; for the more we beat our brains to find out why the slightest allusion to the most distinguished of our ecclesiastical musicians, whose works constitute this volume, had been neglected in so important a page as the title, the less we were able to discover a reason. Advancing a step further, and attempting to learn wherefore the sublime strains of King David and the pious effusion of Nicetius had been assigned to English poets, we were still more at fault. In searching too deeply for causes, those that lie near the surface are often missed. The knight of la Mancha's squire would at once have suggested, that the title-page in question was perhaps engraved before the volume was thought of ; and thus have conquered in half a minute, a difficulty which cost us half an hour to overcome.

Such being, we may fairly presume, the exact state of the case, will account in some measure for the irreconcileable difference betwixt the work and its title. The latter we now leave to the correction of the editor, and proceed to speak of the contents of the former, which consist of a preface, and a selection from the sacred music of Purcell, Weldon, Croft, Greene, Boyce, Blake, Kent, Marcello, and others, abridged and altered so as to be rendered—in Mr. Gardiner's opinion—more fit for general use.

" The anthem," Mr. G. observes, " is too often marked by the same prolixity which characterizes the sermons and disquisitions of the times in which it took its rise ; but as that which was deemed an excellence in the scarcity of musical productions, will now be considered a defect, the author [the *editor*] has used his best judgment in abridging many of the pieces in the present work."

Now we must beg leave to deny this alleged " prolixity." That the censure may attach to some few English anthems we readily admit, but that it cannot justly fall on the vast majority of them, is shewn by their constant performance in an unaltered state, in the principal cathedrals throughout the empire, and without producing any complaint of tediousness from the great bulk of the congregations. Not many anthems exceed a dozen minutes in duration ; many are much less : the two first in Mr. G.'s present volume, " O give thanks," by Purcell, and " God is our hope," by Greene, are about ten minutes each, played from the original scores ; and if a good composition of this class even extended to a quarter of an hour, it would not be thought too long by most of its hearers, were it only tolerably well performed.

" Some passages," says the preface, " having nothing to recommend them but their quaintness, have been removed, and other movements have been supplied, which, it is presumed, will accord better with the improved taste of the age" * * * * *. " In some instances he has ventured to change the course of the harmony. These alterations are confined chiefly to the works of Purcell. In the *Te Deum* [Purcell's] numberless errors have been faithfully copied in every succeeding edition down to the present time. Some of them are doubtless to be attributed to the mistakes of the press, but the same explanation cannot be given of the coarse transitions that occur in " O give thanks," as this anthem was edited by the scientific and careful Dr. Boyce ; its defects must, therefore, be attributed to an idea of modulation less accurate than that which we now possess."

Here is an avowal of practices which, if imitated to any extent, bid fair at no very distant period to mutilate and disfigure every fine composition of every age and school ; for if the principle be once admitted, that passages of classic authors may be " removed" because they seem *quaint* to one critic, and that the " course of the harmony" may be " changed," if not agreeable to the ears of another, there can be no security for the integrity or preservation of any piece of music that already exists, or that may hereafter be produced. In none of the fine arts is there such a diversity of tastes as in music ; it is the youngest of its sisters, and has not yet established a standard of excellence that is universally recognised. Hence every professor, nay, even every amateur, considers his own taste as the true criterion, and condemns, openly or covertly, each other that differs from it. The admirers of Purcell and of his school, at first viewed Handel's compositions with jealousy and dislike. Of this party were Doctors Pepusch and Greene. At the same period the major part of the nobility, and the fashionable world generally, despised both Purcell and Handel, and patronised composers of the most contemptible kind, whose very names are now unknown except to the musical antiquarian. The Handelians of the present day reluctantly hear Haydn and Mozart : to Beethoven they will not listen. On the other hand, the enthusiastic admirers of the latter will not tolerate the music of the "Giant Handel," and already speak with ill-dissembled coolness of the two earliest of the three great symphonists. We do not from this mean to infer that there are no compositions permanently good, or, in other words, that there are not to be found such as have always pleased, and always will continue to please, persons of real judgment : on the contrary, we are persuaded that there is a standard of taste in music as well as in the other liberal arts ; but we do mean to infer that while opinions differ so widely, while capricious fashion exercises so much control, and prejudice influences such numbers, it is inexpedient, it is unsafe, to trust any individual with the discretionary power which the compiler of this volume of "Sacred Melodies" has assumed ; and that it is our duty as critics, it is the interest of all lovers of music, to condemn and resist a practice fraught with so much danger to the art.

"Many of these compositions have hitherto remained unknown," says Mr. G., " except to the learned, chiefly from the obsolete character in which they are written, and partly from the want of an arranged accompaniment for the organ and piano-forte. To render them more easy of performance, the author has compressed those of five and six voices into the compass of four ; and many beautiful duettos and trios, intended originally for altos, he has accommodated to the soprani."

We cannot agree with the editor in thinking that "many" of the pieces now republished by him, are in so unknown a state. Except the *Te Deum* of Purcell, and a few other things, all that appear in the present publication have been often heard by the frequenters of those places of worship where cathedral service is performed. This, however, is not material ; but the reason which Mr. G. assigns for what he supposes to be the case, is not quite intelligible to us. We believe ourselves to be pretty well acquainted with English church music, and know not what obsolete character is employed in its composition, except now and then a *breve*. The mean, or C, clef, cannot be alluded to, for it is still nearly as much used in scores as formerly, and, moreover, Mr G. retains it in this very volume ; though, contrary to all rule and precedent, he places it for the service of the tenor on the third line instead of the fourth. Surely we need not remind him that it is never written on the third line except for the counter-tenor, or alto, and that by putting it on this for the use of the lower voice, he throws a great difficulty in the way of most tenor singers, without gaining a single advantage in favour of the general performer. The occasional change from three-two time to three-four, we do not oppose ; and the reduction from five and six voices, to four, has utility on its side, so far as regards parochial or private performance.

This volume commences with Purcell's much-celebrated anthem, "O give thanks," the duet for the contra-tenor and base, as well as the solo for the former, being omitted, and in lieu of the duet, Mr. G. has reset the words in the form of a base solo ; why, we cannot guess ; for though the original movement has no very powerful charms, we do not perceive more in its substitute. There are some other alterations made in this anthem, of no great moment certainly, except one in the last chorus, the opening of which loses all its solemnity, by being changed from the " slow" of Purcell, to the "allegro" of Gardiner.

The second piece is the duet, " Te ergo quæsumus,"

from Graun's splendid *Te Deum*, judiciously abridged, and with four English lines very well set to it : but the transposing it into F is any thing but an improvement.

The next is Dr. Greene's brilliant and admirable anthem, " God is our hope and strength," very skilfully reduced from six voices to four, but not otherwise curtailed of a note, Then follows an equally fine composition of the same class, " O Lord, thou hast searched me out," written by Dr. Croft for contra-tenor, tenor and base, but arranged by Mr. G. for two sopranos and a base. This is also injuriously transposed into G, and without any motive that we can trace. In the symphony to the lovely air, " Whither shall I go ?" are imprudent alterations of the composer's text, such as would too often occur, should the practice, in its present infant state, be suffered to pass without animadversion.

We now come to the beautiful anthem, " I have set God always before me," by the Rev. Dr. Blake, with which the editor has taken more unwarrantable liberties, than with any piece in the collection. He has transposed it from E to F, a step peculiarly prejudicial to this composition : he has changed the notation ; altered the harmony ; reversed the parts ; interpolated a symphony, in which the rhythm is incorrect ; discarded two admirable movements, full of religious feeling and musical expression, and replaced them by one of his own, that cannot for a single moment stand the test of comparison. This, by curtailing one of the connecting verses of the psalm chosen by the reverend composer, produces a sort of *non sequitur*, and leaves those who have no means of better information, to conclude, that a doctor in divinity did not understand the sacred words which he set to music.

As this movement, so placed, seems to challenge criticism, we have no reluctance in saying that we find in it errors, both in accent and harmony, which the composer should have corrected, ere he had committed it to the press. In the 7th bar, page 302, the emphasis is thrown on " thy" instead of " holy ;" and in the 4th bar, page 303, " thou" is the accented word, instead of " wilt." In the former page, bar 6, is an F, which we must impute to the engraver : but in the latter page is the following harmony, if it can be so named, which we did not expect to meet with in the compositions of one who censures the " quaintness" of some great masters, and complains of the " coarse transitions" of Purcell.

The elegant and sweetly-flowing movement, " Thou shalt show me the path of life," has suffered materially, either from the ill-judged innovations of the editor, or the faultiness of his copy : the subjoined examples will enable the reader to compare the original notes with Mr. Gardiner's version of them, and will prove the danger of attempting to amend what has long been approved by the best judges, and sanctioned by continual use.

We could add other instances from the same, but must think of concluding this article. We cannot, however, resist making one remark on the editor's new reading in the second example. "Fulness of joy," though satisfactory enough to the psalmist, does not, apparently, come up to Mr. G.'s idea of perfect happiness, so be doubles the figure; thus we have "Fulness *and* joy." The emendation would have been worthy of London's most corpulent alderman.

Dr. Blake's anthem is followed by Dr. Boyce's " By

the waters of Babylon," a work which, alone, is sufficient to confer lasting fame on its author. Mr. G. gives it at length, and without any alterations that we have observed. But his arrangement of it for the organ is, in two or three instances, rather faulty, and betrays a want of practical skill in adapting a score. We refer to page 309, bar 14, and page 311, bar 8, where, by a little contrivance, the horrid effect of the uncovered consecutive 5ths might have been avoided. In the first of these, the omission of the author's pause contributes much to the mischief; and in the bar next to it, the added crotchet, c, is little less than vulgar.

The cheerful anthem, "Sing unto the Lord a new song," by Dr. Greene, is given with only the abridgment of a few bars, and very well arranged for the organ. Then come the two pages of Mozart, with English words; "This is the day," by Dr. Croft; Marcello's delightful duet, "Qual anelante," with English words; the first movement of "We will rejoice," Dr. Croft's fine anthem; and "Sing unto God," by the same. The well-known delightful work by Kent, "Hear my prayer," succeeds these, in which we find alterations in the harmony that admit of no excuse, being equally adverse to the composer's intentions, to science, and to good taste.

Dr. Boyce's "Be thou my judge," follows, transposed from E flat into C, by which it loses considerably in effect. Then a fine solemn movement by Haydn, with appropriate words adapted. And after this, Dr. Croft's "God is gone up," with a few useful introductory bars by the editor, and the last part compressed from six to four voices.

The remarkably elegant anthem of Dr. Greene, "O God of my righteousness," which, in its pure state, is as fresh and modern at the present moment, as on the day of its birth, has suffered in more than one place from Mr. G's arrangement. An editor can plead no apology for so decidedly preferring his own opinion and taste to the real author's, in the case of so finished a composition as this. We have no room left for further extracts, therefore must simply refer to the 5th and 6th bars of the third movement, where Dr. Greene's single appoggiatura is converted into a 9th and 4th; and to bar 8 of the same, where two leading notes, without any base, have an accompaniment added to them. But this is not the worst; the last few notes of the verse are entirely changed, and a bar added which, as in a former case, utterly destroys the rhythm. We have not time to dwell on other objectionable points in this, but must pass rapidly on, merely naming part of an anthem by Goldwin, with a very good movement, by Mr. Gardiner, added to it; a charming terzetto by Sarti, from Latrobe's collection; a movement by Ciampi; Broderip's "Awake up, my glory;" and Weldon's masterly anthem, "In thee, O Lord."

These bring us to the last thing in the volume, Purcell's Te Deum in D, originally composed with orchestral accompaniments, but here arranged for the organ, and abridged. We have always thought that this, though a work of genius, has been over-praised. The imperfect manner in which the first edition of it, in type, and also that by Walsh, are published, certainly renders it difficult to make out the composer's meaning; nevertheless there is enough of it discernible to enable a person acquainted with Purcell's style, to judge with tolerable fairness of its merits. Would that Mr. G. had confined his "alterations and omissions" to this Te Deum; and that of the alterations—provided they had been

actually corrections—he had augmented the number; for passages in abundance are left that are amazingly annoying to the ear. But the editor of this portion of the volume has shown us how "confusion" may be "worse confounded" by means of an awkward accompaniment: we name the 12th and 13th bars of page 403, as one example. The editor also is sometimes as untrue to the sense as to the fame of his author; a strong proof of this appears in page 409, where the annexed bar may be found; by the side of which we place the original notes:—

Gardiner.   *Purcell.*

Mr. G. is fond of this dry 4th and 3rd. But we must now be brief.

We have dwelt thus unusually long on this volume on account of the importance of its matter; and of the weight of recommendation which Mr. Gardiner's respectable name will add to it; for, agreeing entirely with its compiler, that "this species of sacred music, is inferior to none in pathos and devotional feeling," and that it "is peculiar to this country," we have felt it a duty to afford it all the protection that we are able to give, and to guard it against those innovations which—whether to be justified or not in other cases—ought only to be suffered under very peculiar circumstances when it forms a part of our church service.

BROKEN PROMISES.

AN OPERA *Performed at the* English Opera House: *The Poetry by* S. J. ARNOLD, Esq., *adapted, and in part composed, by* WILLIAM HAWES. (Welsh and Hawes, 246, *Regent Street*.)

OVERTURE, arranged by Thos. Valentine.
1. BALLAD, "There's a tear."
2. SONG, "Oh, turn again."
3. TRIO, "Absence is over."
4. SONG, "I'm in such a bustle."
5. DUET, "Two orphan girls."
6. BALLAD, "Why didst thou leave me."
7. SONG, "'Tis not her beauty."
8. SONG, "In young life's morning."
9. BALLAD, "Her I love so dearly."
10. SONG, "Oh! I could weep."
11. DUET, "How should language."
12. SONG, "Nor gems, nor wealth."
13. BALLAD, "Though sorrow may come."
14. AIR, "To love, and yet our love conceal."
15. SONG, "My morning prayer to heaven is sewn."
16. CAVATINA, "Ah, why that look of sorrow?"

Every English song, &c., that now-a-days is published, has been performed, somewhere or other, with either

The most enthusiastic
The most rapturous   } Applause;
Or, The most unbounded

or else it has been received with

Universal
With the most unanimous } Approbation :
Or, With distinguished

for nothing of the sort, in the present melodious age, ever appears in print till it has charmed all mankind; nay, worked up many into a delirium of joy. So susceptible now is the whole human race of the effects of our vocal music, that not a tune, old or new, good or bad, can issue from English singers, of any class, without producing effects that are only to be described in the strongest superlatives that language can supply. This is quite sufficient to shew the vast superiority of British over every other species of song, for we never find that German, or Italian, or French, airs excite such truly astonishing results; if they did, their authors would not conceal so flattering a circumstance; unless indeed they are guided by that mistaken modesty, and foolish self-denial, which dictate the title-pages of high literary characters—men otherwise of sound sense. We assert from positive fact, for we see a great deal of foreign music, and never perceive in its titles the remotest allusion to its success. Can any thing be more conclusive? How fortunate then, how rich in genius, are the composers of these happy isles!—there is no monopoly here of the talent for delighting; every professor of the art who can put two or three dozen bars together, is endowed with the power of yielding his fellow creatures the most unlimited pleasure, and of drawing from them in return the most enthusiastic applause. Doubtless, therefore, if the phrenologists were to compare the craniums of—who shall we say?—of Mr. Bishop and Mr. Hawes, they would find the musical bosses of these two gentlemen much alike; for the compositions, or arrangements (we will not dispute about the term) of the latter excite, he tells us, unbounded applause, and those of the former, we are sure, do no more; the genius then for producing such compositions must be equal. *Quod erat demonstrandum.*

These reflections, which had often before occurred to us, were recalled by the titles of the above pieces in the opera of *Broken Promises.* Not one of them, it would appear, was performed without some extraordinary mark of public approbation, a fact which, being in print, must be true; yet we were present at the representation of the said opera, and thought that the musical part of it was received very coldly. Miss Kelly's acting, it seemed to us, was the making of the piece, and her comic song—the merit whereof is Mr. Arnold's—produced a general encore, certainly; so did a Scotish air, sung in Miss Stephens's naïve and charming manner. The rest, according to our opinion at the moment, was ineffective. But there can be no longer any question on the subject, since Mr. Hawes asserts, and asserts in print too, that every thing, with one exception, which we shall notice in its place, was received with some unequivocal testimony of high public approval.

But to business.—

The first of the above we believed to be the Scotish air, " Here's a health to those far awa," on which Mr. Arnold has written a kind of parody, but copied the syllabic quantity with great fidelity, so as to give Mr. Hawes not the smallest trouble in the arrangement of it. This beautiful melody we published, with an accompaniment after our own fancy, in the first number of the Harmonicon, therefore imagined that we had become intimately acquainted with the tune, and entirely supposed when we looked over Mr. Hawes's notation of it, that it was precisely the same as every other edition gives it. But how thoroughly we had deceived ourselves!—for on reading the title, we discovered, to our great amazement, that Mr. Hawes's " favourite ballad" is only *founded* on the melody to which Caledonia lays claim, and therefore differs entirely from it in management and detail : just as Shakspeare *founded* his Hamlet on a story told by Saxo-Grammaticus, but was by no means indebted to the Danish historian for the fine philosophy, the splendid eloquence, and the admirable poetry that shine in every scene of the play.

Still we were unsatisfied on this point, so went to book, and collated the air as given in that excellent work, *The Scotish Minstrel*, by R. A. Smith, with the version of Mr. Hawes, and could not, with all our industry, find out any thing that deserves to be called a difference between them. Nevertheless, as the latter gentleman asserts in print—(who will be hardy enough to doubt what is printed?)—that his ballad is only " *founded* on a Scotish melody," is " newly arranged, and in part composed" by him, we must distrust our own senses, and believe his declaration.

No. 2, is the Romance, " Giovinetto Cavalier," from Meyerbeer's *Crociato in Egitto*, with English words, and is the piece alluded to, as the only one that, judging by Mr. Hawes's silence, did not receive some unequivocal mark of approbation. Now this is also " newly arranged."—Good gracious!—We must absolutely quit our calling as critics, or our poor senses will be in sad disorder. We have compared this with the *arranged* copy published at Milan, by Ricordi, and find it identically the same as Mr. Hawes's: there is not a note, not a tittle of difference, in our eyes. We surely cannot understand the signification of the word *arranged*; what can it mean?

Next comes No. 3, Cherubini's Canon, " *Perfida Clori;*" and here we had vision enough to discover a new accompaniment. Would to Apollo that we had found out no such thing!

No. 4, is " The Dusty Miller," and No. 5, " Gin living worth," the poetry of both " newly arranged *to*—." Here we cannot be mistaken; Mr. H. must positively have intended to write *adapted to;* for never did we see the French verb so used before.

In No. 6, we have " Here awa, there awa,"—" *arranged to*, and in part composed," by Mr. H. Pray do enlighten our dark understandings, good Mr. Hawes: What part of this beautiful air owes its charm to your pen?

But our readers will grow incensed at our unhappy blindness.

Prices are *looking up* in every thing, therefore, it is fair that music, which has hitherto been so dirt cheap, should also mount in value. Mr. Hawes thinks with us, and for some of these songs has charged at the rate of nearly *a penny a bar.* No. 4 will cost to the buyers almost *two-pence per bar*: that is to say, the air and symphony are comprised in fourteen bars; but there are six stanzas: now each of these is engraved with the music over again, at full length, instead of being printed separately from the notes, according to the foolish old fashion; and thus the public will have to pay—that is, if they buy —two shillings for, in reality, fourteen bars of music. It is true that many of these pieces, consisting of three pages, swelled out as we have described, are charged at eight-pence a page. But why not?—Mr. Hawes has not been at the expense of paying for talent, for invention, for composition, we grant; for except two airs by himself, all the above are copies and reprints that cost not a farthing: But then his *arrangements*, and his " partly composed," must be paid for :—aye, sure ; every man must live. And after all, what is five or six hundred per cent. profit on an article?

One word more, to shew how silly such men as Doctors Boyce and Arnold were in their generation. The former published his splendid CATHEDRAL MUSIC, in Royal Folio, on paper which cost at least double what is demanded for the common article now, and it was engraved in a manner equal to copper plate: for this, and for all his learning and research, he charged—seven farthings a page. And Dr. Arnold, for his continuation of Boyce's work, was satisfied with a price, which amounted to very little more than four farthings per page!

In our next we shall print one of these Scotish songs, " Here awa," that we have long had ready, and which will cost our subscribers—not two shillings, but—three halfpence.

1. FISHER'S *Celebrated* RONDO, *in E flat, newly arranged, with an* Introduction, *for the* PIANO-FORTE, *by* J. B. CRAMER. (Cramer, Addison, and Beale, 201, Regent-street.)

2. Cruda Sorte, *Theme favori de* Rossini, *arrangé en* RONDEAU, *pour le* PIANO-FORTE, *par* CAMILLE PLEYEL. (Cocks, 20, Princes-street, Hanover-square, and Pleyel, Paris.)

IT is many years since we heard the present Rondo of Fisher, which was justly celebrated in its day : and how many recollections does the sound of it now awaken! Probably none of the fine arts operates so powerfully by association as music.

The subject of this is animated, the rhythm well marked, and the effect upon the whole uncommonly pleasing ; yet there is a something in it that we would fain not call vulgar, though to our ears bordering closely on it ; and this we apprehend depends not on any inherent defect in the melody, but from its having been so frequently imitated in vulgar compositions. Mr. Cramer has not bestowed a vast deal of thought on it, or extended it beyond a very moderate length ; his object has been to revive a forgotten favourite, and he has given it such a dress as will make it re-appear without a blush for its fashion.

Cruda Sorte is the most admired piece in *Ricciardo e Zoraide* ; it consists of three movements, the first of which M. Camille Pleyel has used as an Introduction, and the last, *Sara l' alma*, is what he has taken, and ought to have named, as his theme. He has executed his task with amazing spirit, and produced an excellent piano-forte rondo ; brilliant in effect, yet simple in construction, and adapted to a large class of performers. We have not often met with a publication that is so likely to succeed, and obtain a general circulation, as the present work.

1. La Salle d'Apollon, *a collection of new and elegant* GERMAN WALTZES, *for the* PIANO-FORTE, *composed by the most esteemed foreign authors,* Nos. 1 to 12. (Wessel and Stodart, 1, Soho Square.)

2. SIX WALTZES, *composed for the* PIANO-FORTE, *by* D. SCHLESINGER. (Cramer and Co., 201, Regent Street.)

THE first of these is one of the neatest publications that ever came under our view. It is in octavo, and each number contains at least one waltz, generally with a trio, and sometimes two, composed by Beethoven, Moscheles, Rossini, Weber, and *Prince Ypsilanti.* From the latter name, are we to learn that the modern Greeks imitate their ancestors in their system of education, and blend the musical with the military art in their schools? The waltz attributed to this Hellenic prince and general, is not likely to work so many wonders as the sounds of Amphion, we fear ; if it would only do as much as the strains of Tyrtæus, we should be satisfied. But do the publishers of this pretty work expect that the masters will recommend so cheap a collection ?—

Mr. Schlesinger dives deeply into the motives which actuate his professional brethren, when he gives only eight pages for four shillings ; but then he has bestowed as much labour upon his waltzes, as would have gone far towards the formation of an overture. Had he been rather less scientific, and a little more melodious, he would have spared himself not only a vast deal of trouble, but also the mortification of seeing the fruits of his industry reposing ingloriously on dusty shelves, instead of finding places on polished music desks.

1. OVERTURE *to the opera of* Tarrare, *or* Axur, Re d' Ormus, *by* SALIERI, *arranged for the* PIANO-FORTE, *with the* Accompaniment *of* FLUTE *or* VIOLIN, *ad lib.* (Ewer and Johanning, Bow Church Yard, and 263, Regent Street.)

2. BRILLIANT OVERTURE *to the opera of* JESSONDA, *composed and arranged for the* PIANO-FORTE *by* LOUIS SPOHR. *(Published by the same.)*

THE overture to *Tarrare* is as weak and vapid as any old Italian orchestral piece we ever heard ; but it is so easy, that any body may execute it, and the accompaniment may give some little interest to it ; at all events, it makes it social ; and then there are but three pages of it. The overture to *Jessonda* claims to be considered as an elaborate, scientific production. Viewed in this light it is unquestionably a clever composition ; but as to effect—at least on the piano-forte—it will disappoint most who undertake it, for it is weighed down by a multitude of notes, having little extricable melody to give it buoyancy.

FOREIGN MUSICAL REPORT.

VIENNA.—The reign of music has been shortened here since our last report, by the closing of the Italian Opera ; and nothing new has appeared on the German stage to compensate for the loss, if we except the revival of the *Ugolino* of Seyfried, which abounds in melodies of a very effective kind, and contains many combined pieces which display the hand of a master. Of the other two pieces, which were called new in the bills, *Jupiter in Wien,* and *Der Zauberguckguck* (the Magic Cuckoo), the music of the former of which is by Ignaz Schuster, and the latter by Kepellmeister Wenzel Müller, we can only say—*Requiescant in pace!*—However, there was an experiment made in another piece, entitled, *König Ottakar's Gluck und Ende,* which if not entitled to our praise and worthy of imitation, proved, at least, a treat in the absence of the music of the great lyric theatre. The piece itself possesses but little merit, and relies for its interest on the selection of instrumental masterpieces interwoven with the subject. The brilliant overture was arranged by Hummel from the most celebrated of Haydn's national melodies. The transition to the second act is formed of Beethoven's charming andante from the symphony in D major. The third opens with a hunting piece, taken from Mehul's spirited overture to *Ariodant ;* the fourth from Mozart's highly tragical quick movement in his sonata in c minor, with an additional accompaniment by Seyfreid ; lastly, the characteristic *entr' acte* from Cherubini's *Medea.* We cannot but acknowledge that the effect of this magnificent *pasticcio* was highly imposing, whatever severer critics may say of the taste by which it was conceived.—But if the theatres here have been inactive, the concert-rooms have been more than usually alive ; we have had no less than twenty concerts, of one kind or another. The two most remarkable were that of Professor Schuppenzih, at which, among other interesting pieces, was given a new double quatuor by Sphor, which was pronounced by all the amateurs to be a masterpiece, and created a very great sensation; the other was a Concert Spirituel, opening with Beethoven's grand spirited symphony in A major, which was performed with admirable taste and expression. 2. Three hymns and an Offertory from Winter's new Mass, which, in spite of their general beauty, struck us as being in a more florid style than is suitable to church music. In the Offertory there was a solo piece of great beauty and power of expression, which was enthusiastically encored; indeed, it is in melodies of the deep and touching kind that the *forte* of this great master lies. One of the movements with a double orchestra was also full of power, and shows that years have quenched nothing of the vigour and fire of this veteran composer. 3. A chorus from Handel's *Timotheus,* which was admirably performed, and created a very lively sensation.

In the musical chit-chat of the town it is said that Barbaja is anxious to become a purchaser of the Karnthuerthor theatre. This is rather a dubious salvation for this declining establishment, for it is not impossible but it may tend to the downfall of German art. The celebrated mechanician Leonard Mälzel is said to have completed his new instrument, called the *Metall-Harmonikon.* We hope soon to be able to give you some particulars of this invention.—The late composer Salieri has left by will the whole of his musical manuscripts to the *Tonkunstler Societät.* Among them is the manuscript of a new *Requiem,* entitled *Messa funebra piccola, da me piccolissimo, Antonio Salieri.* According to the composer's own wish, as expressed in his will, the work is to be performed for the first time on his anniversary, by all his surviving scholars, male and female, who are particularized by name.

BERLIN.—On occasion of the marriage of the Princess Louisa with the Prince of the Netherlands, the long and anxiously-expected opera of Spontini was produced, and by the magnificence of the manner in which it was brought out, but above all, by the power and originality of the music, far surpassed the expectations of the most sanguine. It is entitled *Alcidor,* a grand magic opera, in three acts, the subject of which is taken from that inexhaustible muse of the dramatic poet, the "Arabian Nights' Entertainments." The outline of the subject is this : *Almoran,* the king of the sylphs, is a protector of *Alcidor,* the Lord of the golden island, whose love for *Selaide,* daughter of queen *Oriane* of Lahore, he favours, in opposition to *Ismenor,* prince of the isle of volcanoes, who has learnt from the secrets of fate that their union will prove his ruin. That his malignity is counteracted, and that the lovers are made happy in the possession of each other, may readily be supposed. It would be presumption, after having heard the music but twice, to attempt to form a decided opinion; all we can do is to enumerate the pieces which met with the greatest applause. The short, but rich and expressive introduction, consisting of a chorus of the followers of Ismenor, who are seen forging arms in the caverns of their mountain, gave, in its finely-blended harmonies and melodies, a favourable foretaste of the treat that was to follow. After this came the *scena* of Alcidor,

with a melody of a sweet and original character ; followed by a duet between the same and Almoran, and a chorus of warriors, interrupted by an air of Alcidor. The finale of this act was also much admired. In the second act, the pieces that excited the greatest sensation were, the *scena* of Selaide, with an air of a very sweet and plaintive expression ; then follows a duet between Alcidor and Zelaide, which displays the taste and feeling of the composer to great advantage; after this comes the air of Oriane, and the finale, including a chorus of the female attendants, full of new and charming effects. In the third act the most striking pieces appeared to be the opening chorus of genii and the finale *. We may add that, in scenery and decoration, this fairy-opera surpasses any thing before witnessed in Berlin. In these points, wonders had already been effected in the *Nurmahal* of Sphor, and the *Olympia* of the present composer, but the one before us throws them all into the shade. Before, we were astonished at the view of valleys, landscapes, saloon, and temples, in all the luxury of decoration ; but now we have gardens and structures of gold, aërial palaces, with columns of living fire, &c. &c. The first thing that naturally strikes us, is the reflection that it must require music of a very extraordinary and attractive kind, to counterbalance in some degree the effect of these gorgeous scenic decorations. In order that the ear should obtain an equal impression with the eye, it is requisite not only to employ all the possible strength of the orchestra and chorus, but the composer also found it necessary to avail himself of those great and massive effects, which, of all the composers of the day, Spontini possibly alone possesses the art to employ, without absolutely overwhelming his audience.

We have been fertile in novelty here, for besides the above splendid work, we have had a comic opera in one act, entitled, *Jery and Bätely,* the poetry by Göthe, the music by Adolph Bernhard Marx, editor of the Musical Gazette published in this place. As far back as the year 1801, this same opera was set to music by Reichard, and considerable expectations were excited on the subject, which, however, were disappointed. M. Marx has attempted more appropriate music to the piece, and though he has not entirely succeeded in rendering the spirit of the admirable text, he has thrown so many beauties into the piece, that it is likely to prove a favourite. Among the pieces that most generally applauded were a duet between Jery and Bätely, and a song by Jery of a very pleasing character. We have also, *en passant,* been treated with a little French opera, got up by M. Hyacinthe Brice, first tenor from the French theatre at St. Petersburgh, assisted by his wife, and daughter Rose, a sprightly girl of ten years of age, together with Miss Angely, and Rosicke. The pieces given were *Le Chanteur et Le Tailleur,* an opera in one act, the words by Armand Gouffé, the music by Gaveaux, with various Italian and French airs introduced. *Le vieux Garçon et la petite Fille,* in one act, by Scribe, in which the Rose performed several characters. *L'Actrice en Voyage,* a vaudeville, by Scribe and Melèsville, in which the young lady also distinguished herself; indeed, she gives promise of great future excellence.

We have now among us a musical prodigy of four years of age, of the name of Carl Anton Florian Eckert, born in Potsdam, 1820, whose father is a serjeant-major in the royal guard. Even in its cradle, when only nine months old, this child had no greater enjoyment than to listen to a visitant who played on the flute, accompanied by the father on a guitar. On the passage of a tune into the minor mode, tears were seen to start into its eyes, and if merely a noise was made upon the instrument, it would begin to cry vehemently, place its little hands against its ears, and was with difficulty pacified again. When the child was fifteen months old, the father happened to be playing on an old harpsichord, with his left hand, the favourite German air, *Schöne Minka, ich muss scheiden,* (Beauteous Minka, I must depart), the child began to weep, and expressed great impatience to reach the keys of the instrument. The father took it on his knee, and placing it before the key-board of the harpsichord, the child succeeded in picking out the notes of

---

* We shall have occasion in our next, to give a more minute analysis of the music of this opera.

the air, and those which it could not reach with its fingers, it struck with its knuckles. The first time the child was brought to an organ, it was evidently terrified at sounds strange to its ear, and it required a considerable time to reconcile it to this instrument. At three years of age it was able to play off several pieces from *Die Precioxa* and *Der Freischütz*, and it is now undergoing a course of instructions under a master of eminence.

WEIMAR.—Our opera season here continues in all its vigour; indeed, the theatre has not, for many years, had to boast of so effective a company. The *Ferdinand Cortez* of Spontini continues the great favourite, and affords the amateur a constant opportunity of admiring this composer's profound talent for dramatic music of the higher order. The characters were admirably supported, particularly the principal part, which was sustained by the well-known Madame Steinert, who has also delighted the public in the characters of *Annette* in *Der Freischutz*, and *Myrrha* in *Das Opferfest.*—Under the management of Music-director Eberwein, our church music has received a new impulse. The pieces lately given have been the *Stabat Mater* of Haydn, which was new to this place, a *Te Deum* by Jomelli, an *Offertorio* by Winter, with its delightful oböe obligato, admirably performed by the brother of the director, a *Mass* and admirable *Misericordia* by Mozart, the celebrated 104th Psalm by Naumann, and several sacred cantatas by Homilius. M. Eberwien's zeal and industry are also conspicuous in our Musical Society; a laudable establishment, which affords the friends of the art an admirable opportunity for the display of amateur talents, and of doing justice to some of the great masterpieces, vocal and instrumental.—We have recently had a visit here from the young prodigy of Magdeburg, the pianist Schilling, a youth nine years of age, whose taste and powers of execution are really astonishing at his age.—He executed Mozart's concerto in D minor, and a difficult piece by Moscheles, to the admiration of a numerous meeting of the amateurs of the place. He found here the encouragement which all rising talent merits.

DARMSTADT.—Under the auspices of the Grand Duke, whose zeal in the cause of the art is never seen to relax, music continues to make daily progress in this town. Our opera proceeds with spirit, and can boast of considerable talent. Among other singers of eminence here is the celebrated basist, Fischer, who has delighted the lovers of chaste yet energetic singing, in the characters of *Leporello* in *Don Juan*; *Osmin* in *Der Entführung aus dem Serail*; and *Œdipe* in Sacchini's *Œdipe in Colonne.* This singer, besides an excellent style, possesses the still rarer qualification in a vocalist, of entering perfectly into the sentiments of the composer, and being contented to sing what is set down for him, without any meretricious ornament. Happy would it be for the interest of the art, if he had more imitators! A Madame Schömberger also pleased much in *Sargino*, in Paër's opera of that name. She sings with great taste, and there is a simplicity in her manner and style which is very pleasing, and which is of itself sufficient to atone for a multitude of sins.

KONIGSBERG.—After the Opera of this place had been for a long time in bad hands, it had the good fortune to pass under the direction of the able and active Adolph Schröder, who, among other distinguished singers, succeeded in engaging the celebrated Madame Rosalie Braun, who made her debût as *Julia* in the *Vestalin.* Her reception was flattering in the extreme; her singing shows the goodness of her school, and her style of acting is far superior to that of the generality of singers. Her talents will doubtless be productive of a good effect here; and, to say the truth, we stood much in need of some able artist to direct the public taste. She afterwards filled, with increasing success, the characters of *Elvire* in *Das Opferfest; Constantia* in *Der Enführung aus dem Serail; Agatha* in *Der Freischutz;* in *Die Prinzessin von Navarre;* in *Lodoiska*, &c. The other favourite is M. Geisler, who created a considerable sensation in *Don Juan, Une Follie,* by Mehul, and afterwards in an opera revived here, entitled *Die Wiener in Berlin,* which,

though without any great intrinsic merit, is become a great favourite.—We have lately been visited by several artists their musical travels. Among them was M. Maurer, royal Hanoverian concert master, who delighted the amateurs of the place by two pieces of his own composition, the one a grand violin concerto, in which the air of *God save the King,* with variations, was introduced with great effect; the other was a rondo militaire, of a very brilliant and original kind.—Among sacred music, *Der Tod Jesu,* (the Death of Christ,) by Graun, was admirably given here under the management of music-director Riel, for the benefit of the public charities; and we are happy to say the object was satisfactorily fulfilled.—M. C. Urban, music-director of Elbing, has just published here a work upon which he has' been long engaged, entitled, *Theorie der Musik nach rein Naturgenrässen Gesetzen,* (Theory of Music according to pure Natural Principles; as the work contains many things of value, and of deep importance to the interests of the arts, we shall find an early opportunity of giving some account of its contents.

VENICE.—The *Mose* of Rossini has engrossed the favour of this place; the characters were cast as follows; *Faraone,* Antonio Tamburini; *Amaltea,* Maddalina Massini; *Osiride,* Giovanni David; *Elcia,* Henrietta Maria Lelande; *Arons,* Giuseppe Vaschetti; *Mose,* Ernest Augustus Kellner, from England. The principal singers, Lalande, Tamburini, David, and Kellner, particularly distinguished themselves. But a few days after, the tables were quite turned, for, in the *Zelmira,* David made quite a *fiasco.* The good people of Vienna cannot dream how such an outrage on their favourite could have happened. The privileged Venetian Gazette gave a just and admirable critique respecting David's fall. In the *Mose* his trills and roulades surprised and delighted ears open to be pleased; in the *Zelmira* they no longer possessed the charm of novelty. His own celebrated cavatina, *Cara, deh attendimi,* is said not to have moved a single soul, not even excepting the ladies. A Milanese, near where we sat, looked quite desponding; he confessed that the favourite's voice had really taken its flight. Madame Borgondio also failed in the part of *Emma.—Dardano e Dartala,* a new opera by Pavesi, met with a very lukewarm reception; or, as an Italian journal expresses it, *non fece ne caldo ne freddo.*

PALERMO.—The operas that have been performing here are Morlacchi's *Teobaldo ed Isolina* and Rossini's *Zelmira* and *Semiramis,* but only the latter continued a favourite.

From the above list, added to our preceding report, it will be seen that Italy is not poor in public singers, and then as for dilettanti, how vast is their number! Indeed, it may be said of this land that every one here is a singer. We have been favoured by a list made by a person curious in these particulars, from which it appears, that within the last five years, Italy can reckon above 1100 individuals, who devote their talents to the public amusement on the lyric scene. When classed they run as follows: 230 *prime donne,* (including those who perform male characters,) 250 *seconde donne,* 140 *primi tenori,* 130 *secondi tenori,* 240 *buffi comici* 'and *buffi cantanti* (it may be remarked that an Italian *buffo* and *basso* mean nearly the same thing,) the rest *secondi buffi* and *terzi donne.* Italy can reckon nearly 200 theatres, above 50 living opera composers, and 30 opera poets; but it must be acknowledged that the Peninsula has lost much of its native music, and can no longer boast of the great singers who illustrated their lyric theatre half a century ago. The number of those really entitled to the name of singers, in this age so full of pretension, is comparatively small indeed; and the judicious observer will not allow his judgment to be biassed, but have the resolution to form an opinion of his own. For the rest it must not be omitted, that at no period of the musical history of Italy was such a number of foreign singers seen on the stages of this country, composing a motley group of Italians, Germans, French, Spaniards, English, Poles, &c. The number of the latter, however, sinks into nothing when compared to the number of Italians who exercise this art in foreign counties.

2 G 2

TURIN.—*Teatro Regio.* A furious war of the pen has been carried on here respecting Mercadante's new opera, one party maintaining it to be a masterpiece of the art, and the other denouncing it as a wretched imitation.

Nicolini's new opera, which, from various causes, could not be produced last season, made its appearance this, but did not meet with much success. It is entitled *Teuzzone,* and possesses but little interest either in the story or music. A dancer from Vienna, Signora Heberle (who writes her name Hebèrlè, to give it, we suppose, a French physiognomy,) has obtained great applause here, as well as in the great theatre at Milan.—*Teatro Sutera.* The principal singers of this theatre are, *prima donna,* Maria Castarelli; *tenore,* Enrico Molinello; *bassi,* Filippi Ricci and Pacifico Prosperi. The *Pretendenti Delusi* of Mosca, and the *Amore aguzza l' ingegni,* an opera in one act, by Celli, pleased considerably.

TRIESTE.—Mayerbeer's celebrated opera *Il Crociato in Egitto* was replaced by Rossini's *Barbiere,* and by a new opera, entitled *Aminta,* by a composer residing here, of the name of Antonio D'Antoni; the music is said to bespeak the hand of a master, and to abound with many original ideas.

PARMA.—The great attraction of the season has been Rossini's *Mosè,* which caused a great sensation here. The singers were every evening called upon the scene to receive the congratulations of the public. The talk of the place is the production of Mayerbeer's *Crociato.*

AREZZO—The principal singers at the theatre of this town are, *prima donna,* Adelaide Rinaldi; *musico,* Angelica Corri; *tenore,* Silvano Casini; *basso,* Paulli. *La Gazza Ladra* was the favourite of the season, in which Signora Corri pleased much.

MODENA.—The latest novelty given here was *La Capanna Moscovita,* by Cappaletti, and a new opera by Vicenzo Gabussi, of Bologna, which is said to have been received with great applause, and is spoken of in the journals as containing much new and original music.

REGGIO.—Principal singers, *prima donna,* Catherine Monticelli; a dilettanti tenorist; *bassi,* Michele Cavarra and Vincenzo Pozzi. The operas given were *Matilda Chabran,* and *Elisa e Claudio.*

PIACENZA.—*L'Ajo nell' imbarazzo* (the embarrassed Tutor), compressed into one act, by Il Conte Alberte Scribani, and newly set by Il Conte Daniele Nicelli, both natives of Piacenza, was received with great applause.

CREMONA.—Rossini's ever-pleasing *Barbiere* has been the great attraction of the season. The soprano singer, Signora Rosa Mariani, is the reigning favourite. She has appeared in several pieces of Mosca, Rossini, and Pacini.

CREMA.—The performances here have been a new opera by Signor Cella of Piacenza, entitled, *Il Servo Astuto,* which was favourably received; the other piece was Mecadante's *Elisa e Claudio,* which also pleased considerably.

PAVIA.—After Mercadante's *Elisa,* a piece new to these boards, was produced, composed by Signor Coccia at Lisbon, entitled, *La Festa della Rose,* in which the contralt', Giuditta Favini, performed with great success. The music of this opera is full of pleasing effects, particularly a buffo-terzetto.

BERGAMO.—The opera of the season has been Rossini's *Cenerentola,* which pleased.

BRESCIA and LODI.—The same company and performances as at Bergamo.

VICENZA.—*La Gazza Ladra* satisfied the good people of this place, who are not like some of their neighbours, greedy of novelty.

PARIS, Sept. 23d.—Meyerbeer's opera, *Il Crociato in Egitto,* was produced at the *Théatre Italien* yesterday. It has been about nine months in preparation, though it is said that it was got up in London in four or five weeks. Its success has been brilliant, but we must delay till to-morrow any detailed account of it.

AN ITALIAN OPERA AT NEW YORK.

AN agent of Mr. Price, the active and respectable manager of the Theatre at New York, has been in England, for the purpose of engaging a company of Italian Singers to perform operas in America. He has not been successful in procuring Italians to aid his enterprise, for he has only obtained the younger Crivelli, who took the minor parts at the King's Theatre last season, and a Signor Rosiche, who afforded great amusement for a night or two in 1824, and was in the list for 1825, at a salary of 50l., but never allowed to appear*. But Mr. Price has obtained the Spanish family of the Garcias, consisting of husband, wife, son, and daughter. How an opera is to be got up by such slender means we cannot guess, for though Madlle. Garcia is clever, she possesses a contr' alto voice, not a soprano, though the latter, of course, must be wanted; and the father is liable to such frequent rheums, that he cannot always be counted on: besides which he is no longer young. Madame Garcia, some years ago, in Paris, took the inferior parts, and once made an unsuccessful attempt in the same in London. The son has never appeared. But our trans-atlantic brethren have no experience in this kind of musical representation, and, therefore, will not perhaps be very nice. The sums said to be secured to these persons, are past belief, all circumstances considered. We have hitherto been the laughing-stocks of Europe, for the preposterous manner in which we pay foreign singers, but the ridicule will now be transferred to the Western continent, if the statements put forth—which we cannot credit—should actually prove true.

* Since writing the above, we hear that Signor Angrisani has been induced to join the troop. Madame Caradori declined a large offer; so did the young Signora Marinoni, and others.

THE
HARMONICON.

No. XXXV., November, 1825.

MEMOIR OF JEAN-PHILIPPE RAMEAU*.

JEAN-PHILIPPE RAMEAU, Composer to Louis XV., and Chevalier of the Order of St. Michel, was born at Dijon, 1683. He may be said to have inherited a talent for music, for his father manifested so strong a predilection for the art, that he commenced studying it as a profession after he had passed his thirtieth year, and became organist of the *Sainte-Chapelle* in the above city. He neglected nothing that could tend to inspire his children with a taste for his own favourite pursuit, and taught them to play even before they began to read. The subject of this memoir was the eldest son; he went early in life to Italy, and at his return was appointed organist at Clermont en Auvergne, were his *Traité de la Musique* was written in 1722. He was afterwards elected organist of St. Croix de la Bretonnerie at Paris. Here his time was chiefly employed in teaching; however he published harpsichord lessons and several other theoretical works without distinguishing himself much as a vocal composer till the year 1733, when, at fifty years of age he produced his opera of *Hippolite and Aricie†*. The music of this drama excited professional envy and national discord. Party rage was now as violent between the admirers of Lulli and Rameau, as in England between the friends of Bononcini and Handel, or, in modern times, at Paris, between the Gluckists and the Piccinists.

When the French, during the last century, were so contented with the music of Lulli, it was nearly as good as that of other countries, and better patronised and supported by the most splendid prince in Europe. But that people, so frequently accused of more volatility and caprice than their neighbours, have manifested a steady persevering constancy to their music, which the strongest ridicule and contempt of other nations could never vanquish.

Rameau only answered his antagonists by new productions, by his *Castor and Pollux*, *Dardanus*, and *Zoroaster*, which were still more successful; and at length, he was acknowledged by his countrymen to be not only superior to all competition at Paris, but sole monarch of the musical world. From 1733 to 1760 he composed twenty-one operas and ballets, besides other works, a list of which is subjoined to this memoir.

The successful revival of his opera of *Castor and Pollux* in 1754, after the victory obtained by his friends over the

Italian burletta singers, who had raised such disturbance by their performance of Pergolesi's intermezzo, the *Serva Padrona*, was regarded as the most glorious event of his life. The partisans for the national honour could never hear it often enough. "This beautiful opera," says M. de la Borde, "without any diminution in the applause or pleasure of the audience, supported a hundred representations, charming at once the soul, heart, mind, eyes, ears, and imagination of all Paris."

From this era to the time of his death in 1764, at eighty-four years of age, Rameau's glory was complete. The Royal Academy of Music, who all regarded themselves as his children, performed a solemn service in the church of the Oratory, at his funeral, and M. Philidor had a mass performed at the church of the Carmelites, in honour of a man whose talents he so much revered.

Rameau's style of composition, which continued in favour almost unmolested for upwards of forty years, though formed upon that of Lulli, is more rich in harmony and varied in melody. The *genre*, however displeasing to all ears but those of France, which had been nursed in it, was carried by the learning and genius of Rameau to its acme of perfection; and when that is achieved in any style, it becomes the business of subsequent composers to invent or adopt another, in which something is still left to be done, besides servile imitation.

After frequent perusals and consultations of Rameau's theoretical works, and a long acquaintance with the writings of his learned commentator D'Alembert, and panegyrists the Abbé Roussier, M. de la Borde, &c., if any one were to ask me, says Dr. Burney, to point out what was the *discovery* or *invention* upon which his system was founded, I should find it a difficult task.

The base to a common chord has been known ever since the first attempts at counterpoint; and it only seems as if Rameau had given new names to old and well-known combinations, when he calls the key-note with $\frac{5}{3}$, *Generateur*, *Basse-fondamentale*. But the Italians ever since the time of Zarlino have distinguished this lowest sound by calling it the *first base*, 1*mo. basso*; and the other parts of the chord when made the base, *basso rivoltato*, or 2*do. basso*. But Brossard in his *Musical Dictionary*, published 1702, in defining *Trias Harmonica*, or the three sounds of a common chord in its first state, calls the under-note *basse*, or *son fondamental*, and afterwards remarks that among the three sounds that compose the *Triade Harmonique*, the gravest is called *basis* or *sonus fundamentalis*. And what has Rameau told us more, except that the

* For the greater part of this memoir, we are indebted to Dr. Burney's History of Music.
† The Prince de Conti asked Campra, what he thought of this work? The composer replied; "There is enough music in it to make six operas."

harmonics produced by a string or pipe, which he does not pretend to have first discovered, are precisely the third and fifth in question. This is the practical principle of the fundamental base, the theory was surely known of harmonical, arithmetical, and geometrical proportion, and ratios of sound, with which so many books have been ostentatiously filled ever since the time of Boethius.

The Abbé Roussier, his most learned apostle and able champion, candidly confessed in his first work, that "the system of a *fundamental base* ought not to be regarded as one of those principles which precedes the consequence to be deduced from it." *Le mérite de cette découverte consiste, à avoir réduit en un systéme simple, commode, et facile à saisir, toutes les opérations des grands maîtres de l'harmonie.* Traité des Accords, 1764.

Rameau's system, as compressed and arranged by D'Alembert, is perhaps the shortest, clearest, and best digested, that is extant; and yet, from the geometric precision with which it has been drawn up by that able mathematician, many explanatory notes and examples are wanting to render Rameau's doctrine intelligible to musical students in the first stage of their application; and even after that, the work, to be be rendered a *complete theory* would require many additions of late discoveries and improvements, both in the theory and practice of Harmony.

About the year 1760, the system of a Fundamental Base, by Rameau, gave occasion to much discussion in Germany. By some it was adopted there, as well as in Italy, by others disputed. It seems, however, as if this system, ingenious as it is, were somewhat overrated by French theorists, who would persuade the world that all music not composed on Rameau's principles should be thrown into the flames. *Jusqu'à mon systeme,* says Rameau himself, and M. de la Borde says, that "Music, since the revival of arts, was abandoned to the ear, caprice, and conjecture of composers, and was equally in want of unerring rules in theory and practice, when Rameau appeared, and chaos was no more. He was at once Descartes and Newton, having been of as much use to music as both those great men to philosophy." But were Corelli, Geminiani, Handel, Bach, the Scarlattis, Leo, Caldara, Durante, Jomelli, Perez, &c, such incorrect harmonists as to merit annihilation because they never heard of Rameau or his system? Indeed, it may be further asked, what good music has been composed, even in France, in consequence of Rameau giving a new name to the base of a common chord, or chord of the seventh? The Italians still call the lowest sound of music in parts the base, whether fundamental or derivative; but do the French imagine that the great composers above mentioned, and the little composers who need not be mentioned, were ignorant whence every supposed base was derived? The great harmonists of the sixteenth century seldom used any other than fundamental bases. . And the fundamental base to the hexachords has always been the key-note, and the fifth above and fifth below, just as Rameau has given it in his theoretic tracts.

But though the several merits of this musician have been too much magnified by partisans and patriots in France, and too much depreciated by the abettors of other systems and other styles, as well as patriots of other countries, yet Rameau was a great man; nor can the professor of any art or science mount to the summit of fame, and be elected by his countrymen supreme dictator in his particular faculty, without a large portion of genius and abilities.

CATALOGUE OF THE WORKS OF RAMEAU.

THEORETICAL WORKS.

1. Traité de l'harmonie, réduite à ses principes naturels; 1772, in 4to.
2. Nouveau Système de Musique théorique; 1726, in 4to.
3. Génération harmonique, ou Traité de la Musique théorique et pratique; 1737, in 8vo.
4. Dissertation sur l'accompagnement; 1781, in 8vo.
5. Dissertation sur le principe de l'harmonie; 1752, in 8vo.
6. Nouvelles Réflections sur la démonstration du principe de l'harmonie; 1752, in 8vo.
7. Réponse à une lettre de M. Euler, 1752; in 8vo.
8. Observations sur notre instinct pour la musique; 1754, in 8vo.
9. Erreurs sur la musique dans l'Encyclopédie: 1755, in 8vo.
10. Code de musique pratique; 1760, in 4to.

MUSICAL WORKS.

1. Three books of pieces for the Harpsichord, 1706, 1721, 1726.
2. Hyppolyte et Aricie; opéra, 1733.
3. Les Indes Galantes; ballet, 1735.
4. Castor et Pollux; opéra, 1737.
5. Les Talens lyriques; ballet, 1739.
6. Harpsichord Concertos; about 1740.
7. Dardanus; opéra, 1743.
8. Les Fêtes de Polymnie; ballet, 1745.
9. Le Temple de la Gloire; ballet, 1745.
10. Les Intermedes de la Princesse de Navarre, Comedy; 1745.
11. Samson; opéra, not represented.
12. Pygmalion; opera in one act, 1747.
13. Les Fêtes de l'Hymen et de l'Amour; ballet, 1748.
14. Zaïs; ballet, 1748.
15. Naïs; ballet, 1749.
16. Platée; Comedy-ballet, 1749. ç
17. Zoroastre; opera, 1749.
18. Acante et Céphise; heroic pastoral, 1751.
19. La Guirlande; ballet, 1751.
20. Anacréon, ballet, 1754.
21. La Fête de Pamèlie; ballet, 1754.
22. Les Surprises de l'Amour; opera ballet, 1757.
23. Les Sybarites; ballet, 1759.
24. Les Paladins; Comédy-ballet, 1760.

HIS MAJESTY THE KING OF PRUSSIA AND SIGNOR SPONTINI.

Paris, September 18, 1825.

KINGS do not create men of genius as they distribute titles. They make Lords: a superior power makes great men; but it belongs to those whom society have invested with authority, to encourage talent, to incite by delicate favours those who by their genius throw a real glory round the throne. Such examples as the following are always pleasant to notice. The author of *La Vestale* and of *Ferdinand Cortez,* belongs to France as the first country that adopted his fine talents. He has just received a gold box, enriched with diamonds, from his Majesty the King of Prussia, adorned with his miniature, likewise encircled by brilliants; the whole is of exquisite workmanship, but the design is still more elegant than the execution is delicate and elaborate. This box was accompanied by a medal in gold, struck upon the marriage of his daughter, the Princess of the Low Countries, and also by a note, full of kindness. Several weeks afterwards the same composer received the letter already noticed in the German Journals, which we subjoin to the first. These historical facts are useful to preserve.

"You have added to the fame which your compositions have acquired, by your opera of *Alcidor*; and I join in the approbation testified by the public in so incontestible a manner. I add to the present, the medal in gold struck upon the occasion of

the marriage of Her Royal Highness of the Low Countries, my daughter; and also one other remembrancer, in permitting you to publish these expressions of my satisfaction, if you approve of it.
(Signed) "FREDERIC WILLIAM."
"*Potsdam, June 29,* 1825.

"The opera of *Alcidor* carries with it, as all your operas do, the stamp of original talent, and is as worthy of admiration as are the *Vestale, Cortez, Olympie,* and *Nurmahal.* I accept, with pleasure, the dedication of this opera, and am charmed and delighted thereby to afford a public testimony of the esteem in which I hold the composer, and of the real value I attach to the work. (Signed) "FREDERIC WILLIAM."
"*Berlin, August* 10, 1825."

It is not astonishing that so dazzling a distinction should have fixed the Author of *Vestale* in Prussia. The representations of *Nurmahal* and *Olympie* drew presents of equal value, and as honourable letters. This is truly rewarding the fine arts. It is this union of graciousness and munificence that induces talent to attach itself to courts, and to honour the power which thus renders homage to genius.

THE *MISERERE* OF ALLEGRI.

MUCH has been written, and more said, of the composition by Gregorio Allegri performed in the pontifical chapel during the passion-week: and while all admit that the effect produced by it is most imposing, few seem to be able to account for this in a satisfactory manner.

Andrea Adami,—who may have been a very good singer, but was a feeble writer,—tells us that "it is the wonder of our times, being conceived in such proportions as ravish the soul of the hearer." Upon which Sir. J. Hawkins observes, that this eulogium, hyperbolical as it is, does not equal in warmth of admiration the terms in which many express themselves on the subject; and adds, "that the burial-service of Purcell and Blow may well stand in competition with it." The learned historian might with truth and propriety have expressed his opinion more undisguisedly on the subject, and have said at once that the composition which he names very far surpasses the renowned work of the Italian contrapuntist. But he should not have forgotten Morley, Farrant, and other early harmonists of England, particularly Orlando Gibbons, whose works for the church shew the advanced state of musical genius in this country before the depression of it commenced, shortly after the restoration, by the injurious partiality for foreigners manifested by the French-hearted Charles.

That the effect of the celebrated *Miserere* depends mainly on the theatrical manner in which it is performed, there can be little doubt; though its harmony is pure, and, for the time in which it was written, not without a considerable share of ingenuity, and a peculiar kind of beauty.

Dr. Burney's account of this composition, in his Musical Tour in Italy, is drawn from authentic sources, and partly confirmed by his personal observation. He seems to have discovered the cause of the impression which it makes on its bearers; though he is rather reserved in his mode of explaining the nature and working of the machinery employed in giving action to it.

"Signor Santarelli favoured me with the following particulars relative to the famous *Miserere* of Allegri. This piece, which, for upwards of a hundred and fifty years, has been annually performed in passion-week at the Pope's chapel, on Wednesday and Good-Friday, and

which in appearance, is so simple as to make those, who have only seen it on paper, wonder whence its beauty and effect could arise, owes its reputation more to the manner in which it is performed, than to the composition; the same music is many times repeated to different words, and the singers have, by tradition, certain customs, expressions and graces of convention, which produce great effects; such as swelling and diminishing the sounds altogether; accelerating the measure at some particular words, and singing some entire verses quicker than others. Thus far Signor Santarelli.

"However, some of the greatest effects produced by this piece, may, perhaps, be justly attributed to the time, place, and solemnity of the ceremonials, used during the performance: the pope and conclave are all prostrated on the ground; the candles of the chapel, and the torches of the balustrade are extinguished one by one; and the last verse of this psalm is terminated by two choirs; the *Maestro di Capella* beating time slower and slower, and the singers diminishing or rather extinguishing the harmony, by little and little, to a perfect point*.

"This composition used to be held so sacred, that it was imagined excommunication would be the consequence of an attempt to transcribe it. Padre Martini told me that there were never more than three copies made by authority, one of which was for the Emperor Leopold, one for the late king of Portugal, and the other for himself: this last he permitted me to transcribe at Bologna, and Signor Santarelli favoured me with another copy from the archives of the pope's chapel. Upon collating these two copies, I find them to agree pretty exactly, except in the first verse. I have seen several spurious copies of this composition in the possession of different persons, in which the melody of the soprano or upper part, was tolerably correct, but the other parts differed very much; but this inclined me to suppose the upper part to have been written from memory, which, being so often repeated to different words in the performance, would not be difficult to do, and the other parts to have been made to it by some modern contrapuntist afterwards.

"The Emperor Leopold the First, not only a lover and patron of music, but a good composer himself, ordered his ambassador to Rome, to entreat the pope to permit him to have a copy of the celebrated *Miserere* of Allegri, for the use of the imperial chapel at Vienna: which being granted, a copy was made by the Signor Maestro of the pope's chapel, and sent to the emperor, who had then in his service some of the best singers of the age; but, notwithstanding the abilities of the performers, the composition was so far from answering the expectations of the emperor and his court, in the execution, that he concluded the pope's *Maestro di Capella,* in order to keep it a mystery, had put a trick upon him, and sent him another composition.

"Upon which, in great wrath, he sent an express to his holiness, with a complaint against the *Maestro di Capella,* which occasioned his immediate disgrace, and dismission from the service of the papal chapel; and in so great a degree was the pope offended at the supposed

---

* The original is written in *alla capella* time, two semibreves in each bar. We have subdivided the bars, for the convenience of those who are not accustomed to ancient church music. To such it will be necessary also to observe, that in this species of composition the notes are only half as long as in modern secular music. Paying strict attention to this, the above composition is to be performed *larghetto,* beating twice slowly in each bar.

imposition of his composer, that, for a long time, he would neither see him, nor hear his defence; however, at length, the poor man got one of the cardinals to plead his cause; and to acquaint his holiness that the style of singing in his chapel, particularly in performing the *Miserere*, was such as could not be expressed by notes, nor taught or transmitted to any other place, but by example; for which reason the piece in question, though faithfully transcribed, must fail in its effect, when performed elsewhere.

"His holiness did not understand music, and could hardly comprehend how the same notes should sound so differently in different places; however, he ordered his *Maestro di Capella* to write down his defence, in order to send it to Vienna, which was done: and the emperor, seeing no other way of gratifying his wishes with respect to this composition, begged of the pope, that some of the musicians in the service of his holiness might be sent to Vienna, to instruct those in the service of his chapel how to perform the *Miserere* of Allegri."

Mozart heard this composition twice, in 1769, and such was the impression left by it on his sensitive mind, that he noted it down from memory, in exact conformity to the original manuscript[*]. In 1771, Dr. Burney published a score of it, at Bremner's, of which very few copies were printed, and it is now become extremely rare. In 1810, M. Choron introduced it in his *Collection des Classiques*; and as the work, whatever may be its positive merit, must often have excited the curiosity of lovers of music, and cannot fail to prove interesting to all who seek general information, it is here inserted, but in a very contracted space; though every note is given, except the repetitions.

The *Miserere* is the 51st psalm, whence Allegri has selected part of the 1st verse, and the whole of the 2nd, 4th, 6th, 8th, 10th, 12th, 14th, 16th, 18th verses, and part of the 19th. These are all set to the music now printed; it follows therefore that each of the chants—if they may so be called—is sung five times over, except the last, which is performed but once; for the effect of this, if reiterated as the others, would be lost,—reason would resume its sway,—the illusion would vanish[†].

1ˢᵀ VERSE, 2 *Sopranos, Contratenor, Tenor, and Base.* The 4ᵀᴴ, 8ᵀᴴ, 12ᵀᴴ, and 16ᵀᴴ Verses are sung to the same.

---

* See HARMONICON, No. III., page 32, in Memoir of Mozart, for a circumstantial account of this.

† Adami's instructions are these:—" Averta pure il Signor Maestro che l'ultimo verso del salmo termina a due Cori, e però sarà la Battuta Adagio, per finirlo piano, smorzando a poco a poco l'armonia." *Osserò. per reg. il coro della cap. pont.* p.36.

2ᴺᴰ VERSE, 2 *Sopranos, Contratenor, and Base.* The 6ᵀᴴ, 10ᵀᴴ, 14ᵀᴴ, and 18ᵀᴴ Verses are sung to the same.

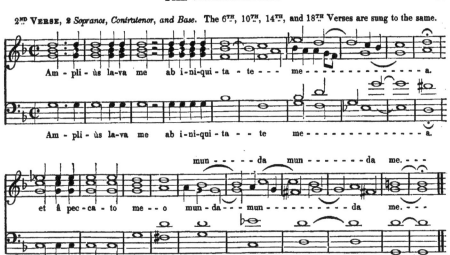

SECOND PART OF 19ᵀᴴ VERSE: two Choirs; the first consisting of 2 *Sopranos, Contratenor, Tenor, and Base;* the second of 2 *Sopranos, Contratenor, and Base.* To be sung *adagio, piano, e smorzando.*

The well-informed and entertaining author of *A Tour in Germany in the years* 1820, 1821, and 1822*, gives the following account of the mode of performing the *Miserere.* " Allegri's famed *Miserere*, as sung in the Sistine chapel

* Published in 1824, in 2 vols. 12mo., by Constable, Edinburgh.

at Rome, during Easter, justifies the belief that, for purposes of devotion, the unaided human voice is the most impressive of all instruments. If such a choir as that of his Holiness could always be commanded, the organ itself might be dispensed with. This, however, is no fair sample of the powers of vocal sacred music; and those who are most alive to the "concord of sweet sounds" forget that, in the mixture of feeling produced by a scene so imposing as the Sistine chapel presents on such an occasion, it is difficult to attribute to the music only its own share in the overwhelming effect. The Christian world is in mourning; the throne of the Pontiff, stripped of all its honours, and uncovered of its royal canopy, is degraded to the simple elbow-chair of an aged priest. The Pontiff himself, and the congregated dignitaries of the church, divested of all earthly pomp, kneel before the cross in the unostentatious garb of their religious orders. As evening sinks, and the tapers are extinguished one after another, at different stages of the service, the fading light falls ever dimmer and dimmer on the reverend figures. The prophets and saints of Michael Angelo look down from the ceiling on the pious worshippers beneath; while the living figures of his Last Judgment, in every variety of infernal suffering and celestial enjoyment, gradually vanish in the gathering shade, as if the scene of horror had closed for ever on the one, and the other had quitted the darkness of earth for a higher world. Is it wonderful that, in such circumstances, such music as that famed *Miserere*, sung by such a choir, should shake the soul even of a Calvinist."

The Reverend GREGORIO ALLEGRI, born at Rome*, was admitted into the pope's chapel 1629, as a contra-tenor. He studied under the famous Nanini, who was cotemporary with Palestrina, and his most intimate friend; both of whom had been fellow-students under Gaudimel, who instituted a music-school at Rome, which produced many eminent professors. Allegri was accounted an admirable master of harmony: many of his works are still preserved and performed in the pope's chapel, particularly the above *Miserere*. His vocal abilities were not great; yet so much was he esteemed by all the musical professors of his time, that the pope, in order to secure his services, appointed him one of the singers of his chapel. He joined to his extraordinary merit an excellent moral character, for he not only assisted the poor, by whom his door was usually crowded, but daily visited the prisons of Rome, in order to bestow his alms on distressed and deserving objects. "Of this," says the author from whom these particulars are extracted, "I was assured by one of the scholars of Allegri, a man of the greatest veracity, who is now (in 1711) alive." He set many parts of the church service with such divine simplicity and purity of harmony, that his loss was much felt, and sincerely lamented, by the whole college of singers in the papal service. He died in 1652, and was buried in the *Chiesa Nuova*, before the chapel of S. *Filippo Neri*, near the altar of the Annunciation, where there is a vault for the reception of deceased singers belonging to the pope's chapel; upon which is the following inscription:

CANTORES PONTIFICII,
NE QUOS VIVOS,
CONCORS MELODIA
JUNXIT:
MORTUOS CORPORIS,
DISCORS RESOLUTIO
DISSOLVERIT.
HIC UNA CONDI
VOLUERE.
ANNO 1640.

* He was a relation of the great painter, Correggio, whose family name was *Allegri*.

AN UNPUBLISHED LETTER OF MOZART.

Translated from the German original.

IN laying before the readers of the *Harmonicon* the subjoined letter of the great Mozart, I beg to observe, that I am indebted for this valuable communication to the kindness of Mr. Moscheles. The authenticity of this document being therefore fully established, and the letter itself bearing such strong internal evidence of its being Mozart's, there cannot remain the slightest doubt on the subject with any one, who has, like myself, had an opportunity of inspecting other letters of that composer. The original is without date, but a Vienna correspondent, through whom it was received, supposes that it was written from Prague in 1788. As to the translation, I have taken the utmost pains to preserve the spirit, and the good humour of the original, but, above all, to render it as faithful and as literal as the idiomatic difference of the two languages would admit.

J. R. S——z.

LETTER OF W. A. MOZART, TO THE BARON V——.

HEREWITH I return you, my good Baron, your scores, and if you perceive, that, in *my* hand, there are more *nota benes** than notes, you will find from the sequel of this letter, how that has happened. Your *symphony* has pleased me, on account of its ideas, more than the other pieces, and yet I think it will produce the least effect. It is much too crowded, and to hear it partially or piecemeal (*stückweise*,) would be, with your permission, like beholding an ant-hill; (*Ameisenhaufen*.) I mean to say that it is, as if Eppes the devil were in it. You must not snap your fingers at me, my dearest friend, for I would not for the world have spoken out so candidly, if I could have supposed it would give you offence. Nor need you wonder at this, for it is so with all composers, who, without having, from their infancy, as it were, been trained by the whip, and the curses (*Donnerwetter*) of the *maestro*, pretend to do every thing with natural talent alone. Some compose fairly enough, but with other people's ideas, not possessing any themselves; others, who have ideas of their own, do not understand how to treat and master them. This last is *your* case. Only do not be angry, pray! for Saint Cecilia's sake, not angry, that I break out so abruptly. But your song has a beautiful cantabile, and your dear Fränzl † ought to sing it very often to you; which I should like as much to see as to hear. The minuet in the quartett is also pleasing enough, particularly from the place I have marked. The coda, however, may well clatter or tinkle, but it never will produce *music*. *Sapienti sat*, and also to the *nihil sapienti*, by whom I mean myself. I am not very expert in writing on such subjects, I rather shew at once how it ought to be done.

You cannot imagine with what joy I read your letter. Only you ought not to have praised me so much. We

* In the original stands *fenster* (windows,) which signify passages marked ♯, for the sake of drawing the reader's attention particularly to them.
† Probably the Baron's daughter.

may get accustomed to the hearing of such things, but to read them is not quite so well. You good people make too much of me, I do not deserve it, nor my compositions either. And what shall I say to your present*, my dearest Baron? that came like a star in a dark night, or like a flower in winter, or like a cordial in sickness. God knows, how I am obliged at times to toil and labour, to gain a wretched livelihood, and Stänerl† too must get something. To him, who has told you, that I am growing idle, I request you sincerely (and a baron may well do such a thing) to give him a good box on the ear. How gladly would I work, and work, if it were only left to me to write always such music as I please, and as I can write; such, I mean to say, as I myself set some value upon. Thus I composed three weeks ago an orchestral symphony, and by to-morrow's post I write again to Hofmeister‡, to offer him three piano-forte quatuors, supposing that he is able to pay. O heavens! were I a wealthy man, I would say: "Mozart, compose what you please, and as well as you can; but till you can offer me something finished, you shall not get a single kreutzer§. I'll buy of you every manuscript, and you shall not be obliged to go about and offer it for sale like a hawker." Good God! how sad all this makes me, and then again how angry and savage, and it is in such a state of mind that I do things which ought not to be done. You see, my dear good friend, so it is, and not as stupid or vile wretches (Lumpen) may have told you. Let this, however, go a cassa del diavolo.

I now come to the most difficult part of your letter, which I would willingly pass over in silence, for here my pen denies me its service. Still I will try, even at the risk of being well laughed at. You say, you should like to know my way of composing, and what method I follow in writing works of some extent. I can really say no more upon this subject than the following; for I myself know no more about it, and cannot account for it. When I am, as it were, completely myself, entirely alone, and of good cheer; say travelling in a carriage, or walking after a good meal, or during the night, when I cannot sleep; it is on such occasions that my ideas flow best and most abundantly. Whence and how they come I know not, nor can I force them. Those ideas that please me, I retain in memory, and am accustomed, as I have been told, to hum them to myself ||. If I continue in this way, it soon occurs to me, how I may turn this or that morsel to account, so as to make a good dish of it, that is to say, agreeably to the rules of counter-point, to the peculiarities of the various instruments, &c. All this fires my soul, and provided I am not disturbed, my subject enlarges itself, becomes methodized and defined, and the whole, though it be long, stands almost finished and complete in my mind, so that I can survey it, like a fine picture or a beautiful statue, at a glance. Nor do I hear in my imagination the parts successively, but I hear them, as it were, all at once (gleich alles zusammen.) What a delight this is I cannot tell! All this inventing, this producing, takes place, as it were, in a pleasing lively dream. Still the actual hearing of the tout ensemble is

after all the best. What has been thus produced I do not easily forget, and this is, perhaps, the best gift I have my Divine Maker to thank for.

When I proceed to write down my ideas, I take out of the bag of my memory, if I may use that phrase, what has previously been collected into it, in the way I have mentioned. For this reason, the committing to paper is done quickly enough, for every thing is, as I said before, already finished; and it rarely differs on paper, from what it was in my imagination. At this occupation I can therefore suffer myself to be disturbed; for whatever may be going on around me, still I write, and even talk, but only of fowls and geese, or of Gretel* and Bärbel, or some such matters. But why my productions take from my hand that particular form and style which makes them Mozartish, and different from the works of other composers, is probably owing to the same cause which renders my nose so-or-so large, so aquiline, or, in short, makes it Mozart's, and different from those of other people. For I do really not study or aim at any originality; I should, in fact, not be able to describe in what mine consists, though I think it quite natural that persons who have really an individual appearance of their own, are also differently organized from others, both externally and internally. At least, I know that I have constituted myself neither one way nor the other.

May this suffice, and never, my best friend, never trouble me again with such subjects. I also beg you will not believe that I break off from any other reason, but because I have nothing further to say on that point. To others I should not have answered, but have thought: "Mutschi, buschi quille. Etche molape newing†!"

In Dresden I have not been eminently successful. The Dresden people fancy themselves to be even yet in possession of every thing that is good, merely because they had formerly to boast of a great deal. Two or three good souls excepted, the people here hardly knew any thing further about me, than that I had been playing at concerts, in Paris and London, in a child's cap. The Italian Opera I did not hear, the court being in the country for the summer season. Naumann‡ treated me in the church with one of his masses, which was beautiful, well harmonized, and in good keeping, though too much spread, and as your C—— would say, rather cold (e bieszle kühlig§.) It was somewhat like Hasse, but without his fire, and with a more modern cantilena. I played a great deal to these gentlemen, but I could not warm their hearts, and excepting Wischi waschi¶, they said nothing at all to me. They asked me to play on the organ, and they have most magnificent instruments. I told them, what is the real truth, that I had but little practice on the organ; notwithstanding I went with them to the church. Here now it shewed itself, that they had in petto another foreign artist, a professed organ-player, who was to kill me, if I may say so, by his playing (todt spielen). I did

---

* Some bottles of wine.
† The diminutive in the upper German dialect, for Constantia, the name of his wife.
‡ A music-seller at Leipzig.
§ A small Austrian coin of the value of a halfpenny.
|| Beethoven does exactly the same thing.—R. S.

* Gretel and Bärbel are again diminutives for Margarethe and Barbara.
† What language this is, or what it means, I am not in the least able to tell.—R. S.
‡ Maestro di Capella, like Hasse, at the Electoral Court of Saxony. Both are known, and even celebrated by their sacred and dramatic compositions.
§ This is in the Austrian idiom, instead of "ein Bischen kühl."
|| These are the very words of the original.

not immediately know him, and he played very well, but without much originality or imagination. I, therefore, aimed directly at this stranger, and exerted myself well. I concluded with a double fugue in the perfectly strict style, and played it very slowly, both that I might conduct it properly to the end, and that the hearers might be able to follow me through all the parts. Now, all was over. No one would play after this. Hässler, however (this was the stranger's name, who has written some good things in the style of the Hambro' Bach *), was the most good-natured and sincere of them all, though it was he whom I had endeavoured to punish. He jumped about with joy, and did not know how to express his delight. Afterwards he went with me to the hotel, and enjoyed himself at my table; but the other gentlemen *excused* themselves when I gave them a friendly invitation; upon which my jolly companion Hässler said nothing, but " *Tausend sapperment !*"

Here, my best friend and well-wisher, the pages are full, and the bottle of your wine, which has done the duty of this day, nearly empty. But since the letter which I wrote to my father-in-law, to request the hand of my present wife, I hardly ever have written such an enormously long one. Pray take nothing ill! In speaking, as in writing, I must shew myself as I am, or I must hold my tongue, and throw the pen aside. My last word shall be: "My dearest friend, keep me in kind remembrance !" Would to God I could, one day, be the cause of so much joy as you have been to me! Well! I drink to you in this glass: Long live, my good and faithful ——. Amen!

W. A. MOZART.

THE HAARLEM ORGAN.

In our two former numbers, were inserted extracts from the interesting account of the York Festival, in 1823, for the purpose of communicating to our readers a history of the origin and present state of that most noble of all musical instruments, the organ. The celebrated one at Haarlem is only cursorily noticed by the indefatigable writer whose labours have furnished us with those two instructive articles; and as it is an instrument more generally spoken of than any other, and, with perhaps one exception, is the largest and most powerful that ever was constructed, a circumstantial account of its component parts cannot but prove acceptable to those who give any attention to the pages of this work. We therefore extract from Dr. Burney's *Tour through the United Provinces*, the following particulars relative to this extraordinary and far-famed organ.

" There were few things that I was more eager to see, in the course of my journey, than this celebrated organ in the great church of this city. Indeed it is the *lion* of the place ; but to hear this lion roar, is attended with more expense than to hear all the lions and tigers in the tower of London. The fee of the *keeper*, or organist, is settled at half a guinea; and that of his assistant keeper, or bellows-blower, at half a crown. Expectation, when raised very high, is not only apt to surpass probability, but possibility. Whether imaginary greatness diminished the real, on this occasion, I know not, but I was somewhat disappointed upon hearing this instrument. In the first place, the person who plays it is not so great a performer as he imagines; and in the next, though the number of stops amounts to sixty, the variety they afford is by no means equal to what might be expected. As to the *vox humana*, which is so celebrated, it does not at all resemble a human voice, though a very good stop of the kind; but the world is very apt to be imposed upon by names; the instant a common hearer is told that an organist is playing upon a stop which resembles the human voice, he supposes it to be very fine, and never inquires into the propriety of the name, or exactness of the imitation. However, with respect to my own feelings, I must confess, that of all the stops I have yet heard, which have been honoured with the appellation of *vox humana*,. no one, in the treble part, has ever reminded me of any thing human, so much as the cracked voice of an old woman of ninety, or, in the lower parts, of Punch singing through a comb.

" As this organ is not only said to be the largest, but the best in Europe, that is in the world, I shall here insert a list of the stops it contains, with equivalent English names, to such as are used in England, and short explanations of the rest.

"*Catalogue of the stops in the great Organ at* HAARLEM, *built by* MULLER, 1738."

GREAT MANUAL †.

No.	Names.	Length.										English Names.
1.	*Prestant* - -	16 feet	-	-	-	-	-	-	-	-	-	Open double diapason
2.	*Bourdon* - -	16 ,,	-	-	-	-	-	-	-	-	-	Stopt ditto
3.	*Octave* - - -	8 ,,										Open diapason
4.	*Viol da Gamba*	8 ,,	A narrow pipe which imitates the whistling of the bow									Unison with ditto
5.	*Roer Fluit* -	8 ,,	With a funnel or small pipe upon the top -									Diapason, half stopt
6.	*Octave* - - -	4 ,,	-	-	-	-	-	-	-	-	-	Principal
7.	*Gem's-Hoorn* -	4 ,,	A kind of flute, the pipes narrow at the top									Unison with ditto
8.	*Roer-Quint* -	6 ,,										Twelfth half stopt
9.	*Quint* - - -	3 ,,	-	-	-	-	-	-	-	-	-	Fifth
10.	*Tertian* - -	2 ranks	-	-	-	-	-	-	-	-	-	Tierce, or 17th
11.	*Mixture* -	6, 8, and 10 ranks										Furniture, or mixture
12.	*Wood Fluit* -	2 feet	Stopt pipe, unison with the -									Fifteenth, or octave flute
13.	*Trumpet* - -	16 ,,										{ Double trumpet
14.	*Trumpet* - -	8 ,,	} Reed stops - - - - -								{ Trumpet
15.	*Trumpet* - -	4 ,,										{ Clarion
16.	*Hautbois* - -	8 ,,										{ Hautbois

---

* C. Ph. E. Bach, the second son of the great Sebastian Bach.   † Key-board, or row of keys.

UPPER MANUAL.

	Names.	Length.		English Names.
1.	*Prestant* - -	8 feet	- - - - - - -	Open diapason
2.	*Quintadeena* -	16 ,,	Breaks into a 5th, which predominates - -	Double diapason
3.	*Gem's-Hoorn* -	8 ,,	- - - - - - -	Unison with stopt diapason
4.	*Baar pyp* - -	8 ,,	A muffled pipe, used with the *vox humana* -	Bear pipe
5.	*Octave* - - -	4 ,,	- - - - - - -	Principal
6.	*Flag Fluit* - -	4 ,,	Derivation unknown - - - - -	Flute
7.	*Nassat* - - -	3 ,,	- - - - - - -	Stopt twelfth
8.	*Nagt-Hoorn* -	2 ,,	{ Night horn, but why so called, no reason can be given - - - - - - -	} Flute
9.	*Flageolet* - -	1½ ,,	- - - - - - -	Octave twelfth
10.	*Sesquialter* - -	2 ranks	Tuned octave and 12th to the diapason - -	Sesquialter
11.	*Cimbaal* - - -	3 ,,	- - - - - - -	Octave to mixture
12.	*Mixture* - - -	4 and 6 ranks	{ A series of eight notes repeated through the instrument - - - - - -	} Mixture
13.	*Schalmay* - -	8 ,,	Reed stop - - - - - -	Bagpipe
14.	*Dultian* - - -	8 ,,	A narrow delicate pipe, unison with diapason -	Dulciana
15.	*Vox humana* -	8 ,,	An imitation of the - - - -	Human voice

POSITIF, OR SMALL ORGAN,—*(Lowest set of Keys.)*

	Names.	Length.		English Names.
1.	*Prestant* - -	8 feet	- - - - - - -	Open diapason
2.	*Holfluit* - -	8 ,,	- - - - - - -	Diapason half stopt
3.	*Quintadeena* -	8 ,,	- - - - - - -	Ditto
4.	*Octave* - - -	4 ,,	- - - - - - -	Principal
5.	*Fluit* - - -	4 ,,	- - - - - - -	Flute
6.	*Speel Fluit* - -	3 ,,	- - - - - - -	Twelfth
7.	*Serquialter* -	2, 3, and 4 ranks		Fifteenth
8.	*Super-Octave* -	2 feet	- - - - - - -	Fifteenth
9.	*Scherp* - -	6, and 8 ranks	- - - - - - -	High mixture
10.	*Cornet* - -	4 ,,		
11.	*Cimbaal* - -	3 ,,	- - - - - - -	Octave mixture
12.	*Fagotte* - -	16 feet	- - - - - - -	Double bassoon
13.	*Trumpet* - -	8 ,,		
14.	*Regaal* - - -	8 ,,	{ Formerly a portable organ, used in processions, was called a *regal;* the stop in this organ is entirely of reeds - - - - -	} Regal

PEDALS·

No.	Names.	Length.		English Names.
1.	*Principal* - -	32 feet	- - - - - - -	Octave below the double diapason
2.	*Prestant* - -	16 ,,	- - - - - - -	Double diapason open
3.	*Subbas* - - -	16 ,,	- - - - - - -	Ditto stopt
4.	*Roer-Quint* -	12 ,,	- - - - - - -	Fourth below the diapason stopt
5.	*Holfluit* - -	8 ,,	- - - - - - -	Diapason half stopt
6.	*Octave* - - -	8 ,,	- - - - - - -	Open diapason
7.	*Quint-prestant* -	6 ,,	- - - - - - -	Fifth
8.	*Octave* - - -	4 ,,	- - - - - - -	Principal
9.	*Ruish-Quint* -	3 ,,	- - - - - - -	Twelfth
10.	*Holfluit* - -	2 ,,	- - - - - - -	Fifteenth
11.	*Bazuin* - - -	32 ,,	By the Germans called *Posaune;* a reed stop -	Double sackbut *
12.	*Bazuin* - - -	16 ,,	- - - - - - -	Sackbut
13.	*Trumpet* - -	8 ,,	- - - - - - -	Trumpet
14.	*Trumpet* - -	4 ,,	- - - - - - -	Clarion
15.	*Cink* - - - -	2 ,,	A cornet, horn, or shawm - - -	Octave clarion

" This organ has sixty stops, two tremulants, two couplings, or springs of communication, four separations or valves to close the wind-chest of a whole set of keys, in case of a *cipher,* twelve pair of bellows, and 5300 pipes.

" Upon the whole, it is a noble instrument, though I think that of the new church at Hamburgh is larger, and that of the old kirk at Amsterdam better toned; but all these enormous machines seem loaded with useless stops, or such as only contribute to augment noise, and stiffen the touch."

---

* The word *sackbut* is now superseded by that of *trombone.*

THE LATE YORKSHIRE MUSICAL FESTIVAL.

To the EDITOR *of the Harmonicon.*

SIR,—In common with all who were present at the York Festival, I was too much gratified with it, as a whole, to indulge any thing like a desire to pick out blemishes. Still it is desirable that such an undertaking should be as perfect as possible, and that those defects (at least as they struck me) should on a future occasion be obviated.

I would recommend the conductor another time to inform every principal singer of the whole of his duty each morning and evening. Had this been the case, Mr. Sapio would have prepared himself for " O thou bright Orb," and for the trio in *Creation*, " The Lord is great," neither of which he sang. Madame Caradori would not have absented herself from the performance of the *Messiah*, believing that she had nothing to sing ; nor would such constant reference to the conductor have been necessary to ascertain who were to perform certain songs, trios, &c., just before their commencement. The conductor, if he neglect so obviously necessary a part of his duty, cannot blame any one but himself should those unpleasant omissions take place, which you have so properly reprehended in your very just and full account of the York Festival. And it is rather too much to expect Miss Stephens, who with every respect for Madame Caradori's talent, is in no respect her inferior as an oratorio singer, to become the mere stop-gap for that lady, or for Mr. Vaughan to volunteer to supply Mr. Sapio's want of ability to sing " O thou bright Orb."

Public singers, Sir, are very well aware how liable their conduct is to misrepresentation from the press, and, had Mr. Vaughan sung the air, Messieurs the Reporters, in the plenitude of their wisdom, would doubtless have indulged in some very shrewd remarks on the reasons, (for they know every thing, and the reason for every thing,) why Mr. Vaughan had been allowed very *unfairly* and *improperly* to *deprive* Mr. Sapio of his song !

Let me here remark on the extreme modesty, as well as superior information, of these individuals. . I happened to take up a Leeds paper—*The Intelligencer*, I think it is called,—wherein are detailed all the particulars of a conversation between some members of the York committee, and the reporter for that paper, in which the reporter claimed, and accompanied his claim with the most insolent threats, tickets of admission to all the performances. This request does not appear to have been complied with by the committee, whereat the gentleman prints the conversation, I suppose " to shame the rogues." Now, Sir, just see what this demand would have drawn from the charity, had it been complied with. There are fifteen papers published in Yorkshire, and there are fourteen London daily papers, every one of which, (to say nothing of the other London papers, or those published in the counties adjoining Yorkshire,) had an equal claim with this Leeds paragraph writer. There were seven performances, without reckoning the balls, so that the committee would have had to distribute among this fraternity 203 tickets, or in other words to have deprived the charities of 152*l.* 5*s.* And for what ? Why, that these gentry might edify the public with their blunders and nonsense. I read, for instance this Leeds man's account of the festival, and it was just what might be expected from one who knew nothing whatever

of the subject on which he wrote. A more wretched, trashy, silly composition never was put upon paper. Only think of a ....., ..., ...,* exercising his critical powers upon the works of Handel and Mozart, and sitting in judgment upon Stephens, Vaughan, and Braham ; and think of the incomparable assurance of such a person's asking to be paid by a free admission for so exercising his vocation ! If indeed men competent to the office of critics were employed by the newspaper proprietors, there might be some reason for their request, but we have only to look at their reports in order to be satisfied that this is not the case.

Your remarks on the engagements of some of the performers are strictly just. Is it possible that the sums stated in the newspapers as their respective amounts can be true ? If so there *must* have been some influence at work, of which the managers ought to be ashamed, and to which they ought not to have submitted. In what respect was Madlle. Garcia Miss Stephens's superior ? I happened to hear her rehearse " Rejoice greatly," and I never heard it so badly sung. She went through it twice, and the second time was worse than the first. Hardly a bar in either time or tune from the beginning to the end. How ill-judged, again, was it to allow her to introduce " Gratias agimus," in the very midst of the selection from *Israel in Egypt.* To have introduced a scene from *Mother Goose* into *Hamlet* would not have been more absurd. We had plenty of introductions that morning, by which the performance was foolishly lengthened till half-past five o'clock. But there was one from which we were happily delivered, viz., a composition of Mr. Cutler's, which Mr. Braham would have favoured us with. Future historians of the York Festival will not be able to record that the Friday morning's selection was from the works of Handel, Mozart, Graun, Croft, and CUTLER ! Nothing certainly was more inexplicable to mere auditors than that Miss Wilkinson should be paid 20*l.* for singing " O thou that tellest," and " Return, O God of Hosts," while Mr. W. Knyvett was sitting in the orchestra. This lady must abate most exceedingly in her terms, or she will attend but few more music meetings I apprehend.

Miss Goodall's song, " The Advent of the Messiah," was utterly unworthy of her powers, and still more unworthy of a place at the York Festival. Vulgar, noisy, commonplace, and of course wholly unlike what a song with such a title ought to have been. I entirely agree with your opinion of this lady's singing " If God be for us." I never heard its beauties so well developed. Mr. Bochsa is quite out of his depth in oratorio music.†.

In the performance of the *Creation* there was constant confusion among the principal singers, from their not having all the same translations of the words. There were three different sets of words in the orchestra at one time. It is much to be regretted that the original translation was not adhered to. In some respects it is faulty, but the ear had got reconciled to now and then an awkward expression, and the new edition is very far from being always an improvement. Why, for instance, is " achieved" altered to so vile a singing word as " accomplished ?"

In the Friday morning's selection, the chorus of " To

---

* We must leave the reader to conjecture what language our correspondent employs in this part of his letter. ED.

† And though he sank, he could not be said to *drown.* Perhaps the old proverb saved him. ED.

the Cherubim," suffered very much from not being done in connexion with the movement which immediately precedes it. There was not time enough to perform the connecting movements between them, though there was time enough to introduce two songs, the singing of which took about four times as long. But the whole of the *Dettingen Te Deum* should have been performed. Perhaps there is hardly a composition existing more worthy the employment of such a band. The *Dead March* was solemn and affecting in the highest degree. It is impossible to feel all that Handel intended, without hearing it played by such a band. It would, however, have been still more effective, had it been introduced in the selection from *Samson*, and preceded by the recitative "The body comes."

The remark of your correspondent CLIO is perfectly just, that the choruses would produce a more powerful effect, if the singers all faced the audience; but I doubt the possibility of constructing an orchestra which should bring such an army of chorus-singers into that situation, without completely burying the organ, and driving the instrumental band too high into the tower. The size of the pillars drew a complete screen before that part of the choral band which was in the side aisles, and rendered them comparatively inaudible to a majority of the company.

Dr. Camidge deserves much credit for the pains he took in getting up for this festival some pieces which have been scarcely, if at all, heard in this kingdom; and where so much was done, it is perhaps hardly fair to expect more. But it is much to be regretted that the *Masses*, both of Haydn and Mozart, should not have been heard at such a festival.

A great part of Mozart's No. 7, of Novello's arrangement, was performed at the Norwich Festival, and formed a very splendid feature in the bill. Great pains had evidently been taken in the preparation of it, and it was sung with as much precision as any of Handel's choruses. Now this is a sort of rivalry which one would be glad to see existing between the managers of the three great meetings. Let them each endeavour to bring into notice those great works of the foreign masters, which are now known only to the classical harmonists. There is an abundant field open for them, if they have but knowledge and perseverance enough to enter upon it.

Having thrown out these hints for the consideration of those to whom they may be of use, I cannot conclude without expressing both my admiration and my thanks to those individuals who had the public spirit to plan, and the perseverance to carry through, such an undertaking. The difficulties and discouragements which they had to overcome seem only to have roused them to fresh exertions, and the triumphant success with which their labours were crowned, must have been a most noble reward. They have raised the character of England as a musical nation. That England is a musical nation is no longer a matter of dispute. If we are asked for proof, we can point to the York Festival, and say "read it there." Read it in the mighty and excellent band there assembled—in the admirable selection of music—in the crowds who daily thronged to witness such a splendid concentration of talent—in the unexampled success of an undertaking—itself unexampled. I am, Sir,

Your obedient Servant,
A HEARER.

London, October 15, 1825.

ADDENDA TO THE ACCOUNT OF THE YORK FESTIVAL, 1825.

THE concert-room newly erected at York, and described in our last, has been made the subject of some animadversions, not altogether unfounded. The steps of the orchestra are undoubtedly most unnecessarily and dangerously high, and must be altered, even if the room be not enlarged. With regard to what has been said as to the light being wholly derived from the roof, and to the squareness of the room, it must be observed, that those arrangements were a matter of necessity, from the ground obtained being no more than was to be entirely occupied by the building; except a projecting portion, by which a separate access was obtained to the orchestra from the street. The purchase of a tenement, as laid down in the plan given in the account of the Festival of 1823, now lying before us, would enable the committee to extend the building some twenty feet or so, at the same time that the orchestra might be remodelled; and thus to improve the proportions of the room, by making it about 115 feet by 60, and to accommodate 3000 persons, as was originally intended. We have been given to understand, that such an alteration is at present in contemplation, along with the provision of retiring rooms, &c. Could one uniform front be given to the whole pile of buildings, from the assembly-room in Blake-street to the concert-room in Lendal-street, the effect would be exceedingly striking.

On the Tuesday after the Festival, a meeting of the Committee of Management was held, at which it was unanimously resolved: "That it is gratifying to this Committee to receive from his Grace the Archbishop, as President of the late Festival, the assurance of his Grace's approbation, and his congratulations on the splendid success of the arrangements which were adopted on the occasion." Separate votes of thanks were also unanimously passed—to the Rev. W. H. Dixon, the Chairman of the Committee, for his able, zealous, and indefatigable exertions, and his conciliatory, unassuming, and independent conduct—to the Lord Mayor, (W. Oldfield, Esq.) for the use of the Guildhall—to the Magistrates for their attention to the police—to the Directors of the Assembly Rooms for allowing a communication with the Concert Room—to the Stewards—the Auxiliary Committee—the Managers of the Balls—and to Mr. Jonathan Gray and Mr. Robert Davies, the Honorary Secretaries, for their respective exertions and attention—to Mr. Wolstenholme for his gratuitous trouble in keeping a register of lodgings; and to Mr. Noke for the use of his room near the Minster. Lastly, it was resolved, "That this Committee do continue in existence no longer than may be necessary for bringing to a conclusion the concerns of the late Festival."

These proceedings strongly mark the interest taken by all classes in the festival. With respect to the period at which another may be expected, although it must always depend, as was officially intimated from the first, upon the pleasure of the Dean and Chapter at the time, yet the present dean, Dr. Cockburn, is stated, in the York papers, to have expressed his approval of an interval of *three* years, keeping clear of the Birmingham meeting in 1829, and leading the public to expect the *third* Yorkshire Festival in 1828.

To the Editor of the HARMONICON.

SIR,—A report having been propagated, that the Committee of the York Musical Festival made an application to Signor Velluti

2 I 2

to sing at those performances, I shall be glad if you will contradict it in your next number, as your work has given us so good and ample an account of the meeting. You may assure your readers that, whatever may be the feeling of London managers on the subject, the thought of engaging that singer never was seriously entertained by any one who was entrusted with the ordering of our Festival. I am, &c.,

Oct. 13th, 1825.   ONE OF THE PATRONIZERS.

Owing to the shortness of time between the Yorkshire Festival and the day of our publication, some errors unavoidably crept into our account of that meeting; which, without being too minute, we are desirous of correcting, in order to render the statements in our pages worthy of future reference.

Page
175, *for* Allison, *read* Atkinson.
—— *for* 85 feet, *read* 95.
—— *for* 484 persons, *read* 734.
177, *for* Military Concerto, *read* Duet, Flute and Harp.
—— *for* Scotch ballad, *read* Song " Lo, here the gentle lark."—
                                                          Bishop.
178, line 24, *for* Madame Caradori, *read* Miss Stephens.
180, *for* Mr., *read* Mrs. Sheridan.
—— *for* Recit. and Air, Mlle. Garcia, *read* Miss Goodall.
—— *for* Trio, Miss Goodall, *read* Miss Travis.
181, In " Ah taci," *for* Sig. De Begnis, *read* Mr. Phillips.
—— *for* Duetto, Flute and Harp, *read* Harp and Horn, Messrs.
                                                  Bochsa and Platt.
—— *for* Duetto ; " Fiero," *read* " Ravvisa qual alma," (*Il Crociato in Egitto,*) Meyerbeer.
182, *for* Decanis, *read* Decani.
184, dele *di* in the autograph of Mozart.
—— *for* eight, *read* seven thousand persons.
Passim, *for* Cosi fan tutti, *read* tutte.
Sheet 3 O, p. 229, (Music) title of National Hymn, in last line of the first stanza, *for* the, *read* thy ; and *for* the, *read* our, as in page 233.

The necessity for some of the above corrections, has arisen from the circumstance of our printer having set up the programme of the performances from copies which did not contain the latest arrangements ; the differences between which, and the books of the words forwarded with our correspondents remarks, escaped our notice until too late. What other variations exist, are sufficiently explained in the course of our observations.

HEREFORD MUSIC MEETING.

THE one hundred and second meeting of the three choirs of Hereford, Worcester, and Gloucester, for the benefit of the widows and orphans of clergymen of the three dioceses, took place on Tuesday, Wednesday, and Thursday, September 16th, 17th, and 18th. The principal performers were

Miss Stephens,	Mr. W. Knyvett,
Miss Paton,	Dr. Chard,
Miss Travis,	Mr. Bellamy, and
Mr. Vaughan,	Signor De Begnis.

Mr. F. Cramer led the band, and the whole was conducted by Dr. Clarke Whitfield, organist of the cathedral.

At an early hour on Tuesday, the doors of the cathedral were besieged by an anxious multitude. The choir was thronged by nearly a thousand auditors, and great numbers were obliged to leave the church, unable to find places. The sermon was preached by Dr. Carr, bishop of Chichester, who delivered a very appropriate and elegant discourse. The music performed during the service consisted of the overture to *Saul*, the Dettingen *Te Deum*, Dr. Boyce's anthem " Here shall soft charity

repair," and the *Coronation anthem*. Mr. Vaughan, unfortunately, could not attend, on account of illness, but the parts assigned to him were obligingly taken by Mr. Bellamy. The collection at the doors, for the charity, amounted to 265l., being 94l. more than was taken on the first day of the meeting in 1822. In the evening, the concert at the spacious and elegant Shire-hall was fashionably, though not numerously, attended. Dr. Clarke Whitfield made an apology for the absence of Mr. Vaughan.

On Wednesday morning the *Messiah* drew a most respectable audience. Dr. Chard opened the oratorio, instead of Mr. Vaughan, whose indisposition still continued. Miss Stephens, Miss Travis, and Mr. Bellamy, distinguished themselves as usual ; but the privation of the tenor was much felt. On Wednesday evening, the concert-room exhibited a brilliant and animated scene : nearly 700 persons, including almost all the principal families of the county, and many distinguished strangers, were present. Amongst the pieces performed, was a new symphony, composed by Dr. C. Whitfield, which was warmly applauded. Miss Stephens and Mr. Bellamy were very successful in their songs ; and Miss Paton and Signor De Begnis were encored in " La ci darem," from *Don Giovanni*.

On Thursday, the company attending the cathedral was nearly as numerous as on the preceding morning. The performances were opened by the overture to the *Crucifixion*, an oratorio by Dr. Whitfield, which was followed by an *Offertorio*, the composition of Dr. Chard, of Winchester, both of which were greatly admired. Of the *Resurrection*, also the production of Dr. Whitfield, which succeeded, we were happy to hear expressions of unqualified approbation, from both the performers and the audience.

A selection from *Samson* formed the second part of the performance. Mr. Vaughan took his place this morning, though evidently suffering under severe indisposition : but he sang " Total eclipse !" in his most finished manner.

In the evening, the Shire-hall was, as on the previous night, crowded with beauty and elegance. The performances commenced with a scena, from the *Freischütz ;* the overture was loudly encored ; and Mr. Vaughan, who was greeted on his appearance with a welcome of applause, sang " Oh ! I can bear my fate no longer," with all the effect which his rich voice is so capable of giving to it. The *Huntsman's* chorus was encored. Instead of a concertante by Messrs. Lindley, Miss Cann, a highly-talented girl, of twelve years of age, the daughter of Mr. John Cann, of Hereford, played Drouet's variations to " God save the king," on the flute ; and her performance excited astonishment and admiration, both in the room and in the orchestra. We were pleased to see the leader, Cramer, nodding mute approbation ; and Lindley, leaning upon his silent violoncello, smiling as the rapidly-executed notes struck on his ear. She concluded amidst a thunder of applause.

The collection at the doors, for the charity, amounted to 910l. 1s. 6d., being very considerably more than has ever been collected, in any of the choirs, since the commencement of the triennial meetings, with the single exception of Worcester, at the time of the king's visit. The sums collected each morning were as follows : first day, 265l. ; second day, 240l. ; third day, 398l. 6s. ; added since, 6l. 15s. 6d. ; total, 910l. 1s. 6d. The amount of tickets sold was 1269l. 19s. 6d., making the total receipts 2180l. 1s.

REVIEW OF MUSIC.

1. FOREIGN MELODIES, *the* words *by* HARRY STOE VAN DYK; *the* symphonies *and* accompaniments *by* T. A. RAWLINGS. (Goulding, D'Almaine, and Co., 20, *Soho Square.*)

2. *Selection of* FRENCH MELODIES, *with* symphonies *and* accompaniments *by* W. EAVESTAFF; *the* words *by* W. H. BELLAMY, ESQ. *Book* 2d. (Eavestaff, 66, *Great Russell Street, Bloomsbury.*)

NOTWITHSTANDING the almost numberless mutations of which the seven sounds, their semitones and various lengths, are capable, melody seems nearly exhausted; or else the art of producing it in any unknown form is, at present, in a dormant state. Foreign airs, therefore, though not very recently composed, with English words united to them, and decked out in fresh accompaniments, carry an appearance of novelty, and satisfy the cravings of those who are continually asking for *something new.* Such publications then as these now before us, answer a temporary purpose at least, and sometimes make the public acquainted with melodies worth knowing, that otherwise might never have come under their observation. The joint work of Mr. Van Dyk and Mr. Rawlings comprises twelve airs; three of them also harmonized, for two sopranos and a base, and one with a short chorus of four voices. The first, *à la polonaise,* is a pretty French melody. The second is Tyrolese, tasty but not uncommon. The third is said to be Portugueze; but, in reality, Sarti's beautiful cavatina, " *Lungi dal caro bene,*" is the parent of it. The fourth is German, a mere waltz. The fifth Mexican!—in fact, Spanish, and a slight alteration of the Cachucha. The sixth is also from the country of romance. The copper-plate engraving to this is well designed, and being printed on a paper tinged with green, produces an evening hue exactly suited to lovers and to serenading. The seventh is called Portugueze. The eight and ninth are expressive German melodies: the former is indebted to Braham's " Beautiful maid," and the latter is attributed to the Portugueze. The tenth, Italian, reminds us of " Life let us cherish." The eleventh—Portugueze again—is very common; and the twelfth is another Spanish air—something like the Cachucha also, but in common time—with a very *John-Bullical* chorus.

The accompaniments to these are ably set, free from affectation, and with the sole intention of aiding the melodies. We do not perceive a single error of accentuation in the whole of the volume. The harmonized airs are not much calculated for effect, and in no way augment the value of the work, though they add very considerably to its bulk. We observe twice in this volume the word *scherzo* used, instead of *scherzoso,* or—to be still more correct—*scherzosamente.* The substantive must not be thus employed; the adjective may, but the adverb is the most grammatical. The work is well brought out, in the form and manner of *Moore's Irish Melodies.*

The *Selection of French Melodies* is the second number of the work mentioned in our review for last April. The present contains three airs, one of them also harmonized

for three voices. Much as we approved the first number, we still more admire the second, which will further corroborate the opinion that we have often ventured to give on the subject of French melody. The second of these is a tune popular all over Europe, and has put into motion the feet of every modern votary of Terpsichore. The symphony to this is admirable as a composition, though far from appropriate to the air; but the word " loneliness" is too drawling. We know, however, by experience, how impossible sometimes it is to adapt words to melodies already written, with the accuracy that is to be wished.

TWENTY-FOUR GRAND STUDIES, *for the* PIANO-FORTE, *in the Major and Minor Keys, Composed and Fingered by* HENRY HERTZ. *Book* 1. (Cocks and Co., 20, *Princes Street, Hanover Square.*)

THE readers of the Harmonicon have often met with the name of this composer in its foreign reports: he is still a youth, and has been performing in most parts of Germany, as well as in Paris, as a prodigy. We opened the present book expecting to see nothing except dull passages of mechanical execution, but have been agreeably surprised at finding an abundance of invention, and as much expression as the nature of the design would admit. That these studies are almost unboundedly and purposely difficult, we admit; we likewise grant that the author has carried this point a great deal too far, injuriously to himself, with respect to the sale of his work: but we consider it as a collection of severe exercises for the practice of a few first-rate performers, not as pieces intended for society, or for individual amusement; and therefore make allowance for what, in any other case, we should at once designate as downright and wanton absurdities. They are quite novel in style, and will enable those who are strangers to the present taste of the ultra-fashionables at Vienna, to become acquainted with the kind of music that is cultivated in the capital of Austria, by a small number of persons who wholly mistake, and thoroughly defeat, the true object of the art. These introduce such compositions as we allude to into the drawing-room, instead of confining them to the solitary closet, or at the most, of now and then producing them to a few curious people, to near relations, or intimate friends, and with the caution that a well-bred private gentleman would observe in exhibiting feats of strength, or of manual dexterity.——We recommend this publication, therefore, to professors, and to such amateurs as rival, in amount, or sometimes go beyond, professors in practical skill: but we exhort all those persons to view them as downright tasks, as no more calculated for amusement than the diophantine problem, or a dissertation on the digamma. It will be seen at once, from what has been said, how much M. Hertz's Studies differ from Mr. Cramer's delightful as well as improving Exercises: but to the latter, the present publication will make a good appendix; not however to be opened till a thorough mastery has been gained over the other unrivalled work.

We would willingly give a specimen of these compositions, but the nature of the music precludes the possibility of this, beyond the annexed fragments; which will only convey an imperfect idea of the whole.

The third study begins thus:

The commencement of the 8th is as follows:

The following excellent passage is in the eleventh, page 21:

The title-page tells us, that Mr. Moscheles has revised this edition, and arranged the passages for the additional keys, so that they may be performed on instruments that only go up to C.

The work is well published, at the reasonable price of one crown for twenty-two pages.

A compendious MUSICAL GRAMMAR, *in which the Theory of Music is completely developed, in a series of Familiar Dialogues, written by* BONIFACIO ASIOLI, *Director of the Royal Conservatorio at Milan. Translated, with considerable additions and improvements, by* J. JOUSSE, *Professor of Music.* (Cramer, Addison, and Beale, 201, *Regent Street.*)

MANY years ago, Bonifazio Asioli published his *Principj Elementari di Musica*, compiled for the use of the Conservatory, of which he had the direction. He was a good musician, though his compositions are light, and not formed of lasting materials. He was also a sensible man, therefore better qualified for the duties of a master than many who possess the higher gift of a genius for invention. The title of his work is simple, short, and in the very words that we have given; hence he is not responsible for that which has been fabricated for him in London: he was too wise a man to suppose that " the theory of music" could be " completely developed" in so small a compass, and too modest to be guilty of such vain boasting, even if he had thought what the English title expresses. Moreover, he never meant to enter at all into the theory—properly so called—in a publication intended to teach the *elementary principles of music* to mere beginners. Thus much we say in vindication of a meritorious artist, who might otherwise appear to have been one of those conceited persons whose auto-eulogy should have been written only in chalk on a brick wall.

The title of M. Jousse's publication would lead most people to conclude that it is translated immediately from the Italian. But in the year 1819, Signor Asioli's *Principj* appeared at Lyons, in a French garb, as a *Grammaire Musicale*, and from this, we shrewdly suspect, the present volume is derived; for the preface, as well as the " additions," are, nearly the same in both; though we must do the Lyons editor the justice to say, that he has introduced no bombast in the title-page.

In the translator's preface he says,

" The theory of the musical art, being chiefly studied by young people, should be written with clearness and precision. The present grammar is divested of all obscure and abstruse definitions."

This is an excellent maxim, and by way of exemplification, we have, page 63, the following question and answer.

" Q. Is there any particular denomination given to these sounds ?—[*i. e.* c sharp and D flat.]

" A. Yes; they are called *homologous.*"

Homologous !—Many will doubt whether so very Greek a term can be made to appear clear to young people of seven or eight years. *Omologo* is not uncommon with Italian writers, but extremely rare in English ones: we never met with it out of the dictionaries, and hope that M. Jousse will retain the undisturbed monopoly of it in his own hands.

In the preface also we learn, that the translator " has occasionally inserted useful and important observations on the text." Amongst these is doubtless to be enumerated the remark in a note, page 50—" the Italian words *al segno,* at the sign, are sometimes written where a repeat is intended."—Thus it is that M. Jousse translates one of the commonest expressions used in music: *Da capo al segno*—(*again, or, from the beginning, to the sign*)—is a phrase continually occurring ; but the performer who construes the dative *al* by the words *at the,* will always misunderstand the composer, and find himself in a state of constant perplexity.

In a chapter which is M. Jousse's own, we are told, that " the principal means of obtaining expression are accent, emphasis, the modification of sound, the legato and staccato." What then, are not accent, emphasis, legato, and staccato, modes of sound ?

As a specimen of the editor's " precision," we offer the following note, page 36. " When a series of triplets occurs, the time changes from simple to compound ; ⁴₄ becomes ⁶₈, and ³₄, ⁹₈." Now this is a complete sophism, which can only puzzle and mislead a learner ; for if the time changes from ³₄ to ⁹₈, the notes—quavers for instance—are, by the definition, no longer triplets : if the notes still remain triplets, the time is unchanged, although the figures ⁹₈ may be written.

The sixteenth lesson, on transposition, added by the Lyons editor, and translated by the present, is founded on an erroneous assumption. To transpose is to change the key, a difficult process, which can only be executed systematically, and with any degree of certainty, by means of a supposed clef. (This rule applies to performers, not to copyists.) To imagine all the notes on other lines and spaces, in order to get rid of a troublesome clef, is not transposition, for in this case the sounds are unaltered ; it is a mere supposition. In real

transposition, we must also observe, it is not enough to place " after the clef the sharps and flats which belong to the new key," and to play or write " the music higher or lower, according to the new key ;" but the rule, a most important one, must be known for the management of the accidental sharps, flats and naturals, for want of which, whoever attempts to transpose by the directions in this grammar, will produce a hideous confusion of sounds.

In all didactic works, definition ought to be a primary consideration. The terms employed in music are chiefly Italian, the language in which Signor Asioli wrote his *Principj* ; it was not therefore incumbent on him to explain them beyond their technical meaning. But to the English student a literal translation of all such words, in addition to their signification as terms of art, would have been a vast improvement of the book.

---

1. CAPRICCIO *for the* PIANO-FORTE, *founded on the* celebrated Round *in the favourite Opera of* Tarrare, *arranged by* J. B. CRAMER. (J. B. Cramer, Addison, and Beale, 201, *Regent Street.*)

2. GIOVINETTO CAVALIER, *with an* INTRODUCTION *and* BRILLIANT VARIATIONS, *composed for the* PIANO FORTE, *by* J. P. PIXIS. (*By the same.*)

3. RONDEAU MIGNON, *pour le* PIANO-FORTE, *composé par* J. P. PIXIS. *Œuvre* 77. (Boosey and Co., 28, *Holles-street.*)

4. INTRODUCTION *and* RONDO BRILLIANT, *for the* PIANO-FORTE, *composed by* D. SCHLESINGER. Op. 2. (*By the same.*)

THE most popular thing in the once celebrated opera of *Tarrare,* and now the only piece in the original work that meets with any portion of the applause which the whole, in days gone by, received, is the *Canone,* as the composer calls it, or round, as it may be named, if more convenient. It is not an easy subject to arrange for keyed instruments ; it has too many breaks for a rondo, or for variations, and the best form in which it could be put for the piano-forte, has been chosen by Mr. Cramer. The introduction to it is exceedingly good ; the air is ingeniously managed, and so distributed to both hands, as to preserve much of the conversational effect of the original. The modulation into E flat, page 6, is bold, and the few succeeding bars, where the subject passes into C minor, is quite in the adapter's good style. This is certainly not to be classed amongst easy music, but in the present age of difficulties, it will excite no alarm in the minds of tolerably good performers.

Pixis is one of the many new names that have appeared in Germany during the last three or four years. He is a very brilliant pianist, and, generally speaking, his music—at least such of it as has come under our view —is calculated chiefly to shew great powers of execution. The present composition, however, is not exactly one of this description, and is, very wisely, better calculated for rational English performers, than for the extravagant— we might almost say, half frantic—amateurs of Vienna. In truth, there is great beauty in parts of this composition by M. Pixis, and merit in the whole of it. It is difficult certainly, but the labour that the practitioner may bestow on it will be well rewarded by the pleasure and improvement which it will afford.

No. 3 is an original composition, by the author of the foregoing. The subject of the rondo is simple and pleasing, and the whole is written in a familiar, easy style, comparatively speaking. Most persons who have made any progress in the instrument, may undertake this piece; which, if not remarkable for any original traits, has no defects, and bears on its title-page a name that is new to the majority of amateurs.

We should be happy could we say so much of M. Schlesinger's rondo. That it shews him to be a good musician, in the common sense of the word, is undeniable ; but it proves also that he composes rather to obtain a certain kind of reputation—a reputation for putting difficulties on paper, and, by inference, of having overcome them—than to consult the public opinion, and circulate his productions. Let us hope, however, that his object is already attained, and that he will now perceive that without taste and feeling, without a melody that all having an ear can make out and understand, music is intolerable ; and that to people of sense and cultivated minds, a brazier hammering on his vessel is quite as entertaining as a performer whose merit consists solely in execution.

1. *The* OVERTURE, *and* SELECT AIRS *in* MEYER-BEER'S *celebrated Opera,* Il Crociato in Egitto, *arranged as* DUETS *for Two Performers on the* PIANO-FORTE, *by* T. ATTWOOD. *Book* 1. (Clementi and Co., *Cheapside.*)

2. *The* OVERTURE *to the same, arranged as a* DUET *for the* PIANO-FORTE, *by* C. DUMON. (Goulding, D'Almaine, and Co., *Soho Square.*)

THE reputation of Meyerbeer's fine opera is increasing every day, as we expected, and is appearing in as many shapes as *Don Giovanni* did half a dozen years ago, and as the *Freischütz* has assumed lately. *Il Crociato in Egitto* is one of those original and masterly works that require to be frequently heard to be thoroughly understood ; it is formed of very uncommon materials, the melodies particularly, and as these become known, by being spread abroad in such various guises, the public opinion is more and more declared in its favour [*]. Both of the above arrangements of the overture, and opening chorus, will add to the popularity of the opera : they are executed with great ability, and give as much effect to the compositions as a single instrument can be made to render. Mr. Attwood, we conclude, means to adapt most of the pieces in the work, many of which, from the fulness of the parts, and the complicated nature of the composition, can only derive the just effect of their harmony from four hands. These arrangements are not difficult in performance; the division of labour facilitates as much in music as in manufactures, and most players may fearlessly undertake either of these publications.

[*] We have learnt lately, from the best authority, that great persuasion was used, and many arts employed, to deter Mr. Ayrton from bringing out this opera last season ; even Signor Velluti himself—who owes every success that he has met with here to the beauty of Meyerbeer's music,—was one of the most strenuous in wishing to appear in an inferior work by Morlacchi!

1. MARTIAL IMPROMPTU, *on the celebrated Song,* "Revenge he cries, and the traitor dies," *for the* PIANO-FORTE, *by* IGNACE MOSCHELES. (Welsh and Hawes, 246, *Regent Street.*)

2. BRILLIANT VARIATIONS *on the favourite Cavatina,* "Serena i vaghi rai", *from* ROSSINI'S *Opera of* Semiramide, *for the* PIANO-FORTE, *composed by* MAYSEDER. (*Published by the same.*)

3. *A Second* RONDINO *on the favourite quintett from* ROSSINI'S *Opera of* Corradino, *for the* PIANO-FORTE, *by* CHARLES CZERNY. (Cocks and Co. *Princes Street, Hanover Square.*)

No. 1, is the melody which Mr. Braham introduced into *Tarrare*, and sang with that effect which his declamatory powers are sure to produce. It is a fine martial air, decided in its rhythm, bold and animating. Mr. Moscheles—who never adopts a subject without improving it—has enlarged it into a very spirited divertisement of two movements. He has also managed to make it as shewy as any ambitious young lady can wish, while he has confined the passages within very moderate bounds, so as to require moderate powers of execution in its performance.

The air in *Semiramide*, selected by M. Mayseder, is deservedly popular. He has certainly added variations to it that are brilliant, and require not only a rapid finger, but a powerful hand. For practice they may be made useful; but we find nothing in the mode of treating the subject that has any pretence to originality, neither do we discover any allurement that it possesses for the true lover of music, except what is to be found in the melody itself.

No. 3 is quite the contrary of the last; the subject is indifferent, but it is improved by the arranger. It will not, however, extend the fame of either Sig. Rossini or M. Czerny : though we must add that, it is not so *outré* as most of the piano-forte productions of the latter.

1. THEMES *from the* Beggar's Opera, *with* VARIATIONS *for the* PIANO-FORTE, FLUTE, *and* VIOLONCELLO, *by* J. MAZZINGHI. (Goulding, D'Almaine, and Co. *Soho Square.*)

2. INTRODUCTION *and* RONDO, *the subject from* "Di tanti palpiti," *for the* ORGAN *or* PIANO-FORTE, *composed, and performed on the Apollonicon, by* THOMAS ADAMS. (Clementi and Co. *Cheapside.*)

MR. MAZZINGHI deserves the thanks of all lovers of ancient English song, for assisting to preserve from oblivion these fine old airs. His talent for such arrangements has long been acknowledged: none ever succeeded better than this gentleman in rendering publications of the present kind popular. This is quite equal to his former adaptations, and will make its way in most places where the three instruments can be collected together, for it is perfectly easy for each, and effective in union.

No. 2 is a very clever arrangement, and shews that knowledge of counterpoint so absolutely necessary to a good organist. But we hardly know what to say further of this: it is too *organic* for the piano-forte, and too much in the piano-forte style for the organ. On the latter instrument rapid notes are out of character, and reiterated staccato semiquavers are intolerable. On the former, fugual imitations, excellent as they are in themselves, are out of fashion. We would therefore advise Mr. Adams to forget the organ when he writes for the piano-forte ; and when he composes for the case of strings, to dismiss the box of whistles from his thoughts.

---

1. GRAND MARCH *for the* PIANO-FORTE *from* MEYERBEER'S Il Crociato, *arranged by* AUG. MEVES. (Clementi and Co. *Cheapside.*)

2. "Soave Immagine," INTRODUCTION *and* POLONAISE, *from the same. Arranged and Published by the same.*

3. The favourite AIRS *in* SPOHR'S *celebrated Opera,* Jessonda, *arranged for the* PIANO-FORTE *by* J. H. GRIESBACH. (Cocks and Co., *Princes Street, Hanover Square.*)

4. The admired AIRS *in* SPOHR'S *celebrated Opera,* Faust, *arranged and published by the same.*

THE March in *Il Crociato in Egitto* appeared in our thirty-first number; both this and the following, No. 2, are well arranged, in a very popular, easy manner, by Mr. Meves, who has followed the original as closely as he found practicable, and where he has deviated for the sake of an accompaniment to suit the instrument, he has shewn great judgment.

Spohr's Opera of Jessonda is not unknown to our subscribers ; the first and best of the airs in the above edition, appeared in the last number of the Harmonicon, and we do not perceive any difference in the copies, except that ours, by means of repeats, and other modes of abbreviation, lies in a smaller compass. Mr. Griesbach has inserted four pieces from this opera. He has published the same number from *Faust.* These are not well contrived for the left hand, which has many awkward passages given to it : neither are they the most striking specimens that might have been selected from the opera ; but they are the most simple in keys and construction, therefore the best adapted for general use.

---

1. LA MISCIA, *for the* PIANO FORTE, *Introducing the favourite subjects and movements in* MEYERBEER'S *admired opera,* Il Crociato in Egitto ; *arranged by* T. A. RAWLINGS. (Goulding, D'Almaine, and Co., *Soho Square.*)

2. L'Eté, DIVERTISEMENT *for the* PIANO FORTE, *with an* Introduction *and* FLUTE *Accompaniment, (ad lib.) by the same. (Published by the same.)*

3. Beau Temps, DIVERTISEMENT *for the* PIANO FORTE, *Introducing the admired* Glee, The Wreath, *with* Variations, *by the same. (Published by the same.)*

4. ARIA ALL' INGLESE, *with* Variations, *for the* PIANO FORTE, *by* JAMES CALKIN. (Clementi and Co., *Cheapside.*)

5. FANTASIA BRILLIANTE, *Introducing the* Waltz *and* Jager chorus *from* Der Freischütz, *composed for the* PIANO FORTE, *by* JAMES CALKIN. (Lindsay, 217, *Regent Street.*)

WHAT *Miscia* signifies, we know not ; possibly it is a misprint for *miscea, baggattella,* though really M. Meyerbeer's airs are neither worn out nor trifling, as the latter word signifies. In the music-plates the piece is named *la Mischia,* the quarrel, the riot. This must be an error :—but perhaps the thing matters not. Mr. Rawlings gives us here the chorus " *Nel Silenzio,*" and the aria " *Giovinetto Cavalier ;*" the first a little enlarged upon, the second very nearly note for note, according to the piano-forte adaptation of the score.

No. 2 is an introduction of about two pages ; the air " Oh ! yes, dear love," by Bishop, *arpeggioed ;* and a waltz, *à la Freischütz.*

No. 3 cannot be better described than in the title-page. All these compilations, or pieces—we must not call them compositions—by Mr. Rawlings, are nearly as easy as piano-forte music can be made, and there is a certain prettiness about them by which they will be recommended to those who have no taste for what they call " learned stuff."

We do not know the melody, No. 4, chosen by Mr. Calkin, but it is exceedingly tender and beautiful : though we cannot conjecture why, being an " old English air," published in England, with an English title-page, it should be metamorphosed into an *Aria all' Inglese.* This is a device which, whatever young composers may think to the contrary, never sells a single copy, and is bordering on the ridiculous. There are seven variations, some of which, inasmuch as they extend a sweet air, will please. Two are quite irrelevant to the subject, and no one of them makes any attempt to move out of the usual track. The publication however is worth having, for the sake of the melody.

The title of No. 5 explains as much as is necessary to know : we can only add a few words to it ; but first, should rather be inclined to ask what claim this publication has to the appellation of Fantasia. It is made up of three movements, an *adagio* as an opening, the well-known waltz, and the chorus ; the latter extended by two or three pages of semiquavers in triplets ; the whole not affording quite so much facility to the performer as the foregoing three pieces, but, nevertheless, adapted to any learner of two years' standing.

---

1. THREE ROUNDS, *with an accompaniment for the* Piano-Forte ; *the Music by* GEORGE B. HERBERT : *the Poetry by* J. R. PLANCHE. *Book 2.* (Goulding and Co., *Soho Square.*)

2. GLEE, 4 Voices, "There is beauty on the mountains," *the Poetry by* BERNARD BARTON ; *the Music by* JOHN GOSS. (Welsh and Hawes, 246, *Regent Street.*)

3. ODE, " Not a drum was heard," *on the Death of Sir* John Moore, *composed by* T. PURDAY. (Clementi and Co., *Cheapside.*)

THE first book of these rounds was mentioned in our thirty-third Number, in those terms of approbation which we think they richly merit. The pieces in the present book are in the same dramatic style as the last, and though upon the whole we prefer those in the first, yet there is enough to praise in the melody, sentiment, and effect of the present. We would, however, call Mr. Herbert's attention to the last bar but one, in page 1, where the c sharp continues too long, and becomes very grating to the ear:—

The sharp 8th is a very dangerous companion, and should only be admitted as a passing acquaintance. Had it been the flat 2d, with the flat 6th and 4th, and falling to its resolution, the case would have been widely different. We are not much better satisfied with the fourteenth bar, page 8, where there are three unnecessary and objectionable octaves.

We hope that these rounds will find their way into drawing-rooms, and boarding-schools, for which they are designed ; so much ingenuity deserves patronage.

Mr. Goss has produced a lovely piece of vocal harmony, under the name of a glee, to which we beg to call the attention of the many societies spread over this island ; for they will now very rarely meet with a composition of the kind that has half its beauty. Does not the last bar of page 2 contain errors of the engraver ?

Mr. Purday's *Ode* must be meant as a burlesque.

---

1. TERPSICHORE, *choix des Pièces tirées des Operas, &c. Composées par* ROSSINI, WEBER, MOZART, *et* BEETHOVEN : *Mises pour le* PIANO-FORTE. Nos. 12 to 14. (Wessel and Stoddart, *Soho Square.*)

2. Ewer and Johanning's *Collection of favourite and modern* MARCHES, WALTZES, POLONAISES, *and* MINUETS, *for the* PIANO-FORTE, *by* GLUCK, MOZART, WEBER, &c., &c. No. 1 to 4. (Ewer and Johanning, *Bow Church Yard, and* 263, *Regent Street.*)

THE first of these is a continuation of the work formerly noticed. The present numbers contain a rondo from Spohr's *Jessonda*, " *Giovinetto Cavalier*," from *Il Crociato*, and a piece from Winter's *Opferfest* ; all well arranged by Diabelli, of Vienna.

No. 2 is a new work, well brought out, at a reasonable price. The above numbers comprise much from the *Freischütz*, marches by Winter and Cherubini, Oginsky's polonaise, and a waltz by Beethoven ; arranged with a view to accommodate moderately qualified performers.

---

1. BALLAD, " Wandering Willy," *sung by Miss Paton, composed by* DR. WILLIAM CARNABY. (Cramer and Co., 201, *Regent Street.*).

2. SONG, " O Erin, the land of the fair and the bold !" *written on the Lakes of Killarney, by* W. F. COLLARD, *the music by* J. C. CLIFTON. (Clementi and Co., *Cheapside.*)

3. SONG, " Farewell," *sung by Mr. Pearman, composed by* J. BLEWITT. (*Published by the same.*)

4. SONG, " Two and twenty miles from town," *a rustic portrait, by* THOMAS DIBDIN. (*Published by the same.*)

5. CANZONET, *sung by Miss Goodall* ; *the poetry by* J. HAN ALLAN, Esq., *composed by* BURFORD G. H.

GIBSON. (Willis and Co., St. James's Street, and Dublin.)

6. SERENADE, " Whilst the moon," *the words by* HARRY STOE VAN DYK, ESQ., *the music by* JOHN BARNETT. (Boosey and Co., 28, *Holles Street.*)

7. CANZONET, " Dear is the blush," *the poetry from Lord Strangford's Cameens, composed by* P. W. HORNCASTLE. (Birchall and Co., *New Bond Street.*)

8. BALLAD, " The blind Boy ;" *words by* Colley Cibber ; *sung by Master Smith, composed by* J. A. TACTET. (Welsh and Hawes, 246, *Regent Street.*)

9. SONG, " Forget me not when beauty's smile," (*Composed and published by the same.*)

DR. CARNABY is one of the few remaining disciples of the good old English school of pure melody ; there is a delightful naiveté in most of his compositions, which reminds us of Arne, Jackson, and Linley, names that will never be strange to those who have an ear for the charms of song, uninfluenced by the voice of fashion, which raises up one day, pulls down the next, and condemns indiscriminately all the past. While, however, simplicity is the leading feature in Dr. Carnaby's productions, he can shew vigour in his style, and richness in his harmony, when he is inclined—witness " I hate that drum's discordant sound," and " The braes of Yarrow."

The present is an extremely pretty, playful ballad ; the air has much originality, and is in the author's most natural manner. The accompaniment is in two parts only, treble and base, and the whole has a very pleasant, and rather novel effect.

No. 2 is indeed a beautiful song, in which the poet and musician have joined their talents to produce one of the most agreeable unions of the two arts that we have met with, in so unpretending a shape, for many a long year. Both verse and melody seem to have been inspired by the scene—are as gentle and elegant as the lake whence they sprang ; and partake largely of that tenderness which so generally characterizes the song of ill-fated Erin.

No. 3 is pretty ; and No. 4 is, like every thing that comes from the pen of Mr. T. Dibdin, good-humoured and entertaining. The air to which he has set his verses is either Scotish, or else an intentional imitation of an ancient Caledonian melody.

No. 5 possesses considerable merit, but the composer has got a little out of his depth, at page 5 of his Canzonet, by plunging into a flood of extraneous harmony.

Mr. Barnett's *Serenade* is a very ingenious composition, shews a great deal of invention, and produces an excellent effect. We have had occasion to point out to this young writer what we considered as errors in his publications, and are persuaded that he now feels indebted to us for our candor. We most unhesitatingly recommend his present production to all vocal performers ; it will gratify them, and do the author much credit.

Nos. 7 and 8 are very much in the style of nineteen out of twenty of the songs that are now published. They are entitled to negative praise.

No. 9 is more aspiring, and shews talent ; but the accompaniments are too laborious for a song, and inappropriate to the sentiment of the words.

FOREIGN MUSICAL REPORT.

BERLIN.—Our German stage can boast of nothing new lately, if we except a comic opera, in two acts, entitled, *Das Fest der Winzer* (the Vintage Feast), the music by M. Kunze, late Royal Kapellmeister to the court of Denmark. Many of the airs are of a very pleasing and original cast, and were loudly encored; also a terzetto, a quartetto, and the finale of the second act, were found to be marked by much that was pleasing, and that bore the stamp of originality. Unfortunately, the story to which this music is attached is of a weak and ineffective nature, and therefore cannot be expected long to survive; such is the unhappy destiny that attaches to many a meritorious piece of music; chained to the perishable material, it is dragged by it into oblivion.—The French company, of which we spoke in our last, still continues to give its representations, and with the same success. The pieces performed by them have been *Le Maître de Chapelle*, the music by Paer; *Adolph et Clara, ou les Deux Prisonniers*, by D'Aleyrac; *Les Amans Protées, ou Qui Compte sans son Hôte, compte deux Fois*, by Patrat; *Les deux Jaloux*, the music by Madame Gail, intermixed with airs from Boieldieu and Isouard.—The celebrated Madame Milder Hauptmann treated us with a musical Soirée, before leaving us for Paris. She was in her usual power, without having lost any thing of the sweetness of her tones, and sung with great feeling and expression C. Blum's song, entitled, *Schweizergruss* (an Address to the Swiss). She also sang two airs from Göethe's *Westostlichem Divan*, the music by F. Schubert, and *Den Erlkönig*, also by Göethe, and the music by Schubert, which pleased extremely. This lady has the judgment and good taste to select such pieces for her performance as are calculated to afford her an opportunity for her powers of expression and of moving the soul, not of showing off the compass of her voice.

There has just appeared in this place *Sonate für Fortepiano und Violine*, comp. von Felix Mendelssohn-Bartholdy, 4th Op. This production of the grandson of the celebrated philosopher of the same name, is hailed by the amateurs of the continent as a presage of great musical excellence. They mention it as a composition, that bespeaks not only the hand of one perfectly versed in all the secrets of the technical branch of his art, but also of one who knows all the avenues to the heart, and all the sources of profound feeling and expression. We trust that judgment will be shown in the completion of this young man's education, and that the failing of others in the same career will be held up to him as a warning beacon[*].

At parting we may remark, that it would appear as if our whole opera were about to be transplanted to Paris. Besides Madame Milder and Madame Schulz, we are to lose Spontini and music-director Möser. The latter, who by his distinguished activity has made his value so much felt here, is said to have proceeded to Paris for the promotion of the objects of his art.

DRESDEN.—One of the great attractions of the day is, the admirable performance of M. Keller in the part of *Die Falche Katalani*, (The False Catalani,) in which his extraordinary falsetto is called so effectively into play, in the imitation of this distinguished singer. The manner in which he imitates the various styles of Italian singing, and particularly the laborious fidelity with which he gives the well-known variations of Rode, as executed by this singer, is altogether marvellous.

---

[*] *Sur les Prodiges à la mode.*

Plus merveilleux que nos ancêtres,
On peut-être plus singuliers,
À dix ans nous avons des maitres,
Qui sont à vingt des écoliers.—FAYOLLE.

On the Prodigies à la mode.

Ours is an age of wonders—we behold
Precocious talents budding forth in plenty;
We have our masters now at ten years old,
Who sink to humble scholars when they're twenty.
W. J. W.

Besides this comic opera, the pieces given at the German Theatre have been *Der Friessnkütz*, which was honoured for the first time by the presence of the Grand Duchess of Tuscany; Weigl's *Nachtigall und Rabe* (Nightingale and Raven,) Mozart's *Entfuhrnng aus dem Serail*, and the *Don Juan* of the same.— The Italian Opera Establishment has for the present limited its representations to once a week, which is on the Saturday, and is always numerously attended, though nothing in the shape of novelty has been produced, unless we rank as an exception the *Elisa e Claudio* of Mercadante, which is heard alternately with *Le Nozze di Figaro, Tancredi*, and *Cenerentola*.

We hear that Moriacchi, the celebrated composer, still continues in a delicate state of health; the last we heard of him was, that he was on a visit to the waters at Marienbad.

WEIMAR.—We have not for many years had to boast of so successful a season, so effective a company, and so varied and judicious a choice of musical pieces, for all which advantages we are indebted in a great degree to the zeal and industry of our music-director, Kapellmeister J. N. Hummel. The following is a list of the pieces performed: 1. *Il Matrimonio Secreto*, by Cimarosa, twice; 2. *Cenerentola*, by Rossini, once; 3. *La Folle*, once; 4. *Libussa*, by Kreutzer, twice; 5. *Die Schwestern von Prague*, (The Sisters of Prague) once; 6. *Der Freischütz*, six times; 7. *Bär und Bassa*, twice; 8. *Der Wassertrager*, (The Water-carrier) once; 9. *Das neue Sonntagskind*, seven times; 10. *La Molinara*, by Paisiello, twice; 11. *Tancredi*, twice; 12. *Die Zauberflöte*, twice; 13. *Jean de Paris*, once; 14. *Graf von Gleichen*, twice; 15. *Das Opferfest*, by Winter, once; 16. *Die Saalnixe*, (The Snow-storm) twice; 17. *Fanchon*, once; 18. *Die Entfuhrung aus dem Serail*, twice; 19. *Euryanthe*, three times; 20. *Ferdinand Cortez*, twice; 21. *Le Nozze di Figaro*, twice; 22. *Richard, Cœur de Lion*, twice; 23. *La Clemenza di Tito*, twice; 24. *Den neuen Gutsherrn*, twice; 25. *Camilla*, by Paer, twice; 26. *Il Don Giovanni*, once.

In a theatre of a moderate compass like ours, the talents of the artist are developed in an effective and yet pretensionless manner; none of those violent efforts are necessary, which are not less painful to the singer than to the hearer; this is a blessing which we still enjoy, but which most of the larger cities of Europe have either lost, or are getting rid of as quickly as they can. The great favourite of the season has been a Madlle. Heygendorf, whose voice is said to be of the first-rate quality, and who displays an excellent school. Not only is the lightness and grace with which she gives the ornamental passages excellent, and a proof of the best taste; but the power of her recitative and declamatory song is not less admirable. The only point on which the public is divided, is whether she excels most in comic or serious characters. She appeared as Fiordaligi in *Il Matrimonio Secreto*; as Libussa; in the opera of the same name; as the daughter in *La Molinara*; as Amenaide in *Tancredi*; as Chadija, in *Graf von Gleichen*; as Susanna in *Figaro*; Sextus in *La Clemenza di Tito*; as Camilla, in the opera of the same name; and Donna Anna in *Il Don Giovanni*.

HAMBURG.—Before giving an account of the state of music in this place, I shall beg leave to premise a few observations.

Among all the fine arts, practical music possesses this disadvantage, to which the rest are not subject, viz., that it requires an assemblage of artists for its perfect display. Now, how many difficulties are presented by such an assemblage, through the variety of their capacities and peculiarities of view, as well as through all those weaknesses incident to humanity, and from which artists are as little exempt as any of the other children of Adam, such as vanity, which prides itself on its own talents and opinions alone; self-interest, collateral views, &c; Singular as it may appear, these feelings are found to be not less predominant in self-created establishments, than in those where talents are rated at a certain estimate, and paid by the government. But music not only requires effective artists, but also hearers gifted with the means of enjoying it; for all steal for the art will cool, if there is not a due degree of interest displayed in its behalf, and encouragement bestowed upon it. Now this, perhaps, is the principal reason, why music does not prosper to such a degree in commercial towns such as our own, as in places graced by the presence of a court, and where the interest of the nobility is exerted in favour of the art. Not that our town is wanting in warm and zealous supporters of music among the mercantile classes; all that we say is, that not all is done which even the modest friends of the art could wish. The truth is, we want an effective orchestra, and till that deficiency be made good, we can never hope to see music make that progress which its friends could wish. But in spite of these defects, we have had Handel's *Judas Maccabeus,* as well as an oratorio by a composer of our town, of the name of M. Grund, entitled, *Die Auferstehung und Himmelfahrt Jesu,* (The Resurrection and Ascension of Jesus,) a work of great power and spirit, and which was spoken of with great applause. After this were given Handel's *Samson,* and *The Alexander's Feast,* and which, considering the limited means of the place, were astonishingly well and correctly performed. These were followed by Schicht's oratorio, *Das Ende des Gerechten,* (The End of the Just.)

DANTZIC.—The samemusical activity which reigns through the principal towns of Germany, is also, perhaps with some little deductions, prevalent in our own. We have various newly established institutions for music, vocal and instrumental, where numerous amateurs assemble to exercise their talents, and derive instruction from their mutual observations. We cannot, however, abstain from a remark in this place, which we deem important; it is, that no amateur efforts can reach the effects of primitive instruction, as imparted in early years, when the mind is fresh and open to those impressions which are generally denied at a later period of life, and best suited to receive and nourish the seeds of instruction. We hope, however, to see this evil remedied in part by the efforts of music-director Urban, of Elbing, who has recently published his practical work, *Ueber die Musik, deren Theorie und den Musik unterricht,* (on Music, its Theory, and mode of Instruction,) according to which, he intends giving a series of lessons on elementary principles, to a class of his friends and others; we have no doubt but this will lead to beneficial results. Among the most zealous promoters of music in this place is Professor Kniewel, head-director of the Musical Institution. His efforts are highly praiseworthy, and deserving of acknowledgment. He gives from time to time grand oratorios, which are performed in the great Music Hall, among which we have to reckon *Das Weltgericht,* by Schneider, *Das befreite Jerusalem,* (Jerusalem Delivered,) by the Abbé Stadler, and *Die Sündfluth,* (The Deluge,) also by Schneider. The latter was again recently performed for the benefit of the public charities of the place, the object of which, we are happy to say, was fulfilled.

HALLE.—The highest treat of music that this town has enjoyed for a considerable time, was the grand anniversary concert, given in honour of the King of Prussia's birth-day. It was conducted by the university music-director, M. Naue, whose zeal and perseverance cannot be too highly commended. In order to give every possible eclat to this occasion, he, with great sacrifices on his own part, assembled from 70 to 80 musicians from all the neighbouring towns. With this strength of orchestra, he was enabled to give us a chorus of his own composition, in sixteen parts, as well as different specimens of Hallelujahs of various ages, of the 9th, 13th, and 15th centuries, terminating with Handel's celebrated composition of the same name. In the course of the selection was also given, the finale of the second act, and the triumphal march of *Olympia,* as well as the celebrated duet from the opera of *Nurmahal,* by the same composer. When I inform you that the lovers of music here had never heard any of the compositions of Spontini, except with a meagre violin or piano accompaniment, you will easily form an idea of their surprise and delight at hearing these grand compositions of this master given with dne power and effect. It was universally acknowledged that such vigour and passion, as predominate in

this finale, were never found united with such clearness and ease of conception. The effect which this produced is still the subject of every conversation, and every one is anxious to hear, sing, or play something of Spontini's. Such, indeed, is the general encouragement which M. Naue has experienced, that it is said we are shortly to have a second concert, when doubtless Spontini will not be neglected.

MAINZ.—The following announcement has recently appeared in this place: Prospectus of a publication by subscription of the three latest grand works of Beethoven:—

1. *Missa Solennis,* D major.
2. Grand Overture, C major, and
3. Symphony with chorus.

The genius of harmony has been particularly propitious to our times. Scarcely has one brilliant star set beneath the musical hemisphere, when another genius rises in his brilliancy to replace the loss. No sooner had a Mozart and a Haydn quitted this earthly sphere, when Heaven gave us a Beethoven, whose works are of a character to stand by the side of those of his great competitors, and with them to share the admiration of the latest posterity. The originality of his harmony, the ever-varied and all-expressive power of his modulations are inimitable, and emanate from the pure fount of genius. The publishers are proud to have it in their power to afford the public an opportunity of possessing these last, and perhaps, most original of this great man's productions. They will appear in the following form:

I. The Grand *Missa Solennis.*
    1st. In full score; 2nd. In separate pieces for the orchestra and voice; and 3dly, In pieces arranged for the voice, with piano accompaniments.

II. The Overture for a Grand Orchestra.
    1st. In score; 2nd. In Orchestral pieces.

III. The Grand Symphony, with chorusses and solo pieces on Schiller's *Song of Joy.*
    1st. In score; 2nd. In Orchestral pieces.

FRANKFORT.—Two numbers of Shakspeare's songs have appeared here, set to music, with a piano-forte accompaniment, by Fr. von Boyneburgk. The text is selected from the best German translations of Voss, Kessler, Krausse, and particularly Schlegel. The foreign critics speak of this composer as having entered into the spirit and character of his author, and rendered his ideas with force and simplicity. Above all, they represent him as being particularly happy in his short chorusses and interlocutory passages. Each number contains six pieces. The author receives every encouragement to proceed.

NANTES.—*Der Freischütz* was lately produced here under the name of *Robin des Bois,* and gave rise to a singular discussion. It was thus announced on the bills of the opera:—"Robin des Bois, opera en trois actes, de Castilblaze, et Sauvage." The question was, why the name of the author did not precede the opera, according to usage immemorial. The poets thought that the name of Castilblaze ought not to stand first, as he was only the compiler of the work; the musicians maintained that M. Sauvage was nothing more than an arranger, since he did nothing else than adjust the German text, and hitch it into short verses according to the pleasure of M. Castilblaze. At last the important dispute was thus decided: as the piece was not from the pen of M. Castilblaze, any more than from that of M. Sauvage, therefore the bill should run thus: "Opera in three acts, words by M. Castilblaze, music by M. Sauvage, or words by M. Sauvage, music by M. Castilblaze." By-the-by, the manner and form in which this opera is brought out here is whimsical enough. In the first place, the scene of the action is transposed to England, to the county of Kent, and amidst the ruins of St. Dunstan's Abbey. The black huntsman is transformed into Robin Hood, and Max into *Tony!* The magic balls are diminished to three, but by way of making up for the diminution, the first is of gold, the second of silver, and the third of lead. The rest of the changes and substitutions are equally bright and judicious.

FLORENCE.—There has recently appeared here a work, entitled, *Offertori a due, tre, quattro, sei e otto voci, con Organo solo obligato, del Sig. Franc. Basili, compositore e Maestro di Capella dell' insigne Basilica di Loretto.* The composer here mentioned is a pupil of the celebrated Zingarelli, but, though he has produced several works of merit, his name is as yet little known. Though fame is tardy in doing justice to his merits, yet, as they are of a class far above the common, they will not fail to shine forth in their due time. A matured is frequently much better than a precocious renown. Besides the work above-mentioned, I have now lying before me the original M.S. of a *Kyrie* for eight voices, with organ accompaniment, which shews no less masterly knowledge of the fundamental principles of the art, than grace and beauty of manner. The present *Offertorios* are in the same pleasing and effective style, without having any great difficulties to overcome. We should think they were of a nature likely to become popular, though it might certainly be objected to some of them, that they are in too secular a style for church music. It should, however, be remembered, that in music of this kind, the same as in the anthem, a certain latitude should be given to the fancy of the composer, beyond the parts strictly belonging to the church service.

No. 1. *Justorum animæ in manu Dei sunt.* This is perhaps the most beautiful of all the set; a lovely and expressive melody runs throughout the whole, and there is a tone and finish in the piece which is not less rare than delightful.

No. 2. *Justus ut palma florebit,* a terzetto for soprano, alto, and bass, a movement of a sprightly and vigorous kind, and admirably suited to the expression of the text. Add to this, it is far from being difficult of performance, and the melody is of a kind which is easily retained.

No. 3. *Exultabant sancti in gloria,* for two basses, both of which are equally well wrought as to the subject, and the rhythm is of a peculiar character that imparts a charm to the whole.

No. 4. *Ave Maria,* for a soprano and tenor voice. Care is required to give this piece with the effect which it is intended to produce. The melody is particularly expressive, and yet of a peculiar cast, which marks an original mind.

But this author has not been successful in smaller compositions only; he has also produced an oratorio, entitled *Il Sansone,* of which the foreign journals have spoken in terms of very great praise.

[We have been so fortunate as to procure a copy of a ROMANCE from this composition, which our readers will find at page 254 of the Music of the present Number, with an accompaniment for the piano-forte.]

MUSICAL HOSTILITIES COMMENCED IN PARIS.

MADAME FODOR is arrived in the capital of France. She no sooner made her entrance, than the horizon of the *Théâtre Italien* began to assume a threatening aspect. *Semiramide* had been granted to Madame Pasta for her benefit; this concession unavoidably implied that she was to perform the principal part in the opera, the character in which she shone so brightly last season at the King's Theatre. But by an evasion, too common in opera management, and not, it seems, beneath a Viscount, though utterly unworthy of a gentleman, when the moment for commencing the rehearsals was come, the part of *Arsaces*—(performed here by Madame Vestris)— was allotted to Pasta, and the principal character given to

Fodor. This proceeding of the *noble* Director produced the following advertisement:—

"Various reports spread by some journals might make it believed that I have no right to fill the character of Semiramis, at the first representation of the opera of that name, which has been set apart for my benefit of the year 1824. I think it my duty therefore to lay before the public, whose suffrages have been always so precious to me, the supplementary article which was added to my act of engagement the 2nd of May last, by Mr. Plantys, director of the Italian theatre-royal. This article, written entirely with his own hand, is as follows:

"'It is well understood that the words *primo musico* which Madame Pasta has consented to insert in the first article of this engagement will not oblige her to perform the part of Arsaces in Semiramis, which opera is reserved for her benefit.
(Signed)   'R. DU PLANTYS.
'Paris, May 2, 1824.'

"If any objection could still be made to a right so clearly stated, I shall find myself under the necessity of publishing a letter which has been written to me on the 22nd of November, 1824. This document, by the authority whence it emanates, the date which it bears, and the precision of its terms, will certainly leave room for no ambiguity.

"*Paris, Sept. 28, 1825.*   JUDITH PASTA."

Madame Fodor lost no time in replying, in the annexed letter to the journalists.

"I have read, in a journal of this morning, a letter signed by Madame Pasta, in which she quotes an article of her engagement, which provides that she shall not be obliged to play the part of Arsaces in Semiramis, an opera which is reserved for her benefit.

"This letter lays me under the obligation,—a very painful one for me,—of informing the public of the following facts.

"When, almost a year ago, the management thought fit to testify a desire of re-attaching me to the Italian theatre-royal, I authorized my agent (*fondé de pouvoirs*) to make some concessions, as far as my interests were concerned: but I strongly insisted on a clause which would guarantee me the choice of parts.

"It is in consequence of this wish that the following article was inserted in my contract of engagement, signed at Paris, on the 20th of February, by the Viscount Rochefoucault on one side, and on the other by my agent.

"'Art. 9. The two works in which Mad. Mainvielle Fodor is to make her *début* shall be chosen by her; and she therefore will inform the management, before the 1st of July next, what two works she has chosen, in order that they may be ready to be brought on the stage when she arrives in Paris.'

"In consequence, therefore, of this liberty to choose my parts, which is guaranteed to me by this article, I had the honour of announcing to the Viscount de la Rochefoucault, that I should choose those of *Semiramis* and *Elisabeth.*

"This choice was agreed to by the Viscount, who, in the letter which he did me the honour of writing to me, made use of the following words:

"'As a matter of course, nothing can hinder Madame Fodor from *debuting* in the operas she has chosen.'

"This is all that is of any importance for the public to know. Madame Pasta is perfectly at liberty to play or not play Arsaces, as she pleases; and if she is determined that Semiramis shall be for her benefit, I shall deem myself happy to be able to assist in it.

"I have the honour to be, &c.,
"MAINVIELLE FODOR.

"P. S. Let me add, that if Madame Pasta desires, after my *debut,* to sing the character of Semiramis, I shall with the greatest alacrity yield it to her.

"*Paris, Sept. 29, 1825.*"

Which produced the subjoined pungent epistle. How LE VISCOUNT DE LA ROCHEFOUCAULT, and M. DU

PLANTYS, looked, after reading it, we cannot guess, not knowing what command the parties have acquired over their countenances.

" TO THE EDITOR OF THE JOURNAL DES DEBATS.

" *Paris, Oct. 8.*

" SIR—Sensible of the injustice which I am to suffer by being deprived of the part of *Semiramis* the day of the first representation of that Opera, I am obliged to publish the letter in which Viscount De la Rochefoucault, Director of the Department of Fine Arts, confirmed the promise of my having this part for my benefit. This letter is dated November 22, 1824. On my return from London, where I performed the part of *Semiramis* in August, 1824, I obtained a promise from Viscount de la Rochefoucault that this Opera should be given for my benefit. *Semiramis* was to be substituted for the *Donna del Lago*, which I had at first chosen, and which I had subsequently given up to the administration. I have now learnt that the first representation of *Semiramis* has been promised to M. Rossini for his benefit. It was in answer to my respectful representations on this subject, that the Viscount de la Rochefoucault wrote me the following letter, with his own hand, and signed by his initials:—

" 'How could Madame Pasta suppose that I should commit an injustice with regard to her? This is to misconceive my character—to doubt the enthusiasm which is inspired by her talents, and the esteem which I personally have for her. M. Rossini gives up *Semiramis* to her—he only requests that she will postpone the moment of representation. If Madame Pasta will be so kind as to think of me one of these days, I shall be delighted to speak to her.—I have the honour to be,

" '*Her very humble servant,*   L. R.'

" 'Nov. 22, 1824.—To Mad. Pasta.'

" I waited on M. de la Rochefoucault, to thank him for the decision in my favour. The Director of the Fine Arts asked me, in the name of M. R. to await the arrival of M. Galli, who was expected in April, before *Semiramis* was given. In April, M. de la Rochefoucault proposed to me to give up the part of *Semiramis*, and to take that of *Arsaces*, which is in no respect suitable to me. He admitted the impossibility of my taking this part, and to prevent all further discussion, he ordered that an additional article should be added to my engagement. It is this article which M. du Plantys, with a hastiness which I will not describe, accuses me of inaccurately copying. Indignant at such a reproach, which casts a doubt on my veracity, I add the article; the word *reserve*, denied by M. du Plantys, is written by the hand of this administrator.

" ' It is understood that the words *e primo musico*, which Madame Pasta has consented to insert in the first article of this engagement, is not to oblige her to play the part of *Arsaces* in *Semiramis*, an opera which is reserved for her benefit.

" ' The Administrator, R, DU PLANTYS.
" ' Paris, May 2, 1825.'

" What prevents me from despairing of obtaining justice is, that a De la Rochefoucault is both judge and party in this business,

" JUDITH PASTA."

The Parisians are all on the side of Pasta, and it is pretty evident that she has been unhandsomely treated. The French journals insinuate that Signor Rossini is at the bottom of the affair; we should, however, be cautious how we condemn him unheard, or without evidence equally convincing as the above letters contain against the other branches of the *administration*,—as our neighbours term the theatrical management.

But passing from the *Théâtre Italien* to our own Opera-House, we are constrained to say that occasionally some

of the leading singers amongst the Italian performers shew a daring intrepidity in their conduct, which at once proves their want of sense, and the enduring apathy of the English public. How often has this been exhibited in London, and how seldom has it been properly resented! But at the King's Theatre the crowd of foreigners who are now admitted by the orders of their vocal friends, are sufficient to bear down all opposition, even if the audience had energy enough to shew their resentment when displeased. We have heard it stated, that a kind of servant of one of the singers engaged at the opera last season, had the audacity to declare, that he would place himself in the pit, and challenge—aye, challenge!—any person that should hiss his employer.

But while we admit and condemn the absurd pretensions, the intolerable exactions, and the glaring misbehaviour of a few of these performers, let us do justice to the others, by adding, that most of them are reasonable, polite, and obliging. It must also be confessed, that they are too often provoked by vexatious delays in the payment of their salaries, by dishonoured bills, and by the necessity to which they are sometimes reduced, of sacrificing part of their just demands, in order to secure the remainder. A pamphlet will appear shortly, it is said, on operatic affairs, and, by disclosing a vast deal of the private history of the establishment, open the eyes of the subscribers to the real state of that hot-bed of folly, meanness, and prodigality, the Italian theatre in London. Our space will not allow us to go further into this matter at present, but we shall return to the subject.

THE DRAMA,

COVENT-GARDEN THEATRE.

ON the 21st of last month, a new " Operatic Drama," named *Lilla*, was produced for the first time, from the pen of Mr. Planché, who has produced several successful pieces at this theatre.

Brenhold (a Silesian Farmer)	Mr. Fawcett.
Ehrenberg	Mr. Cooper.
Martin Brand	Mr. Connor.
Victor St. Phar	Mr. Power.
Jacob Grotsen	Mr. J. Isaacs.
Fritz Flacksen	Mr. Keeley.
Joseph	Mr. Chapman.
Peter	Mr. Meadows.
Lilla (Brenhold's Daughter)	Miss Paton.
Antonette	Miss Love.

The dramatic part, which is of the serious cast, excites a considerable share of interest; for it is extremely well written, though a little extravagant, and displays not only Mr. Fawcett's superior talent in scenes of strong parental feeling, but brings to light Miss Paton's powers as a sensible actress; while it gives her nothing to do worth notice, in her own immediate department.

The musical part is selected and arranged by Barham Livius, Esq., from *Weigl's Schweizerfamilie*, according to the announcement; but there is so little music of any kind in the piece, and what is introduced is so perfectly insignificant, that, except a dance of a very common manufacture, it excited no notice whatever.

THE

HARMONICON.

No. XXXVI., December, 1825.

MEMOIR OF THOMAS LINLEY.

THOMAS LINLEY, the composer of some of our most popular operas, received the foundation of his musical education in Bath, from Thomas Chilcot, organist to the Abbey-church of that city; but it was reserved as a lasting honour to Paradies, a Venetian, and known for his twelve Sonatas, to complete an education so well begun.

Mr. Linley having established himself in Bath, conducted during many seasons the concerts which were regularly performed there, and through the fascinating talents of his two daughters, Eliza and Mary—afterwards Mrs. Sheridan * and Mrs. Tickell—joined to his own accurate discrimination and excellent management, music became the predominant amusement of the *Western metropolis*, as it was once called, at that time the most fashionable place of resort, during the winter months, in England. At those concerts, and at the oratorios subsequently performed under his direction in London, he revived a taste for Handel's compositions—then falling into neglect—which has never since deserted those true lovers of the art who are not infected by the senseless inconstancy of fashion.

Both as a teacher and composer, Mr. Linley had a style and taste entirely his own, although it may be said

---

* Of ELIZA LINLEY, the beautiful and accomplished *Maid of Bath*, the following particulars, from Mr. Moore's Life of the Right Hon. R. B. Sheridan, cannot but prove interesting to our readers :—

"Her personal charms, the exquisiteness of her musical talents, and the full light of publicity which her profession threw upon both, naturally attracted round her a crowd of admirers, in whom the sympathy of a common pursuit soon kindled into rivalry, till she became at length an object of vanity as well as of love. Her extreme youth, too,—for she was little more than sixteen when Sheridan first met her,—must have removed, even from minds the most fastidious and delicate, that repugnance they might justly have felt to her profession, if she had lived much longer under its tarnishing influence, or lost, by frequent exhibitions before the public, that fine gloss of feminine modesty, for whose absence not all the talents and accomplishments of the sex can atone.

"She had been, even at this early age, on the point of marriage with Mr. Long, an old gentleman of considerable fortune in Wiltshire, who proved the reality of his attachment to her in a way which few young lovers would be romantic enough to imitate. On her secretly representing to him that she never could be happy as his wife, he generously took upon himself the whole blame of breaking off the alliance, and even indemnified the father, who was proceeding to bring the transaction into court, by settling 3000l. upon his daughter. Mr. Sheridan, who owed to this liberal conduct not only the possession of the woman he loved, but the means of supporting her during the first years of their marriage, spoke invariably of Mr. Long, who lived to a very advanced age, with all the kindness and respect which such a disinterested character merited.

"It was about the middle of the year 1770 that the Sheridans took up their residence in King's Mead-street, Bath, where an acquaintance commenced between them and Mr. Linley's family, which the kindred tastes of the young people soon ripened into intimacy. It was not to be expected,—though parents, in general, are as blind to the first approach of these dangers, as they

---

are rigid and unreasonable after they have happened,—that such youthful poets and musicians should come together, without Love very soon making one of the party. Accordingly, the two brothers became deeply enamoured of Miss Linley. Her heart, however, was not so wholly un-preoccupied, as to yield at once to the passion which her destiny had in store for her. One of those transient preferences, which in early youth are mistaken for love, had already taken lively possession of her imagination ; and to this the following lines, written at that time by Mr. Sheridan, allude :—

'TO THE RECORDING ANGEL.

Cherub of Heaven, that from thy secret stand,
    Dost note the follies of each mortal here,
Oh, if Eliza's steps employ thy hand,
    Blot the sad legend with a mortal tear.

Nor, when she errs, through passions wild extreme,
    Mark then her course, nor heed each trifling wrong ;
Nor when her sad attachment is her theme,
    Note down the transports of her erring tongue.

But when she sighs for sorrows not her own,
    Let that dear sigh to Mercy's cause be given ;
And bear that tear to her Creator's throne,
    Which glistens in the eye up-raised to Heaven !'

"But in love, as in every thing else, the power of a mind like Sheridan's must have made itself felt through all obstacles and difficulties. He was not long in winning the entire affections of the young 'Syren,'—though the number and wealth of his rivals, the ambitious views of her father, and the temptations to which she herself was hourly exposed, kept his jealousies and fears perpetually on the watch. He is supposed, indeed, to have been indebted to self-observation, for that portrait of a wayward and morbidly sensitive lover, which he has drawn so strikingly in the character of Falkland.

"Miss Linley went frequently to Oxford, to perform at the oratorios and concerts ; and it may easily be imagined that the ancient allegory of the Muses throwing chains over Cupid was

---

2 L

that it was modelled on the purest principles of the English school, a school which, however obscured at present, by the blaze of foreign genius that has poured over England of late years, can never be totally eclipsed, while there is one musical man living who loves his country and its reputation in science and the arts. The

nation which has produced a Purcell, an Arne, a Boyce, an Arnold, a Dibdin, a Shield, and names equally illustrious, but now neglected, except by the discerning few, need never bow its head, but may start once again into musical existence, and raise its crest higher than ever among the musical nations.

---

here reversed, and the quiet shades of learning not a little disturbed by the splendour of these 'angel visits.'"

At Oxford, "the rivals most dreaded by her admirers were, Norris, the singer, whose musical talents, it was thought, recommended him to her, and Mr. Watts, a gentleman-commoner, of very large fortune."

"While all hearts and tongues were thus occupied about Miss Linley, it is not wonderful that rumours of matrimony and elopement should, from time to time, circulate among her apprehensive admirers; or that the usual ill-compliment should be paid to her sex of supposing that wealth must be the winner of the prize. But, to the honour of her sex, which is, in general, more disinterested than the other, it was found that neither rank nor wealth had influenced her heart in its election; and Sheridan (whose advances in courtship and in knowledge seem to have been equally noiseless and triumphant) was the chosen favourite of her, at whose feet so many fortunes lay."

"In the year 1771, Miss Linley suffered from the persecution of a Captain Matthews, who, though a married man, so continually annoyed her by his addresses, that the disgust thus excited, and "an increasing dislike to her profession, which made her shrink more and more from the gaze of the many, in proportion as she became devoted to the love of one, she adopted, early in 1772, the romantic resolution of flying secretly to France, and taking refuge in a convent,—intending, at the same time to indemnify her father, to whom she was bound till the age of 21, by the surrender to him of part of the sum which Mr. Long had settled upon her. Sheridan, who, it is probable, had been the chief adviser of her flight, was, of course, not slow in offering to be the partner of it. His sister, whom he seems to have persuaded that his conduct in this affair arose solely from a wish to serve Miss Linley, as a friend, without any design or desire to take advantage of her elopement, as a lover, not only assisted them with money out of her little fund for house expenses, but gave them letters of introduction to a family with whom she had been acquainted at St. Quentin. On the evening appointed for their departure,—while Mr. Linley, his eldest son, and Miss Maria Linley, were engaged at a concert, from which the young Cecilia herself had been, on a plea of illness, excused,—she was conveyed by Sheridan in a sedan-chair from her father's house in the Crescent, to a post-chaise which waited for them on the London road, and in which she found a woman whom her lover had hired, as a sort of protecting Minerva, to accompany them in their flight. They were married at a little village not far from Calais, about the latter end of March, 1772, by a priest well known for his services on such occasions."

"So soon as Miss Linley's marriage was avowed, Mr. Sheridan withdrew her not only from public performance, but altogether from her profession; she, however, continued, upon the terms of friendship, to charm, by her exquisite vocal powers, the circles in which she moved; where her other delightful qualities appear to have been equally conspicuous as her musical talents.

"Mrs. Sheridan, now retired into private life, was the soul of every society in which she mixed, and in her domestic relations was not less respected than beloved. Of her attainments and elegant turn of mind, many proofs might be adduced; but the following from Mr. Moore's second volume, will be sufficient to shew that her genius and taste were not limited to a single art; that more than one of the Muses presided over her birth. The verses were written on the death of her favourite sister, Mrs. Tickell. Mr. Moore has thus prefaced them:—

"The passionate attachment of Mrs. Sheridan to this sister, and the deep grief with which she mourned her loss, are expressed in a poem of her own so touchingly, that, to those who love the language of real feeling, I need not apologise for their introduction here. Poetry, in general, is but a cold interpreter of sorrow; and the more it displays its skill, as an art, the less it is likely to

do justice to nature. In writing these verses, however, the workmanship was forgotten in the subject; and the critic, to feel them as he ought, should forget his own craft in reading them.

Written in the Spring of the Year 1788.

" The hours and days pass on ;—sweet Spring returns,
And whispers comfort to the heart that mourns ;
But not to mine, whose dear and cherished grief
Asks for indulgence, but ne'er hopes relief.
For, ah, can changing seasons e'er restore
The lov'd companion I must still deplore ?
Shall all the wisdom of the world combin'd
Erase thy image, Mary, from my mind,
Or bid me hope from others to receive
The fond affection thou alone could'st give ?
Ah no, my best belov'd, thou still shalt be
My friend, my sister, all the world to me.
" With tender woe and memory wooes back time,
And paints the scenes when youth was in its prime ;
The craggy hill, where rocks, with wild flowers crown'd,
Burst from the hazel copse or verdant ground ;
Where sportive Nature every form assumes,
And, gaily lavish, wastes a thousand blooms ;
Where oft we heard the echoing hills repeat
Our untaught strains and rural ditties sweet,
Till purpling clouds proclaim'd the closing day,
While distant streams detain'd the parting ray.
Then, on some mossy stone we'd sit us down,
And watch the changing sky and shadows brown,
That swiftly glided o'er the mead below,
Or in some fancied form descended slow.
How oft, well pleas'd each other to adorn,
We stripp'd the blossoms from the fragrant thorn,
Or caught the violet where, in humble bed,
Asham'd of its own sweets it hung its head.
But, oh, what rapture Mary's eyes would speak,
Through her dark hair how rosy glow'd her cheek,
If in her playful search, she saw appear
The first-blown cowslip of the opening year.
Thy gales, oh Spring, then whisper'd life and joy ;—
Now mem'ry wakes, thy pleasures to destroy,
And all thy beauties serve but to renew
Regrets too keen for reason to subdue.
Ah me ! while tender recollections rise,
The ready tears obscure my sadd-en'd eyes,
And, while surrounding objects they conceal,
Her form belov'd the trembling drops reveal.
" Sometimes the lovely, blooming girl I view,
My youth's companion, friend for ever true,
Whose looks, the sweet expressions of a heart
So gaily innocent, so void of art,
With soft attraction whisper'd blessings drew
From all who stopp'd her beauteous face to view.
Then, in the dear domestic scene I mourn,
And weep past pleasures never to return !
There, where each gentle virtue lov'd to rest,
In the pure mansion of my Mary's breast,
The days of social happiness are o'er,
The voice of harmony is heard no more ;
No more her graceful tenderness shall prove
The wife's fond duty or the parent's love.
Those eyes that brighten'd with maternal pride,
As her sweet infants wanton'd by her side,
'Twas my sad fate to see for ever close
On life, on love, the world, and all its woes ;
To watch the slow disease, with hopeless care,
And veil in painful smiles my heart's despair ;
To see her droop, with restless languor weak,
While fatal beauty mantled in her cheek,
Like fresh flow'rs, springing from some mouldering clay,
Cherish'd by death, and blooming from decay.
Yet, though oppress'd by ever-varying pain,
The gentle sufferer scarcely would complain,

In 1774, Mr. Christ. Smith, once the friend and amanuensis of Handel, declared his intention of retiring from the management of the oratorios; on which occasion Mr. Sheridan thus wrote to his father-in-law, Mr. Linley:—

" Mr. Stanley was with me a day or two ago on the subject of the oratorios. I find Mr. Smith has declined, and is retiring to Bath. Mr. Stanley informed me that on his applying to the king for the continuance of his favour, he was desired by his majesty to make me an offer of Mr. Smith's situation and partnership in them, and that he should continue his protection, &c.—I declined the matter very civilly and very peremptorily. I should imagine that Mr. Stanley would apply to you;—I started the subject to him, and said you had twenty Mrs. Sheridans more. However, he said very little :—if he does, and you wish to make an alteration in your system at once, I should think you may stand in Smith's place. I would not listen to him on any other terms, and I should think the king might be made to signify his pleasure for such an arrangement. On this you will reflect, and if any way strikes you that I can move in it, I need not add how happy I shall be in its success."

In consequence of this Mr. Linley joined Mr. Stanley in carrying on these performances during the Lent season.

We shall here again avail ourselves of Mr. Moore's recently-published biography of Mr. Sheridan—a work of great interest, and inimitably executed—for the purpose of giving some account of the *Duenna*, for which Mr. Linley, in conjunction with his son Thomas, selected and composed the music.

" As every thing connected with the progress of a work, which is destined to be long the delight of English ears, must naturally have a charm for English readers, I feel happy in being enabled to give, from letters written at the time by Mr. Sheridan himself to Mr. Linley, some details relating to their joint adaptation of the music, which, judging from my own feelings, I cannot doubt will be interesting to others.

Hid every sigh, each trembling doubt reprov'd,
To spare a pang to those fond hearts she lov'd.
And often, m short intervals of ease,
Her kind and cheerful spirit strove to please;
Whilst we, alas! unable to refuse
The sad delight we were so soon to lose,
Treasur'd each word, each kind expression claim'd,—
' 'Twas me she look'd at,'—' it was me she nam'd.'
Thus fondly soothing grief, too great to bear,
With mournful eagerness and jealous care.
" But soon, alas ! from hearts with sorrow worn
Ev'n this last comfort was for ever torn :
That mind, the seat of wisdom, genius, taste,
The cruel hand of sickness now laid waste;
Subdued with pain, it shar'd the common lot,
All, all its lovely energies forgot!
The husband, parent, sister, knelt in vain,
One recollecting look alone to gain :
The shades of night her beaming eyes obscured,
And Nature, vanquish'd, no sharp pain endur'd;
Calm and serene—till the last trembling breath
Wafted an angel from the bed of death !
Oh, if the soul, releas'd from mortal cares,
Views the sad scene, the voice of mourning hears,
Then, dearest saint, didst thou thy heav'n forego,
Lingering on earth in pity to our woe.
'Twas thy kind influence sooth'd our minds to peace,
And bade our vain and selfish murmurs cease ;
'Twas thy soft smile, that gave the worshipp'd clay
Of thy bright essence one celestial ray,
Making e'en death so beautiful, that we,
Gazing on it, forgot our misery.
Then—pleasing thought !—ere to the realms of light
Thy franchis'd spirit took its happy flight,
With fond regard, perhaps thou saw'st me bend
O'er the cold relics of my heart's best friend,
And heard'st me swear, while her dear hand I prest,
And tears of agony bedew'd my breast,
For her lov'd sake to act the mother's part,
And take her darling infants to my heart,
With tenderest care their youthful minds improve,
And guard her treasure with protecting love.
Once more look down, blest creature, and behold
These arms the precious innocents enfold ;
Assist my erring nature to fulfil
The sacred trust, and ward off every ill !
And, oh, let *her*, who is my dearest care,
Thy blest regard and heavenly influence share ;
Teach me to form her pure and artless mind,
Like thine, as true, as innocent, as kind,
That when some future day my hopes shall bless,
And every voice her virtue shall confess,
When my fond heart delighted hears her praise,
As with unconscious loveliness she strays,
' Such,' let me say, with tears of joy the while,
' Such was the softness of my Mary's smile ;

' Such was *her* youth, so blithe, so rosy sweet,
' And such *her* mind, unpractis'd in deceit ;
' With artless elegance, unstudied grace,
' Thus did *she* gain in every heart a place!'·
    " Then, while the dear remembrance I behold,
    Time shall steal on, nor tell me I am old,
    Till, nature wearied, each fond duty o'er,
    I join my Angel Friend—to part no more !"

" In the year 1792, after a long illness, which terminated in consumption, Mrs. Sheridan died at Bristol, in the thirty-eighth year of her age.

" There has seldom, perhaps, existed a finer combination of all those qualities that attract both eye and heart than this accomplished and lovely person exhibited. To judge by what we hear, it was impossible to see her without admiration, or know her without love ; and a late Bishop used to say that ' she seemed to him the connecting link between woman and angel[a].'

" The devotedness of affection, too, with which she was regarded, not only by her own father, and sisters, but by all her husband's family, shewed that her fascination was of that best kind which, like charity, ' begins at home;' and that, while her beauty and music enchanted the world, she had charms more intrinsic and lasting for those who came nearer to her. We have already seen with what pliant sympathy she followed her husband through his various pursuits,—identifying herself with the politician as warmly and readily as with the author, and keeping Love still attendant on Genius through all his transformations. As the wife of the dramatist and manager, we find her calculating the receipts of the house, assisting in the adaptation of her husband's opera, and reading over the plays sent in by dramatic candidates. As the wife of the senator and orator we see her, with no less zeal, making extracts from state-papers, and copying out ponderous pamphlets,—entering with all her heart and soul into the details of elections, and even endeavouring to fathom the mysteries of the Funds. The affectionate and sensible care with which she watched over, not only her own children, but those which her beloved sister, Mrs. Tickell, confided to her, in dying, gives the finish to this picture of domestic usefulness. When it is recollected, too, that the person thus homelily employed was gifted with every charm that could adorn and delight society, it would be difficult, perhaps, to find any where a more perfect example of that happy mixture of utility and ornament, in which all that is prized by the husband and the lover combines, and which renders woman what the Sacred Fire was to the Parsees,—not only an object of adoration on their altars, but a source of warmth and comfort to their hearts."

---

[a] Jackson of Exeter, too, giving a description of her, in some Memoirs of his own Life that were never published, said that to see her, as she stood singing beside him at the piano-forte, was " like looking into the face of an angel."

" Mr. Linley was at this time at Bath, and the following letter to him is dated in October, 1775, about a month or five weeks before the opera was broughtout :—

"DEAR SIR,—We received your songs to-day, with which we are exceedingly pleased. I shall profit by your proposed alterations ; but I'd have you to know that we are much too chaste in London to admit such strains as your Bath spring inspires. We dare not propose a peep beyond the ancle on any account: for the critics in the pit at a new play are much greater prudes than the ladies in the boxes. Betsey intended to have troubled you with some music for correction and I with some stanzas, but an interview with Harris to-day has put me from the thoughts of it, and bent me upon a much more important petition. You may easily suppose it is nothing else than what I said I would not ask in my last. But, in short, unless you can give us three days in town, I fear our opera will stand a chance to be ruined. Harris is extravagantly sanguine of its success as to plot and dialogue, which is to be rehearsed next Wednesday at the theatre. They will exert themselves to the utmost in the scenery, &c., but I never saw any one so disconcerted as he was at the idea of there being no one to put them in the right way as to music. They have no one there whom he has any opinion of—as to Fisher (one of the managers) he don't choose he should meddle with it. He entreated me in the most pressing terms to write instantly to you, and wanted, if he thought it could be any weight, to write himself. Is it impossible to contrive this ? couldn't you leave Tom to superintend the concert for a few days ? If you can manage it, you will really do me the greatest service in the world. As to the state of the music, I want but three more airs, but there are some glees and quintetts in the last act, that will be inevitably ruined, if we have no one to set the performers at least in the right way. Harris has set his heart so much on my succeeding in this application, that he still flatters himself we may have a rehearsal of the music in Orchard-street to-morrow se'nnight. Every hour's delay is a material injury both to the opera and the theatre, so that if you can come and relieve us from this perplexity, the return of the post must only forerun your arrival ; or (what will make us much happier) might it not bring you ? I shall say nothing at present about the lady ' with the soft look and manner,' because I am full of more than hopes of seeing you. For the same reason I shall delay to speak about G—— ; only this much I will say, that I am more than ever positive I could make good my part of the matter ; but that I still remain an infidel as to G.'s retiring, or parting with his share, though I confess he seems to come closer to the point in naming his price,

" Your ever sincere and affectionate
" R. B. SHERIDAN."

" On the opposite leaf of this letter is written, in Mrs. S.'s hand writing—

"Dearest father, I shall have no spirits or hopes of the opera, unless we see you.
" ELIZA ANN SHERIDAN."

" In answer to these pressing demands, Mr. Linley, as appears by the following letter, signified his intention of being in town as soon as the music should be put in rehearsal. In the instructions here given by the poet to the musician, we may perceive that he somewhat apprehended, even in the tasteful hands of Mr. Linley, that predominance of harmony over melody, and of noise over both, which is so fatal to poetry and song, in their perilous alliance with an orchestra. Indeed, those elephants of old, that used to tread down the ranks they were brought to assist, were but a type of the havoc that is sometimes made both of melody and meaning by the overlaying aid of accompaniments.

"DEAR SIR,—Mr. Harris wishes so much for us to get you to town, that I could not at first convince him that your proposal of not coming till the music was in rehearsal was certainly the best, as you could stay but so short a time. The truth is, that what you mention of my getting a master to teach the per-

formers is the very point where the matter sticks, there being no such person as a master among them. Harris is sensible there ought to be such a person ; however, at present, every body sings there according to their own ideas, or what chance instruction they can come at. We are, however, to follow your plan in the matter ; but can at no rate relinquish the hopes of seeing you in eight or ten days from the date of this ; when the music (by the specimen of expedition you have given me) will be advanced as far as you mention. The parts are all writ out and doubled, &c., as we go on, as I have assistance from the theatre with me.

"My intention was to have closed the first act with a song, but I find it is not thought so well. Hence I trust you with one of the enclosed papers ; and, at the same time, you must excuse my impertinence in adding an idea of the cast I would wish the music to have ; as I think I have heard you say you never heard Leoni, and I cannot briefly explain to you the character and situation of the persons on the stage with him. The first (a dialogue between Quick and Mrs. Mattocks), I would wish to be a pert, sprightly air ; for, though some of the words mayn't seem suited to it, I should mention that they are neither of them in earnest in what they say. Leoni takes it up seriously, and I want him to show himself advantageously in the six lines, beginning ' Gentle maid.' I should tell you, that he sings nothing well but in a plaintive or pastoral style ; and his voice is such as appears to me always to be hurt by much accompaniment. I have observed, too, that he never gets so much applause as when he makes a cadence. Therefore my idea is, that he should make a flourish at ' Shall I grieve thee ?' and return to ' Gentle maid,' and so sing that part of the tune again After that, the two last lines, sung by the three, with the persons only varied, may get them off with as much spirit as possible. The second act ends with a slow glee, therefore I should think the two last lines in question had better be brisk, especially as Quick and Mrs. Mattocks are concerned in it.

"The other is a song of Wilson's in the third act. I have written it to your tune, which you put some words to, beginning, ' Prithee, prithee, pretty man !' I think it will do vastly well for the words: Don Jerome sings them when he is in particular spirits ; therefore the tune is not too light, though it might seem so by the last stanza—but he does not mean to be grave there, and I like particularly the returning to ' O the days when I was young !' We have mislaid the notes, but Tom remembers it. If you don't like it for words, will you give us one ? but it must go back to ' O the days,' and be funny. I have not done troubling you yet, but must wait till Monday."

" A subsequent letter contains further particulars of their progress.

"DEAR SIR,—Sunday evening next is fixed for our first musical rehearsal, and I was in great hopes we might have completed the score. The songs you have sent up of ' Banna's Banks,' and ' De'il take the Wars,' I had made words for before they arrived, which answer excessively well ; and this was my reason for wishing for the next in the same manner, as it saves so much time. They are to sing ' Wind, gentle evergreen,' just as you sing it (only with other words), and I wanted only such support from the instruments, or such joining in, as you should think would help to set off and assist the effort. I enclose the words I had made for ' Wind, gentle evergreen,' which will be sung, as a catch, by Mrs. Mattocks, Dubellamy, and Leoni. I don't mind the words not fitting the notes so well as the original ones. ' How merrily we live,' and ' Let's drink and let's sing,' are to be sung by a company of friars over their wine. The words will be parodied, and the chief effect must arise from their being known ; for the joke will be much less for these jolly fellows to sing any thing new, than to give what the audience are used to annex the idea of jollity to. For the other things Betsy mentioned, I only wish to have them with such accompaniment as you would put to their present words, andI shall have got words to my liking for them by the time they reach me.

"My immediate wish at present is to give the performers their parts in the music (which they expect on Sunday night), and for any assistance the orchestra can give to help the effect of the glees, &c., that may be judged of and added at a rehearsal, as you say, on inquiring how they have been done; though I don't think it follows that what Dr. Arne's method is must be the best. If it were possible for Saturday and Sunday's post to bring us what we asked for in our last letters, and what I now enclose, we should still go through it on Sunday, and the performers should have their parts complete by Monday night. We have had our rehearsal of the speaking part, and are to have another on Saturday. I want Dr. Harrington's catch, but, as the sense must be the same, I am at a loss how to put other words. Can't the under part ('A smoky house,' &c.) be sung by one person and the other two change? The situation is—Quick and Dubellamy, two lovers, carrying away Father Paul (Reinold) in great raptures, to marry them:—the Friar has before warned them of the ills of a married life, and they break out into this. The catch is particularly calculated for a stage effect; but I don't like to take another person's words, and I don't see how I can put others, keeping the same idea ('of seven squalling brats,' &c.) in which the whole affair lies. However, I shall be glad of the notes, with Reinold's part, if it is possible, as I mentioned.

"I have literally and really not had time to write the words of any thing more first and then send them to you, and this obliges me to use this apparently awkward way.

* * * * * *

"The enclosed are the words for "Wind, gentle evergreen;' a passionate song for Mattocks, and another for Miss Brown, which solicit to be clothed with melody by you, and are all I want. Mattocks's I could wish to be a broken, passionate affair, and the first two lines may be recitative, or what you please, uncommon. Miss Brown sings hers in a joyful mood; we want her to show in it as much execution as she is capable of, which is pretty well; and, for variety, we want Mr. Simpson's hautboy to cut a figure, with replying passages, &c., in the way of Fisher's 'M'ami, il bel idol mio,' to abet which I have lugged in 'Echo,' who is always allowed to play her part. I have not a moment more. Yours ever sincerely."

" The next and last extract I shall give at present is from a letter, dated November 2, 1775, about three weeks before the first representation of the opera."

"Our music is now all finished and rehearsing, but we are greatly impatient to see you. We hold your coming to be necessary beyond conception. You say you are at our service after Tuesday next; then 'I conjure you by that you do possess,' in which I include all the powers that preside over harmony, to come next Thursday night (this day se'nnight), and we will fix a rehearsal for Friday morning. From what I see of their rehearsing at present, I am become still more anxious to see you.

"We have received all your songs, and are vastly pleased with them. You misunderstood me as to the hautboy song; I had not the least intention to fix on 'Bel idol mio.' However, I' think it is particularly well adapted, and, I doubt not, will have a great effect. * * * * *"

" On the 21st of November, 1775, The Duenna was performed at Covent-garden, and the following is the original cast of the characters :—

Don Ferdinand	. . . .	*Mr. Mattocks.*
Isaac Mendoza	. . . .	*Mr. Quick.*
Don Jerome	. . . .	*Mr. Wilson.*
Don Antonio	. . . .	*Mr. Dubellamy.*
Father Paul	. . . .	*Mr. Mahon.*
Lopez	. . . .	*Mr. Wewitzer.*
Don Carlos	. . . .	*Mr. Leoni.*
Francis	. . . .	*Mr. Fox.*
Lay Brother	. . . .	*Mr. Baker.*
Donna Louisa	. . . .	*Mrs. Mattocks.*
Donna Clara	. . . .	*Miss Brown.*
The Duenna	. . . .	*Mrs. Green.*

" The run of this opera has, I believe, no parallel in the annals of the drama. Sixty-three nights was the career of The Beggars' Opera; but The Duenna was acted no less than seventy-five times during the season, the only intermissions being a few days at Christmas, and the Fridays in every week;—the latter on account of Leoni, who, being a Jew, could not act on those nights."

It was about this time, that Mr. Linley became a joint-patentee of Drury-lane theatre, with his son-in-law, Mr. Sheridan; and in consequence of this weighty enterprise, it became necessary for him to quit his occupations at Bath, and reside in London. Here, for several years, he had the sole conducting of the operatic department in that concern, and the public were every season gratified with fresh productions of his genius.

The history of Mr. Linley's purchase of a share in the first of our national theatres, particularly in junction with so distinguished a character as Mr. Sheridan, is too interesting to require any apology for introducing it here, in the words of Mr. Moore.

" Towards the close of the year 1775, it was understood that Garrick meant to part with his moiety of the patent of Drury-lane theatre, and retire from the stage. He was then in the sixtieth year of his age, and might possibly have been influenced by the natural feeling, so beautifully expressed for a great actor of our own time by our greatest living writer :—

——"Higher duties crave
Some space between the theatre and the grave;
That, like the Roman in the Capitol,
I may adjust my mantle, ere I fall."

" The progress of the negotiation between him and Mr. Sheridan, which ended in making the latter patentee and manager, cannot better be traced than in Sheridan's own letters, addressed at the time to Mr. Linley, and most kindly placed at my disposal by Mr. William Linley :—

" Sunday, Dec. 31, 1775.

"DEAR SIR,—I was always one of the slowest letter-writers in the world, though I have had more excuses than usual for my delay in this instance. The principal matter of business, on which I was to have written to you, related to our embryo negotiation with Garrick, of which I will now give you an account.

"Since you left town, Mrs. Ewart has been so ill, as to continue near three weeks at the point of death. This, of course, has prevented Mr. E. from seeing any body on business, or from accompanying me to Garrick's. However, about ten days ago, I talked the matter over with him by myself, and the result was, appointing Thursday evening last to meet him, and to bring Ewart, which I did accordingly. On the whole of our conversation that evening, I began (for the first time) to think him really serious in the business. He still, however, kept the reserve of giving the refusal to Colman, though at the same time he did [not hesitate to assert his confidence that Colman would decline it. I was determined to push him on this point, (as it was really farcical for us to treat with him under such an evasion,) and at last he promised to put the question to Colman, and to give me a decisive answer by the ensuing Sunday (to-day). Accordingly, within this hour, I have received a note from him, which (as I meant to show it my father) I here transcribe for you.

" 'Mr. Garrick presents his compliments to Mr. Sheridan, and as he is obliged to go into the country for three days, he should be glad to see him upon his return to town, either on Wednesday about 6 or 7 o'clock, or whenever he pleases. The party has no objection to the whole, but chooses no partner but Mr. G.—Not a word of this yet. Mr. G. sent a messenger on purpose (i. e. to Colman). He would call upon Mr. S. but he is confined at home. Your name is upon our list.'"

"This decisive answer may be taken two ways. However, as Mr. G. informed Mr. Ewart and me, that he had no authority or pretensions to treat for the whole, it appears to me that Mr. Garrick's meaning in this note is, that Mr. Colman declines the purchase of *Mr. Garrick's share*, which is the point in debate, and the only part at present to be sold. I shall, therefore, wait on G. at the time mentioned, and, if I understand him right, we shall certainly without delay appoint two men of business and the law to meet on the matter, and come to a conclusion without further delay.

"*According* to his demand, the whole is valued at 70,000*l.* He appears very shy of letting his books be looked into, as the test of the profits on this sum, but says it must be, in its nature, a purchase on speculation. However, he has promised me a rough estimate, of *his own*, of the entire receipts for the last seven years. But, after all, it must certainly be a *purchase on speculation* without *money's worth* being *made out*. One point he solemnly avers, which is, that he will never part with it under the price above-mentioned.

"This is all I can say on the subject till Wednesday, though I can't help adding, that I think we might *safely* give five thousand pounds more on this purchase than richer people. The whole valued at 70,000*l.* the annual interest is 3,500*l.*; while this is *cleared*, the proprietors are *safe*,—but I think it must be *infernal* management indeed that does not double it.

"I suppose Mr. Stanley has written to you relative to your oratorio orchestra. The demand, I reckon, will be diminished one-third, and the appearance remain very handsome, which, if the other affair takes place, you will find your account in ; and, if you discontinue your partnership with Stanley at Drury Lane, the orchestra may revert to whichever wants it, on the other's paying his proportion for the use of it this year. This is Mr. Garrick's idea, and, as he says, might in that case be settled by arbitration.

"My best love and the compliments of the season to all your fire-side. Your grandson is a very magnificent fellow.

"Yours ever sincerely,   R. B. SHERIDAN."

"January 4, 1776.

"DEAR SIR,—I left Garrick last night too late to write to you. He has offered Colman the refusal, and showed me his answer ; which was (as in the note) that he was willing to purchase the whole, but would have no partner but Garrick. On this, Mr. Garrick appointed a meeting with his partner, young Leasy, (Lacy,) and, in presence of their solicitor, treasurer, &c., declared to him that he was absolutely on the point of settling, and, if *he* was willing, he might have the same price for his share ; but if he (Leasy) would not sell, Mr. Garrick would, instantly, to another party. The result was, Leasy's declaring his intention of not parting with his share. Of this Garrick again informed Colman, who immediately gave up the matter.

"Garrick was extremely explicit, and, in short, we came to a final resolution. So that, if the necessary matters are made out to all our satisfactions, we may sign and seal a previous agreement within a fortnight.

"I meet him again to-morrow evening, when we are to name a day for a conveyancer on our side, to meet his solicitor, Wallace. I have pitched on a Mr. Phips, at the recommendation and by the advice of Dr. Ford. The three first steps to be taken are these,—our lawyer is to look into the titles, tenures, &c. of the house and adjoining estate, the extent and limitations of the patent, &c. We should then employ a builder (I think, Mr. Collins) to survey the state and repair in which the whole premises are, to which G. entirely assents. Mr. G. will then give us a fair and attested estimate from his books of what the profits have been, at an average, for these last seven years. This he has shewn me in rough, and valuing the property at 70,000*l.*, the interest has exceeded ten per cent.

"We should, after this, certainly, make an interest to get the king's promise, that while the theatre is well conducted, &c., he will grant no patent for a third,—though G. seems confident that he never will. If there is any truth in professions and appearances, G. seems likely always to continue our friend, and to give every assistance in his power.

"The method of our sharing the purchase, I should think, may be thus,—Ewart to take 10,000*l.*, you 10,000*l.*, and I 10,000*l.*—Dr. Ford, agrees, with the greatest pleasure, to embark the other five ; and, if you do not choose to venture so much, will, I dare say, share it with you. Ewart is preparing

his money, and I have a certainty of my part. We shall have a very useful ally in Dr. Ford ; and my father offers his services on our own terms. We cannot unite Garrick to our interests too firmly ; and I am convinced his influence will bring Leasy to our terms, if he should be ill-advised enough to desire to interfere in what he is totally unqualified for.

"I am exceeding hurried at present, so excuse omissions, and do not flag, when we come to the point. I'll answer for it, we shall see many golden campaigns.

"Yours ever,   R. B. SHERIDAN.

"You have heard, I suppose, that Foote is likely never to show his face again."

"January 31st, 1776.

"DEAR SIR,—I am glad you have found a person who will let you have the money at 4 per cent. The security will be very clear ; but, as there is some degree of risk, as in the case of fire, I think 4 per cent. uncommonly reasonable.—It will scarcely be any advantage to pay it off, for your houses and chapel, I suppose, bring in much more. Therefore, while you can raise money at 4 per cent. on the security of your theatrical share *only*, you will be right to alter, as little as you can, the present disposition of your property.

"As to your quitting Bath, I cannot see why you should doubt a moment about it. Surely, the undertaking in which you embark such a sum as 10,000*l.* ought to be the chief object of your attention—and, supposing you did not choose to give up all your time to the theatre, you may certainly employ yourself more profitably in London than in Bath. But, if you are willing (as I suppose you will be) to make the theatre the great object of your attention, rely on it you may lay aside every doubt of not finding your account in it ; for the fact is, we shall have nothing but our own equity to consult in making and obtaining any demand for exclusive trouble. Leasy is utterly unequal to any department in the theatre. He has an opinion of me, and is very willing to let the whole burthen and ostensibility be taken off his shoulders. But I certainly should not give up my time and labour (for his superior advantage, having so much greater a share) without some exclusive advantage. Yet, I should by no means make the demand till I had shewn myself equal to the task. My father purposes to be with us but one year ; and that only to give me what advantage he can from his experience. He certainly must be paid for his trouble, and so certainly must you. You have experience and character equal to the line you would undertake ; and it never can enter into any body's head that you were to give your time or any part of your attention gratis, because you had a share in the theatre. I have spoke on this subject both to Garrick and Leasy, and you will find no demur on any side to your gaining a *certain* income from the theatre—greater, I think, than you could make out of it—and in this the theatre will be acting only for its own advantage. At the same time you may always make leisure for a few select scholars, whose interest may also serve the greater cause of your patentee-ship.

"You must not regard the reports in the paper about a third theatre—that's all nonsense.

"Betsey's and my love to all. Your grandson astonishes every body by his vivacity, his talents for music and poetry, and the most perfect integrity of mind.

"Yours most sincerely,   R. B. SHERIDAN."

"In the following June the contract with Garrick was perfected ; and, in a paper drawn up by Mr. Sheridan, many years after, I find the shares of the respective purchasers thus stated :—

Mr. Sheridan, two-fourteenths of the whole	10,000*l.*
Mr. Linley, ditto	10,000*l.*
Dr. Ford, 3 ditto	15,000*l.*

"Mr. Ewart, it will be perceived, though originally mentioned as one of the parties, had no concern in the final arrangement."

The success of the *Duenna* was a sufficient inducement to Mr. Linley to strike the lyre again ; and in a few years he produced, in his own theatre, the following pieces, all of which had their due share of popularity: *The Carnival of Venice; Selima and Azor* (from the French); *The Camp*, one of Sheridan's best operas, and, we believe, his second production; *The Spanish Maid; The Stranger at Home; Love in the East*; and several other works of less reputation, and less pretensions to it. All these productions, but more especially the *Duenna, Selima*, and the *Carnival*, exhibited every proof that the most fastidious criticism could require of the abundant fancy, judgment, and skill of the composer. His minor pieces we have not thought it necessary to enumerate; but the music of one of them, *Robinson Crusoe*, that delight of the young and the old, we must mention; it is not easy to forget the accompaniments to the business of the first part of that popular piece, which are at once so appropriate, original, and effective in elucidating the dramatic action of that best of ballets. Another of the delightful effects of Mr. Linley's unwearied industry, was his adding harmonies and orchestral accompaniments to the songs of *The Beggar's Opera*. Before this admirable improvement, the treble only, and a weak and often incorrect bass were all that accompanied those beautiful specimens of simple English song; but from his labours they have now all the advantages of a full orchestra, and every variety of instrumental illustration.

Mr. Linley's next work was his *Six Elegies*, produced while he was residing at Bath. Dr. Burney, in his history, has especially pointed out these to the notice of the cognoscenti: no small compliment from a man who certainly had not a very strong predilection for the English school.

Twelve ballads by the subject of this Memoir were published a short time after the untimely death of his favourite son Thomas. The first of them, " I sing of the days that are gone," evidently refers to that mournful loss. These are, perhaps, too decidedly and purely English in their simplicity of construction, to suit the taste of the present day; but it would be difficult to select any compositions in so unpretending a style, which could compare with them in spirit, simple pathos, and originality.

The works left at the death of the son and the father, were collected and published a few years after the decease of the latter. They are in two volumes, and consist of a rich assemblage of songs, madrigals, elegies, &c. It is surprising that they remain almost entirely unknown. One of these productions, however, by the elder Linley, no lapse of time or change of taste will ever consign to oblivion—his madrigal on Cowley's thoughtful and delicious words, full of the very spirit and essence of poetical idleness, and philosophical enjoyment of retreat from the stir of this busy world:—

" Let me, careless and unthoughtful lying,
   Hear the soft winds above me flying:"

This was evidently designed to display all the peculiar excellences of Miss Linley's style of singing. It may be affirmed that there is not any madrigal superior, and it is equally certain that there are few pieces, in that peculiar style of composition, which are equal to this delicious native specimen of vocal harmony. This delightful effort of his genius is still performed at the Ancient Concerts, and occasionally at the Catch and Glee Clubs, and is heard with the same admiration which it originally commanded.

Mr. Linley died in 1795, at his house in Southampton-Street, Strand, and was buried in the same family vault where his beloved and most celebrated daughters lie, under the Cathedral of Wells: a monument, erected by William Linley, his youngest son, points out the spot where rests all that remains, save his works, of Thomas Linley the Elder.

As the untimely death of his eldest son, at the early age of twenty-two, spread a melancholy gloom over the remaining period of his father's life, we will briefly relate the circumstances of it. The late Duke of Ancaster had extended his patronage to this promising young man even from his childhood, and on his returning from the Continent, he used occasionally, with his sisters, to visit the Duke and Duchess at their seat at Grimsthorpe, in Lincolnshire. During one of those visits, on the 7th of August, 1778, it was proposed by some of the young people who were there assembled, to enjoy the pleasure of sailing on a canal in the park, in a boat belonging to his Grace. Neither the Duke, the Duchess, nor his sisters, were acquainted with this project, or their prudence might have instilled some caution into the young men. They went on board; the wind was not high, but came in sudden gusts, and by one of these the boat, before they could take in the sail, was upset. Some of the young gentlemen saved themselves by clinging to the keel, whilst Thomas Linley, who was reputed a fine swimmer, made for the bank, to procure such aid as might succour them. It was too fatal an experiment! Encumbered by his clothes, and deceived as to the width of the canal, the bank of which he had nearly gained, he sank exhausted in the sight of his young companions. The unhappy father's grief at this afflicting termination of all his long-cherished hopes of a favourite son, produced a brain fever, from which he ultimately recovered, but was never restored again to the health and happiness he had till then enjoyed. His son had been the pride of his existence, the partner of his studies; his name had mingled with the father's in a united reputation; he was the " admired of all observers" of his growing genius [*]; and these were bereavements which an affectionate father did not, and which indeed he could not, cease to mourn to the last hour of his life. Thomas Linley the younger was buried in the ancestorial vault of the Duke, and was deeply lamented by him, as well as by all who were acquainted with his worth.

William Linley, Esq., the youngest son, is living. When young he was appointed, by Mr. Fox, to a writership at Madras, and subsequently filled the responsible situations of provincial paymaster at Vellore, and sub-treasurer at the presidency, Fort St. George. He returned early, with an easy independence, and is known to the public by many ingenious productions; the chief of which is, his " *Dramatic Songs of Shakspeare*," a work that shews not only great musical invention and taste, but that clear perception of the meaning and beauties of the great bard, which is but rarely to be traced in those composers who have attempted to set his poetry to notes. Mr. W. Linley is also the author of some literary works; and part of a very feeling elegy written by him on the death of his sister, Mrs. Sheridan, appears in the 2d volume of Mr. Moore's recent work.

---

[*] He had made himself exceedingly beloved and esteemed, during his travels in Italy and Germany: Mozart knew him well, and never spoke of him but with admiration and regard. We may also add here that the younger Linley composed the Overture to the *Duenna*, as well as the opening song, " Tell me, my lute," and, we believe, one or two other pieces.

A CHARACTER.

The *world's* abused by *a* most villainous knave,
A base notorious knave, *a* scurvy fellow——
      *   *   *
O put in every honest hand a whip,
To lash the rascal naked through the world.

To the EDITOR *of the Harmonicon.*

SIR,

I HAVE long witnessed with equal surprise and indignation the unchecked career of a foreign knave, who by means of impudence, intrigue, and quackery, has contrived to palm himself on the musical world. So daring is the audacity with which he obtrudes himself on the public, that there is scarcely a musical assemblage of a public kind which he does not infest; and, to the great disgrace of the Directors, with—I blush when I insert so respectable a name in a narrative of such atrocities—with the Archbishop of York at their head, he was suffered to insult by his presence the large portion of the rank and wealth of our country, assembled at the recent Festival at York; chilling by his daring hardihood the pious and benevolent sentiments which the solemn scene was otherwise so well calculated to inspire.

I had reason to believe that the blasted character, innate viciousness, and confirmed villany of this man, had been pretty notorious; but it appears that I have been mistaken—for who, knowing such facts, would tolerate in public, or admit into their houses, the branded convict and runaway galley-slave? Who, with their eyes open, would suffer the exulting bigamist to approach their daughters in the sacred and confidential character of an instructor? Who, that had undertaken the awful responsibility of forming the youthful mind, would depute their high and solemn functions to one of an outcast felon?

Allow me, therefore, very briefly, to recapitulate some of the pretensions of this notorious swindler.

Passing over, for the present, his earlier pursuits abroad, (to which he will probably have no objection,) be it remembered that for his residence, here we are indebted to the discovery of a series of forgeries committed by him on his most intimate friends, for whom he thus procured the blessings of poverty, and the comforts of a prison. Between the period of disclosure, and the visit of the officers of police, a short interval occurred, which he employed in stealing a horse and carriage, and started off to Calais, where he sold his stolen goods, and shortly afterwards appeared in London, as a professional gentleman; setting up (in compliment, I presume, to our morality) as an instructor of our sons and daughters. When cited before his own criminal tribunals, he, of course, did not appear; but he was tried, *par contumace*, found guilty, sentenced to be branded, condemned to the galleys for life, and, being absent, his name was publicly nailed to the pillory, in which he would have figured had he been present.

Soon after his settlement in this country, he must be married, forsooth; and married he was: and the *caste* from which he made his selection was, perhaps, of all others, the most proper for such a character to choose from. To be sure, he had left a wife behind him; a virtuous, accomplished, and (notwithstanding her unfortunate connexion with a scoundrel) a respectable lady, to whom, and to her distinguished relative, he is indebted for what professional knowledge he possesses. That, however,

signified nothing; when remonstrated with on the cruelty of deserting his wife, and informed that bigamy is by the laws of England punishable with transportation, the moral logician ably answered all scruples, by reminding his informant that, being a *condemned felon*, he was dead by the laws of his own country, and consequently no longer liable to his marriage engagements! The appearance in London of his deserted wife certainly, for a moment, deranged his philosophy; but he turned upon his pursuer, and, by threats of immuring her in a mad-house, and other expedients, he so scared the poor woman, that she was glad to escape from a country in which she doubted her personal safety.

I forbear following this depraved, this heartless, this profligate wretch through the details of his subsequent conduct in London, lest in so doing I should remove the veil that has hitherto concealed some of the painful consequences resulting from misplaced and imprudent confidence. But his attempts to deceive and impose upon the world by the agency of an anonymous writer, specially retained to puff him off, to raise for him a pretension to professional excellence, by writing down artists as immeasurably above him in talent as in character, must be still in the recollection of most persons connected with the musical world; and still more recent is his audacious attempt to influence and dictate to the whole metropolis, relative to one of our national entertainments. A grand crash soon after followed—the carriage and country-house were suspended during the short period prescribed by law for a convenient whitewash, and the old bird is again upon the wing, looking out for new fools to become the dupes of his incurable villany. * * * *

I will not, at present, Mr. Editor, trespass further on your patience with this disgusting subject, but should circumstances require it, I will at a future time furnish you with a few details and authentic documents, to fill up the outline I have here sketched, together with a clue to the names of some parties whom it will surprise the world to hear have been his associates and employers.

I remain, your constant reader,
DETECTOR.

A VISIT TO BEETHOVEN.

[Extract from a letter written by an English lady; dated Vienna, October, 1825.]

* * * *

——The imperial library is the finest room I ever saw, and the librarian very agreeable and obliging. What will you say when I tell you, that, after taking an infinity of trouble, he succeeded in obtaining for me an introduction to BEETHOVEN,—who is exceedingly difficult of access; but, in answer to the note requesting that I might be allowed to visit him, wrote—

" *Avec le plus grand plaisir, je recevrai une fille de* * * * * * BEETHOVEN."

We went to Baden, a pretty little town in the Archduchy of Austria, about fifteen miles S.W. of Vienna, much frequented for its hot baths, (whence it derives its name, similarly to our Bath), where *the giant of living composers*—as Mr. **** always pleases me by calling him—retires during the summer months.

The people seemed surprised at our taking so much trouble; for, unaccountable as it may seem to those who have any knowledge of, or taste for music, his reign in Vienna is over, except in the hearts of a chosen few, with whom, by-the-by, I have not yet met*; and I was even taught to expect a rough unceremonious reception. When we arrived, he had just returned home, through a shower of rain, and was changing his coat. I almost began to be alarmed—after all that I had heard of his *brusquerie*, —lest he should not receive us very cordially: when he came forth from his *sanctum*, with a hurried step, and apparently very nervous; but he addressed us in so gentle, so courteous, so sweet a manner, and with such a truth in his sweetness, that I only know Mr. ****† with whom he can be compared; whom he much resembles, in features, person, address, and also in opinions. He is very short, extremely thin, and sufficiently attentive to personal appearance. He observed, that **** was very fond of Handel; that he himself also *loved* him; and proceeded for some time in eulogizing that great composer. I conversed with him in writing, for I found it impossible to render myself audible; and though this was a very clumsy mode of communicating, it did not much signify, as he talked on freely and willingly, and did not wait for questions, or seem to expect long replies. I ventured to express my admiration of his compositions, and, amongst others, praised his *Adelaide*, in terms by no means too strong for my sense of its beauties. He very modestly remarked, that the poetry was beautiful.

Beethoven speaks good French—at least by comparison with most other Germans—and conversed a little with **** in Latin. He told us that he should have *spoken* English, but that his deafness had prevented his acquiring more of our language than the power of reading it. He said that he preferred English to French writers, because "*ils sont plus vrai*." Thomson is his favorite author, but his admiration of Shakspeare is very great indeed.

When we were about to retire, he desired us to stop— "*Je veux vous donner un souvenir de moi*." He then went to a table in an adjoining room, and wrote two lines of music—a little fugue, for the piano-forte,—and presented it to me in a most amiable manner. He afterwards desired that I would spell my name to him, that he might inscribe his impromptu to me correctly. He now took my arm, and led me into the room where he had written, that I might see the whole of his apartment, which was quite that of an author, but perfectly clean; and though indicating nothing like superfluity of wealth, did not shew any want of either useful furniture, or neatness in arrangement. It must be recollected, however, that this is his country residence, and that the Viennese are not so costly or particular in their domestic details as we English. I led him back very gently to a room on the other side, in which was placed his grand piano-forte, presented to him by Messrs. Broadwood: but he looked, I thought, melancholy at the sight of it,

and said that it was very much out of order, for the country tuner was exceedingly bad. He struck some notes to convince me; nevertheless I placed on the desk the page of MS. music which he had just given to me, and he played it through quite simply; but prefaced it by three or four chords—such handfuls of notes!—that would have gone to Mr. ****'s heart. He then stopped; and I would not on any account ask for more, as I found that he played without any satisfaction to himself.

We took leave of each other in a tone of, what in France would be called, confirmed friendship; and he said, quite voluntarily, that if he came to England, he would certainly pay us a visit.

ON ENGLISH OPERAS.

To the EDITOR *of the Harmonicon.*

THE revival of Arne's opera of *Artaxerxes* at Coventgarden theatre, during the present month, has given rise to a variety of curious speculations and conjectures with regard to the success of operas brought before the English public. I am fully aware that no composer was ever so mad as to say to himself, upon completing a composition for the theatre,—"This is good music; I am sure the harmonies are sound, and the melodies flowing and natural, and therefore it must succeed." Such sentiments as these (although the conclusion might be warranted from the premises) would display total ignorance of the nature of a theatrical audience. It is a complete fallacy to suppose that the success of an English opera is entirely owing to the goodness or badness of the composition: and if in fact, that rather important feature of an opera, the music, have any thing at all to do with its success, we may attribute it rather to the latter than the former quality. Few of your musical readers who are frequenters of the theatre will be inclined to doubt what I have advanced, when they reflect upon the motley assemblage of compositions brought forward for the entertainment of the town, from the positively good to the absolutely execrable. We have had at short intervals, in the full possession of musical popularity, *Der Freischütz, Artaxerxes, Rob Roy, Lilla,* and *The Coronation.* Perhaps it would not be possible to find a greater contrast than these pieces present to one another; and I will answer for it, that those parts which should have been "damned beyond redemption," have received the greatest share of applause. When I hear of the musical taste of the public, I cannot help smiling at such a misapplication of the term. The *taste* of the public is a mere chimera; it is true that boxes, pit, and gallery, have their enthusiasm desperately excited by a long shake on the octave-flute; but further than this, deponent saith not. The aforesaid shake on the octave-flute is a most invaluable requisite in modern operatic compositions; and my advice to a young composer is, that if he have a cultivated shaker in the orchestra for which he writes, that he make him shake through the whole of the first act. This will procure a favourable hearing for the second; and if his invention then begin to flag, what an invaluable and never-failing resource he will find in the carillons. I must not be accused of insensibility in indulging a little merriment on so melancholy an

---

* The taste of the *people of fashion* at Vienna is worthy of their government; they at this moment prefer C. Czerny to Beethoven. —When Mozart was alive, and his operas were performing in that city, the court and beau-monde actually patronised Salieri, in opposition to him!—(*Editor*.)

† A literary character, remarkable for the goodness of his heart, and the naïveté of his manners.

occasion as that which will be the downfall of the hopes of every legitimate musical aspirant. It is the tendency of human nature to extract as much pleasure as possible from things which lead rather the contrary way; and when the prospect is so very deplorable, the only refuge is laughter.

We have seen in a late opera, *(Der Freischütz,)* that good music may be inveigled on the stage, and by the assistance of a dexterous machinist may keep its place there: but can any one be found so hardy as to affirm that the incantation scene in that opera would have been tolerated for a quarter of an hour, unaccompanied by the extraordinary exhibition of imps, devils, &c., with which the stage is crowded?

In *Artaxerxes* the whole dialogue is carried on in recitative, accompanied by the orchestra. There is not a single chorus in the original opera; and the interpolations consist of a quartetto from *Kais,* and a finale by Bishop. Is it an old prejudice in favour of Arne's opera, as genuine English music, which procures it so patient a hearing? or is it the appearance of Madame Vestris in male attire, or some other adventitious and inexplicable circumstance? It is not quite reasonable to suppose that the same audience which applauds the "White Cockade," will very much admire the delightful modulation in the recitatives in *Artaxerxes:* to my taste those fine chords holding on the stringed instruments are the best part of the opera.

The whole end of my inquiry is, to be satisfied on what grounds a composer may think himself ensured of success with the public, seeing that he is debarred from the only rational one—the merit of his composition as music. The little encouragement which is given to a good style of composition, and the applause which follows the most frivolous songs, are sufficient to make him adopt other methods of pleasing an audience instead of writing merely good music:—he must contrive that there shall be some pageant or mummery passing on the stage, something to amuse the gaping multitude, and his performance will probably become a stock piece.

The operas of the present day are not required to possess any peculiar musical merit; they are mere accompaniments to something of more interest which is to be passing on the stage. Hence, at Covent-garden, with the help of two hacks an *opera* may be manufactured on the shortest notice, and the said musical cobblers pass for composers. For my own part, I rejoice when it is possible to have any thing like sound harmony and flowing melody, as in *Der Freischütz,* brought before the town; every thing of this sort is something gained on the side of good taste; and as it is not to be supposed that the public ear was always as depraved as it is in our day, the ignorant composers of modern sing-song have much to answer for in helping to spoil that which was at no time very good—the taste of a theatrical audience. It is to the frequent hearing of melodies accompanied with bad and ignorant harmonies, that we may in great part attribute the abhorrence which is entertained of a good chord.

A. B. *

---

* We give our correspondent's letter, without pledging ourselves to agree with him in all he advances.—(*Ed.*)

DON SANCHE, ou *LE CHATEAU D'AMOUR,*

AN OPERA IN ONE ACT,

THE MUSIC BY FRANTZ LISZT.

Produced at the *Académie Royale de Musique.*

(*From a German Correspondent* *.)

THE extraordinary youth, the composer of this Opera, has but just entered his thirteenth year. He has been acknowledged by some of the first connoisseurs of Germany and France, to merit a place among the principal pianists of Europe; nay, some have gone so far as to say, that he yields the palm to Hummel only, whose immense talent as an improvvisatore, undoubtedly stands as yet alone and unrivalled. But the youthful Liszt is also a composer, and gifted with the talent of improvisation in a high degree. Aware of this, and wishing early—we trust not too soon—to develop his talents, the admirers of the youthful compatriot of Mozart, desired him to try his strength on a wider field; they procured a poem adapted, as they supposed, to his powers: he has for some time been diligently engaged upon it, and the present is the result of his labours.

* * * *

But the authors of the poem have afforded but little scope for the exercise of his talents. We will allow them to explain their own views.

"Our sole object in composing this lyric work, was to furnish the astonishing child, to whom we are indebted for the score, with a certain number of scenes, the variety of which might afford his talent the means of shewing itself under a variety of aspects. . . We think it necessary to offer this remark to the critic, who may find but little connexion between certain scenes of this unassuming opera. Here poetry has entirely renounced her pretensions in favour of the music, and the interest which attached to the name of the celebrated Liszt, imposed silence on our vanity as authors."

We have here a very humble confession; one capable of disarming the rigours of criticism. But criticism has also its duties to fulfil, and one of the first is to be impartial. In what respect, it might be asked, could a regular action, all the scenes of which were in perfect accordance; in what could a lively and interesting poem, affording a series of situations of a contrasted character, have proved injurious to the varied talent of our youthful composer? How, in this case, could the genius of music have had reason to complain of any undue pretensions on the part of her sister, poetry? Is not the poetry of an opera the natural auxiliary of the music? Has the latter any advantages to exercise in employing its powers upon unconnected scenes and a dull subject? You may reply, that your only object was to produce a *libretto,* to arrange, without much attention to order or connexion, a series of images and passions, by turns gay and serious: but have you forgotten that, at the present day, a more serious attention has been paid to this subject, and that masters have laboured upon works not unworthy of the public sanction. Instead of lowering your subject to what you conceived to be the level of the talents of the young-

---

* In our Paris report will be found another account of this opera. From all that we have heard, from various quarters, we are inclined to believe, that Liszt's friends have not acted with judgment in persuading him to bring his work before the public at present.—(*Ed.*)

and gifted artist, you would, had you been consistent, have aided his inspirations with all the powers of theatrical combination, and all the authority of poetic composition.

The subject of the opera is taken from a tale of Florian, entitled *Don Sanche*, one of the feeblest of all this author's works. It is a kind of allegory, in which love appears in person, armed with his bow and arrows. The little god is the lord and master of an almost inaccessible castle, the gate of which can be entered only by two and two at a time. The draw-bridge is never let down, save to a knight accompanied by his lady. Elvira, persecuted by one whom she detests, and who is attempted to be forced upon her as a husband, disguises herself as a knight, and finding a favourable moment for escape, sallies forth alone from the castle of the king her father. In the midst of a forest, she meets with Don Sancho; who being in quest of adventures, is desirous of entering into conversation with the unknown. Piqued at being answered only in monosyllables, he finds means to excite a quarrel. A combat ensues, Elvira, as every child could have foreseen, is vanquished, she sinks to the earth, and her helmet falling off discovers the features of a beauteous female. The victor is on his knees before his lovely foe; Elvira no longer merits that title; she also is in love with Don Sancho at first sight. But a fearful storm comes on, and they hasten to the Castle of Love *(le Château d'Amour,)* which is seen in the distance. On the way they are encountered by Rostubalde—for such is the name of the odious rival—who wishes to prevent their entrance into the castle. Don Sancho rushes upon him, but is wounded; Elvira avenges the wound of her lover by the death of Rostubalde. At length the two lovers are at the gates of the castle; the winged god appears upon one of the towers; "Open to us," cries Elvira, "we are two faithful ones who love, and will love for ever." At this magic word *ever*, the gates fly open; Cupid with a single touch heals the wound of Don Sancho; Elvira returns with him to the court of the good-natured king her father, who asks not a word of explanation relative to the absence of his blooming daughter from her home, but hastens to unite the two lovers.

In the outline here given of this dull and insipid pastoral, will, with a very few exceptions, be found that of the opera in question. The principal change is that of the person of Rostubalde into an enchanter, of the name of Alidor; but even this resource, such as it is, the authors have turned but to little account. In a word, we consider our young artist as dragged to the earth by the dead weight of this mass, which he has attempted in vain to leaven by his genius.

But we must now speak of the music. The overture contains many happy motivos, and passages of great beauty and effect. If it fails in being strongly characteristic, we should impute the fault in a great measure to the subject. An overture should be the preface to the work, but what must be the preface to a work without interest? Among the airs, the most admired was that of the magician, and above all, two romances, one sung by Don Sancho and the other by the page. Many of the orchestral parts are treated with a vigour and intelligence which would do honour to composers long disciplined in their art.

Upon a cool and dispassionate view of the whole composition, we must remark, that the young Liszt ought to view this his first dramatic work only in the light of an experiment on the extent of his powers. Mozart was only twelve years of age when he composed his *Finta*

Semplice for the theatre of Vienna. The distance is immense, indeed, between that essay and his *Don Giovanni;* but the question is whether he would ever have created the latter wondrous opera, if his first steps in the career of excellence had been inhumanly arrested?

DERBY FESTIVAL.

THE fifth Derby Triennial Festival, for the benefit of the County Hospital, was held on the 4th, 5th, 6th, and 7th of October. President, Earl Howe. Patrons, thirty-four noblemen and gentlemen of the county. The Dukes of Devonshire and St. Albans, the Marquis and Marchioness of Hastings, the Earls of Rawdon, Chesterfield, &c., were present. Mr. F. Cramer led, and Mr. Greatorex conducted, as on former occasions.

On the first day a sermon was preached by the Bishop of Lichfield, accompanied with full cathedral service, in the fine church of All Saints, which is admirably adapted for musical purposes. Orlando Gibbons's "Hosanna," Dr. Croft's *Te Deum* and *Jubilate*, with Dr. Cooke's "Amen;" Dr. Greene's anthem "O Lord give ear," "Pious orgies," by Miss Stephens, "Holy, holy," by Miss Wilkinson. The duet "O never, never bow we down," by Misses Stephens and Travis, with the chorus; and the 32d psalm, harmonized by Mr. Greatorex, formed the selection.

The second morning's performance opened with the *Coronation Anthem*, "The king shall rejoice." "Qual anelante" was next sung by Madame Caradori and Miss Wilkinson, in a chaste and pleasing manner. Mozart's motett in B flat, performed at York to the words "Lord, have mercy," &c., was done with those beginning "Hail, O Lord Jehovah," written by Hampden Napier, Esq. There are now two editions of this splendid composition, published in separate vocal parts: the York edition, including also the *instrumental* ones. "Ye guardian saints," from Dr. Crotch's *Palestine*, and "Golden columns," from *Solomon*, with a quartett of Haydn's, "O Lord, call to remembrance," from Gardiner's *Judah*, were in a great measure new to the audience; the first was not very happily sung by Mr. Bellamy. In the second Miss Wilkinson appeared to advantage, although it is rather a heavy song. The quartett was doubled. "O magnify," by Miss Travis, in which she has scarcely any rival. The choruses from *Israel in Egypt*, and Croft's "Sing unto God," are sufficiently well known. The chorus "He sent a thick darkness," was, as usual, far from being mastered by the singers. The second part, after a symphony of Gluck, consisted wholly of a selection from *Jephthah*, which does great credit to the judgment of Mr. Greatorex, and comprises the choicest pieces in the oratorio, preserving at the same time the unity of the story, and doing away with the unpleasant impression, too commonly entertained, as to the actual sacrifice of *Iphis*. Miss Stephens, Miss Wilkinson, Messrs. Knyvett, Vaughan, and Bellamy, sustained the respective parts, except that the recitative of "Glad tidings," which belonged to *Hamor*, (Mr. Knyvett), was given to *Storge*, (Miss Wilkinson.) The message of the angel was delivered with great truth and animation by Miss Travis, and the concluding chorus, "Theme sublime," was very fairly executed, which is more than can be said for all the choruses of this day. The singers were not all perfect, nor had they always copies sufficient. The third part opened with the well-known scene from *Belshazzar*, and closed with the no less known "Gloria Patri," of Leo. Madame Caradori in "Ah! parlate," and Mr. Phillips in "The Lord worketh wonders," were both highly successful. The other pieces consisted of "Lord, to thee," by Miss Wilkinson, and the two fine and contrasted choruses of "Glory to God," by Beethoven, and "See the proud chief," from Handel's *Deborah*.

The Messiah was performed on Thursday, and opened by Vaughan in his ablest manner. Miss Wilkinson in "O thou that tellest," and "He shall feed," certainly exceeded any thing we have previously heard from her; and the size of the building, as well as its acknowledged adaptation to sound, was as much in her favour, as the size of York Minster had been against her. Madame Caradori acquitted herself very respectably in the difficult song of "Rejoice greatly:" and that of "If God be for us," which we mentioned as having been raised into greater estimation than it previously was held in, by Miss Goodall at York, had quite as much prominence given to it now by Miss Travis. Of the other pieces, allotted as usual, it is unnecessary to speak in commendation.

The selection of Friday opened with the first movement of the Dettingen *Te Deum*. "Tears such as tender fathers shed," by Mr. Phillips; "What though I trace," by Miss Travis; "Gentle airs," by Mr. Vaughan; and "Gratias agimus," by Miss Stephens, presented nothing new. Lindley's cadence in one, and the double cadence with the clarionet in another, were both sadly too long, and it is creditable to the improved taste of the audience that, notwithstanding the excellence of their execution, they were generally thought to be both absurd and tire-

some. The choruses were "Let none despair," "Then round about," and the "Hallelujah" from the *Mount of Olives*. The concluding quartett and chorus "Our soul with patience," by Marcello, is, we presume, one of Mr. Greatorex's recent adaptations from that author.

Handel's 1st Grand Concerto finely introduced the second part, and was followed by "Return, O God,"—one of the songs best suited to Miss Wilkinson's powers— Haydn's magnificent motet, "The arm of the Lord," the "Recordare" from the *Requiem*, doubled; the chorus "Immortal Lord," "Shall I in Mamre's," given with good effect by Mr. Bellamy, and the difficult chorus "O God, who in thy heavenly hand."

A short selection from *The Creation* next exhibited Madame Caradori in "With verdure clad," and Mr. Vaughan in "In splendour bright" to the best advantage, and closed with the appropriate chorus "The heavens are telling." Part the Third commenced with the chorus "Ye sons of Israel," succeeded by "Agnus Dei," sweetly sung by Miss Travis, and Jomelli's "Sanctus." Pergolesi's "Cum sancto," Boyce's fine duet "Here shall soft charity," by Vaughan and Phillips, followed next. Luther's hymn was then allotted to Miss Wilkinson, an arrangement which appears to us rather singular, and not well adapted to her powers; the ornaments introduced in the execution, moreover, were sadly out of place, and what we should not have expected from such a quarter. "Let the bright seraphim," by Miss Stephens and Mr. Harper in their usual perfection, and the march and double chorus from *Solomon*, "From the censer curling rise," formed a magnificent termination to the morning's performance, and to the festival.

REVIEW OF MUSIC.

A COLLECTION *of* MOTETTS, *for the* Offertory, *and other Pieces, principally adapted for the Morning Service. The whole composed, selected, and arranged, with a separate Accompaniment for the Organ or Piano-Forte, and respectfully inscribed to* M. W. Troy, Esq.: *by* VINCENT NOVELLO, Organist to the Portuguese Embassy in London. (Faulkner, 3, *Old Bond-street*.)

THE first six books of this collection appeared before our work had commenced, they therefore have not been publicly noticed by us, though well worthy of attention.

The latter four books, however, resemble so much, in every feature, the former six, that our present review may almost be considered as embracing the whole work. Mr. Novello has prefixed to his seventh book an *Ordo Missæ*,—or precise succession of verse and response, as delivered by the priest, and returned by the choir or congregation, throughout the mass—for the guidance of young organists and cantors, or choir-masters, of Catholic establishments. The responses are given with full harmonies, but of appropriate simplicity. We think, with Mr. Novello, that the omission of the organ in these responses, where the choir is competent to go alone, would prove an accep-

table relief from its general introduction through the service.

No. 1. Of the Motetts, Book VII., is an elegant flowing Quartett, by Haydn: the words "In devicto mortis aculeo," are from the Te Deum, but whether an extract from the original of Haydn, or an adaptation, we are not informed.—No. 2. is a very pretty airy duet— afterwards a quartett—from a manuscript mass of Naumann, not having much of the sacred character about it, but still nothing to violate devotional feeling. The words "Deus noster" are an invocation to the Saviour, which, although certainly proper for Christian devotion, appears to us to have been in this portion of the collection, too often repeated; not fewer than one in every three motetts being set to similar invocations, differing from each other only in a transposition of the various designations employed, and which are more remarkable for fervour than dignity;—at one time "Amator noster," "Fili Mariæ," "Jesu mi;" at another, "Jesu mi," "Fili Mariæ," "Amator noster." It is to be regretted that the second line of this duo was not assigned to a soprano. It is disagreeably high for an Alto.

No. 3, and No. 7, are immediate extracts from a

To Deum by Schicht, " Salvum fac populum tuum," a treble solo of much beauty and delicacy, and " Et rege eos," a chorus, terminating with a fugue, " In Te Domine."—We should have been glad to have had the same bold trumpet-like motion, that twice fills up the half-bar of interval for the voices in the first movement of the chorus, continued in the corresponding intervals that follow.

The intermediate motetts have all great merit; but we have not space to go minutely into them.

No. 4.—"O Jesu," &c. terzetto, Winter,— has some errors which we must impute to the engraver: " Fili *Maria Virgine*," for " *Mariæ Virginis*," and " *Exemplar Virtutem*" for " *Virtutum*."

In the first page of No. 5, last bar but one, an imperfect 5th (a minor 9th fundamentally) is left unresolved, although the quaver in the accompaniment beginning the next bar affords a convenient opportunity.

No. 6. Quartett " Jesu Deus," &c, by Naumann, brings to mind both Pleyel's Hymn, as it is called, and " *Ah perdonna*." It is very pretty.

The first bar, bottom staffs, second page of the fugue, requires the inner part to fall a fifth in order to preserve the course of the subject; and we think the advantage of facility in the way it is set, thus,

over *that* above described, thus,

is so small, that this sacrifice need not have been made; especially when it is considered that to accompany, at all, many of the movements occurring in Mr. Novello's collection, requires more command of the instrument than the point in question.

The VIIIth book opens with an original composition by Mr. Novello, an air and quartett, the beauty and delicacy of which leave us only to regret that he has not recourse to himself as an author more frequently. In the second bar, tenor part, we should have wished for a passing note, as at once getting rid of an unmelodious progression, and forming a response to the base, in the former bar.

This is a most interesting air throughout; but we are especially delighted with the frequent recurrence, under a variety of forms, of the following sweetly emphatic passage:

No. 2. Is a soothing, elegant air, by Himmel, divided into solo, duet, and quartett; the minor passage upon " Consolatrix afflictorum," and the bold unison immediately following are very impressive.

We are rather annoyed by the mis-accentuation of the word " Nobis," that occurs a few bars beyond, and which we think might be easily obviated. It is set thus:

O - ra pro no - - bis O

We would correct it thus,

O - ra pro no - bis O

No. 3. Is a quartett by Haydn.

One important characteristic in Mr. Novello's mode of conducting this and his former works, is the instruction occasionally given for the use of the stops on the organ, and for which all young organists must befor ever grateful to him.

In No. 4, the value of this instruction is strikingly exemplified. It is grateful even to the eye of the tasteful organist, who hears " with his mind's ear," the delicate opening, the solemn advance, and the thrilling swell upon the change of chord at the third bar; the subsequent relief of four detached notes on a different stop; and then the resumption of the sweet sostenuto swelling onward to the introduction of the voice ! This solo and chorus of Righini, is one of the most truly devotional pieces throughout the collection. The author is indebted to Mr. Novello for enriching his harmony in the fourth bar of the chorus by a ninth before the plain chord. Thus also preserving, from bar to bar, the train of dissonance, which would be otherwise interrupted.

The movement of the base in the concluding bars of this motett is peculiarly striking and impressive, beginning with the fall of a flat seventh, and diminishing that fall by half a tone at each return, during the tranquil and lengthened course of the three voices above. The resolution however of the flat sixth which is omitted, we conceive to be quite necessary, and we are not aware why it should not, accordingly, have terminated thus—

O - - ris tu - i

No. 5. A quartett, by Weigl, " Jesu Deus pacis," is marked as proper " for solemn occasions," and to be sung " at the Benediction:" but why the many other motetts, set to words of similar import, are not marked in like manner, does not appear.

No. 6. An alto solo, which, being likewise of excessive altitude for that voice, (as remarked of a former in the VIIth book,) should also 'have been assigned to a soprano. The steady march of the base in diatonic solemnity, though three different keys, in the symphony, p. 18, and then 'sliding quietly back into its original key, is certainly a very prominent and effective feature.

·No. 7. A noble solo, quartett, and chorus, by Himmel, much in the same rich, elegant, and flowing strain as others of the same author before noticed, but which we incline to consider of rather an *ultra*-refinement,—too much luxuriating in the rich pastures of *the diminished Seventh* for genuine *church style*, the dignity of which is much more allied to simplicity than to chromatic combinations.

Nos. 8 and 9, are manuscripts by Caldara, both of which are marked by the gravity and sobriety of the ecclesiastical character, but have very little pretension to melody. We are not aware whether the various points in these two motetts, that are led off by a single voice, the others following also one at a time, are harmonized by Mr. Novello, or the author himself; but if the accompaniment had only come in with the voices, we should have preferred such arrangement.

No. 10. A chorus by Hummel,—in the first bar of which, Mr. Novello's arrangement of the harmonies is obviously better than that of the author. In the fourth bar of the accompaniment, middle staffs, p. 29, Mr. Novello has added to the chord,—which in the voice parts, has only 6th and 3rd,—a 4th. This, we think would have been better omitted. The chorus is of considerable grandeur and effect, and worthy the great master from whom it emanates.

No. 1. Book IX.—" O Crux benedicta" is a quartett by Haydn, elegant and airy, yet perfectly simple and appropriate.

No. 2. " Inclina ad me," &c., base, solo and quartett, by Himmel, is a most impressive and truly devotional composition, the awkward accent on the preposition *ad* might have been obviated thus,

in - - cli - - na ad   me

No. 3. A trio, by Cherubini, has much beauty, especially the following passage, in which the ascending progression of treble and tenor against the descending base, is extremely effective; rather in the manner of Mozart.

It is used twice.

The crude modulation that occurs in the next passage is not less distressing to the ear than the foregoing is gratifying. In the leading subject, which is several times repeated, the words, forming the substance of the angelic salutation to the Virgin, are certainly not applied with propriety. The pronoun, *tu*, should not have been set to a short note; nor should it be suffered to follow in repetition after *inter*, as it cannot but appear to be connected with it. The defect would have been obviated thus,

Be - ne - - dic - ta, be - nedicta. Tu, &c.

Signor Cherubini's air would not be injured, we think, by the extra F.

No. 4, duo, by Novello, has much sweetness, but not much originality. Its principal feature is the pretty passage first led off in the symphony, at the end of the fourth bar, and frequently reiterated by the way. In the symphony, where the semiquaver motion in this passage is transferred to the base, the binding curves on the D spoil its conformity with the other places where it occurs.

No. 5, quartett, from a " Benedictus" of Hummel, is a delicate flowing pastorale. The term *allegretto*, even with the qualifying *poco*, is certainly not appropriate: the coda, from the " Dolce," is the most striking point.

No. 6. Quartett, and chorus by Andreas Romberg, is a composition of superior order, and which Mr. Novello has further enriched by his organ accompaniment. It is full of devotion. We wish that the point " miserere" upon the last page had been led off without the two octave notes below, as these injure the imitation.

&c.

In the concluding pianissimo, Mr. N. has, during two bars, trusted the alto to move without the organ; why has he not ventured to do the same by the tenor, for the one bar that follows?

No. 7. Adoramus—" a rare manuscript by Antonio Benelli," is also of rare beauty and merit, and well worthy its place in this charming collection. The words which are supplicative, are finely set.

No. 8. An original " Tantum ergo" by Mr. N. who has several times before set the same hymn; always well, but perhaps never more charmingly than in this instance. The first portion consists of a most elegant and interesting air, and the second " Genitori," is a quartett and chorus, beginning with a few bars, in a bold dignified strain, upon even chords, and proceeding at the words " Laus et jubilatio," with a firm *fugato* point, followed up by that close interweaving of four parts, without ever coming in collision by the way, which so eminently displays skill in counter-point.

The Tenth Book begins with a beautiful, well-known air of Gluck, arranged also in quartett, to one of those hymns addressed to the Virgin which engross an unreasonable portion of the collection, considering that the Scripture furnishes an exhaustless store of fine passages. The Roman Breviary itself would prove also a never-failing source of variety.

No. 2. Quartett, Beethoven, an airy, graceful composition, but possessing no stamp of this extraordinary man's originality.

No. 3, duo, Pergolesi, is a good specimen of old style, gracefully smooth, and sedately devout; but tiresome, from its paucity of *materiel*, though well employed. The opening of Rossini's *Mosè* is forcibly brought to mind by the main point in this motett. It is to be remarked, that the words of this duet, which appear to be a part of a "Gloria in excelsis," have no verb, and, of course, do not form a phrase. We doubt the legitimacy, therefore, of considering it as a detached piece. The sequel of the "Gloria" is given at No. 5, as a distinct motett.

No. 4. Alto solo and quartett. This is one of the least interesting of Signor Novello's productions, and the voice is again carried unmercifully high.

No. 5. "Gratias agimus," chorus, Pergolesi. The sequel, apparently, to the passage from his "Gloria" above. (No. 3).

No. 6. Quartett, by Haydn, which name at once marks its excellence; but, containing nothing uncommon for that great author, it requires no comment.

In No. 7, Mr. N. has furnished another "Tantum ergo," by the adaptation of Gluck's fine march from his *Alceste*. In the second verse he has varied the harmonies, and introduced some rich combinations; but we should have preferred,—with the varied effect of the chorus,—the repetition of the simpler harmonies, with the exception of two chords upon the second inversion in succession, "*cedat ritui*," which are bad in effect.

No. 8 is another original composition of Mr. N., to the hymn "O Sacrum," which he has also set repeatedly before, but most successfully as a duet for tenor and base, followed by a chorus, which is inserted in an early volume of his works. Mr. N. has terminated his tenth book with a most magnificent composition.

No. 9, of A. Romberg. The first movement consists of a few bars of a very solemn and dignified character. This is followed by a bold and noble fugue, in which this admirable author has, in a distinguished manner, displayed his great powers. This motett is probably set in the original to the same words. We are, however, pleased that Mr. N. should have again introduced this clause of truly dignified devotion from the Te Deum, which is worthy of the fine music here set to it. It is remarkable that Mr. N. has also concluded both his seventh and ninth books with this same passage.

The length to which this article has extended, will prove that our delay in noticing the present collection has not arisen from the slightest doubt as to its merit and importance: it is a publication not only for the present, but for the future, generation ;—a classical work, interesting to musical amateurs, whatever creed they may profess; and of course doubly so to those of the Catholic church, by whom, we should imagine, it will be considered as an invaluable means of diversifying such parts of their religious service as admit of variety, and also as a delightful occupation for some of their leisure hours. We will but add, that we most unfeignedly congratulate

not only Mr. N. on his access to the rich stores of harmony, both ancient and modern, whence he has drawn these volumes, but likewise the public that such treasures should have fallen into hands so capable of converting them to the best possible use.

---

1. VARIATIONS *pour le* PIANO-FORTE, *sur la Marche de l'opera*, Les deux Journées, *par* Cherubini, *composées par* J. N. HUMMEL. (Cocks and Co., *Princes Street, Hanover Square*.)

2. BRILLIANT RONDO *for the* PIANO-FORTE, *on an air from* Mercadante's Elisa e Claudio, *composed by* C. CZERNEY. (Welsh and Hawes, 246, *Regent Street*.)

3. INTRODUCTION *and* RONDO *on an air in* La Gazza Ladra, *composed for the* PIANO-FORTE *by* CAMILLE PLEYEL. (Cocks and Co.)

4. MARCH *in* Mose in Egitto, *arranged as a* RONDO *for the* PIANO-FORTE, *by the same*. (Cocks and Co.)

M. HUMMEL composes with extraordinary facility, and gets a good price for his labours, therefore writes abundantly. The majority of his latest productions are addressed to the many, and do not alarm by an appearance of discouraging difficulties, whether of rapidity or unusual combinations of notes. Of the latter we have not recently had much reason to speak—on behalf of those who love their ease—for M. H. seems at this moment in a state of exhaustion, arising from over-production, and not very fertile in invention; of which fact the present variations bear evidence. They shew the contrapuntist, but want spirit and novelty, and more than once betray haste or carelessness; the third bar from the end of page 5 for instance. The subject from Cherubini's French opera, is animated and popular.

M. Charles Czerney is now a fashionable piano-forte composer in Vienna; for genius is not in vogue at present in the Austrian dominions. Open as we are to conviction, and anxious to praise, we should be most truly thankful for a view of some production by this artist, that would enable us to ascribe to him an original idea. That he is a very brilliant performer, we have no doubt; that he occasionally displays elegance, we admit; but as to the power of creating, we cannot discover a trace of it in his publications. This now under notice shews some good taste, mixed up with much of an opposite kind: it is flowing and graceful where the theme prevails, but laboured yet ineffective when the subject is diversified. At the 7th page is a descending semitonic passage of semiquavers, in thirds, running through no less than three octaves! This is not melody; it is not harmony; but it is detestable, and only to be matched by the howling of wolves. The theme of the Rondo has been borrowed without any scruple from the well-known Tyrolian, or Bavarian air; for Mercadante is one of the non-inventors of the day, and very much addicted to poaching. M. Czerney has drawn this through twenty and one pages, and though its difficulty will prevent the performer from sleeping, it has no quality that will deter the hearer from nodding.

We turn with pleasure to M. Camille Pleyel's two arrangements, because from him we expect at least good sense.—He chooses his subjects well, and in an instrumental dress sets them off to advantage. He consults the powers of the vast majority of those who ought to be esteemed good amateur performers, and studies to please all who really have an ear for music, and do not affect to admire a bustling among the notes, and a rattling of the keys. Both of his present publications are highly deserving of praise; his themes are beautiful, he has treated them well, and not diluted them to insipidity, as is too commonly the case. The first consists of five, and the second of six pages, lengths that will assist in recommending them to the public.

———

1. ARIA, alla Scozzese, *with* Introduction *and* Variations *for the* PIANO-FORTE, *by* T. A. RAWLINGS. (J. B. Cramer, Addison, and Beale, 201, *Regent Street.*)

2. POLONAISE *on the march in the Opera of* Das Rosenhutchen, *for the* PIANO-FORTE, *composed by* DE WINKHLER, *and performed before* HIS MAJESTY, GEORGE IV., *by* EDWARD SCHULTZ, *of Vienna, aged 11 years.* (Wessel and Stodart, 1, *Soho Square.*)

3. ANDANTE and BRILLIANT RONDO *for the* PIANO-FORTE, *composed by* W. WILKINSON. (*By the same.*)

4. FANTASIA, *in which are introduced a Scotch and Irish Air, composed for the* PIANO-FORTE, *by* T. S. ROBBENS. (*For the Author, Bath.*)

5. FANTASIE ALLA RONDO, *in which is introduced the* Jager Chorus, *from* Der Freischütz, *composed by* E. SOLIS. (Clementi and Co., *Cheapside.*)

6. OPERATIC RONDO, *on an air in* Elisa e Claudio, *arranged for the* PIANO-FORTE, *by* J. SALMON. (Blackman, 5, *Bridge Street, Southwark.*)

7. RONDINO, *for the* PIANO-FORTE, *composed by* S. GODBE. (Wheatstone, 436, *Strand.*)

8. SWISS MELODY, Fleuve du Tage, *with* Introduction *and* Variations, *by the same.* (*Published by the same.*)

THE Introduction to Mr. Rawlings's air is in the excellent style of Dussek and Cramer, and many passages among the Variations also remind us of both; the latter particularly. There is a good deal of display for the performer in this publication, though nothing very difficult to execute. The air itself does not strike us much, but the third variation is clever. In the multitude of compositions, adaptations, arrangements,—or by whatever name they are to be called,—which are daily issuing, it is not to be expected that much originality can be found, and therefore in such productions, which have but a temporary purpose to answer, we are now never surprised at its absence, and try to content ourselves with good taste and an exemption from errors. On this principle we have every reason to be satisfied with the present composition. The young Schultz, who, with his brother, astonished many people here last season, and had previously excited some surprise in Germany, is certainly a very extraordinary player, his age being considered, for he seems to have no small share of musical feeling blended with his powers of execution. This composition does credit to its author,—whose name is unknown to us,—but is rather in the style of the concertos of thirty years ago, than of the modern polonaise, which is indeed its recommendation; for these reminiscences are exceedingly agreeable, when they do not betray servile imitation, or undisguised pla-

giarism. There is a great deal for the performer to do in this, and his left hand is called into severe duty; but it is a good piece for practice, to which all the passages will submit, without any uncommon devotion of labour; provided the player is of a superior class, and possesses a powerful hand.

No. 3 is, we are given to understand, by an amateur, and as such he is entitled to praise for this effort, which exhibits marks of some musical taste: but it likewise proves, incontestably, that dilettante composers should never venture before the public, till they have submitted their manuscript to the correction of a competent judge. The Fantasia of Mr. Robbens proves that he respects the style of some very good piano-forte composers, which he has followed without much admixture of the modern school. We do not perceive in this piece any attempt to move out of the frequented track; we rarely find a passage in it which has any claim to novelty, though it is not meant to be considered as unpretending. Viewing it then in the light of a work which the author intends to be examined, we must say, that its merit is by no means proportioned to its bulk; that in playing through nineteen pages, we expected to meet with more to reward our pains, but were disappointed by the result. The Introduction is spirited, but common, and the variations to " Scots, wha hae," are devoid of error, and equally free from originality. In the former, 3d bar, 4th treble staff, is a D flat, which should be a C sharp. The same sort of mistake occurs again at the bottom of the fifth page, where the E flat should have been written as a D sharp. In the fourth page is an instance of what the Italians term *rosalia*,—the repetition of a passage, one note higher or lower at each recurrence,—which is very tiresome to the ear, and betrays a want of resource. We have said thus much, because, judging from a former publication by Mr. R., we think him equal to better things than the multitude of *soi-disant* composers produce, and that therefore he has not sufficiently exerted himself in his present work.

The title of No. 5, *Fantasie alla Rondo*, is quite worthy of the piece. Mr. Salmon, No. 6, has chosen a very unpolished subject, which may be " popular" in one sense of the word, but not in the sense in which *it is* intended to be understood. Nos. 7 and 8 evince some fancy, and also a want of a very careful revision.

———

1. Useful Extracts, *for the* PIANO-FORTE, *consisting of* SCALES *and* EXERCISES, *intended as an Introduction to the celebrated Studies of* Clementi, Cramer, Woelfl, &c., *arranged and fingered by* J. B. CRAMER. Book 1. (J. B. Cramer, and Co., 201, *Regent Street.*)

2. PRELUDES *for the* PIANO-FORTE, *in the keys most generally used, Major and Minor, composed by* T. A. RAWLINGS. (Welsh and Hawes, 246, *Regent Street.*)

3. EXERCISES *for the* PIANO-FORTE *for beginners, composed and arranged in progressive order, with a preface, by* CH. H. RINK. *With some additions by* William Clark. (Goulding and Co., *Soho Square.*)

4. The Piano-Forte Student's Companion, *containing all the* SCALES *in four positions,* &c., &c., *by* J. H. GRIESBACH. (Cocks and Co.)

Mr. CRAMER has published a useful work, a great part of which is adapted to beginners, and may beneficially be placed before them so soon as they have passed through an elementary book. The six first pages contain scales in eleven keys, for both hands, and fingered. Then follow passages to improve the strength of the third finger : others for reiterated notes, the shake, skips, &c., all of which are well calculated to improve the learner who will *regularly*, even if but for a very short time, practice one of them every day. The title might have run thus,—*the celebrated Studies of some great masters,*—leaving out all names, which omission would have been in better taste. Or else to have added a few more, that ought not to have been rejected, if any had been inserted.

The Preludes by Mr. Rawlings are, beyond compare, the best we have ever seen ; there is a spontaneousness in their character which will gain for the performer,—if he play them accurately by memory, and freely,—all the credit of an unpremeditated effusion. Most of the things of this kind that have fallen into our hands, are too formal for the intended purpose, and sound more like the ceremonious opening of the piece, than a flight of notes as preliminaries to it. These are elegant and natural ; taste and expression predominate, but not to the exclusion of many brilliant passages to shew off the finger, and to prepare it for what is immediately to follow.

The Exercises of Rink (a German), now published in England for the first time we believe, differ from all others that we have met with, in being written as duets for two performers on one instrument ; the great advantage of which is, the steadiness in time acquired by the learners. The author tells us, that " the scholar ought to be accompanied by the master as soon as possible," and that " it is quite practicable to teach two at one time by this method." To the first proposition we agree ; but on the second we must remark, that however desirable it may be, and really is, to let children play duets, yet they must be *taught* to perform them one at a time, and accompanied only by the master. This is also a most useful book ; and in schools will prove particularly inviting and serviceable.

Mr. Griesbach's work is also a collection of Exercises in the major and minor scales, but for one performer. Also of passages, of double notes, chords, &c. all fingered, preceded and interspersed by a number of explanatory and other remarks, many of which will be acceptable to those who possessed no previous information on the subject. We conjecture, by what we can collect from Mr. G.'s observations, that Mr. Kalkbrenner's method is followed and inculcated in this publication ; and though we differ from it in some points, respecting fingering, yet on the whole, the rules are unimpeachable. Mr. Kalkbrenner's mode of playing octaves, by using the third finger on the black keys, is worthy of particular notice, he being remarkable for the rapidity and neatness with which he executes passages of this kind.

Mr. G. is rather prolix, and forgets that, in writing to be read, the art of condensing is of inestimable value. His book however, taken altogether, shews that he thinks, and that he has at least spared no pains in endeavouring to make it useful.

1. DUET *for the* PIANO-FORTE, *selected and arranged from* Der Freischütz, *by* SAMUEL WEBBE, No. 1. (Cramer and Co., 201, *Regent-Street.*)

2. *Ditto, from* Pietro l'Eremita, *by ditto.*

VOL. III.

3. DUETS. Amusement *on the* PIANO-FORTE, *composed by* J. N. Hummel, *arranged for* TWO PERFORMERS. *by* FRED. JOS. HOFFMAN. Books 1, 2, and 3. (Welsh and Hawes, 246, *Regent-Street.*)

4. DUETS. Select Airs *from* SPOHR'S Jessonda, *arranged for Two Performers on the* PIANO-FORTE. (Boosey and Co., 28, *Holles-Street.*)

MR. WEBBE's two duets are easy to execute, yet brilliant in effect. The parts taken from Weber's opera are not, in our opinion, the best that he might have chosen from that work ; but his selections from the *Most*, —or *Pietro l'Eremita*, as named in England,—are excellent, and including the original and splendid march. The whole are arranged with the skill of an experienced piano-forte master.

No. 3, are the *Trois Amusemens en forme des Caprices*, (reviewed in our twenty-second number,) exceedingly well arranged as duets ; in which form the difficulties which they presented in their original state, being divided, are much diminished, and an effect is now given to them by four hands, which they cannot derive from two.

The arrangements from Spohr's opera might have been rendered more easy, without the smallest diminution of effect, by a retrenchment of notes not at all essential, and by giving passages now allotted to the left hand of the first part, to the right hand of the second. Herein is shewn the judgment of an adaptor, which is only acquired after much experience. The third of these, *alla marcia*, is scientific and grand ; and the fourth—given in our Thirty-fourth Number for one performer,—is new, full of melody, and extremely brilliant.

INSTRUCTIONS *for the* PIANO-FORTE, *with Popular National Airs arranged as Lessons, by* A. BENNETT, *Organist of New College, Oxford.* (J. B. Cramer and Co., 201, *Regent Street.*)

IN a book of elementary instruction, the utmost correctness and clearness of definition are indispensible. The want of these essential qualities has rendered nine-tenths of the works of the present kind useless, and has condemned them, after a short, ineffectual struggle, to be sold at *per* pound.

In the very first page of these Instructions we find the following :—

" In music the different sounds are expressed by characters called notes.

" These notes (of which there are seven) are called A, B, C, &c."

In the next page we learn that

" Six notes are used in music, *viz.*, a semibreve, minim," &c.

Now how is a child to reduce to any order such confusion as this ? And yet Mr. Bennett may plead many precedents.

In the first page we see *stave*, for staff ; *ledger*, for *leger* ; *space*, for *interval*. In the next we read, " the length of *each note*, and the proportion *they* bear to each other, *is* as follows."

We have searched no further ; but if Mr. B. will revise his work, we shall be most happy to look it through, and give our opinion of it in a corrected edition.

2 N

HARP, New Preceptor for, *including a Series of Exercises, and succeeded by Preludes and Progressive Lessons, with the Method of Tuning, &c. &c. by* T. H. WRIGHT. (Cramer and Co., 201, *Regent-Street*.)

" As it very rarely occurs," says Mr. Wright, " that the learner commences the study of the harp without having a previous knowledge of the piano-forte, the primary rudiments of music are in consequence omitted."— His work therefore is entirely devoted to the practice of the instrument, and his directions are given with clearness; though they certainly admit of many verbal emendations, which would render them still more perspicuous. The rules laid down are unexceptionable, and the annotations which accompany the lessons, explanatory of the different terms and characters used, are correct and intelligible ; though, in point of definition they might have been rendered much more serviceable. The lessons are well chosen, and consist principally of the airs which are now most popular ; fingered in a very accurate manner. And though the author almost gives us to understand, in his preface, that such a work was unnecessary,—for he says that he " is aware of the excellent publications already in circulation for the harp,"—yet we hope that his present production will be successful, for it deserves to meet with an extensive circulation.

GUITAR.

1. Twelve original Venetian CANZONETS, *arranged with an Accompaniment for the* SPANISH GUITAR, *by* J. A. NUSKE. Book 1. (Boosey and Co., *Holles-Street*.)

2. A Selection of Scottish MELODIES, *arranged by the Voice and Spanish Guitar, by* M. HOLST. Nos. 1 and 2. (Bedford Repository, *Southampton-Row*.)

M. NUSKE is, we believe, a native of St. Petersburg, and well known in private society, as an excellent performer on the Spanish Guitar. His present publication comprises six canzonets, or, ballads, out of the twelve intended to be printed, of undoubted Venetian birth. They are very light and pretty, offering great temptation in point of facility, to both singer and accompanist. No. 2 is a very neat little work, well arranged and published. Each number contains six airs, in thirteen octavo pages, at a most reasonable price.

FLUTE.

1. OVERTURE *and* AIRS *in* Weber's Preciosa, *arranged as* DUETS' for two Flutes. (Ewer and Co., *Bow-Church-Yard, and* 263, *Regent-Street*.)

2. Thirty-three Petits DUOS, *composés par* T. BERBIGUIER. Op. 72. *(The same.)*

3. KUFFNER's Adagio and Polonoise, *with* Piano-Forte accompaniment, *arranged by* Rud**. Wessel. (Wessel and Stodart, 1, *Soho-Square*.)

4. Flora, RECUEIL, &c., *pour le* FLUTE *seule*. No. 5. *(The same.)*

5. Themes, BERBIGUIER, *varied* ; *with an accompaniment* for the Piano-Forte. No. 5. (Cocks and Co., *Princes-Street, Hanover-Square*.)

6. Twenty-four STUDIES, *or Exercises on both Scales and Chords, calculated for all degrees of proficiency; composed by* RAPHAEL DRESSLER. Op. 54. *(The same.)*

7. The Maid of Lodi, *varied, with* Piano-Forte *accompaniment by* L. DROUET. *(The same.)*

8. POLACCA *from* Tancredi, *arranged for* TWO FLUTES *and* PIANO-FORTE, *by* TOLOU. *(The same.)*

9. Cocks's FOREIGN MELODIES, *selected from* BERBIGUIER, &c. &c., *by* CHARLES SAUST. Book 12. *(The same.)*

10. " Di tanti palpiti," *with* brilliant Variations *by* W. GABRIELSKY, *to which a* Piano-Forte *accompaniment is added*. (Lindsay, 217, *Regent-Street*.)

11. SELECT FLUTE SOLOS, No. 4. *(The same.)*

12. BRILLIANT FANTASIA, *by* RAPHAEL DRESSLER. Op. 50. (Paine and Hopkins, 69, *Cornhill*.)

13. " Home !" *with* Variations, *and a* Piano-Forte *accompaniment, by* BERNARD LEE. (Balls, 408, *Oxford-Street*.)

No. 1 are published without any name. They form a pleasing work, requiring a moderate degree of proficiency.

No. 2 is a useful publication for young performers ; the melodies are good, and the author's name alone is sufficient to recommend them.

No. 3 is superior in point of composition, but demanding no great powers of execution. The accompaniment is quite adapted to a young player.

No. 4 is a continuation of the work before mentioned in the *Harmonicon*. This contains an air, " Mariendel, Zuckerkandel," composed by Klingenbrunners : but the melody has more of music in it than the title-page.

No. 5 contains an air with some difficult variations.

No. 6 is a valuable publication for students, containing, intermixed with the studies, some excellent instructions. This is a very desirable work for those who have not access to a good master.

No. 7 is short, brilliant, difficult, and without any attraction.

No. 8 is also brief, but more easy, and pretty.

No. 9 is the twelfth number of this agreeable work, which is now completed.

No. 10 is well arranged for moderately good performers on the flute : but the air has been so often in every body's hands, that it should be allowed to rest for a time.

No. 11 is by the same composer, containing some good variations for practice.

No. 12 wants an accompaniment ; seven pages for the flute alone will not command many listeners.

No. 13 is the pretty Sicilian air, arranged with some variations that are good, in one sense, but not very appropriate to the melody. The accompaniment is well arranged, and exceedingly simple.

FOREIGN MUSICAL REPORT.

BERLIN.—Jacob Hertz Beer, the great banker, died lately at this place. A more than common interest is now attached to his name, as being the father of the celebrated author of ' *Il Crociato in Egitto.*' At the commencement of his illness, his son was in a distant part of Germany, but he hastened to watch at the death-bed of his father, and had the melancholy satisfaction of being able to hold him in his arms when he breathed his last. The charitable deeds of this worthy man are proverbial in this place, and no more honourable testimony can be rendered to his memory than to record that his earthly remains were attended to the grave by at least six thousand persons, all anxious to pay their last tribute of respect to worth and virtue.

———— A concert was lately given here for the benefit of the charitable institutions of the place; the novelty on this occasion was, Pergolesi's far-famed *Stabat Mater*, which was performed with words that the celebrated poet Klopstock had adapted to the music, as also with additional accompaniments, and parts for the oboe and flute, by J. Adam Hiller. This latter was a delicate and arduous task to perform, but we must do this composer the justice to observe that has executed it in a superior manner, and in unison with the spirit and character of the composition of this greatest of the Italian masters.

———— It has been remarked, that at the two last representations at the opera, his majesty the king [of Prussia] walked in the saloon, amidst a respectful crowd, who appeared anxious to see a sovereign that had so highly noticed the author of *La Vestale* and *Ferdinand Cortes.* His Majesty conversed for a long time with Spontini on the resources which the Royal Academy possesses to enable it to rank amongst the first theatres of Europe, blending in his discourse the most flattering and well-merited praises on the personal talents of the composer. A grand circle was formed around the royal interlocutor, and every body heard this interesting conversation, wherein talent was treated by majesty as its equal.

———— The Superintendent-general of the music of his majesty, (M. Spontini) enjoys the most transcendent favour of his sovereign.

His majesty has honoured by his presence the Castle of La Muette, which belongs to M. Erard, a relation of M. Spontini. After having admired the beautiful gallery of pictures, and the almost boundless view that the eye commands from the top of a lofty turret, the monarch testified, in the most flattering terms, the pleasure which this visit had afforded him, and complimented M. Erard on his possession of so charming a place, and on the reputation that he had obtained throughout Europe, as the manufacturer of such celebrated harps and pianos.

VIENNA.—Two grand masses have appeared here by the Abbé Maximilian Stadler, which are spoken of by the critics as containing much that is sublime and beautiful, and which breathe the true character of animated church music.—There has also appeared a piece entitled, *Rimembranze di Napoli, composizione per Piano-forte sopra motivi Neapolitani,* by a young composer of the name of Dessauer, and which is marked as his Op. 1. It has become a great favourite in all our musical circles. It is a kind of Pot-pourri, consisting of a variety of motivos from Neapolitan national songs and dances. The arrangement is good and highly commendable; in the first place, the composer gives the melody in its native simplicity, exactly as he heard it on the spot, and afterwards introduces it with an appropriate and characteristic accompaniment. The melodies here introduced are six in number; among which the most striking are *La Musica di Zambogna* (a pretty pastoral melody for the bagpipe,) the *Tarantella,* and the singular melody (a kind of monkish chant,) with which the *Improvvisatori* usually accompany their poetical effusions. These form the ground-

work of M. Dessauer's composition, by a happy interchange of which and appropriatness of introduction, they produce a very pleasing and characteristic effect. We learn that M. Dessauer is a pupil of the Musical Conservatory at Prague, and his pleasing little work is dedicated to his master, D. Weber.

HAMBURG.—Madame Mara, the once celebrated singer, who has for some time past resided at Revel, has announced her intention, through the medium of our journals, of publishing her own Memoirs, which are to include the period of her whole musical career. She states, that her principal inducement for doing this, is to correct a variety of inaccurate statements which have been circulated among the public respecting her. We may reasonably anticipate much that will prove highly gratifying to the lovers of music, in the journal of the life of so eminent an artist: we make no doubt that the public will hasten to patronise a work, which to many will be full of pleasing reminiscences, and to all of interest.

PARIS.—The new Italian theatre was opened with *Tancredi.* With respect to the house, its form is elegant, its ornaments rich and in excellent taste, and it is lighted in a manner to display the beauties of its interior to the highest advantage. The eye was enchanted; can we say as much of the ear? Mesd. Pasta and Cinti, and the singers Bordogni and Levasseur, were in their characters; they were accompanied by the usual orchestra, and the piece performed was once held in high estimation. All this, added to the novelty of the occasion, was surely sufficient to waken the attention of the public. Yes, doubtless; but one of the first wishes of these artists must be to be heard, and to say the truth, their voices were so lost, that but little could be enjoyed of those delightful effects, of that vigour and force of expression, which we admire in the Italian opera. The walls, the ceilings, the numerous friezes, absorbed the greater part of the sounds; the orchestra itself appeared dull and heavy; one was half tempted to believe that the diapason of the *Academie Royale* had stolen into the interior of the new Italian theatre, to give one the horrors with its lugubrious drone. The singers, astonished at being able to produce so little effect, re-doubled their efforts to make themselves heard, and these efforts were injurious to the execution and even to the *ensemble* of *Il Tancredi.* All the favourite pieces terminated with scarcely a hand raised to applaud them, and the Cavatina of Pasta, which always drew down a triple round of applause, was allowed to pass with one cold salute only. It struck me that the sounds of approbation might also be swallowed up by the interior; I looked around me to ascertain the fact, and saw the *dilettanti* all sitting in cold inaction. The interior of the Italian theatre is deaf; I will not say,—as a wicked wag did the other day relative to that of the *Academie Royale,*—"Yes, and a lucky thing for the interior." As to the latter theatre, at all times have the shafts of satire been aimed against it; it has lately been pronounced by a musical man, whose authority is of some weight, to be the last theatre in Europe of which barbarity and bad taste have kept undisturbed possession. And to say the truth, into such discredit has it fallen—so greatly have its receipts diminished—in such horror are its screams and howlings held, that the greater part of its most zealous defenders have joined the ranks of the opposition.

Tancredi was followed by *La Donna del Lago,* in which a singer of celebrity, from Germany, named Schütz, made her first appearance in the character of *Malcolm.* This lady is an excellent musician; her execution is decided and full of power; the quality of her voice is good, and it possesses no less justness than flexibility; but she is not a contr'alto, as was announced. Madame Schütz has nothing of the *musico,* whose place she fills, saving the cuirass and the helmet. The latter, with its towering plumes, was really a remarkable object, from the active part which it took, or seemed to take, in the execution of the music, by picturing as it were to the eye the triolets that glided from the lips of *Malcolm.* It cannot be denied that female characters would be better suited to Madame

Schütz, as her general appearance has but little of the heroic. It should be remembered that it is the voice, and not the helmet and sword, that constitutes the office of a *musico*. The lady should also remember that large boots with spurs must be a nuisance instead of an ornament to a hero who necessarily travels on foot.

Rubini performed the part of *Uberto* in a manner deserving of all praise. Signor Zucchelli, who personated the character of *Rodrigo*, acquitted himself admirably of his part, and sang with great effect and justness of expression. One word more of Rubini, his voice possesses an inconceivable charm, and, without effort, is capable of the most surprising effects. The manner in which he sung the Romance, *Aurora sorgerai*, was altogether enchanting; he threw numberless charming graces into it, without injuring the original air, or at all altering its character. He is one of the most valuable acquisitions which the French theatre has had for years.

PARIS.—The opera of *Il Crociato* has obtained a brilliant and merited success. It drew a very large audience on its first performance, and the richness of the score justified this eagerness of the public to hear it in action. It abounds in pieces replete with grace and force, in vigorous movements, full of charms and sweetness. The music of this opera speaks; it is the expression of sentiment and passion; it nearly stands in lieu of words, by the correctness of its declamation; it occupies and fills the scene; it portrays the situations sufficiently, and makes them comprehensible to those who do not even understand Italian. One feels in listening to this work all that M. Meyerbeer might do for a poem well written. The drama is not without some interest, but offers nothing determined: it has too many unmeaning scenes, which the art alone of the musician has rendered tolerable.] Madame Pasta is excellent in her soliloquy in the first act: she sung and acted this admirably: she has a warmth and expression which exceeds all praise, and we sincerely regret to see her pass from a scene where she is sublime, both as a singer and actress, to others that are frivolous and insignificant, where the poet affords her nothing to express. She is charming in her costume of the young Turk, and one may, in beholding her, yield oneself up to the illusion, that, in spite of her feminine beauty, she is a young and handsome lover of the Houri of Mahomet: but when she returns in the costume of a Crusader, her sex betrays her. She resembles rather *Jeanne d'Arc* than a Knight-Templar. Under a Christian clothing she accuses the conscience of a Christian, and despite of the magnanimous jerk with which she draws the sword, one is tempted to exclaim—

" Pour des combats plus doux, l'Amour forma vos charmes."

—— The reputation which Meyerbeer has acquired by his *Crociato*, is beginning to call public attention to his other productions. His opera entitled *Margherita d'Anjou*, which was brought out at Milan nearly three years since, is preparing for representation at the Odeon. At the *Academie Royale*, they are about to produce Meyer's *Rosa bianca, e Rosa rossa*, an opera which has long been highly popular in Germany. Signor Rubini is to perform the principal character. It is no unfavourable omen of the return of the reign of good taste, that the public attention is thus directed to the land of genuine music, and that the productions of the German school are thus deservedly becoming popular.—The King of Prussia, at the liberal suggestion of Spontini, who fills the place of superintendent of his music, was pleased to confer an honour of a very gratifying kind on four of the composers of this capital. He has given orders that the *Abencerages* of Cherubini, and the *Pharamond* of MM. Boieldieu, Martin, and Kreutzer, should be prepared for representation at the Theatre Royal of Berlin. There is no way in which the works of composers of merit can be made known to other countries at once so effectually and so agreeably, as at the generous and disinterested suggestion of a brother composer. Such acts, too, will do much towards removing an unfavourable impression from the public mind, relative to the jealousies that are found to prevail among the members of this profession. It is said that, in return, the *Academie Royale* has

solicited M. Spontini to superintend the production of his two operas, *Olympia* and *Alcidor*, on that Theatre.

—— October 15th. Yesterday the orchestra of the Comic Opera performed, between the two pieces, the overture to *Jeune Henri* of Méhul. This composition might stand in the place of a piece, from its length, and from the effect it produces. We listen to it with real interest, so entirely has the composer painted the circumstances of a chase. We follow the rapid steps of the hounds, hear the trampling of horses, and the sound of the hunter's horn: we are present, as it were, at the last moments of the stag, who expires shedding tears. Imitative music cannot be carried to a greater degree of perfection. This chef-d'œuvre is always received with enthusiasm. The orchestra, filled by first-rate talent, and one of the finest in the capital, performed the overture with a vigour and precision most remarkable, and worthy of the highest praise.

—— October 18th. The opera by young Liszt, *Don Sanche*, ou le Chateau d'Amour, was performed at the Académie Royale yesterday, and in no way answered to the magnificent and absurd praises which had previously been bestowed on it. It merited the encouragement of his friends in private, and the praises of his family, but not the ill-judged honour of a public representation on a stage where has been produced the works of a Gluck, a Piccini, a Mozart. No one more than we can applaud the brilliant execution and precose merits of this child: but at the same time, none can be more deeply interested for the character of a theatre, the dignity of which ought not to be compromised by such experiments.

—— October 21. A new opera, *Don Sanche, ou le Chateau d'Amour*, by Master Liszt, has been performed here. The whole thing turned out to be of an exceedingly childish nature, and the great majority of the audience looked, on the dropping of the curtain, very like persons painfully conscious of having been very completely mystified.

—— Mademoiselle Cinti has just contracted an engagement of ten years with the administration of the Academy Royal of Music. She will appear before the first of January. The parts she will fill are *Amazili; Antigone; Aglaure*, in the opera *Aristipe; Philis*, in *le Rossignole;* and *Collette*, in *Le Devin du Village*. They likewise talk of a very brilliant part in the new opera of Rossini. The *rapidity* with which the celebrated Maestro has worked for some time past, leads one to surmise that this opera will be published towards the conclusion of the engagement of Mademoiselle Cinti.

—— Madame Catalani is deigning at present to give some concerts at Toulouse; but we do not learn that the public there deign to attend them.

—— The third representation of the *Berg Geist*, an opera by Spohr, has been given at Leipzig, with little success, notwithstanding the superb decorations by M. Gropius. This failure is imputed to the poem itself, which has not common sense. It is to be hoped, however, that the composer of *Faust* and of *Jessonda* will soon redeem his name.

—— The composer of the *Freischütz* is occupied in setting an English opera, named *Oberon*, which is to be given at London in the month of March. It is said that M. de Weber, in passing through Paris, will get up his *Euryanthe*, of which a skilful translator has made, we are told, a charming drama.

—— *Robin des Bois*, [the French name for the *Freischütz*,] is in a fair way to travel through France. It has been performed at Tours, where, as in Paris, the famous hunter's chorus is always encored.

—— Madame Szymanowska, the celebrated Polish pianiste, who was applauded excessively here lately, and who has since travelled through England and Italy, is returning to us. We have not forgotten her graceful, easy, and brilliant execution; and it is probable that her concerts will not be less thronged, than at the period of her first visit.

Paris.—On the 4th of last month, the distinguished harpist, Madame Hendal-Pouneze had her benefit at the *Theatre de Madame.* The choice she made of two Concertos by Bochsa, *the fugitive,* was considered by the critics to be injudicious; the artist is to be pitied when, instead of being content to touch the heart by effective melody, he is ambitious to surprise by the conquest of mechanical difficulties; how often in this manner, is the hearer made the martyr of the vanity of the composer. The public received with particular marks of favour Zuchelli, whose admirable voice and manner seemed to impart a fresh charm to that most familiar of familiar airs *Non più andrai.* Indeed, it may be remarked, that a concert would scarcely be worthy of the name, unless enlivened by that sweetest and most perfect of all instruments, the human voice. And here we cannot but express a regret, in which we are sure that many will join us, that instead of a judicious selection from the great master-pieces of the old school, we are condemned to an eternal repetition of airs, &c., which are daily heard in the theatres. What happy occasions would these be of making the public acquainted with numerous treasures of art which may be said to be lost to posterity. But we think it requires no prophetic spirit to see that the dawn of good taste is near at hand, that a disgust at the tinsel and extravagant ornaments of the Rossinian school, is rapidly spreading among us, and that this will naturally lead to a wish to bring to light the *chefs-d'œuvres* of expression and melody, and vigorous and classic productions of a better age. Music, the most delightful of the arts, has a manifest disadvantage over the rest: paintings, or statues, are exposed to the eyes of all, and continue to command admiration from age to age, while the productions of the great masters are condemned to sleep in dull oblivion, covered with dust and neglect. The glorious creations of a Pergolesi, a Vinci, a Leo, a Durante, a Porpora, a Jomelli, a Majo, will for ever remain unknown in our regard; we are taught to admire the genius of these illustrious masters, but our admiration is but ignorance, for we are unable to fathom the secrets of their mighty art.

Musical Obituary.

FRANCIS SERAPHICUS IGNATIUS LAUSKA, better known to the English public as the master of the two great modern geniuses, Von Weber and Meyerbeer, than from an acquaintance with his own works, died during the present year at Berlin. He was born at Brünn in Moravia, the 13th of January, 1764, where his father held an official situation of great respectability. He gave his son a very liberal education in the collegiate school of that town, where he made a considerable progress in languages, mathematics, and metaphysics, and was honoured with the degree of Bachelor of Arts. He was destined for the civil law, but his great love for music predominated, and he quitted the study of Justinian and Grotius, for that of Haydn and Mozart. He had the good fortune to enjoy the instructions of the celebrated Albrechtsberger, under whom he made a rapid progress in the study of harmony. He then visited Milan and Rome, and afterwards filled the situation of chamber-musician in the Palatinate of Bavaria. As a pianoforte player, Lauska particularly distinguished himself by his uncommon ease and finish in extempore performance. He composed numerous works for the piano, which in his travels through Europe were everywhere received with the most lively interest, not to say enthusiasm. Hamburg, Copenhagen, Petersburg, Riga, Konigsberg, and Berlin, were successively the witnesses of his triumphs. His *Fantasias* were universally acknowledged as master-pieces of their kind. There never had been a pianist who so perfectly understood the powers of his instrument as Lauska; and he is said by amateurs, who remember him at this period, to have anticipated many of the more refined modes which have recently conferred such celebrity on some distinguished masters.

As a teacher of the piano, Lauska united every requisite, and in the midst of all his vivacity, his patience and perseverance were eminently conspicuous. He passed many years at Berlin; and, after visiting most of the cities of Europe, at length finally settled there. His fame spread daily. He had the honour of instructing nearly the whole of the Princes and Princesses of the royal family of Prussia, by whom he was treated with every respect and esteem for his worth and talents.

Of his merits as a composer, his numerous works, among which not the least valuable are his posthumous productions, will stand as the most enduring testimonial. In his private character Lauska was much esteemed for his excellent qualities, and particularly for his freedom from those little arts of jealousy and intrigue, which—it is with pain we are obliged to confess it—but too often disgrace the profession: extremely alive to a sense of right and wrong, he always manifested this feeling without respect to persons. As a companion he possessed a fund of humour and merriment, though of a serene and gentle kind.

After a residence of more than twenty years in Berlin, where he had the happiness of uniting himself to a lady of great beauty and rare talent in his own art, in the year 1821, he revisited Italy, and passed a considerable time at Rome and Naples, an object for which he had sighed for years; indeed ever since the visit in his youth, he had frequently been heard to express it as his most fervent wish that he might once again be permitted to behold the favoured land of music and the arts. Shortly after his return in 1824, he fell into a state of debility, which increased till his death, which took place immediately after Easter of the present year.

He died in the house of his friend M. Schlesinger, the publisher of many of his works; and every honour was done to his memory. An appropriate piece of his own composition was performed on occasion of his funeral, which was numerously attended by many of the principal people of the town, and by all his friends and brother artists. The composition selected for this occasion, was a solemn movement from his Requiem to the words *Quando corpus morietur,* with the concluding passage *Pie Jesu dona eis requiem.*

PETER WINTER. To the Memoir of this eminent composer and excellent man, given in another part of the present volume*, we have now to add the termination of his earthly career. He died at Munich on the 17th of August, at the good old age of 71, universally esteemed both as a man and as an artist. He continued to the last to draw on the abundant stores of his genius, having very shortly before his death composed a Mass for the chapel of his royal protector the King of Bavaria, who has since paid the debt of nature, and followed his favourite musician to the tomb.

In October last died, at his house in Berners-Street, JOHN CROSDILL, Esq., *Violist* in ordinary to the late King, and to his present Majesty. He received the early part of his education as a chorister in Westminster Abbey, and in 1782 was appointed chamber musician to Queen Charlotte; about which time he had the honour of instructing the Prince of Wales,— our reigning Monarch—on the Violoncello. Mr. Crosdill was

* Page 49.

the principal Violoncello at the commemoration of Handel; also at the Professional Concert, so long as it continued, and likewise at the Ancient Concerts, till he withdrew from his profession, about five and thirty years ago, upon entering into wedlock with a lady of considerable fortune. But after this, he continued to delight his friends in private by his admirable performances, which had never been excelled. His tone, whereby he was particularly distinguished, survives in Lindley; though the latter far surpasses him in point of execution.

Mr. Crosdill was born in London, in 1755, and has left a son, Lieut. Col. Crosdill, of the East India Company's Service, to inherit his property. He was 57 years a member of the Royal Society of Musicians, and by his direction his successor has presented that body with the liberal donation of 1000l.

Mr. Crosdill was exceedingly beloved by all who knew him. He was a sensible, but unassuming, man; full of good humour, and even playfulness, to the last hour of his life; qualities which, combined with a personal appearance that tended to conceal his age, made him pass for young, till within a very few years of his death. He was a most honourable man, and dignified the profession to which he once belonged.

M. Le Comte de Lacepede, member of the Academy of Sciences, and Ancient Grand Chancellor of the Legion of Honour, died October 7th, at his country-house at Epinay, of the small-pox. The count was born at Agen, in Guienne, in 1756. In 1785 appeared at Paris his *Poétique de la Musique*, in two volumes 8vo., a work which displays a lively imagination, and an active spirit of metaphysical inquiry; though unfortunately having chosen most of his examples from operas composed by himself, but never performed, and therefore unknown, his arguments want that illustration which might have rendered them convincing, had he availed himself of the works of Gluck.

In science and letters, his deep knowledge and talent for writing placed him on a rank with Buffon: as a man, he was equally distinguished by justice and probity in his public capacity, and by his rare virtues in private society, which rendered him one of its most valuable members.

Mr. D. P. Bruguier, a violin-player and teacher of the Piano-Forte, also died in October. He was an associate of the Philharmonic Society, and published many arrangements of overtures, &c., as well as a number of easy lessons. He was much respected by his professional brethren.

THE DRAMA.

KING'S THEATRE.

The following letter has appeared in the daily papers: we offer no comment on it, as it speaks plainly enough for itself:

"Sir,—Observing in a paper of yesterday that a Mr. Bochsa is announced as Director of the Musical Department at the King's Theatre, you will much oblige me by publicly stating, that I have been for some time past engaged by Mr. Ebers, as sole Director of all Operas which will be given at the theatre during the season, and that no other person can assume to himself a title which only belongs to me. This I should not have considered necessary publicly to announce, but to remove the impression which would otherwise fall upon that establishment by the promulgation of the above-mentioned statement.

"I am, Sir, yours, very obediently,
"Nov. 10.   "G. B. Velluti."

But hereupon some noble influence was immediately used,—the cause being so noble—and the next day the subjoined was published, through the same channel as the former.

"Sir,—I have been informed by some friends, that in the letter which I addressed to you yesterday, I had made use of expressions which might be considered personal and offensive. If I have done so, my ignorance of the English language must plead my excuse; for neither my education nor my principles have ever permitted me to insult any one.

"I remain, Sir, your obedient Servant,
"Nov. 11.   "G. B. Velluti."

But though Signor Velluti had no occasion to boast of the literary assistance of the first scribe, he has less cause to be satisfied with the second writer, who has made him endeavour to explain away language that, at least, expressed an honest indignation; and has also furnished him a little indiscreet boasting about education, together with two grammatical errors, in the short compass of six lines.

DRURY-LANE THEATRE.

Mrs. Inchbald's two-act piece, *The Midnight Hour*, which she translated from the French with admirable humour, was revived at this house on the 23rd of last month, enlarged into an opera of three acts, under the name of *The Wager*, or *The Midnight Hour*. Mr. T. Cooke has selected, for the piece, some favourite music from the works of the popular foreign composers of the day; and, thus brought forward, assisted by the good acting of Miss Kelly, Dowton and Harley, a favourite old farce, in an exalted state, has proved successful, and is likely to be often performed during the season. This is the only musical attempt that has been made since the re-opening of the house.

COVENT-GARDEN THEATRE.

The imitations of M. Mazurier, so flattering to our nature, and so creditable to a patent theatre, continue, and are sufficiently successful to render any new effort of a musical kind, at present, unnecessary.

HAYMARKET THEATRE.

This House closed on the 15th of October, after a very prosperous season; in which, however, music had very little share. We suppose it to be almost an understood thing, that the English Opera House is to have the musical field to itself during the summer months.

Lightning Source UK Ltd.
Milton Keynes UK
UKHW020826260119
336152UK00008B/462/P